Design for Trustworthy Software

Design for Trustworthy Software

Tools, Techniques, and Methodology of Developing Robust Software

Bijay K. Jayaswal
Peter C. Patton

Upper Saddle River, NJ • Boston • Indianapolis • San Francisco
New York • Toronto • Montreal • London • Munich • Paris
Madrid • Cape Town • Sydney • Tokyo • Singapore • Mexico City

Many of the designations used by manufacturers and sellers to distinguish their products are claimed as trademarks. Where those designations appear in this book, and the publisher was aware of a trademark claim, the designations have been printed with initial capital letters or in all capitals.

The author and publisher have taken care in the preparation of this book, but they make no expressed or implied warranty of any kind and assume no responsibility for errors or omissions. No liability is assumed for incidental or consequential damages in connection with or arising from the use of the information or programs contained herein.

The publisher offers excellent discounts on this book when ordered in quantity for bulk purchases or special sales, which may include electronic versions and/or custom covers and content particular to your business, training goals, marketing focus, and branding interests. For more information, please contact:
U.S. Corporate and Government Sales
800-382-3419
corpsales@pearsontechgroup.com
For sales outside the United States, please contact:
International Sales
international@pearsoned.com

 This Book Is Safari Enabled

The Safari® Enabled icon on the cover of your favorite technology book means the book is available through Safari Bookshelf. When you buy this book, you get free access to the online edition for 45 days. Safari Bookshelf is an electronic reference library that lets you easily search thousands of technical books, find code samples, download chapters, and access technical information whenever and wherever you need it.
To gain 45-day Safari Enabled access to this book:
• Go to http://www.phptr.com/safarienabled
• Complete the brief registration form
• Enter the coupon code B3JD-ZRJL-STW2-ZXKJ-62AE
If you have difficulty registering on Safari Bookshelf or accessing the online edition, please e-mail customer-service@safari-booksonline.com.

Visit us on the Web: www.prenhallprofessional.com
Library of Congress Cataloging-in-Publication Data:
Jayaswal, Bijay K., 1949-
  Design for trustworthy software : tools, techniques, and methodology of developing robust software / Bijay K. Jayaswal, Peter C. Patton.
    p. cm.
  Includes index.
  ISBN 0-13-187250-8 (hardback : alk. paper)
1. Computer software—Reliability. 2. Computer software—Quality control. 3. Computer software—Development. I. Patton, Peter C. II. Title.
  QA76.76.R44J39 2006
  005—dc22
                       2006016484

ISBN 0-13-187250-8
Text printed in the United States on recycled paper at R.R. Donnelley in Crawfordsville, IN.
First printing, September 2006

Contents

PART II   TOOLS AND TECHNIQUES OF DESIGN FOR TRUSTWORTHY SOFTWARE

CHAPTER 6   The Seven Basic (B7) Tools of Quality   193

PART IV   PUTTING IT ALL TOGETHER: DEPLOYMENT OF A DFTS PROGRAM

PART V   SIX CASE STUDIES

CHAPTER 22   Cost of Software Quality (CoSQ) at Raytheon's Electronic Systems (RES) Group   633

CHAPTER 23   Information Technology Portfolio Alignment   643

Foreword

I have spent my career writing business enterprise software, but I can foresee the day when application software will no longer be written by programmers like myself. For more than twenty years, my advanced development team and I have been working on realizing the Holy Grail of programming—specification-based software. This is application software generated automatically from a very precise specification written by a domain expert rather than a system analyst or a programmer. Today's business application programmers will become either domain experts or the system programmers who create the metacompilers for the specification languages or Domain-Specific Design Languages (DSDLs) that will automatically generate full application systems. After years of research, we at Lawson have announced such a tool, called Landmark™, which is being used to prepare our new application software releases.

It is impossible to automate any process that cannot be done manually in a reliable and repeatable way. The unfortunate reliability situation with computer software historically has retarded its automation for years. The sort-merge generator is more than fifty years old, but this achievement has not been repeated for more-complex applications. It is one thing to write a precise, unambiguous specification for a sort-merge program and quite another to write one for even a piece of an HR or supply/chain application. The first problem is to develop a specification language that has the unambiguous expressive power to do for any application what a sort-merge specification does for its application. Considerable progress has been made with this issue in recent years with the advent of Pattern Languages and the DSDLs that implement them. The second problem is understanding the software development process in a prescriptive rather than a merely descriptive way. The five design technologies described and presented in both theory and example in this book are one of the first attempts to do that with software. They are tried and tested in the hardware manufacturing process and product design but have yet to be applied to software development in any systematic way. This book represents a first attempt to do so, as a combined primer and handbook. The fact that this book incorporates as a case study almost every published example of the application of these design technologies to software design and development identifies it as a pioneering work.

I agree with the authors that the future of business application software lies in specification-based languages. I also think that their book will be a bridge from today's untrustworthy, manually created software to tomorrow's automatically generated, fully trustworthy software. I recommend this book very highly.

H. Richard Lawson
Vice Chairman, Lawson Software

Preface

The fastest-growing phenomenon in the world today is computer end-user expectation. The computer revolution that began with the announcement of the ENIAC on Valentine's Day 1946 in the *New York Times* has completely changed the world. Computer hardware has become so reliable that we cast it in silicon microchips and even embed it in other machines. We assume that if hardware survives its "infant mortality" period, it will never need to be repaired, as do other machines. (Frequently upgraded to meet demand, perhaps!) Software has likewise come a long way, but it remains the Achilles' heel of truly trustworthy computing. No hard-goods manufacturer today would deliberately ship goods with known defects into a high-tech market, yet software vendors do so routinely. They simply have no other choice given the relentless demand of computer end-user expectation, software's inherent complexity, and the general lack of the kind of strong "quality cultures" that pervade high-tech hard-goods manufacturing.

The authors bring more than 30 years of quality experience and 50 years of software development experience to bear on the problem of designing software to be inherently trustworthy. We were inspired by Craig Mundie's Trustworthy Computing Initiative at Microsoft Corporation. After reading the literature on software quality and attending numerous conferences, we were convinced that Taguchi Methods had much to offer. We were further emboldened to find that Taguchi Methods had been recommended for such applications by none other than Dr. Taguchi himself. They had been applied in only a half-dozen cases, and all successfully. The major premise of this book is that although software is *designed* like hardware, nothing in its development process is akin to the *manufacturing* of hardware. Therefore, any quality method employed to improve software reliability and hence trustworthiness would have to be applied *as far upstream as possible*. The genius of Taguchi Methods is that they can treat both *controllable* (inherent design) factors and uncontrollable *noise* (exogenous) factors *at design time*. By using a statistical experiment technique employing orthogonal matrices or Latin Squares, Taguchi Methods can consider *all factors simultaneously*. This means the end of downstream testing, bottleneck analysis, and finding and fixing one bug at a time in software products. The goal of software quality now becomes preventing bugs in implementation rather than finding and eliminating them during and after implementation. Like other quality methods, Taguchi Methods are not a "black box" that you simply insert into the software development process. Nor are they used alone. They are used in the context of other upstream customer-oriented methods, such as Analytic Hierarchy Process (AHP), Quality Function Deployment (QFD), TRIZ, Pugh Concept Selection, and Failure Modes and Effects Analysis (FMEA), all of which may be applied before a single line of code is written!

The essence of Taguchi Methods is listening to the "voice of the customer." By listening carefully, the software architect or designer can get in front of computer end-user expectation and guide it to realizable and reliable products. This is better than being dragged behind end-users in an endless cycle of product "fix and repair" without any hope of ever catching up. This book offers a framework of tools, techniques, and methodologies for developing *robust software*. This framework is an integrative technology based on the principles of transformational leadership, best practices of learning organizations, management infrastructure, and quality strategy and systems, all blended into the unique context of software development milieu. We call it *Design for Trustworthy Software* (DFTS).

This book is intended to meet the needs of software development organizations, big and small, that want to build the kind of trustworthy or highly reliable software demanded by today's increasingly sophisticated computer user. It is designed to be a resource for organization-wide learning that helps you understand, implement, improve, and maintain a trustworthy software development system. It is meant for organizations that are led by visionary leaders who understand and value such user needs and who are ready to lead their organizations to develop such robust capability. Although we have emphasized enterprise software, this book can be used by any organization in which software development is an important activity for developing proprietary software, providing internal software support, or imparting outsourcing vendor service. Organizations can use it for formal DFTS black belt, master black belt, and other certifications. Such formal certification can greatly enhance organization-wide DFTS learning and deployment. This book can also be used as a practical reference by software developers as well as quality professionals and senior management, who play a crucial role in such organizations.

This book is equally useful for students of software development technology, MIS, product design and development, operations, quality management, and technology management, at both undergraduate and graduate levels. It particularly complements Master of Science programs in engineering, MIS, IT, and computer science, as well as MBA programs that focus on operations, product development, and technology. It also is a useful resource for the American Society for Quality's (ASQ's) Certified Software Quality Engineer (CSQE) examination.

This book contains examples, sidebars, and case studies. It is supported by key points, review questions, discussion questions, projects, exercises, and problems. It is further supported by additional learning material on the Internet to provide intensive and continually updated material for learning in corporate settings or classrooms or for self-study.

The book is not a "handbook" in the classic sense. Instead, it is an exposition of the principles and practices involved in several proven quality methodologies that interact well and that are suitable for software development. They are particularly applicable at design time, before implementation begins. Smaller software and other engineering design case studies and examples are presented throughout the book to illustrate the application of the principles. Software architects will find examples that support their design concepts. Software engineers will find examples that support building in quality at the detailed design stage. Although all the DFTS techniques are applicable throughout the development process, the emphasis changes as a product goes from end-user need to concept, architecture, engineering design, implementation, testing, and finally support in the field. All five parts deal with relevant leadership and management infrastructure for successful learning and deployment of DFTS technology.

How This Book Is Organized

The book is organized into five parts. Part I, containing Chapters 1 through 5, presents contemporary software development practices, with their shortcomings and the challenges of and framework for developing trustworthy software. This is supported by chapter length treatment of two critical software quality issues, namely, *software quality metrics* and *financial perspectives on trustworthy software*. Part II, containing Chapters 6 through 14, presents the tools and techniques advocated by the authors for developing trustworthy software and is the primary focus of the book. Part III, containing Chapters 15 through 19, shows you how to apply these tools and techniques upstream in the design process before program implementation even begins. Part IV, containing Chapters 20 and 21, lays the groundwork for deploying a DFTS initiative in your organization. Like all quality initiatives, DFTS must be supported from the top to succeed and must become a part of the organization's "culture." Part V, containing Chapters 22 through 27, presents six major case studies of the software quality techniques presented in Parts I and II. We have sought out world-class practitioners of these techniques, and they have generously contributed their leading examples for your consideration and study.

Useful Software

You can benefit from using several software packages that facilitate learning and the deployment of quality methodologies such as AHP, Taguchi Methods, and QFD. A number of Web sites provide free limited-use/limited-time downloads. In particular, the following software is available:

- **AHP:** You can find a free 15-day trial version of Expert Choice at http://www.expertchoice.com/software/grouptrialreg.htm

  Special prices are available for students, instructors, and corporate bulk purchases. Call 1-888-259-6400 for pricing details.

- **QFD:** Modern Blitz QFD® templates for Microsoft Excel are included in QFD Institute training programs. Details are available at http://www.qfdi.org

- **Taguchi Methods:** Qualitek-4 DEMO software lets you review over 50 examples and use an L_8 array to design your own experiments. It can be downloaded from http://www.nutek-us.com/wp-q4w.html

  You may also want to visit the following Web sites that we found useful:
  http://www.nutek-us.com/wp-q4w-screen.html
  http://www.nutek-us.com/wp-q4w-eval.html

  You may try the DEMO version for experiments involving L_8 arrays. The full version may be negotiated with the vendors.

This Book's Web Site

This book's Web site keeps the book current between editions, providing new material, examples, and case studies for students and instructors. The Web site also provides materials for other users of this book—quality professionals and corporate leaders who play a crucial role in the DFTS process. The book's two websites are:

http://www.prenhallprofessional.com/title/0131872508

http://www.agilenty.com/publications

Instructors may contact the publisher for answers to the exercises and problems. We look forward to comments and feedback on how the material can be further enhanced and continually improved. Tell us about your experience, what you like about the book, how it has been useful, and, above all, how we can improve it. We trust that you will.

Bijay Jayaswal   Peter Patton
Minneapolis, MN   St. Paul, MN
bijay.jayaswal@agilenty.com   peter.patton@agilenty.com

Acknowledgments

We are indebted to many individuals who have contributed to the development of this book over the last few years.

We want to thank the reviewers and critics of various drafts:

Richard A. DeLyser, University of St. Thomas

Paul Holser

Steve Janiszewski, PS & J Software Six Sigma

Patrick L. Jarvis, University of St. Thomas

H. Richard Lawson, Lawson Software, Inc.

Bhabani Misra, University of St. Thomas

Richard D. Patton, Lawson Software, Inc.

German J. Pliego, University of St. Thomas

In particular, we would like to express our deepest gratitude to Prof. C. V. Ramamoorthy of the University of California, Berkeley for his wise and patient counsel throughout the last three years. This book would have been a very different product without his guidance.

We are grateful to two generations of scholars who have influenced our work. In particular, we would like to mention Yoji Akao, Genrich Altschuller, Philip Crosby, W. Edwards Deming, Eliyahu Goldratt, Hiroyuki Hirano, Kaoru Ishikawa, Joseph Juran, Shigeru Mizuno, Taichi Ohno, Stewart Pugh, Thomas L. Satty, Walter A. Shewhart, Shigeo Shingo, and Genichi Taguchi. We would also like to thank Barry W. Boehm, Maurice H. Halstead, and B. Kanchana, whose work we have cited extensively. The number of scholars are too numerous for us not to miss any. We acknowledge the work of all of them.

Numerous practitioners have inspired us too. We want to mention Craig Mundie of Microsoft Corporation, whose white paper on trustworthy computing triggered our own thought process on the formidable challenges of trustworthy software. We thank Craig for his work and friendship over the years. Two corporate titans we have never met or discussed our project with were inspirational to our work—the late Eiji Toyoda of Toyota Motor Corporation and Jack Welch, the former chairman of General Electric. Their work and able stewardship of two of the world's foremost corporations are great examples of leadership by quality. We have extensively quoted GE and Toyota in this book. We thank both of them.

We would like to express our gratitude to Glenn Mazur, Mike Jones of Expert Choice, Inc. and Ranjit Roy of Nutek, Inc. for software support for the book. We would like to thank Paul O'Mara and Alice Haley of ASQ, Linda Nicol and Linda Hart of Cambridge University Press, Peter O'Toole of GE, Tina B. Gordon of Johnson & Johnson, Michelle Thibodeau of Pearson Education, Lia Rojales of Productivity Press, and Richard Zultner of Zultner & Co. for permission to use relevant copyrighted material.

It is a great pleasure to express our great appreciation to the Prentice Hall team led by Bernard Goodwin, who is simply the best. He, Michelle Housley, Stephane Nakib, and Beth Wickenhiser were just wonderful. The project editor Andrew Beaster and copy editor Gayle Johnson have indeed done a superb job. A big thank you to all of them!

Finally, we would like to thank the contributing authors: Andrew Bolt, Jack Campanella, Ernest Forman of George Washington University, Herb Krasner of the University of Texas at Austin, Glenn Mazur of QFD Institute, and Richard Zultner of Zultner and Co. They have enriched the book with their contributions. We are forever indebted to them for their insight, wisdom, and generosity.

About the Authors

Bijay K. Jayaswal holds a B.Eng. (Hons.) degree in electrical engineering from the Birla Institute of Technology and Science, Pilani, India, and an MBA and a master's degree in electrical engineering from Aston University in England. He is the CEO of Agilenty Consulting Group, LLC. He has held senior executive positions and has consulted in quality and strategy for the last 25 years. His consulting and research interests include value engineering, process improvement, and product development. He has taught engineering and management at the University of Mauritius and California State University, Chico and has directed MBA and Advanced Management programs. He has helped introduce corporate-wide initiatives in reengineering, Six Sigma, and Design for Six Sigma and has worked with senior executive teams to implement such initiatives. He can be contacted at bijay.jayaswal@agilenty.com.

Dr. Peter C. Patton is Professor of Quantitative Methods and Computer Science at the University of St. Thomas, St. Paul, Minnesota. He also is Chairman of Agilenty Consulting Group. He has taught at the Universities of Minnesota, Paris, and Stuttgart and has held the position of Chief Information Officer at the University of Pennsylvania. He has engineering and mathematics degrees from Harvard, Kansas, and Stuttgart. He was Chief Technologist at Lawson Software from 1996 to 2002. He was Lawson's representative on the Technical Advisory Committee of IBM's SanFrancisco™ Java Framework project. He has been involved in computer hardware and software development since 1955. He can be contacted at peter.patton@agilenty.com.

PART I

Contemporary Software Development Process, Their Shortcomings, and the Challenge of Trustworthy Software

CHAPTER 1

Software Development Methodology Today

Cease dependence on inspection to achieve quality.
—W. Edwards Deming

Quality is a many-splendored thing, and every improvement of its attributes
is at once an advance and an advantage.
—C. V. Ramamoorthy

Overview

Both personal productivity and enterprise server software are routinely shipped to their users with defects, called *bugs* from the early days of computing. This error rate and its consequent failures in operation would not be tolerated for any manufactured or "hardware" product sold today. But software is not a manufactured product in the same sense as a mechanical device or household appliance, even a desktop computer. Since programming began as an intellectual and economic activity with the ENIAC in 1946, a great deal of attention has been given to making software programs as reliable as the computer hardware they run on. Unlike most manufactured goods, software undergoes continual redesign and upgrading in practice because the system component adapts the general-purpose computer to its varied and often-changing, special-purpose applications. As needs change, so must the software programs that were designed to meet them. A large body of technology has developed over the past 50 years to make software more reliable and hence trustworthy. This introductory chapter reviews the leading models for software development and proposes a robust software development model based on the best practices of the past, while incorporating the promise of more recent programming technology. The *Robust Software Development Model (RSDM)* recognizes that although software is designed and "engineered," it is not manufactured in the usual sense of that word. Furthermore, it recognizes an even stronger need in software development to address quality problems upstream, because that is where almost all software defects are introduced. *Design for Trustworthy Software (DFTS)* addresses the challenges of producing trustworthy software using a combination of the iterative *Robust Software Development Model, Software Design Optimization Engineering,* and *Object-Oriented Design Technology*.

Chapter Outline

- Software Development: The Need for a New Paradigm
- Software Development Strategies and Life-Cycle Models
- Software Process Improvement
- ADR Method
- Seven Components of the Robust Software Development Process
- Robust Software Development Model

- Key Points
- Additional Resources
- Internet Exercises
- Review Questions
- Discussion Questions and Projects
- Endnotes

Software Development: The Need for a New Paradigm

Computing has been the fastest-growing technology in human history. The performance of computing hardware has increased by more than a factor of 10^{10} (10,000 million times) since the commercial exploitation of the electronic technology developed for the ENIAC 50 years ago, first by Eckert and Mauchly Corp., later by IBM, and eventually by many others. In the same amount of time, programming performance, a highly labor-intensive activity, has increased by about 500 times. A productivity increase of this magnitude for a labor-intensive activity in only 50 years is truly amazing, but unfortunately it is dwarfed by productivity gains in hardware. It's further marred by low customer satisfaction resulting from high cost, low reliability, and unacceptable development delays. In addition, the incredible increase in available computer hardware cycles has forced a demand for more and better software. Much of the increase in programming productivity has, as you might expect, been due to increased automation in computer software production. Increased internal use of this enormous hardware largesse to offset shortcomings in software and "manware" have accounted for most of the gain. Programmers are not 500 times more productive today because they can program faster or better, but because they have more sophisticated tools such as compilers, operating systems, program development environments, and integrated development environments. They also employ more sophisticated organizational concepts in the cooperative development of programs and employ more sophisticated programming language constructs such as Object-Oriented Programming (OOP), class libraries, and object frameworks. The first automation tools developed in the 1950s by people such as Betty Holburton[1] at the Harvard Computation Laboratory (the sort-merge generator) and Mandalay Grems[2] at the Boeing Airplane Company (interpretive programming systems) have emerged again. Now they take the form of automatic program generation, round-tripping, and of course the ubiquitous Java Virtual Machine, itself an interpretive programming system.

Over the years, a number of rules of thumb or best practices have developed among enterprise software developers, both in-house and commercial or third-party vendors. Enterprise software is the set of programs that a firm, small or large, uses to run its business. It is usually conceded that it costs ten times as much to prepare (or "bulletproof") an enterprise application for the marketplace as it costs to get it running in the "lab." It costs another factor of 2 from that point to market a software package to the break-even point. The high cost of software development in both time and dollars, not to mention political or career costs (software development is often referred to as an "electropolitical" problem, and a high-risk project as a "death march"), has encouraged the rise of the third-party application software industry and its many vendors. Our experience with leading both in-house and third-party vendor enterprise software development indicates that the cost of maintaining a software system over its typical five-year life cycle is equal to its original development cost.

Each of the steps in the software life cycle, as shown in Figure 1.1, is supported by numerous methods and approaches, all well-documented by textbooks and taught in university and industrial courses. The steps are also supported by numerous consulting firms, each having a custom or proprietary methodology, and by practitioners well-trained in it. In spite of all of this experience supported by both computing and organizational technology, the question remains: "Why does software have bugs?" In the past two decades it has been popular to employ an analogy between hardware design and manufacture and software design and development. Software "engineering" has become a topic of intense interest in an effort to learn from the proven practices of hardware engineering—that is, how we might design and build bug-free software. After all, no reputable hardware manufacturer would ship products known to have flaws, yet software developers do this routinely. Why?

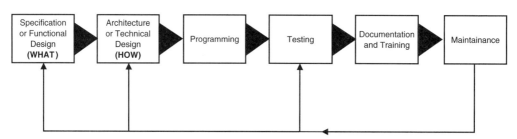

FIGURE 1.1
Essential Steps in the Traditional Enterprise Software Development Process

One response is that software is intrinsically more complex than hardware because it has more states, or modes of behavior. No machine has 1,000 operating modes, but any integrated enterprise business application system is likely to have 2,500 or more input forms. Software complexity is conventionally described as proportional to some factor—say, *N*—

depending on the type of program, times the number of inputs, I, multiplied by the number of outputs, O, to some power, P. Thus

software complexity $= N*I*O^P$

This can be thought of as increasing with the number of input parameters but growing exponentially with the number of output results.

Computers, controlled by software, naturally have more states—that is, they have larger performance envelopes than do other, essentially mechanical, systems. Thus, they are more complex.

Sidebar 1.1: Computer Complexity

When one of the authors of this book went from being an aircraft designer to a computer architect in 1967, he was confronted by the complexity of the then newly developing multiprocessor computer. At the time, Marshall McLuhan's book *Understanding Media* was a popular read. In it, this Canadian professor of English literature stated that a supersonic air transport plane is far simpler than a multiprocessor computer system. This was an amazing insight for a professor of English literature, but he was correct.

One of the authors of this book worked on the structural optimization of the *Concorde* and on a structural aspect of the swing-wing of the Boeing SST. In 1968 he was responsible for making the Univac 1108 function as a three-way multiprocessor. Every night at midnight he reported to the Univac test floor in Roseville, Minnesota, where he was assigned three 1108 mainframe computers. He connected the new multiprocessor CRT console he had designed and loaded a copy of the Exec 8 operating system modified for this new functionality. Ten times in a row the OS crashed at a different step of the bootstrap process. He began to wonder if this machine were a finite automaton after all. Of course it was, and the diverse halting points were a consequence of interrupt races, but he took much comfort from reading Marshall McLuhan. Today, highly parallel machines are commonplace in business, industry, and the scientific laboratory—and they are indeed far more complex than supersonic transport aircraft (none of which are still flying now that the *Concorde* has been taken out of service).

Although software engineering has become a popular subject of many books and is taught in many university computing curricula, we find the engineering/manufacturing metaphor to be a bit weak for software development. Most of a hardware product's potential problems become apparent in testing. Almost all of them can be corrected by tuning the hardware manufacturing process to reduce product and/or process variability. Software is different. Few potential problems can be detected in testing due to the complexity difference between software and hardware. None of them can be corrected by tuning the manufacturing process, because *software has no manufacturing process*! Making copies of eight CD-ROMs for shipment to the next customer along with a box of installation and user manuals offers little chance for fine-tuning and in any case introduces no variability. It is more like book publishing, in which you can at most slip an errata sheet into the misprinted book before shipping, or, in the case of software, an upgrade or fix-disk.

So, what is the solution? Our contention is that because errors in software are almost all created well upstream in the design process, and because software is all design and development, with no true manufacturing component, everything that can be done to create bug-free software must be done as far upstream in the design process as possible. Hence our advocacy of Taguchi Methods (see Chapters 2, 15, and 17) for robust software architecture. Software development is an immensely more taxing process than hardware development. Although there is no silver bullet, we contend that the Taguchi Methods described in the next chapter can be deployed as a key instrument in addressing software product quality upstream at the design stage. Processes are often described as having upstream activities such as design and downstream activities such as testing. This book advocates moving the quality-related aspects of development as far upstream in the development process as possible. The RSDM presented in this book provides a powerful framework to develop *trustworthy software* in a time- and cost-effective manner.

This introductory chapter is an overview of the software development situation today in the view of one of the authors. Although he has been developing both systems and applications software since 1957, no single individual's career can encompass the entire spectrum of software design and development possibilities. We have tried in this chapter to indicate when we are speaking from personal experience and sharing our personal opinions, and when we are referring to the experience of others.

Software Development Strategies and Life-Cycle Models

Here we will describe from a rather high altitude the various development methods and processes employed for software today. We focus on designing, creating, and maintaining large-scale enterprise application software, whether developed by vendors or in-house development teams. The creation and use of one-off and simple interface programs is no challenge. Developing huge operating systems such as Microsoft XP with millions of lines of code (LOC), or large, complex systems such as the FAA's Enroute System, bring very special problems of their own and are beyond the scope of this book. This is not to say that the methodology we propose for robust software architecture is not applicable; rather, we will not consider their applications here. The time-honored enterprise software development process generally follows these steps (as shown in Figure 1.1):

- Specification or functional design, done by system analysts in consort with the potential end users of the software to determine *why* to do this, *what* the application will do, and *for whom* it will do it.

- Architecture or technical design, done by system designers as the way to achieve the goals of the functional design using the computer systems available, or to be acquired, in the context of the enterprise as it now operates. This is *how* the system will function.

- Programming or implementation, done by computer programmers together with the system designers.

- Testing of new systems (or regression testing of modified systems) to ensure that the goals of the functional design and technical design are met.

- Documentation of the system, both intrinsically for its future maintainers, and extrinsically for its future users. For large systems this step may involve end-user training as well.

- Maintenance of the application system over its typical five-year life cycle, employing the design document now recrafted as the Technical Specification or System Maintenance Document.

This model and its variations, which we overview in this chapter, are largely software developer-focused rather than being truly customer-centric. They have traditionally attempted to address issues such as project cost and implementation overruns rather than customer satisfaction issues such as software reliability, dependability, availability, and upgradeability. It may also be pointed out that all these models follow the "design-test-design" approach. Quality assurance is thus based on fault detection rather than fault prevention, the central tenet of this book's approach. We will also discuss—in Chapters 2, 4, and 11 in particular—how the model that we propose takes a fault-prevention route that is based not only on customer specifications but also on meeting the totality of the user's needs and environment.

A software development model is an organized strategy for carrying out the steps in the life cycle of a software application program or system in a predictable, efficient, and repeatable way. Here we will begin with the primary time-honored models, of which there are many variants. These are the build-and-fix model, the waterfall model, the evolutionary model, the spiral model, and the iterative development model. Rapid prototyping and extreme programming are processes that have more recently augmented the waterfall model. The gradual acceptance of OOP over the past decade, together with its object frameworks and sophisticated integrated development environments, have been a boon to software developers and have encouraged new developments in automatic programming technology.

These life-cycle models and their many variations have been widely documented. So have current technology enhancements in various software development methods and process improvement models, such as the *Rational Unified Process (RUP)*, the *Capability Maturity Model (CMM)*, and the *ISO 9000-3 Guidelines*. Therefore, we will consider them only briefly. We will illustrate some of the opportunities we want to address using the RSDM within the overall framework of DFTS technology. It is not our purpose to catalog and compare existing software development technology in any detail. We only want to establish a general context for introducing a new approach.

Build-and-Fix Model

The *build-and-fix* model was adopted from an earlier and simpler age of hardware product development. Those of us who bought early Volkswagen automobiles in the 1950s and '60s remember it well. As new models were brought out and old models updated, the cars were sold apparently without benefit of testing, only to be tested by the customer. In every case, the vehicles were promptly and cheerfully repaired by the dealer at no cost to their owners, except for the inconvenience and occasional risk of a breakdown. This method clearly works, but it depends on having a faithful and patient customer set almost totally dependent on the use of your product! It is the same with software. A few well-known vendors are famous for their numerous free upgrades and the rapid proliferation of new versions. This always works best in a monopolistic or semimonopolistic environment, in which the customer has limited access to alternative vendors. Unfortunately in the build-and-fix approach, the product's overall quality is never really addressed, even though some of the development issues are ultimately corrected. Also, there is no way to feed back to the design process any proactive improvement approaches. Corrections are put back into the market as bug fixes, service packs, or upgrades as soon as possible as a means of marketing "damage control." Thus, little learning takes place within the development process. Because of this, build-and-fix is totally reactive and, by today's standards, is not really a development model at all. However, the model shown in Figure 1.2 is perhaps still the approach most widely used by software developers today, as many will readily, and somewhat shamefully, admit.

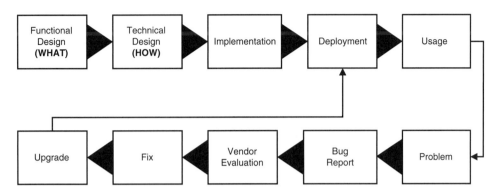

FIGURE 1.2
Build-and-Fix Software Development Model

Waterfall Model

The classic waterfall model was introduced in the 1970s by Win Royce at Lockheed. It is so named because it can be represented or graphically modeled as a cascade from establishing requirements, to design creation, to program implementation, to system test, to release to customer, as shown in Figure 1.3. It was a great step forward in software development as an engineering discipline. The figure also depicts the single-level feedback paths that were not part of the original model but that have been added to all subsequent improvements of the model; they are described here. The original waterfall model had little or no feedback between stages, just as water does not reverse or flow uphill in a cascade but is drawn ever downward by gravity. This method might work satisfactorily if design requirements could be perfectly addressed before flowing down to design creation, and if the design were perfect when program implementation began, and if the code were perfect before testing began, and if testing guaranteed that no bugs remained in the code before the users applied it, and of course if the users never changed their minds about requirements. Alas, none of these things is ever true. Some simple hardware products may be designed and manufactured this way, but this model has been unsatisfactory for software products because of the complexity issue. It is simply impossible to guarantee correctness of any program of more than about 169 lines of code by any process as rigorous as mathematical proof. Proving program functionality *a priori* was advantageous and useful in the early days of embedded computer control systems, when such programs were tiny, but today's multifunction cell phones may require a million lines of code or more!

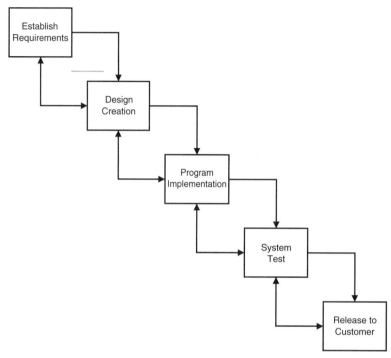

FIGURE 1.3
Waterfall Model for Software Development

Rapid Prototyping Model

Rapid prototyping has long been used in the development of one-off programs, based on the familiar model of the chemical engineer's pilot plant. More recently it has been used to prototype larger systems in two variants—the "throwaway" model and the "operational" model, which is really the incremental model to be discussed later. This development process produces a program that performs some essential or perhaps typical set of functions for the final product. A throwaway prototype approach is often used if the goal is to test the implementation method, language, or end-user acceptability. If this technology is completely viable, the prototype may become the basis of the final product development, but normally it is merely a vehicle to arrive at a completely secure functional specification, as shown in Figure 1.4. From that point on the process is very similar to the waterfall model. The major difference between this and the waterfall model is not just the creation of the operational prototype or functional subset; the essence is that it be done very quickly—hence the term *rapid* prototyping.[3]

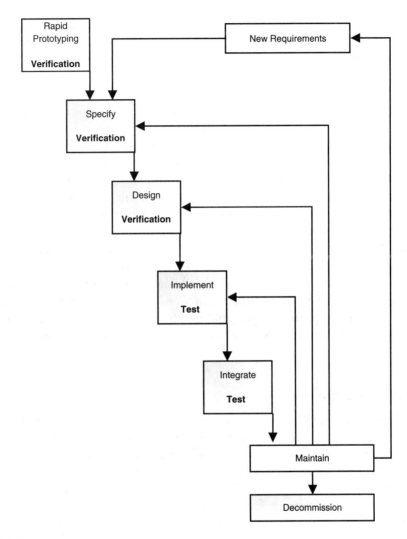

FIGURE 1.4
Rapid Prototyping Model

Incremental Model

The incremental model recognizes that software development steps are not discrete. Instead, Build 0 (a prototype) is improved and functionality is added until it becomes Build 1, which becomes Build 2, and so on. These builds are not the versions released to the public but are merely staged compilations of the developing system at a new level of functionality or completeness. As a major system nears completion, the project manager may schedule a new build every day at 5 p.m. Heaven help the programmer or team who does not have their module ready for the build or whose module causes compilation or regression testing to fail! As Figure 1.5 shows, the incremental model is a variant of the waterfall and rapid prototyping models. It is intended to deliver an operational-quality system at each build stage, but it does not yet complete the functional specification.[4] One of the biggest advantages of the incremental model is that it is flexible enough to respond to critical specification changes as development progresses. Another clear advantage is that analysts and developers can tackle smaller chunks of complexity. Psychologists teach the "rule of seven": the mind can think about only seven related things at once. Even the trained mind can juggle only so many details at once. Users and developers both learn from a new system's development process, and any model that allows them to incorporate this learning into the product is advantageous. The downside risk is, of course, that learning exceeds productivity and the development project becomes a research project exceeding time and budget or, worse, never delivers the product at all. Since almost every program to be developed is one that has never been written before, or hasn't been written by this particular team, research program syndrome occurs all too often. However, learning need not exceed productivity if the development team remains cognizant of risk and focused on customer requirements.

Extreme Programming

Extreme Programming (XP) is a rather recent development of the incremental model that puts the client in the driver's seat. Each feature or feature set of the final product envisioned by the client and the development team is individually scoped for cost and development time. The client then selects features that will be included in the next build (again, a build is an operational system at some level of functionally) based on a cost-benefit analysis. The major advantage of this approach for small to medium-size systems (10 to 100 man-years of effort) is that it works when the client's requirements are vague or continually change. This development model is distinguished by its flexibility because it can work in the face of a high degree of specification ambiguity on the user's part. As shown in Figure 1.6, this model is akin to repeated rapid prototyping, in which the goal is to get certain functionality in place for critical business reasons by a certain time and at a known cost.[5]

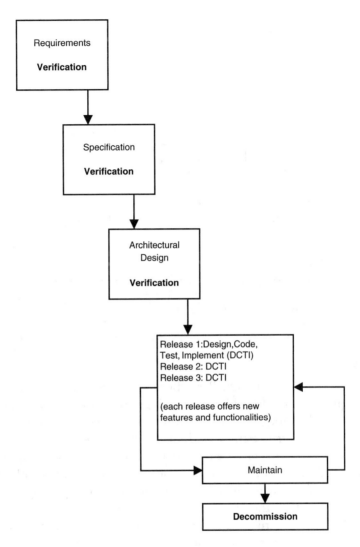

FIGURE 1.5
Incremental Model

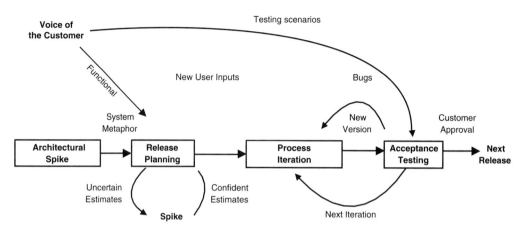

FIGURE 1.6
Extreme Programming Model

Adapted from Don Wells: www.extremeprogramming.org. Don Wells XP website gives an excellent overview of the XP development process. A more exhaustive treatment is given in Kent Beck. *Extreme Programming Explained* (Boston: Addison-Wesley, 2000)

Spiral Model

The spiral model, developed by Dr. Barry Boehm[6] at TRW, is an enhancement of the waterfall/rapid prototype model, with risk analysis preceding each phase of the cascade. You can imagine the rapid prototyping model drawn in the form of a spiral, as shown in Figure 1.7. This model has been successfully used for the internal development of large systems and is especially useful when software reuse is a goal and when specific quality objectives can be incorporated. It does depend on being able to accurately assess risks during development. This depends on controlling all factors and eliminating or at least minimizing exogenous influences. Like the other extensions of and improvements to the waterfall model, it adds feedback to earlier stages. This model has seen service in the development of major programming projects over a number of years, and is well documented in publications by Boehm and others.

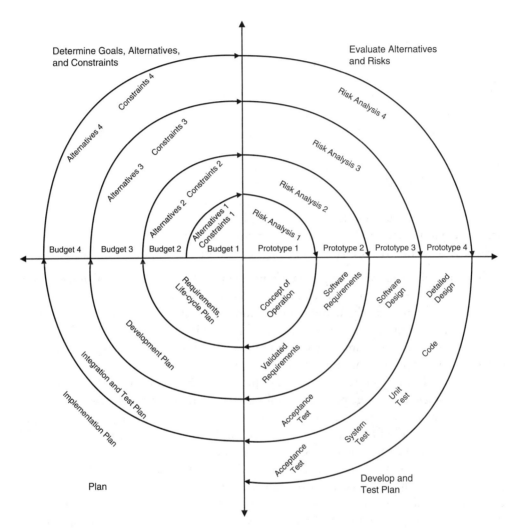

FIGURE 1.7
Spiral Model

Adapted from B. W. Boehm, "A Spiral Model of Software Development and Enhancement," *IEEE Computer*, 21 (May 1988), pp. 61–72.

Object-Oriented Programming

Object-Oriented Programming (OOP) technology is not a software development model. It is a new way of designing, writing, and documenting programs that came about after the development of early OOP languages such as C++ and Smalltalk. However, OOP does enhance the effectiveness of earlier software development models intended for procedural programming languages, because it allows the development of applications by slices rather than by layers. The central ideas of OOP are encapsulation and polymorphism, which dramatically reduce complexity and increase program reusability. We will give examples of these from our experience in later chapters. OOP has become a major development technology, especially since the wide acceptance of the Java programming language and Internet-based application programs. OOP analysis, design, and programming factor system functionality into objects, which include data and methods designed to achieve a specific, scope-limited set of tasks. The objects are implementations or instances of program classes, which are arranged into class hierarchies in which subclasses inherit properties (data and methods) from superclasses. The OOP model is well supported by both program development environments (PDEs) and more sophisticated team-oriented integrated development environments (IDEs), which encourage or at least enable automatic code generation.

OOP is a different style of programming than traditional procedural programming. Hence, it has given rise to a whole family of software development models. Here we will describe the popular Booch Round-Tripping model,[7] as shown in Figure 1.8. This model assumes a pair of coordinated tool sets—one for analysis and design and another for program development. For example, you can use the Uniform Modeling Language (UML) to graphically describe an application program or system as a class hierarchy. The UML can be fed to the IDE to produce a Java or C++ program, which consists of the housekeeping and control logic and a large number of stubs and skeleton programs. The various stub and skeleton programs can be coded to a greater or lesser extent to develop the program to a given level or "slice" of functionality. The code can be fed back or "round-tripped" to the UML processor to create a new graphical description of the system. Changes and additions can be made to the new UML description and a new program generated. This general process is not really new. The Texas Instruments TEF tool set and the Xcellerator tool set both allowed this same process with procedural COBOL programs. These tools proved their worth in the preparation for the Y2K crisis. A working COBOL application with two-digit year dates could be reverse-engineered to produce an accurate flowchart of the application (not as it was originally programmed, but as it was actually implemented and running). Then it could be modified at a high level to add four-digit year date capability. Finally, a new COBOL program could be generated, compiled, and tested. This older one-time reverse engineering is now built into the design feedback loop of the Booch Round-Trip OOP development model. It can be further supported with code generators that can create large amounts of code based on recurring design patterns.

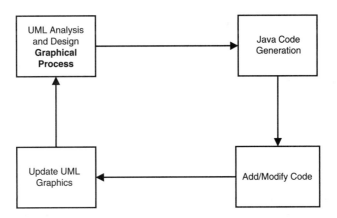

FIGURE 1.8
Round-Tripping Model

Iterative Development or Evolutionary Model

The iterative development model is the most realistic of the traditional software development models. Rather than being open-loop like build-and-fix or the original waterfall models, it has continuous feedback between each stage and the prior one. Occasionally it has feedback across several stages in well-developed versions, as illustrated in Figure 1.9. In its most effective applications, this model is used in an *incremental iterative* way. That is, applying feedback from the last stage back to the first stage results in each iteration's producing a useable executable release of the software product. A lower feedback arrow indicates this feature, but the combined incremental iterative method schema is often drawn as a circle. It has been applied to both procedural and object-oriented program development.

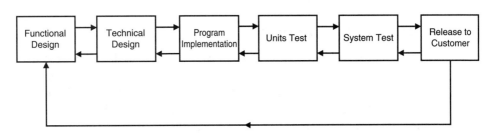

FIGURE 1.9
Iterative Model of Software Development

Comparison of Various Life-Cycle Models

Table 1.1 is a high-level comparison between software development models that we have gathered into groups or categories. Most are versions or enhancements of the waterfall model. The fundamental difference between the models is the amount of engineering documentation generated and used. Thus, a more "engineering-oriented" approach may have higher overhead but can support the development of larger systems with less risk and can support complex systems with long life cycles that include maintenance and extension requirements.

TABLE 1.1
Comparison of Traditional Software Development Models

Model	Pros	Cons
Build-and-fix	OK for small one-off programs	Useless for large programs
Waterfall	Disciplined, document-driven	Result may not satisfy client
Rapid prototyping	Guarantees client satisfaction	May not work for large applications
Extreme programming	Early return on software development	Has not yet been widely used
Spiral	Ultimate waterfall model	Large system in-house development only
Incremental	Promotes maintainability	Can degenerate to build-and-fix
OOP	Supported by IDE tools	May lack discipline
Iterative	Can be used by OOP	May allow overiteration

Software Process Improvement

Although the legacy models for software development just discussed are honored by time and are used extensively even today, they are surely not the latest thinking on this subject. We will describe only briefly RUP, CMM, and ISO 9000 software process improvement development models, because they will receive attention in later chapters. These are very different things but are considered here as a diverse set of technologies that are often "compared" by software development managers. RUP and CMM are the result of considerable government-sponsored academic research and industrial development. When rigorously applied, they yield good, even excellent, results. They also provide a documentation trail that eases the repair of any errors and bugs that do manage to slip through a tightly crafted process net. These newer methods are widely used by military and aerospace contractors who are required to build highly secure and reliable software for aircraft, naval vessels, and weapons systems. In our experience they have had relatively little impact on enterprise software development so far, whether internally or by way of third-party vendors.

Rational Unified Process

The Rational Unified Process (RUP) is modeled in two dimensions, rather than linearly or even circularly, as the previously described models are. The horizontal axis of Table 1.2 represents time, and the vertical axis represents logical groupings of core activities.[8]

TABLE 1.2
A Two-Dimensional Process Structure—Rational Unified Model

Workflow	Phase			
	Inception	Elaboration	Construction	Transition to Next Phase
Application model	Definition	Comparison	Clarification	Consensus
Requirements	Gathering	Evaluation	User review	Approval
Architecture	Analysis	Design	Implementation	Documentation
Test	Planning	Units test	System test	Regression testing
Deployment	User training	User planning	Site installation	User regression testing
Configuration management	Long-range planning	Change management	Detailed plan for evolution	Planning approvals
Project management	Statements of work	Contractor or team identification	Bidding and selection	Let contracts or budget internal teams
Environment	Hiring or relocation	Team building	Training	Certification

The Rational Model is characterized by a set of software best practices and the extensive application of use cases. A use case is a set of specified action sequences, including variant and error sequences, that a system or subsystem can perform interacting with outside actors.[9] The use cases are very effective at defining software functionality[10] and even planning to accommodate error or "noise." However, the RUP's most important advantage is its iterative process that allows changes in functional requirements also to be accommodated as they inevitably change during system development. Not only do external circumstances reflect changes to the design, but also the user's understanding of system functionality becomes clearer as that functionality develops. The RUP has been developing since 1995 and can claim well over 1,000 user organizations.

Capability Maturity Model

The Capability Maturity Model (CMM) for software development was developed by the Software Engineering Institute at Carnegie Mellon University. CMM is an organizational maturity model, not a specific technology model. Maturity involves continuous process improvement based on evaluation of iterative execution, gathering results, and analyzing metrics. As such, it has a very broad universe of application. The CMM is based on four principles:[11]

- Evolution (process improvement) is possible but takes time. The process view tells us that a process can be incrementally improved until the result of that process becomes adequately reliable.

- Process maturity has distinguishable stages. The five levels of the CMM are indicators of process maturity and capability and have proven effective for measuring process improvement.

- Evolution implies that some things must be done before others. Experience with CMM since 1987 has shown that organizations grow in maturity and capability in predictable ways.

- Maturity will erode unless it is sustained. Lasting changes require continued effort.

The five levels of the CMM, in order of developing maturity, are as follows:

- **Level 1** (Ad Hoc): Characterized by the development of software that works, even though no one really understands why. The team cannot reliably repeat past successes.

- **Level 2** (Repeatable): Characterized by requirements management, project planning, project tracking, quality assurance, configuration management.

- **Level 3** (Defined): Organization project focus and project definition, training program, integrated software management, software product engineering, intergroup coordination, peer reviews.

- **Level 4** (Managed): Quantitative process management, software quality management.

- **Level 5** (Optimizing): Defect prevention, technology change management, process change management.

Note that level 3 already seems to be higher than most software development organizations attain to, and would seem to be a very worthy goal for any development organization. However, the CMM has two levels of evolutionary competence/capability maturity above even this high-water mark. CMM as well as Capability Maturity Model Integration (CMMI) and PCMM (People Capability Maturity Model) have had enthusiastic acceptance among software developers in India. In 2000, the CMM was upgraded to CMMI. The Software Engineering Institute (SEI) no longer maintains the CMM model. IT firms in India accounted for 50 out of 74 CMM level 5-rated companies worldwide in 2003.[12] They are also leading in other quality management systems, such as Six Sigma, ISO 9001, ISO 14001, and BS 7799. It would seem that embracing a multitude of systems and models has helped software developers in India take a rapid lead in product and process improvement, *but still there is no silver bullet!*

ISO 9000-3 Software Development Guidance Standard

This guidance standard is a guideline for the application of standards to the development, supply, and maintenance of computer software. It is not a development model like RUP or even a organization developmental model like CMM. Neither is it a certification process. It is a guidance document that explains how ISO 9001 should be interpreted within the software industry (see Figure 1.10). It has been used since 1994, having been introduced as ISO 9001 Software Quality Management.[13] It was updated in 2002 as ISO 9000-3. Prudent compliance of ISO 9000-3 may result in the following benefits:

- Increases the likelihood of quality software products

- Gives you a competitive advantage over non-ISO 9000 certified development vendors

- Assures customers of the end product's quality

- Defines the phases, roles, and responsibilities of the software development process

- Measures the efficiency of the development process

- Gives structure to what is often a chaotic process

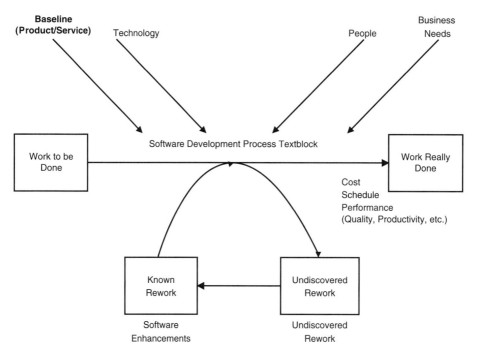

FIGURE 1.10
ISO 9000-3 Software Development Model

The document was designed as a checklist for the development, supply, and maintenance of software. It is not intended as a certification document, like other standards in the ISO 9000 series. Copies of the guideline can be ordered from the ISO in Switzerland. Also, many consulting firms have Web sites that present the ISO 9000-3 guidelines in a cogent, simplified, and accessible way.[14]

The Tickit process was created by the British Computer Society and the United Kingdom Department of Trade and Industry for actually certifying ISO 9000-3 software development.[15] This partnership has turned the ISO 9000-3 guideline standard into a compliance standard. It allows software vendors to be certified for upholding the ISO 9000-3 standard after passing the required audits. As with other ISO 9000 standards, there is a great deal of emphasis on management, organization, and process that we will not describe in this brief overview. Rather, we will emphasize the ISO development procedures that control software design and development. These include the use of life-cycle models to organize and create a suitable design method by reviewing past designs and considering what is appropriate for each new project. The following three sets of issues are addressed:

- Preparation of a software development plan to control:
  - Technical activities (design, coding, testing)
  - Managerial activities (supervision, review)
  - Design input (functional specs, customer needs)
  - Design output (design specs, procedures)
  - Design validation
  - Design verification
  - Design review
  - Design changes
- Development of procedures to control the following documents and data:
  - Specifications
  - Requirements
  - Communications
  - Descriptions
  - Procedures
  - Contracts
- Development of procedures to plan, monitor, and control the production, installation, and service processes for managing the following:
  - Software replication
  - Software release
  - Software installation
  - Develop software test plans (for unit and integration testing)
  - Perform software validation tests
  - Document testing procedures

Much of this sounds like common sense, and of course it is. The advantage of incorporating such best practices and conventional wisdom into a guidance standard is to encourage uniformity among software vendors worldwide and leveling of software buyers' expectations so that they are comfortable with purchasing and mixing certified vendors' products.

Comparison of RUP, CMM, and ISO 9000

A brief comparison of these process improvement systems is provided in Table 1.3. Such a comparison is a bit awkward, like comparing apples and oranges, but apples and oranges are both fruit. In our experience, software development managers often ask each other, "Are you using RUP, CMM, or ISO 9000?" as if these were logically discrete alternatives, whereas they are three different things.

TABLE 1.3
Comparison of RUP, CMM, and ISO 9000

Method	Pros	Cons
RUP	Well supported by tools Supports OOP development More than 1,000 users	Expensive to maintain High training costs Used downstream with RSDM
CMM	Sets very high goals Easy to initiate Hundreds of users	Completely process-oriented Requires long-term top management support
ISO 9000-3	Provides process guidelines Documentation facilitated Comprehensive, detailed	Some firms may seek to gain certification without process redesign

The RUP is very well supported by an extensive array of software development and process management tools. It supports the development of object-oriented programs. It is expensive to install and has a rather steep learning curve with high training costs but is well worth the time and cost to implement. RUP is estimated to be in use by well over 1,000 firms. Its usability with RSDM will be detailed later. The CMM sets very high ultimate goals but is easy to initiate. However, it does require a long-term commitment from top management to be effective over time and to be able to progress to maturity level 3 and beyond. It is estimated to have well over 400 users in the United States. As stated earlier, it is very popular in India, where the majority of CMM user firms are located. ISO 9000-3 was updated in 2002. It is essential for the development of third-party enterprise software to be sold and used in the EEC. A large number of consulting firms in both Europe and North America are dedicated to training, auditing, and compliance coaching for ISO 9000. Users report that it works quite well, although at first it appears to be merely institutionalized common sense. Perhaps the only downside is, because it is a required certification, some firms may just try to get the certification without really redesigning software development processes to conform to the guidelines.

Table 21.4 in Chapter 21 compares different quality systems currently common in software companies. These systems serve different needs and can coexist. The need for integration is discussed in Chapter 21 (see Case Study 21.1) and Chapter 27.

ADR Method

ADR stands for assembly (A), disassembly (D), and reassembly (R)—the major aspects of component-based software development.[16] Software components in enterprise systems are fairly large functional units that manage the creation and processing of a *form*, which usually corresponds to an actual business form in its electronic instance. For example, a general ledger (GL) system may consist of 170 components, some 12 or more of which must be used to create a general ledger for a firm from scratch. Each component in the GL application corresponds to an *accounting* function that the application is designed to perform. This approach arose in the early days of 4GL (Fourth-Generation Language) software development and has continued to be popular into the OOP era. OOP components tend to be somewhat smaller than 4GL components due to the class factoring process that naturally accompanies Object-Oriented Analysis and Design. In the cited paper,[16] Professor Ramamoorthy describes the evolution of software quality models and generalizes and classifies them.

Seven Components of the Robust Software Development Process

Software has become an increasingly indispensable element of a wide range of military, industrial, and business applications. But it is often characterized by high costs, low reliability, and unacceptable delays. Often, they are downright unacceptable (see Sidebar 1.2). Software life-cycle costs (LCC) typically far exceed the hardware costs. Low software quality has a direct impact on cost. Some 40% of software development cost is spent testing to remove errors and to ensure high quality, and 80 to 90% of the software LCC goes to fix, adapt, and expand the delivered program to meet users' unanticipated, changing, or growing needs.[17] While the software costs far exceed hardware costs, the corresponding frequency of failure rate between software and hardware could be as high as 100:1. This ratio can be even higher for more advanced microprocessor-based systems.[18] Clearly, these are huge issues that cannot be addressed effectively by continuing to deploy traditional software development approaches.

It is well known that various quality issues are interrelated. Moreover, high costs and delays can be attributed to low software reliability.[18] Thus, it is conceivable that several objectives may be met with the correct strategic intervention. Quality has a great many useful attributes, and you must clearly understand the customer perspectives throughout the software life cycle. This helps you not only understand the changing user needs but also avoid cost escalation, delays, and unnecessary complexity. You need to deploy a multipronged strategy to address quality issues in large and complex software such as enterprise applications. The Seven Components of a Robust Software Development Process are shown in Figure 1.11. They are as follows:

1. A steadfast development process that can provide interaction with users by identifying their spoken and unspoken requirements throughout the software life cycle.

2. Provision for feedback and iteration between two or more development stages as needed.

3. An instrument to optimize design for reliability (or other attributes), cost, and cycle time at once at upstream stages. This particular activity, which addresses software product robustness, is one of the unique features of the RSDM, because other software development models do not.

4. Opportunity for the early return on investment that incremental development methods provide.

5. Step-wise development to build an application as needed and to provide adequate documentation.

6. Provision for risk analyses at various stages.

7. Capability to provide for object-oriented development.

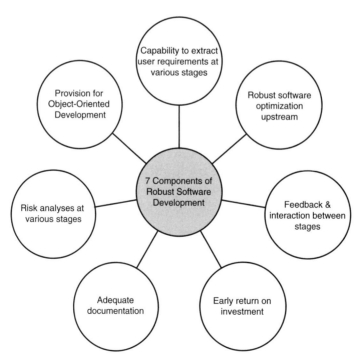

FIGURE 1.11
Seven Components of the Robust Software Development Process

Robust Software Development Model

Our proposed model for software development is based on DFTS technology, as shown in Figure 2.6 in Chapter 2. DFTS technology consists of Robust Software Development Model, Software Design Optimization Engineering, and Object-Oriented Design Technology. As you will soon see, it is a more elaborate combined form of the cascade and iterative models with feedback at every level. In fact, it attempts to incorporate the best practices and features from various development methodologies and collectively provides for a customer-focused robust software technology. It is intended to meet all seven key requirements for a robust software architecture development method just identified. Although Taguchi Methods have been applied to upstream software design in a few cases,[19, 20] there is not yet an extensive body of literature devoted to this area.

The primary focus of this book is to explain this model in the context of robust software design and to show you how you can use it for DFTS. The purpose of this book is to give you a map for robust software design from the hardware design arena to that of software design and development. We will also establish a context for methodologies such as Taguchi Methods and Quality Function Deployment (QFD) in the software arena. We will show you how they can be used as the upstream architectural design process for some of the established software quality models using Professor Ramamoorthy's taxonomy, as well as the software quality management processes that will allow the development organization using it to become a learning organization.

Sidebar 1.2: Mission-Critical Aircraft Control Software

The control computer of a Malaysian Airlines Boeing 777 seemed intent on crashing itself on a trip from Perth to Kuala Lumpur on August 1, 2005. According to *The Australian* newspaper, the Malaysian flight crew had to battle for control of the aircraft after a glitch occurred in the computerized control system. The plane was about an hour into the flight when it suddenly climbed 3,000 feet and almost stalled. The Australian Air Transport Safety Bureau report posted on its Web site said the pilot was able to disconnect the autopilot and lower the nose to prevent the stall, but the auto throttles refused to disengage. When the nose pitched down, they increased power.[a] Even pushing the throttles to idle didn't deter the silicon brains, and the plane pitched up again and climbed 2,000 feet the second time. The pilot flew back to Perth on manual, but the auto throttles wouldn't turn off. As he was landing, the primary flight display gave a false low airspeed warning, and the throttles jammed again. The display also warned of a nonexistent wind shear. Boeing spokesman Ken Morton said it was the only such problem ever experienced on the 777, but airlines have been told via an emergency directive to load an earlier software version just in case. The investigation is focusing on the air data

---

[a]http://www.atsb.gov.au/aviation/occurs/occurs_detail.cfm?ID=767

inertial data reference unit, which apparently supplied false acceleration figures to the primary flight computer.

More recently, a JetBlue Airbus 320 flight from Burbank, California to New York on September 21, 2005 attracted several hours of news coverage when the control software locked its front landing gear wheels at a 90-degree angle at takeoff. After dumping fuel for three hours, the plane landed without injuries at LAX. However, the front landing gear was destroyed in the process in a blaze of sparks and fire. An NTSB official called the problem common[b]. A Canadian study issued last year reported 67 nose wheel incidents with Airbus 319, 320, and 321 models. The NTSB official leading the investigation said that "If we find a pattern, we will certainly do something." (From the *Los Angeles Times*, September 22, 2005)

Software failures in aircraft control systems are likely to incur a much higher social and economic cost than an error in a client's invoice, or even an inventory mistake. Unfortunately they are much harder to find and correct as well.

---

[b]http://www.airweb.faa.gov/Regulatory_and_Guidance_Library/rgad.nsf/0/25F9233FE09B613F8625706 C005D0C53?OpenDocument

Key Points

- In spite of 50 years of software development methodology and process improvement, we need a new paradigm to develop increasingly complex software systems.

- Productivity gains in software development have not kept up with the performance increases in hardware. New hardware technology enables and encourages new applications, which require much larger and more complex programs.

- Perhaps a dozen models of software development aim to improve development productivity and/or enhance quality. They all work reasonably well when faithfully and diligently applied.

- The Department of Defense has sponsored a number of software development process improvement initiatives as a leader in the use of sophisticated computer applications and dedicated or embedded applications.

- The Design for Trustworthy Software (DFTS) technology addresses challenges of producing trustworthy software using a combination of the iterative Robust Software Development Model, Software Design Optimization Engineering, and Object-Oriented Design Technology.

Additional Resources

http://www.prenhallprofessional.com/title/0131872508

http://www.agilenty.com/publications

Internet Exercises

1. Search the Internet for U.S., Canadian, and Australian government reports on failure in aircraft control software. Is this problem getting better or worse?

2. Search the Internet for sites dedicated to the Rational Unified Process. How would you present an argument to your management to employ this process for software development in your own organization?

3. Look at the CMM site at the Software Development Institute. Can you see how this complex model could be applied in your organization?

4. What is the current status of the ISO 9000-3 Software Development Model, and what firms are supporting its use by software developers?

Review Questions

1. The CEO of the company for which you are MIS director asks why the new enterprise software for which he paid millions still has bugs. What do you tell him?

2. Which software development model does your organization or an organization you are familiar with employ? Do you consider it successful? If not, what does it lack, and where does it fail?

3. If a computer program is algorithmically similar to a mathematical theorem, why can't the person who designed it prove it will work properly before it is run?

4. How is object-oriented programming fundamentally different from earlier procedural programming technology? What promise do these differences hold for future software trustworthiness?

Discussion Questions and Projects

1. Create a table that shows the benefits and costs of using RUP, CMM, and ISO 9000-3 development models in terms of the size of the programs an organization develops and the number it completes per year.

2. Does your organization's software development process fit into the table you just created? If so, estimate the one-time costs and continuing costs of introducing the new model. Also estimate the benefits, long-term cost savings, and competitive advantages of using it.

Endnotes

[1] P. C. Patton, "The Development of the Idea of Computer Programming," QMCS White Paper 2003.3, St. Thomas University, June 2003, p. 4.

[2] Ibid, p. 6.

[3] S. R. Schach, *Object-Oriented and Classical Software Engineering* (Boston: McGraw-Hill, 2002), p. 71.

[4] Ibid, p. 73.

[5] K. Beck, "Embracing Change with Extreme Programming," *IEEE Computer*, 32 (October 1999), pp. 70–77.

[6] B. W. Boehm, "A Spiral Model of Software Development and Enhancement," *IEEE Computer*, 21 (May 1988), pp. 61–72.

[7] G. Booch, *Object-Oriented Analysis and Design with Applications*, 2nd Ed. (Menlo Park, CA: Addison-Wesley, 1994).

[8] P. Krutchen, *The Rational Unified Process* (Boston: Addison-Wesley, 2000), p. 23.

[9] J. Rumbaugh, I. Jacobson, G. Booch, *The Uniform Modeling Language* (Boston: Addison-Wesley, 1998).

[10] A. Cockburn, *Writing Effective Use Cases* (Boston: Addison-Wesley, 2001).

[11] K. M. Dymond, *A Guide to the CMM* (Annapolis, MD: Process Transition International, 2002), pp. 1–4.

[12] http://www.nasscom.org/artdisplay.asp?Art_id=3851

[13] M. G. Jenner, *Software Quality Management and ISO 9001* (New York: Wiley, 1995).

[14]http://www.praxiom.com/

[15]M. Callahan, *The Application of ISO 9000 to Software*, Team 7, 2002.

[16]C. V. Ramamoorthy, *Evolution and Evaluation of Software Quality Models*, Proceedings. 14th International Conference on Tools with Artificial Intelligence (ICTAI '02), 2002.

[17]W. Kuo, V. Rajendra Prasad, F. A. Tillman, Ching-Lai Wang. *Optimal Reliability Design* (Cambridge: Cambridge University Press, 2001), p. 5.

[18]D. Simmons, N. Ellis, H. W. Kuo. *Software Measurement: A Visualization Toolkit for Project Control and Process Improvement* (Englewood, NJ: Prentice-Hall, 1998).

[19]B. Kanchana, *Software Quality and Dependability Issues for the Airborne Surveillance Platform*, Doctoral Dissertation, Indian Institute of Science, Bangalore, India, Dec. 1998.

[20]G. Taguchi, S. Chowdhury, Yuin Wu, *Taguchi's Quality Engineering Handbook* (Boston: Jossey-Bass, 2004).

CHAPTER 2

The Challenge of Trustworthy Software: Robust Design in Software Context

Design products not to fail in the field; you will simultaneously reduce defectives in the factory.

—*Genichi Taguchi*

To improve is to change; to be perfect is to change often.

—*Winston Churchill*

Overview

A multifaceted view of quality is essential in identifying numerous requirements of customers and other stakeholders. There are remarkable similarities between quality issues pertaining to software and those of manufactured products, but important differences must be taken into account as well. The cost implications of poor software quality are becoming increasingly critical as the software life-cycle costs of a typical system exceed hardware costs. Improved software quality reduces costs dramatically, because 80 to 90% of costs go toward maintenance to fix, adapt, and expand the delivered software. Some 40% of software development cost today is incurred for testing to remove errors. Software reliability too is critical, because the software-to-hardware failure frequency rate could be 100:1, or even higher. This chapter discusses the fallacies of traditional quality systems in the context of delivering trustworthy software. It proposes an integrated software development technology, Design for Trustworthy Software (DFTS), based on three key elements: an iterative Robust Software Development Model, Software Design Optimization Engineering, and Object-Oriented Design Technology. DFTS focuses quality efforts on upstream phases of the development process; enables continual interaction with users and between associates in different phases; helps capture the voice of customers; and provides for early and continual risk analysis, design optimization, and use of appropriate software development technology. This chapter emphasizes the criticality of genuine management involvement for producing trustworthy software.

Chapter Outline

- Software Reliability: Myth and Reality

- Limitations of Traditional Quality Control Systems

- Japanese Quality Management Systems and the Taguchi Approach

- The Nitty-Gritty of Taguchi Methods for Robust Design

- The Challenge of Software Reliability: Design for Trustworthy Software

- A Robust Software Development Model: DFTS Process in Practice

- Key Points

- Additional Resources

- Internet Exercises

- Review Questions

- Discussion Questions and Projects

- Endnotes

Software Reliability: Myth and Reality

Quality is a multifaceted concept in software, just as in hardware. In fact, taking a multi-sided view of quality is essential to understanding and creating product value and to satisfy an assortment of stated and unstated customer requirements. The producer also has to meet the requirements of a multitude of other stakeholders, such as regulators, suppliers, trade associations, media, and other interest groups. Last, but not least, every producer has to ensure that its products are cost-effective and competitive to respond to the needs of the enterprise's owners. Quality encompasses all such needs and requirements.

One often hears that quality issues are different in software, but that has to be taken with a grain of salt. Generally, quality principles, systems, and methodologies applicable to manufactured products are equally valid in software, hardware, and other products and services. However, software products have their own design and development environments that must be understood. Furthermore, you must recognize the specific challenges associated with the discrete nature of digital systems and the complexities associated with many software products given the novelty and difficulties of the tasks they are often designed to handle.

We believe that for software enterprises, and in organizations where software development is an important activity, the issues of software architecture and design are central to the enterprises' long-term viability and success. In all such organizations, these tasks are too important to be left to software engineers only. The task of producing trustworthy software is truly challenging and calls for total management involvement. This book presents a philosophical base, a management system, and a technology for managing software quality in both large and small enterprises, with particular reference to enterprise software.

Similarities and Differences Between Software and Manufactured Products

Understanding similarities between software and manufactured products is essential in designing a robust software quality management system. Only then can you adapt systems and methodologies that have made such a remarkable contribution to improving quality of all kinds of manufactured products, as well as other products and services, over the last 50 years. Important differences, however, must be taken into account to develop valid software quality systems. The following are some pertinent issues:

- Software and manufactured products differ regarding the significance of various phases in their development process (see Figures 2.1 and 2.2). Software development is characterized by the centrality of design. Software is in fact a case of pure design in which all activities are design-related. Thus, its quality and reliability issues are always the result of design faults that are, in turn, the deficiencies often caused by some cognitive failure.

- In software, nothing is comparable to manufacturing and assembly, in which design lapses can be compensated for or even corrected. Essentially, software has no fabrication; the program code itself is but a further level of design. Furthermore, software has nothing like a product's "done and delivered." It can always be redesigned, modified, or upgraded and thus changed. This flexibility in software often breeds an attitude of "Let's deliver now; we can always fix it later."

- Unlike a manufactured product, software does not have any equivalent design analysis. Most analysis (testing) has to be done on program code. Hence, design problems or lapses may not be detected until late in the development process or during usage.

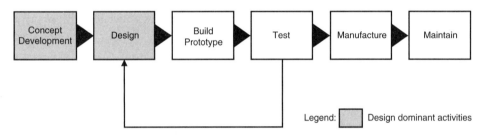

FIGURE 2.1
Basic Steps in the Development of Manufactured Goods

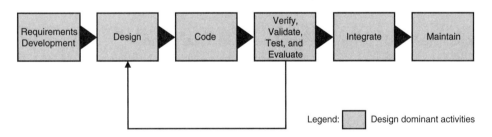

FIGURE 2.2
Basic Steps in Software Development

It may also be noted that today many hardware products are increasingly dependent on software for their functioning. These complex systems present another level of challenge for software design.

Comparing Software and Hardware Reliability

Hardware unreliability is dominated by random physical failure of individual components, which are often a consequence of the perversity of nature. Software, on the other hand, is characterized by the discrete behavior of digital systems. Hardware design and engineering knowledge are more easily documented to prevent failure than is the case in software. Furthermore, reliability theories for hardware have been developed over the years and have enabled very high reliability in manufactured products.[1] By comparison, very little knowledge base is available for software reliability—thus the inherent difficulty in software reliability assurance.

Software is always accompanied by hardware. However, when you know the reliability of the hardware component in the system, you can optimize the system's reliability by including only software components.[2] Any system consisting of software and hardware may fail due to the incapability of the software executed by external commands. A software failure is defined as a departure from the expected external result or as an output of the program that differs from the stated requirements. Software may fail when it is used in an unexpected situation. Generally, a failure may be caused by a software fault or by some other cause in a new user environment or an unanticipated usage condition. In other words, the program must be run for a failure to occur.

The current hardware/software system cost trend is approaching software domination disproportionately. A typical software life-cycle cost (LCC) exceeds hardware cost, with 80 to 90% of these costs going into software maintenance to fix, adapt, and expand the delivered program to meet the users' changing and growing needs. Some 40% of software development cost is spent on testing to remove errors and to ensure high quality.[3]

The software-to-hardware failure frequency could be as high as 100:1 for typical integrated-circuit computers.[4] For more complicated chips, it may be even higher and thus carries critical cost and quality imperatives. Table 2.1 summarizes the major differences in hardware and software reliability.

TABLE 2.1
Differences and Similarities Between Hardware and Software Reliability[5]

Category	Hardware Reliability	Software Reliability
Fundamental concept	Due to physical effects	Due to programmer errors (or program defects or faults)
Life-cycle causes		
Analysis	Incorrect customer understanding	Incorrect customer understanding
Feasibility	Incorrect user requirements	Incorrect user requirements
Design	Incorrect physical design	Incorrect program design
Development	Quality control problems	Incorrect program coding
Operation	Degradation and failure	Program errors (or remaining defects or faults)
Use effects		
Function of design		
Domains	Hardware wears out and then fails	Software does not wear out but fails from unknown defects or faults
Time relationships		
Math models	Physics of failure	Programmer skill
	Time (t)	Time and data
Time domain	Bathtub curve	Decreasing function
	Theory well-established and accepted	Theory well-established but not well-accepted
Functions	$R = f(\lambda,t)$, λ = failure rate	$R = f$(failure [or defects or faults], t)
	Exponential (constant λ)	
	Weibull (increasing λ)	
Data domain	No meaning	No agreement among the various time function models that have been proposed
		Failures = f(data tests)
Growth models	Several models exist	Several models exist
Metric	λ, MTBF (mean time between failures)	Failure rate, number of defects (or faults) detected or remaining
	MTTF (mean time to failure)	

Category	Hardware Reliability	Software Reliability
Growth application	Design, prediction	Prediction
Prediction techniques	Block diagram, fault trees	Path analysis (actual analysis of all paths is an unsolvable problem, because the number of possible dynamic paths for even simple programs can be shown to be infinite), complexity, simulation
Test and evaluation	Design and production acceptance	Design acceptance
Design	MIL-STD-781C (exponential) Other methods (nonexponential)	Path testing, simulation, error, seeding Bayesian
Operation	MIL-STD-781C	None
Use of redundancy Parallel	Can improve reliability	Need to consider common cause
Standby	Automatic error detection and correction, automatic fault detection and switching	Automatic error detection and correction, automatic audit software and software reinitializing
Majority logic	m-out-of-n	Impractical

[5]Reproduced with permission from W. Kuo, V. Rajendra Prasad, F. A. Tillman, and Ching-Lai Wang. *Optimal Reliability Design.* Cambridge University Press, Cambridge, 2001, section 13.5.1, p. 4.

Causes of Software Unreliability

Software reliability is a major societal issue. In fact, it is assuming global significance, and considerable resources are being committed to address it. The following are major causes of software unreliability:

- **Lack of management commitment:** The most common causes of quality problems are lack of management commitment, involvement, and support. Deming[6] once estimated that causes attributable to management comprised some 85% of the overall quality problems in an organization; he later revised that estimate upward to 94%. This is applicable to both software and manufactured goods.

- **Inadequate interaction with users:** The user environment and requirements are not properly understood. It is implied that the voice of customer should be sought and that their stated and unstated requirements are adequately understood and interpreted. Unfortunately, software development often entails little user involvement after specifications are written and agreed upon. This lack of ongoing interaction with the users and their changing and evolving requirements is not always recognized in the software development process. This is a major cause of software quality problems and must be addressed.

- **Increasing complexity:** Software systems are being called upon to handle increasingly difficult problems. Often, no equivalent manual solutions are available to help you understand the nature of the difficulty involved. Software empowers the designer to undertake unsurpassed levels of difficulty and to provide additional features and convenience that may or may not create bona fide value. Complex software systems used for automatic flight control, massive search engines, e-commerce, and global multicurrency fund-transfer management have no manual equivalents for comparison. Furthermore, such novel applications may have no prior experience to compare with. Both difficulty and novelty lead to complexity and consequent design and cognitive challenges, with resultant reliability, safety, and security challenges in software development.

- **Lack of agreed-upon criteria:** In novel complex systems, the developer often ends up setting reliability criteria that may or may not meet user requirements.

- **Competitive time pressure:** The competitive need for short development cycle time ("We can fix it later, but not deliver later") almost inevitably results in design and other faults. Very often, the time needed for comprehensive testing and debugging is just not made available.

- **Limited scope of automation:** Software development and usage are intensely human-interactive. Automation tools such as CASE and Object-Oriented Design have certainly helped but the scope of automation in software is limited compared to manufactured products.

- **Linkage with the Internet:** The increasing use and integration of software systems with the Internet makes the system vulnerable to accidental and malicious risks. Such risks can be enormous. They range from identity theft to massive financial fraud to national security threats.

- **Discrete behavior of digital systems:** Given the inherently discrete behavior of digital systems, it is difficult to provide quality assurance in a software product.

- **Lack of adequate incentives:** Often, there are inadequate market and regulatory incentives for software reliability, but there are plenty of inducements for innovative features, convenience of use, and rapid development cycle time.

Limitations of Traditional Quality Control Systems

Quality assurance practice has traditionally focused on downstream activities such as production and testing (see Figures 2.1 and 2.2). Such an approach may not result in an optimal design, even with a large number of repetitive design-prototype-test cycles that may essentially be a trial-and-error approach. This has consequent impact on cost, cycle time, and customer quality if the product is released for production without adequate performance characteristics. Very often this is the case because product managers run out of time and budget and have to release the design for production. Further downstream, products are inspected and screened to identify units that are not within specifications. Such units are repaired, recycled, or rejected. Such quality control systems are based on two basic premises:

- Customer requirements are met as long as the product is within the agreed-upon specification limits.

- Business implications of the product performance or quality being "barely within specification limits" and those of "right on target" are the same.

As you will see, none of these is a valid assumption. W. Edwards Deming[7] was among the first management thinkers to realize the inadequacy of a quality system depending on inspection. But it was the Japanese industrial engineer Genichi Taguchi who came up with an alternative quality management system known as Taguchi Methods. It emphasizes the value of "right on target" and the need to address quality effectively upstream at R&D, design, and engineering phases of the product development cycle, rather than depending on inspection to detect and correct faults.

Japanese Quality Management Systems and the Taguchi Approach

Taguchi Methods are a collection of design principles and methodologies aimed at improving product and process quality. These constitute a body of knowledge variously known as quality engineering, robust engineering, or, particularly in the United States, Taguchi Methods, after its exponent, Dr. Genichi Taguchi (see Sidebars 2.1, 2.2, and 2.3).

Sidebar 2.1: The Life and Times of Dr. Genichi Taguchi[8,9]

Dr. Genichi Taguchi has had a profound effect on the emergence of design-focused quality management methodologies. He was born in 1924 in Japan. After serving in the Astronomical Department of the Navigation Institute of the Imperial Japanese Navy in from 1942 to 1945, he worked in the Ministry of Public Health and Welfare and at the Institute of Statistical

Mathematics, Ministry of Education. He learned much about experimental design techniques and the use of orthogonal arrays from the prize-winning Japanese statistician Matosaburo Masuyama, whom he met while he was working at the Ministry of Public Health and Welfare. This also led to his early involvement as a consultant to Morinaga Pharmaceuticals and its parent company, Morinaga Seika.

In 1950 Taguchi joined the newly founded Electrical Communications Laboratory of the Nippon Telephone and Telegraph Company with the purpose of increasing the productivity of its R&D activities by training engineers in effective techniques. He stayed for more than 12 years, during which time he began to develop his methodology, which is now known as Taguchi Methods or robust engineering (see Sidebar 2.2). While working at the Electrical Communications Laboratory, he consulted widely in Japanese industry. Accordingly, Japanese companies began applying Taguchi Methods extensively from the early 1950s, including Toyota and its subsidiaries. Taguchi's first book, which introduced orthogonal arrays, was published in 1951.

In 1954 and 1955, Taguchi was a visiting professor at the Indian Statistical Institute in Calcutta (now named Kolkata), India. During this visit he met the famous statisticians Ronald A. Fisher and Walter A. Shewhart. In 1957 and 1958 he published the first version of his two-volume book *Design of Experiments*. His first visit to the United States was in 1962 as a visiting research associate at Princeton University, during which he visited AT&T Bell Laboratories. At Princeton, Taguchi was hosted by the eminent statistician John Tukey, who arranged for him to work with the industrial statisticians at Bell Laboratories. In 1962 Taguchi received a PhD from Kyushu University.

In 1964 Taguchi became a professor at Aoyama Gakuin University in Tokyo, a position he held until 1982. In 1966 Taguchi and several coauthors wrote *Management by Total Results*, which was translated into Chinese by Yuin Wu, his collaborator on a number of later publications. At this stage, Taguchi Methods were still essentially unknown in the West, although applications were taking place in Taiwan and India. In this period and throughout the 1970s, most applications of Taguchi Methods were on production processes; the shift to product design began later. In the early 1970s Taguchi developed the concept of Quality Loss Function. He published two other books in the 1970s and the third edition of *Design of Experiments*. By the late 1970s Taguchi had earned widespread recognition in Japan, having won the Deming Application Prize in 1960 and Deming awards for literature in 1951, 1953, and 1984.

In 1980 Taguchi was invited to the United States and arranged to revisit AT&T Bell Laboratories. Despite communication problems, successful experiments were run that established Taguchi Methods within Bell Laboratories. Following his 1980 visit to the United States, more and more American manufacturers implemented Taguchi's methodology. Despite an adverse reaction to the Taguchi Methods among a few American statisticians, possibly because of how they were being marketed, major U.S. companies became involved in Taguchi's methodology.

In 1982 Taguchi became an advisor at the Japanese Standards Association. He has received numerous recognitions for his contributions to industries worldwide:

- The Deming Prize on three separate occasions for his contributions to the field of quality engineering
- The Willard F. Rockwell Medal for combining engineering and statistical methods to achieve rapid improvements in cost and quality by optimizing product design and manufacturing processes
- The Shewhart Medal from the American Society for Quality Control
- The Blue Ribbon Award from the Emperor of Japan in 1990 for his contribution to industry
- Honorary membership in the American Society for Quality Control
- Induction into the Automotive Hall of Fame and the World Level of the Hall of Fame for Engineering, Science, and Technology

---

Sidebar 2.2: Quality Engineering Methodology at a Glance[8, 9]

Taguchi methodology is concerned with optimizing product and process at the design and R&D stages before manufacturing. It is a quality methodology applied at the early stages of product or process development, rather than focusing on achieving quality through inspection. This is an efficient technique involving design tests before entering the manufacturing, fabrication, or assembly phase. Quality thus becomes a function of sound design rather than of test and inspection, however rigorous. Taguchi's approach can also be used as a troubleshooting methodology to address production and process problems in manufacturing and increasingly in other industries, including software.

In contrast to the Western concept of quality, Taguchi methodology perceives quality in terms of *quality loss* rather than quality itself. *Quality loss* is defined as "loss imparted by the product to society from the time the product is shipped." This loss includes loss to the company through costs of reworking or scrapping, maintenance costs, and downtime due to equipment failure and warranty claims. It also includes costs to the customer through poor product performance and reliability, leading to further losses to the manufacturer as its market share falls. Taking a target value for the quality characteristic under consideration as the best possible value of this characteristic, Taguchi associates a simple quadratic loss function with deviations from this target. The quality loss function shows that a reduction in variability about the target leads to a decrease in loss and a subsequent increase in quality.

With this concept of quality loss, a loss will occur even when the product is within the allowed specification limits but is minimal when the product is on target. In real life, users do not care for product specifications—do they? All they want is for the product to perform even when the voltage is slow, the road is slippery, or the operator at the terminal is new on the job. The product must perform on target under varied user conditions. In other words, *design for variations in customer use*. It is in the producer's interest to attain product or process performance as close to target as economically possible. The loss function may be used to evaluate design decisions on a financial basis. It helps you decide whether additional costs in improving tolerance and production improvement are justified and whether they will actually prove worthwhile in the marketplace.

Taguchi Methods can be applied "offline" in design or "online" in production.

Taguchi breaks offline quality control into three stages:

1. **System Design** involves creating a design concept by using brainstorming, research, and other techniques. System design as a whole also includes other tools, techniques, and methodologies, particularly Analytic Hierarchy Process (AHP), Quality Function Deployment (QFD), Theory of Inventive Problem Solving (TRIZ), and Failure Modes and Effects Analysis (FMEA) (see Chapters 8, 11, 12, and 13, respectively).

2. **Parameter Design** is at the heart of Taguchi Methods. This is where the Japanese have traditionally excelled and have achieved high quality levels without an increase in costs—a major source of their competitive advantage. The nominal design features or process factor levels selected are tested. The combination of product parameter levels or process operating levels that are least sensitive to changes in environmental conditions and other uncontrollable (noise) factors are determined (see Chapters 16 and 17).

3. **Tolerance Design** applies to product or process design if the variation reduction from parameter design is insufficient. It tightens the tolerance further on factors shown to have a large impact on variation. Using the loss function, more money is spent *only if necessary*. You may tighten tolerance or buy better materials or equipment if necessary, which emphasizes the Japanese philosophy of invest last, not first, as has been the practice in the West.

Sidebar 2.3: Taguchi on Taguchi Methods[10]

- Quality losses result mainly from product failure after sale; product "robustness" is more a function of product design than of online control, however stringent, of manufacturing processes.

- Design products not to fail in the field; you will simultaneously reduce defectives in the factory.

- You gain virtually nothing in shipping product that just barely satisfies the corporate standard over a product that just fails. Get on target; don't just stay in-spec.

- Quality Engineering (Taguchi Methods) is a technology to forecast and prevent quality problems at the early stages of product development and product design, including the troubles associated with a product's function, pollution, and other costs that occur downstream in manufacturing and in the market place.

- Do not use customer-based quality measures (such as fraction of defects or reliability) as the upstream measure of quality in R&D. Instead, use the dynamic SN ratio as the performance index to evaluate the robustness of a product's function.

- Robust products deliver a strong "signal" regardless of external "noise" and with a minimum of internal "noise." Any strengthening of a design, that is, any marked increase in signal-to-noise ratios of component parts, will simultaneously improve the robustness of the product as a whole.

- Work consistently to achieve designs that can be produced consistently; demand consistently from the factory.

- Catastrophic stack-up is more likely from scattered variation within specifications than from consistent deviation outside. Where deviation from target is consistent, adjustment to the target is possible.

- Ambient conditions in the factory are rarely as damaging as variations in customer use.

Taguchi Methods have been hailed as being among the major engineering accomplishments of the 20th century. Although the statistical techniques employed by Taguchi have their origins in experimental design practices developed by the English statistician Sir Ronald Fisher, their philosophical underpinnings are unmistakably Japanese. Taguchi Methods and other Japanese quality management systems such as *Kaizen* (continuous improvement), *Kanban* (Just in Time), *Total Quality Control*, and *Lean Manufacturing* all were inspired by the teachings of American quality guru W. Edwards Deming, as propounded in his *14 Points for Management, Seven Deadly Diseases*, and *Obstacles to Quality Products*. (Richard Zultner's adaptations of Deming's principles to software development are presented in Chapter 5.) Taguchi Methods and other quality management systems provided the foundations for Japan's remarkable rise as an industrial power in the decades after the World War II.

Deming's impact on Taguchi's work can hardly be overestimated. Like other Japanese quality gurus, Taguchi was deeply influenced by Deming. To understand Taguchi's particular approach, it is important to examine its context and roots. Taguchi Methods and the modern Japanese quality systems all had their beginnings in the aftermath of World War II. Deming, often referred to as the father of the modern quality movement, first visited Japan in 1946. He continued to work with the Japanese government and industries during the next decades and trained thousands of Japanese managers and engineers. The Japanese managers were interested in contemporary American management principles. However, Deming offered them something totally innovative that he believed would help transform Japan into a prosperous society and rebuild it as a major industrial power.

The essence of Deming's management principles are well known (see Sidebar 2.4), although they are not as widely assimilated outside Japan. These principles include *voice of the customer, reduction of variation, use of statistical measures, winning the confidence and respect of coworkers*, and *continual improvement* in processes as well as in products and services. Deming's approach was enthusiastically studied and applied in Japan. It has had a profound impact on the Japanese industries. In 1951, the Japanese Union of Scientists and Engineers (JUSE) honored Deming by naming its prestigious quality award the Deming Prize. In the United States, however, Deming's theories were largely ignored for almost 30 years. It is widely believed that this might have led to loss of competitiveness in a score of American industries such as automobiles and consumer electronics, where Japanese corporations have made huge strides.

Sidebar 2.4: The Essence of Deming's 14 Points[11]

1. Create constancy of purpose toward improving products and services. The aim is to become competitive, to stay in business, and to provide jobs.

2. Management must awaken to the challenge of quality, must learn their responsibilities, and must take on leadership for change.

3. Cease dependence on inspection to achieve quality. Eliminate the need for inspection on a mass basis by building quality into the product in the first place.

4. End the practice of awarding business on the basis of price. Instead, minimize total cost. Move toward a single supplier for any one item, creating a long-term relationship of loyalty and trust.

5. Improve constantly and forever the system of production and service, to improve quality and productivity and thus constantly decrease costs.

6. Institute training on the job. If people are inadequately trained, they will not all work the same way, and this will introduce variation.

7. Institute leadership. Deming makes a distinction between leadership and mere supervision. The latter is quota- and target-based. The aim of supervision should be to help people, machines, and gadgets do a better job. Supervision of management is in need of overhaul, as well as supervision of production workers.

8. Drive out fear so that everyone may work effectively for the company.

9. Break down barriers between departments. People in research, design, sales, and production must work as a team to foresee problems of production and problems with usage that may be encountered with the product or service.

10. Eliminate slogans, exhortations, and targets for the workforce that ask for zero defects and new levels of productivity. Such exhortations only create adversarial relationships.

Most causes of low quality and low productivity belong to the system and thus are beyond the workforce's control.

11a.   Eliminate work standards (quotas) on the factory floor. Substitute leadership.

11b.   Eliminate management by objective. Eliminate management by numbers (numerical goals). Substitute leadership.

12a.   Remove barriers that rob the hourly workers of their right to pride of workmanship. The responsibility of supervisors must be changed from sheer numbers to quality.

12b.   Remove barriers that rob people in management and engineering of their right to pride of workmanship. This means, among other things, abolishing the annual merit rating and managing by objective.

13.   Institute a vigorous program of education and self-improvement.

14.   Put everybody in the company to work to accomplish the transformation. The transformation is everyone's job.

Much of Taguchi's work was inspired by Deming's 14 Points for Management—in particular the dictum *Cease dependence on inspection to achieve quality.* Taguchi took a step back in the product development process from emphasis on inspection to R&D, design, and engineering. He emphasized the value of a product's performing consistently and on target, rather than being merely within specifications. As illustrated in Figures 2.3, 2.4, and 2.5, this is achieved in two steps. First, you reduce the variability, and then you adjust an appropriate design factor to achieve the performance as close as possible to the target customer requirement, taking into account cost, design, and other constraints.

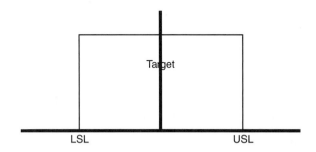

FIGURE 2.3
Performance Distribution Within Specification Limits but Inconsistent and Off Target

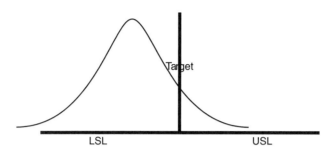

FIGURE 2.4
Performance Distribution Consistent but Off Target

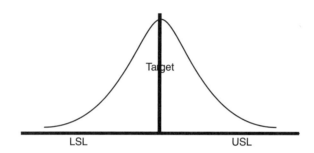

FIGURE 2.5
Performance Distribution Consistent and Around Target

Furthermore, Taguchi underscored the merit of making design robust against variability in both production and user environments. It will be useful to introduce here the major imperatives of the Taguchi quality philosophy:

1. *Continual quality improvements* and *cost reductions* are necessary for business survival.

2. An important measurement of product quality is the total loss generated by that product to society—the *quality loss function*.

3. Change the preproduction experimental procedure from varying one factor at a time to *varying many factors simultaneously*. (This is known as Statistical Design of Experiments [SDE] or simply Design of Experiments [DOE].) Thus, quality can be *built into* the product and the process.

4. The customer's loss due to poor quality is approximately proportional to the square of the deviation of the performance characteristic from its target or nominal value. Taguchi changes the objectives of the experiments and the definition of quality from *achieving conformance to specifications* to *achieving the target and minimizing the variability.*

5. Product (or service) performance variation can be reduced by examining the nonlinear effects of *control factors* (parameters) on its performance characteristics. Any deviation from a target leads to poor quality.

One of the major Taguchi objectives is to improve product and process design by identifying controllable factors and their settings, which minimize variation from a target response. By setting controllable factors to their optimal levels, a product can be made more robust to changes in operation, usage, and environmental conditions. A major element of Taguchi Methods is removing the bad effect of the cause rather than the cause of a bad effect. Thus, you obtain a higher-quality product at the lowest possible cost. This strategy of neutralizing just the effect rather than the cause is the smart thing to do, because it may be easier as well as more cost-effective and time-saving. The Taguchi Methods have two key design objectives:

- Reduce and minimize product and process variability and achieve the target economically.

- Ensure that the product robustness measured at the design and prototype stages is maintained downstream in the manufacturing and user environments.

The Nitty-Gritty of Taguchi Methods for Robust Design

Robustness is a key concept in Taguchi Methods. Being "robust" may mean healthy, hefty, vigorous, strong, sturdy, and stout. Taguchi defines robustness as "the state where the technology, product, or process performance is minimally sensitive to factors causing variability (either in the manufacturing or user's environment) at the lowest unit manufacturing cost." It is the capability of a product or process to perform and meet customer requirements (for reliability, safety, security, and so on) despite the presence of various noise factors that may cause variability. A robust process or product performs as intended regardless of any harmful factors, called noise, that may be present. Noise is caused by variations of various kinds: environmental variation during customer usage of the product, manufacturing variation of individual units and components, and component variation due to aging and deterioration.

The Concept of Signal-to-Noise Ratio

According to Taguchi, robustness should be addressed at the design and R&D stages. It implies a specific philosophical premise that true robustness can only be designed and built into a product or process rather than inspected and repaired. In other words, prevention—rather than cure—is its basic tenet. It also requires that quality problems be addressed upstream at the R&D, advanced engineering, and design stages, rather than during manufacturing and inspection, or, worse, after delivery to the customer. Taguchi Methods provide a cost- and time-efficient methodology to design and test products for robustness prior to manufacturing. These methods are also used for troubleshooting, redesigning defective processes, and problem solving of various kinds.

We will now define some basic terms used in Taguchi Methods:

Signal is what the product (or part or subassembly) is meant to deliver as its performance/functional characteristics. In a TV or phone, signals are what the product (TV or phone) delivers as picture or voice. A good signal is one that retains its quality despite noise (internal and external electromagnetic interference in a TV or phone).

Noise is all the various factors that cause variation. Taguchi recognized that many noise factors such as customer usage (the single most common cause of variability), road conditions, and weather cannot always be controlled or eliminated. Noise is what causes performance/functional characteristics to deviate from their target quality. In general, there are three types of noise factors:

- **Outer noise:** Also called *external noise* or *environmental noise*. This includes external/environmental factors such as thermal or electromechanical interference, mechanical/electrical shocks, dust, and customer abuse during product use. In the case of a car, these factors would include temperature, snow, road, driving conditions, dust, and so on.

- **Inner noise:** Also called component variation or internal deterioration of the parts due to wear and aging.

- **Between-product noise:** Also called *manufacturing variation* or *piece-to-piece variation* between various product units themselves, even though they are produced under the same manufacturing specifications. This may be due to tolerances in materials and processes.

Noise causes products to operate out of specification or to fail completely. Product performance is dominated by unit-to-unit (inner) noise in early phases of the product life cycle, external (outer) noise in midlife, and deterioration (between-product) noise at the end of life. Robustness and Robust Design imply lack of sensitivity to noise factors in different phases of the product life cycle, even though these noise factors may not have been eliminated, only their effects neutralized. In a TV, some common noise is "snow" on the screen, lightning, a storm, fluctuating voltages, and other "nasty" operating conditions.

In case of software, some key noise factors that cause variability are erratic customer usage, attackers and hackers, worms and viruses, accidental and malicious security breaches, lack of documentation, inadequate training, procedural breakdown, unauthorized access and use, and subjecting the system to uses that it was not designed for.

Taguchi suggests that **signal-to-noise (SN) ratio** be used as a measure of quality.[12] He argues that SN ratio

- May be used to evaluate the robustness of a product's function as it represents functionality.

- Represents the ratio of sensitivity (or "average" in nondynamic terminology) to variability.

- When applied to evaluate the robustness of a product or process is referred to as transformability (into energy, power, information, image, data, and so on).

For example, in an electromechanical device such as an electric motor, the SN ratio can be expressed as follows:

$$S/N = \frac{\text{Electrical energy conversion to meet desired mechanical function}}{\text{Energy conversion resulting into unintended wasteful functions}}$$

$$= \frac{\text{Energy conversion into useful torque}}{\text{Energy conversion resulting in wasteful heat, sparks, vibrations, screech, etc.}}$$

In general, SN ratio in an engineering system such as a motor or generator can be expressed as follows:

$$S/N = \frac{\text{Energy transformation into desired output functions}}{\text{Energy transformation into undesired output functions}}$$

For software, it's transformation of information, data, images, and so on instead of energy/power. Robust Design in both software and hardware attempts to maximize the SN ratio for optimal design.

The Concept of Quality Loss Function

As stated earlier, this concept is a major departure from the Western approach to quality. Taguchi addresses loss of quality, rather than the quality itself, and the implications of such loss to the customer, producer, and society at large. It is clearly implied that product quality incorporates more than reliability and that product cost incorporates more than just manufacturing and bill of materials costs. The customers expect reliability throughout the product life cycle, and cost optimization for the product life cycle is what matters eventually. Customers are increasingly demanding failure-proof delivery and performance. They expect various additional functional and convenience features. Finally, they are increasingly seeking consistent, high-quality, "on-target" performance, rather than accepting inconsistent performance within specifications. On-target performance may provide considerable cost and performance advantages for both the producer and customer. This constitutes one of the fundamental tenets of the Taguchi methodologies.

Fowlkes and Creveling classify the life-cycle cost with respect to the following: [13]

- Cost of goods includes bill of materials and manufacturing costs.

- Costs associated with maintenance support, warranty, repair, replacement, scrap, and recycling.

- Customer costs include downtime, operating cost, and troubleshooting.

- Marketing costs include time to market, sales campaigns, incentives, and customer retention and replacement.

Quality loss is defined as "loss imparted by the product to society from the time the product is shipped." This includes the loss to the company through costs of reworking, scrapping, maintenance, and downtime due to equipment failure and warranty claims. It also includes costs to the customer through poor product performance and reliability, leading to further losses to the manufacturer as its market share falls. There may be further loss to society if the product or service involves waste disposal, pollution, crime, safety, security, or health hazards.

Taking a target value for the quality characteristic under consideration as the best possible value of this characteristic, Taguchi associates a simple quadratic loss function with deviations from the target value. The quality loss function shows that a reduction in variability about the target leads to a decrease in loss and a subsequent increase in quality. This function is used for design decisions on financial grounds to decide whether additional costs of improved quality will actually prove worthwhile in the marketplace. To the producer, the total costs can be expressed as follows:

total costs incurred due to deviation from quality = factory loss + quality loss

Factory loss consists of scrap, rework, delay, and so on. Quality loss (QL) is the cost of product failure; it comes into the picture after products are shipped. It includes losses due to return, warranty, and repair, and loss of goodwill, resulting in loss of market share. QL can be huge even if the product is within specifications. It is 0 only if the product performance is exactly on target.

Taguchi provides a rough-and-ready estimate for the quality loss function (QLF):

$L = D^2C$, where

D = deviation from the target

C = cost of countermeasures to get the product performance on target

This expression is an approximation, not a "law of nature."[10] It is an engineer's tool, not a scientific law. It just implies that there is a "law of increasing costs" as the product performance deviates from the target. A general and accurate cost model is difficult to construct. One of the reasons for this difficulty is that a product may have different users and usage under differing environmental conditions. Taguchi suggests that individual corporations having better cost estimates may use those. But the preceding estimate of QLF is valuable as it is for the following practical purposes:

- It offers engineers and managers a simple cost estimate of deviation from target.

- It sets tolerance and quality targets that are based on such a cost estimate.

- It provides an estimation process for the optimal design that is time- and cost-effective. (In other words, the design process for a better product is cheaper and faster than that provided by traditional design of experiments and other methods.)

QLF and SN ratio are two measures of quality in Taguchi Methods. Both emphasize upstream/design activities, and both use customer measures such as dollar cost and performance/functional characteristics as evaluators of quality. As you will see in Chapters 16 and 17, they are related, and that provides a useful measurement in Taguchi methodologies.

The Concept of Robust Design

Taguchi recommends the following strategy for Robust Design:

- Use *orthogonal arrays* to conduct *offline* experiments. The orthogonal array is a matrix that is an integral part of Taguchi Methods. Analyzing a product or a process for robustness involves identifying the noise factors that cause deviations. This could be a tedious and costly exercise. Taguchi devised orthogonal arrays to isolate these noise factors from all others in a time- and cost-effective way. We will discuss their application in software development in Chapter 17.

- *Maximize performance measures and SN ratio* with respect to the control factors to optimize the design.

Robust Design using Taguchi Methods is carried out in the following three stages:

- **System design** has to do with developing a design concept or prototype. This is essential for the purpose of defining the initial product/process characteristics. It's essentially similar to system design practiced in the West.

- **Parameter design** is the crucial stage of Robust Design, in which the Japanese excel at achieving robust products at lower cost. It is essentially a methodology that reduces variation by reducing the performance sensitivity of a product or process design to the sources of variation rather than by trying to control or eliminate these sources. Here you test the nominal design features or the selected process factor levels and the combination of product parameter levels or process operating levels that are least sensitive to changes in environmental conditions and other uncontrollable (noise) factors. This is the heart of Taguchi Methods for Robust Design.

- **Tolerance design** is employed to reduce variation further, if required, by tightening the tolerance on factors shown to have a large impact on variation. Here you use the quality loss function to determine if the cost of enhanced quality is market-viable. Investments are made to improve tolerance by using better materials and equipment if required by the market, and not as the first resort.

Chapters 16 and 17 discuss the Taguchi methodologies and how they can be adapted to software development. Their applications in the downstream phases of software development are presented in Chapters 18 and 19.

The Challenge of Software Reliability: Design for Trustworthy Software

Software is the most treacherous component of any information system. The other two components, hardware and communications networks by themselves, have attained a far higher level of performance and reliability over the last 50 years. Microprocessor performance, for example, has increased by a factor of some 200 million times over software during this period. Modern communications networks provide means to move and access colossal volumes of data, images, and voice across an organization and globally. However, modern communications networks and especially the Internet have also created the potential for malicious and accidental accesses and other security vulnerabilities. But it is the design weaknesses in software that for the most part make information systems vulnerable and unreliable. Even while hardware performance has attained amazing performance levels, the ultimate promise of any information system depends on the dependability of its software—which is the subject of this book.

Table 2.2 describes some common software quality definitions and attributes. Software metrics are discussed in some detail in Chapter 3, but it will be helpful to identify a few basic concepts here. The most fundamental concept is the notion of quality itself. We define software quality as the degree to which a system, component, or process meets customer or user needs or expectations. This may have several components. of which software dependability is the most commonly cited deficiency. It encompasses various user requirements, including reliability, safety, security, and availability.[14] This is close to our concept of trustworthy software, except that for trustworthy software, we add and emphasize the capability of meeting *customer trust* and developing the *capability to meet their stated, unstated, and even unanticipated needs.* The five major challenges of trustworthy software are as follows:

- **Reliability** is the ability of software to perform its required functions under specified conditions for a specified time. It is essentially a software design quality and has to do with detecting errors rather than correcting errors.

- **Safety** refers to freedom from conditions that can cause death, injury, illness, damage to, loss of access to, or control over data, privacy, equipment, or property or environmental harm.

- **Security** pertains to the software's resilience to attack, thus providing protection of confidentiality, data integrity, and system availability.

- **Maintainability** refers to the ease with which a software system or component can be modified after delivery to correct faults, improve performance or other attributes, or adapt to a changed environment.

- **Customer responsiveness** is the ability of the software vendor to solicit, interpret, and respond to the preceding customer requirements. It also implies the possession of corresponding robust software design capabilities, the ability to train and transfer knowledge, the ability to help integrate existing systems, providing post-implementation support, the ability to provide upgradeable software and systems, and meeting the customers' cost and delivery schedule requirements. In particular, we emphasize the ability to meet *customer trust* and *meeting their stated, unstated, and even unanticipated needs.*

TABLE 2.2
Selected Software Quality Attributes

Quality and Quality Attributes and Systems	Description
Quality	The degree to which a system, component, or process meets (1) the customer's or user's stated, unstated, and unanticipated needs or expectations and (2) specified and implied requirements of other stakeholders.
Design for Six Sigma	A system to design and develop (new) products, processes, and services that meet customer requirements while being defect-free at the same time.
Design for Trustworthy Software (DFTS)	A system to design and develop software that is dependable (inclusive but not limited to reliability, safety, security, availability, and maintainability) and customer-responsive at various stages of the software life cycle.
Robust architecture (also called the Robust Software Development Model [RSDM])	A software development model for developing trustworthy software (see Figure 2.6).
Robust Design	A methodology developed by Genichi Taguchi to develop products and processes that perform on target as per customer requirements despite the presence of factors that cause variability in user and manufacturing environment at the lowest possible cost.
Six Sigma	A philosophy, system of management, and methodology deployed to improve (existing) product, process, and service performance that are defect-free and that meet customer requirements in a cost-effective manner.
Software	Computer programs, procedures, and (possibly) associated documentation and data pertaining to the operation of a computer system.
Software availability	The ability of the software to provide functions of a type when the user needs them. Often expressed as uptime/(uptime + downtime).

Quality and Quality Attributes and Systems	Description
Software capability	The degree to which a software vendor's systems, components, or processes can meet specified requirements and user needs and expectations.
Software dependability	Encompasses, among other attributes, reliability, safety, security, and availability.
Software design	Architecture and code of a software program to perform the required function.
Software maintainability	The ease with which the software system or component can be modified after delivery to correct faults, improve performance or other attributes, or adapt to a changed environment. Often expressed as MTBF/(MTBF + MTTR).
Software quality	The fitness of use of a software product. The degree to which a software product possesses a specified set of attributes necessary to fulfill stated or implied customer needs and satisfaction. (Program correctness is essential but insufficient if the software fails to satisfy the customer.)
Software quality attributes	Various requirements in software, such as reliability, safety, security, and availability, to fulfill stated or implied needs.
Software reliability	Essentially concerned with software design quality. Has to do with detecting errors rather than correcting errors. It is the ability of a software system or component to perform its required functions under specified conditions for a specified time.
Software safety	Freedom from conditions that can cause death, injury, illness, damage to or loss of access to and control over data, privacy, equipment, or property, or environmental harm.
Software scalability	The ability of a computer application to run on a larger machine or a parallel processor to handle a larger transaction volume or throughput in such a way that performance scales linearly or nearly linearly with volume. That is, if an application can handle a certain transaction volume on a given size of server, it should scale to handle four times that volume on a server that is four times larger.

TABLE 2.2
Continued

Quality and Quality Attributes and Systems	Description
Software security	The software's attributes pertaining to its resilience to attack, and providing protection of confidentiality, data integrity, and system availability.
Software transaction speed	The rate at which an application handles transactions on a given computer, usually measured in thousands of completed transactions per minute.
Software upgradeability	The ability of software to be easily reconfigured to handle more, larger, or more complex transactions.
Trustworthy computing	A hardware-software-network system that is dependable (inclusive but not limited to reliability, safety, security, availability, and maintainability) and customer-responsive at various stages of the system life cycle.
Trustworthy software	Software that is dependable (inclusive but not limited to reliability, safety, security, availability, and maintainability) and customer-responsive at various stages of its life cycle.

These are the primary aspects of trustworthy software, but they are required to varying degrees depending on the software category and its application. For example, *customer responsiveness* is a particularly critical element in enterprise software. The important point here is that the software maker knows and listens to the *voice of the customer (VOC)*, interprets it correctly, and can develop trustworthy software accordingly.

An observation on the use of the word trustworthy may be in order. In a quality management context, the word trustworthy was first used by Deming. He used it to mean a determining factor in supplier selection, in the context of "driving out fear" from employees. We found Deming's use of the word and its context profoundly meaningful for the message we ourselves wanted to convey: Trustworthy and dependable software, or, for that matter, any product and service, can be provided consistently only by people who are trustworthy. This word also was used in Microsoft's "Trustworthy Computing" (TWC) initiative launched in 2002. In his landmark memos of January and July 2002,[15] addressed to the company's 50,000 employees worldwide, Microsoft Chairman Bill Gates wrote, "In the past, we've made our software and services more compelling for users by adding new features and functionality, and by making our platform richly extensible ... we've done a terrific job at that, but all those great features won't matter unless customers trust our software. So now, when we face a choice between adding features and resolving security issues, we need to choose security." Gates further stated that he believed that TWC was "the highest priority for the company and for our industry over the next decade: building a Trustworthy Computing environment for customers that is as reliable as the electricity that powers our homes and businesses today." Making software as reliable as electricity is an enormous challenge to the software industry. There is a clear need for collaboration between the software industry, software professionals, software users, regulatory agencies, and research institutions worldwide. DFTS, proposed in this book, provides a coherent structure and technology for addressing these software quality issues.

A Robust Software Development Model: DFTS Process in Practice

Software, compared to other engineered products, is a case of pure design. As we have stated, software unreliability is always the result of design faults and human intellectual failures.[16] Therefore, it is even more critical that that is where the quality issues are addressed. The philosophy and systems proposed in this book provide an upstream methodology for software developers to identify optimal features and settings for robust (trustworthy) software. The elements of the system just discussed are depicted in our proposed Robust Software Development Model (RSDM) created to help develop trustworthy software (see Figure 2.6). It meets *the seven key requirements* of the Robust Software Development Process that we discussed in Chapter 1. It is based on sound management principles and proven tools, techniques, and methodologies characterized by the following key elements:

- An infrastructure providing required leadership and a communication, training, and reward system across the organization that is unambiguously supportive of the DFTS process (see Chapter 5).

- A reliable data collection system that can correctly identify user requirements (the VOC) on an iterative basis throughout the various phases of the software development cycle (see Chapter 11).

- Deployment of Taguchi Methods to optimize software design and addresses various customer requirements, such as reliability, cost, and cycle time at the same time (see Chapters 16 and 17).

- Establishing a concurrent coding and testing practice and providing for adequate debugging time. This strategy provides a cost- and time-efficient debugging process because information about software failure intensity or failure rate is more readily available at this time (see Chapter 18).

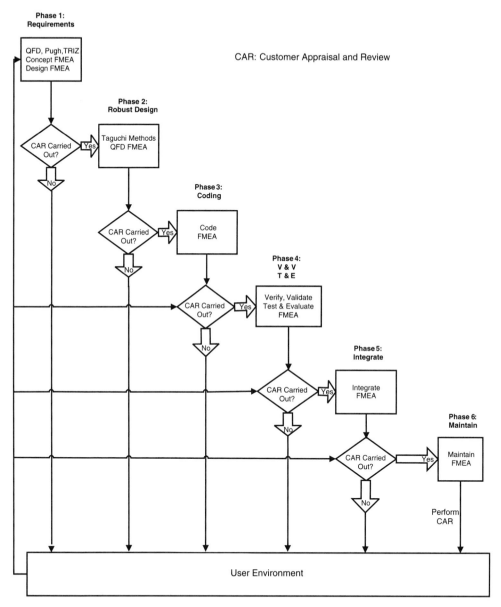

FIGURE 2.6
A Robust Software Development Model

- Using N-version programming[17] in case redundant software is required. This makes the failures of redundant copies statistically as independent as possible by applying different computer languages, development tools, development methodologies, and testing strategies to different redundant programs (see Chapter 14).

- Benchmarking best practices and deploying appropriate quality and planning tools such as QFD, TRIZ, Pugh, and FMEA, which have been used widely in manufacturing (see Chapters 11, 12, and 13, respectively).

- Using innovative software development tools such as Object-Oriented Design (OOD), Extreme Programming (XP), and appropriate CASE tools.

We will refer to the RSDM and DFTS process interchangeably: The model depicts the process, and the process is illustrated by the model. A number of software development models have evolved over the last few decades. Many of these, such as the Waterfall Model, Phased Life-Cycle Models, the Spiral Model, and the V-Model, have their origins in aerospace and other manufacturing industries and do not always reflect the realities of the software development process. RSDM is an iterative model and provides for interaction with internal as well as external customers and capturing VOC throughout the development process. Furthermore, it is robust and flexible and can be tailored for any software development process. The following chapters discuss the application of this model and its various elements, particularly in an enterprise software development context.

We would like to reiterate that in a software development organization or any enterprise where software technology is an important activity, software development is too important to be left to software engineers alone. It is ultimately the responsibility of the CEO and the top executive team. They must provide the required leadership, create the right management infrastructure, and foster the enabling environment for developing trustworthy software.

Key Points

- Taking a multisided view of quality is essential to understand and satisfy an assortment of stated and unstated customer requirements and those of other stakeholders.

- Generally, quality principles, systems, and methodologies applicable to manufactured products are equally valid in software. However, software products have their own design and development environments. The complexities associated with many software products must be understood, given the novelties and difficulties of the tasks they are often designed to handle.

- The task of producing trustworthy software is truly challenging and calls for genuine management involvement.

- Traditional quality control systems are based on two fallacies: First, customer requirements are met as long as the product is within the specification limits, and second, business implications of the quality being "barely within specification limits" and those of "right on target" are the same.

- Deming's 14 Points for Management for improving quality include listening to the voice of the customer, reduction of variation, use of statistical measures, winning the confidence and respect of coworkers, and continual improvements. He pointed out the inadequacy of a quality system depending on inspection.

- The Japanese industrial engineer Genichi Taguchi developed an alternative quality management system, Taguchi Methods. It emphasizes the value of "right on target" and addresses quality effectively upstream rather than depending on inspection to detect and correct faults downstream.

- The Taguchi quality philosophy can be summarized as follows:

  - Continual quality improvements and cost reductions are necessary for business survival.

  - An important measurement of quality is the total loss generated by that product to the society—the quality loss function.

  - Build quality into the product or process by design using Statistical Design of Experiments.

  - The customer's loss due to poor quality is nonlinear and can be approximately quantified as proportional to the square of the deviation of the performance characteristic from its target.

  - Product performance variation can be reduced by examining the nonlinear effects of "control factors" on performance characteristics.

- Robust Design using Taguchi Methods is carried out in three stages: System Design, Parameter Design, and Tolerance Design.

- Trustworthy software meets a variety of spoken and unspoken customer needs and must be customized. In an enterprise software context, a trustworthy software meets, at least, the following requirements: reliability, safety, security, maintainability, and customer responsiveness.

- The DFTS process is characterized by the following:

  - Genuine leadership commitment and a supportive infrastructure

- The ability to identify spoken and unspoken requirements using QFD

- Optimization of customer requirements deploying Taguchi Methods

- Establishing a concurrent coding and testing practice

- Use of redundant software if required

- Deploying appropriate quality and planning tools such as TRIZ, Pugh, and FMEA

- Use of innovative software development tools such as OOD

Additional Resources

http://www.prenhallprofessional.com/title/0131872508

http://www.agilenty.com/publications

Internet Exercises

http://www.asiusa.com/publications/images/HBR.pdf

After reading the article by Taguchi and Clausing on the preceding site, come to class prepared to discuss your conclusions.

1. Discuss the problems associated with the "in spec/out of spec" style of thinking associated with "Zero Defects" in software development contexts. What remedy does the Taguchi methodology offer?

2. Give three examples of "signals" and "noise" in the software development context.

3. Propose a set of recommendations to improve the software development process.

This article is also available from the following:

- Genichi Taguchi and Don Clausing, "Robust Quality," *Harvard Business Review*, January–February 1990.

- http://harvardbusinessonline.hbsp.harvard.edu/b01/en/common/item_detail. jhtml?id=90114&referral=8636&_requestid=9765

Review Questions

1. Describe how a multifaceted view of quality helps serve the needs of diverse stakeholders. Illustrate your answer with examples related to a software product you are familiar with.

2. Are quality issues in software fundamentally different from those of manufactured products? What are the similarities and differences between software and manufactured products with regard to their development process?

3. Compare and contrast software and hardware reliability. Explain their implications on three complex systems consisting of software and hardware.

4. List major causes of software unreliability. Which of these do you consider to be the most critical?

5. Describe the two major fallacies of traditional quality control systems and their implications for a software product.

6. Describe the essence of Deming's 14 Points for Management, and explain their relevance today.

7. Explain how Taguchi Methods relate to and support Deming's teachings as listed in the 14 Points.

8. What are the five philosophical imperatives of Taguchi philosophy? Explain their relevance to software development. Are they different for hardware? How?

9. Summarize the key concepts of Taguchi Methods and the three stages of Robust Design. Describe how they can support a software development process.

10. List and explain five major challenges of trustworthy software. Illustrate your answer with two specific software products you are familiar with.

11. Describe the features of the Robust Software Development Model. Explain how these and the model as a whole compare with two comparable models described in Chapter 1.

Discussion Questions and Projects

1. How do Deming's 14 Points for Management address the limitations of traditional quality control systems? You may also refer to Tables 5.2, 5.3, and 5.4 in Chapter 5. How might Deming's teachings be applied to a software enterprise? Present your answers to the class.

2. Discuss and contrast application of Taguchi methodologies in an enterprise software and in a manufactured product. You may refer to Chapters 16 through 19. Present your answers to the class.

3. Discuss the merits and challenges of introducing a Design for Trustworthy Software (DFTS) methodology in an organization. What are the possible sources of resistance in introducing it? How will you address them? Present your answers to the class.

4. Consider yourself a member of the top management team headed by the CEO. The team has been assigned by the board of a software development company to identify the major causes of software quality problems and to recommend a framework to address them. Write a memo to the board after your initial assessment. Present the memo to the class.

Endnotes

[1] Bev Littlewood and Lorenzo Strigini, "Software Reliability and Dependability: A Roadmap," Proc. ICSE 2000, the 22nd International Conference on Software Engineering, p. 2.

[2] W. Kuo, V. Rajendra Prasad, F. A. Tillman, Ching-Lai Wang, *Optimal Reliability Design* (Cambridge: Cambridge University Press, 2001), section 13.5.1, p. 325.

[3] Ibid. Section 1.3.3, p. 5.

[4] D. Simmons, N. Ellis, H. W. Kuo, *Software Measurement: A Visualization Toolkit for Project Control and Process Improvement* (Prentice-Hall, 1998).

[5] Adapted with permission. Op cit, Kuo et al., p. 4.

[6] N. Logothetis, *Managing for Total Quality* (London: Prentice-Hall International, 1992), p. 27.

[7] W. Edwards Deming, *Out of the Crisis* (Cambridge, MA: MIT Press, 2000). See in particular Point 3 of 14 Points for Management.

[8]http://www.asiusa.com/about/asi_thought_genichi.aspx

[9]http://www.dti.gov.uk/mbp/bpgt/m9ja00001/m9ja0000111.html

[10] Genichi Taguchi and Don Clausing, "Robust Quality," *Harvard Business Review*, January-February 1990, p. 68.

[11]Adapted from *Out of the Crisis* by Deming.

[12]Yuin Wu and Alan Wu, *Taguchi Methods for Robust Design* (New York: ASME, 2000), pp. 13–28.

[13]William Y. Fowlkes and Clyde M. Creveling, *Engineering Methods for Robust Product Design: Using Taguchi Methods in Technology and Product Development* (Reading, MA: Addison-Wesley, 1997).

[14]Op cit Littlewood and Strigini, p. 1.

[15]http://www.microsoft.com/mscorp/execmail/2002/07-18twc-print.asp

[16]Op cit Littlewood and Strigini, p. 2.

[17]N. Ashrafi, O. Berman, M. Cutler, "Optimal design of large software-systems using N-version programming," *IEEE Transactions on Reliability*, R-43 (2): 344-350, 1994.

CHAPTER 3

Software Quality Metrics

*Software cost overruns, schedule delays, and poor quality have been endemic
in the software industry for more than 50 years.*

—*Capers Jones*

The system is stable; let's just document the known problems.

—*Quality control manager of a tier-one application vendor*

Overview

A large body of literature has appeared over the past three or four decades on how developers can measure various aspects of software development and use, from the productivity of the programmers coding it to the satisfaction of the ultimate end users applying it to their business problems. Some metrics are broader than others. In any scientific measurement effort, you must balance the sensitivity and the selectivity of the measures employed. Here we are primarily concerned with the quality of the software end product as seen from the end user's point of view. Although much of the software metrics technology used in the past was applied downstream, the overall trend in the field is to push measurement methods and models back upstream to the design phase and even to measurement of the architecture itself. The issue in measuring software performance and quality is clearly its complexity as compared even to the computer hardware on which it runs. Managing complexity and finding significant surrogate indicators of program complexity must go beyond merely estimating the number of lines of code the program is expected to require.

Chapter Outline

- Measuring Software Quality
- Classic Software Quality Metrics
- Total Quality Management
- Generic Software Quality Measures
- Current Metrics and Models Technology
- New Metrics for Architectural Design and Assessment
- Common Architectural Design Problems

- Pattern Metrics in OOAD
- Key Points
- Additional Resources
- Internet Exercises
- Review Questions
- Discussion Questions and Projects
- Endnotes

Measuring Software Quality

Historically software quality metrics have been the measurement of exactly their opposite—that is, the frequency of software defects or bugs. The inference was, of course, that quality in software was the absence of bugs. So, for example, measures of error density per thousand lines of code discovered per year or per release were used. Lower values of these measures implied higher build or release quality. For example, a density of two bugs per 1,000 lines of code (LOC) discovered per year was considered pretty good, but this is a very long way from today's Six Sigma goals. We will start this chapter by reviewing some of the leading historical quality models and metrics to establish the state of the art in software metrics today and to develop a baseline on which we can build a true set of upstream quality metrics for robust software architecture. Perhaps at this point we should attempt to settle on a definition of *software architecture* as well. Most of the leading writers on this topic do not define their subject term, assuming that the reader will construct an intuitive working definition on the metaphor of computer architecture or even its earlier archetype, building architecture. And, of course, almost everyone does! There is no universally accepted definition of software architecture, but one that seems very promising has been proposed by Shaw and Garlan:

> Abstractly, software architecture involves the description of elements from which systems are built, interactions among those elements, patterns that guide their composition, and constraints on those patterns. In general, a particular system is defined in terms of a collection of components, and interactions among those components.[1]

This definition follows a straightforward inductive path from that of building architecture, through system architecture, through computer architecture, to software architecture. As you will see, the key word in this definition—for software, at least—is *patterns*. Having chosen a definition for software architecture, we are free to talk about measuring the quality of that architecture and ultimately its implementations in the form of running computer programs. But first, we will review some classical software quality metrics to see what we must surrender to establish a new metric order for software.

Classic Software Quality Metrics

Software quality is a multidimensional concept. The multiple professional views of product quality may be very different from popular or nonspecialist views. Moreover, they have levels of abstraction beyond even the viewpoints of the developer or user. Crosby, among many others, has defined software quality as conformance to specification.[2] However, very few end users will agree that a program that perfectly implements a flawed specification is a quality product. Of course, when we talk about software architecture, we are talking about a design stage well upstream from the program's specification. Years ago Juran[3] proposed a generic definition of quality. He said products must possess multiple elements of fitness for use. Two of his parameters of interest for software products were quality of design and quality of conformance. These separate design from implementation and may even accommodate the differing viewpoints of developer and user in each area.

Two leading firms that have placed a great deal of importance on software quality are IBM and Hewlett-Packard. IBM measures user satisfaction in eight dimensions for quality as well as overall user satisfaction: capability or functionality, usability, performance, reliability, installability, maintainability, documentation, and availability (see Table 3.1). Some of these factors conflict with each other, and some support each other. For example, usability and performance may conflict, as may reliability and capability or performance and capability. IBM has user evaluations down to a science. We recently participated in an IBM Middleware product study of only the usability dimension. It was five pages of questions plus a two-hour interview with a specialist consultant. Similarly, Hewlett-Packard uses five Juran quality parameters: functionality, usability, reliability, performance, and serviceability. Other computer and software vendor firms may use more or fewer quality parameters and may even weight them differently for different kinds of software or for the same software in different vertical markets. Some firms focus on process quality rather than product quality. Although it is true that a flawed process is unlikely to produce a quality product, our focus here is entirely on software product quality, from architectural conception to end use.

TABLE 3.1
IBM's Measures of User Satisfaction

	Capability	Usability	Performance	Reliability	Instability	Maintainability	Documentation	Availability
Capability								
Usability								
Performance	●	●						
Reliability	●	○	●					
Instability		○	○	○				
Maintainability	●	○	●	○				
Documentation	●	○				○		
Availability	●	○	○	○	○	○		

●: Conflict One Another

○: Support One Another

Blank: Not Related

Total Quality Management

The Naval Air Systems Command coined the term *Total Quality Management* (TQM) in 1985 to describe its approach to quality improvement, patterned after the Japanese-style management approach to quality improvement. Since then, TQM has taken on many meanings across the world. TQM methodology is based on the teachings of such quality gurus as Philip B. Crosby, W. Edwards Deming, Armand V. Feigenbaum, Kaoru Ishikawa, and Joseph M. Juran. Simply put, it is a management approach to long-term success that is attained through a focus on customer satisfaction. This approach requires the creation of a quality culture in the organization to improve processes, products, and services. In the 1980s and '90s, many quality gurus published specific methods for achieving TQM, and the method was applied in government, industry, and even research universities. The Malcolm Baldrige Award in the United States and the ISO 9000 standards are legacies of the TQM movement, as is the Software Engineering Institute's (SEI's) Capability Maturity Model (CMM), in which organizational maturity level 5 represents the highest level of quality capability.[4] In 2000, the SW-CMM was upgraded to Capability Maturity Model Integration (CMMI).

The implementation of TQM has many varieties, but the four essential characteristics of the TQM approach are as follows:

- **Customer focus:** The objective is to achieve total customer satisfaction—to "delight the customer." Customer focus includes studying customer needs and wants, gathering customer requirements, and measuring customer satisfaction.

- **Process improvement:** The objective is to reduce process variation and to achieve continuous process improvement of both business and product development processes.

- **Quality culture:** The objective is to create an organization-wide quality culture, including leadership, management commitment, total staff participation, and employee empowerment.

- **Measurement and analysis:** The objective is to drive continuous improvement in all quality parameters by a goal-oriented measurement system.

Total Quality Management made an enormous contribution to the development of enterprise applications software in the 1990s. Its introduction as an information technology initiative followed its successful application in manufacturing and service industries. It came to IT just in time for the redevelopment of all existing enterprise software for Y2K. The efforts of one of the authors to introduce TQM in the internal administrative services sector of research universities encountered token resistance from faculty oversight committees. They objected to the term "total" on the curious dogmatic grounds that nothing is really "total" in practice. As CIO, he attempted to explain TQM to a faculty IT oversight committee at the University of Pennsylvania that this name was merely a phrase to identify a commonly practiced worldwide methodology. But this didn't help much. However, he persevered with a new information architecture, followed by (totally!) reengineering *all* administrative processes using TQM "delight-the-customer" measures. He also designed a (totally) new information system to meet the university's needs in the post-Y2K world (which began in 1996 in higher education, when the class of 2000 enrolled and their student loans were set up).[5]

Generic Software Quality Measures

Metrics Methodology

In 1993 the IEEE published a standard for software quality metrics methodology that has since defined and led development in the field. Here we begin by summarizing this standard. It was intended as a more systematic approach for establishing quality requirements and identifying, implementing, analyzing, and validating software quality metrics for software system development. It spans the development cycle in five steps, as shown in Table 3.2.

TABLE 3.2
IEEE Software Quality Metrics Methodology

Software Quality Activity	Development Cycle Phasing
Establish software quality requirements	⎯⎯⎯
Identify software quality metrics	⎯⎯⎯
Implement software quality metrics	⎯⎯⎯⎯⎯⎯
Analyze results of these metrics	⎯⎯⎯⎯⎯
Validate the metrics	⎯⎯⎯

A typical "catalog" of metrics in current use will be discussed later. At this point we merely want to present a gestalt for the IEEE recommended methodology. In the first step it is important to establish direct metrics with values as numerical targets to be met in the final product. The factors to be measured may vary from product to product, but it is critical to rank the factors by priority and assign a direct metric value as a quantitative requirement for that factor. There is no mystery at this point, because Voice of the Customer (VOC) and Quality Function Deployment (QFD) are the means available not only to determine the metrics and their target values, but also to prioritize them.

The second step is to identify the software quality metrics by decomposing each factor into subfactors and those further into the metrics. For example, a direct final metric for the factor reliability could be faults per 1,000 lines of code (KLOC) with a target value—say, one fault per 1,000 lines of code (LOC). (This level of quality is just 4.59 Sigma; Six Sigma quality would be 3.4 faults per 1,000 KLOC or *one million lines of code*.) For each validated metric at the metric level, a value should be assigned that will be achieved during development. Table 3.3 gives the IEEE's suggested paradigm for a description of the metrics set.[6]

TABLE 3.3
IEEE Metric Set Description Paradigm[7]

Term	Description
Name	Name of the metric
Metric	Mathematical function to compute the metric
Cost	Cost of using the metric
Benefit	Benefit of using the metric
Impact	Can the metric be used to alter or stop the project?
Target value	Numerical value to be achieved to meet the requirement
Factors	Factors related to the metric
Tools	Tools to gather data, calculate the metric, and analyze the results
Application	How the metric is to be used
Data items	Input values needed to compute the metric
Computation	Steps involved in the computation
Interpretation	How to interpret the results of the computation
Considerations	Metric assumptions and appropriateness
Training	Training required to apply the metric
Example	An example of applying the metric
History	Projects that have used this metric and its validation history
References	List of projects used, project details, and so on

To implement the metrics in the metric set chosen for the project under design, the data to be collected must be determined, and assumptions about the flow of data must be clarified. Any tools to be employed are defined, and any organizations to be involved are described, as are any necessary training. It is also wise at this point to test the metrics on some known software to refine their use, sensitivity, accuracy, and the cost of employing them.

Analyzing the metrics can help you identify any components of the developing system that appear to have unacceptable quality or that present development bottlenecks. Any components whose measured values deviate from their target values are noncompliant.

Validation of the metrics is a continuous process spanning multiple projects. If the metrics employed are to be useful, they must accurately indicate whether quality requirements have been achieved or are likely to be achieved during development. Furthermore, a metric must be revalidated every time it is used. Confidence in a metric will improve over time as further usage experience is gained.

In-Process Quality Metrics for Software Testing

Until recently, most software quality metrics in many development organizations were of an in-process nature. That is, they were designed to track defect occurrences during formal machine testing. These are listed here only briefly because of their historical importance and because we will be replacing them with upstream quality measures and metrics that will supersede them.

Defect rate during formal system testing is usually highly correlated with the future defect rate in the field because higher-than-expected testing defect rates usually indicate high software complexity or special development problems. Although it may be counterintuitive, experience shows that higher defect rates in testing indicate higher defect rates later in use. If these appear, the development manager has a set of "damage control" scenarios he or she may apply to correct the quality problem in testing before it becomes a problem in the field.

Overall defect density during testing is only a gross indicator; the pattern of defect arrival or "mean time between defects" is a more sensitive metric. Naturally the development organization cannot fix all of the problems arriving today or this week, so a tertiary measure of *defect backlog* becomes important. If the defect backlog is large at the end of a development cycle, a lot of prerelease fixes have to be integrated into the system. This metric thus becomes not only a quality and workload statement but also a predictor of problems in the very near future.

Phase-based defect removal uses the defect removal effectiveness (DRE) metric. This is simply the defects removed during each development phase divided by the defects latent in the product, times 100 to get the result as a percentage. Because the number of latent defects is not yet known, it is estimated to be the defects removed during the phase plus the defects found later. This metric is best used before code integration (already well downstream in the development process, unfortunately) and for each succeeding phase. This simple metric has become a widely used tool for large application development. However, its ad hoc downstream nature naturally leads to the most important in-process metric as we include in-service defect fixes and maintenance in the development process.

Four new metrics can be introduced to measure quality after the software has been delivered:

- Fix the backlog and the backlog management index (BMI)
- Fix the response time and responsiveness
- Percentage of delinquent fixes
- Fix quality (that is, did it really get fixed?)

These metrics are not rocket science. The monthly BMI as a percent is simply 100 times the number of problem arrivals during the month divided by the number of problems closed during the month. Fix responsiveness is the mean time of all problems from their arrival to their close. If for a given problem the turnaround time exceeds the required or standard response time, it is declared delinquent. The percentage of delinquent fixes is 100 times the number that did not get fixed in time divided by the number that did. Fix quality traditionally is measured negatively as lack of quality. It's the number of defective fixes— fixes that did not work properly in all situations or, worse, that caused yet other problems. The real quality goal is, of course, zero defective fixes.

Software Complexity Metrics

Chapter 1 pointed out that computer systems are more complex than other large-scale engineered systems and that it is the software that makes them more complex. A number of approaches have been taken to calculate, or at least estimate, the degree of complexity. The simplest basis is LOC, a count of the executable statements in a computer program. This metric began in the days of assembly language programming, and it is still used today for programs written in high-level programming languages. Most procedural third-generation memory-to-memory languages such as FORTRAN, COBOL, and ALGOL typically produce six executable ML statements per high-level language statement. Register-to-register languages such as C, C++, and Java produce about three. Recent studies show a curvilinear relationship between defect rate and executable LOC. Defect density, or defects per KLOC, appears to decrease with program size and then increase again as program modules become very large (see Figure 3.1). Curiously, this result suggests that there may be an optimum program size leading to a lowest defect rate—depending, of course, on programming language, project size, product type, and computing environment.[8] Experience seems to indicate that small programs have a defect rate of about 1.5 defects per KLOC. Programs larger than 1,000 lines of code have a similar defect rate. Programs of about 500 LOC have defect rates near 0.5. This is almost certainly an effect of complexity, because small, "tight" programs are usually intrinsically complex. Programs larger than 1,000 LOC exhibit the complexity of size because they have so many pieces. This situation will improve with Object-Oriented Programming, for which there is greater latitude, or at least greater convenience of choice, in component size than for procedural programming. As you might expect, interface coding, although the most defect-prone of all programming, has defect rates that are constant with program size.

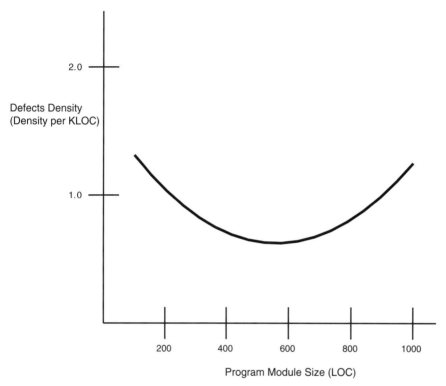

FIGURE 3.1
The Relationship Between LOC and Defect Density

Software Science

In 1977 Professor Maurice H. Halstead distinguished software science from computer science by describing programming as a process of collecting and arranging software tokens, which are either operands or operators. His measures are as follows:

n_1 = the number of distinct operators in a program

n_2 = the number of distinct operands in a program

N_1 = the number of operator occurrences

N_2 = the number of operand occurrences

He then based a set of derivative measures on these primitive measures to express the total token vocabulary, overall program length, potential minimum volume for a programmed algorithm, actual program volume in bits, program level as a complexity metric, and program difficulty, among others. For example:

Vocabulary (n) $n = n_1 + n_2$

Length (N) $N = N_1 + N_2 = n_1 \log_2 (n_1) + n_2 \log_2 (n_2)$

Volume (V) $V = N \log_2 (n) = N \log_2 (n_1 + n_2)$

Level (L) $L = V^*/ V = (2/n_1) \times (n_2/N_2)$

Difficulty (D) $D = V / V^* = (n_1/2) \times (N_2/n_2)$

Effort (E) $E = V / L$

Faults (B) $B = V / S^*$

V^* is the minimum volume represented by a built-in function that can perform the task of the entire program. S^* is the mean number of mental discriminations or decisions between errors—a value estimated as 3,000 by Halstead.

When these metrics first were announced, some software development old-timers thought that Halstead had violated Aristotle's first law of scientific inquiry: "Don't employ more rigor than the subject matter can bear." But none could gainsay the accuracy of his predictions or the quality of his results. In fact, the latter established software metrics as an issue of importance for computer scientists and established Professor Halstead as the founder of this field of inquiry. The major criticism of his approach is that his most accurate metric, program length, is dependent on N_1 and N_2, which are not known with sufficient accuracy until the program is almost done. Halstead's formulas fall short as direct quantitative measures because they fail to predict program size and quality sufficiently upstream in the development process. Also, his choice of S^* as a constant presumes an unknown model of human memory and cognition and unfortunately is also a constant that doesn't depend on program volume. Thus, the number of faults depends only on program size, which later experience has not supported. The results shown in Figure 3.1 indicate that the number of defects is not constant with program size but may rather take on an optimum value for programs having about 500 LOC. Perhaps Halstead's elaborate quantifications do not fully represent his incredible intuition, which was gained from long experience, after all.

Cyclomatic Complexity

About the same time Halstead founded software science, McCabe proposed a topological or graph-theory measure of cyclomatic complexity as a measure of the number of linearly

independent paths that make up a computer program. To compute the cyclomatic complexity of a program that has been graphed or flow-charted, the formula used is

$$M = V(G) = e - n + 2p$$

in which

      V(G) = the cyclomatic number of the graph G of the program

        e = the number of edges in the graph

        n = the number of nodes in the graph

        p = the number of unconnected parts in the graph

More simply, it turns out that M is equal to the number of binary decisions in the program
plus 1. An n-way case statement would be counted as n – 1 binary decisions. The advantage
of this measure is that it is additive for program components or modules. Usage recommends
that no single module have a value of M greater than 10. However, because on average every
fifth or sixth program instruction executed is a branch, M strongly correlates with program
size or LOC. As with the other early quality measures that focus on programs per se or even
their modules, these mask the true source of architectural complexity—interconnections
between modules. Later researchers have proposed structure metrics to compensate for this
deficiency by quantifying program module interactions. For example, fan-in and fan-out
metrics, which are analogous to the number of inputs to and outputs from hardware circuit
modules, are an attempt to fill this gap. Similar metrics include number of subroutine calls
and/or macro inclusions per module, and number of design changes to a module, among
others. Kan reports extensive experimental testing of these metrics and also reports that,
other than module length, the most important predictors of defect rates are number of
design changes and complexity level, however it is computed.[9]

Function Point Metrics

Quality metrics based either directly or indirectly on counting lines of code in a program
or its modules are unsatisfactory. These metrics are merely surrogate indicators of the number of opportunities to make an error, but from the perspective of the program as coded.
More recently the *function point* has been proposed as a meaningful cluster of measurable
code from the user's rather than the programmer's perspective. Function points can also be
surrogates for error opportunity, but they can be more. They represent the user's needs and

anticipated or *a priori* application of the program rather than just the programmer's *a posteriori* completion of it. A very large program may have millions of LOC, but an application with 1,000 function points would be a very large application or system indeed. A *function* may be defined as a collection of executable statements that performs a task, together with declarations of formal parameters and local variables manipulated by those statements. A typical function point metric developed by Albrecht[10] at IBM is a weighted sum of five components that characterize an application:

$4 \times$ the number of external inputs or transaction types

$5 \times$ the number of external types or reports

$10 \times$ the number of logical internal files

$7 \times$ the number of external interface files

$4 \times$ the number of external (online) inquiries supported

These represent the average weighting factors w_{ij}, which may vary with program size and complexity. x_{ij} is the number of each component type in the application.

The function count FC is the double sum:

$$FC = \sum_{1}^{5} \sum_{1}^{3} w_{ij} * x_{ij}$$

The second step employs a scale of 0 to 5 to assess the impact of 14 general system characteristics in terms of their likely effect on the application:

- Data communications
- Distributed functions
- Performance
- Heavily used configuration
- Transaction rate
- Online data entry
- End-user efficiency
- Online update
- Complex processing
- Reusability
- Installation ease
- Operational ease
- Multiple sites
- Facilitation of change

The scores for these characteristics c_i are then summed based on the following formula to find a value adjustment factor (VAF):

$$VAF = 0.65 + 0.01 \sum_1^{14} c_i$$

Finally, the number of function points is obtained by multiplying the number of function counts by the value adjustment factor:

FP = FC × VAF

This is actually a highly simplified version of a commonly used method that is documented in the *International Function Point User's Group Standard* (IFPUG, 1999).[11]

Although function point extrinsic counting metrics and methods are considered more robust than intrinsic LOC counting methods, they have the appearance of being somewhat subjective and experimental in nature. As used over time by organizations that develop very large software systems (having 1,000 or more function points), they show an amazingly high degree of repeatability and utility. This is probably because they enforce a disciplined learning process on a software development organization as much as any scientific credibility they may possess.

Availability and Customer Satisfaction Metrics

To the end user of an application, the only measures of quality are in the performance, reliability, and stability of the application or system in everyday use. This is "where the rubber meets the road," as users often say. Developer quality metrics and their assessment are often referred to as "where the rubber meets the sky." This book is dedicated to the proposition that we can arrive at *a priori* user-defined metrics that can be used to guide and assess development at all stages, from functional specification through installation and use. These metrics also can meet the road *a posteriori* to guide modification and enhancement of the software to meet the user's changing needs. Caution is advised here, because software problems are not, for the most part, valid defects, but rather are due to individual user and organizational learning curves. The latter class of problem calls places an enormous burden on user support during the early days of a new release. The catch here is that neither alpha testing (initial testing of a new release by the developer) nor beta testing (initial testing of a new release by advanced or experienced users) of a new release with current users identifies these problems. The purpose of a new release is to add functionality and performance to attract new users, who initially are bound to be disappointed, perhaps unfairly, with the software's quality. The DFTS approach we advocate in this book is intended to handle both valid and perceived software problems.

Typically, customer satisfaction is measured on a five-point scale:[11]

- Very satisfied

- Satisfied

- Neutral

- Dissatisfied

- Very dissatisfied

Results are obtained for a number of specific dimensions through customer surveys. For example, IBM uses the CUPRIMDA categories—capability, usability, performance, reliability, installability, maintainability, documentation, and availability. Hewlett-Packard uses FURPS categories—functionality, usability, reliability, performance, and serviceability. In addition to calculating percentages for various satisfaction or dissatisfaction categories, some vendors use the *net satisfaction index* (NSI) to enable comparisons across product lines. The NSI has the following weighting factors:

- Completely satisfied = 100%

- Satisfied = 75%

- Neutral = 50%

- Dissatisfied = 25%

- Completely dissatisfied = 0%

NSI then ranges from 0% (all customers are completely dissatisfied) to 100% (all customers are completely satisfied). Although it is widely used, the NSI tends to obscure difficulties with certain problem products. In this case the developer is better served by a histogram showing satisfaction rates for each product individually.

Sidebar 3.1: A Software Urban Legend

Professor Maurice H. Halstead was a pioneer in the development of ALGOL 58, automatic programming technology, and ALGOL-derived languages for military systems programming at the Naval Electronics Laboratory (NEL) at San Diego. Later, as a professor at Purdue (1967–1979), he took an interest in measuring software complexity and improving software quality. The legend we report, which was circulated widely in the early 1960s, dates from his years at NEL, where he was one of the developers of NELIAC (Naval Electronics Laboratory

International ALGOL Compiler). As the story goes, Halstead was offered a position at Lockheed Missile and Space Systems. He would lead a large military programming development effort for the Air Force in the JOVIAL programming language, which he also helped develop. With messianic confidence, Halstead said he could do it with 12 programmers in one year if he could pick the 12. Department of Defense contracts are rewarded at cost plus 10%, and Lockheed had planned for a staff of 1,000 programmers, who would complete the work in 18 months. The revenue on 10% of the burdened cost of 1,000 highly paid professionals in the U.S. aerospace industry is a lot of money. Unfortunately, 10% of the cost of 12 even very highly paid software engineers is not, so Lockheed could not accept Halstead's proposition. This story was widely told and its message applied for the next 20 years by developers of compilers and operating systems with great advantage, but it has never appeared in print as far as we know. Halstead did leave the NEL to join Lockheed about this time. They benefited from his considerable software development expertise until he went to Purdue.

Current Metrics and Models Technology

The best treatment of current software metrics and models is *Software Measurement: A Visualization Toolkit for Project Control and Process Measurement*,[12] by Simmons, Ellis, Fujihara, and Kuo. It comes with a CD-ROM that contains the Project Attribute Monitoring and Prediction Associate (PAMPA) measurement and analysis software tools. The book begins with Halstead's software science from 1977 and then brings the field up to date to 1997, technologically updating the metrics and models by including later research and experience. The updated metrics are grouped by size, effort, development time, productivity, quality, reliability, verification, and usability.

Size metrics begin with Halstead's *volume*, now measured in source lines of code (SLOC), and add *structure* as the number of unconditional branches of control loop nesting and module fan-in and fan-out. The newly added *rework* attributes describe the size of additions, deletions, and changes made between versions. Combined, they measure the *turmoil* in the developing product. The authors have also added a new measure of code functionality smaller than the program or module, called a *chunk*. It is a single integral piece of code, such as a function, subroutine, script, macro, procedure, object, or method. Volume measures are now made on functionally distinct chunks, rather than larger-scale aggregates such as programs or components. Tools are provided that allow the designer to aggregate chunks into larger units and even predict the number of function points or object points. Furthermore, because most software products are not developed from scratch but rather reuse existing code chunks with known quality characteristics, the toolkit allows the prediction of *equivalent volume* using one of four different algorithms (or all four, if desired) taken from recent software science literature. A new volume measure called *unique SLOC* has been added. It evaluates new LOC on a per-chunk basis and can calculate unique SLOC for a developing version of the product.

Naturally, volume measures are the major input for *effort* metrics. Recent research adds five categories of 17 different *dominators*, which can have serious effort-magnifying effects. The categories into which dominators fall are project, product, organization, suppliers, and customers. For example, potential dominators in the product category include the amount of documentation needed, programming language, complexity, and type of application. In the organization category, they include the number of people, communications, and personnel turnover. Customer includes user interface complexity and requirements volatility, which are negative, but then the dominators are all basically negative. Their name signifies that their presence may have an effort-expansion effect as large as a factor of 10. But when their influence is favorable, they generally have a much smaller positive effect. A range of effort prediction and cost forecasting algorithms based on a variety of theoretical, historical/experiential, statistical, and even composite models are provided.

The third measure category is *development time*, which is derived from effort, which is derived from size or volume. The only independent new variable here is schedule. Given the resources available to the project manager, the toolkit calculates overall minimum development time and then allows the user to vary or reallocate resources to do more tasks in parallel. However, the system very realistically warns of cost runaways if the user tries to reduce development time by more than 15% of the forecast minimum.

Because effort is essentially volume divided by productivity, you can see that *productivity* is inversely related to effort. A new set of cost drivers enters as independent variables, unfortunately having mostly negative influences. When cost drivers begin to vary significantly from nominal values, you should take action to bring them back into acceptable ranges. A productivity forecast provides the natural objective function with which to do this.

The *quality* metrics advocated in Simmons, et al. are dependent on the last three metric sets: *reliability*, *verification*, and *usability*. Usability is a product's fitness for use. This metric depends on the product's intended features, their verified functionality, and their reliability in use. Simply stated, this metric means that all promises were fulfilled, no negative consequences were encountered, and the customer was delighted. This deceptively simple trio masks evaluation of multiple subjective psychometric evaluations plus a few performance-based factors such as learnability, relearnability, and efficiency. Much has been written about measures of these factors. To sell software, vendors develop and add more features. New features contain unique SLOCs, and new code means new opportunities to introduce bugs. As might be expected, a large measure of customer dissatisfaction is the result of new features that don't work, whether due to actual defects or merely user expectations. The only thing in the world increasing faster than computer performance is end-user expectations: *A product whose features cannot be validated, or that is delivered late or at a higher-than-expected price, has a quality problem.* Feature validation demands that features be clearly described without possible misunderstanding and that metrics for their measurement be identified.

The last point in the quality triangle is *reliability*, which may be defined as defect potential, defect removal efficiency, and delivered defects. The largest opportunity for software defects to occur is in the interfaces between modules, programs, and components, and with databases. Although the number of interfaces in an application is proportional to the program's size, it varies by application type, programming language, style, and many other factors. One estimate indicates that 70% or more of software reliability problems are in interfaces. Aside from the occurrence of errors or defects, and their number (if any), the major metric for quality is the mean time between their occurrence. Whether you record time to failure, time intervals between failures, cumulative failures in a given time period, or failures experienced in a given time interval, the basic metric of reliability is *time*.

Chapter 2 defined software quality as the degree to which a system, component, or process meets specified requirements, and customer or user needs and requirements. It also introduced software dependability, which includes reliability, safety, security, and availability. Our definitions incorporate Kan's multifactor software quality definition[13] and our definition of trustworthy software. The latter includes the ability to meet customer trust *as well as unstated and even unanticipated needs*, including the emphasis by Simmons, et al. on features.[14]

New Metrics for Architectural Design and Assessment

A new science of software architecture metrics is slowly emerging, amazingly in the absence of any generally accepted definition of software architecture. Software engineers have been coasting on the metaphor of building architecture for a long time. Some clarity is developing, but it is scarcely more than extending the metaphor. For example, an early (1994) intuitive definition states the following:

> There is currently no single, universally accepted definition of software architecture, but typically a systems architectural design is concerned with describing its decomposition into components and their interconnections.[15]

Actually, this is not a bad start. When one of the authors became manager of a large-scale computer design at Univac as chief architect in 1966, this was the operative definition of computer (hardware) architecture. It was sufficient only because of the tradition of hardware systems design, which had led to the large-scale multiprocessor computer system.[16]

But to be more precise for software that comes later to this tradition, software architecture is "the structure of the components of a program/system, their interrelationships, and principles and guidelines governing their design and evolution over time."[17] While descriptive, these definitions still do not give us enough leverage to begin defining metrics for the architectural assessment of software. We would like to again quote Shaw and Garlan's more recent definition:

> Abstractly, software architecture involves the description of elements from which systems are built, interactions among those elements, patterns that guide their composition, and constraints on those patterns. In general, a particular system is defined in terms of a collection of components and the interactions among those components.[18]

A software *design pattern* is a general repeatable solution to a commonly occurring problem in software design. It is not a finished design that can be transformed directly into program code. Rather, it is a description of or template for how to solve a problem that can be used in many different situations. Object-oriented design patterns typically show relationships and interactions between classes or objects, without specifying the final application classes or objects that are involved. Algorithms are not thought of as design patterns, because they solve computational problems rather than design problems.

In practice, architectural metrics are involved not only upstream in the software development process and *architecture discovery* but also further downstream before coding begins as *architectural review*. These terms were introduced by Avritzer and Weyuker[19] for use at AT&T and will be used here as well.

Common Architectural Design Problems

The most commonly occurring architectural design problems can be grouped into three categories: *project management*, *requirements*, and *performance*. The following list describes problems affecting *project management*.[20] It's an excellent list that we have reordered to reflect our own experiences with software development management:

- The stakeholders have not been clearly identified.

- No project manager has been identified.

- No one is responsible for the overall architecture.

- No project plan is in place.

- The deployment date is unrealistic.

- The independent requirements team is not yet in place.

- Domain experts have not been committed to the design.
- No software architect(s) have been assigned.
- No overall architecture plan has been prepared.
- No system test plan has been developed.
- No measures of success have been identified.
- No independent performance effort is in place.
- No contingency plans have been written.
- No modification tracking system is in place.
- Project funding is not committed.
- No quality assurance team is in place.
- No hardware installation schedule exists.

Here are the most common issues affecting the definition of *requirements* for a software development project (again in order of importance according to our experience):

- The project lacks a clear problem statement.
- No requirements document exists.
- The project lacks decision criteria for choosing the software architecture.
- Outputs have not been identified.
- The size of the user community has not been determined.
- Data storage requirements have not been determined.
- Operational administration and maintenance have not been identified.
- Resources to support a new requirement have not been allocated.

Here are the most common *performance* issues affecting the architecture of a software development project (priority reordered):

- The end user has not established performance requirements.
- No performance model exists.
- Expected traffic rates have not been established.
- No means for measuring transaction time or rates exists.

- No performance budgets have been established.

- No assessment has been made to ensure that hardware will meet processing requirements.

- No assessment has been made to ensure that the system can handle throughput.

- No performance data has been gathered.

In our experience, the leading critical quality issues in each category are either *customer requirements issues* or aspects of the *project management team's commitment to the customer's requirements*. This leads to our focus on QFD as a means of hearing the voice of the customer at the beginning of the software development project rather than having to listen to their complaints after the software has been delivered.

Pattern Metrics in OOAD

Object-Oriented Analysis and Design (OOAD) has at last come of age; it is the preferred software development technology today. Sophisticated online transaction-oriented applications and systems in aerospace and medical technology have been using C++ for years. The emergence of Java as the preferred language for Internet application development has established OOAD and Object-Oriented Programming (OOP) as major players. Many college and university computer science programs are Java-based nowadays, and many application groups are busy converting COBOL and PL/1 applications to Java. The use of OOAD both in the development of new systems and in their conversion from legacy procedural language implementations favors the discovery and use of design patterns. A design pattern is a microarchitecture that provides a proven solution to design problems that tend to recur within a given application or software development context. A design pattern includes its static structure as the hierarchy of classes and objects in the pattern and their relationships. It also includes the behaviors (to use the Java term) or dynamic relationships that govern how the objects exchange messages. Design patterns are classified by their users into three groups; they are either creational, structural, or behavioral. Creational patterns concern object creation. Structural patterns capture class or object composition. Behavioral patterns deal with how classes and objects interact. Most patterns are discovered in existing software packages when they are either modified or rewritten by very senior programmers or software architects who notice their repetitive occurrences. A research group at the Institute for Scientific and Technical Research in Trento, Italy has developed a set of metrics for OO software applications that allow them to extract design patterns automatically.[21]

Ostensibly the major benefit of understanding and using repeating design patterns in OOP is to enhance code reusability. However, software quality enhancement has significant benefits as well. Not only do patterns reduce the unique SLOC in an application, they also reduce its effective volume, increase development productivity, and simplify later enhancement and maintenance. The technology frontier in software development today is learning how to break high-level architectural design into its architectural components. This is similar to how a building architect breaks his or her overall design into horizontal micro-architectures such as stories and plazas and into vertical micro-architectures or infrastructure components such as HVAC, plumbing, power, elevators, and stairways.

The future of software quality is further automation by automatic program generation. This means the ability to break the overall customer-responsive architecture (form follows function) into successively lower levels of architecture, down to micro-architectures such as design patterns from which quality application software can be generated automatically.

Key Points

- Historically software quality metrics have measured exactly the opposite of quality—that is, the number of defects or bugs per thousand lines of code.

- Software is a multidimensional concept that can be viewed from many professional and user viewpoints.

- Two leading firms in customer-focused software quality are IBM and Hewlett-Packard.

- IBM has a proprietary measure set, whereas HP uses five Juran quality parameters.

- The Naval Air Systems Command coined the term Total Quality Management (TQM) in 1985 to describe its own quality improvement program. It soon spread worldwide.

- The four essential characteristics of a TQM program in any field are customer focus, process improvement, quality culture, and measurement and analysis.

- TQM made an enormous contribution to the quality of enterprise software in the early 1990s, just in time for the Y2K transition.

- Until recently, most software quality metrics were of an in-process nature; metrics to support DFTS must be applied upstream in the development process.

- Small programs (less than 100 LOC) exhibit 1.5 defects per KLOC. Large programs (more than 1,000 LOC) exhibit 1.5 defects per KLOC. Medium-sized programs often have only 0.5 defects per KLOC.

- Sophisticated software tools for measuring software quality, such as PAMPA, are beginning to appear.

- OOP goals in software reusability tend to enhance software quality as well.

Additional Resources

http://www.prenhallprofessional.com/title/0131872508

http://www.agilenty.com/publications

Internet Exercises

1. Look up Maurice Halstead on the Internet, and summarize his contributions to software development technology.

2. Look up the PAMPA product and describe its capability for software measurement.

3. See if you can find products similar to PAMPA. Compare them according to functionality, price, and applicability to upstream DFTS.

4. Investigate the current status of the IEEE Software Quality Metrics Methodology.

Review Questions

1. Distinguish between software science, cyclomatic complexity, and function point analysis.

2. Define the term software function point.

3. Why do OOP goals for software reusability tend to enhance software quality as well?

4. Review Table 3.1. Which CUPRIMDA factors compete with each other, and why?

5. Compare IBM's CUPRIMDA with HP's FURPS. Which IBM quality factors map to the HP schema, and which ones do not?

Discussion Questions and Projects

1. Explain why small programs (less than 100 LOC) exhibit 1.5 defects per KLOC and large programs (more than 1,000 LOC) exhibit 1.5 defects per KLOC but medium-sized programs often have only 0.5 defects per KLOC.

2. Why do Halstead's formulas fail to predict program size and hence quality upstream in the development process? How would you change his methodology to enhance its upstream use for DFTS?

3. IBM and HP are recognized leaders in software quality. How do their customer-focused quality measures support this perception?

Endnotes

[1]M. Shaw and D. Garlan, *Software Architecture: Perspectives on an Emerging Discipline* (New Jersey: Prentice Hall, 1996), p. 1.

[2]P. B. Crosby, *Quality Is Free: The Art of Making Quality Certain* (New York: McGraw-Hill, 1979).

[3]J. M. Juran and F. M. Gryna, Jr., *Quality Planning and Analysis: From Product Development Through Use* (New York: McGraw-Hill, 1970).

[4]S. H. Kan, *Metrics and Models in Software Quality Engineering* (Singapore: Pearson Education, 2003), p. 7.

[5]P. C. Patton and L. May, "Making Connections: A five-year plan for information systems and computing," ISC, University of Pennsylvania, 1993.

[6]IEEE, *Standard for a Software Quality Metrics Methodology* (New York: IEEE, Inc., 1993).

[7]Ibid, p. 10.

[8]Op cit Kan, p. 312.

[9]Op cit Kan, p. 327.

[10]S. D. Conte, H. E. Dunsmore, V. Y. Shen, *Software Engineering Metrics and Models* (Menlo Park, CA: Benjamin/Cummings, 1986).

[11]IFPUG, *International Function Point User's Group Standard* (IFPUG, 1999).

[12]D. B. Simmons, N. C. Ellis, H. Fujihara, W. Kuo, *Software Measurement: A Visualization Toolkit for Project Control and Process Measurement* (New Jersey: Prentice-Hall, 1998).

[13]Op cit Kan, p. 55.

[14]Op cit Simmons, et al., p. 250.

[15]Ibid, p. 257.

[16]D. Garlan, R. Allen, J. Ockerbloom, "Architectural mismatch: why reuse is so hard," *IEEE Software*, Nov. 1995, pp. 17–26 (p. 20).

[17]D. Garlan and D. Perry, "Introduction to the special issue on software architecture," *IEEE Transactions on Software Engineering*, April 1995, pp. 269–274 (p. 269).

[18]Op cit Shaw and Garlan, p. 1.

[19]G. Avritzer and E. J. Weyuker, "Investigating Metrics for Architectural Assessment," Proceedings of the Fifth International Software Metrics Symposium, pp. 2–10.

[20]Ibid, p. 8.

[21]G. Antoniol, R. Fiutem, L. Cristoforetti, "Using Metrics to Identify Design Patterns in Object-Oriented Software," Proceedings of the Fifth International Software Metrics Symposium, pp. 23–34.

CHAPTER 4

Financial Perspectives on Trustworthy Software

The important thing is not to stop questioning.
—Albert Einstein

Price has no meaning without quality.
—Walter A. Shewhart

Overview

Financial analyses of a DFTS process are meant to provide visibility and control for effective decision-making. Important nonfinancial metrics and control mechanisms also are needed. However, you shouldn't lose sight of customer requirements. Sound financial return is one of the desired outcomes of a DFTS initiative that is designed to meet customer requirements while also meeting the software developer's internal objectives. This chapter discusses four financial approaches to evaluating economic imperatives of a DFTS deployment: Cost of Software Quality (CoSQ), Activity-Based Costing (ABC), Taguchi's Quality Loss Function (QLF), and financial evaluation of a DFTS investment. This chapter illustrates the need to address quality problems upstream and the cost advantage of doing so. Investments made in upstream preventive measures provide a much higher payoff than development models that rely on corrective measures downstream, or worse, on corrective measures that follow failure during customer usage. This chapter discusses the classification, implementation, payback, benefits, and pitfalls of CoSQ. Then it covers the relevance, establishment, and benefits of ABC in a software context. This is followed by life-cycle costs and QLF in a software context. Finally, financial evaluation of a DFTS investment is presented, together with other financial and nonfinancial metrics required for effective visibility, accountability, control, and decision-making.

Chapter Outline

- Why DFTS Entails Different Financial Analyses

- Cost and Quality: Then and Now

- Cost of Software Quality

- Cost of Software Quality Over the Life Cycle

- CoSQ and Activity-Based Costing

- Quality Loss Function in Software

- Financial Evaluation of a DFTS Investment

- Key Points

- Additional Resources

- Internet Exercises

- Review Questions

- Discussion Questions

- Problems

- Endnotes

Why DFTS Entails Different Financial Analyses

This chapter discusses economic imperatives of a DFTS initiative using a set of financial approaches. But while carrying out financial analyses, you should not lose sight of the objectives of such an exercise, as often happens. The key objectives here are delivering customer requirements as trustworthy software. Chapter 2 identified five key elements of trustworthy software: *reliability, safety, security, maintainability,* and *customer responsiveness.* Delivering these objectives should remain the focus of such analyses. Appropriate financial analyses provide visibility and control for effective decision-making. In this regard, we underline, equally, the need for nonfinancial control mechanisms presented in Chapter 21.

From another perspective, sound financial return is one of the desired outcomes of a DFTS initiative that is designed to meet customer requirements while also meeting the software developer's internal objectives. It is just that customer requirements rather than short-term financial return are the primary focus of DFTS. Therefore, this implies that before financial return of a DFTS initiative is evaluated, you must answer the question "Did we deliver trustworthy software in the first place?" If the answer is "yes," the next question is "Do the customers concur with this answer?" If the answer is "no" to either of these questions, financial evaluation is not one for trustworthiness, and you must go back to the drawing board. Any financial evaluation of DFTS deployment without due consideration of customer requirements is largely a pointless exercise in a DFTS context and is of limited value. For one thing, it may lead to wrong decision-making regarding the initiative's cost and quality implications. Ignoring customer requirements may also impair financial performance in the long term. This is due to higher life-cycle costs associated with defective software as well as loss of customer confidence and competitiveness due to poor quality. High costs and poor quality constitute the double whammy of a flawed software development process.

Because regular accounting data is inadequate, we recommend using the following four approaches, as needed, to evaluate economic imperatives of a DFTS deployment:

- Cost of Software Quality (CoSQ)
- Activity-Based Costing (ABC) in software development
- Application of Taguchi's Quality Loss Function (QLF) to evaluate software quality
- Financial evaluation of a DFTS intervention

Cost and Quality: Then and Now

Traditionally, quality initiatives have been viewed as adversarial to cost-reduction objectives. Even today, goal-directed managers continue to consider quality-related expenditures a cost rather than an investment, despite the crusades of Deming, Taguchi, and Crosby.

The idea that improved quality can improve cost-effectiveness is not totally new, but it has been gaining ground only in recent years. Growing acceptance of quality as an investment can be attributed to several factors:

- **The success of Six Sigma, DFSS, and other initiatives:** Several U.S. corporations, such as GE, Motorola, Allied Signal, and a score of companies worldwide, have deployed Six Sigma and Design for Six Sigma (DFSS) successfully and have delivered remarkable results in product and service quality while realizing enormous savings and other benefits.[1] (Table 4.1 compares Six Sigma/DFSS deployments at GE, DuPont, and Caterpillar with the Toyota Production System [TPS].) These initiatives have been the focus of much corporate, academic, and media attention in recent years, leading to greater awareness of quality as an essential component of business strategy.

- **The Japanese miracle:** We have witnessed the emergence of Japan as a major industrial power following the devastation of World War II. It is better understood now how Japanese corporations such as Toyota, Honda, and Sony have deployed Total Quality Management (TQM), Lean Production, and Taguchi Methods to gain quality and cost advantages.

- **Congruence with the CEO's concerns:** Management practices in the West have gradually adopted TQM and Lean Production systems. For example, Six Sigma, a variant of TQM, places much more emphasis on the bottom line and measurable short-term results on a project-by-project basis than the traditional TQM that has been practiced in Japan. A major factor in Six Sigma's attractiveness in the West is its record of delivering short- as well as long-term bottom-line improvements. The CEOs in the West can hardly ignore the stock market's short-term expectations. Jack Welch describes this challenge succinctly: "The only reason anyone has the title of manager is to manage short and long. ... Anybody can manage short. All you do is go in and for two years squeeze everything and look like a hero. Anybody can also manage for the long term, go in and say I'm going to deliver in 1995 and don't bother me until then. The hard game is balancing it."[2]

- **Customer expectations:** Customers in any industry can hardly be satisfied with offerings based on cost or quality alone. They ask for both. This doesn't mean that the product has to be all things to all people; it implies understanding the customer's cost and quality requirements and responding intelligently to those requirements.

- **Competitive advantage:** Even though a quality product can command a premium price, a cost advantage provides competitive cover, better margin, or both. In software development, the right strategy is to design software such that it optimizes both the customer's trustworthiness requirements (quality) and the software developer's cost requirements (Route C in Figure 4.1). For example, DFTS provides a systematic methodology to optimize various requirements at the lowest cost. In the absence of such a development model, software developers try to fulfill customer requirements first and then attempt to lower development costs (Route A) or, worse still, develop at a low cost first and then seek to meet customer requirements (Route B). Both these approaches are difficult to pursue and fail to deliver trustworthy software at the lowest cost. So here is the amazing revelation: *Find a way to deliver as per the customer requirements, or it will cost you more!*

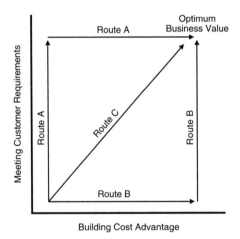

FIGURE 4.1
Alternative Routes to Creating Optimum Business Value

TABLE 4.1
Examples of Corporate-Wide Quality Deployments: Lean, Six Sigma, DFSS, and TPS

Company	Initiatives and Scope	Results
GE	**Six Sigma, DFSS, and Lean Six Sigma** 10,000 black belts and 100,000 green belts in 2000 Expects to train up to 30,000 black belts 50,000 projects in 2002 Six Sigma assistance to customers in 2003 All new products to be developed using DFSS Initiated Lean Six Sigma in 2004 Six Sigma consulting service to suppliers worldwide Innovative across-the-board applications	$6.6 billion in savings in five years During the years 2002–2004, GE Transportation improved inventory turns from seven to nine, and GE Advanced Materials improved accounts receivable by six turns $2.7 billion in improvements in working capital in 2003–2004 Expects to save $7 to $10 billion annually in the long term $1.5 million in annual savings per black belt $1.0 addition to EPS Improvement in operating profit margins from 13.6% in 1995 to 16.7% in the third quarter of 1999 Huge reduction in the need for capital investments due to improved plant utilization
DuPont	**Six Sigma and DFSS** 250 master black belts 1,200 black belts 10,000 green belts One of every four employees participates in a Six Sigma project Completed 11,000 projects 4,000 projects with increased safety and reduced environmental impact Over 12,000 projects underway around the world in all regions and lines of business	More than $1.6 billion in cost savings in four years 50% of projects focus on cost reduction, 25% on transactions, and 25% on revenues, including top-line customer-related More than 1,000 top-line growth (TLG) projects were active in 2002 More than 500 financial analysts and managers have been trained in the specifics of Six Sigma financial metrics and reporting

Company	Initiatives and Scope	Results
Caterpillar	**Lean Six Sigma and DFSS** Leveraged across the value chain as a broad cultural philosophy to drive continuous process improvement, promote teamwork, process information, solve problems, and manage business First company to launch Six Sigma at all business units simultaneously—10 manufacturing facilities in 24 countries worldwide concurrently 2,000 black belts, 14,000 green belts, 2,000 sponsors More than 25,000 employees and 15,000 projects in 2003 97 dealers and 240 suppliers	$138 million quarterly bottom-line improvement directly attributed to Six Sigma $1.6 billion cost reduction target $30 billion revenue target for 2010 from 2003 revenue of $20 billion Objective of 35% reduction in warranty-related costs
Toyota	**Toyota Production System (TPS)** aims to eliminate all kids of waste and improve productivity and quality. It's a way of life in Toyota and uses a number of quality systems and tools: *Kanban* (Just In Time) *Jidoka* (quality in the process) Small-lot delivery Deming's Plan, Do, Check, Act (PDCA) cycle and *kaizen* (continuous improvement) *Heijunka* (leveling of demand) Visual control 5S, or clean, orderly workplaces	Quality consistently ranks among the world's best More profitable than GM, Ford, DaimlerChrysler, and Volkswagen combined Lexus is the top luxury brand in the United States Lexus dealerships are the second most profitable Camry is the best-selling car The Toyota brand sells more than the Ford and Chevrolet brands Toyota, Lexus, and Scion outsell Chrysler, Dodge, and Jeep Surpassed Ford as the world's No. 2 automaker 11.7% of the world auto market in 2003 (10% in 2001 and has a goal of 15 % by 2010—equal to that of GM)

Cost of Software Quality

Philip Crosby, in *Quality Is Free*,[3] argues that the cost of quality (CoQ) is "the expense of nonconformance—the cost of doing things wrong." Some call it the "cost of poor quality" (CoPQ) or the "price of nonconformance" (PoNC). Determining CoQ is important, because it reveals how much you expend on prevention, appraisal, inspection, discovering, analyzing, scrapping, and correcting defects, faults, and errors. Software process maturity and quality levels lag hardware by a factor of 20 to 1. The cost of poor quality (CoPQ) related to software bugs, development cost overruns, botched implementation, and canceled projects is astronomical. A recent study puts one aspect of CoPQ, canceled projects, in excess of $300 billion in the United States alone.[4]

Cost of software quality (CoSQ) can be defined as the total cost of conformance and nonconformance to the customer's quality requirements. It consists of various direct and indirect expenses incurred when preventing, appraising, testing, discovering, analyzing, and fixing software faults, including maintenance. As we discuss in Chapters 1 and 2, some 40% of software development cost is spent on testing alone to remove errors and ensure adequate quality. Further, some 80 to 90% of the total software life-cycle cost (LCC) goes into software maintenance to fix, adapt, and expand the delivered program to meet users' changing and growing needs.[5]

Benefits of Cost-of-Quality Analysis

Identifying, understanding, and managing the cost of software quality are crucial components of a DFTS initiative for the following reasons:[6]

- Cost-of-quality analysis helps the software team focus on discovering, and correcting, the *root causes* of software defects.

- Root-cause analysis allows the project personnel to determine how the development process can be improved to prevent further defects—and thus improve quality.

- This visibility also provides a vehicle for effective communication across all functions supporting the project, regardless of the organizational structure.

Traditional cost-evaluation metrics, generally associated with manufactured products, have focused on internal costs of rework, rejects, and returns; therefore, they have focused just on "failure-related activities."[7] They emphasize inspection and cost minimization by taking corrective measures following inspection. Although the need for corrective measures cannot be eliminated, an enlightened approach emphasizes preventive interventions so that corrective measures are unneeded in the first place, or can be minimized.

It should be emphasized that quality can be "free" only if the cost of quality improvement tasks is less than the consequent cost of not undertaking such tasks. This is possible only if adequate quality tasks are actually performed and are targeted at failure reduction. Such reduction can be dramatically enhanced by employing ways and means to move failure prevention, detection, and removal activities closer to the front end of the development process—to the upstream stages of requirements planning, concept development, and design. Only in this way can the cost of performing quality tasks become less than the cost of not performing quality tasks.[8]

Evaluating the costs of not performing quality tasks is always challenging, because so many intangible factors are related to customer expectations and competitive factors that are in play in a particular industry. Often, conservative estimates are the only way to come up with a workable figure. This issue is discussed further when we cover Taguchi's Quality Loss Function (QLF) later in this chapter. Two sets of measures are involved in cost benefits related to quality tasks: the costs associated with quality tasks, and the cost savings from performing quality tasks.

Cost of Quality Tasks

Figure 4.2 shows the relationships between the cost components of various quality tasks. They can be summarized as follows:

$$\text{cost of performing quality tasks} = \text{cost of conformance} + \text{cost of nonconformance}$$
$$\text{cost of conformance} = \text{preventive costs} + \text{appraisal costs}$$
$$\text{cost of nonconformance} = \text{cost of internal failure} + \text{cost of external failure}$$
$$\text{cost of internal failure} = \text{cost of upstream internal failure} + \text{cost of downstream internal failure}$$

It's important to understand this cost structure and its implications for overall quality and product cost for three reasons:

- Emphasizing interventions upstream ensures much lower downstream and overall costs than would be the case otherwise.

- These costs are interrelated. For example, high external failure costs may be due to lack of attention to upstream preventive measures. Thus, external failure costs may be avoided or reduced drastically as a result of taking appropriate preventive measures upstream.

- Increased expenditure on inspection and testing without addressing the root cause of failure at upstream stages may just increase the cost of quality without any long-term improvement in overall quality.

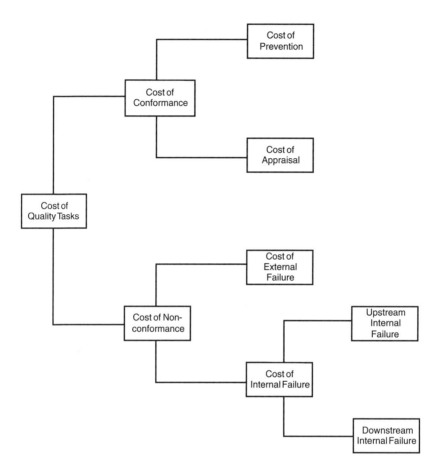

FIGURE 4.2
Cost Breakdown of Software Quality Tasks

The following example illustrates the points we want to make:

Experts estimate that 60 to 90 percent of the total quality costs are the result of internal and external failure and are the responsibility of, but not easily controllable by, the management ... an increase in prevention usually generates larger savings in all other cost categories.... In a typical scenario, the cost of replacing a poor-quality component in the field might be $500; the cost of replacement after assembly might be $50; the cost of testing and replacement during assembly might be $5; and the cost of changing the design to avoid the problem might be only 50 cents.[9]

The objective should be to reverse this process. The majority of quality costs should be incurred at prevention, some in appraisal, perhaps a few in upstream and downstream internal failures, and virtually none in external failure. Thus, the software developer should first attempt to reduce external failure costs to zero by investing in preventive and appraisal activities to design bug-free software in the first place. Then he or she should discover sources of design and coding failure, if any, and take corrective actions consequently. As quality improves, failure costs decrease, and the amount of appraisal can be reduced with the shift of emphasis to prevention activities.[10] Determining cost of quality is a first step in identifying and removing the root causes of failure.

Classification of Cost of Software Quality

The profile of software quality costs differs from that of manufactured products. The costs reflect the manpower intensity, service orientation, and more intense customer interaction of a software development process. Because much of the work is intellectual, it lacks the visibility of a manufacturing process. The required visibility must be "created" by appropriate documentation. Just like in other service organizations, user interaction, or the lack thereof, is a crucial element of overall costs. CoSQ can be classified into five major categories:

- Prevention costs

- Appraisal costs

- Upstream internal failure costs

- Downstream internal failure costs

- External failure costs

Prevention Costs

This category includes various costs associated with equipment, systems, and manpower associated with preventive upstream activities to ensure that nonconforming software products are not designed in the first place. These costs can be broken down as follows:

- **Quality planning and development costs:** Personnel costs of quality professionals involved in developing new systems.

- **Information systems costs:** The costs associated with equipment and organization of data and measurements required for making various quality-related decisions.

- **Training and administrative costs:** Training, administrative, and communication-related costs.

- **Quality initiative implementation costs:** Various costs associated with implementing quality initiatives.

- **Risk assessment:** Cost of risk appraisal, such FMEA.

Appraisal Costs

This category includes various costs associated with activities carried out to ensure that the software designed and developed meets customer requirements. This includes salaries, equipment, measurement and analysis, customer interaction, and equipment costs. The activities involved are

- Review and inspection

- Test and evaluation

- Verification and validation costs

- Risk appraisal at downstream stages

Upstream Internal Failure Costs

Includes all costs related to manpower and equipment incurred in detecting and correcting defects and faults associated with requirements identification, design, and coding. This involves self-debugging your own unit and components. All this may also require interacting with the customer and user domains and carrying out risk analysis.

The formal testing by the independent test team is done in the following stage and is identified as part of downstream internal failure costs. Failure costs escalate after self-debugging, because it involves the following steps:

- The test engineer researches and reports the failure.

- The coder receives the failure report and fixes the fault.

- The release engineer comes up with a new release.

- The system administrator installs the new release in the test environment.

- The tester tests the new release to confirm the fix and to check again for regression.

It helps a great deal if self-debugging can detect and fix faults.

Downstream Internal Failure Costs

This category includes all costs related to manpower and equipment incurred in detecting and correcting defects and faults associated with review, test and evaluation, and verification and validation. Testing at this stage involves an independent test team. As just mentioned, the internal failure costs in the downstream stages may be much higher than in the previous stage. These activities also require interacting with the customer and user environments and carrying out risk analysis.

External Failure Costs

Here the costs may be even higher than those incurred at the two internal failure stages just discussed. The faults in this case are found by the customers and not by self-debugging or by the internal test engineer. The whole cycle of fault fixing has to be undertaken. The costs include all manpower as well as equipment-related costs associated with detecting and correcting faults and complaints following release to customers. This category also includes

- Testing and fault-correction costs following complaints, returns, or any other usage-related problems
- Warranty and litigation costs following customer usage that are covered by warranty and product liability clauses

As stated earlier, the cost of software quality can be minimized dramatically by taking preventive measures, and corrective measures, if needed, upstream. (Table 4.2 lists essential activities at various stages.) The investments made in upstream preventive measures provide a much higher payoff than development models that rely on corrective measures downstream, or worse, corrective measures following failure during customer usage. External failures involve numerous unforeseen and intangible costs. In extreme cases, the potential damage may cripple the business. In addition to a sound preventive system, provisions must be made for costs related to insurance, product liability, and legal defense. The best strategy is, of course, prevention.

TABLE 4.2
Conformance and Nonconformance Quality Activities at Various Software
Development Stages

	Cost of Conformance		Cost of Nonconformance		
Cost Classification	Prevention Costs	Appraisal Costs	Upstream Internal Failure Costs	Downstream Internal Failure Costs	External Failure Costs
Quality activities associated with the cost	Activities designed to prevent faults throughout the development process, especially internal upstream	Activities to ensure conformance, especially internal downstream	Activities at upstream stages to self-debug before downstream stages	Activities at downstream stages to debug before release to customers	Activities to fix errors after release to customers
Typical breakdown of quality activities	Training Management Infrastructure Preventive quality initiative DFTS, including QFD, Robust Design, FMEA, poka yoke, customer appraisal, requirements, design and code review, customer appraisal and review (CAR), and training	Review Inspect Test Evaluate Verify Validate CAR Corrective measures	Design Review Detect Design and coding corrections CAR Corrective measures	Review Inspect Test and evaluate Validate and verify Coding and design corrections CAR Detect Corrective measures	Returns All internal activities for the first four stages CAR Detect Corrective measures during integration, expansion, and maintenance Complaints compliance Expedited delivery Legal issues

Cost-reduction potentials are realized only if quality-related activities are based on clear analysis and understanding of root causes of faults, which a CoSQ analysis helps reveal. A CoSQ quality matrix points out quality problems and associated costs, as shown in Table 4.3. It is important not to get into a futile discussion about a particular item's cost categorization. Certain items could be considered either a development activity or a quality-related one. It is best to exclude debatable items in CoSQ reporting. Similarly, a cost item may belong to one category or another, depending on a particular perspective. However, major cost items are not difficult to categorize. In all such cases, it is best to be consistent so that improvements and opportunities for improvements are clearly identified.

CoSQ reporting is the first step in identifying the root causes that need to be addressed by the software developer and outsourcing firms if they are involved. Various tools such as *process mapping, cause-and-effect diagrams,* and *brainstorming* can be used to identify the root causes (see Chapter 6).

Establishing a CoSQ Reporting System

The first requirement of a CoSQ program is to establish a reporting system that identifies costs incurred due to poor quality. Establishing such a reporting system is a major initiative and must be carefully planned. Evans and Lindsay[11] have summarized a 12-step implementation plan based on the recommendations of the Institute of Management Accountants:

1. **Obtain management commitment and support.** The ideal milieu in which to launch such a system is created only if it's initiated by top management. If it's prompted by accounting or quality personnel, it is wise to secure management commitment. An estimate of the cost of poor quality and its sheer magnitude may encourage management's commitment and support. It is advisable not to embark on such a system without management support. It is also critical that accounting executives support and "own" the system. The accounting department should be involved in and responsible for CoQ operations for several reasons: They have access to primary data, they are used to evaluating processes in monetary terms, they are seen as neutral, and their results are trusted. Moreover, their involvement ensures that they will be active participants in the process to make it work.

TABLE 4.3
Establishing a CoSQ Reporting System

Phase Quality Tasks	Requirements Costs	Design Costs	Code Costs	Test, Evaluation, Validation, and Verification Costs	Integration Costs	Maintenance Costs	Total Costs	Explanation of Cost and its Implications
Prevention Costs								
Quality planning and management								
Information systems for quality								
Training for quality								
Quality initiatives such as DFTS (QFD, TRIZ, Pugh, risk analysis, Taguchi Methods)								
Design review								
Customer appraisal and review								
Any other preventive measures								

Phase Quality Tasks	Requirements Costs	Design Costs	Code Costs	Test, Evaluation, Validation, and Verification Costs	Integration Costs	Maintenance Costs	Total Costs	Explanation of Cost and its Implications
Appraisal Costs								
Inspect								
Test and evaluation								
Validate and verify								
Equipment for the preceding								
Design review								
Risk analysis								
Customer appraisal and review								
Any other appraisal measures								

TABLE 4.3
Continued

Phase Quality Tasks	Requirements Costs	Design Costs	Code Costs	Test, Evaluation, Validation, and Verification Costs	Integration Costs	Maintenance Costs	Total Costs	Explanation of Cost and its Implications
Upstream Internal Failure Costs								
Detect design/coding correction								
Risk analysis								
Customer appraisal and review								
Any other upstream failure-related measures								

Phase Quality Tasks	Requirements Costs	Design Costs	Code Costs	Test, Evaluation, Validation, and Verification Costs	Integration Costs	Maintenance Costs	Total Costs	Explanation of Cost and its Implications
Downstream Internal Failure Costs								
Test and evaluation								
Detection and coding/design correction								
Risk analysis								
Design review								
Validate and verify								
Customer appraisal and review								
New release								
Any other downstream failure-related measures								

TABLE 4.3
Continued

Phase Quality Tasks	Requirements Costs	Design Costs	Code Costs	Test, Evaluation, Validation, and Verification Costs	Integration Costs	Maintenance Costs	Total Costs	Explanation of Cost and its Implications
External Failure Costs								
Returns								
All internal activities in the first four stages								
Complaints								
Expedited delivery								
Legal issues								
CAR								
Corrective measures (during integration, expansion, and maintenance)								
New release								
Any other external failure-related measures								
Total Costs								

2. **Establish an installation team.** A credible team is essential in establishing such a system. It should consist of software professionals, test and sales engineers, quality professionals, and an accounting cadre. It should be headed by a senior accounting executive as champion. It is important to provide the best resources and personnel for such an initiative. If it is part of a DFTS initiative, a trained black belt who is well-versed in CoSQ and DFTS may be an excellent candidate to coordinate this assignment.

3. **Select an organizational segment as a prototype.** It is best to launch such an initiative as a prototype in a small software project in the early planning stages. It can be launched as a stand-alone initiative, but the payoff is substantially higher if it is part of a larger initiative, such as DFTS.

4. **Obtain the cooperation of users and suppliers of information.** It is critical that both users and suppliers of CoSQ information have a stake in the initiative's success and are adequately represented on the implementation team. Management should provide encouragement and incentives to ensure its success.

5. **Define quality costs and quality cost categories.** It must be understood that quality data is secondary or derivative data, not the primary fiduciary data. It is important that various costs are defined properly (see Tables 4.2 and 4.3) and are clearly understood. Explanations should be provided for various conformance and nonconformance costs and their implications. Such documentation identifies necessary follow-up.

6. **Identify quality costs within each category.** A brainstorming meeting of users and providers of information is an effective way to recognize the costs incurred at various phases of the software life cycle. The objective is not to seek consensus but to come to agreement with a view to identifying quality cost items correctly.

7. **Determine the sources of quality cost information.** Certain data may not be readily obtainable or may not be useful in the form available. In such cases, considerable effort may be needed to uncover quality costs from aggregate accounting data. But a good estimate—rather than rigorous accuracy—may be all that is required at this stage. Accuracy of data collection as well as estimates improve as the system is implemented, used, and documented correctly over a period of time.

8. **Design quality cost reports and graphs.** Reports and graphs should be user-friendly in terms of details, the type of information needed, and timely availability. They should be accurate and have a simple presentation. In this regard, the value of appropriate visual aids cannot be overemphasized.

9. **Establish procedures to collect quality cost information.** Best practices from within and across industries should be identified. Involvement of accounting professionals can be extremely useful. Only individuals who understand the process of data collection and who have been trained in the CoSQ process should be responsible for collecting cost information. Proper procedures should be established and supported by adequate forms, personnel, and computer systems.

10. **Collect data and prepare and distribute reports.** The team should ensure that this step is carried out in a manner that is based on a sound reporting system developed as a result of following the preceding steps diligently. By doing so, the team will inspire confidence and prepare the organization to use data and facts to manage its quality initiatives.

11. **Eliminate bugs from the system.** The whole system should be monitored by running trial runs. People must learn and develop confidence in collection and use of data. The issues related to reliability of data should be addressed. The focus should be on the value of data from the users' perspective, with a view toward helping them improve the quality of the software development process.

12. **Expand the system.** As soon as the system is up and running, this practice can be expanded to other segments of the organization in a planned manner. It is important to maintain proper records for the existing reporting system so that best practices can be established internally. The reporting system should be evaluated regularly for continuous improvement.

Payback from Investment in Quality

Quality initiatives are actually investments in future benefits and cost savings. They are like investments in preventive health care with a view to enjoying the benefits of good health (the quality). They also prevent catastrophic health-care expenses (costs) that may have to be incurred if prevention is ignored. The benefits or savings to be realized are not always apparent. For, example although certain internal cost savings are identifiable, costs of external failures associated with regulation, litigation, bad publicity, loss of customer or market share, and bankruptcies are difficult to estimate. Equally, the impact of quality on future revenue and business growth is difficult to estimate. Dollar estimates are just that—estimates. Being obsessed with absolutely measurable costs and benefits is counterproductive to any quality initiative. This mind-set of absolute accuracy and measuring everything often becomes a major irritant. If past records are available, they should be used. But it is impossible to get all the data on costs and benefits. It is best to take a practical approach toward these matters: make a conservative estimate of costs and benefits, and take appropriate measures upstream to prevent external failures. As a CoSQ system is established and up and running, such data is available more readily.

The payback from investment in various quality tasks can be expressed as follows:

$$\text{Payback from quality investments} = \text{benefits realized} - \text{investments in quality tasks}$$

The Return on Quality Investments (ROQI) is calculated as follows:

$$\text{ROQI} = \frac{\text{Payback from quality investments}}{\text{Investments in quality tasks}} \times 100, \%$$

Discounted Cash Flow Approach

ROQI normally is discounted using Net Present Value (NPV)/Internal Rate of Return (IRR) analysis. Another important Discounted Cash Flow (DCF) metric is the payback period. ROQI with discounted return is

$$\text{ROQI} = \frac{\text{NPV of payback from quality investments}}{\text{Investments in quality tasks}} \times 100, \%$$

Value of CoSQ Analysis

Quality initiatives very often emanate from quality professionals. Management may not be fully aware of the benefits to be realized. A good CoSQ analysis invariably reveals surprising, even shocking, facts to upper management. They are likely to understand and respond to such revelations because CoSQ is expressed in the language they understand best—dollars. It uncovers the cost of not paying attention to quality and helps identify activities that need to be addressed. A CoSQ metric program thus plays a critical role in successful execution of a DFTS initiative from both quality and cost perspectives.

It may be added that normally an appropriate quality task saves more than it costs. At times, a quality task may cost more than it saves, but it may satisfy a critical customer requirement. Customer requirements and not cost alone should be the determining factor in initiating a quality task. Equally, customer requirements may necessitate cost, quality, and schedule optimization, a basic precept of DFTS. The important thing about DFTS is that it helps you understand customer requirements throughout the software life cycle. Such understanding of various customer requirements provides the need and opportunity for *robust optimization*. We discuss this in Chapters 16 and 17.

Pitfalls of a CoSQ Program

A CoSQ initiative is too critical to be allowed to go astray. It is therefore important to be aware of the following potential pitfalls:

- **Lack of management support:** Ideally the initiative should be initiated by top management, with specific objectives of improving quality and customer satisfaction. If it is initiated by quality professionals or the accounting department, they must make sure that top management is committed to it. Without management's support, the initiative is likely to fail and should not be attempted.

- **Treating the CoSQ data as financial data:** CoSQ is not regular financial data that is prepared for financial reporting. The quality of CoSQ data is determined by whether it leads to addressing the root causes of failures effectively rather than by their absolute accuracy. Absolute accuracy of cost of quality is difficult to ensure and may be costly because many intangibles exist. Furthermore, you're not looking for absolute accuracy.

- **Emphasizing cost reduction, not customer requirements:** The emphasis should always be on improving product or process quality, and meeting customer requirements and not treating CoSQ primarily as a cost-reduction exercise.

- **Using the initiative for performance appraisal:** The initiative should not be used as an instrument for personnel evaluation, because it is not. It will end up giving you wrong information if used for that purpose. As a rule, it is precarious to use any kind of quality management data for individual performance appraisal. Effective quality improvement is an organizational process and is the outcome of many cooperating individuals. Rewarding them individually results in local optimization. Further, as Deming has said, performance evaluation, merit rating, and annual reviews have devastating effects on individuals and quality.

Cost of Software Quality Over the Life Cycle

As we've discussed, various software activities can be broadly classified as follows:

- Productive activities
- Preventive activities

- Appraisal activities

- Corrective activities: debugging internal upstream and downstream failures and external failures

Only productive activities create value for the customers. The rest constitute the costs of quality that should be minimized. These costs are interrelated in that the better the job done upstream, the lower the downstream and, consequently, overall costs. In a typical software project, as much as 80 to 90% of the time and costs are incurred downstream. Figure 4.3 shows a situation in which conformance-related activities have not been carried out well and consequently result in unacceptably high internal and external failures. But the whole picture changes if preventive and appraisal activities are performed well so that just a few minor internal failures and virtually no external ones exist (see Figure 4.4).

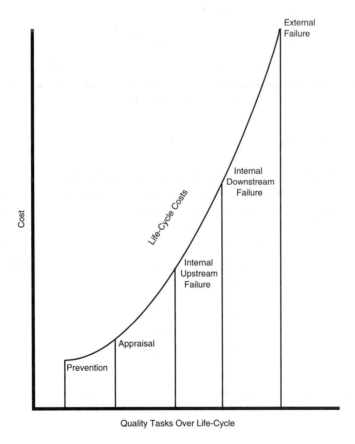

FIGURE 4.3
CoSQ Over the Life Cycle of a Traditional Software Development Process

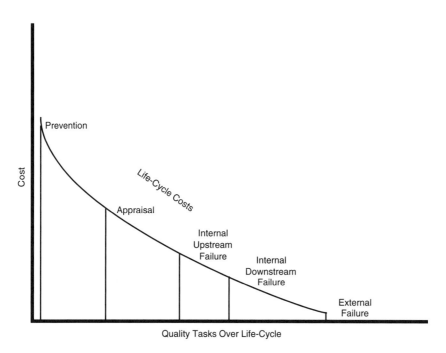

FIGURE 4.4
CoSQ Over the Life Cycle of a DFTS Development Process

This approach requires more time, cost, and attention upstream to reduce overall cost and cycle time while meeting customer requirements throughout the software life cycle. Taguchi recommends that about 80% of product development time and cost should be dedicated to the upstream stages of product development—namely, advanced engineering and design. This is compared to the 20% that is usually the case. This line of thinking requires greater time and cost expended upstream, resulting in dramatically lower downstream and overall life-cycle costs. Obviously, this requires totally new thinking and novel approaches:

- From thinking based on the cost of the initial release to a mind-set of life-cycle cost

- From an orientation toward testing and inspection to focusing on customer requirements and design

- From an approach based on corrective actions to a strategy of prevention

This is the essence of DFTS deployment. Chapter 5 discusses the need for management support and infrastructure in a DFTS process. Chapters 15 through 19 discuss deploying DFTS methodology for requirements and cost optimization.

Case Study 4.1: CoSQ at Intents Software

Intents Software is an enterprise software vendor. It is proposing to establish a CoSQ system as part of the proposed DFTS initiative. Top management is contemplating deploying DFTS to a selected software development project and eventually expanding it organization-wide.

The discussion is still in the preliminary stages. The current practice involves 18 months of development time and uses the typical build-and-repair development model, with little effort and money spent to prevent and appraise errors. Management has set up a CoSQ team with the task of recommending a framework for establishing it. As the first step, the team is expected to come up with a memo supported by appropriate data, facts, and assumptions on the financial and nonfinancial benefits of CoSQ and DFTS initiatives. The team has collected data on sales and development costs. They have placed costs of quality-related activities into five categories: prevention, appraisal, upstream internal failure, downstream internal failure, and external failure. This data has been compiled for the current software development practice and has been estimated for the proposed DFTS initiative, as shown in Table 4.4.

Based on the available data and estimates, the CoSQ team has analyzed the financial implications of the proposed quality initiative. What should be the highlights of such an analysis?

Case Analysis

The preceding case is a common decision situation involving the introduction of quality initiatives. We will analyze the case using the Discounted Cash Flow method.

Step 1: Tabulate Period Cash Flows

You compile the quality costs and total costs by adding the various costs shown in Table 4.4. The period cash flow is simply the difference between sales revenue and total costs for each year. These are compiled for both the current practice and the proposed practice, as shown in Table 4.5.

TABLE 4.4
Sales Revenues and Development, Marketing, and Quality Costs

Cost	Current Development Practice (in Dollars)					With Proposed DFTS Initiative (in Dollars)				
	Year 1	Year 2	Year 3	Year 4	Year 5	Year 1	Year 2	Year 3	Year 4	Year 5
Development cost	1M	500k	0	0	0	1M	500k	0	0	0
Marketing cost	50k	100k	250k	400k	200k	50k	100k	250k	400k	200k
Prevention cost	20k	10k	0	0	0	150k	60k	0	0	0
Appraisal cost	20k	10k	0	0	0	80k	40k	0	0	0
Upstream internal failure cost	80k	40k	0	0	0	20k	10k	0	0	0
Downstream internal failure cost	0	60k	0	0	0	0	20k	0	0	0
External failure cost	0	0	120k	80k	30k	0	0	30k	20k	10k
Total quality costs	120k	120k	120k	80k	30k	250k	130k	30k	20k	10k
Sales revenue	0	2M	5M	8M	4M	0	2M	5M	10M	5M

TABLE 4.5
Period and NPV Cash Flows

Cost	Current Development Practice (in Dollars)					With Proposed DFTS Initiative (in Dollars)				
	Year 1	Year 2	Year 3	Year 4	Year 5	Year 1	Year 2	Year 3	Year 4	Year 5
Development cost	1M	500k	0	0	0	1M	500k	0	0	0
Marketing cost	50k	100k	250k	400k	200k	50k	100k	250k	400k	200k
Total quality costs	120k	120k	120k	80k	30k	250k	130k	30k	20k	10k
Total costs	1.17M	0.72M	0.37M	0.48M	0.23M	1.57M	0.73M	0.28M	0.42M	0.21M
Sales revenue	0	2M	5M	8M	4M	0	2M	5M	10M	5M
Period cash flow	−1.17M	1.28M	4.63M	7.52M	3.77M	−1.57M	1.27M	4.72M	9.5 8M	4.79M
NPV cash flow **r = 0.12**	11.44M					13.23M				

Step 2: Compute the NPV Cash Flow

You compute the NPVs of cash flows of the current practice and the proposed initiative—NPV_{CP} and NPV_{PI}, respectively—by discounting the period cash flows by 12% per year:

$$NPV_{CP} = -1.17 + \frac{1.28}{(1+.12)} + \frac{4.63}{(1+.12)^2} + \frac{7.52}{(1+.12)^3} + \frac{3.77}{(1+.12)^4} = \$11.44 \text{ million}$$

$$NPV_{PI} = -1.57 + \frac{1.27}{(1+.12)} + \frac{4.72}{(1+.12)^2} + \frac{9.58}{(1+.12)^3} + \frac{4.79}{(1+.12)^4} = \$13.23 \text{ million}$$

Step 3: Compute the Quality Cost Differential

The discounted differential between the quality costs in the proposed initiative and the existing system provides the difference in investments in quality costs, I_{QCD}. It is computed as follows:

$$I_{QCD} = (250-120) + \frac{(130-120)}{(1+.12)} + \frac{(30-120)}{(1+.12)^2} + \frac{(20-80)}{(1+.12)^3} + \frac{(10-30)}{(1+.12)^4} = \$11,700$$

Step 4: Compare the NPV Cash Flows and Compute the ROQI

The NPV cash flows of the current practice and the proposed initiative have been computed and are as follows:

NPV_{CP} = $11.44 million

NPV_{PI} = $13.23 million

Difference in NPVs = $ 1.79 million

Based on the preceding analysis, because the NPV cash flow of the proposed quality initiative is higher than that of the existing system, the proposal seems financially attractive.

ROQI, based on cash flow, is computed as follows:

$$ROQI = \frac{\text{Payback from proposed initiative}}{\text{Investment in quality}}$$

$$= \frac{\text{Difference in NPVs}}{\text{Difference in investment}}$$

$$= \frac{1,790,000}{11,700}$$

$$= 153 \text{ times}$$

Step 5: Benefits of CoSQ

CoSQ helps you see the costs incurred at various stages of the development process. It is usually followed by cause-and-effect analysis to identify root causes of poor quality and taking remedial measures to remove them. It also lets you measure the costs of the current system and compare them to the cost of quality of the proposed initiative or benchmark costs. Finally, CoSQ provides data for the quality initiative, budgeting trade-offs at various stages of the software development cycle. Thus, no quality initiative can be financially assessed without the CoSQ measurement system, as the preceding analysis illustrates.

Step 6: Statement on Assumptions and Qualitative Factors

Although NPV and ROQI of cash flows both support the proposed initiative, they are based on cash flow estimates of the proposed initiative. The estimates should be conservative, which is what was done in the preceding case. Numerous cost factors are difficult to estimate, especially those involving the long-term impact of poor quality on the enterprise's market share and competitiveness. Therefore, it is critical that quality efforts be focused upstream.

It has been assumed that improved quality as a result of a DFTS initiative will result in improved sales. In the present analysis, the marketing costs are assumed to be the same in the two cases, but a more aggressive approach to emphasize improved quality can be undertaken. This may help improve sales figures further.

Any decision should also take into account the expected qualitative improvements in software from customer perspectives. Trustworthy software can be delivered only by deploying preventive and upstream quality initiatives such as DFTS.

CoSQ and Activity-Based Costing

A good estimate of quality costs is crucial to the success of a CoSQ program. With custom-built software, costs were much easier to estimate, because the cost of software development was pretty much the cost of the hours of labor used in the software's development. With the advent of reusable components and object-oriented and other software development tools, this direct relationship based on custom-built single-use development has broken down.[12]

These tools and applications include not only program code, but also a range of analysis, design, and test programs. Given the growing emergence of such reusable software, one particular project need not recover all the costs the first time it is used. Also, the team assembling the application is likely to be encouraged to carefully consider its own development cost for similar applications, especially if proper incentives are provided for reusing components and tools. With all this, the ballgame changes, and software development becomes more like manufacturing as far as accurate cost allocation of overheads and other shared resources. Traditional financial accounting fails to allocate the cost correctly. What we need is Activity-Based Costing (ABC) to help identify the actual cost of various software development activities, just like in manufacturing, where it is used rather widely.

ABC in a Software Organization

You should carefully consider the following issues before introducing ABC and its variant, Activity-Based Management (ABM), in a software organization:[13]

- **Extent of reuse:** In a systematic reuse environment, indirect costs and overhead associated with reuse can become a significant portion of software development costs, possibly approaching 50%. Traditional methods of accounting tend to under-cost projects that are comparatively heavy consumers of reuse activities and over-cost projects that are light consumers of reuse activities. This leads to inappropriate conclusions about the true cost of those projects. Furthermore, traditional methods provide no systematic means for assessing and improving the efficiency and effectiveness of reuse activities. ABC methods and associated ABM principles provide a means to address both of these shortcomings of traditional approaches. In a heavy reuse environment, costing anomalies resulting from traditional accounting can defeat a CoSQ program. They can also lead to poor decisions in any domain where accurate knowledge of costs is the key factor, especially product pricing and product mix decisions.

- **Cost categorization:** ABC provides a systematic method for mapping resource costs to various software development activities and from activities to products.

- **Conditions of ABC application:** Although ABC was originally developed for repetitive manufacturing environments, it has since been generalized as a means to map true resource costs to any *cost object* of interest. This includes not just products, but also services, such as health care, education, customers, branch offices, and projects. However, to apply ABC, three conditions must be met:

  - Indirect and overhead costs must be substantial and must be poorly accounted for by traditional means.

  - Objects (such as products, customers, and projects) must exist for which management cares about knowing the true costs.

  - Repetitive activities must exist that can serve as the basis for mapping indirect overhead costs to cost objects.

The systematic reuse environment, such as component-based software, meets these criteria. Such environments are characterized by high overhead costs associated with centralized reuse teams and infrastructure.

Starting ABC in a Software Organization

The cost assignment view of an ABC model can be developed according to the following seven-step procedure (see Turney[14] for more detailed guidance):

1. Identify the repetitive activities to define within the scope of the ABC effort.

2. Group the activities into activity centers—collections of activities that share the same overhead cost pools.

3. Identify the resources used in overhead work, and aggregate them into pools by activity center.

4. Identify resource drivers—those that determine the relative share of each overhead cost pool attributable to each activity.

5. Determine the basis for calculating unit costs of each activity.

6. Identify cost objects, such as products and customers.

7. Determine the cost drivers—those that define the extent of consumption of each activity by cost objects of interest.

Benefits of ABC

ABC can provide three kinds of benefits to software organizations practicing systematic reuse:

1. Because it supports more accurate allocation of overhead costs, ABC can lead to more accurate conclusions about the cost-effectiveness of individual projects. When the result of a project is a product sold to others, it can provide the basis for pricing and judging profitability.

2. Equally important, ABC can help you assess and improve the productivity and effectiveness of indirect reuse activities.

3. ABC assists in various quality initiatives by providing a more accurate costing of activities. It can clearly reveal what the costs are and which of the following categories the costs are absorbed into:

   - **Productive activities:** Identifying customer requirements, designing, and coding. These are the useful activities that "customers pay for," and they must be carried out to produce the desired software.

- **Preventive activities:** Making sure that software development processes and procedures will lead to conformance to customer requirements.
- **Appraisal activities:** All activities carried out to ensure that the software developed meets customer requirements.
- **Internal upstream corrective activities:** All activities associated with detecting and correcting defects and faults associated with the requirements identification, design, and coding stages.
- **Internal downstream corrective activities:** All activities related to detecting and correcting defects and faults associated with the downstream stages of test and evaluation, and verification and validation.
- **External corrective activities:** All activities associated with detecting and correcting faults and complaints following release to customers.

ABC, if applicable, goes hand-in-hand with CoSQ. Like CoSQ, ABC does not provide financial data. Therefore, it does not need the accuracy and rigor associated with financial reporting. The pitfalls associated with CoSQ are largely applicable to ABC as well. It is absolutely critical to involve financial professionals in managing and supporting ABC and CoSQ. ABC can be easily adapted to the software development process and is well documented.[15, 16, 17]

Sidebar 4.1: ABC for Service Industries

Two fields in which cost increases have been hyper-inflationary over the past three decades are health care and higher education. Every nursing station in a hospital has been a "profit center" for years, but without ABC, it made no sense to ask a question such as "What is the average cost of a heart bypass procedure?" Or, in higher education, "What is the marginal cost of allowing 10 more students to enroll in Psychology 101?" Although the "data" is available in principle, it's inaccessible without ABC. ABC has allowed significant improvements in controlling runaway costs in health care and higher education since it was first applied nearly a decade ago.

Quality Loss Function in Software

The concept of Quality Loss Function is a central tenet of Taguchi Methods. As discussed in Chapter 2, Taguchi argues around "loss of quality" rather than quality itself, and the implications of such loss to the customer, producer, and society at large. Quality loss is defined as "loss imparted by the product to society from the time the product is shipped." This includes the following:

- Loss to the company through the costs of preventive, appraisal, and various internal and external software failure and debugging activities

- Costs to the customer through poor software product performance and reliability

- Further losses to the company if it loses customers as a result of poor product performance

- Probable losses to society if the software causes cost, crime, safety, security, health, or environmental hazards to society at large

Taking a best-possible target value for the quality characteristic, Taguchi associates a simple quadratic loss function with deviations from the target value. QLF shows that a reduction in variability about the target leads to a disproportionate decrease in various losses and a subsequent increase in quality. This function is used for design decisions on financial implications of quality investments to decide whether additional costs of improved quality will actually prove to be worthwhile in the marketplace. The important difference between the traditional approach and Taguchi's approach is that in Taguchi Methods, the product quality is determined by lack of variability from the target value as opposed to quality acceptance within specifications (see Figures 2.3, 2.4, and 2.5 in Chapter 2).

QLF, along with the signal-to-noise ratio, constitutes one of the two measures of quality in Taguchi Methods. It helps you make a sound financial decision on improved performance that comes from tighter tolerance. QLF is discussed further in Chapters 16 and 17.

Financial Evaluation of a DFTS Investment

The most common financial evaluation emphasizes just the dollar savings or ROQI following the introduction of a quality initiative, as discussed earlier in this chapter. This is absolutely inadequate, even from a financial perspective. Due emphasis should be given to other financial metrics, such as cash flow, sales growth, productivity gains, and Return on Equity (ROE), that quality improvements create in successive years. Equally important are nonfinancial metrics with regard to *customer satisfaction*, *process improvement*, and *leadership development* that are critical in creating sustainable value. A set of financial and nonfinancial metrics should be used for evaluation in an ongoing manner, rather than using just ROQI following the initial deployment. Sound development practice over a period of time creates sustainable results. The improved results are also made possible by addressing root causes of deficiencies that robust nonfinancial metrics reveal. So both are important: financial and nonfinancial metrics, one no more than the other. Such an approach based on Kaplan and Norton's *balanced scorecard* leads to improved decision-making and problem-solving.[18]

Metrics for DFTS Evaluation

The following metrics can be used to evaluate the DFTS intervention in various stages of the software life cycle:

- **Financial performance:** ROQI, CoSQ, cash flow, sales growth, profitability, life-cycle cost, market share, productivity, ROE

- **Customer satisfaction:** Software trustworthiness (including reliability, safety, security, maintainability, and customer responsiveness, as well as cost and delivery time)

- **Software process capability:** Improvement in understanding user domain, dealing with software complexity, schedule deviation, delivered defects, test defects, final testing time, user-reported defects, development cost, process predictability

- **Leadership and quality of work life (QWL):** Individual capability, team and leadership development, hiring and retaining talent, innovation capability, QWL

These measures are obviously interrelated. A broad evaluation enables sound performance monitoring, which helps you initiate appropriate corrective measures with a view to improving the DFTS process. In the absence of nonfinancial metrics, organizations may not be able to measure the impact on *customer satisfaction*, *process improvement*, and *leadership capability*. Many organizations get into the trap of just chasing financial returns following a quality initiative, without ascertaining its impact on other aspects. Such an approach inevitably leads to missed opportunities.

Establishing a Financial Evaluation Framework for a DFTS Initiative

The following list discusses some broad issues for financial evaluation of a DFTS intervention that you must keep in mind:

- **Obtain management commitment and support.** The top management team, including the CEO, CFO, and senior executives in charge of software development and DFTS, must support the establishment of financial metrics for the software development process. The value of establishing various financial metrics should be obvious to them before they commit resources and use them in decision-making.

- **Do not use just ROQI.** ROQI plays an important but essentially limited role. First, it helps in the initial decision-making to introduce DFTS. Second, it identifies the initial investment. Because initial investments are relatively small, organizations need to consider other financial objectives, such as *growth* and *market share*, that may be strategic. Other financial metrics also need to be considered in financial evaluation: *cash flow*, *profitability*, *life-cycle cost*, *productivity*, *ROE*, and *CoSQ*.

- **Establish the cost** of various quality-related activities in the software development process. Most software organizations do not have them, but it is essential to identify them to create useful and reliable financial metrics.

- **Establish a financial evaluation team.** The evaluation exercise should be headed by an accounting professional and should be adequately supported by the DFTS black belt, master black belt if available, DFTS champion, and software developers who are participating in the initiative. It is important to provide the best resources and personnel for this task.

- **Provide training and incentives.** All these personnel need to undergo training as part of the DFTS implementation process. (Chapter 5 discusses training and incentive issues.)

- **Select financial measures and the DCF approach.** Decide which of the financial metrics you will use. For ROI, select the appropriate Discounted Cash Flow (DCF) approach between IRR, NPV, and payback period that will be applied.[19] These require that future savings or revenue streams be forecast and a system for tracking costs be established. Life-cycle costs (see Figures 4.3 and 4.4) should be taken into account, not just internal development costs. Estimating various savings—especially on failure costs, one of the main areas of cost savings and quality improvement—is not easy. You must use historical data whenever possible. It is important to be conservative on estimates of future savings. You will have an opportunity to revise the estimates as the project progresses (which should be done in any case).

- **Start with a small software project.** It is advisable to launch a DFTS initiative on a small software project. This approach lets you introduce change without major disruption. (However, a roll-out plan for expanding DFTS to the rest of the organization should be carefully developed and communicated. All important development and learning should be documented for future learning and communicated to sustain interest and support.)

- **Integrate the CoSQ team.** If a CoSQ team exists, it may be advisable to integrate them in one unified team to establish financial information required for DFTS. Care should be taken to ensure that the team does not duplicate work and compile data that is readily available elsewhere.

- **Identify savings and costs.** Determining the savings from a DFTS intervention is an important step in the evaluation process. The net savings in an activity from DFTS can be calculated from the following equation:

    net savings in an activity = costs without DFTS − costs with DFTS

Here all the direct and indirect recurring costs are identified. If historical and valid data is available, costs without DFTS can be established relatively easily; otherwise, an estimate of various costs should be made. It may be easier to cost certain activities than others. The all-important external failure costs are the most difficult to estimate. These include costs that have not yet been encountered but that are plausible. It is advisable to estimate on the worst case.

- **Monitor and improve.** It is important to monitor for accuracy of data and value and validity of metrics from user perspectives. Steps should be taken to improve the cost and quality of data collection and presentation. A tracking system should be established to keep records.

- **Expand the system as needed.** After the system is debugged and documented, it can be expanded to the rest of the organization systematically.

Chapter 22 illustrates an excellent CoSQ program at Raytheon's Electronic Systems (RES) Group. It captures the essence of a sound CoSQ initiative and is highly recommended reading for software developers and quality professionals. Chapter 3 discussed software quality metrics. Chapters 5 and 20 cover individual, team, and leadership capability metrics. Chapters 6 through 21 discuss various software trustworthiness issues. They all contribute to delivering trustworthy software. A software organization embarking on a quality initiative must rely on a balanced set of financial and nonfinancial metrics covering various spheres. Many quality issues do not lend themselves to quantitative evaluation. "Everything must be measured before we move" is a wrong mind-set. Often, sound estimates may be just fine. The idea that a sound process creates value by itself should not be ignored. Most significantly, the prime focus should always be on meeting customer requirements. In the absence of that, financial evaluation may not even be carried out. In any case, you need nonfinancial metrics to understand and respond to customer needs, improve the software development process, and fortify your organization's software development capability. A sole focus on financial results is inevitably dysfunctional. As Walter A. Shewhart said, "Price without quality has no meaning." Such clarity and the implied self-discipline are essential for an organization embarking on a robust software development process. Without such commitment, it is difficult to see how the much-needed internal transformation for customer and process focus can be pulled off.

Key Points

- Financial analyses of a DFTS process are meant to provide visibility and control for effective decision-making. Equally, various nonfinancial control mechanisms are needed in this regard. These analyses should not, however, lose sight of customer requirements.

- Sound financial return is one of the desired outcomes of a DFTS initiative that is designed to meet customer requirements while also meeting the software developer's internal objectives. It is just that the focus is on customer requirements.

- The idea that improved quality can improve cost-effectiveness is not totally new. It has been gaining ground only in recent years, following the enormous success of Six Sigma, DFSS, and Lean.

- Cost of quality (CoQ) analysis is important, because it reveals how much you expend on prevention, appraisal, inspection, discovering, analyzing, scrapping, and correcting defects, faults, and errors.

- CoSQ can be defined as the total cost of conformance and nonconformance to the customer's quality requirements. It consists of various direct and indirect expenses incurred when preventing, appraising, testing, discovering, analyzing, and fixing software faults, including maintenance.

- Determining CoQ is a first measure in identifying and removing the root causes of failure.

- Monetary evaluation of not performing quality tasks is challenging, because many intangible and competitive factors come into play. Often, conservative estimates are the only way.

- Self-debugging can detect and fix faults. Failure costs can escalate if this is not done.

- Given the growing emergence of reusable software, one particular project doesn't need to recover all the costs the first time it is used. ABC can be used to identify the correct cost of use, just as in manufacturing.

- Three conditions must be met before ABC is initiated: indirect and overhead costs must be substantial and poorly accounted for by traditional means, cost objects must exist that management cares about, and repetitive activities must exist to serve as the basis for cost mapping.

- CoSQ requires a new line of thinking: from cost of initial release to a mind-set of life-cycle cost, from an orientation toward testing and inspection to focusing on customer requirements and design, and from an approach based on corrective actions to a strategy of prevention.

- QLF shows that a reduction in variability about the target leads to a disproportionate decrease in various losses and a subsequent increase in quality.

- ROQI emphasizes return on quality investment following initial introduction. This is inadequate, so due emphasis should be given to other financial metrics, such as cash flow, sales growth, productivity gains, and ROE. Equally important are nonfinancial metrics with regard to customer satisfaction, process improvement, and leadership development.

Additional Resources

http://www.prenhallprofessional.com/title/0131872508

http://www.agilenty.com/publications

Internet Exercises

Go to http://lifelong.engr.utexas.edu/pdf/sqi/xtalk98.pdf and read the article by Herb Krasner.

1. Come to class prepared to discuss your conclusions about this article.

2. Why is CoSQ important in software development?

3. What are important issues in adapting and applying CoQ to software?

4. What are the various ways in which a CoSQ approach can be used?

5. How can you improve a CoSQ program following initiation?

This article is also available from Herb Krasner, "Using the Cost of Quality Approach to Software," *CROSSTALK: The Journal of Defense Software Engineering*, November 1998, pp. 6–11.

Review Questions

1. What are the objectives of financial analyses in a DFTS process? Do they by themselves suffice in meeting those objectives? What should such analyses focus on?

2. What are the desired outcomes of a DFTS initiative? Give five specific examples in a software development context.

3. How have views on quality and cost evolved in recent years? What are the major causes of the change in thinking?

4. Explain what CoSQ means. List three benefits of cost-of-quality analysis.

5. Explain how payback and Return on Quality Investments (ROQI) are determined. Why should you consider NPV and IRR in evaluating ROQI? What should be the determining factor in initiating a quality task?

6. List and explain five major CoSQ categories. How are they related, and what are the implications of their relationships?

7. Explain, with examples, how failure costs escalate if self-debugging by the programmer fails to detect a fault.

8. What are the pitfalls of a CoSQ program?

9. What major factors should you consider before initiating ABC and ABM programs in a software environment? List and explain the steps involved in initiating such programs.

10. What are the benefits of ABC? What are its pitfalls?

11. Explain and differentiate between "productive activities" and "cost-of-quality activities." How are they related? How will you spread your quality efforts and costs over the software life cycle?

12. Explain "loss of quality" in the context of Taguchi's QLF. What are the components of such losses? How is QLF used in a product design?

13. List six financial metrics in evaluating a quality investment and explain their importance.

14. Why don't financial metrics suffice in evaluating a quality investment? How can this be addressed?

Discussion Questions

1. What are the limitations of financial analyses as control mechanisms in a DFTS process? Give some examples of nonfinancial control mechanisms. What can go wrong when such analyses lose sight of customer requirements and focus only on the software developer's internal objectives?

2. Discuss the need for visibility and control in a software development process. Specify with examples the challenges of providing visibility and control. What are their implications?

3. Discuss the limitations of the CoSQ approach given the difficulties of knowing and estimating even the most important costs. How much can you depend on quantitative analysis for taking quality initiatives? What else should you consider?

4. Explain the need to incorporate ABC into the software development process. When is it most recommended? When is it not?

5. Explain the limitations of financial metrics in evaluating a quality initiative. How can they be addressed?

6. Interview the appropriate managers in a software development company to determine if and how they measure the cost of quality. If they do, find out how useful their experience has been. If they don't, ask why not.

7. Explain the difference between the "specification-based" approach to quality loss and Taguchi's concept of Quality Loss Function. Illustrate with specific examples in a software development context.

8. What does Taguchi mean by "loss to society"? Is it possible to measure all these losses? What does Taguchi propose in this context?

Problems

1. A software developer has identified the following costs of quality at three development centers:

Center	Development Center 1	Development Center 2	Development Center 3
Sales revenue	$15M	$7.9M	$2M
Total quality costs	$5.4M	$ 1.4M	$5.M
Prevention	3%	52%	15%
Appraisal	12%	22%	30%
Upstream internal failure	15%	12%	27%
Downstream internal failure	28%	9%	15%
External failure	42%	5%	13%

What conclusions can management draw from these figures? Explain with appropriate analysis.

2. The following table shows estimates for development, marketing, and various quality costs with respect to the current practice and a proposed quality initiative in a software organization. What are the financial implications of the proposed initiative? What is your recommendation for the company?

Cost	Current Development Practice (in Dollars)					Proposed Quality Initiative (in Dollars)				
	Year 1	Year 2	Year 3	Year 4	Year 5	Year 1	Year 2	Year 3	Year 4	Year 5
Development Cost	2M	1.5M	0	0	0	2M	1.3M	0	0	0
Marketing Cost	75k	150k	300k	450k	250k	90k	200k	350k	500k	300k
Prevention Cost	5k	10k	0	0	0	200k	90k	0	0	0
Appraisal Cost	20k	10k	0	0	0	90k	50k	0	0	0
Upstream Internal Failure Cost	90k	60k	0	0	0	40k	20k	0	0	0
Downstream Internal Failure Cost	0	90k	0	0	0	0	20k	0	0	0
External Failure Cost	0	0	180k	90k	60k	0	0	40k	30k	10k
Sales Revenue	0	2M	5M	8M	4M	0	2M	7M	10M	7M

Endnotes

[1]See, for example, Noel M. Tichy and S. Sherman, *Control Your Destiny or Someone Else Will* (New York: Harper Business, 2001), pp. 13, 334–336, 507–513, 518–524.

[2]http://www32.brinkster.com/unaweb/work_examples/GE1990.htm provides a pretty good evaluation of Jack Welch's stewardship of GE, particularly his strategic initiatives during his two decades as its CEO.

[3]Philip Crosby, *Quality Is Free* (New York: McGraw-Hill, 1979).

[4]http://www.motorola.com/content/0,,2514,00.html.

[5]W. Kuo, V. Rajendra Prasad, F. A. Tillman, Ching-Lai Wang, *Optimal Reliability Design* (Cambridge, MA: Cambridge University Press, 2001), 1.3.3 on p. 5.

[6]James H. Dobbins in G. Gordon Schulmeyer and James I. McManus, *Handbook of Software Quality Assurance* (Upper Saddle River, NJ: Prentice-Hall PTR, 1999), p. 196.

[7]Ibid, p. 195.

[8]Ibid, p. 215.

[9]James R. Evans and William M. Lindsay, *The Management and Control of Quality* (Cincinnati, OH: South-Western College Publishing, 1999), p. 487.

[10]Ibid, p. 490.

[11]Ibid, p. 490.

[12]Robert G. Fichman and Chris F. Kemerer, "Activity Based Management of Component-based Software Development," www.pitt.edu/~ckemerer/ieeesoft.htm.

[13]Op cit Evans and Lindsay, pp. 490–491.

[14]P. B. Turney, *Common Cents* (Hillsboro, OR: Cost Technology, 1991), as cited in reference 10.

[15]Robert S. Cooper and Robert S. Kaplan, *The Design of Cost Management Systems: Text, Cases and Readings* (Englewood Cliffs, NJ: Prentice-Hall, 1991).

[16]Robert S. Kaplan, Ed., *Measures for Manufacturing Excellence* (Boston, MA: Harvard Business School Press, 1990).

[17]H. Thomas Johnson, "Activity-Based Information: A Blueprint for World-Class Management Accounting," *Management Accounting*, June 1988, pp. 23–30.

[18]Robert S. Kaplan and David P. Norton, "Balanced Scorecard: Measures That Drive Performance," *Harvard Business Review*, May–June 1994.

[19]Charles T. Horngren, Srikant M. Datar, George Foster, *Cost Accounting: A Managerial Emphasis*, 11th Ed. (Englewood Cliffs, NJ: Prentice-Hall, 2000), pp. 720–726.

CHAPTER 5

Organizational Infrastructure and Leadership for DFTS

There is nothing more difficult to take in hand, more perilous to conduct or more uncertain in its success than to take the lead in the introduction of a new order of things.

—*Niccolo Machiavelli*

…no mere process can turn a poor performer into a star. Rather, you have to address employees' fundamental way of thinking.

—*Fujio Cho, Former President, Toyota Motor Corporation*

Overview

Quality challenges in software are not unique. Much can be gained by adapting quality system best practices from manufacturing and hardware and using them in the software development environment. Because DFTS requires major changes in the typical software development process, organizations that anticipate these changes and provide required leadership benefit in quality, customer satisfaction, cycle times, costs, and quality of work life. The underlying causes of failures of quality initiatives such as Six Sigma, Business Process Reengineering (BPR), and Total Quality Management (TQM) are just as pertinent to a DFTS initiative. All successful quality initiatives are invariably led by CEOs. This chapter describes a 15-step implementation framework, PICS, for deploying a DFTS initiative. It is based on Deming's quality philosophy, Kurt Lewin's Force Field Analysis Model for introducing and integrating desired social change, and other organizational best practices. Organizations embarking on DFTS should understand the magnitude of the tasks ahead if they are seeking transformative and lasting results.

Chapter Outline

- Organizational Challenges of a DFTS Deployment

- DFTS Implementation Framework

- Putting It All Together

- Key Points

- Additional Resources

- Internet Exercises

- Review Questions

- Discussion Questions and Projects

- Endnotes

Organizational Challenges of a DFTS Deployment

Software quality problems are not unique or unusual. This is despite design and intellectual predominance of software development processes and, to be sure, these must be taken into account in a DFTS deployment. However, much can be gained by adapting quality system best practices from manufacturing and hardware to software development environments. This is a basic precept of DFTS technology and is emphasized throughout this book. What is crucial for a successful deployment is to recognize that a DFTS initiative requires major changes in how organizations typically go about their software development process. The challenge is to understand the change process and lead it proactively to achieve both the short- and long-term objectives of the DFTS initiative.

The underlying causes of failure of quality initiatives such as Six Sigma, BPR, and TQM are just as pertinent to a DFTS initiative. There is much to learn from the implementation experiences of these interventions since the 1980s, when TQM and subsequently BPR and Six Sigma were introduced in corporations worldwide. But benchmarking best practices is insufficient (see Edgar H. Schein's article cited in the "Internet Exercises" section). The organizational preparedness and cultural fit are equally crucial. One lesson is clear: All successful quality initiatives are invariably led by CEOs. CEOs understand the business value of these initiatives, communicate them earnestly across their organizations to secure understanding and commitment, and provide necessary training and resources throughout the process. The role of the CEO and the senior management team cannot be overemphasized. As Deming said, "Either management does it, or it does not happen."

Before embarking on the DFTS process, an organization should assess its preparedness to make sure that it is indeed ready for a robust deployment. Even organizations with a formidable quality culture will do well to carry out such an appraisal. We discuss organizational preparedness later in this chapter and more fully in Chapter 20.

DFTS Implementation Framework

This chapter presents the DFTS implementation framework as a 15-step process, as shown in Table 5.1.

TABLE 5.1
DFTS Implementation Steps

Step #	Description
1.	Creating management awareness and buy-in
2.	Communicating top management's commitment
3.	Recognizing pitfalls
4.	Laying philosophical foundations for a quality-focused enterprise
5.	Building the organizational infrastructure
6.	Understanding roles and responsibilities of the key players
7.	Designing a supportive organizational structure
8.	Establishing an effective communication system
9.	Creating an appropriate reward system
10.	Establishing a Cost of Software Quality (CoSQ) reporting system
11.	Planning and launching organization-wide learning
12.	Implementing the DFTS process
13.	Monitoring and feedback for learning and improvement
14.	Freezing improvements and gains
15.	Integrating and expanding the initiative

The DFTS implementation model, shown in Figure 5.1, is a four-phase PICS framework consisting of Plan, Implement, Control, and Secure. The first ten steps relate to planning, Steps 11 and 12 represent implementing, Step 13 controlling, and Steps 14 and 15 securing. The framework emphasizes the importance of planning to prepare the organization for this major initiative. The time and resources committed to sound planning are essential and invariably pay off in successful outcomes. Even organizations with an established quality culture will do well to go through this process step by step. It provides an opportunity to address issues that are not always obvious. It is a systematic methodology for not only implementing the initiative soundly but also for sustaining it long-term and continually improving it. The two feedback loops provide opportunities for learning, corrective measures, and continual improvement. The framework consists of a variety of tools, systems, and models that constitute the subject of this book.

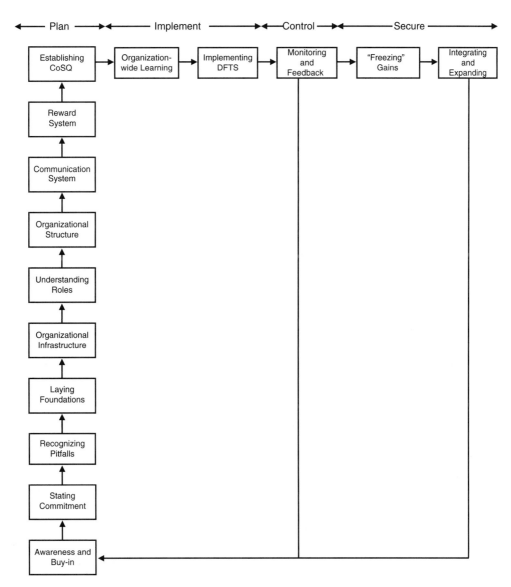

FIGURE 5.1
The PICS Implementation Model

The implementation framework can be customized for particular software development contexts. A powerful feature of this framework is that it helps you understand evolving and changing user needs throughout the development process (see Figures 5.6 and 2.6).

The feedback loops also provide updates for continual product and process improvements. The 15 steps are described next.

Step 1: Creating Management Awareness and Buy-in

This is obviously the essential first step. Nothing this significant can be undertaken successfully unless the top management team understands the initiative's business values. The business values most easily grasped by the CEO and top management team often relate to cost reduction, bottom- and top-line growth, market share, and Return on Investment (ROI). Often they are interested not only in DFTS's long-term promise but also in what it delivers in the short term. This is especially true of publicly traded corporations, where the CEOs cannot ignore financial returns beyond a few quarters. This may be a serious impediment to quality initiatives.

The initial interest is usually instigated when the CEO or a member of the top management team becomes aware of DFTS, either from an industry colleague, an academic, or a software professional. Whatever the source of the initial idea, any follow-up depends entirely on the top management team led by the CEO buying in. It happens only if DFTS's potential to create business values involving significant improvements in cost, cycle time, and expanded business opportunities is clearly grasped. This process takes place over a series of formal and informal meetings involving the CEO, the top management team, and, often, other business contacts and consultants.

The DFTS implementation process is essentially an exercise in corporate leadership. Successful implementation depends largely on how well the CEO understands various social forces involved in the implementation process. The *Force Field Analysis Model* developed by Kurt Lewin[1] is a powerful tool to diagnose major social forces that could be in play when embarking on a DFTS initiative. Figure 5.2 shows some common restraining and driving forces in this context: The restraining forces identified here are *fear of change*, *lack of skills*, and *peer pressure*. The driving forces are *incentives*, *training*, *management support*, and addressing quality problems generally by *focusing upstream*. Theoretically, the desired changes may be attained by either increasing the driving forces or diminishing the restraining forces. However, it is desirable to introduce changes by strengthening the driving forces (see Figure 5.3) rather than diminishing the restraining ones. The secondary effects of opposing restraining forces often result in higher organizational tension. This may carry unacceptable dysfunctional consequences that may best be avoided.

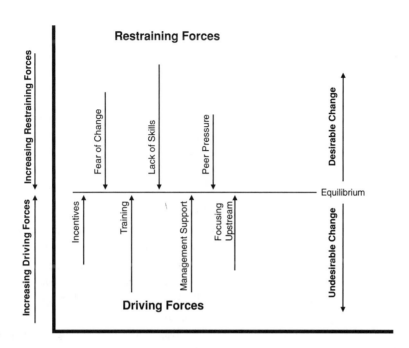

FIGURE 5.2
The Force-Field Analysis Model: Driving and Restraining Forces of Change

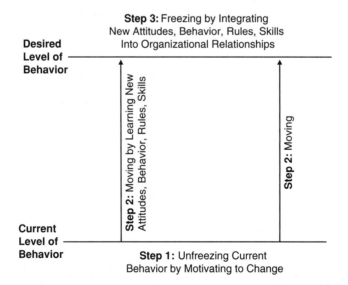

FIGURE 5.3
Lewin's Three-Step Model of Permanent Social Change

The objective of the buy-in process is for the top management team to understand that trustworthy software creates not only immense customer value but also bottom-line, growth, and other opportunities for the business. The team may deliberate on major challenges involved in a DFTS initiative using Lewin's twin models—the *Force Field Analysis Model* and the *Three-Step Model of Permanent Social Change*, shown in Figures 5.2 and 5.3, respectively. If the decision to go ahead has been made, management must set some broad goals at this stage that are primarily customer-focused. Goal refinement can be achieved gradually through the implementation process. Any goal that emphasizes just the software developer's short-term cost or growth objectives is not likely to contribute to the development of trustworthy software. *Start with customer in mind!* Other objectives will inevitably follow.

At this stage, it may be best to set up a DFTS Steering Committee. This group is responsible for policy guidelines, preparing an implementation plan, mobilizing resources, and overseeing the overall implementation. If the organization already has an equivalent body, these tasks may also be assigned to it to avoid duplication. The committee should have five or six members. It should be chaired by the Vice President of Software Development or the Chief Software Architect and assisted by a DFTS Implementation Project Manager. The CFO, CIO, CTO, Chief Quality Officer (CQO), and Vice President of Human Resources should be the other committee members. We discuss their roles later in this chapter. Additionally, we strongly believe that the CEO should be not only a member of the committee but also an active participant. This is a powerful signal to other senior executives that DFTS is a big deal. The overall direction for the successful implementation can only be provided by the CEO, who should make sure that the committee is up to the task. It is important for the CEO to remain engaged, attend committee meetings regularly, and demand results.

The committee must immediately undertake two important tasks:

- Assess any existing quality systems, resources, and initiatives within the organization with a view to preparing a DFTS implementation plan. This is part of organizational preparedness, as discussed in Chapter 20. Many valuable resources, ideas, and systems may already be available. For example, if a Cost of Software Quality (CoSQ) reporting system is in place, it could provide quite a jump start.

- Prepare an outline plan and budget in consultation with the executives concerned and consultants, if any. This is essential to get things started.

It must be emphasized that the CEO and top management do not perceive DFTS as a program to be implemented. It should be thought of more as an initiative undertaken, and then continuously improved as an ongoing process, perfected, and finally expanded and integrated with the rest of the organization. Following that, other quality improvement opportunities might require new initiatives as the organization evolves. "A target to be achieved" or "a program to be completed" mind-set often leads to burnouts and frustrations even if the "program" is successful. As Deming says, quality management requires "constancy of purpose" and should be an integral part of an organization's business process. The senior management team should be active participants in the process rather than being mere observers and auditors. In Toyota, when the president of the company comes to a training session, he has come to learn the role he has to play rather than attending merely as an observer or a ceremonial figurehead. At General Electric, Jack Welch brought similar commitment to Six Sigma. This level of involvement can be powerful and makes a huge difference. The CEO and senior management team must grasp this reality early in the process.

Step 2: Communicating Top Management's Consensus and Commitment

After the top management team has been sold on the value of DFTS and has decided to proceed, it is important to build consensus and communicate it organization-wide. The CEO should communicate the decision to launch the DFTS initiative, its rationale, and its broad objectives and expectations. Such a communique should also mention the creation of the steering committee and its membership. All those who are crucial to the initiative's success should not only understand its benefits but also be its vocal champions. This process of building consensus should be actively led by the CEO, or it runs the risk of being sabotaged. At this stage, there may be noticeable or subtle resistance that must be addressed. A clear communication plan should involve the whole organization so that people clearly understand what's being initiated and how both they and the organization will benefit from it.

Step 3: Recognizing Potential Pitfalls of a DFTS Initiative

Examining and understanding the potential pitfalls of a DFTS intervention is an extremely valuable exercise. It provides a cost-effective opportunity to foresee what could go wrong and how to avoid these potential problems. We strongly believe that this exercise should be carried out by the senior management team before the initiative begins. It should not be avoided, because a failure of even a pilot project can be fatal for the initiative's overall success. The following sections discuss some of the most common pitfalls.

Lack of Management Support

DFTS is a major corporate initiative. As such, it depends particularly on the involvement and enthusiasm of the CEO and the senior management team for its successful execution. It offers the potential for breakthrough results but can easily be derailed by lack of leadership support. The corporate world is ever abuzz with stories of countless failures of otherwise-sound initiatives, such as TQM, BPR, Lean Enterprise, and, of late, Six Sigma and DFSS. For every successful implementation, numerous cases of failures exist. The single most significant cause of such failures is lack of CEO support. Behind every successful initiative, on the other hand, has been a CEO who believed in it, communicated it with the organization as a whole, made the needed resources available, and provided unwavering support and enthusiasm throughout. Clearly, successful deployment of a DFTS initiative calls for similar commitment and support on the part of management. Often the CEO and the senior management team underestimate the time and commitment required for such initiatives. The vital role the CEO plays can hardly be overemphasized. We discuss this further later in this chapter.

Middle Management Antipathy

In spite of delayering and downsizing in recent years, middle management remains a vital building block in the organizational pyramid. These managers are known by a range of designations, from vice presidents, directors, general managers, senior managers, project managers, and supervisors to simply managers, or all of these, depending on the organization's size. In recent years, middle managers have been given additional appellations such as sponsors, champions, black belts, and master black belts, representing their roles and responsibilities in quality initiatives such as Six Sigma and DFSS. Whatever their titles or position in the hierarchy, middle managers play important roles throughout the DFTS process. There are several reasons for middle management antipathy. They may not understand the DFTS process, they have not been sold on its value, they do not believe that the CEO and top management are serious about it and will provide the needed support and resources, they may have had a bad experience in the past, or they are insufficiently motivated to embrace the change because they do not have a personal stake in its success. All this invariably leads to reluctance, fear, and antipathy that may be fatal for the initiative.

Empty Quality Slogans

Often organizations indulge in slogans and catchphrases as motivating and cheerleading doodads. These simplistic exhortations create the wrong impression about the hard tasks and challenges involved in a quality initiative. They can be especially frustrating if the slogans do not reflect the volume and complexities of the tasks involved. Such slogans become inevitable if the initiative is driven by the desire to win an external award rather than produce measurable results. Empty slogans can, in fact, be the only result if the quality initiative is not integral to the enterprise's day-to-day operations. Only when an organization is free of such slogans can it identify real challenges, address them meaningfully, and begin to communicate them effectively and credibly with the various stakeholders. Deming strongly advises against such meaningless buzzwords: "Eliminate slogans, exhortations, and targets for the workforce that ask for zero defects and new levels of productivity. Slogans do not build quality systems." See point 10 in Table 5.2. (Tables 5.2, 5,3 and 5.4 are Zultner's adaptations of Deming's "14 Points," "Seven Deadly Diseases," and "Obstacles to Quality" to software context.)

TABLE 5.2
The Fourteen Points for Software Managers[2]

1.	Create constancy of purpose for the improvement of systems and service, with the aim to become excellent, satisfy users, and to provide jobs.
2.	Adopt the new philosophy. We are in a new age of software engineering and project management. Software managers must awaken to the challenge, learn their responsibilities, and take on leadership for change.
3.	Cease dependence on mass inspection (especially testing) to achieve quality. Reduce the need for inspection on a mass basis by building quality into the system in the first place. Inspection is not the answer. It is too late and unreliable—and does not produce quality.
4.	End the practice of awarding business on price alone. Minimize total cost. Move toward a single supplier for any one item or service, making them a partner in a long-term relationship of loyalty and trust.
5.	Constantly and forever improve the system development process, to improve quality and productivity, and thus constantly decrease the time and cost of systems. Improving quality is not a one-time effort.
6.	Institute training on the job. Everyone must be well trained, as knowledge is essential for improvement.
7.	Institute leadership. It is a manager's job to help their people and their systems do a better job. Supervision of software managers is in need of an overall, as is supervision of professional staff.
8.	Drive out fear, so that everyone may work effectively. Management should be held responsible for faults of the organization and environment.
9.	Break down barriers between areas. People must work as a team. They must foresee and prevent problems during systems development and use.
10.	Eliminate slogans, exhortations, and targets for the work force that ask for zero defects and new levels of productivity. Slogans do not build quality systems.
11.	Eliminate numerical quotas and goals. Substitute leadership. Quotas and goals (such as schedules) address numbers—not quality and methods.
12.	Remove barriers to pride of workmanship. The responsibility of project managers must be changed from schedules to quality.
13.	Institute a vigorous program of education and self-improvement for everyone. There must be a continuing training and education commitment to software managers and professional staff.
14.	Put everyone to work to accomplish the transformation. The transformation is everybody's job. Every activity, job, and task is part of a process. Everyone has a part to play in improvement.

TABLE 5.3
The "Seven Deadly Diseases" of Software Quality[3]

1.	Lack of constancy of purpose to plan systems that will satisfy users, keep software developers in demand, and provide jobs.
2.	Emphasis on short-term schedules—short-term thinking (just the opposite of constancy of purpose toward improvement), fed by fear of cancellations and layoffs, kills quality.
3.	Evaluation of performance, merit rating, and annual reviews—the effects of which are devastating on individuals, and therefore, quality.
4.	Mobility of software professionals and managers. Job hopping makes constancy of purpose, and building organizational knowledge, very difficult.
5.	Managing by "visible figures" alone—with little consideration for figures that are unknown or unknowable.
6.	Excessive personnel costs. Due to inefficient development procedures, stressful environment, and high turnover, software development person-hours are too high.
7.	Excessive maintenance costs. Due to bad design, error ridden development, and poor maintenance practices, total lifetime cost of software is enormous.

Copyright © 1988 by Zultner & Co. Reprinted with permission.

TABLE 5.4
The Obstacles to Software Quality[3]

1.	Hope for instant solutions. The only solution that works is knowledge—solidly applied, with determination and hard work.
2.	The belief that any new hardware or packages will transform software development. Quality (and productivity) comes from people, not fancy equipment and programs.
3.	"Our problems are different." Software quality problems aren't unique—or uncommon.
4.	Obsolescence in schools. Most universities don't teach software quality—just appraisal techniques.
5.	Poor teaching of statistical methods. Many software groups don't have good statistical-oriented training in quality or project management.
6.	"That's good enough—we don't have time to do better"—but time will be spent later to fix the errors. Doing the right things right the first time (and every time) is fastest.
7.	"Our quality control people take care of all quality problems." Quality is management's responsibility, and cannot be delegated. Either management does it or it does not happen.

8.	"Our troubles lie entirely with the programmers." Who hired the programmers? Trained them (or not)? Manages them? Only management can do what must be done to improve.
9.	False starts with quality (and productivity). Impatient managers who don't understand that quality is a long term proposition quickly lose interest.
10.	"We installed quality control." Quality is a never-ending task of management. Achieve consistency (statistical control)—then continuously improve.
11.	The unmanned computer—such as CASE package used without solid knowledge of software engineering.
12.	The belief that it is only necessary to meet specifications. Just meeting specifications is not sufficient. Continue to improve consistency and reduce development time.
13.	The fallacy of zero defects. Constant improvement does not end with zero defects (all specs met). The mere absence of defects is no guarantee for user satisfaction.
14.	Inadequate testing of prototypes. The primary purpose of testing prototypes is to learn— and then apply that knowledge to a robust production system.
15.	"Anyone that comes to help us must understand all about our systems." Software managers may know all there is to know about their systems and software engineering— except how to improve.

Copyright © 1988 by Zultner & Co. Reprinted with permission.

Lack of Team Cohesiveness

Organization-wide quality initiatives such as DFTS can be marred irreparably for lack of team cohesiveness. The need for team cohesiveness is profound both within and across various software development teams. Software design and development, especially in large projects such as enterprise software, is a uniquely team-based process. Creating an organization that embraces inherent change with one voice and as a committed team is a challenging task and can hardly be overestimated.

Wrong Implementation Strategies

Wrong implementation strategies can be fatal for a quality initiative. Three strategic issues must be addressed diligently:

- Strategic clarity
- Scope of the initiative
- "Buy or build"

Strategic Clarity

Management may not have thought through the initiative's strategic rationale. It may not have addressed some basic questions, such as the following: Are the current processes first-rate? Can they meet customer requirements consistently? Are we actually listening to the customers? How are our quality, cost, and cycle time vis-à-vis customer expectations? How do these compare with competitors' products and services? Finally, how would the proposed initiative help us enhance customer satisfaction and improve our competitive situation, market share, and the bottom line? In the absence of such analyses, it's difficult to provide commitment, justify resources, and extend support in a sustainable manner. It's critical that not only the top management team but also the board should deliberate these issues and be totally supportive. Decisions resulting from these deliberations must be unequivocal. For corporations that have done their homework, these initiatives have clear strategic value. Many companies, such as General Electric and Caterpillar, are not only implementing Six Sigma and DFSS throughout the organization but also are involving their customers and suppliers in their Six Sigma initiatives, thus extending them further in the supply chain (see Table 5.5). Among Japanese corporations, it's a common practice to engage suppliers in the firm's quality initiative. Failures of many initiatives can be traced to the absence of a *raison d'etre*. Often, external factors such as awards, certificates, or public relations, not an actual business need, drive a quality initiative. It's impossible to sustain such an initiative if external factors do not create genuine value for the business. Furthermore, even great initiatives must be integrated with the organization's day-to-day work and not be mere add-ons. Toyota's quality management system, for example, is simply known as the Toyota Production System and has become a way of life for the corporation's operations worldwide.

TABLE 5.5
Implementation Strategies for a Software Quality Initiative

Strategy	Pros	Cons
Incremental	Avoids organization-wide risk Less disruptive and risky Opportunity to perfect the process on a small scale Mistakes are contained	May compete with current practice Organizational politics and resistance to change may result in suboptimization One project failure may derail the whole initiative Overall cost may be higher Opportunity for transformative results may be lost May not get top management's attention

Strategy	Pros	Cons
Concurrent	Focuses on one approach improves the odds of eventual success Less resistance to change Cost and time savings Transformative and faster results Benefits from top management's attention and support	Risky if the initiative is inappropriate or is not managed well May be disruptive if not planned and executed well The opportunity for debugging on a smaller scale is lost Errors and wrong practices may be cumulative
Staggered incremental	Planned for organization-wide implementation but introduced incrementally Avoids organization-wide risk Less disruptive and risky Opportunity to perfect the process on a small scale Mistakes are contained Opportunity for debugging on a smaller scale Greater chances of success than with the other two May still produce transformative results	May compete with current practice Organizational politics and resistance to change may result in suboptimization One project failure may derail the whole initiative Opportunity for transformative results may be lost May not get top management's full attention May take much longer than concurrent implementation

Scope of the Initiative

"What should the scope of the initiative be? How deep should it be? Will we deploy a single quality system such as DFTS or an integrated system that includes Six Sigma and the Capability Maturity Model (CMM)? Will we address just software development issues, or will we include transactional processes such as recruitment, marketing, and billing? How wide will the implementation be? Will it be deployed divisionally or enterprise-wide? How should the new initiative be introduced: as a pilot project, on a one-project-at-a-time basis, or enterprise-wide concurrently? What are the trade-offs?" These may seem like perennial questions, but they have important implications and must be addressed. The reasoning for pilot-project incremental deployment is that it provides an opportunity for experimentation, learning, and debugging. It also eliminates the risks of costly mistakes if the initiative is inappropriate. Its downside is that it sends a mixed signal that management is not fully committed, and the existing practice may be reverted to, or some other alternatives may be explored. This may be fatal for the new initiative. Resistance to change may be more entrenched and costly in terms of time, cost, and morale. It may also lead to a situation of two practices competing for resources and attention. This often leads to unwarranted rivalry between the two teams, two agendas, and two sets of development methodologies. Such a situation does not bode well for the new initiative. The alternative to a pilot project is an enterprise-wide concurrent implementation. This may be especially challenging in large organizations and calls for careful planning. In spite of the common belief that this is the norm for successful interventions, many successful quality initiatives have started on a divisional basis or a subsidiary level and gradually expanded to include the rest of the organization. This includes General Electric, DuPont, and Motorola. Caterpillar, on the other hand, introduced Lean, Six Sigma, and DFSS across 110 manufacturing facilities in 24 countries worldwide concurrently. In fact, it was the first company to launch Lean, Six Sigma, and DFSS in all business units simultaneously. Caterpillar is now also committed to helping its suppliers.

The common denominator for successful interventions is the commitment of the top management team—either concurrently or incrementally—across the organization as a whole. Some corporations, like GE, given their sheer size, have introduced Six Sigma and DFSS, but one initiative at a time, incrementally. The initial focus was on manufacturing activities. Service activities were included only later, where the opportunities are even greater. Jack Welch has often regretted not introducing DFSS and Six Sigma for service activities earlier than he did. The current trend is to go for all-inclusive, organization-wide initiatives that include both manufacturing and service activities. Typically, companies go for one initiative, such as Six Sigma or DFSS, at a time. But Caterpillar, as just stated, introduced Lean, Six Sigma, and DFSS concurrently.

In an enterprise software context, where projects tend to be large, it may be just fine to introduce DFTS on a new software development project and gradually expand it to all incoming projects. There is an alternative to *incremental* and *concurrent* approaches; we call it the *staggered incremental* approach (see Table 5.5). Here management has decided on an organization-wide implementation, has a clear plan to that effect, and introduces it incrementally as appropriate. What's important is that management knows the initiative's business value and has a clear plan for the organization as a whole. This conveys an unmistakable message: "This is what we will do; there's no turning back."

"Buy or Build"

This deals with the issue of whether the expertise for initiating and implementing the quality initiative should be outsourced or provided internally. Most companies in the West have sought outside help in their Six Sigma and DFSS initiatives. Also, all of them seek knowledge transfer and build internal capabilities to sustain these initiatives or expand them further following initial outside help; this is called *buy-to-build*. The most notable exception is Motorola, the inventor of the Six Sigma methodology, which did everything internally. Many companies, such as General Electric, Motorola, and Honeywell, have developed a high degree of internal competence and now not only drive these initiatives internally but also offer these services to their suppliers, customers, and other potential clients. It may be sensible to go for buy-to-build to jump-start the process and build internal competencies concurrently. "Do it yourself" doesn't always work. General Electric reaped returns of $7.1 billion over five years since its Six Sigma initiative was launched in 1996.[4] However, Xerox's tentative Lean and Six Sigma initiatives since the late 1990s produced only modest results and had to be relaunched in 2003.[5] Competent consultants not only enhance the speed of execution but also bring cross-industry best practices. In addition to creating competitive value, speed and robust deployment are crucial for successful implementation. The extent of initial outside help is contingent on the organization's needs and should be customized accordingly. It's critical to make knowledge transfer and help with building internal capabilities part of any outsourcing engagement. Although considerable cost savings may result, the overriding reason for outsourcing is not one of cost; it's more a question of effectiveness. As Peter Drucker said, "Most look at outsourcing from the point of view of cutting costs, which I think is a delusion. What outsourcing does is greatly improve the quality of the people who still work for you."[6]

Inadequate Reward and Incentives for Change

One major reason quality initiatives fail is an inadequate reward system. Deming has stated clearly on this issue, "Evaluation of performance, merit rating, and annual reviews...are devastating on individuals, and therefore, quality" (see point 3 in Table 5.3). Individual rewards have three negative consequences for quality. First, they undermine teamwork, which is crucial to quality, especially in team-based processes such as enterprise software development. Second, they may encourage short-term goal orientation. Third, they deprive the participants of pride of ownership for a job well done. This topic is discussed further in the section "Step 9: Creating an Appropriate Reward System."

Wrong Success Indicators

Quality initiatives must drive desirable results. It's important that the key objectives and success metrics be correctly identified. These objectives are based on customer requirements, not just the internal organizational goals. Wrong indicators can lead to wrong decisions and can disrupt a quality initiative. In a DFTS methodology, for example, upstream costs typically are higher than in traditional software development systems. The higher initial cost shouldn't bear an adverse judgment on DFTS, because it optimizes overall life-cycle costs.

Wasting Resources on Inconsequential Issues

Often quality initiatives become bureaucratic, paper-driven instruments that are of little relevance to the business. Many quality initiatives document every process—even those that may never be used. Thus, they become cumbersome and expensive, with little quality value. This issue must be addressed carefully.

Failure of Communication

In any major corporate initiative, effective communication is absolutely crucial for a successful implementation. A communication plan should take into account the diverse information needs of various stakeholders; a "one-size-fits-all" approach does not work. The section "Step 8: Establishing Effective Communication" discusses elements of a communication system and roles of various players in the communication process.

Inadequate Training

The importance of training cannot be overemphasized in a DFTS initiative. It's the basis for acquiring best practices and value creation. A learning organization develops the capacity of "generative learning."[7] This means being able to deal continually with changing customer needs and market and competitive environments. The learning should therefore include creative thinking as well as problem solving at all levels of the organization. Furthermore, training and learning should include everyone, including the top management team. The training content and objectives, however, must be differentiated according to the participants' roles and responsibilities.

No Clue About Costs

Finally, the worst offense is failing to measure cost savings correctly. When this is the case, it becomes difficult to justify ongoing costs. Therefore, it's an excellent idea to establish a cost of poor quality (CoPQ) system in any organization that is serious about quality management. (See Chapter 4 for details on CoPQ.)

Sidebar 5.1: Virtuous Teaching Cycle and TPOV

Training and teaching have played a crucial role in GE's massive Six Sigma deployment. Tichy characterizes GE's Six Sigma program as a "Virtuous Teaching Cycle" where teacher and learner roles are intertwined. The roles get continually reversed and enhance learning: "The Six Sigma program is a Virtuous Teaching Cycle, with the black belts teaching quality tools to the workforce, who then use them to generate new ideas and, in turn, teach the black belts."[8]

The "Virtuous Teaching Cycle" can be a powerful instrument of change and leadership development and can be established in any organization where leaders have strived to develop a "Teachable Point of View" (TPOV). Jack Welch saw the virtue of teaching and its potent role in leadership development. He taught at GE's Crotonville Leadership Development Institute throughout his stint as its CEO for two decades. Tichy describes General Electric's as the world's largest teaching infrastructure: "More than 15,000 high-potential middle managers are assigned for two full-time years as 'black belt' teachers of Six Sigma. They are teaching all 300,000+ employees at General Electric and leading over 20,000 Six Sigma projects." The other elements of the teaching infrastructure are quarterly Corporate Executive Council (CEC) meetings, Work-Out program, Change Acceleration program, Crotonville Leadership Development Institute, and GE Operating Mechanism.[9]

Source: Noel M. Tichy, *The Cycle of Leadership*, HarperBusiness, New York, 2002.

Step 4: Laying Foundations for a Quality-Focused Enterprise

We have witnessed with distress how certain enterprises go about their quality initiatives. Certain gimmicks are downright laughable, like the CEO of a company on the verge of financial collapse talking about a TQM initiative. It's also important to understand that major quality initiatives can be successful only in a stable climate that is free of immediate risks. Another annoying stunt that we recall pertains to a TQM initiative launched as part of a corporation's centennial celebration. In both cases, the CEOs and the senior management team had not invested enough time and commitment. Both the initiatives perished and might have left bad legacies in their wake. This kind of amateurish approach to quality does much harm to meaningful initiatives later. Organizations embarking on major quality initiatives need strong, shared beliefs to which everyone can relate. "Why do we need to embark on this journey?" must be answered.

Deming sought a major transformation of Western management practice in his book *Out of the Crisis*.[10] (See also Tables 5.2, 5.3, and 5.4 for Zultner's adaptation of Deming's philosophy: "14 Points for Software Managers," "The Seven Deadly Diseases of Software Quality," and "Obstacles to Software Quality.") It can help tremendously in the successful implementation of a DFTS or other quality initiatives. A practical framework for implementing Deming principles is discussed next.

Awareness of Shortcomings of Current Practices

The organization might want to start by organizing a one-day seminar to discuss its current practices for customer satisfaction and product and process development capabilities.

Adequate preparation is absolutely crucial so that the seminar discussion is based on a real assessment of the organization's quality challenges. It may be a good idea to seek help from a competent facilitator to help prepare for the seminar. As with any major issue, CEOs play a crucial role in leading such seminars. For the seminar to be successful, they understand the issues, have discussed the implications with the key lieutenants, and bring their commitment and energy. The key to a positive outcome is solid preparation and prior consultation among the senior management team. That's why you need a competent facilitator. We have seen too many corporate seminars on quality turn into a benevolent but detached discussion of everything under the sun. Quality-related issues should be deliberated just like any other important business function, such as finance and marketing, and the CEOs and senior management team should have a clear outcome in mind. In such cases, CEOs very often know or determine the outcome of such conferences. This is not to suggest that the discussions are phony. Only such results-oriented meetings led by the CEOs will bring to light real issues with a view toward addressing them. People will act real because the stakes are high. Such a results-oriented approach to quality is typical of Japanese organizations, in which the CEOs lead the process.

The facilitator works closely with the CEO and the top management team and prepares them for the seminar. A great deal of consensus will be built before the formal seminar. The morning session could start with a presentation on the cost of quality, yield, cycle time, and return and warranty costs if a formal CoSQ is already established or if such data is available. This may be followed by a presentation of Deming's principles, particularly The 14 Points, Seven Deadly Diseases, Obstacles to Quality (see Tables 5.2, 5.3, and 5.4), and a discussion of possible causes. The identified causes may very well resemble the "diseases" and "obstacles." Such a discussion may also reveal some additional obstacles to quality, such as the following:[11]

- Hope of instant pudding

- Asking for quantification of every improvement

- Search for examples elsewhere

- "Our problems are different/our culture is different"

- Poor teaching of statistical methods

- "We installed quality control"

- Specifications and the fallacy of zero defects

- Inadequate testing of prototypes

An honest discussion will help identify real issues and how they relate to Deming's teachings, a consensus on their meanings, and implications for the organization.

Contemplate and Adopt Deming's Teachings

The afternoon session could focus on adopting Deming's teachings and identifying the new challenges and responsibilities. Honest discussion leads to shared ownership and pride. The CEOs again play a crucial role. They lead the discussion and want a meaningful outcome. They may choose to announce major decisions such as the appointment of a senior corporate executive as Chief Quality Officer (CQO) and the setting up of a Corporate Quality Council (CQC) consisting of the senior corporate officers. The message that the top management team is committed to quality helps build credibility. The operational responsibility for implementation should be with the CQO.

Organization-Wide Consultation and Communication

After the decision to implement Deming has been made, the rest of the organization should be consulted through a series of seminars and other forms of communication. People should be genuinely consulted rather than just informed. This will help gain acceptance for the initiative, channel valuable ideas, and enhance motivation. Rushing to implement without consultation across the organization is often costly in terms of time and effectiveness.

Plan and Implement Deming's Principles

Although Deming's teachings often seem to be common sense, a closer look reveals that his philosophy is a major departure from contemporary management practice in the West. Appropriate integration with DFTS methodology must be carried out if the implementation is part of a DFTS initiative. The plan should clearly identify responsibilities, milestones, datelines, and monitoring and appraisal mechanisms. It should also identify potential pitfalls, countermeasures, and incentives for change across the organization. Successful implementation of the change process requires considerable time and attention on the part of the top management team. Its challenges can hardly be overestimated. Only the strategy of permanently securing the new level can ensure that the organization will not revert to old ways. This requires cultivating new attitudes, behavior, and skills by deploying various interventions such as training and a reward system. There are numerous examples of organizational life gravitating back to old ways after the "shot in the arm" effect of the initial thrust is gone.

A successful change is carried out in three steps (see Figure 5.3, shown earlier):

1. Unfreezing the present level (gaining acceptance for the need to change)

2. Moving to the new level (putting the needed changes into effect)

3. Freezing the new level (consolidating the changes to guard against reversion)

The essentials of Deming's philosophy can be grouped into three broad issues:

- Management's commitment to quality (points 1, 2, and 14 in Table 5.2)

- Application of fact-based (statistical) methodology (points 3, 5, 6, and 13 in Table 5.2)

- Improve teamwork and be customer-responsive (points 4, 7, 8, 9, 10, 11, and 12 in Table 5.2)

Deming's approach is not a program; it's a philosophy and a system of management. If it's initiated with genuine management support, it will build the foundations of a high-performance organization. Recent quality movements such as Six Sigma and DFSS have tended to touch on Deming as a historic reference and emphasize just the tools and methodologies, such as DMAIC and IDDOV. Effective use of tools can certainly help in individual process improvement and problem-solving, but it can hardly suffice in creating irreversible change and transformative leadership. In the absence of the sound anchoring that Deming's philosophy provides, it is all too easy to revert to old ways. This happens often with a change in leadership, during emergencies, and following temporary setbacks. Several models exist for building transformative organizations. Use them if they work for you. We believe that Deming's model is inherently sound, practical, and time-tested. It can help you lay the foundation for a quality- and customer-driven enterprise. DFTS can deliver truly transformative results only in such organizations. The basic requirement is a change in people's thinking.

Step 5: Building the Organizational Infrastructure

A supportive organizational infrastructure is crucial for a successful DFTS implementation. The following are the key elements:

- Quality of leadership

- Strategic planning

- Operations and process management

- Management information system

- Accounting and financial management

- Human resources management

It is beyond the scope of this book to delve deeper into these issues. Corporations such as Toyota and GE, which have benefited enormously from various quality initiatives, have had excellent organizational infrastructures and best practices in place. The need for a strong organizational infrastructure cannot be overemphasized for a DFTS initiative.

Step 6: Understanding the Roles of the Key Players

DFTS is a transformative process that involves the organization as a whole. The following sections discuss the roles of certain key personnel in implementing and sustaining DFTS. It is possible to combine certain roles, depending on the organization's size and structure and other contingencies. The following key roles and responsibilities identify the leadership challenges in a DFTS process.

Role of the CEOs

The role of the CEOs in a successful implementation of a major quality initiative such as DFTS can hardly be overemphasized. Lack of CEO support will most definitely result in failure. The following are the key roles that the CEOs play in a DFTS initiative:

- **Provide unfailing leadership.** CEOs must be the driving force of DFTS. They must, above all, create a sense of ownership and pride in what is being initiated. They recognize that to attain great results the organization as a whole must not only possess technical and leadership skills but also live the DFTS quality philosophy in letter and spirit. They understand that Deming's quality philosophy is essential in such an endeavor and that it requires a new way of looking at things.

- **Ensure involvement of senior management.** It's absolutely critical that the CEOs take their senior management teams into their confidence and ensure that they understand the business stakes in the DFTS initiative and support it enthusiastically. The CEOs know that any transformative change requires everyone in senior management to support it. They make that possible by making it absolutely clear that the change is a requirement, that there is no going back to old ways, and that everyone must be onboard. They communicate this with clarity and conviction. Either the CEOs do it, or it doesn't happen.

- **Appoint a senior executive to oversee the implementation process.** Appointing the right person to be the CQO may be the CEOs' single most important decision as far as DFTS's eventual success. The person selected must be business-savvy and possess leadership qualities to help implement the DFTS process. He or she will be responsible for the overall quality of the organization's products and services. The CQO reports directly to the CEOs and works in close consultation with them.

- **Chair the CQC.** The CEOs should be active participants in the quality process. They should chair the CQC and provide leadership for the initiative through this and other forums as required. The CEOs should also lead the DFTS steering committee. Many corporations also have corporate board committees on quality in which the CEOs must lead as well. Their message and support must be unwavering and well-communicated throughout the organization.

- **Provide resources and unwavering support.** The CEOs ensure that financial and personnel resources are made available in a timely manner. They make sure that the most talented people are brought in to launch and lead the initiative. They must talk about it earnestly and enthusiastically whenever possible. In a successful quality initiative, the CEOs become its chief spokespersons. They are genuine, enthusiastic, and direct.

- **Insist on training and continuous learning.** The CEOs should understand the value of training across the organization for the success of the DFTS initiative. They need to undergo appropriate training covering both leadership and technical aspects of the initiative. The CEOs also ensure that their top management team undergoes training. They should be enthusiastic about learning and may conduct certain seminars themselves and teach important issues (see Sidebar 5.1). CEOs finding the time to train and teach sets a great example in a learning organization, especially for the black belts (BBs) and master black belts (MBBs). In a software development enterprise, training should be less differentiated because the organizational hierarchy itself is likely to be less differentiated. CEOs and the top management team must understand the DFTS process in its entirety. It will be great asset if they have undergone the black belt training. CEOs and members of their senior management team who are likely to be in concept development and high-level design should undergo black belt training.

- **Provide appropriate incentives.** The CEOs should understand that software development is a collaborative effort. As such, the reward system should reinforce teamwork in line with long-term objectives of the DFTS initiative, as opposed to traditional performance evaluations, merit ratings, and annual reviews (see points 2 and 3 in Table 5.3).

- **Simply be in charge.** The CEOs must be aware of the enormous payoff from the DFTS initiative, be up-to-date with the progress, and be enthusiastic about its prospects. They have high expectations but should make sure that occasional setbacks do not derail the initiative. They should be seen as the initiative's principal proponents.

Role of the Corporate Quality Council

The role of the corporate council is crucial. It can become a forum for sharing information, making honest appraisals of progress, and creating much-needed top management team cohesiveness for successful implementation. The CEO should chair the CQC and should make sure its smooth and effective functioning becomes the standard by which other executives in the council manage their own DFTS teams. The CQC is responsible for all strategic and policy matters and plays the following crucial roles:

- **Crafts a quality vision.** The CQC should be responsible for crafting the organization's quality vision. It should also state clearly whether and how the DFTS initiative confirms and contributes to realizing that vision.

- **Decides on introducing the initiative.** Although the CEO may have initially made the first move and has the final say, the CQC must collectively and enthusiastically agree. It should also provide the rationale and go-ahead after an honest deliberation of its potential and challenges. Because DFTS requires commitment from across the organization, the CEO must ensure that the CQC understands the stakes involved and that the buy-in is honest.

- **Approves plans and budgets.** The line managers prepare plans and budgets for the quality initiatives. The CQC should approve them only after careful and candid discussion of viability, cost, and benefits of the initiative.

- **Appraises progress.** The CQC should be a forum where tough questions are asked and serious business conducted. All the participants should know this and come totally prepared. The CQC should be collectively accountable to produce desired results. Honest discussion of results—good and bad—should be seen as a crucial part of the process. To fulfill this and other responsibilities, the CQC must meet regularly—at least once every quarter.

- **Provides support.** The CQC and the senior managers as a team must provide steadfast support to the initiative and should be vocal about it. Furthermore, they should provide resources and show personal interest in the results on a regular basis.

Role of Chief Quality Officer

Chief Quality Officer (CQO) is an emerging position in many organizations where managing quality is considered essential to organizational success. Such organizations totally believe that quality must be led from the highest levels in the organization, and they live that premise in practice.

The CQO should be a member of the top management team, along with the CEO, CFO, CTO, and CIO, and other senior executives in charge of operations, marketing, and R&D. The decision to appoint a CQO should be made after careful deliberations at the highest levels and only after a clear need has been identified. The appointment itself should be made after the organization has embarked on a major quality initiative or is contemplating one. The CEO and the board of such organizations consider quality the primary building block. They do not seek cosmetic touch-ups but instead look for breakthrough and transformative results through quality. Quality is not seen as a problem to be fixed but as an enabling instrument for attaining corporate ambitions.

The CQO should be someone with great promise and a proven track record. Such a person should be a consummate software engineer with considerable experience with end-user needs as well as senior customer executives. This person should understand the value of software quality—not only from the customer perspective but also from the standpoint of business success. The CQO needs to understand various quality management systems, but it's even more important that he or she possess leadership qualities. If the person does not possess technical skills of quality management, he or she may seek help from internal or external consultants as needed. The important thing is to learn quickly and be involved in the DFTS process.

Although the CQO primarily serves a leadership role, we foresee an emerging and pressing need for CQOs to be technically savvy as well. Many quality problems can be attributed to senior mangers lacking software development and quality management skills. In the future, more quality professionals—those with MBB and BB backgrounds—will be called on to undertake greater leadership responsibilities, including that of CEO. Jack Welch believes that future CEOs at General Electric will most likely be those who currently work as an MBB or BB. Their specific training and experience provide an excellent vehicle for developing future leaders within an enterprise. The CQO shouldn't be hired for just the DFTS initiative. After DFTS is successfully assimilated, the CQO should identify other quality challenges. This should be a permanent senior position vested with authority and resources. The CQO's major roles are as follows:

- **Help create strategic awareness about quality.** The most important role of the CQO is to help create a quality vision and awareness about its strategic significance. Quality should be seen as crucial to business success and not as a problem to be fixed. This is no minor task; it requires a CQO who is respected as a leader and business-savvy. DFTS should be seen as part of an ongoing quality process geared toward helping organizations achieve their corporate ambitions.

- **Lead the change process.** DFTS constitutes a major change in organizational practice. The CQO is the key change agent in this process. This person works closely with the Executive Champions (ECs) of the DFTS initiative. This often requires waking up the organization: no more of the same old practices. The organization must shed its tolerance for defects as a cost of doing business. Changing this mind-set is formidable. The CQO must have a clear understanding of organizational politics and processes and be able to analyze the quality challenges and communicate them coherently. Above all, this person must be able to address and allay the fear that accompanies any major change. This role can best be played by a company veteran who has earned "capital" and staying power. If the only choice is to hire someone from outside, the person must have a proven record and must be given the required support by the CEO and the senior management team. They must want him or her to succeed.

- **Lead organization-wide learning.** The CQO should work closely with the EC, human resources (HR), and consultants to devise an effective and relevant learning program in line with the organization's needs. The training should be organization-wide and differentiated. This learning includes senior executives, including the CEO.

- **Build a quality information system.** DFTS relies on a culture of fact-based decision-making. Therefore, it's important that valid measures be available to initiate, manage, and appraise various activities, processes, and decisions. A range of customer and process-centric measures are needed that deal with cost, quality, and delivery schedules. Savvy quality professionals sense intuitively sound decisions and support them even if a valid measurement is not possible. Quality management often requires serious consideration of things that are unknown or unknowable.

- **Communicate effectively.** The CQO should establish an effective and fact-based communication plan that is designed to inform and educate various constituents and thus strengthen the DFTS initiative. This topic is discussed further in the section "Step 8: Establishing Effective Communication."

- **Liaise with customers and outsourcing partners.** Software development is becoming more like manufacturing in yet another sense: Customers may be end users or software developers themselves who have outsourced all or part of their software development activities. On the other hand, the software developers may outsource some of their activities to an outsourcing partner. This kind of supply chain in software development is now a common industry practice and may have a profound effect on software quality. It needs to be coordinated and integrated with the customer and supplier (outsourcing partner) software quality. DFTS CQOs and ECs should make sure that they have an adequate framework to address such issues.

- **Advise the CEO and the board.** The CQO is the chief advisor to the CEOs and the board on quality matters. To do that, he or she must understand how the DFTS initiative fits into the larger scheme of things and how it will help the company attain its short- and long-term objectives. For this reason, many companies choose a seasoned company veteran to be the first CQO. This is probably smarter than hiring a quality professional from outside. CQOs may not be quality professionals themselves, but to be viable, such appointees must master the operational and strategic context of quality management quickly. They should clearly understand the benefits and strategic value of the DFTS initiative and how it can best be implemented, integrated, and expanded within the enterprise smoothly and profitably. They should also be able to advise on all policies and initiatives related to process improvement vis-à-vis competition and evolving customer needs and demands.

Role of DFTS Executive Champion

The Executive Champions (ECs) of the DFTS initiative are usually the executive heads of software development (variously known as Vice President/Senior Vice President of Software Development, Chief Software Architect, and so on). Having line responsibility for software development, they are better placed to fulfill the additional roles of EC. Thus, they are the principal process owner, internal customer, and beneficiary of the DFTS initiative. Being EC has little to do with being a cheerleader. It requires being a strong leader with staying power and conviction to stay the course. ECs provide the support system and motivation to the Project Leaders (PLs) and project teams. They work closely with CQOs, software PLs, and external and internal consultants to ensure that the whole initiative is conceived, planned, and executed flawlessly. Above all, they are accountable to produce results, rather than look for scapegoats at the first setback. ECs play the following crucial roles:

- **Provide implementation leadership.** ECs understand the enormous value of DFTS as well as the challenges involved in its implementation. They motivate their team to embrace the change. They lead a team of PLs who, in turn, lead various software development teams. ECs address their concerns and help them with conflict resolution. They communicate with the CEOs and CQOs to ensure that the DFTS project teams have the necessary tools, training, and resources to do the job—well. They are called on to play a political role of ensuring that organizational power and politics do not impugn the desired change and instead are channeled to help the process. They should possess qualities to steer through ups and downs.

- **Select talented people to be Project Leaders.** ECs pick the most talented leaders to be the PLs. It is at this level that success is accomplished, one project at a time. ECs should be provided with BB and eventually MBB training. Another reason for MBB training for PLs in an enterprise software organization is that they often manage large projects in terms of team size, duration, and dollars. ECs along with CQOs must provide PLs with adequate support all through the implementation process. DFTS also provides an excellent opportunity to train future leaders for the organization as PLs and team members work together through various stages.

- **Organize learning.** ECs understand that learning, teaching, and mentoring are essential aspects of improvement and change, and they prepare the organization as a whole for training and learning. They insist that the senior management team, including the CEO, sign up for adequate DFTS training. They also make sure that various project team members are trained to be BBs. In a typical Six Sigma or DFSS initiative in a manufacturing environment, team members are trained to be green belts (GBs), and the PLs are trained to be BBs. In a DFTS context, however, various members of the software development team work both within a team as well as individually. They should therefore be better equipped to understand and deal with quality challenges in a DFTS process. Hence, we recommend BB training for all the members of the project team. Furthermore, PLs should be trained to be BBs initially but should be provided with additional training and coaching rapidly so that they can transition to MBBs. They can then also assume mentoring and teaching responsibilities with greater confidence. The senior management team may undergo BB, MBB, or GB training as appropriate. In an enterprise software context, we recommend that senior software professionals undergo at least BB training, with the exception of CQOs, who should train to be MBBs. More advanced training for the senior executives will enable them to deal with the upstream phases of the DFTS process more competently (see Figure 5.4). This will also equip them to lead the overall DFTS initiative knowledgeably. As is well-known, most quality problems can be attributed to lack of top management competence and understanding quality issues. Therefore, top management learning DFTS is even more important. These issues are discussed further in Chapters 20 and 21.

- **Provide a strong support system.** DFTS PLs and individual team members require adequate support from senior management, especially during the early stages of the DFTS implementation process. Glitches, unforeseen difficulties due to inadequate planning, or other problems may occur. DFTS is a major departure from the conventional software development process. It requires more time and resources at upstream stages (so that quality issues are addressed early rather than having to be fixed later). This requires a change in mind-set. There could be major frustrations if the ECs don't get it. They must understand the process and its eventual value and must be patient and provide steady leadership. The support system requires involvement, appraisal, mentoring, and adequate time and resources.

- **Liaise with customers and outsourcing partners.** As stated earlier in this chapter, ECs along with the CQOs work with customers and outsourcing partners to address relevant quality issues. They make sure that these are dealt with within a framework that is consistent with the organization's DFTS philosophy. They develop long-term partnerships that provide an opportunity for mutual learning and support. The emphasis should be on upstream activities, prevention, long-term relationships, and customer needs.

- **Ensure management commitment to the quality philosophy.** As senior executives with line responsibility, ECs make sure that DFTS is not perceived merely as a set of tools and techniques. They must emphasize Deming's teachings about the role of management (points 1, 2, and 14 in Table 5.1) and not resort to shortcuts and ad hoc measures that may jeopardize the initiative (see Tables 5.2 and 5.3). Successful ECs understand that the Deming management philosophy is meant to be a way of life and not a one-time intervention.

- **Help create a fact-based decision-making culture.** Understanding the causes of variation and eliminating or reducing them is crucial to any sustainable quality management system. Such systems depend on a culture of statistical thinking and getting to the bottom of the source of variation, which often leads to the top management team. These must be addressed upfront rather than swept aside.

- **Emphasize the value of people and a team-based quality system.** ECs understand that it's people who are at the core of quality management. As such, they emphasize the need to continuously improve skills and capabilities of people across the organization, beginning with the top management team. They understand the value of teamwork in software development. They should work tirelessly to break down barriers; drive out fear; eliminate meaningless slogans, arbitrary targets, and quotas; and improve relationships with customers and suppliers (see Table 5.2).

- **Liaise with the CEO and top management team.** ECs make sure that the CEO, CQO, and other senior executives are duly briefed about the progress of the DFTS initiative, as well as its challenges. They are willing to take responsibility in case of setbacks and ask for help, if needed. They work with the top management team to ensure their continued support.

Role of Software Engineers (DFTS Black Belts)

Software engineers who work individually and those who are members of software project teams should be trained to be DFTS black belts. Their roles and responsibilities are broader and deeper than those of team members in a typical Six Sigma/DFSS project in manufacturing organizations. They require both leadership and quality management capabilities in addition to being technically skilled as software engineers. They must be able to develop trustworthy software individually and as members of project teams and be able to identify user requirements; conceive of and design robust software; and code, test, integrate, and maintain it. For a successful DFTS implementation and integration, the traditional roles of the software engineers should be broadened to include critical additional skills:

- **DFTS process competence:** Software project team members should be savvy enough to understand the whole DFTS methodology rather than just the individual pieces of the development process they may be involved in at a given time. By understanding methodologies and tools such as QFD, FMEA, and Taguchi Methods, they can contribute more effectively at a particular stage of the development process, work without a glitch with those working upstream or downstream, and be moved across various stages if needed. Furthermore, with DFTS black belt proficiency, they are better equipped to work as members of a software development team and individually. In a software development team, the members are both its workhorses and technical experts.

- **Understanding and anticipating user requirements:** This is a crucial requirement for developing trustworthy software. Software engineers should be able to converse with the system's users in terms of the application and inform them of the trade-offs among the various requirements that often conflict. This requires technical knowledge, critical thinking, and competence with tools such as TRIZ, QFD, and FMEA.

- **Leadership and interpersonal flair:** Software engineers should be able to work in a team, coordinate their own pace with that of others, and possess communication and interpersonal skills critically needed in a software development environment.

- **Design and programming deftness:** Software engineers should certainly be gifted as programmers, well-versed in data structures and algorithms, and fluent in several programming languages as required. They should also understand various design alternatives and their implications for meeting user requirements in their particular environments.

Role of Project Leaders (DFTS Master Black Belts)

Project Leaders (PLs) are the front-end leaders in a DFTS initiative. PLs lead a team of talented people who might have undergone DFTS training. The PL role in DFTS is essentially that of a leader who can extract the best from a group of educated and accomplished people who may or may not have the natural instincts to be team players. This leadership role can be challenging and requires a person who is a natural leader and who is proficient in software engineering, DFTS methodology, and project management.

PLs are the linchpin between the project teams and the senior management team, reporting to ECs. PLs should be able to work with these people and help shape project objectives. They also coordinate with marketing personnel and customers, as well as the CQOs and their team. The selection of PLs is a critical decision on the part of the ECs. As stated, PLs should be trained to be DFTS master black belts because they need technical expertise as well as leadership and DFTS process competence. PLs play a crucial role, especially in an enterprise software context, where the projects are large in terms of manpower, cost, and duration. Chapter 21 discusses the training needs of MBBs.

The preceding sections have described a variety of roles and responsibilities in a software organization embarking on a DFTS process. DFTS requires the organization as a whole to be up to the task. It needs the involvement and commitment of senior executives from supporting functions such as finance, HR, and sales and marketing. Certain responsibilities can be modified, enlarged, or combined, depending on the organizational contingencies. But every software enterprise, irrespective of its size and needs, must address the issues implied in these roles and responsibilities. One important difference in the DFTS system is the need for greater depth of process expertise among software team members, team leaders, and the executive management team. Hence, we have recommended more intense training and learning than is the case with equivalent DFSS training in a manufacturing organization. Understanding these roles provides the basis for training and building the competence of the personnel needed for the process.

Step 7: Designing a Supportive Organizational Structure

Figure 5.4 shows a typical structure of an enterprise software development organization. It also shows the likely roles of various players along the different phases of the software development process. A well-designed structure must support the organization's key business processes, especially the ones that are crucial to meeting customer requirements. An appropriate organizational structure depends on a number of contingency factors, such as management style, size of the organization, its product and geographic diversity, the availability of managerial and technical skills, and user needs for supportive services.

DFTS requires a structure that is user- and process-focused. In particular, we emphasize three basic requirements:

- The structure must provide for robust communication between users and software development personnel as well as between various personnel within the organization throughout the development process. It should thus enable a network of internal and external constituents.

- The structure must be process-based, reflecting the DFTS methodology.

- The structure must be team-based, the way enterprise software is developed.

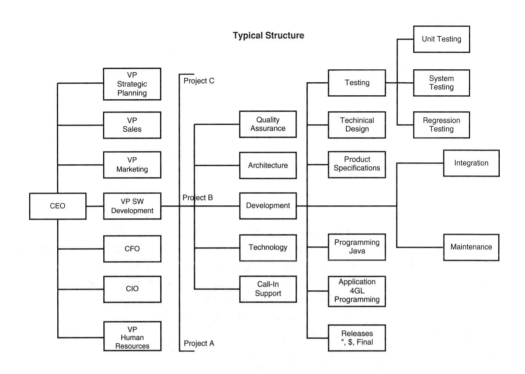

Typical Structure

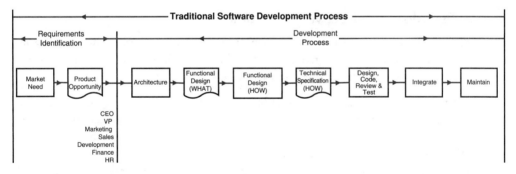

Traditional Software Development Process

A Simplified Robust Software Development Process

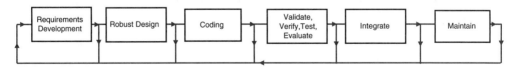

FIGURE 5.4
Form Versus Function in a Software Enterprise

Figure 5.5 shows a simple structure based on these basic requirements. The CQC or its subcommittee, the DFTS Steering Committee, is the apex body responsible for the initiative's successful implementation and ongoing improvement. It consists of all the senior executives, chaired by the CEO, and jointly coordinated by the Vice President of Software Development and CQO. The supporting services and systems are a crucial part of the structure and are provided by departments such as Quality, HR, IT, Finance, and Sales and Marketing. CQOs or their representatives coordinate these supporting roles. It's important that all the personnel involved understand user needs as they evolve during the development process. CQOs make sure that an adequate communication mechanism is made available to ensure robust communication with the users.

Software development is a creative process, but it also involves a lot of labor-intensive mechanical work at downstream stages that must be carried out equally well. The software development process thus can benefit from creativity as well as standardization. Both are needed to meet customer requirements. The structure must provide for both. But it can hardly suffice by itself. It must be supplemented by effective communication and documentation to handle coordination between customers and various personnel involved in different phases of the development process. DFTS methodology provides a number of tools and techniques, such as TRIZ, Pugh, FMEA, and QFD, that help address communication challenges related to evolving needs typical in enterprise software development.

Step 8: Establishing Effective Communication

As stated, a DFTS process has two kinds of communication challenges. The first, relating to communication between the users/customers and the organization, is covered in Chapter 11. The second pertains to communication within the organization.

CQOs and the executive leadership should understand the critical role of communication and ensure that the organization has a sound communication plan in place. It should be planned, monitored, and improved continuously rather than set up as an afterthought. The CQO should work with the ECs and various departments to ensure that appropriate information is made available in a timely manner. It is important that raw data is collected, analyzed, and presented as per the recipients' information needs. The communication system should provide for and encourage information up, down, and across the organization as appropriate.

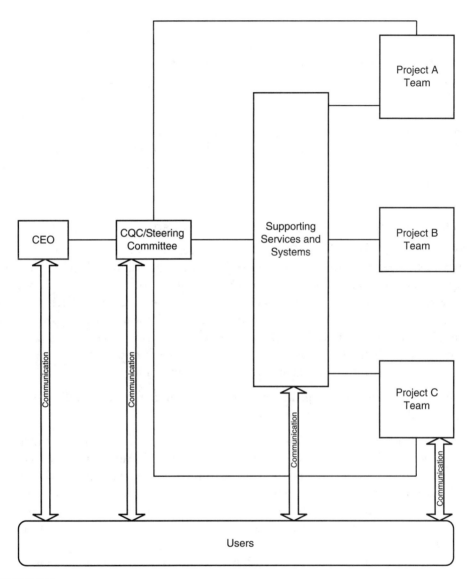

FIGURE 5.5
A Process-Based Organizational Structure

It may be best to set up a committee to come up with a robust communication plan. This will ensure participation and creativity. Every organization is unique, so it's important to customize the communication plan accordingly. Lack of effective communication can seriously mar the initiative. We cannot overemphasize the importance of robust communication as an integral part of the DFTS initiative. The most important communication tool is personal meetings, including one-on-one, in a problem-solving manner. The decisions and follow-ups are crucial to meaningful communication. A variety of other tools, such as e-mails, bulletin boards, company newsletters, and posters, may be used. Innovative use of the Internet, as well as various formal and informal meetings, media events, books, and publications, can be powerful too.

Step 9: Creating an Appropriate Reward System

A reward system is the totality of reinforcement processes that encourage individuals and teams to believe and behave in a manner that helps the organization achieve its most crucial goals and ambitions. As such, it is more than salary, compensation, and monetary incentives. In fact, monetary rewards may fail to secure the desired results. There is no one best way to reward people. A reward system's effectiveness depends on the type of organization, its culture and beliefs, the goals that the reward system is seeking to achieve, and desired actions, beliefs, and behaviors that need to be reinforced. Involvement, commitment, and a stake in the outcome are essential ingredients for high performance.[12]

The reward system for an organization-wide quality initiative such as DFTS should be designed carefully and should be the following:

- **Assimilated with the DFTS process:** The reward system should support and assimilate with the DFTS model. It should reinforce the DFTS learning process, its objectives, and its subsequent integration and expansion. It should be organization-wide in that it involves everyone, from newly recruited software engineers, to HR personnel helping with designing the reward and communication systems, to ECs, the CQO, and the CEO. The surest way to ensure that the reward system will work is to link the reward system for the CEO and senior management to the rigorous and timely implementation of the DFTS initiative and its integration and expansion.

- **Customer-focused:** The goals and metrics must be customer-focused. They measure whether the initiative has met or exceeded the customers' spoken and unspoken needs and expectations. That's the crux of trustworthiness. The members of the project team should be taught to interact with external and internal customers on an ongoing basis and understand their evolving needs, concerns, and challenges in measurable terms.

- **Team-based:** Enterprise software development is a particularly collaborative process. The reward system should be structured to encourage teamwork and collaboration. This can be achieved by a variety of instruments, such as team-based incentives and feedback on teamwork, process defects, and goals rather than feedback on individual performance. Often, root-cause analysis reveals causes relating to management polices and decisions rather than individual performance.

- **Goal-focused:** The reward system should have clear, measurable goals with consistent short-term (quarterly) and long-term (yearly/three-times-yearly) elements. Furthermore, goals should be gradually linked to the ultimate objective of integrating and expanding the DFTS initiative beyond the initial projects. The rewards should be clear, and individuals should be able to redeem them either quarterly or yearly. The rewards should not be part of yearly performance evaluations, merit ratings, or annual reviews—the effects of which are devastating on individuals and, therefore, quality (see point 3 in Table 5.3).

- **Communicated effectively:** Teams and individuals should understand what their roles and contributions are. But the emphasis should always be on how the team can address individual shortcomings. They should be provided with the required skills and resources. Team members must be encouraged and respected for improvement ideas. The PLs and others should be required to regularly provide accurate feedback on team and individual performance. It's important that leaders take an interest in individuals and their teams and encourage team-based high performance.

- **Supported by genuine appreciation:** The reward system should be organized so that feedback and rewards are frequent and linked. The value and type of rewards should be tied to the performance and value created by the teams. These should be decided after careful deliberation, should be in line with the organizational culture, and must be substantial and meaningful. They may be gifts for the family, vacations, or financial rewards, including stock options for outstanding performance.

Step 10: Establishing Cost of Software Quality

This is the last of the planning steps before the DFTS initiative is launched. In the absence of Cost of Software Quality (CoSQ), the organization may be ill-equipped to identify various improvement opportunities that pop up during the implementation process. CoSQ serves four useful purposes in a software quality initiative:

- It helps you focus on activities that discover and correct the root causes of software defects.

- It helps you determine how you can improve the development process to prevent further defects.

- It provides a vehicle for communication across all functions supporting the project, regardless of the organizational structure.

- It communicates in a language that's easily understood: dollars.

CoSQ was discussed in Chapter 4, along with other financial evaluation tools such as ROQI using NPV and IRR, Quality Loss Function (QLF), and Activity-Based Costing (ABC). It is important to establish both CoSQ and financial evaluation metrics before the DFTS initiative so that opportunities for improvement are measured and identified during the implementation process.

Step 11: Planning and Launching Organization-Wide Learning

This is the first step in the implementation process that involves planning, designing, and imparting formal DFTS learning and training for the organization as a whole. Training programs should be customized and differentiated according to the roles and training needs of the people concerned. It takes place in two stages and is described briefly in this step and the next. The details of various DFTS training schedules are provided in Chapter 21.

Step 11 is concerned with imparting learning to all those who will largely be in supportive roles, such as the senior executives, ECs, and various personnel in sales, marketing, finance, and HR. These personnel provide important help in software development, documentation, costing, customer liaison activities, and training and other HR-related matters. They must understand the DFTS process to contribute to its implementation and integration. DFTS training is a lot more inclusive than that for a DFSS program because of the unique design predominance of the software development process. In the preimplementation stage (Step 11), two customized training programs are scheduled. Senior executives and ECs undergo senior executives and champions training, and other support personnel undergo white belt training. Step 12 training involves software developers and PLs. They receive intensive training interspersed with the actual development process. It is scheduled as part of the implementation of the DFTS model, which enables effective learning through project implementation and classroom learning.

The two training schedules in Step 11 are part of preimplementation planning:

- **Senior executives and champions training:** This three-day executive seminar provides an overview of opportunities, benefits, and leadership challenges in developing trustworthy software. It's meant for the CEO and senior executives from software development, quality, finance, planning, sales, marketing, internal IS, and HR. The roles and responsibilities of various players in a DFTS process are clarified. It also creates awareness about how DFTS works and how it can help the organization with its business objectives and, subsequently, securing genuine buy-in, commitment, and support. A major outcome of this seminar is identifying the software project(s) that black belt and master black belt trainees will work on.

- **White belt training:** White belt training is meant for everyone who supports software developers at the front end. This includes personnel from HR, from sales and marketing who interact with the customers, from finance who help with cost data, and from systems support personnel who provide support for the internal information system. This two- or three-day training introduces them to the basics of the DFTS process and equips them to help software development teams across various stages of the process. White belt participants should be introduced to the metrics, tools, and techniques of the DFTS process and acquire an awareness of the methodology and its immense value.

Step 12: Implementing the DFTS Model

This step is essentially learning and applying the DFTS model (see Figure 2.6) to an actual software development project. Its success depends on how the previous Steps 1 through 11 are planned and implemented. It's the responsibility of the senior management team led by the CEO, CQO, and EC to ensure that these have indeed been carried out carefully. These steps lay the ground-work for successful implementation of the DFTS model. In absence of this preparation, one can hardly realize its full potential. Step 12 consists of training the team members and leaders by having them use the DFTS model in an actual software development project. It consists of DFTS Black Belt Training and DFTS Master Black Belt Training.

DFTS Black Belt Training

All software professionals, from Vice President of Software Development down to young software engineers, must acquire black belt expertise. It should also be required training for all quality professionals, from CQO downward. The need for such organization-wide training is obvious. A rigorous quality management program is hardly ever a part of software engineering curricula in colleges or graduate schools. Furthermore, DFTS covers critical software development activities that provide a solid basis for quality management in the organization as a whole. The team undergoing black belt training should have an approved software development project already assigned to it, together with a project charter. As far as possible, the first project should be small in scope and development time so that it's manageable as a first DFTS project. Classroom learning and its successful application on a real software development project comprise the basic black belt training and are at the heart of the DFTS implementation process.

Black belt training constitutes the core body of knowledge for the DFTS process. We emphasize the importance of acquiring Personal Software Process (PSP) and Team Software Process (TSP) skills.[13] These skills contribute immensely to the DFTS process and also enhance the overall process and people maturity in CMM/CMMI and People Capability Maturity Model (PCMM) contexts. The training is designed as a sandwich program in the implementation process. It consists of five weeks of classroom learning followed by five software development activities that take four to eight weeks each (see Figure 5.6). The actual duration of the development activities between training sessions depends on the specific project. Correctly applying what has been learned during the training seminars is an integral part of the learning process.

It is important to develop, apply, and document best practices during the development activity. Knowledge transfer from the classroom to the actual development process is critical and should be carefully planned and monitored. CQOs and ECs work closely with trainers/coaches to ensure effective learning and knowledge transfer.

DFTS Master Black Belt Training

PLs are trained to be MBBs, who provide technical, teaching, coaching, mentoring, and leadership support to the project team. We discussed the roles and responsibilities of PLs earlier. MBB training and certification are also recommended for all software professionals above the PL level, as well as for quality professionals such as CQOs and their direct reports in the quality department. The training and certification plan for DFTS MBBs is discussed in Chapter 21, along with those of other cadres.

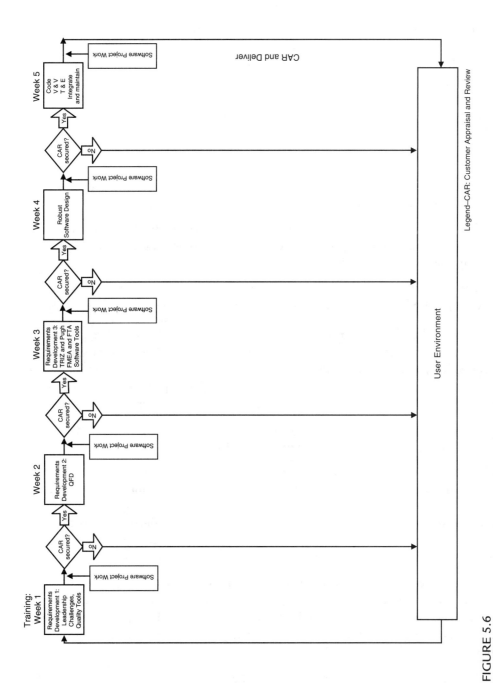

FIGURE 5.6
DFTS Black Belt Training and Project Work Schedule

Step 13: Monitoring and Feedback for Learning and Improvement

Learning from process and customer feedback is an important aspect of a learning enterprise. Steps 11 and 12 constitute the two-step implementation of the PICS model. These result in delivering the software product to the customer after the project team has carried out Customer Appraisal and Review (CAR) and has complied with predelivery customer requirements (see Figure 5.6). This is an excellent opportunity to get customer feedback upon actual delivery. Here are some important questions to ask at this stage:

- **Have** we specifically met the customer's cost, quality, and delivery schedule, as measured by pertinent metrics? Have we exceeded them or fallen short?

- **How** capable is our process, as determined by the process feedback loop, in meeting stated and unstated customer requirements, as determined by CAR?

- **What** are the opportunities for improvement, as measured by the gap between customer needs and process performance? (Process capability improves as the gap diminishes; this also implies less room for improvement.)

- **What** steps should we take to improve the process capability before integrating the revamped DFTS process and expanding it further?

Checking how the plan was implemented and is evolving is a crucial part of the PICS model. Here you use actual data, analyze it to discover the root causes of deviations, and take corrective actions to strengthen the process. To do so, appropriate metrics must be developed as part of the CoSQ initiative taken during the planning stage. Corrective actions complete the Deming cycle. All this must be properly documented.

Step 14: Freezing the Improvements and Gains

In this important stage, the organization takes the necessary steps to solidify the gains from the DFTS initiative (see Figure 5.3). This requires a planned effort aimed at changing people's attitudes, behavior, and beliefs. It should not only encourage the converts but also address the skeptics. You might have diehards who remain unconvinced. Such persons may have valid grounds for doubts, which must be given due consideration. You also might have downright cynics; it may be best to take appropriate remedial measures in such cases.

A variety of measures, such as counseling, a reward system, and training, can be deployed to encourage people to embrace the change. Freezing the gains invariably necessitates new roles and rules, and, above all, leadership that is visibly and vocally supportive of transformation. Many organizations find it crucial to create a strong quality culture, as discussed in Step 4.

Step 15: Integrating and Expanding the Initiative

The success of the DFTS initiative ultimately lies in its seamless integration with the rest of the organization beyond the initial project. This can happen successfully only if the initial project has been planned and executed systematically. We believe that the 15-step implementation framework proposed in this chapter provides a systematic methodology. It will help you successfully execute your first project. It also helps you develop the capability and knowledge base to expand the project further in your organization. Your objective should be for your next projects to be even more successful than the first one. This continuous improvement project after project will have a profound effect on customer satisfaction and corporate performance.

The task of organization-wide deployment can be a lot more challenging and risky. It is therefore critical that a tentative integration plan be prepared and updated as the first project is being implemented. The first project provides a unique opportunity to learn various "dos" and "don'ts." These should be properly documented and can help you develop a repertoire of best practices. The CQO and ECs should work closely and set up a "DFTS Integration and Expansion Task Force" when the first project is being planned. The best guarantee of subsequent success is a successful and systematic implementation of the first project, and learning from it. It is therefore critical that the organization mobilize its resources, including the most talented people, to be involved in the first project.

Finally, there should be a road map and a game plan if the first project does not produce the expected results. Instead of indulging in blame and finding scapegoats, management should analyze the implementation process and find the root causes and take appropriate measures. It's important to remain steadfast in the face of temporary setbacks. Certain setbacks are inevitable when implementing large projects; they are part of the learning process. Chapter 21 discusses DFTS integration and expansion further. Case Study 21.2 deals with integrating a new initiative with an organization's other quality platforms. Glenn Mazur provides a framework for integrating QFD and other quality methods to improve the new-product development process in Chapter 27.

Putting It All Together

A breakthrough improvement in quality never happens by itself. Neither is it the result of incremental learning from your past experience alone or because everyone works harder and faster. As Deming said, "The fact is that management cannot learn by experience alone what they must do to improve quality." It is invariably the result of fundamental and irreversible changes directed by the CEO and the top management team. These changes are planned and transformative as opposed to haphazard and incremental. At the end of all the talk, it is all about leadership. We have emphasized Deming and Kurt Lewin's models for introducing and leading change. If you have more effective models, use them. GE, for example, has its Operating System and other models that are very different from what Deming preached all his life. But it works for GE's culture. We believe that Deming and Lewin offer formidable models to lead change systematically. These are time-tested and proven and can be adapted across organizations, industries, and cultures.

All organizations embarking on DFTS should understand the magnitude of the tasks ahead, especially if they are seeking transformative and lasting results. As Fujio Cho, President of Toyota Motor Company, said in a recent interview,[14] "Some people think that if they just implement our techniques, they can be as successful as we are. But those that try often fail. That's because no mere process can turn a poor performer into a star. Rather, you have to address employees' fundamental way of thinking." The DFTS model and its methodology can be deployed successfully only alongside a broader change process to produce desired results.

Key Points

- Software quality problems are not unique or unusual, despite the design and intellectual predominance of the software development process.

- Quality system best practices from manufacturing and hardware are largely applicable to software development environments as well.

- DFTS requires major changes in the typical software development process. The underlying causes of failure for quality initiatives such as Six Sigma, BPR, and TQM are just as pertinent to a DFTS initiative.

- All successful quality initiatives are led by the CEOs, who understand their business value, communicate them, and provide resources.

- Before embarking on the DFTS initiative, an organization should assess its preparedness.

- The PICS framework, a 15-step implementation process, emphasizes the importance of planning to prepare the organization for the major initiative. It consists of a variety of tools, systems, and models that constitute the subject of this book.

- Even organizations with an established quality culture can benefit from the step-by-step PICS process. Time and resources spent on sound planning are essential and pay off in terms of successful execution. It helps implement the initiative soundly and ensure its long-term sustenance and continual improvement. The two feedback loops provide opportunities for learning, corrective measures, and continual improvement.

Step 1: Creating management awareness and buy-in. It's important to recognize that top management is interested in long-term as well as short-term results.

Use Lewin's Force Field Analysis Model to understand social forces in play in a major initiative such as DFTS. It is desirable to introduce changes by strengthening driving forces rather than diminishing restraining ones.

Set up a "DFTS Steering Committee."

Step 2: Communicating top management's consensus and commitment. The CEO should communicate the decision to launch the DFTS initiative, its rationale, and the broad objectives and expectations. There should be clarity on how the organization and individuals will benefit. The CEO also creates the steering committee.

Step 3: Recognizing potential pitfalls of a DFTS initiative. Examining and understanding the potential pitfalls of a DFTS intervention is an extremely valuable exercise. It provides a cost-effective opportunity to foresee what problems could occur and how to avoid them. The most common pitfalls of a major quality initiative such as DFTS are lack of management support, middle management antipathy, empty quality slogans, lack of team cohesiveness, wrong implementation strategies, inadequate rewards and incentives for change, wrong success indicators, wasting resources on inconsequential issues, failure of communication, inadequate training, and no clue about costs.

Step 4: Laying foundations for a quality-focused enterprise. This step includes awareness of shortcomings of current practices, contemplating and adopting Deming's teachings, organization-wide consultation and communication, and planning and inducting Deming's Principles.

Step 5: Building the organizational infrastructure. A supportive organizational infrastructure consists of the following key elements:

Quality of leadership

Strategic planning

Operations and process management

Management information system

Accounting and financial management

Human resources management

Step 6: Understanding the roles of the key players. DFTS requires the organization as a whole to be up to the task. It needs the involvement and commitment of the CEO and senior executives, including those from supporting functions such as finance, HR, and sales and marketing. Certain responsibilities can be modified, enlarged, or combined, depending on the organizational contingencies. But every software enterprise, irrespective of its size and needs, must address the issues implied by these roles and responsibilities. One important difference in the DFTS system is the need for greater depth of process expertise among software team members, team leaders, and the executive management team. Understanding these roles provides the basis for training and building the competence of personnel needed for the process.

Step 7: Designing a supportive organizational structure. Software development is a creative process, but it also involves a lot of labor-intensive, mechanical work at downstream stages that must be carried out equally well. The software development process thus can benefit from creativity as well as standardization. Both are needed to meet customer requirements. The structure must provide for both. But it can hardly suffice by itself. It must be supplemented by effective communication and documentation to handle coordination between customers and various personnel involved in different phases of the development process.

Step 8: Establishing effective communication. There are two kinds of communication challenges in a DFTS process: communication between the users/customers and the organization, and communication within the organization. The executive leadership should understand the critical role of communication and ensure that the organization has a sound communication plan in place.

Step 9: Creating an appropriate reward system. A reward system encourages individuals and teams to believe and behave in a manner that helps the organization achieve its most crucial goals and ambitions. As such, it is more than salary, compensation, and monetary incentives. There is no one best way to reward people. A reward system's effectiveness depends on the type of organization, its culture and beliefs, the goals of the reward system, and the desired actions, beliefs, and behavior that need to be reinforced. Involvement, commitment, and a stake in the outcomes are essential ingredients for high performance.

Step 10: Establishing Cost of Software Quality. CoSQ serves the following purposes in a software quality initiative:

Helps you focus on activities that discover and correct the root causes of software defects.

Helps you determine how the development process can be improved to prevent further defects.

Provides a vehicle for communication across all functions supporting the project, regardless of the organizational structure.

Communicates in a language that's easily understood: dollars.

Step 11: Planning and launching organization-wide learning. This is the first part of organization-wide learning. It involves supportive roles such as the senior executives, ECs, and various personnel in sales, marketing, finance, and HR. These personnel provide help in software development, documentation, costing, customer liaison, and training and other HR-related matters.

Step 12: Implementing the DFTS model. This step involves learning and applying the DFTS model to an actual software development project. It includes training the team members and leaders and having them use the DFTS model in an actual software development project. It consists of DFTS black belt training and master black belt training.

Step 13: Monitoring and feedback for learning and improvement. Important issues addressed at this stage include the following:

Have we specifically met the customer's cost, quality, and delivery schedule, as measured by pertinent metrics?

How capable is our process, as determined by the process feedback loop, in meeting stated and unstated customer requirements, as determined by CAR?

What are the opportunities for improvement, as measured by the gap between the customer needs and process performance?

What steps should we take to improve the process capability before integrating the revamped DFTS process and expanding it further?

Step 14: Freezing the improvements and gains. Here the organization takes necessary steps to solidify the gains from the DFTS initiative and requires a planned effort aimed at changing people's attitudes, behavior, and beliefs. A variety of measures, such as counseling, a reward system, and training, can be deployed to encourage people to embrace the change. Freezing the gains invariably necessitates new roles, rules, and leadership that is visibly and vocally supportive of transformation.

Step 15: Integrating and expanding the initiative. It is critical that an integration plan be prepared and updated as the first project is being implemented. The first project provides a unique learning opportunity that should be properly documented and can help develop a repertoire of best practices. The CQO and ECs should work closely and set up a DFTS integration and expansion task force when the first project is being planned. The best guarantee of subsequent success is successful and systematic implementation of the first project, and learning from it. It is therefore critical that the organization mobilize its resources, including the most talented people to be involved in the first project. Finally, there should be a road map if the first project has not produced the expected results. Instead of indulging in blame and finding scapegoats, management should analyze the implementation process and find the root causes and take appropriate measures. It is important to remain steadfast in the face of temporary setbacks.

Additional Resources

http://www.prenhallprofessional.com/title/0131872508

http://www.agilenty.com/publications

Internet Exercises

Read the article "Kurt Lewin's Change Theory in the Field and in the Classroom: Notes Toward a Model of Managed Learning" by Edgar H. Schein on the following site:

http://mitpress.mit.edu/catalog/item/default.asp?ttype=6&tid=6106

and then do the following:

1. Prepare a one-page executive summary of the article, and come to class prepared to discuss it.

2. Explain Lewin's dictum "There is nothing so practical as a good theory" in a context you are familiar with. According to Schein, what are the attributes of a good theory of change, and how does Lewin's basic change model fit the bill?

3. Explain what the author means by "...learning and change start with some form of dissatisfaction or frustration." What does the author mean by "disconfirming information"? Is it sufficient to cause motivation to change?

4. Describe how Schein proposes to reconcile the conflicting needs of individuals and teams. What are its implications in managing and rewarding individuals on a team?

5. What possible difficulties are associated with role models and consultants? Why might benchmarking not be effective? How will you address these challenges?

6. What is meant by personal and relational refreezing? Explain how to attain these in a context you are familiar with.

(This article is also available from *Reflections: The SoL Journal*, Volume 1, Number 1, 1 August 1999, pp. 59–74(16), Society of Organizational Learning.)

Review Questions

1. Do we need a totally different approach to software quality as compared to manufacturing? Why or why not?

2. Who should lead DFTS initiatives? What do they do in particular?

3. Explain the PICS framework. Why is it important to use a step-by-step approach? What are the benefits of the PICS framework?

4. Why is management buy-in important? What are the typical interests of the CEO and top management team regarding a major initiative?

5. Explain how Lewin's Force Field Analysis Model helps you understand the process of introducing a major change.

6. What are the outcomes of a successful management buy-in process? What can go wrong if DFTS is perceived as a program to be implemented?

7. How should an organization go about communicating its decision to launch a DFTS initiative?

8. Why is it important to understand the pitfalls of a DFTS initiative? Briefly discuss some common pitfalls.

9. Why is laying foundations of a quality-focused organization critical in a successful implementation? How can an organization initiate a quality culture through its ranks?

10. What are the key elements of an organizational infrastructure? Why are they important in a quality initiative?

11. Critically appraise the roles of the key players in a DFTS initiative presented in this chapter.

12. What are the key requirements of an organizational structure that is supportive of a DFTS initiative? Draw an organizational chart that meets these requirements.

13. Identify the key elements of a reward system that is supportive of a DFTS initiative. What are some important nonfinancial rewards? How important are they?

14. What is the significance of CoSQ in a DFTS initiative? Would you launch one without it?

15. What is the importance of training support personnel in the DFTS process? What can go wrong if they are not trained?

16. Compare and contrast the training of black belts and master black belts. Why should DFTS team members possess black belt skills rather than just green belt?

17. What do you monitor following a DFTS implementation? What are the benefits of a strong monitoring system?

18. Using Lewin's Three-Step Model, explain what measures an organization can take to "freeze" and sustain the gains of a DFTS initiative.

19. What key measures can be taken to ensure smooth integration and expansion of the DFTS initiative? What can go wrong in the absence of such measures?

Discussion Questions and Projects

1. What are the key differences in hardware and software development processes? How do they matter in an effective quality management system?

2. An organization has just undertaken a DFTS initiative under the leadership of the newly recruited quality executive, because the CEO and top management team are occupied with another task. Discuss the possible outcomes of such a decision.

3. Can any of the steps in the PICS framework be skipped? Do you think any steps are missing?

4. What are the risks involved in the absence of the implementation framework that PICS provides?

5. Is the top management team typically a cohesive group? Explain with examples.

6. How may conflicting long-term and short-term objectives impede a DFTS initiative?

7. What can CEOs do to avoid possible pitfalls of a DFTS initiative? Can they pull it off themselves? Do a literature survey, including an Internet search, on Jack Welch's Six Sigma initiative at GE in support of your answer.

8. How relevant are Deming's teachings today (see Tables 5.2, 5.3, and 5.4)? Can you suggest some possible adaptations? What are they?

Endnotes

[1]K. Lewin, "Resolving Social Conflicts and Field Theory in Social Science," American Psychological Association, Washington, D.C., 1997.

[2]R. Zultner, "The Deming Way: A Guide to Software Quality (Adapted by Richard Zultner)," "Fourteen Points for Software Managers," brochure from Zultner & Co., 12 Willingford Dr., Princeton, NJ 08540, copyright 1988, Zultner & Co., reprinted with permission.

[3]R. Zultner, "The Deming Way: A Guide to Software Quality (Adapted by Richard Zultner)," "Obstacles to Software Quality" and "Seven Deadly Diseases of Software Quality," brochure from Zultner & Co., 12 Willingford Dr., Princeton, NJ 08540, copyright 1988, Zultner & Co., reprinted with permission.

[4]N. M. Tichy and S. Sherman, *Control Your Destiny or Someone Else Will* (New York: HarperBusiness, 2001), p. 13.

[5]A. Fornari and G. Maszle, "Lean Six Sigma Leads Xerox," *Six Sigma Forum*, Volume 3, Number 4, August 2004, p. 11.

[6]B. Schlender, "Gurus: Peter Drucker Sets Us Straight," *Fortune*, 12 January 2004.

[7]P. M. Senge, *The Fifth Discipline: The Art and Practice of Learning Organization* (New York: Doubleday Currency, 1990), p. 4.

[8]N. M. Tichy, *The Cycle of Leadership* (New York: HarperBusiness, 2002), p. 8.

[9]Ibid.

[10]W. E. Deming, *Out of the Crisis* (Cambridge, MA: MIT Press, 2000).

[11]N. Logothetis, *Managing for Total Quality* (London: Prentice-Hall International, 1992), p. 51.

[12]T. B. Wilson, *Rewards That Drive High Performance* (New York: AMACOM, 1999), p. 2.

[13]W. Humphrey, *Winning with Software: An Executive Strategy* (Boston: Addison-Wesley, 2002), pp. 77–104.

[14]A. Tilin, "The Smartest Company of the Year," *Business 2.0*, January–February 2005, p. 72.

PART II

Tools and Techniques of Design for Trustworthy Software

CHAPTER 6

The Seven Basic (B7) Tools of Quality

As much as 95% of quality-related problems in the factory can be solved with seven fundamental quantitative tools.

—Kaoru Ishikawa

There is nothing so practical as a good theory.

—Kurt Lewin

Overview

Although DFTS is a design-focused quality technology, it also includes problem-solving/process-improvement capabilities and can benefit from the deployment of the Seven Basic (B7) Tools, widely used in manufacturing. In a DFTS context, B7 tools can be of great value in project management, inspection, and testing and in analyzing software metrics. They can also be used in upstream design phases, except for statistical tools such as control charts, histograms, and scatter diagrams that require larger volumes of data to be statistically significant. The most frequently used B7 tools, such as cause-and-effect and Pareto diagrams, are not quantitative, let alone statistical. B7 thus constitutes a useful toolkit in the software development context both in process improvement and design tools, of which a few are indispensable.

It is important to use them in the wider context of DFTS technology, which includes a number of quality methodologies, such as QFD, TRIZ, Pugh, Taguchi Methods, and FMEA, which are discussed later in this book. Additionally, techniques such as systems thinking, process management, standardization, and adequate documentation, which are an integral part of DFTS technology, must be included in process improvement.

A flowchart graphically represents various activities in a sequential manner. Identifying such activities and their causes can help eliminate or minimize redundancies and wasteful activities as well as strengthen those that help achieve process goals and create customer value. It also serves as a communication tool.

Cause-and-effect diagrams are also called fishbone diagrams, because of their structure, or Ishikawa diagrams, for Kaoru Ishikawa, who developed this tool. These are among the most widely used tools in quality management; they are used for the following purposes: *identifying causes of variation and taking countermeasures, process classification, Pareto-Ishikawa, generating data needed for FMEA, identifying possible "noise" and "control factors" in Taguchi Methods, as a visible communication tool*, and *categorizing various inputs (causes) and outputs (effects)*.

A scatter diagram seeks to establish whether a relationship exists between two variables and the strength of the relationship. Establishing relationships can be particularly useful in cause-and-effect analysis. A strong correlation may help identify possible countermeasures to address a particular quality problem.

A check sheet is a paper form that lists items to be measured, checked, and recorded. It makes data collection easy, usable, and standardized by the form's particular design. Various check sheets are possible, depending on the objective of the data collection exercise, such as measuring process variation, analyzing types of defects, and identifying causes of defects. They are often coupled with histograms to display visualization and use of data collected in histograms.

A histogram is used to analyze variation in a set of data. It helps you understand how the data collected from a particular development or production process is distributed in terms of frequency of occurrences of a particular value in the set. The key objective is to look for stability and predictability.

Graphs are useful tools in software quality and project management. Among the most commonly used graphs are run charts, pie charts, and bar charts. They help you monitor time variation and understand causes of defects in a process.

Control charts are among the most important quality tools. They measure process variation periodically to check whether it is within acceptable limits. Processes whose variation is within such limits are said to be "in control." "Out-of-control" processes lead to defective work with adverse cost, quality, and schedule implications. Statistical Process Control (SPC) deploys control charts to prevent defective work by focusing efforts on process quality rather than the final product. It thus lets the enterprise take preventive and process improvement initiatives instead of just appraising the final product. XmR charts and average (X-bar) and range (R) charts have been found to be most useful to measure software process.

This chapter introduces B7 in a software development context and is a precursor to Chapter 15.

Chapter Outline

- The Seven Basic (B7) Tools
- B7 in a DFTS Context
- Other DFTS Tools, Techniques, and Methodologies
- Flowcharts
- Pareto Charts
- Cause-and-Effect Diagrams
- Scatter Diagrams
- Check Sheets
- Histograms
- Graphs
- Control Charts
- Key Points
- Additional Resources
- Review Questions
- Discussion Questions
- Endnotes

The Seven Basic (B7) Tools

This chapter introduces a set of quality tools that are particularly useful in process improvement and problem-solving aspects of the software development process. A few of these tools are also useful in many design-related activities. These tools are popularly known as the *Seven Basic (B7) Tools of Quality*: *flowcharts, Pareto diagrams, cause-and-effect diagrams, scatter diagrams, check sheets, histograms,* and *control charts* (see Table 6.1).[1, 2, 3] These tools were originally developed by Kaoru Ishikawa, one of the pioneers of the Japanese quality movement (see Sidebar 6.1). Ishikawa's original list did not include flowcharts; instead, it had *graphs* as one of the tools. B7 has been part of SPC, a quality management system that uses a set of tools to analyze, control, manage, and improve process quality. But not all seven tools are quantitative, let alone statistical. The flowchart is simply a visual description of a process. A cause-and-effect diagram is a brainstorming-based problem-solving procedure. Check sheets and Pareto diagrams are simply commonsense tools. Histograms, scatter diagrams, and control charts are the only statistical tools in the list.

B7 has been widely used in manufacturing in process-improvement initiatives such as Total Quality Management (TQM) and Six Sigma. They can also be used in upstream design phases, except for statistical tools such as control charts, histograms, and scatter diagrams, which require a larger volume of data to be statistically significant. The most frequently used B7 tools, such as cause-and-effect and Pareto diagrams, are not quantitative, let alone statistical. The tools were originally meant to make process analysis less complicated for the average factory worker in Japan, but now they constitute standard analytical tools to analyze quality problems and develop and identify solutions. Ishikawa believed that some 95% of quality-related problems can be solved with these tools. Their application has not yet been as extensive in software development. They are excellent in analyzing software measures and metrics, as discussed further in Chapter 15. They can and should be used in statistical control and process improvement of medium-size and large projects. Statistical tools are of comparatively limited value in upstream design and implementation activities, but other tools, such as cause-and-effect diagrams and Pareto analysis, are widely used throughout the DFTS process. For example, the cause-and-effect brainstorming procedure is widely used to generate data needed in QFD and FMEA (see Chapters 11 and 13, respectively). Table 6.1 lists a few typical applications of various B7 tools.

TABLE 6.1
Process Improvement Tools and Their Applications

Quality Tool	What It Addresses	Major Application in a DFTS Process
Flowchart/ process map	How can all the process steps and sequences be described visually?	Process improvement Fine-tuning a process before automating it Auditing Communication tool
Pareto chart	Which problems matter most?	Fault analysis Peer review Program maintenance Root-cause analysis Requirements development (QFD) FMEA Robust Design
Cause-and-effect diagram	What are the root causes of these problems?	Root cause analysis Cause-and-effect graphing Requirements development (QFD) FMEA Robust Design
Scatter diagram	What are the relationships between factors?	Requirements development (QFD) Robust Design
Check sheet	How frequently does the problem occur, and how do you record it?	Everywhere

TABLE 6.1
Continued

Quality Tool	What It Addresses	Major Application in a DFTS Process
Histogram	What do the variations look like?	Process improvement Requirements development (QFD) Robust Design
Control chart	Which variations should be controlled, and in what manner	Process improvement Requirements development (QFD) Robust Design
Graph	What are the trends, over time, and fraction-wise distribution pattern of important variables?	Line charts in SPC/control charts Pie and bar charts everywhere

Sidebar 6.1: Kaoru Ishikawa: Developing a Specifically Japanese Quality Strategy*

The career of Kaoru Ishikawa in some ways parallels the economic history of contemporary Japan. Ishikawa, like Japan as a whole, learned the basics of statistical quality control from Americans. But just as Japan's economic accomplishments are not limited to imitating foreign products, so the country's quality achievements—and Ishikawa's in particular—go well beyond the efficient application of imported ideas.

Perhaps Ishikawa's most important contribution has been his key role in the development of a specifically Japanese quality strategy. The hallmark of the Japanese approach is broad involvement in quality—not only top to bottom within the organization, but also from start to finish in the product life cycle.

The bottom-up approach is best exemplified by the quality circle. As a member of the editorial board of *Quality Control for the Foreman*, as chief executive director of Quality Control Circle Headquarters at the Union of Japanese Scientists and Engineers (JUSE), and as editor of JUSE's two books on quality circles (*QC Circle Koryo* and *How to Operate QC Circle Activities*), Ishikawa played a major role in the growth of quality circles.

One of Ishikawa's early achievements contributed to the success of quality circles. The cause-and-effect diagram—often called the Ishikawa diagram and perhaps the achievement for which he is best known—has provided a powerful tool that can easily be used by nonspecialists to analyze and solve problems.

Although the quality circle was developed in Japan, it spread to more than 50 countries, a development Ishikawa never foresaw. Originally, Ishikawa believed circles depended on factors unique to Japanese society. But after seeing circles thrive in Taiwan and South Korea, he theorized that circles could succeed in any country that used the Chinese alphabet. Ishikawa's reasoning was that the Chinese alphabet, one of the most difficult writing systems in the world, can be mastered only after a great deal of study. Thus, hard work and a desire for education became part of the character of those nations. Within a few years, however, the success of circles around the world led him to a new conclusion: Circles work because they appeal to the democratic nature of humankind. "Wherever they are, human beings are human beings," Ishikawa wrote in a 1980 preface to the English translation of the *Koryo*.

In *How to Operate QC Circle Activities,* Ishikawa calls middle and upper management the parent-teacher association of quality control circles. Although circles were one of the earliest Japanese ideas about quality to be popularized in the West, Ishikawa was always aware of the importance of top management support. Support from the top is a key element in Japan's all-encompassing quality strategy: company-wide quality control (CWQC), perhaps best described in Ishikawa's *What Is Total Quality Control? The Japanese Way*. Ishikawa's work with top management and CWQC covered decades. In the late 1950s and early 1960s, he developed quality control courses for executives and top managers. He also helped launch the Annual Quality Control Conference for Top Management in 1963.

As a member of the committee for the Deming Prize, Ishikawa developed the rigorous audit system that determines whether companies qualify for the prize. That audit requires the participation of the company's top executives. According to Ishikawa, that active, visible participation—rather than the acclaim that goes with the prize—is the biggest benefit a winner receives.

If top-down, bottom-up involvement is one axis of CWQC, the other is an emphasis on quality throughout the product life cycle. Here, too, Ishikawa was involved starting in 1959, particularly in the development of a quality control system for new-product development.

Ishikawa was also involved in efforts to promote quality ideas throughout Japan, both in industry and among consumers. As chairman of the quality control National Conference committee for over 30 years, Ishikawa played a central role in the expanding scope of those conferences.

Ishikawa was also active in other efforts to promote quality. For example, he wrote several books explaining statistics to the nonspecialist. One of these, the *Guide to Quality Control*, was translated into English and became a staple in the quality training programs of corporations in the United States.

In addition, Ishikawa served as chairman of the editorial board of the monthly *Statistical Quality Control* and the quarterly *Reports of Statistical Applications Research*. As chairman of Japan's Quality Month committee, Ishikawa was involved in the selection of Japan's quality mark and quality flag.

Ishikawa was involved in Japanese and international standardization activities beginning in the 1950s. In his Shewhart Medal acceptance speech, Ishikawa called standardization and quality control "two wheels of the same cart." His emphasis might be surprising to some who think of standards as rigid and unchanging, but Ishikawa stressed the need for standards to change, and the dangers of clumsy enforcement of standards. In his view, effective standards must be built on a quality analysis of customer needs. When the analysis had not been conducted—as is often the case with national and international standards—Ishikawa recommended reliance on consumer needs rather than standards.

ASQ established the Ishikawa Medal in 1993 to recognize leadership in the human side of quality. The medal is awarded annually in honor of Ishikawa to an individual or team for outstanding leadership in improving the human aspects of quality.

Throughout his career, Ishikawa worked on very practical matters, but always within a larger philosophical framework. In its broadest sense, Ishikawa's work was intended to produce what he called a "thought revolution"—new ideas about quality that could revitalize industry. The wide acceptance of many of Ishikawa's ideas—and the numerous honors he has received from around the world—show how successful his revolution has been.

* Reprinted with permission from www.asq.org. © 2006 American Society for Quality.

B7 in a DFTS Context

As we explained in Chapter 2, Design for Trustworthy Software (DFTS) is essentially a design technology. It emphasizes upstream activities and employs specific tools, techniques, and methodologies to deliver trustworthy software. In this respect, it is akin to design-focused quality initiatives such as Design for Six Sigma (DFSS). However, software development must also provide problem-solving/process-improvement opportunities, as manifested in various iterative loops of the DFTS model (see Figure 2.6 in Chapter 2). Without such iteration providing internal feedback as well as customer interaction and consequent opportunities for process improvement, the model will have a severe deficiency. Process improvement capabilities are an integral part of the DFTS technology and its accompanying process. In this sense, DFTS is not unlike TQM/Six Sigma, which are process-focused quality management systems. DFTS thus must possess design as well as process improvement capabilities to be effective; one is seriously handicapped without the other. But given the *predominance of design* in the software development process, an effective software development technology comprises process improvement capabilities that are a subliminal part of the design process and deployed as required. In particular, B7 tools can be of great value in project management, inspection, and testing and in analyzing software metrics. But statistical tools generally are of relatively limited use in upstream design phases given the lack of volumetric data. However, as we stated earlier, not all B7 tools are quantitative, let alone statistical. All nonstatistical tools can be used in upstream phases too.

B7 tools become even more effective when used as part of the systematic DFTS framework. In Chapters 2 and 5 (see Figures 2.6, 5.1, and 5.6), DFTS was presented as a step-by-step technology deployment that includes organizational learning, human competence building, and problem-solving subprocesses. Such a step-by-step approach is crucial for three reasons:[4]

- It makes the decision process explicit.

- By acting as a "checklist" of the key steps in a development activity, it ensures that important issues are not overlooked.

- The structured methods can be made self-documenting. In the process of executing the method, the team creates a record of the decision-making process for future reference and to educate newcomers.

Other DFTS Tools, Techniques, and Methodologies

DFTS technology also includes a number of quality approaches and methodologies such as QFD, TRIZ, Pugh, Taguchi Methods, and FMEA. Additionally, the following set of techniques complement the DFTS technology and are an integral part of every successful deployment:

- **Systems thinking:** A fundamental tenet of quality management is to view an organization as a set of interconnected elements formed with the purpose of pursuing certain objectives. A change in one element has repercussions on others and the system as a whole. These elements are typically grouped and analyzed as input-process-output parts of a system.

- **Process management:** This is based on Deming's approach of measuring the variances in processes, finding the causes of variances, and eliminating or reducing them to improve quality.

- **Standardization:** After the DFTS has been customized to the organization's needs and internalized, it must be embraced as a standard software development technology for the organization. Any deviation must be justifiable, approved, and documented by appropriate authorities. This standardization must be supported by appropriate control and documentation. Organizations with ISO 9001 and other certifications would integrate DFTS into their procedures and control systems.

- **Adequate documentation:** Systematic process management requires documentation as an essential part of the development technology. What is not documented has not been recognized!

- **Statistical thinking:** Statistical thinking is an integral part of process management. Data on variances must be measured, deploying a set of tools to make fact-based decisions. Statistical tools are invaluable when appropriate and are discussed in Chapter 15. In process improvement, the B7 tools are extremely useful and constitute the subject matter of this chapter. But as you will see in Chapter 9, undue reliance on statistical tools is not always warranted and may even be counterproductive. That chapter also shows the limitations of statistical tools and their irrelevance at upstream stages, where crucial software quality issues such as complexity are addressed.

Flowcharts

A flowchart, also called a process map, is used to visually describe a process. It is a graphical representation of various activities in a sequential manner. It includes various operations, inspections, delays, and decision loops involved in a process.

A properly drawn flowchart shows important activities that may result in desirable or undesirable process outcomes. Identifying such activities and their causes can help you eliminate or minimize redundancies and wasteful activities as well as strengthen activities that help achieve process goals and create customer value. A flowchart also serves as a communication tool. Thus, it is the foundation of effective process improvement initiatives such as Six Sigma. It is also useful in DFTS technology in that it helps define and improve the software development process. In general, flowcharts serve the following purposes:

- They help you understand how a particular process is carried out.

- They help you recognize unnecessary steps in the process or sources of poor quality.

- They help you decide whether the process creates customer value or meets some other requirement.

- They simplify the process to make it more reliable, safer, faster, or cheaper.

- They identify various stakeholders in a process.

- They help you plan required product and process improvement initiatives.

Flowcharts use a variety of symbols. The most common ones are shown in Figure 6.1.

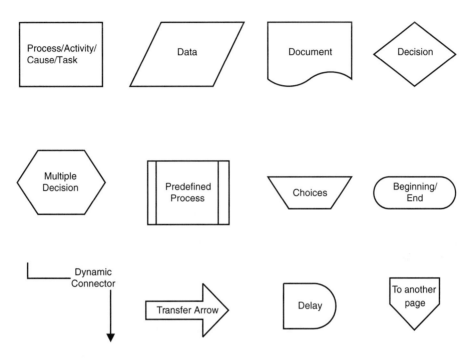

FIGURE 6.1
Commonly Used Flowchart Symbols

The following are the typical eight steps in making a flowchart:

1. Understand the process by visiting the workplace/domain of process activities.

2. Observe the activities, and talk to those who carry them out, not the managers.

3. Identify what is causing the process to start and what it leads to.

4. Observe the sequence of activities leading to the end of the process.

5. Identify "yes/no" decision loops, if any, and the consequent activity.

6. Write down a description of each activity from beginning to end.

7. Draw the chart, and check with the participants and process owner for accuracy.

8. Reconcile discrepancies, if any.

Three types of flowcharts provide different levels of details, as discussed next.

High-Level Flowcharts

This kind of flowchart, also called a *top-down* flowchart, provides a broad view of the process by showing just its major steps. The high-level flowchart shown in Figure 6.2 shows a simple process involving fixing a software defect. It does not deal with various substeps and feedback loops that accompany decision boxes. High-level flowcharts can be used to describe the major sequence of steps that link inputs and outputs in a process. It is useful for identifying various intermediate stages in the process and thus opportunities for monitoring indicators and for grouping individuals involved in similar activities. Usually fewer than ten major steps are required to construct a high-level flowchart.

Detailed Flowcharts

A detailed flowchart, shown in Figure 6.2, is a thorough portrayal of a process; it usually includes various substeps and activities. It also includes various loops that accompany decision boxes. They identify opportunities for improvement from the customer's perspective and show ways to eliminate waste. The detailed flowchart identifies waiting and other routines that do not necessarily create value for the customer. Such activities should be eliminated or minimized to make the process better, cheaper, and faster.

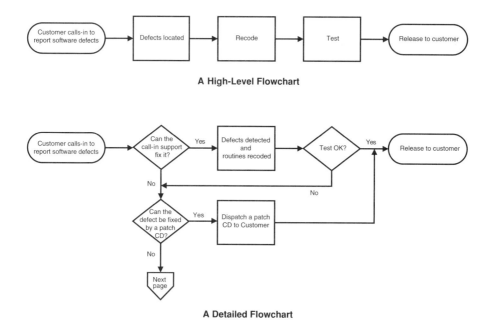

FIGURE 6.2
Two Examples of Flowcharts

Swim Lane Flowcharts

This is a detailed flowchart in which the participants in a particular group of activities such as testing or coding are shown in identifiable horizontal or vertical lanes. It is particularly useful in designing an improved or new process where the roles need to be clearly identified.

Pareto Charts

Quality problems may be the result of any number of root causes that may be too numerous in any given situation. In such situations, it is important to prioritize the critical few causes and focus on them from time, resource, and customer perspectives. It would be beneficial to isolate areas or issues that will lead to the most significant improvements in terms of quality, schedule, and cost. Pareto charts are a series of bar charts with a cumulative line graph arranged in descending order. They indicate the diminishing importance of a series of activities or entities. They are named after 19th century Italian economist/mathematician Vilfredo Pareto, who hypothesized that 20% of the population had 80% of the wealth. He also said that even if the wealth were redistributed equitably to the whole population, a similar proportion would result over time.

A Pareto diagram may look simple, but it is an extremely useful tool. It helps users focus on big issues. As such, it can be used to address any kind of concern that can be measured, such as cost, defects, faults, failures, complaints, returned items, repairs and fixes, risks, safety, and security. You can construct a diagram based on either measurements or estimates.

Figure 6.3 shows a simple Pareto diagram with the underlying causes of defects during different phases of a software life cycle. The most common cause can be attributed to design creation. Furthermore, upstream activities constitute the bulk of the causes. However, the symptoms (effects) are manifested only downstream during testing and maintenance. The implication is that an effective solution is not to deploy an army of engineers in testing and fixing, but to design the product properly at the upstream stages. Experience shows that the strategy of focusing upstream lowers overall life-cycle costs, although the costs at individual upstream phases may go up.

To link causes and effects, cause-and-effect diagrams are often used, as described in the next section.

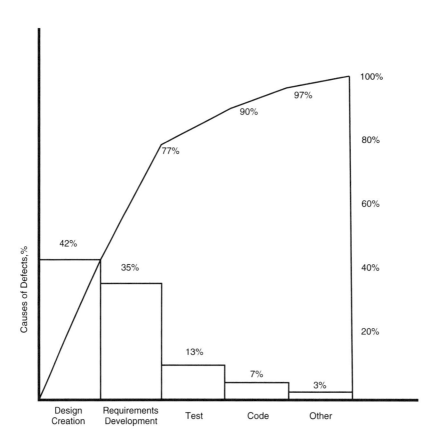

FIGURE 6.3
A Pareto Chart

Cause-and-Effect Diagrams

Cause-and-effect diagrams are also called fishbone diagrams, because of their structure, or Ishikawa diagrams, after Kaoru Ishikawa, who developed this tool. Kinds of Ishikawa diagrams include standard, process, and Pareto, to name a few. They are among the most widely used tools in quality management and are used for the following purposes:

- To identify causes of variation and to take countermeasures
- Process classification
- Pareto-Ishikawa
- To generate data needed for FMEA

- To identify possible "noise" and "control factors" in Taguchi Methods
- As a visible communication tool
- To categorize various inputs (causes) and output (effects)

The cause-and-effect diagram consists of the following three elements (see Figure 6.4):[5]

- **Effect or characteristic:** It is best to find some way to express how bad the problem really is—quantitatively, if possible. It is important to focus on one target at a time. Therefore, you need a cause-and-effect diagram for each characteristic that is being addressed.

- **Major branches:** The major branches are identified by a brainstorming process that discusses what the major branches (also called the big bones) are. The major branches follow certain criteria, such as 4Ms (man, materials, machines, and methods), 5Ms-1E (the 4Ms plus measuring method and environment), related departments, and functions. In the case of software, we suggest 3Ms-SHE, which is defined as follows:

  Man: Includes software engineers, managers, support staff, and management

  Methodology: Includes procedures; methods such as QFD, FMEA, and Taguchi Methods; statistical and nonstatistical tools; techniques such as systematic processes, standardization, and documentation; policies; and the overall methodology, such as DFTS

  Measurement: Equipments and techniques used for measurement

  Software, such as OOD, CASE tools, and software development partner issues

  Hardware: Computer and other hardware used in development process

  Environment: Customer/user as well as internal work environments

- **Midsize, minor, and offshoot branches:** You continue asking "Why?" after identifying the major branches. This leads sequentially to midsize branches (also called medium-sized bones), to minor branches (small bones), and then to offshoots of root causes. The exercise of looking for root causes continues until the group identifies an actionable countermeasure.

The structured brainstorming process, invented by American advertising executive Alex Osborn, is at the heart of the cause-and-effect diagram. Creativity should be encouraged by not allowing ideas to be evaluated or discussion to take place until everyone has had a chance. All ideas, even wild ones, are entertained so long as they relate, even remotely, to the topic in question.

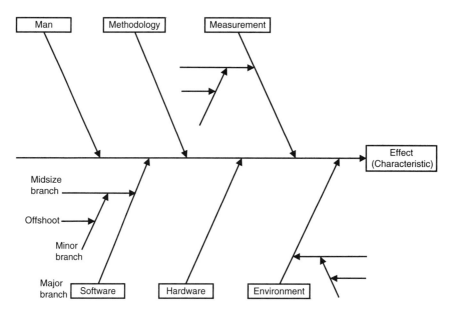

FIGURE 6.4
Elements of a Cause-and-Effect Diagram

Creating Cause-and-Effect-Diagrams to Identify Causes

The procedure described here is used to identify and classify possible causes of a problem. It is also called the generic or standard type. It involves *dispersion analysis* and asking "Why does dispersion occur?" five times. It is a brainstorming tool and therefore should be built on broad discussion and consensus. The objective should be to generate a lot of ideas rather than a few "great" ones. No idea is stupid to start with. The bad ideas are eliminated in due course. The following steps are employed in conducting brainstorming:

1. Assemble the group concerned with the problem. The group size should ideally be six but no larger than ten.

2. Define the effect/characteristic or problem as precisely as possible in a problem statement.

3. Have a skeleton diagram handy on a flip chart, and write the purpose, as defined by the problem statement, as the effect at the "head of the fish" (see Figure 6.4).

4. Ask each person to come up with six major causes of the effect (the major branches along 3Ms-SHE or any other agreed-on grouping). Give them no more than a couple of minutes to write down their ideas on sticky notes before they are asked to read them for the group.

5. Stick the notes from each individual on another flip chart.

6. Discuss and combine common ideas. If grouped properly, they will fall into no more than six major branches. Record those on the diagram.

7. Taking one major cause at a time, ask "Why?", and let each individual come up with the causes (minor branches) for each major cause.

8. Discuss and agree on minor causes, and record them on the diagram.

9. Taking one minor cause at a time, ask for offshoot causes. Repeat steps 7 and 8.

10. Follow the preceding steps until all the actionable causes are identified and agreed on.

11. Assign an importance to each cause ("important," "less important," and "trivial"), and identify those that are particularly significant in their impact on the effect.

12. Collect data on as many causes as possible, particularly the "important" ones. Analyze them further to support the earlier brainstorming analysis and to identify the problem's root causes. Measure data in all cases where importance cannot be ascertained.

13. Document your findings. Revise and upgrade the diagram as warranted.

Figure 6.5 shows a cause-and-effect diagram developed to identify causes.

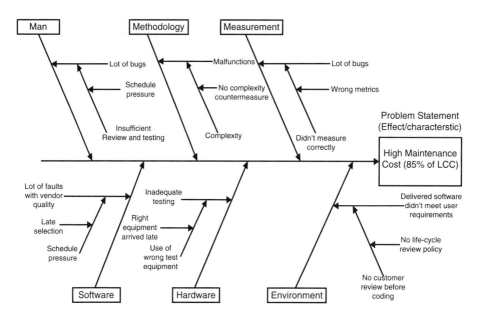

FIGURE 6.5
A Cause-and-Effect Diagram for Identifying Causes

Cause-and-Effect-Diagrams for Process Classification

The purpose of process classification is to identify key factors that influence quality throughout the development process. The end product is an expanded view of the development process as a whole. It is a detailed analysis of the process that also reveals the implications of wrong or inadequate practice upstream on overall cost, quality, and schedule. The weak point of this kind of diagram is that similar causes may be cited repeatedly, as shown in Figure 6.6.

As stated earlier, cause-and-effect diagrams have numerous applications. The basic approach is one of consensus building by structured brainstorming, in which the first and essential step is to agree on the "central question" or "effect." This must be followed by a broader discussion, including identifying the importance of various factors. That is followed by data collection and analyses of the supposed causes. The analyses often involve scatter diagrams and correlation analysis, which are discussed in the next section.

We suggested a 3Ms-SHE format for identifying major branches in a software process, but other formats may be equally applicable. It is wise to include as many ideas as possible initially. *What is included can always be eliminated, but what's not included never gets considered.* It is also smart to discuss "man" (people-related causes) last, for obvious reasons.

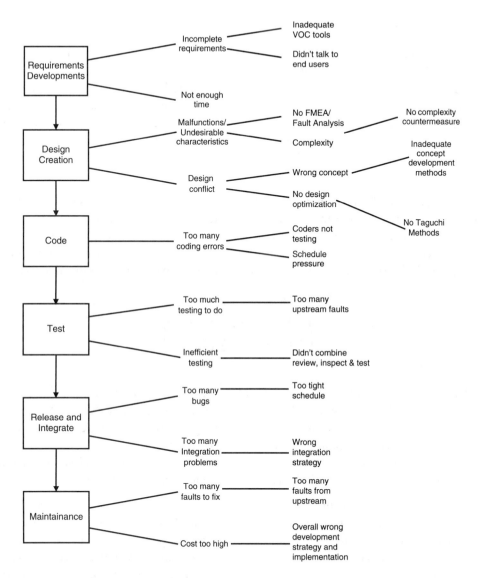

FIGURE 6.6
A Cause-and-Effect Diagram for Process Classification

These diagrams are often used with other tools. For example, Pareto charts (see Figure 6.3) can be used to identify the major branches, which in this case are *design creation, requirements development, testing,* and *coding.* Such use of Pareto is called Pareto-Ishikawa. Similarly, these diagrams can be used in FMEA and Taguchi Methods, as discussed in Chapters 13, 16, and 17.

Scatter Diagrams

A scatter diagram seeks to establish whether a relationship exists between two variables, and the strength of the relationship (if there is one). Establishing relationships can be particularly useful in cause-and-effect analysis. Typically, the variables in question—the independent variable (x) and the dependent variable (y)—represent cause and effect. A strong correlation may help identify possible countermeasures to address a particular quality problem. But a strong correlation is insufficient to establish a relationship. Common sense must never be abandoned to avoid establishing associations that may be pure coincidence. Figure 6.7 illustrates a number of scatter plots.

Although scatter diagrams provide a strong visual display of the relationship between two factors, they do not provide any formal measurement of the strength. Nor can they explain that any apparent visible relationship may be just coincidence. A formal, albeit indirect, measurement of linear association is provided by the correlation coefficient. It measures the strength of the linear relationship between two random variables and is defined as follows:

$$r_{xy} = \frac{\sum_{i=1}^{n}\left(X_i - \bar{X}\right)\left(Y_i - \bar{Y}\right)}{\sqrt{\left[\sum_{i=1}^{n}\left(X_i - \bar{X}\right)^2\right]\left[\sum_{i=1}^{n}\left(Y_i - \bar{Y}\right)^2\right]}}$$

The value of r_{xy} must be between $--1$ and $+1$, inclusive. $+1$ represents a perfect positive correlation if all the points in the plot fall on a straight line that has a slope of 1. Similarly, $--1$ represents a perfect negative correlation. But $r_{xy} = 0$ (see Figure 6.7c) does not mean that there is no relationship, just that there is no linear relationship. Figures 6.7a and 6.7d represent strong positive and negative correlations, respectively. Figures 6.7b and 6.7e indicate the possibility of comparatively weak positive and negative correlations, respectively.

Scatter plot analysis normally should be deployed only after cause-and-effect brainstorming has already identified a possible association. As such, the plots and correlation coefficients constitute confirmatory analysis. If a strong positive or negative correlation exists, causal factors can help identify strong countermeasures. Weaker associations, on the other hand, can be used for taking additional measures for process improvement, in risk analysis and Robust Design as required.

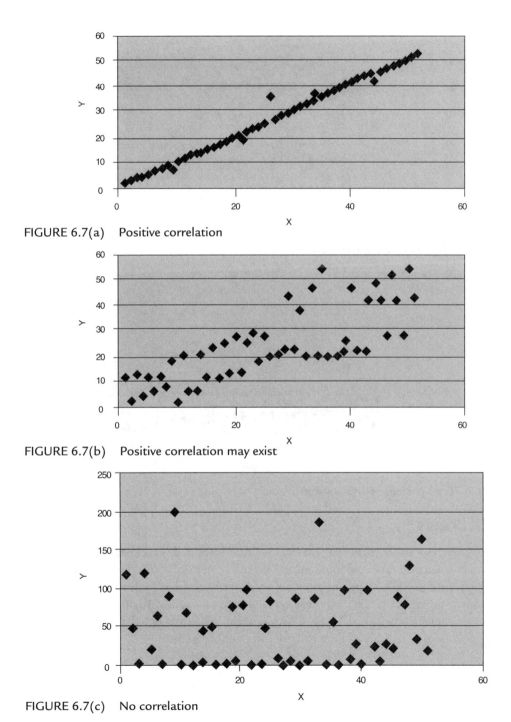

FIGURE 6.7(a)   Positive correlation

FIGURE 6.7(b)   Positive correlation may exist

FIGURE 6.7(c)   No correlation

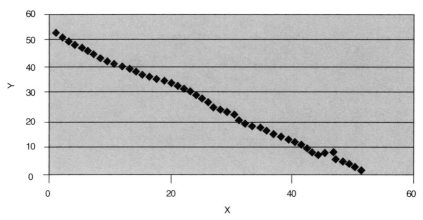

FIGURE 6.7(d)   Negative correlation

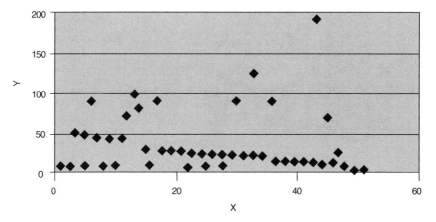

FIGURE 6.7(e)   Negative correlation may exist

Check Sheets

A check sheet is a paper form that lists items to be measured, checked, and recorded. It makes data collection easy and standardized through the form's particular design. Various check sheets are possible, depending on the objective of the data collection exercise, such as measuring process variation, analyzing types of defects, and identifying causes of defects (see, for example, Kume, pp. 10–16). Check sheets are often coupled with histograms to display visualization and use of data collected in the histograms.

It makes sense to start with check sheets to determine if the data collected is feasible and useful for the intended purpose in a software context. Figure 6.8 shows a typical example of a check sheet for a software development process.

	Defect Type	Module 1	Module 2	Module 3	Module 4	Total
Number of Defects	A	III	IV	II	I	X
	B	I	VI	I	III	XI
	C	II		I		III
	D	I				I
Total		VII	X	IV	IV	XXV

FIGURE 6.8
An Example of a Check Sheet

Histograms

Every process has variation and often displays some pattern. A histogram is one of the basic quality tools used to analyze variation in a set of data. It helps you understand how the data collected from a particular development or production process is distributed in terms of frequency of occurrences of a particular value in the set. The key objective is to look for stability and predictability.

A histogram provides a quick look at how the process data is distributed. So-called normally distributed histograms, also called Gaussian histograms, are bell-shaped and display distinct statistical properties. Such unimodal curves are associated with stable processes that are predictable in their variation. Such variation around the bell shape is called chance or natural variation. The variations that are not characterized by a bell shape may be due to various process defects that can be attributed to special and identifiable causes, and may be associated with unstable processes. However, several "exotic" distributions, such as exponential, gamma, beta, Weibull, binomial, and Poisson, are not bell-shaped but are associated with stable and predictable processes. These and other distributions are well-known and statistically characterizable.

An inspection of histograms can provide clues to problems in the process, data sampling, or data collection methodology. It reveals possible problem areas that may be difficult to figure out from mere tabulation of data. The following sections briefly cover various uses of histograms in data analysis, as described by Ozeki, Asaka, and Kume.[6, 7]

Determining the Distribution Pattern

A normal distribution indicates a stable process and data integrity. Within normal distributions, histograms reveal variability differences between two plots (see Figure 6.9). "Double peak" (see Figure 6.10) and "isolated island" indicate mixing of data. A steep "cliff" may be due to including items that do not meet specifications.

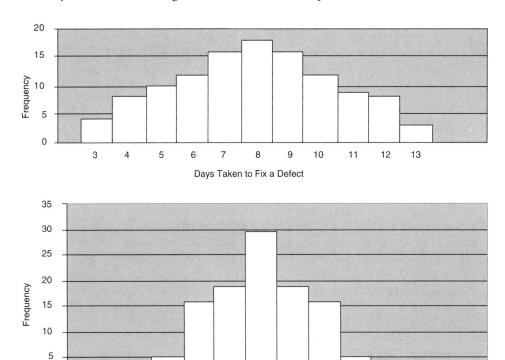

FIGURE 6.9
Examples of Histograms with Normal Distributions but Different Variabilities

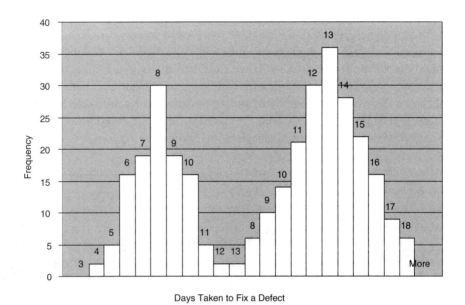

FIGURE 6.10
An Example of a Histogram with Double Peak

Determining Whether Specifications Are Satisfied

A normal distribution in which the center is equidistant from specified limits with room to spare represents a stable system that is easy to maintain. Distributions with centers closer to one or the other limit, and distributions outside the limits, may require corrective measures to bring the mean closer to the center and the need to reduce variation.

Comparing Data by Stratifying

To find the causes of defects, it is useful to divide the data into groups (stratas) by equipment used, shift worked, procedure deployed, or developers involved. The method of grouping by common characteristics is called stratification. By comparing the groups, it may be possible to discover the causes and structure of variability.

Graphs

Graphs are useful tools in software quality and project management. Among the most commonly used graphs are run charts, pie charts, and bar charts (see Figures 6.11, 6.12, and 6.13). They help you monitor time variation and understand causes of defects in a process. Control charts, discussed next, are based on run charts. They constitute the most fundamental tool of statistical process control. Process data can be analyzed using graphs plotted with statistical tools such as Minitab or Microsoft Excel.

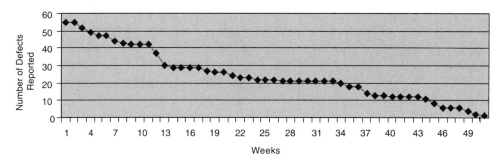

FIGURE 6.11
A Run Chart of the Number of Defects Reported Over Time

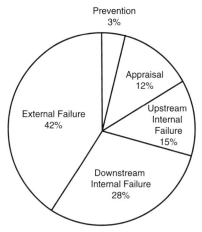

FIGURE 6.12
A Pie Chart of Costs of Quality

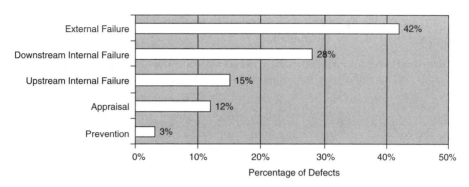

FIGURE 6.13
A Bar Chart of Costs of Quality

Control Charts

Control charts are among the most important quality tools. They have been used exten-sively in a variety of manufacturing industries as part of SPC. Control charts were intro-duced by Walter Shewhart of Bell Laboratories and were strongly supported by Deming while he was in Japan and subsequently the United States. Deming believed control charts were an indispensable tool of process improvement. Conceptually they are pretty straight-forward. SPC concedes that every process has variation. The key to managing a process effectively and efficiently is to measure its variation periodically to check whether it is within the acceptable limits. Processes whose variation is within such limits are said to be "in control." "Out-of-control" processes lead to defective work, with adverse cost, quality, and schedule implications. SPC deploys control charts to prevent defective work from being produced by focusing efforts on the process quality rather than the final product. Thus, it lets the enterprise take preventive and process improvement initiatives rather than just appraising the final product.

There are many types of control charts,[8] but all are characterized by two statistically determined *control limits*: the upper control limit (UCL) and the lower control limit (LCL), which define the upper and lower limits of deviation, respectively. Control charts require some 100 data points to calculate UCL and LCL but only periodic small subgroups to con-tinue monitoring the process. Control charts for attributes data require 25 or more sub-groups to calculate UCL and LCL. A process in statistical control has most of the data points distributed randomly around the mean. Control limits are determined statistically such that there is a high probability (normally greater than 99%) that data will fall between these limits if the process is in control.

Although all types of charts can be used to measure the software process, XmR charts and average (X-bar) and range (R) charts have been found to be the most useful, according to Florac and Carleton (Figures 6.14 and 6.15).[9] This reference provides a step-by-step presentation of implementing statistical process control in the software development process. We consider it an excellent resource on the subject.

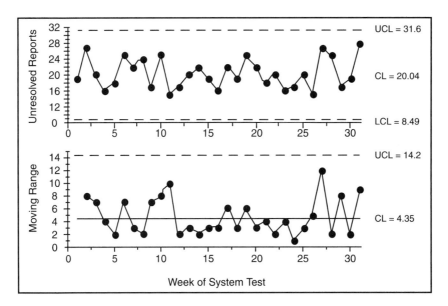

FIGURE 6.14
XmR Charts for Unresolved Critical Problem Reports

W. A. Florac and A. D. Carleton, *Measuring the Software Process*, p. 101, Fig. 5.16. © Pearson Education, Inc. Reprinted by permission of Pearson Education, Inc. All rights reserved.

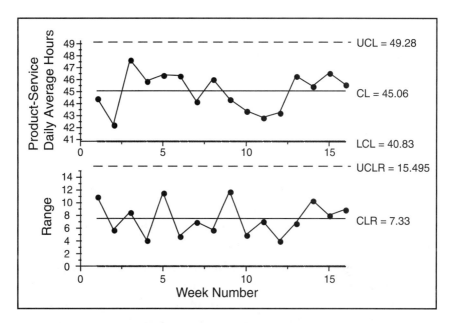

FIGURE 6.15
X-Bar and R Charts for Daily Product Service Effort

W. A. Florac and A. D. Carleton, *Measuring the Software Process*, p. 89, Fig. 5.4. © Pearson Education, Inc.
Reprinted by permission of Pearson Education, Inc. All rights reserved.

This chapter has presented the seven basic tools of quality (B7) in a software development context. These tools provide problem-solving/process-improvement capabilities to DFTS technology in addition to design capabilities. B7 tools can be of great value in project management, inspection and testing, and analyzing software metrics. Statistical tools generally are of relatively limited use in upstream design phases given the lack of volumetric data. But as you have seen, not all the tools are quantitative, not even the most frequently used B7 tools such as cause-and-effect diagrams. These are equally applicable to and used in upstream phases. It is important to use them in the wider context of DFTS technology, which includes a number of quality methodologies, such as QFD, TRIZ, Pugh, Taguchi Methods, and FMEA. Additionally, techniques such as systems thinking, process management, standardization, and adequate documentation, which are integral parts of DFTS technology, must be included in process improvement. This chapter introduced B7 in a software development context and is a precursor to Chapter 15, which discusses quality measures and statistical methods for trustworthy software.

Key Points

- Although DFTS is a design-focused quality technology, it also includes problem-solving/process-improvement capabilities and can benefit from the deployment of the Seven Basic (B7) Tools, widely used in manufacturing.

- Additionally, techniques such as systems thinking, process management, standardization, and adequate documentation, which are integral parts of DFTS technology, must be integral parts of process improvement. These tools can be of great value in project management and in analyzing software metrics.

- They can also be used in upstream design phases, except for statistical tools, which require larger volumes of data to be statistically significant. It is important to use them in the wider context of DFTS technology, which includes quality methodologies such as QFD, TRIZ, Pugh, Taguchi Methods, and FMEA.

- A flowchart is a graphical, sequential representation of various activities. Identifying such activities and their causes can help you eliminate or minimize redundancies and wasteful activities as well as strengthen those that help achieve process goals and create customer value. A flowchart also serves as a communication tool.

- Pareto charts are a series of bar charts with a cumulative line graph arranged in descending order. It indicates the diminishing importance of a series of activities or entities. It helps users focus on big issues. It can be used to address any concern that can be measured, such as cost, defects, faults, failures, complaints, returned items, repairs and fixes, risks, safety, and security.

- Cause-and-effect diagrams are also called fishbone diagrams, for their structure, or Ishikawa diagrams, after their creator. Ishikawa diagrams include standard, process, and Pareto, to name a few. Cause-and-effect-diagrams are among the most widely used tools in quality management. They are used to identify causes of variation, to take countermeasures, for process classification, for Pareto-Ishikawa, to generate data needed for FMEA, to identify possible "noise" and "control factors" in Taguchi Methods, as a visible communication tool, and to categorize various inputs (causes) and output (effects).

- A scatter diagram seeks to establish whether there is a relationship between two variables and the strength of that relationship. Establishing relationships can be particularly useful in cause-and-effect analysis. A strong correlation may help identify possible countermeasures to address a particular quality problem.

- A check sheet is a paper form that lists items to be measured, checked, and recorded. It makes data collection easy, usable, and standardized. Various check sheets are possible, depending on the objective of the data collection exercise—measuring process variation, analyzing types of defects, identifying causes of defects. A check sheet is often coupled with histograms to display visualization and use of data collected in histograms.

- A histogram is used to analyze variation in a set of data. It helps you understand how the data collected from a particular development or production process is distributed in terms of frequency of occurrences of a particular value in the set. The key objective is to look for stability and predictability.

- Graphs are useful tools in software quality and project management. Among the most commonly used graphs are run charts, pie charts, and bar charts. They help you monitor time variation and understand causes of defects in a process.

- Control charts are among the most important quality tools. They have been used extensively in a variety of manufacturing industries as part of statistical process control (SPC). They measure a process's variation periodically to check whether it is within acceptable limits. Processes whose variation is within such limits are said to be "in control." "Out-of-control" processes lead to defective work, with adverse cost, quality, and schedule implications. SPC deploys control charts to prevent defective work from being produced by focusing efforts on the process quality rather than the final product. It thus lets the enterprise take preventive and process improvement initiatives rather than just appraising the final product. XmR charts and average (X-bar) and range (R) charts have been found to be most useful to measure the software process.

- This chapter introduced B7 and some other process improvement tools in the software development context and is a precursor to Chapter 15.

Additional Resources

http://www.prenhallprofessional.com/title/0131872508

http://www.agilenty.com/publications

Review Questions

1. List the three advantages of step-by-step methodologies.
2. List the five techniques that complement the DFTS technology. Describe their significance in a successful DFTS deployment.

3. What is a flowchart, and what purpose does it serve? What steps are required to make a flowchart? Describe the three types of flowcharts and their use.

4. What is the underlying principle of Pareto charts? Describe a Pareto chart, and discuss its use in software quality management.

5. What are the typical applications of cause-and-effect diagrams? Describe their structure and the steps required for making a cause-and-effect diagram for identifying causes.

6. Describe how a scatter diagram is plotted. What are its typical uses and possible pitfalls?

7. Describe a check sheet and its use in quality management.

8. Describe a histogram and how it portrays variability. State what you mean by stability and predictability. What are the various uses of histograms?

9. What is the purpose of graphs? Provide typical plots to illustrate your answer.

10. What purpose does a control chart serve? Describe a typical control chart, and state which control charts are most useful in software development.

Discussion Questions

1. Discuss the application of B7 tools in various phases of the DFTS process (see Figure 2.6 in Chapter 2).

2. Suggest three specific uses for each of the seven B7 tools in a software development process you are familiar with.

Endnotes

[1] K. Ishikawa, *What is Total Quality Control? The Japanese Way* (D. J. Lu, Trans.) (Englewood Cliffs, NJ: Prentice-Hall, 1985).

[2] K. Ishikawa, *Guide to Quality Control*, Asian Productivity Organization (White Plains, NY: Kraus International Publications, 1982).

[3] H. Kume, *Statistical Methods for Quality Improvement*, The Association of Overseas Technical Scholarship (AOTS), Japan, 1985.

[4] K. T. Ulrich and S. D. Eppinger, *Product Design and Development* (New York, NY: McGraw-Hill/Irwin, 2002), p. 7.

[5] S. Moriguchi, *Software Excellence: A Total Quality Management Guide* (Portland, OR: Productivity Press, 1997), p. 52.

[6] K. Ozeki and T. Asaka, *Handbook of Quality Tools: The Japanese Approach* (Portland, OR: Productivity Press, 1990), pp. 175–178.

[7] Op cit Kume, pp. 49–53.

[8] Ibid, pp. 94–95. This reference also provides a pretty good presentation on construction, application, and interpretation of control charts, pp. 92–141.

[9] W. A. Florac and A. D. Carleton, *Measuring the Software Process* (Boston: Addison-Wesley, 1999), p. 207. This book is a great reference for SPC in a software development context.

CHAPTER 7

The 7 MP Tools: Analyzing and Interpreting Qualitative and Verbal Data

Disputes are often nothing more than a mutual misunderstanding of nuances of words, and the seven new tools of QC can prevent this.

—*Shigeichi Moriguchi*

He who would run a company on visible figures alone, will in time have neither a company nor figures.

—*W. Edwards Deming*

Overview

Many quality characteristics, especially those related to innovation, customer needs, and product development issues upstream, are not easily quantifiable. The seven new (N7) tools of quality control (QC), developed by the Union of Japanese Scientists and Engineers (JUSE), were devised to aid in organizing, analyzing, and interpreting qualitative and worded data. These tools were subsequently modified and adapted to American industrial practices by Goal/QPC to a similar set of management and planning tools, called *Seven Management and Planning Tools (7 MP Tools): affinity diagram, interrelationship diagraph (I.D.), tree diagram, prioritization matrices, matrix diagram, process decision program chart (PDPC)*, and *activity network diagram*. The 7 MP tools are by and large qualitative and preventive; B7 tools, on the other hand, are essentially quantitative and diagnostic.

An *affinity diagram* is a set of ideas about the topic in question that are grouped based on their similarity. It is a problem-solving tool for chaotic, difficult, and complex problems.

An *interrelationship diagraph (I.D.)* is a tool that helps explore and identify causal relationships between various ideas. It is thus an extension of an affinity diagram and is often drawn after an affinity diagram has been constructed.

The *tree diagram* is a technique to identify the most important, appropriate, and effective means of attaining a given set of objectives. It charts various paths in increasingly unfolding details to achieve a principal objective and other related goals.

Prioritization matrices prioritize tasks, issues, or product characteristics based on known weighted criteria using a combination of tree and matrix diagram techniques.

A *matrix diagram* displays complex relationships involving two or more sets of ideas. A number of forms have been used, but the L-shaped form is the most common.

A *PDPC* is like a tree diagram that seeks to identify all the things and tasks that can possibly go wrong and specifies necessary countermeasures to prevent or correct them.

The *activity network diagram* is essentially a combination of Program Evaluation and Review Technique (PERT) and Critical Path Method (CPM). It also includes other network diagrams such as node diagram, activity on node diagram (AON), and precedence diagram (PDM). This tool is used to plan the most appropriate schedule for a complex task when the task at hand is a familiar one.

These tools deal with qualitative and verbal data. They are valuable in the planning, design, and development phases, which have a profound effect on overall software quality. Affinity, tree, and matrix diagrams are relatively simple and remain popular as powerful quality tools. Brassard has purposed a set of behavioral skills that must be mastered too to be truly effective in using these tools: *trust the process*; *value brainstorming*; *observe discipline*; *be patient*; *trust in your initial gut reaction*; *treasure listening skills*; *know when to stop*; *recognize when the tools are inappropriate*; *bring integrity*; *respect flexibility and creativity and tolerate ambiguity*; and *value, don't simply tolerate, the different perceptions of others*.

Chapter Outline

- The N7 and 7 MP Tools
- Typical Applications of 7 MP Tools
- Affinity Diagram
- Interrelationship Diagraph (I.D.)
- Tree Diagram
- Prioritization Matrices
- Matrix Diagram
- Process Decision Program Chart (PDPC)
- Activity Network Diagram
- Behavioral Skills for 7 MP Tools
- Key Points
- Additional Resources
- Review Questions
- Discussion Questions and Projects
- Endnotes

The N7 and 7 MP Tools

The previous chapter introduced B7: The Seven Basic Tools of Quality. B7 came out of Statistical Process Control (SPC), based on Shewhart's control chart and its subsequent refinements in Japan. Although not all the tools used in SPC are quantitative, SPC as a whole deals with quality issues and characteristics that are more easily quantifiable. But many quality characteristics, especially those related to innovation, customer needs, and product development issues upstream, are not as quantitative. The major portion of the problems that must be solved by managers and staff makes use of worded data.[1] The seven new tools of QC (N7), developed by the QC Techniques Development Committee of the Union of Japanese Scientists and Engineers (JUSE), were devised to aid in organizing, analyzing, and interpreting qualitative and worded data.[2, 3] JUSE announced the N7 tools in 1977. These tools were subsequently modified and adapted to American industrial practices by Goal/QPC to a similar set of management and planning tools. It called them *Seven Management and Planning Tools*, and they became known as *the 7 MP Tools*. They are as follows:[4, 5]

1. Affinity diagram

2. Interrelationship diagraph

3. Tree diagram

4. Prioritization matrices

5. Matrix diagram

6. Process decision program chart (PDPC)

7. Activity network diagram

Although not all the tools in the N7 kit were novel, two things were totally new when introduced:

- These tools have been combined into a cycle of activity that illustrates the output of one tool into the input of a related technique. This creates a continuous flow of analysis that really focuses any planning process.

- The 7 MP tools, which have been used in isolation by planning specialists in the past, are now available to mainstream managers.[4]

The 7 MP tools are by and large qualitative and preventive; B7 tools, on the other hand, are essentially quantitative and diagnostic. N7 as well as the modified 7 MP tools help you plan for quality, design new products and processes, and reengineer existing ones. This book emphasizes the 7 MP tools, the modified version of the original 7N. These tools, as well as the original N7, work in conjunction with B7, not as their replacement, as the word "new" may imply. B7 and 7 MP tools constitute powerful problem-solving techniques when used in tandem. Table 7.1 summarizes the major differences between B7 and 7 MP tools.

TABLE 7.1
Differences Between B7 and 7 MP Tools

Category	B7 Tools	7 MP Tools
Problem definition	Define problem after data collection	Define problem before data collection
Basic approach	Analytic	Idea generation, brainstorming, and planning
Typical uses	Data analysis, process control, and continual improvement	New product/process design and reengineering existing ones
Data type	Numeric, hard	Worded, soft
Major capability	Corrective, known/knowable	Preventive, unknown/ unknowable
Overall	Quantitative	Qualitative

Typical Applications of 7 MP Tools

As you will see, the processes involved in 7 MP tools enhance teamwork, communication, and understanding. These tools, when used properly, can explain multifaceted issues and help solve new and complex problems in a planned and systematic manner. They also emphasize managing change systematically and getting the product concept right the first time. Although they can be used separately to address specific issues, they were primarily designed to provide an integrated planning system to identify requirements and develop designs for new and complex products. They are also useful as powerful problem-solving tools. Table 7.2 lists the major applications of these tools.

TABLE 7.2
Typical Applications of 7 MP Tools

Tool	Application Recommended
Affinity diagram	Widely applicable in problem solving, requirements identification, and design when only worded data are available, especially when • You need breakthrough results because old solutions will not work • You're dealing with difficult, large, or complex issues • Team contribution and support are crucial for implementation success • Applying Quality Function Deployment (QFD) (see Chapter 11)
Interrelationship diagraph (I.D.)	Valuable if quantitative data are unavailable. It overcomes the weakness of a cause-and-effect diagram because it can handle interrelationships and can rank the importance of various issues analyzed. But it requires a lot of time to analyze the problem carefully. Helps in cause-and-effect and goals/means analysis, particularly for: • Clarifying complex, difficult, intertwined relationships • Identifying most crucial issues and underlying causes • Charting correct sequencing of issues with a high degree of uncertainty • Establishing facts when historical data are unavailable • QFD
Tree diagram	The tree diagram has wide applications in planning, design, and problem-solving related to complex tasks when details are important for success. It is recommended when risks are anticipated but not easily identifiable and when knowing the sequence of activities in a given task is crucial to success. Specific applications are in • Decomposing the problem to be solved into logical components • Determining the feasibility and complexity of a possible solution • Product development and design • Process improvement • Quality assurance • Analysis of cause-and-effect diagram • Problem solving related to cost, quality, efficiency, schedule, and production • Developing policy, goals, objectives, tasks, and budget • Assigning and prioritizing tasks • QFD

Tool	Application Recommended
Prioritization matrices[1]	• Options generated need to be narrowed down • Disagreement exists over the relative importance of solution criteria • Limited resources • Options generated have strong interrelationships • Ranking options and not merely sequencing tasks to be done • QFD
Matrix diagram	• New product/service/process design • Problem solving • Various quality assurance activities • Prioritizing among various tasks • QFD/Voice of Customer (VOC)
PDPC	• Complex, high-risk/stakes tasks • Interdependency of tasks • Quality Control (QC) activities • New product or process launch • Demanding customer schedule • FMEA, FMECA, and FTA
Activity network diagram[a]	• Complex tasks • Subtasks are known • Project is a critical organization target • Simultaneous implementation paths must be coordinated • Little margin for error in the actual versus estimated time

[a]Adapted from Michael Brassard, *Memory Jogger Plus* + (Methuen: Goal/QPC, 1989), p. 214.

As stated earlier, 7 MP tools are essentially planning tools. Figure 7.1 shows the three different levels of planning and corresponding application of 7 MP tools.

These tools are not recommended in the following circumstances:

• Problems/tasks are relatively simple and routine.

• Effective solutions are known and are in use.

• Quantitative data are available, reliable, and cost-effective.

• The problem requires a quick solution.

• A lack of management support for follow-up exists.

- There's not enough time for analysis.

- Cost, quality, customer, and risk implications are marginal.

The 7 MP tools are explained in the following sections.

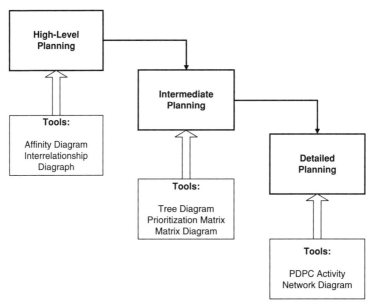

FIGURE 7.1
Levels of Planning and Deployment of 7 MP Tools

Affinity Diagram

An *affinity diagram* is a set of ideas about the topic in question that are grouped based on their similarity. It is a problem-solving tool for chaotic, difficult, and complex problems. This method helps you better understand the problem from a number of diverse, piecemeal, and fragmented verbal data. It can be especially useful in requirements development and design stages of a software development process. Creating an affinity diagram basically has three stages:

1. Generate verbal data by encouraging people to express their ideas, wants, perceptions, and opinions.

2. Group data into clusters of similar ideas.

3. Analyze, clarify, and agree on the problem to be addressed.

Generating valid worded data, spoken as well as written, in people's own words, is crucial. Several sources should be used for this purpose—the more sources, the better. Formal and informal meetings, correspondence, interviews, responses to survey questionnaires, and complaints from customers can all be valuable sources of customer data. In a software development process, end users are not the only sources. Valuable data can also be obtained from the management in the customer organization, software developers, outsourcing partners, and the management team in software development organization. Regulatory requirements should also be used as sources of data. But the focus of any requirements development and design data should be the customers and users. Even in new product development, the voice of potential customers is a required input.

After the written data have been obtained, further data can be generated by a brainstorming process involving a group that has some prior experience with working together effectively. Ideally, they should also possess knowledge to deal with the issues to be discussed. The brainstorming format is similar to the one we discussed in cause-and-effect diagrams, described in Chapter 6. Four basic rules should be observed:[6]

- Criticism is forbidden.
- Wild abandon is encouraged.
- Repetition is acceptable.
- Synergy with the ideas of the other participants should be encouraged.

The pace of brainstorming should be swift and answers and statements should be short to maintain the tempo. This way, you can generate a lot of data without getting bogged down in a particular issue at this stage. It is not uncommon to come up with dozens of ideas within an hour. The following are typical steps in constructing an affinity diagram:

1. **Form a brainstorming team** of five to nine people, selecting members who fit the profile just mentioned. Appoint an experienced person as the moderator.

2. **Announce/agree on the topic issue in question (problem statement).** It's a good idea for the participants to know the topic in advance. The topic, not the solution, should be stated. It should be something in broad terms, such as "What factors affect total life-cycle costs?" This may be decided in a preparatory meeting. It is important that members undergo training on 7 MP tools before beginning to construct the affinity diagram.

3. **Have the participants record their ideas** concisely on sticky notes, no more than one idea per note. The ideas should be written in large letters, each with a noun and a verb, so that they are unambiguous. Mix up the notes and then stick them on the wall, a whiteboard, or a flip chart so that everyone can see them.

4. **Put the ideas into groups** by asking everyone to come to the wall and move the notes together to where they fit best, *without talking*. Some notes may have to be duplicated because they may belong to more than one group. Some items might not belong to any group, but that's fine. The groupings should be done quickly to maintain the pace of creativity. In case of disagreements, just move the notes. Eventually consensus will be attained, because the exercise of groupings is pretty simple. The number of groupings works out to be between six and ten if the exercise is carried out by experienced people.

5. **Divide large groups** into subgroups if needed.

6. **Write appropriate headings** for each group and subgroup, describing the intent of that group. Each heading is an affinity card. Use clear and concise words for headings. This requires time, patience, and creativity. The moderator plays an important role here, ensuring that creative juices keep flowing and that disagreements are encouraged until consensus is reached.

An affinity diagram is the end product of the collection of these groups and subgroups with appropriate headings. It may be ready for the next step in the planning process or used for further discussion and refinement. The affinity diagram is among the most widely used 7 MP tools. It is basically a team-based creative exercise that uses logical groupings to identify and group major issues related to a problem. These groupings, after they are correctly identified, can lead to innovative solutions. The affinity diagram can be used either as a stand-alone tool or preferably as part of a problem-solving process using other 7 MP tools as needed. Figure 7.2 depicts a typical affinity diagram.

How to reduce high software life-cycle Cost?

Management Support for Quality	User environment	Design Complexity	Personnel	Development Model	Test and Maintenance	Technology	Schedule	Documentation
Understand that "software management is not different"	Work with users to prevent open-ended requirements	Understand that complexity may cause malfunction	Emphasize "fixing it now rather than later"	Pay attention to requirements & design issues	Assume only proven reliability theories	Don't depend on "magic of advanced tools"	Make realistic schedules	Inadequate software code documentation
Understand that basic challenges are managerial, not technical	Control change adequately	Understand that high complexity may inhibit comprehension	Coordinate team(s)	Use adequate prototyping if required	Provide sufficient test time	Use suitable automation tools	Provide resources to meet schedules	Inadequate external documentation
Provides sincere commitment to improvement	Understand that requirements are not just "customer's job"	Observe discipline to stick to requirements	Provide adequate training	Focus on upstream phases	Don't base quality on tests alone	Develop suitable higher-order languages		
Define and understand software process	Interpret and trace user needs correctly	Do not add unnecessary features	Provide experienced people as required	Uses methodologies irrespective of group size	Use appropriate quality measures	Use upstream technology like DFTS		
Manage process and quality initiatives competently	Provide training to comprehend user needs	Measure complexity	Provide appropriate incentives	Coordinate between design and code changes	Deploy adequate review and inspection			
Develop and observe appropriate standards	Provide sufficient design tolerance for user errors	Provide counter measure for complexity	Debunk the myth of super-programmers	Observe process discipline	Use appropriate methodology for maintenance			

FIGURE 7.2
An Affinity Diagram

Interrelationship Diagraph (I.D.)

An interrelationship diagraph (I.D.) helps you explore and identify causal relationships between various ideas. Thus, it is an extension of an affinity diagram and is often drawn after an affinity diagram has been constructed. In the original JUSE list of new tools, it was called a relations diagram.[2, 3] I.D. is used to further clarify complex and intertwined cause-and-effect or means and goals relationships among various groups of ideas identified in an affinity diagram, cause-and-effect diagram, tree diagram, or ideas developed by brainstorming. In contrast to an affinity diagram, which displays natural or logical groupings, I.D. shows logical relationships between ideas. It also reveals patterns and sequencing of ideas. The relationships are shown by one-way arrows and can be further clarified with words and phrases in rectangles or ovals. They often get too complicated and may be of little use if poorly constructed. Usability of the diagraph depends on involvement of key personnel who can identify relationships between ideas correctly.

It may be helpful to use cause-and-effect diagrams and tree diagrams, discussed next, in addition to affinity diagrams, as sources of data. In a design context, I.D. helps identify key design elements to meet a particular set of user requirements. An I.D. has various formats, but we will discuss just the centrally converging type.[7] Here the goal/problem being discussed is written on a sticky note and placed on a flip chart. It should be a different color than the other notes. Similarly, in a completed diagraph, the goal/problem should be stated in a larger, shaded rectangle. The arrow is one-sided and points from cause/means to effect/goal. The following are the typical steps in creating an I.D.:

1. **Form a team of five to nine people** to brainstorm about the problem. Persons selected should have worked successfully as a team in the past and should have intimate, firsthand knowledge of the problem or opportunity to be discussed.

2. **Describe the problem to be solved:** "What key issues are related to reducing software complexity?" Write it on a sticky note, and place it on the display board. This may be done as part of a preparatory meeting where members are also briefed about the approach. It is important that members have undergone training on the 7 MP tools.

3. **Generate ideas** by brainstorming, use a tree diagram (discussed next), or use the ones created as idea notes in an affinity diagram, which is the most common source of ideas used to create an I.D. If affinity diagram notes are used, all the note items except the headers can be used. If the problem to be solved relates to a particular header, additional ideas may have to be generated, because the notes related to all the other headers

would be discarded. There should be between 9 and 50 idea items for the problem to be addressed by I.D. Otherwise, the problem is either too simple or too complex to be addressed by this method.[8] Brassard suggests that the number of ideas to be pursued be kept between 5 and 25 to keep them manageable.

4. **Place all the idea notes** randomly on a flip chart. Remember to remove the header cards and mix up the rest of the idea notes thoroughly before placing them on the flip chart. Random placement forces you to think in multiple directions, because there is no choice.[9] When the notes are all on display, the team agrees on which of the items have cause/means-effect/goal relationships and connects all these by one-way arrows. It is best to go card by card to determine cause/effect relationships with all the other cards: "What idea(s) have a major influence on the outcome of this particular item?" Two-way questions and two-way arrows should be avoided. Instead, just repeat a "cause-out" (cause-effect) question for each card, and decide on the major influencer item in each case.[10] Unlike an affinity diagram, some discussion will be needed to reach a consensus, but too much discussion may be dysfunctional. Too much discussion isn't really warranted, because there will be an opportunity for revisions in subsequent meetings. Revisions are essential when dealing with any complex issue.

5. **Copy the I.D., and distribute it to members.** Several important tasks, such as further investigation and review based on realistic data, are carried out between meetings. The whole exercise should be fast-paced. Therefore, the next meeting should be convened fairly soon—within a week or so if practical.

6. **Revise the I.D. in subsequent meetings** as new facts emerge and further interactions are identified. Discuss, agree on, and choose the follow-up projects from the key items and factors identified in the I.D. Count the number of outgoing and incoming arrows for each idea. The item with the most inward arrows (the outcome) is the most crucial issue. The item with the most outward arrows (the driver) has the most influencing factors. It is shown with a bold and broken border in Figure 7.3. Similarly, the next few levels of note items should be identified. The ones with the largest number of outgoing arrows represent some *key issues* that must be addressed to correct a large number of problems or desired outcomes. Similarly, the largest number of incoming arrows represents *secondary issues* involving important problems or bottlenecks that must be

addressed. It is important to continue to work on consensus in identifying the items to be addressed; it should not be on the basis of number of arrows alone. In the interest of manageability, choose a maximum of five to seven items (projects) to pursue further.[11] It is possible to have more than one key and one secondary issue. These issues are often examined using a tree diagram, as discussed next.

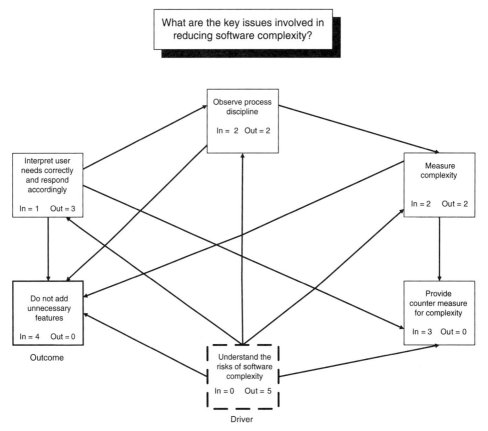

FIGURE 7.3
An Interrelationship Diagraph

Tree Diagram

The tree diagram, called the systematic diagram in the original 7N tools, is a technique to identify the most important, appropriate, and effective means of attaining a given set of objectives. It charts various paths in increasingly unfolding details to achieve a principal objective and other related goals. It deals with details. This type of diagram is used to draw family trees and organization charts. It is based on a logic that Mizuno describes as follows:

> When means to achieve a goal are selected, secondary means are necessary to secure primary means; thus the principal means become the goal of the secondary means.[12]

This logic is illustrated in Figure 7.4. It results in various levels of means for a given objective on the logic of *what/goal* leads to *how/means*.

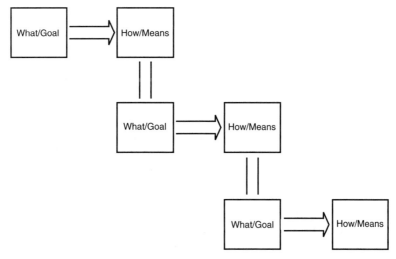

FIGURE 7.4
The Logic of a Tree Diagram

Tree diagrams are among the three most used 7 MP tools, along with affinity diagrams and matrix diagrams. Although the tree diagram can be used as a stand-alone tool, it is much more powerful when used together with other 7 MP tools. When used as part of the MP tool kit, it is deployed after the key issues have been identified following the construction of the affinity diagram and I.D. Tree diagrams have numerous applications. A few typical examples are identifying various tasks to be carried out to achieve an objective, carrying out a cause-and-effect analysis, converting customer desires into product features and characteristics in a QFD application, and identifying the steps needed to implement a project. The typical steps of constructing a tree diagram are as follows:

1. **Assemble the team.** It is best to have the same team that constructed the affinity diagram and I.D. If this is an original problem, the team members should have worked successfully as a team in the past and should have firsthand knowledge of the problem or opportunity to be discussed.

2. **Agree on the problem statement.** Define the effect, characteristic, or problem as precisely as possible. The statement often comes from the I.D.'s *key issue* (the one with the most arrows coming from it) or the *secondary issue* (the one with the most arrows going into it). It is advisable to choose the *key issue* as the statement as the team gets to the heart of the problem, but sometimes the secondary issue puts the original problem in a whole new light.[13] Other sources of the statement are one of the header notes or the affinity diagram's problem statement. Or it could be a new or stand-alone problem that has not been analyzed before. Write the problem statement on a sticky note and place it on the left side of the flip chart or board. This is the objective or target to be achieved.

3. **Identify the primary means.** In case of a new problem, the team members brainstorm the primary means to achieve the objective: "How can we achieve the objective/target?" The team should be focused on the basic objective rather than subsidiary objectives that very often get cited during discussion. There's almost always more than one primary means, and they should all be written on sticky notes and placed to the right of the objective. Draw lines connecting the roots (objective) and branches (primary means). If the problem has been analyzed before, here are the two possibilities:

   • If an affinity diagram was constructed, and one of the header notes was used as the objective of the tree diagram, use the various notes to identify secondary means. Brainstorm further on these notes. If the affinity diagram's problem statement is also the tree diagram's objective, use all the header notes as the first set of brainstorming ideas to identify the primary means.
   • Alternatively, if an I.D. has been constructed and the tree diagram's objective has been chosen from the key or secondary issue, all the notes connecting to the chosen issue make the first pack of brainstorming ideas.

4. **Identify the secondary means.** Proceed by asking: "How can we achieve the primary means?" for each of the primary means identified in the earlier brainstorming session. When agreement is reached on various secondary means following brainstorming, write them on sticky notes and place them on the flip chart to the right of the primary means. Do this for each of the primary means, and connect all the primary and secondary means.

5. **Identify the third and higher-order means.** Repeat step 4 for the second and higher-order means. Usually this process is carried out to the fourth order when actionable and specific means may be identified.

6. **Check the logic of relationships between objectives and means.** You confirm the validity of each objective/means relationship by asking: "Will this means lead effectively to this objective?" This should be done for each order, from right to left. Do it all again in reverse, from left to right: "Will the objective be achieved if we implement these means?" Identify corrective steps by further brainstorming if the answer to any of the questions is "no."

Figure 7.5 shows a simple tree diagram.

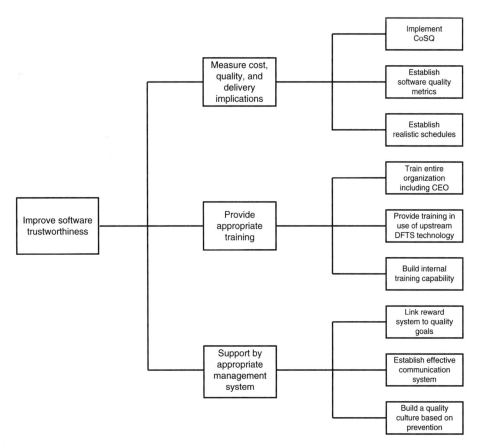

FIGURE 7.5
A Tree Diagram

Prioritization Matrices

In the original Japanese N7 tools, the equivalent of this tool is Matrix Data Analysis. Although Matrix Data Analysis is an excellent tool, it is not easy to use given its heavy statistical emphasis. It has applications in other areas of process and product design, such as QFD, but it does not quite fit with the rest of the tools. Mizuno provides excellent coverage of Matrix Data Analysis.[14]

Michael Brassard has come up with three alternatives to Matrix Data Analysis that he calls prioritization matrices. He defines them as follows:

> These tools prioritize tasks, issues, product/service characteristics, etc., based on known weighted criteria using a combination of Tree and Matrix Diagram techniques. Above all, they are tools for decision making.[15]

Brassard provides the following three prioritization matrices as part of the 7 MP tools:

- **The Full Analytical Criteria Method** is pretty much based on the Analytic Hierarchy Process (AHP). Chapter 8 introduces AHP and its deployment using Expert Choice software.

- **The Consensus Criteria Method** is pretty similar to the Full Analytical Criteria Method in that both assume that the criteria for prioritization are known. The major difference, however, is that in the Full Analytical Criteria Method, the prioritization matrix consists of numbers that represent pair-wise comparison, and the relative rankings are obtained by summing the scores for the various components. In comparison, the Consensus Criteria Method does not use pair-wise comparison and thus is simpler and saves time. For issues that are not absolutely critical, the Consensus Criteria Method can be used.

- **The Combination I.D./Matrix Method** is used simply to prioritize various options to eliminate root problems and bottlenecks. I.D. does not distinguish the strength of the cause-and-effect relationship. This method is designed to overcome this weakness by determining an influence's direction and strength.

Although these three methods are useful and historically significant, they are tedious, time-consuming, and less accurate than AHP. We therefore emphasize AHP as a multiple-objective decision-making methodology (see Chapter 8).

Matrix Diagram

As stated, the matrix diagram is among the three most commonly used 7 MP tools. It displays complex relationships involving two or more sets of ideas, environments, objectives, means, projects, and so on. A number of forms have been used—C-shaped, L-shaped, T-shaped, X-shaped, Y-shaped.[2, 3, 4] L-shaped matrices are the most common.

Matrix diagrams have wide applications in product and process design and problem-solving (see Table 7.2). They are particularly useful in translating user functional quality into quality characteristics for product and process design. QFD provides an excellent example of a composite matrix diagram and is among its most common applications (see Chapter 11).

Process Decision Program Chart (PDPC)

PDPC is like a tree diagram that seeks to identify all the things that can possibly go wrong and the necessary countermeasures to prevent or correct them. It has its roots in operations research and has been developed as a preventive and corrective tool in quality control and product and process design.

PDPC lists undesirable events and corresponding contingency measures. Its power lies not only in anticipating upcoming risk conditions but also in planning to respond adequately to such conditions. You should use it when you have serious concerns about the likelihood of adverse and unpredictable outcomes.

PDPC has no definite structural rules. Mizuno suggests the following guidelines:[16]

- Start with the present.

- Suggest a possible solution under a conceivable future.

- Anticipate undesirable outcomes.

- Present a way to reach a better result.

- Decide on a course of action.

- Review the process in a flexible manner that accommodates new conditions.

PDPC is similar in appearance to the tree diagram, except that it is dynamic and characterized by flow lines chronologically (see Figure 7.6). The steps for constructing a PDPC are as follows:

1. **Form a team** that represents the tasks involved.

2. **Present a basic solution** to the problem in question. It can begin with the tree diagram of the process or product if available. Draw it on a flip chart or whiteboard.

3. **Discuss the challenges.** These should be broad and should not only address current issues but also anticipate unforeseen issues and risks.

4. **Ask** "What can possibly go wrong at this step?" and "What other paths might it take?", starting with the first step. Discuss each answer in terms of likelihood, risk implications, and countermeasures. Write them all down.

5. **Prioritize the issues and countermeasures.** Consider them all together, because information related to one set of possibilities can influence another set.[17] Record all the problems and the countermeasures. Set a date for completing the process.

6. **Review and follow up on the due date.**

PDPC is essentially a method to resolve system failures. But unlike the other well-known methods, such as Failure Modes and Effects Analysis and Fault Tree Analysis (see Chapter 13), PDPC can reveal not only logical phenomena but also those expressed in light of new ideas. Used in addition to these methods, PDPC enhances reliability markedly.[18]

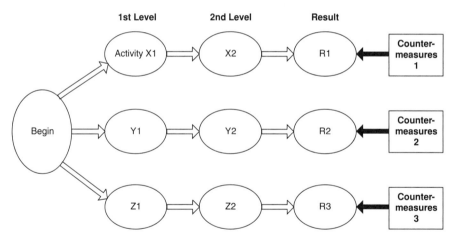

FIGURE 7.6
A Process Decision Program Chart

Activity Network Diagram

The Activity Network Diagram was called the *arrow diagram* in the original N7 tools. Brassard renamed it to include other formats for modeling network activity. This tool is essentially a combination of Program Evaluation and Review Technique (PERT) and

Critical Path Method (CPM), which were developed for operations research. PERT and CPM constitute important areas in project management. You can refer to a number of excellent texts on project management that cover this subject (see, for example, Kerzner).[19] An activity network diagram also includes other network diagrams, such as node diagram, activity on node diagram (AON), and precedence diagram (PDM). This tool is used to plan the most appropriate schedule for a complex task when the task is a familiar one.[20]

This chapter has introduced some very useful tools that deal with qualitative and verbal data. They are particularly valuable in planning, design, and development phases that have a profound effect on overall software quality. As we have stated, not all the tools are equally effective or even applicable in the contemporary software development environment. For example, prioritization matrices have been rendered redundant in light of AHP and accompanying software such as Expert Choice (see Chapter 8). Similarly, many users may prefer PERT and CPM rather than an activity network diagram. Effective use of appropriate tools can be powerful indeed. Affinity, tree, and matrix diagrams are relatively simple and remain popular as powerful quality tools.

Behavioral Skills for 7 MP Tools

Brassard has prepared a checklist of behavioral skills that must be mastered, in addition to technical skills, if you want to be really effective in using these tools:[21]

- Trust the process.
- Value brainstorming.
- Observe discipline.
- Be patient.
- Trust your initial gut reactions.
- Treasure listening skills.
- Know when to stop.
- Recognize when the tools are inappropriate.
- Bring integrity: people commit to use the outcome of the process.
- Respect flexibility and creativity, and tolerate ambiguity.
- Value, don't simply tolerate, the different perceptions of others.

Key Points

- Many quality characteristics, especially those related to innovation, customer needs, and product development issues upstream, are not easily quantifiable.

- Most problems that must be solved by managers and staff use verbal data.

- The seven new tools of QC (N7), developed by the Union of Japanese Scientists and Engineers (JUSE), were devised to aid in organizing, analyzing, and interpreting qualitative and worded data. These tools were subsequently modified and adapted to American industrial practices by Goal/QPC to a similar set of management and planning tools, called the Seven Management and Planning Tools (7 MP Tools): affinity diagram, interrelationship diagraph (I.D.), tree diagram, prioritization matrices, matrix diagram, process decision program chart (PDPC), and activity network diagram.

- The 7 MP tools are by and large qualitative and preventive; B7 tools, on the other hand, are essentially quantitative and diagnostic.

- An affinity diagram is a set of ideas about the topic in question that are grouped based on their similarity. It is a problem-solving tool for chaotic, difficult, complex problems.

- An interrelationship diagraph (I.D.) is a tool that helps explore and identify causal relationships between various ideas. It is thus an extension of an affinity diagram and is often drawn after an affinity diagram has been constructed.

- The tree diagram is a technique to identify the most important, appropriate, and effective means of attaining a given set of objectives. It charts various paths in increasingly unfolding details to achieve a principal objective and other related goals.

- Prioritization matrices prioritize tasks, issues, or product characteristics based on known weighted criteria using a combination of tree and matrix diagram techniques.

- A matrix diagram displays complex relationships involving two or more sets of ideas. A number of forms have been used, but L-shaped is the most common.

- A PDPC is like a tree diagram that seeks to identify all the things that can possibly go wrong. It also specifies necessary countermeasures to prevent or correct them.

- An activity network diagram is essentially a combination of Program Evaluation and Review Technique (PERT) and Critical Path Method (CPM). It also includes other network diagrams such as node diagram, activity on node diagram (AON), and precedence diagram (PDM). This tool is used to plan the most appropriate schedule for a complex task when the task at hand is a familiar one.

Additional Resources

http://www.prenhallprofessional.com/title/0131872508

http://www.agilenty.com/publications

Review Questions

1. What are the benefits of deploying 7 MP tools? What are their typical applications?

2. What are the three distinct levels in a planning process? Which 7 MP tools apply at each level?

3. Describe the circumstances in which 7 MP tools are not recommended.

4. What four basic rules should be observed when constructing an affinity diagram? Describe the steps involved in constructing it.

5. Describe the benefits of developing an interrelationship diagraph (I.D.). What are its deficiencies?

6. What are various sources of ideas for constructing an I.D.? Describe typical steps in constructing one. List a few typical applications.

7. Describe the reasons for drawing a tree diagram. Describe the steps involved.

8. List the three prioritization matrices and the different purposes they serve. Which of the original N7 tools do they replace? Why are they being increasingly replaced by AHP?

9. What is the purpose of drawing matrix diagrams? Which form is the most commonly used?

10. Explain the difference between a PDPC and a tree diagram. List Mizuno's guidelines for drawing a PDPC.

11. What is the purpose of drawing an activity network diagram? List the project management and network techniques it includes.

12. List Brassard's checklist of behavioral skills for effective deployment of 7 MP tools.

Discussion Questions and Projects

1. Discuss the fundamental differences between B7 and 7 MP tools.

2. Describe some typical applications of 7 MP tools in a software development context.

3. Apply appropriate 7 MP tools to the planning stages of a software development project, and present it to the class.

Endnotes

[1]S. Moriguchi, *Software Excellence: A Total Quality Management Guide* (Portland, OR: Productivity Press, 1997), p. 64.

[2]T. Asaka and K. Ozeki, *Handbook of Quality Tools: The Japanese Approach* (Portland, OR: Productivity Press, 1990).

[3]S. Mizuno, *Management for Quality Improvement: The Seven New QC Tools* (Cambridge, MA: Productivity Press, 1988).

[4]M. Brassard, *The Memory Jogger Plus* + (Methuen: Goal/QPC, 1989).

[5]E. R. Domb, "7 New Tools," *Quality Digest*, December 1994.

[6]Op cit Moriguchi, p. 64.

[7]Op cit Mizuno, p. 94.

[8]L. J. Arthur, *Improving Software Quality: An Insider's Guide to TQM* (New York: John Wiley & Sons, Inc., 1993), p. 61.

[9]Op cit Brassard, p. 53.

[10]Ibid, p. 57.

[11]Ibid, p. 64.

[12]Op cit Mizuno, p. 143.

[13]Op cit Brassard, p. 82.

[14]Op cit Mizuno, pp. 197-215.

[15]Op cit Brassard, p. 99.

[16]Op cit Mizuno, p. 221.

[17]Ibid, p. 229.

[18]Ibid, pp. 224–225.

[19]H. Kerzner, *Project Management: A Systems Approach to Planning, Scheduling, and Controlling* (New York: John Wiley & Sons, Inc., 2003).

[20]Op cit Brassard, pp. 201–233.

[21]Op cit Brassard, pp. 235–241.

CHAPTER 8

The Analytic Hierarchy Process

Humans are not often logical creatures. Most of the time we base our judgments on hazy impressions of reality and then use logic to defend our conclusions.

—Thomas Saaty

Not everything that counts can be counted and not everything that can be counted counts.

—Albert Einstein

Overview

The 7 MP tools, introduced in Chapter 7, are invaluable in analyzing and interpreting qualitative and verbal data. A typical challenge in such an analysis is prioritizing various tasks and characteristics identified in affinity and tree diagrams. This can be done using prioritization matrices. However, they have limitations in dealing with high-level complexities. This problem can be obviated by using the Analytic Hierarchy Process (AHP), which helps you prioritize complex architectural and design issues in the software development process. AHP is particularly applicable in QFD, presented in Chapter 11. AHP and its supporting software, Expert Choice (EC), can handle much higher levels of complexities than the tools introduced in Chapter 7. In addition to solutions facilitated by EC, this chapter also illustrates two known approximations to AHP solutions using manual calculations. Manual calculations can be used to solve relatively less-complex problems. They are presented in this chapter to illustrate the first principles and the steps involved in AHP. We emphasize EC as a powerful companion to AHP.

This chapter was written by Ernest H. Forman of George Washington University, along with Bijay K. Jayaswal and Peter C. Patton.

Chapter Outline

- Prioritization, Complexity, and the Analytic Hierarchy Process

- Multiobjective Decision-Making and AHP

- Case Study 8.1 Solution Using Expert Choice

- Approximations to AHP with Manual Calculations

- Conclusion

- Key Points

- Additional Resources

- Internet Exercises

- Review Questions

- Discussion Questions and Projects

- Problems

- Endnotes

Prioritization, Complexity, and the Analytic Hierarchy Process

The preceding chapter discussed the 7 MP tools, which are invaluable in analyzing and interpreting qualitative and verbal data. One typical challenge in such an analysis is prioritizing various tasks, issues, and characteristics that are identified in affinity and tree diagrams. This may be done using *prioritization matrices*, which were introduced as part of the 7 MP tools. However, prioritization matrices have limitations when it comes to dealing with a high level of complexity involving multicriteria decision problems. This limitation can be obviated by using a powerful technique, the *Analytic Hierarchy Process (AHP)*. It helps you solve complex problems involving multiple goals, objectives, criteria, competitors, and other factors.[1] AHP can be used to address important architecture and design prioritization issues in the software development process. As you will see, AHP and its supporting software, *Expert Choice (EC)*, can handle much higher levels of complexities than the tools introduced in Chapter 7. In addition to solutions facilitated by EC, we will also illustrate two known approximations to AHP solutions using manual calculations. Manual calculations can be used to solve relatively less-intricate problems. We therefore emphasize EC as an important companion to AHP.

Our interest in AHP goes beyond prioritization. AHP has a wide range of applications as a multiobjective decision technique in which qualitative factors are present along with quantitative factors or are dominant. AHP has an important application in Quality Function Deployment (QFD), as discussed in Chapter 11. AHP lets you structure complexity and measure and synthesize it. It uses ratio scale measures that can be meaningfully synthesized to arrive at not only a ranking of alternatives, but assign true proportions that can be used to optimally allocate resources. AHP has a variety of applications in economics, business, agriculture, engineering, social sciences, politics, and numerous other fields. In software development it can be used for decision-making in various phases of the software development process, from requirements development to design to review, test, and evaluation to maintenance and decommissioning, involving situations with multiple objectives.

AHP is essentially a theory of measurement and decision-making developed by Thomas L. Saaty when he was at the Wharton School of the University of Pennsylvania. The real value of AHP lies in its ability to combine, or synthesize, quantitative as well as qualitative considerations in an overall evaluation of alternatives. As such, it can be especially applicable when you evaluate complex system designs involving software, hardware, and humanware that can easily include hundreds of system quality indicators.[2] AHP has emerged as a powerful technique for determining relative worth and ranking among a set of elements. You can use it to make design, evaluation, and benefit/cost or optimal resource allocation decisions throughout the software development process.

Multiobjective Decision-Making and AHP

Software development includes numerous situations involving multiple factors, criteria/objective, and metrics. Depending on size, complexity, and level of analysis, there could be dozens of quality characteristics. Our definition of trustworthy software contains five major customer requirements—reliability, safety, security, maintainability, and customer responsiveness; each of these comprises several quality characteristics at various levels of analysis. Add to this the cost and schedule requirements, and we have a high degree of problem intricacy from decision and design perspectives. Figure 8.1 illustrates the point we are making: just two customer-demanded quality characteristics, maintainability and usability, result in 15 characteristics from the developer's perspective. Furthermore, quality metrics based on these characteristics would result in dozens of characteristics. The Walter and McCall Model identifies (at a minimum) a three-level hierarchy in quality characteristics:[3]

- The first level includes quality characteristics from the perspective of users. These are called *factors*.

- The second level comprises quality characteristics from the perspective of developers. These are called *criteria*.

- The third level includes quality characteristics that are further deployments of criteria to a level where qualities can be measured. These are called *metrics*.

Figure 8.1 illustrates just the simplest hierarchy of software quality characteristics. It is not uncommon to have subcriteria and sub-subcriteria in large and complex software. Given the complexity caused by a large number of variables, intuitive decision-making is insufficient to make the best design choices. Littlewood and Strigini articulate the challenges of software complexity:[4]

> Great complexity brings many dangers. One of the greatest is difficulty of understanding: it is common to have systems that no single person can claim to understand completely, even at a fairly high level of abstraction. This produces uncertainty about the properties of the program—particularly its reliability and safety.

Managing complexity remains a critical design challenge, especially in a large software development process. This can be addressed by a two-pronged strategy:

- Deploy a strategy for minimizing complexity (also discussed in Chapter 3).

- Use AHP as a decision tool in a complex multiple-objective decision environment. This can be done throughout a software development process that involves both quantitative data and qualitative judgments, beginning with the requirements development phase through decommissioning, wherever software complexity is an issue.

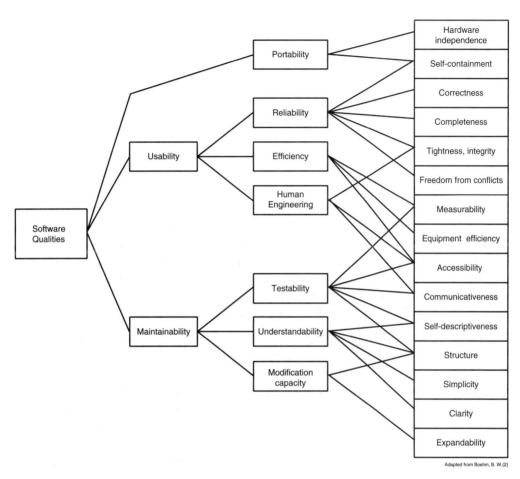

Adapted from Boehm, B. W.(2)

FIGURE 8.1
Hierarchical Structure of Software Product Quality Characteristics

The Gartner Group offers a line of Decision Engine Products,[5] as well as a best practice for technology selection called Refined Hierarchical Analysis. They are based on AHP and Expert Choice (EC), a computerized implementation of AHP and extensions to AHP.

This chapter uses a relatively simple decision situation (Case Study 8.1) to describe the application of AHP as a practical decision theory and then illustrates the use of Expert Choice.

Terminology

The terminology used in decision-making can be confusing, as evidenced by some of the terms used. We read and speak of factors, characteristics, attributes, criteria, objectives, requirements, pros, cons, metrics, musts, and wants. The formal decision-making literature includes three different descriptions of what some might consider the same endeavor:

- Multiattribute decision-making

- Multicriteria decision-making

- Multiobjective decision-making

Although some subtle differences exist, these differences are basically historical and academic in nature and serve to confuse rather than enlighten. We have found that most or all of the confusion can be removed by *focusing on objectives*. Doing so leads to decisions that best align an organization's actions with what it is trying to achieve. In contrast, focusing on competing vendor attributes, characteristics, or other factors that may or may not be relevant to the organization's objectives increases confusion and can lead to actions that are not well-aligned with an organization's objectives.

Focusing on objectives makes it clear when you are erroneously "double counting" (considering an attribute as it relates to more than one objective) and when you *should* double count. For example, a car's size might be included just once in a hierarchy of attributes. But in making a *decision*, you should focus on what you *want* from a car. You should ask, "Why do I care about the car's size?" A large car might be more comfortable, carry more passengers, and have a larger cargo capacity, but it might be less fuel-efficient than a small car. So rather than including the *attribute* size just once in an *attribute* hierarchy, you should include the multiple *objectives* related to size (comfort, safety, passenger capacity, cargo capacity, and perhaps ease of parking) in an *objectives* hierarchy.

Structuring an Objectives Hierarchy

We recommend using both a *top-down* and *bottom-up* approach to identify the objectives of an objectives hierarchy, as illustrated in Figure 8.2. The top-down approach elicits objectives directly. For example, the objectives in choosing from a set of alternative designs for a software product might include ease of use, ease of learning, functionality, and reliability. The subobjectives for ease of learning might be different for casual users and power users. The process can continue to include a lower level of subobjectives.

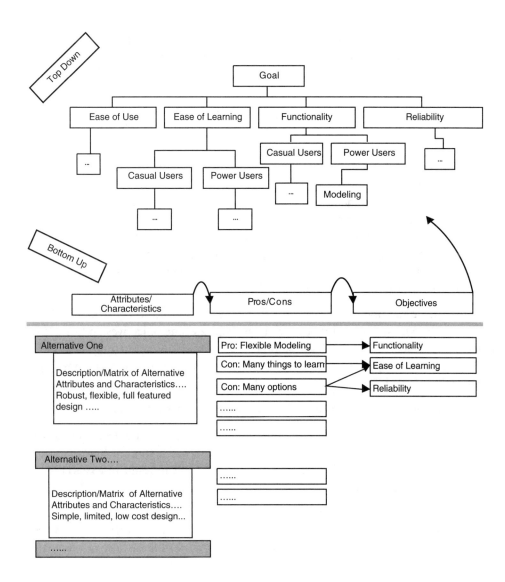

FIGURE 8.2
Structuring an Objectives Hierarchy

The bottom-up approach elicits objectives indirectly, by articulating the *pros* and *cons* of each alternative, some of which emerge from the alternatives' characteristics or *attributes*. For example, in looking at the description and matrix of attributes for Alternative One in Figure 8.2, you can see that this alternative provides very flexible modeling capabilities (a pro). However, this would require the user to learn many things (a con), and a large number of combinations of paths will need to be tested (a con). Each pro and con points to one or more objectives or subobjectives to be included in the hierarchy. A pro for one alternative may be a con for another alternative. At this point, it doesn't matter whether something is a pro or con. The relative preference for the former alternative will be greater than that for the latter alternative when judgments are made to derive priorities later in the AHP process.

You don't need to identify *all* the pros and cons for *each* alternative under consideration. The focus at this point is on identifying objectives for the objectives hierarchy. However, it may be worth the time to identify and document all the pros and cons so that a clear audit trail exists. If a decision is at all political (the more important the decision, the more likely it is political as well as technical) any conclusion is likely to be challenged by someone who feels that another alternative is better. If these "reasons" are already documented as pros and cons and are represented by objectives in the decision hierarchy, it's easy to see how the person's concern is addressed in the evaluation.

If the person identifies some concerns that were overlooked in constructing the objectives hierarchy, and others feel that they are appropriate, the objectives and/or judgments should be included or modified and another iteration of the evaluation performed. The results will either convince everyone that the original selection was best, or a possibly costly mistake will be avoided.

To best model complex decisions, Expert Choice provides two guidelines:[6]

- It is advisable to include no more than nine objectives or subobjectives in any cluster. Experiments have shown that it is cognitively challenging for humans to deal with more than nine factors at once. Trying to do so can result in less accurate priorities and higher inconsistencies.

- Cluster objectives and subobjectives so that they are comparable or so that they do not differ by orders of magnitude. In other words, try not to include objectives or subobjectives of very small importance in the same cluster as those of much greater importance.

AHP software such as Expert Choice can help with structuring. It provides functionality to help you record pros and cons for each alternative, convert them to objectives, and view and manipulate affinity diagrams to cluster objectives according to the two guidelines using drag-and-drop capabilities.

Decision Hierarchy

A decision hierarchy contains the objectives hierarchy and the alternatives under consideration, as shown in Figure 8.2. We will call the lowest-level objectives (or subobjectives) of the objectives hierarchy *covering objectives* because they cover the alternatives. This terminology is concise, unambiguous, and can be extended as necessary. For example, the objectives hierarchy can, in some cases, include other factors, such as scenarios or "players." You can also readily "map" the terminology to other terminologies, such as The Walter and McCall three-level model discussed earlier. The first-level quality characteristics from the perspective of the users that they would call factors, we will call objectives. The second-level quality characteristics from the perspective of developers that they would call criteria, we will call subobjectives. The third-level deployment of criteria that they would call metrics, we will call sub-subobjectives. Because they are the lowest level of this model, we will also call them covering objectives. Because we will be evaluating the alternatives with respect to these covering objectives, we may in fact be employing metrics in the process.

Case Study 8.1: MIS Director's IT Dilemma

A U.S. software vendor had gone from version 5 of its enterprise business software to version 6 to add (currency) internationalization, electronic funds transfer (EFT), and electronic data transfer (EDT). A Canadian user of this software release had used it successfully for years but did not see the need to upgrade to version 6 and therefore did not do so. Meanwhile, the vendor released version 7 and announced that version 5 would soon go off support. The Canadian customer was doing business with American firms that were beginning to require EDT of business documents. The firm also had acquired a U.S. subsidiary and now had to do a two-currency payroll and roll up monthly books in two currencies. The company asked the software vendor if it could upgrade to from version 5 to version 7 but was told that this was not possible. It would have to upgrade in two steps—from version 5 to 6 and then 6 to 7.

The cost of the software was not an issue, because upgrades were free to any customer who kept its support subscriptions up to date, which the company had done. Its problem was that the training and infrastructure upgrade cost from one version to the next was estimated to be $1.9 million. The choices were as follows (see Table 8.1):

- To stay on version 5, forgo support, and write its own new technology software.
- Upgrade to version 6 and get the new features but face another expensive upgrade in a year or so.
- Do a double upgrade from 5 to 6 and 6 to 7 over a short period to save time and money and to stay current, but incur risk.

TABLE 8.1
Information for the MIS Director's IT Dilemma (Overall Goal: Select the Best
Upgrade Path)

Alternative	Implementation Cost	Technical Risk	Business Risk	Competitive Advantage	Time to Implement
A: Modify version 5 with outside help	$900k	High	Moderate	Temporary loss	8 months
B: Upgrade to version 6 now and go to version 7 later	$2.7M	Low	Very low	High	3 months
C: Do a double upgrade now: version 5 to 6 to 7	$1.9M	Moderate	Low	Highest	6 months

These choices illustrate what is known as the MIS director's dilemma. Should the company be conservative and cautious? If so, its users might lose competitive advantage because they lack state-of-the-art software functionality. Or should the company be aggressive and install the latest software? The software might be failure-prone and thus might cause its users to lose competitive advantage. For example, most CIOs installed new Microsoft versions only after Service Pack 2 was released. This may seem too conservative, but this policy saved them from the "screaming blue death" that accompanied Service Pack 1 of NT 4.0.

Case Study 8.1 Solution Using Expert Choice

The MIS director's IT dilemma is a relatively simple case, with a three-level hierarchy, that we are using to illustrate how AHP works. The decision-maker(s) must make judgments about the relative importance of each objective in paired comparisons with each of the other objectives. They also must judge the relative merits of the alternatives with respect to each of the objectives. This is called relative measurement as opposed to absolute measurement, such as arbitrarily assigning a priority to each of the objectives, or stating that an alternative is 'high,' 'moderate,' or 'low' and then arbitrarily assigning priorities to 'High' 'Moderate', and 'Low.' AHP uses hierarchic or network structures to represent a decision problem and then develops priorities for the alternatives based on the decision-makers' judgments throughout the system.[7] The end product of the process is a prioritized ranking of the alternatives available to the decision-maker(s).

We will illustrate the process using Expert Choice software as well as explain some of the subtleties of the AHP process. Later, we also illustrate two approximate solution methods without Expert Choice.

The Expert Choice step-by-step solution for Case Study 8.1 is illustrated next.

Step 1: Brainstorm and Construct a Hierarchical Model of the Problem

The first step in the AHP process is to construct the decision hierarchy. Level 1 of any such hierarchy (see Figure 8.3) is a statement of the overall goal—in this case, "Select the Best Upgrade Path." The goal statement is rather general. Additional specificity is achieved by articulating objectives and subobjectives.

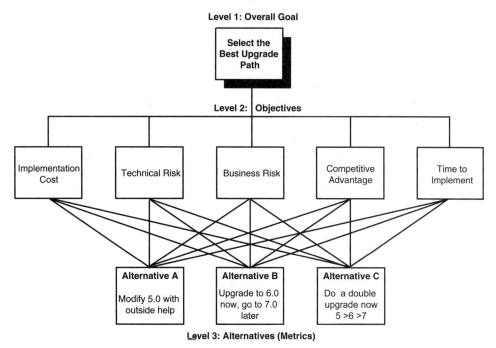

FIGURE 8.3
A Three-Level Hierarchical Model of the MIS Director's IT Dilemma

We will keep this example simple by including only one level of objectives and not doing a thorough top-down and bottom-up evaluation. Instead, we will just include the obvious objectives suggested by Table 8.1—(low) Implementation Cost, (low) Technical Risk, (low) Business Risk, (high) Competitive Advantage, and (low) Time to Implement. (It really is not necessary to specify the low, moderate, and high labels. We will ask which alternative is preferable with respect to each of the objectives. It is obvious that, when considering cost, risk, and time to implement, the alternative that has a lower cost, risk, or time is preferable to one with a higher cost, risk, or time. An alternative with a higher competitive advantage is preferable to one with a lower competitive advantage.)

The third "level" of the hierarchy, as illustrated in Figure 8.3, contains the three decision alternatives:

- Modify version 5 with outside help

- Upgrade to version 6 now and go to version 7 later

- Do a double upgrade now: go from version 5 to 6 to 7

Step 2: Derive Ratio Scale Priorities for the Objectives

Some people will favor Alternative A, some will favor Alternative B, and some will favor Alternative C. The worst thing to do is to decide by voting. A well-known book by Fisher and Ury called *Getting to YES*[8] makes strong arguments for focusing on *interests* rather than *positions*. However, when confronted with difficult choices, most people focus on positions (what we call alternatives), debating why their favored alternative is better than someone else's. The debate can be never-ending and often not very productive. In contrast, a *rational* decision can be defined as one that best achieves your *objectives*, or, in Fisher and Ury's terminology, interests. This can be done by determining the relative importance of each objective (and subobjective in the general case) as well as determining the relative preference of each alternative with respect to each objective. Although we often recommend doing the latter first, for reasons that will be explained shortly, we will first derive the priorities of our objectives using a process of *pairwise comparisons*.

Instead of arbitrarily *assigning* priorities to our objectives, we will *derive* them using relative pairwise comparisons. This process is more accurate and more defensible. (It does not mean that the results are any more "objective." The relative importance of objectives is *subjective*, but it does mean that they will more accurately reflect the insight, knowledge, and experience of those doing the evaluation.)

If we were to use absolute measurement and say that the Implementation Cost objective equals .7 on a scale of 0 to 1, how would we justify this? What does .7 mean to us or to someone else? Instead, we will ask which is more important, Implementation Cost or Technical Risk? (much like an optometrist asks with which eye you can see an image more clearly). But we also ask for a ratio of intensity, not just a direction. This intensity can be expressed numerically, verbally, or graphically. Expressing the intensity of a judgment in the form of a numerical ratio is exact, but it might not be reasonable when comparing high-level objectives—the importance of which are often, if not always, qualitative and subjective. For example, if we were to say that Competitive Advantage is 4.5 times more important than Implementation Cost, how do we justify such a judgment? Why not 4.4 or 4.6 or 6.0? If we were to express the ratio using words, such as "Competitive Advantage is strongly more important," it is easier to support such an inexact judgment. But how do we quantify such a judgment? Saaty developed a "verbal" scale (see Table 8.2)[9] and a process of calculating ratio scale priorities from a set of verbal judgments based on what is essentially ordinal input. These priorities can be astoundingly accurate *if* there is enough variety and redundancy in the cluster of items being compared, *even if* there is some inconsistency in the judgments. Research and experience have confirmed the nine-point scale as a reasonable basis for discriminating between the preferences for two items.[10]

TABLE 8.2
The Fundamental Verbal Scale for Pairwise Comparison

Expressed Judgment of Preference	Numerical Value
Extremely preferred	9
Compromise between very strongly and extremely	8
Very strongly preferred	7
Compromise between strongly and very strongly	6
Strongly preferred	5
Compromise between moderately and strongly	4
Moderately preferred	3
Compromise between equally and moderately	2
Equally preferred	1

Figure 8.4 shows a pairwise verbal judgment expressing that Technical Risk is moderately more important than Implementation Cost. The grid shown at the bottom of Figure 8.4 shows the pairwise comparison for each pair. The judgments are represented numerically, according to Saaty's fundamental verbal scale (refer to Table 8.2). However, you shouldn't say that Technical Risk was judged to be three times as important as

Implementation Cost. The evaluator did not say three times, but said "moderate". "Moderate" to the evaluator might not mean three times. A black entry in the grid indicates that the objective in the cell's row is more important than the objective in the cell's column. A red entry indicates that the objective in the cell's column is more important than the objective in the cell's row. (These entries are actually inverse judgments, such as 1/5, when the eigenvector[11] calculation is performed. This explanation is more easily grasped in the manual solutions presented later in this chapter.)

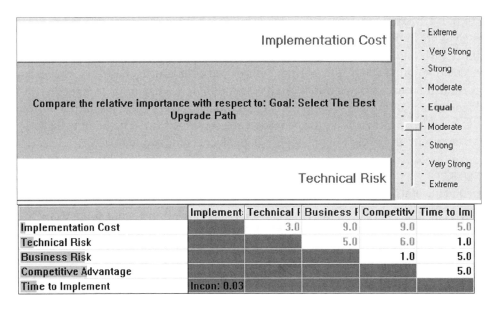

FIGURE 8.4
Pairwise Verbal Judgments for the Importance of Objectives in the MIS Director's
IT Dilemma

Figure 8.5 shows the priorities resulting from this set of judgments. The priorities are a function of the entire set of judgments, not any one judgment. Notice that the ratio of priorities for any pair of objectives is *not* the same as the numerical value of the verbal judgment. This is to be expected, because the words are essentially an ordinal scale, whereas the priorities are ratio scale measures. Expert Choice has many other options for making such judgments, such as being able to compute priorities when some of the judgments are missing. The inconsistency ratio (.03 in this case) is the ratio of the inconsistency index (as defined by Saaty) to the average inconsistency index of sets of random judgments for a similar-size matrix with the same number of missing judgments. The inconsistency ratio is not relevant unless it is larger than about 10% or so, in which case the judgments should be reviewed. Reasons for a high inconsistency ratio include lack of information, lack of concentration, clusters with elements that differ by more than an order of magnitude, and real-world inconsistencies.

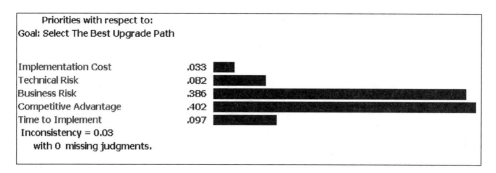

FIGURE 8.5
Derived Objective Priorities and Inconsistency Ratio

When there is not enough redundancy or variety (for example, when there are only two elements in a cluster), or when the evaluator feels that the resultant priorities do not represent what he or she has in mind, pairwise graphical judgments can be made. The evaluator pulls two bars until the ratio of their lengths best describes his or her judgment of the relative importance of the objectives being compared (see Figure 8.6).

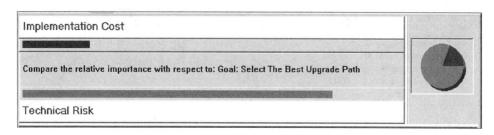

FIGURE 8.6
A Pairwise Graphical Judgment

Step 3: Derive Priorities for the Alternatives with Respect to Each Objective

This step involves making pairwise comparisons of the relative preference of the alternatives with respect to each objective. The judgments, derived priorities, and global priorities of the alternatives with respect to the specific covering objective are shown in Figures 8.7 through 8.11.

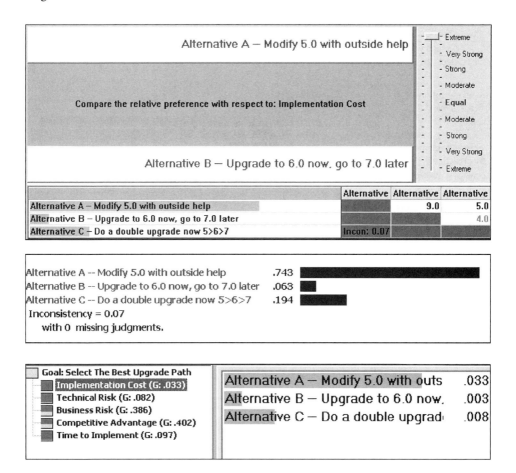

FIGURE 8.7
A Pairwise Comparison Matrix, Derived Priorities, and Global Priorities for the Alternatives Vis-à-Vis Implementation Cost

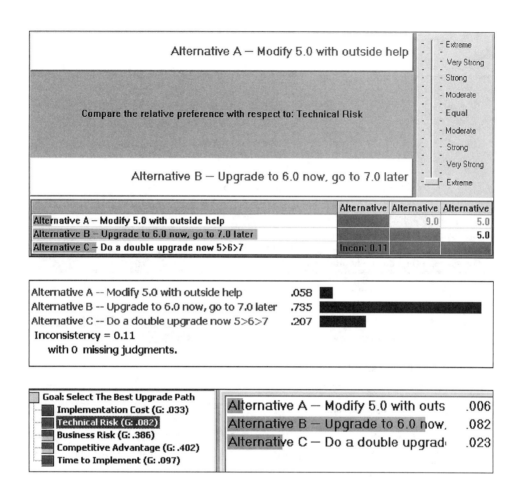

FIGURE 8.8
A Pairwise Comparison Matrix, Derived Priorities, and Global Priorities for the Alternatives Vis-à-Vis Technical Risk

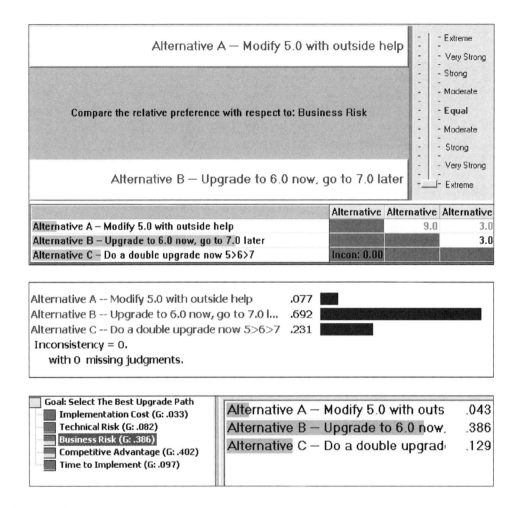

FIGURE 8.9
A Pairwise Comparison Matrix, Derived Priorities, and Global Priorities for the Alternatives Vis-à-Vis Business Risk

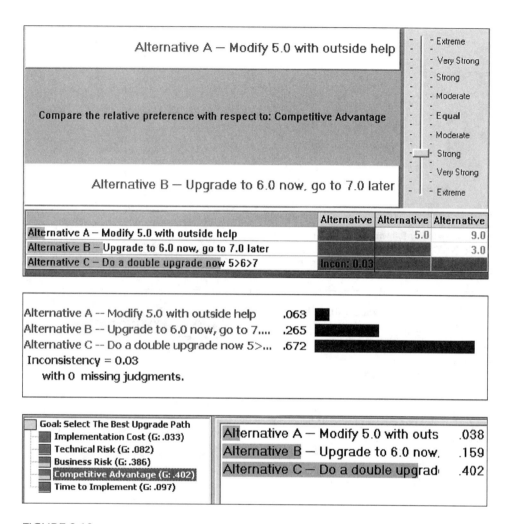

FIGURE 8.10
Judgments and Priorities for the Alternatives Vis-à-Vis Competitive Advantage

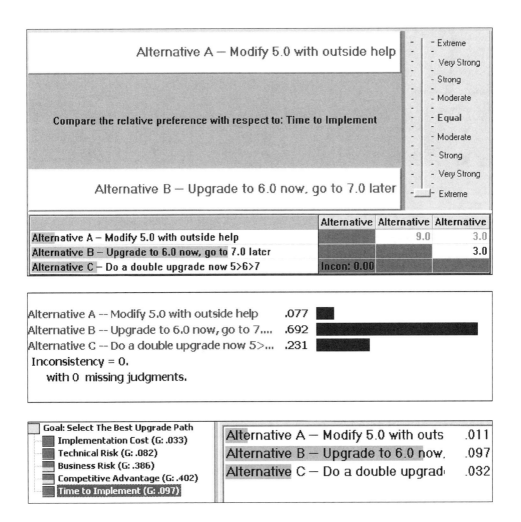

FIGURE 8.11
A Pairwise Comparison Matrix, Derived Priorities, and Global Priorities for the Alternatives Vis-à-Vis Time to Implement

Local and Global Priorities

The G designation in Figure 8.7 stands for "global." Expert Choice can display both local and global priorities. Local priorities add up to 1 in any cluster. Global priorities of elements in the hierarchy add up to their parent's priority. Thus, the priorities of the objectives under the goal add up to 1.

Distributive and Ideal Synthesis Modes

AHP originally had only one synthesis mode, which we now call a *distributive* synthesis. This mode is fine for prioritization where there is "scarcity." This can occur in forecasting applications where the consideration of a new possible outcome means that existing outcomes must be less probable, and in elections (as was the case in the last few U.S. presidential elections). However, the distributive synthesis mode can result in the reversal of ranks when alternatives are added to or removed from consideration. There was much debate in the literature about this. AHP was modified to include an *ideal* synthesis that precludes rank reversal and is appropriate when no scarcity exists.[12, 13] Because this choice decision has no scarcity, the ideal mode is appropriate, and instead of the global priorities of the alternatives adding up to the global priority of the parent or covering objective, you can see in Figure 8.7 that the global priority of the most preferred alternative under the covering objective has the same priority as the covering objective priority (.033 in this case). The other alternatives have priorities determined by the ratios of their local priority to that of the most preferred alternative. For example, the priority of Alternative B is (.063/.743) × .033, or about .0028, which is displayed as .003. When the global priorities are added up for the alternatives under all the covering objectives, they are renormalized so that they add up to 1.

Step 4: Synthesis

The overall synthesis results in the priorities shown in Figure 8.12. Alternative B is clearly the most preferred overall.

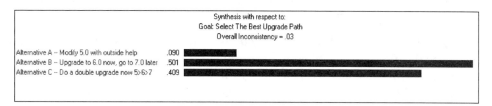

Synthesis with respect to:
Goal: Select The Best Upgrade Path
Overall Inconsistency = .03

Alternative A -- Modify 5.0 with outside help	.090
Alternative B -- Upgrade to 6.0 now, go to 7.0 later	.501
Alternative C -- Do a double upgrade now 5>6>7	.409

FIGURE 8.12
Ideal Mode Synthesis

Expert Choice has numerous sensitivity plots. Figure 8.13 shows a *dynamic* sensitivity plot. Although it's not dynamic on a printed page, when displayed on a computer screen, it allows the user to drag bars on the left pane. You can see, if any of the objectives were to increase or decrease, how the lengths of the alternative priority bars change in the right pane. Even on the printed page, you can see the relative priorities of the top-level objectives as well as the alternatives.

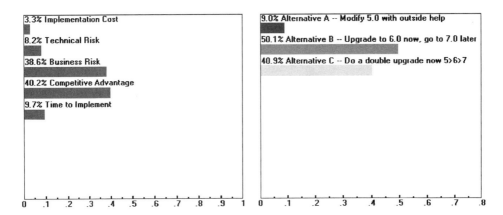

FIGURE 8.13
Dynamic Sensitivity Analysis

The *performance* sensitivity plot shown in Figure 8.14 shows not only the objectives' relative importance (represented by the heights of the histogram bars), but also how well each alternative performs relative to each of the objectives. The overall results are shown on the right. The performance sensitivity plot is the best way to visualize the decision's trade-offs. For example, Alternative C, which is second overall, performs best with respect to Competitive Advantage. So if the relative importance of this objective were to increase, so would the overall priority of Alternative C. Similarly, because Alternative B, which is best overall, is also best with respect to Business Risk, a decrease in the importance of Business Risk would decrease the overall priority of Alternative B. This is also shown in the gradient sensitivity plot shown in Figure 8.15.

Dragging the bars in any of the sensitivity plots causes an immediate and corresponding change to all the other sensitivity plots. For example, if the vertical line in the gradient sensitivity plot shown in Figure 8.15 were dragged to the left so that the priority of Business Risk is decreased to about 10 percent, the bars would automatically change in the dynamic sensitivity plot (see Figure 8.16), showing that Alternative C would become the preferred alternative.

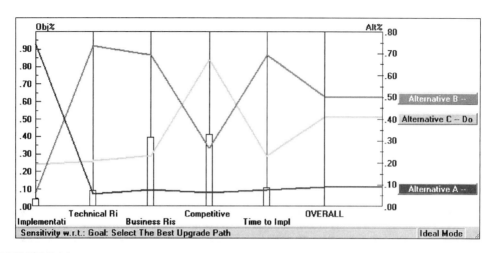

FIGURE 8.14
Performance Sensitivity Analysis

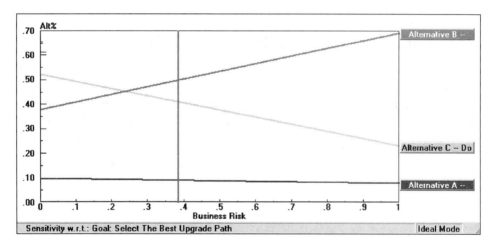

FIGURE 8.15
Gradient Sensitivity Analysis

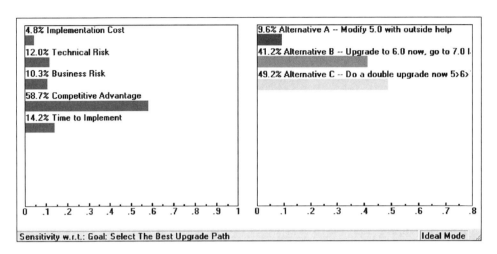

FIGURE 8.16
Dynamic Sensitivity Analysis After Decreasing Business Risk to About 10%

Approximations to AHP with Manual Calculations

The following two solutions illustrate approximations to some of the AHP calculations that are performed with Expert Choice. Although these approximate calculations can be somewhat tedious and may not produce the same results, particularly when there are some inconsistencies in judgments, they give you a more detailed look at some of AHP's intricacies.

We will illustrate two approximate methods for arriving at an AHP solution to Case Study 8.1. The approximations can be good in some cases but not so good in others. In general, the smaller the clusters in an AHP model and the more consistent the judgments, the more accurate the approximate calculations will be. Following this approximate solution, we will present another variation—the one by Michael Brassard.

Approximate Solution Method 1

Step 1: Brainstorm and Construct a Hierarchical Model of the Problem

Step 1 in the solution derivation is same as the one used earlier, in the section "Case Study 8.1 Solution Using Expert Choice."

Step 2: Construct a Pairwise Comparison Matrix for the Objectives

To establish the priority ranking among the three alternatives, AHP uses pairwise relative comparisons. A decision-maker stipulates his or her judgments regarding the relative importance of the objectives in attaining the overall goal.

The decision-maker's judgments are entered into the elements above the diagonal in Table 8.3 using the numeric representation of Saaty's verbal scale. The diagonal elements of Table 8.3 are all 1 because an element's importance when compared to itself is 1. The elements below the diagonal are the reciprocals of the elements above the diagonals, as per Axiom 2 of AHP (if A is $n \times$ B, B is $1/n \times$ A). A fractional judgment, such as 1/3 when comparing the row element Implementation Cost to the column element Technical Risk, means that the column element is more important than the row element—in this case, moderately more important.

Because it is not easy to calculate the principal right eigenvector manually, an approximate technique is used in which the priorities are approximated by the normalized sum of the judgments in each of the rows (or columns). For example, in Table 8.3, the pairwise judgments are summed for each row. The sums are then normalized, as shown in the last column of Table 8.3. The "weights" represent an approximation to the relative importance or priorities of the objectives. For example, the priority of Implementation Cost using this approximate technique is .031, and the exact solution, computed by Expert Choice, is .033. Similarly, the approximate priority for Competitive Advantage is .383, and the exact solution is .402. The more consistent the judgments, the closer the approximate solution is to the exact solution.

TABLE 8.3
Pairwise Comparison Matrix for the Objectives

	Implementation Cost	Technical Risk	Business Risk	Competitive Advantage	Time to Implement	Approximate Weight	Eigenvector Weight
Implementation Cost	1	1/3	1/9	1/9	1/5	1.756 (**.031**)	**.033**
Technical Risk	3	1	1/5	1/6	1	5.367 (**.093**)	**.083**
Business Risk	9	5	1	1	5	21.000 (**.364**)	**.386**
Competitive Advantage	9	6	1	1	5	22.000 (**.383**)	**.402**
Time to Implement	5	1	1/5	1/5	1	7.400 (**.129**)	**.097**
Total						**57.523**	

Step 3: Construct a Pairwise Comparison Matrix for the Alternatives

This step involves pairwise comparisons of the alternatives with respect to each objective in separate matrices, one for each objective. The procedure is similar to the one used for constructing pairwise matrix for objectives. The question to ask here is, which alternative is relatively more important than the other in terms of its contribution toward achieving the particular objective being considered? The five matrices are constructed as shown in Tables 8.4 through 8.8.

TABLE 8.4
Pairwise Comparison Matrix for the Alternatives Vis-à-Vis Implementation Cost

	Alternative A	Alternative B	Alternative C
Alternative A	1	9	5
Alternative B	1/9	1	1/4
Alternative C	1/5	4	1

TABLE 8.5
Pairwise Comparison Matrix for the Alternatives Vis-à-Vis Technical Risk

	Alternative A	Alternative B	Alternative C
Alternative A	1	1/9	1/5
Alternative B	9	1	5
Alternative C	5	1/5	1

TABLE 8.6
Pairwise Comparison Matrix for the Alternatives Vis-à-Vis Business Risk

	Alternative A	Alternative B	Alternative C
Alternative A	1	1/9	1/3
Alternative B	9	1	3
Alternative C	3	1/3	1

TABLE 8.7
Pairwise Comparison Matrix for the Alternatives Vis-à-Vis Competitive Advantage

	Alternative A	Alternative B	Alternative C
Alternative A	1	1/5	1/9
Alternative B	5	1	1/3
Alternative C	9	3	1

TABLE 8.8
Pairwise Comparison Matrix for the Alternatives Vis-à-Vis Time to Implement

	Alternative A	Alternative B	Alternative C
Alternative A	1	1/9	1/3
Alternative B	9	1	3
Alternative C	3	1/3	1

Step 4: Approximate the Priorities from the Judgments

After the various matrices have been constructed, we need to determine the alternatives' priorities with respect to each of the covering objectives. As mentioned earlier, this involves a mathematical computation of eigenvalues and eigenvectors that is beyond the scope of this book. We will use the following procedure, which is a good approximation of the synthesized priorities:[14]

1. Sum the values of the elements in the pairwise comparison matrix.

2. Divide each element in the pairwise comparison matrix by its column total. The resulting matrix is called the *normalized pairwise comparison matrix.*

3. Compute the average of the elements in each row of the normalized matrix. These averages provide an estimate of the relative priorities of the elements being compared.

This three-step procedure is carried out for the pairwise comparison matrix for the alternatives vis-à-vis Implementation Cost (see Table 8.4). It results in the *normalized pairwise comparison matrix* shown in Table 8.9. The three-step construction of the normalized matrix is shown in Tables 8.9 through 8.11.

280

TABLE 8.9
Sum the Values in Each Column

	Alternative A	Alternative B	Alternative C
Alternative A	1	9	5
Alternative B	1/9	1	1/4
Alternative C	1/5	4	1
Totals	59/45	14	25/4

TABLE 8.10
Divide Each Matrix Element by Its Column Total

	Alternative A	Alternative B	Alternative C
Alternative A	45/59	9/14	20/25
Alternative B	5/59	1/14	1/25
Alternative C	9/59	4/14	4/25

TABLE 8.11
Average the Elements in Each Row

	Alternative A	Alternative B	Alternative C	Row Average
Alternative A	.763	.643	.800	.735
Alternative B	.085	.071	.040	.065
Alternative C	.152	.286	.160	.200
				Total = 1.000

The preceding calculations provide the priorities for the three alternatives vis-à-vis the Implementation Cost objective.

The priority vector with respect to Implementation Cost is

$$\begin{bmatrix} .735 \\ .065 \\ .200 \end{bmatrix}$$

compared to the exact solution obtained with Expert Choice:

$$\begin{bmatrix} .743 \\ .063 \\ .194 \end{bmatrix}$$

Similarly, the priority vectors for the other objectives are calculated and are as follows:

Technical Risk	Business Risk	Competitive Advantage	Time to Implement
$\begin{bmatrix} .061 \\ .723 \\ .216 \end{bmatrix}$	$\begin{bmatrix} .077 \\ .692 \\ .231 \end{bmatrix}$	$\begin{bmatrix} .064 \\ .267 \\ .669 \end{bmatrix}$	$\begin{bmatrix} .077 \\ .692 \\ .231 \end{bmatrix}$

The exact solution obtained with Expert Choice is

$$\begin{bmatrix} .058 \\ .735 \\ .207 \end{bmatrix} \quad \begin{bmatrix} .077 \\ .692 \\ .231 \end{bmatrix} \quad \begin{bmatrix} .063 \\ .265 \\ .672 \end{bmatrix}$$

Because the inconsistencies of the judgments are rather small for these matrices, the approximate priorities are close to those obtained with Expert Choice. In fact, they are exactly the same for the two matrices that are perfectly consistent. You will next see how to manually approximate the calculations of the judgment consistencies.

Step 5: Estimate the Consistency Ratio

AHP does not require perfectly consistent judgments, but it provides an index for measuring consistency for each matrix and for the entire hierarchy. Thus, it is possible to find where the inconsistent judgments are. You can change them if you want to, although this is not required. The goal is not to be perfectly consistent, but to be as accurate as possible. A certain amount of inconsistency is required to learn new things.[15] A inconsistency index of .10 or less is usually considered reasonable.

An approximate computation of consistency index and consistency ratio (or what Expert Choice calls the inconsistency ratio, because the higher the value, the more inconsistent the judgments) is as follows:[16]

1. Multiply each value in the first column of the pairwise comparison matrix by the relative priority of the first item considered. Multiply each value in the second column of the matrix by the relative priority of the second item considered. Multiply each value in the third column of the

matrix by the relative priority of the third item considered. Sum the values across the rows to obtain a vector of values labeled "weighted sum." This computation for the MIS director's IT dilemma case is as follows:

$$.735\begin{bmatrix}1\\1/9\\1/5\end{bmatrix}+.065\begin{bmatrix}9\\1\\4\end{bmatrix}+.200\begin{bmatrix}5\\1/4\\1\end{bmatrix}=\begin{bmatrix}.735\\.082\\.147\end{bmatrix}+\begin{bmatrix}.585\\.065\\.260\end{bmatrix}+\begin{bmatrix}1.000\\.050\\.200\end{bmatrix}=\begin{bmatrix}2.320\\.197\\.607\end{bmatrix}$$

2. Divide the elements of the vector of weighted sums you just obtained by the corresponding priority value. You obtain the following:

2.320/.735 = 3.156
.197/.065 = 3.030
.607/.200 = 3.035

3. Compute the average of the three:

λ_{max} = (3.156 + 3.030 + 3.035)/3 = 3.074

4. Compute the consistency index (CI):

CI = $(\lambda_{max} - n)/(n - 1)$

where n = the number of items being compared.
For the MIS Director's IT Dilemma case, with n = 3, you obtain the following:
CI = (3.074 − 3)/2 = .037

5. Compute the consistency ratio (CR):

CR = CI/RI

where the random index (RI) is the average consistency index of many simulated pairwise comparison matrices of random judgments. The RI, which depends on the number of elements being compared, takes on the following values:

n	3	4	5	6	7	8
RI	.58	.90	1.12	1.24	1.32	1.41

For the MIS Director's IT Dilemma case, when n = 3 and RI = 0.58, we get
CR = .037/0.58 = .064
This value for CR, less than .1, is acceptable.

Step 6: Develop the Overall Priority Ranking

Following the preceding computations, the priority vectors for all the objectives are tabulated as shown in Table 8.12.

TABLE 8.12
The Priority Vectors for the MIS Director's IT Dilemma

Objective Alternative	Implementation Cost	Technical Risk	Business Risk	Competitive Advantage	Time to Implement
Alternative A	.735	.061	.077	.064	.077
Alternative B	.065	.723	.692	.267	.692
Alternative C	.200	.216	.231	.669	.231

Table 8.12 reveals the following priorities:

- Alternative A is most preferable for Implementation Cost.

- Alternative B is most preferable for Technical Risk, Business Risk, and Time to Implement.

- Alternative C is most preferable for Competitive Advantage.

No alternative is most preferred for all the objectives. Therefore, to make a choice, we need to look at the relative importance of all the alternatives computed in Table 8.3. The objective priorities from that table appear in Table 8.13.

TABLE 8.13
Relative Ranking of Various Objectives

Objective	Weight
Implementation Cost	.031
Technical Risk	.093
Business Risk	.364
Competitive Advantage	.383
Time to Implement	.129
	Total = 1.000

The overall priority of each alternative can be calculated by summing the products of the objective priority and multiplying by the priority of its decision alternative, as shown in Table 8.13. We can compute overall ranking priority as follows:

Alternative A = .031(.735) + .093(.061) + .364(.077) + .383(.064) + .129(.077) = .091

Alternative B = .031(.065) + .093(.723) + .364(.692) + .383(.267) + .129(.692) = .513

Alternative C = .031(.200) + .093(.216) + .364(.231) + .383(.669) + .129(.231) = .396

This gives us the overall rankings shown in Table 8.14.

TABLE 8.14
Overall Priorities and Rankings of the Three Alternatives

Alternative	Priorities from Approximate Calculations (Method 1)	Priorities from Exact Calculations (Distributive Mode)	Priorities from Exact Calculations (Ideal Mode)
Alternative A	.091	.091	.090
Alternative B	.513	.504	.501
Alternative C	.396	.405	.409

The preceding provides the following rankings:

Rank 1: Alternative B

Rank 2: Alternative C

Rank 3: Alternative A

You can see that, for this simple example, the priorities from the approximate calculations are very close to the Ideal Mode exact calculations produced by Expert Choice. (The Distributive and Ideal synthesis modes are explained in the Expert Choice solution arrived at earlier in the chapter.)

Approximate Solution Method 2: Brassard's Full Analytical Criteria Method for Prioritization

You may recall that this method was introduced in Chapter 7, along with other prioritization matrices—namely, the *Consensus Criteria Method* and the *Combination I.D./Matrix Method*. Of the three prioritization matrices developed by Brassard, the Full Analytical

Criteria Method is the most rigorous and time-consuming. Although it is based on Saaty's AHP methodology, it is not nearly as accurate and can lead to different results. Nevertheless, the following sections describe the steps required to construct a Brassard Full Analytical Criteria Method.[17]

Step 1: Agree on the Ultimate Goal to Be Achieved

We will use the MIS Director's IT Dilemma case for our analysis. This step has to do with clearly stating the ultimate goal of the prioritization process. In this case it is the "overall goal" of Case Study 8.1: "Select the best upgrade path."

Step 2: Create a List of Criteria to Be Applied to the Options Generated

The criteria or objectives are Implementation Cost, Technical Risk, Business Risk, Competitive Advantage, and Time to Implement.

Step 3: Judge the Relative Importance of Each Criterion as Compared to Every Other Criterion

Here each criterion is rated against every other criterion in a paired comparison using the following scale:

    1/10 = Much less important/preferred

    1/5 = Less important/preferred

    1 = Equally important/preferred

    5 = More important/preferred

    10 = Much more important/preferred

Table 8.15 shows the pairwise comparison for the preceding criteria. It is an L-shaped matrix. A criterion when compared to itself results in a numerical score of 1. If it is more important than the criterion it is compared to, it gets a numerical score of 5. When it's less important than the criterion it is compared to, it gets a numerical score of 1/5. If it is much more important than the criterion it is compared to, it gets a numerical score of 10. If it's much less important than the criterion it is compared to, it gets a numerical score of 1/10. The individual comparative scores for each criterion are added and their proportionate weights are calculated, as shown in the last column of Table 8.15. The weights represent the relative importance or priorities of various criteria. The overall pairwise comparison is tabulated in Table 8.15.

TABLE 8.15
Weighing Importance of Criteria: Criterion Versus Criterion Matrix

	Implementation Cost	Technical Risk	Business Risk	Competitive Advantage	Time to Implement	Rows Total (Weights; Total % of Grand Total)
Implementation Cost		1/5	1/10	1/10	1/5	.600 (.010)
Technical Risk	5		1/5	1/5	1	6.400 (.116)
Business Risk	10	5		1	5	21.000 (.379)
Competitive Advantage	10	5	1		5	21.000 (.379)
Time to Implement	5	1	1/5	1/5		6.400 (.116)
Column Total	30	11.2	1.5	1.5	11.2	55.400 (1.000)

The row weights represent the criteria's relative importance. Of the five criteria, Business Risk and Competitive Advantage are significantly more important than Implementation Cost, Technical Risk, and Time to Implement: scores of .379 and .379 compared to .010, .116, and .116, respectively. Given such dramatic differences, the less-important criteria can be dropped from any further analysis.[18] Therefore, we'll use just Business Risk and Competitive Advantage as the criteria against which the three alternatives (A, B, and C) will be compared to achieve the overall goal of selecting the best upgrade path.

Step 4: Compare All the Alternative Solutions to the Individual Criteria

This step involves pairwise comparison of the alternative solutions with respect to each criterion in separate matrices, one for each criterion. The procedure is similar to the one used to construct a pairwise matrix for objectives (Table 8.15). The question to ask here is, which alternative solution has a relatively greater impact than the other in terms of its contribution toward achieving the particular criterion being considered? The rows and columns are summed to get the totals, and the relative weights of each alternative solution are calculated as a percentage (fraction) of the total. The two matrices are constructed as shown in Tables 8.16 and 8.17.

TABLE 8.16
Solution Alternatives Versus Each Criterion Comparison Matrix: Business Risk

	Alternative A	Alternative B	Alternative C	Rows Total (Weights; % of Grand Total)
Alternative A		1/5	1	1.2 (.097)
Alternative B	5		5	10 (.806)
Alternative C	1	1/5		1.2 (.097)
Column Total	6	.4	6	12.4 (1.000)

1/10 = Much less impact

1/5 = Less impact

1 = Equal impact

5 = More impact

10 = Much more impact

TABLE 8.17
Solution Alternatives Versus Each Criterion Comparison Matrix: Competitive Advantage

	Alternative A	Alternative B	Alternative C	Rows Total (Weights; % of Grand Total)
Alternative A		1/10	1/5	.3 (.014)
Alternative B	10		5	15 (.732)
Alternative C	5	1/5		5.2 (.254)
Column Total	15	.3	5.2	20.5 (1.000)

1/10 = Much less impact

1/5 = Less impact

1 = Equal impact

5 = More impact

10 = Much more impact

Step 5: Compare All the Alternative Solutions Based on All Criteria Combined

This is the summary matrix and is prepared by using an L-shaped matrix (see Table 8.18). All the alternative solutions are listed on the vertical side of the matrix. All the criteria considered previously (see Tables 8.16 and 8.17) are listed on the horizontal side. All the percentage scores for the two criteria are recorded as shown. All these scores are multiplied by the weighted score of each criterion in Table 8.15.

TABLE 8.18
Summary Matrix Table: Alternative Solutions Versus All Criteria

Alternative	Business Risk (.379)	Competitive Advantage (.379)	Rows Total (Weights; % of Grand Total)
Alternative A	.097 × .379 = .037	.014 × .379 = .005	.042 (.055)
Alternative B	.806 × .379 = .305	.732 × .379 = .277	.582 (.769)
Alternative C	.097 × .379 = .037	.254 × .379 = .096	.133 (.176)
Column Total	.379	.378	.757 (1.000)

The totals of rows and columns are calculated, as are the weights. This provides the following ranking:

Rank 1: Alternative B

Rank 2: Alternative C

Rank 3: Alternative A

The most preferable alternative overall is alternative B. For this simple example, the ranking results from Brassard's Full Analytical Criteria Method are the same as from the AHP deployments presented earlier in the chapter. As you can see from Table 8.19, alternative B has a much higher relative priority ranking using Brassard's Full Analytical Criteria Method than from Approximate Solution Method 1 and from Expert Choice, both of which are pretty close. As a manual calculation, Method 1 provides a solution that is much closer to the one obtained from Expert Choice than the one obtained from Brassard's Method. For accuracy of results, additional analytical features, and sheer convenience of use, we emphasize Expert Choice.

TABLE 8.19
Comparison of Priorities from AHP Exact, AHP Approximate, and Brassard's Method

Alternative	Exact Priorities from Expert Choice Software (Ideal Mode)	Priority Ranking from Approximate Calculations (Method 1)	Priority Ranking from Approximate Calculations (Brassard's Method)
Alternative A	.090	.091	.055
Alternative B	.501	.513	.769
Alternative C	.409	.396	.176

Conclusion

The three sample solutions used a three-level hierarchy. This example can easily be extended to software quality models involving many more levels and numerous decision-makers.

In an enterprise software context, in addition to its usefulness as a decision tool, AHP can also be deployed as part of an overall complexity management strategy involving both complexity reduction and enabling the right design choices to address those complexities. AHP can be powerful in both these aspects. We believe that AHP, along with accompanying software such as Expert Choice, can be used throughout the enterprise software development process as a decision-support tool. AHP applications are well documented.[2, 19, 20, 21] Chapter 23 describes how AHP is used to determine an optimum portfolio of IT projects using the resource aligner extension to Expert Choice.

Key Points

- Prioritization matrices have limitations in dealing with complexities associated with multicriteria decision problems. This can be obviated by using the Analytic Hierarchy Process (AHP).

- AHP and its supporting software, Expert Choice (EC), can handle much higher levels of complexity and have applications as a multiobjective decision technique involving both qualitative and quantitative factors. It has important applications in the software development process, including Quality Function Deployment, presented in Chapter 11. AHP uses ratio scale measures that can be used to rank alternatives and for optimal allocation of resources.

- AHP can be used for decision-making in various phases of the software development process involving multiple objectives. It can be especially applicable in the evaluation of complex system designs involving software, hardware, and humanware that can include hundreds of system quality indicators. AHP can also be used to measure and manage complexity in large software development projects.

- This chapter illustrated prioritization of alternatives in a multiobjective decision situation using AHP. It discussed the limitations of the two manual solutions and emphasized Expert Choice software as a powerful tool in AHP deployment.

- Chapter 23 describes how AHP is used in determining an optimum portfolio of IT projects using the resource aligner extension to Expert Choice.

Additional Resources

http://www.prenhallprofessional.com/title/0131872508

http://www.agilenty.com/publications

Internet Exercises

1. Read the following Web sites, which describe Expert Choice applications in IT portfolio management and new-product development. Come to class prepared to describe the two applications and their merits.

   http://www.expertchoice.com/epfa/default.htm
   http://www.expertchoice.com/npd/default.htm

2. Read the article "Application of the Analytic Hierarchy Process to Complex System Design Evaluation" on the following Web site. Present a summary of it to the class.

   http://eprints.cs.vt.edu:8000/archive/00000399/

Review Questions

1. Explain what is meant by the hierarchy of software quality characteristics. What is the practical implication of such a hierarchical structure?

2. What challenges are associated with software complexity? Describe a strategy to address them.

3. Explain how focusing on objectives improves the quality of decision-making. What is the significance of pairwise comparison?

4. Describe how a multiobjective decision problem is structured in AHP.

Discussion Questions and Projects

1. Describe AHP as a multiobjective decision-making methodology in a software development context. What are its merits vis-à-vis traditional decision-making approaches?

2. The spectrum of complexity in software has two poles or extremes, as shown in the following figure. The left side of the figure shows high complexity due to fewer but multifunction or multioutput components. The right side shows high complexity due to too many single-function or single-output components. Experience and the limited use of Taguchi Methods to date (see the Kanchana example in Chapter 17) indicates that complexity in an enterprise software application may lie somewhere between these extremes, as shown by the catenary curve between the two poles or complexity extremes.

In software, complexity is proportional to the sum of the power of the number of outputs each component has. It is also proportional to some power of the number of components making up the application. Thus, at design time a trade-off must be made between these implementation alternatives. For example, in the C language, it is most convenient to program in single-output functions, which produces a huge number of small, hierarchically organized single-output modules. In C++ or Java, it is more convenient to program in small or large hierarchically organized classes, which may have multiple outputs. As an example of inherent or intrinsic complexity for these two extremes, consider a jigsaw puzzle that has only 100 pieces but no picture to guide assembly. Compare this to the external or extrinsic complexity of a jigsaw puzzle with 1,000 pieces that comes with a picture of what it will look like when assembled. Describe a possible decision or design procedure to find the "golden mean" between these extremes shown by the dip in the curve. Describe one or more systems in your experience that show type A complexity (such as IBM's SanFrancisco middleware) or type B complexity (such as Microsoft COM+ middleware). Can you summarize your consideration of this issue by a single "rule of thumb" that tends to reduce complexity to a minimum for any given enterprise application?

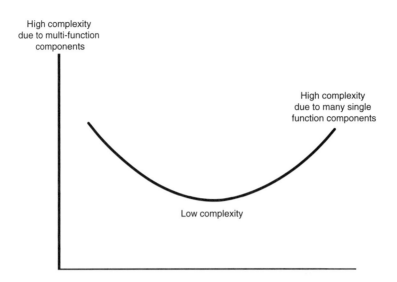

Problems

Problem 1: Managing Complexity in System Conversion

A major research university began preparing for Y2K in 1991. Y2K became an issue in 1996 in higher education due to the need to enroll the class of 2000 and prepare their student loans. The university's long-term goal was to develop a new Y2K-compliant client/server enterprise administrative application suite sharing a common base of data. The new system would serve several thousand PC-based clients and several thousand Mac-based clients. It would include applications such as purchasing that hitherto had eluded automation. Unfortunately, in the early '90s no software vendor could supply software to handle a research university with 24,000 students. The existing student registration and enrollment systems were no longer supported by their vendors, which had been merged into larger companies. The research university market in the United States amounts to perhaps 50 to 75 institutions. It has not been pursued as a viable market by software firms, which target smaller, nonresearch institutions with enrollments of 1,500 to 6,000 students.

The university's choices were as follows, in order of developmental complexity:

- Reverse-engineer all mainframe applications using Texas Instruments TEF and make them Y2K-compliant by "windowing." In other words, let xx = 19xx if xx>50 and 20xx if xx<50. Make code fixes at the flowchart level without changing the individual application databases. This is a labor-intensive but "quick and dirty" solution and is the least complex.

- Replace all mainframe applications with new client/server applications having a common base of data, using third-party software firms. Exclude the critical non-Y2K-compliant (and highly customized) student registration and student finance systems, which are unavailable from third-party vendors for a university with an enrollment of more than 20,000 students. These applications will be reengineered by consultant contract programmers using Xcellerator four-digit year dates incorporated using COBOL filler columns in their individual databases. The code will be redocumented and reimplemented to use these noncontiguous four-digit year dates.

- Replace all mainframe applications with Y2K-compliant client/server applications. Contract for new student systems with a vendor willing to develop or enhance smaller applications at the required scale to meet the university's enrollment. Two vendors made offers to do so, but neither had actually produced systems like these at the required scale. (Complexity prevents many enterprise software applications from being scaled up by a factor of 2 or more.)

The following table summarizes the factors involved in this decision. The first choice was a low-cost but labor-intensive approach that would further customize mainframe applications that are no longer supported by their vendors. Although this could be done between 1992 and 1996 using advanced COBOL software reengineering tools, it would do absolutely nothing for the longer-term goal of achieving a new client/server system with a single base of data. In this case the goal would be reduced to meeting only the near-term necessity of being Y2K-compliant by 1996.

The second choice was to install a completely new suite of client/server apps from one or more vendors all using the same relational database system. The most flexibility was obtained by choosing Oracle as the RDBMS (relational database) because it has 70% market share in this market. Because software at the proper scale was not available for student registration and finance, those applications would be reverse-engineered as Y2K-compliant client/server apps until they could be replaced with commercially available software when it became available.

The third choice would require trusting a vendor that had never built a registration system that could handle 24,000 students. One vendor was testing a system that could handle 11,000 students, and the other had never produced such a system. Both eagerly sought a contract with the university. The CIO thought this approach was too risky. The former system appeared to be unable to scale by a factor of more than 2, and the second firm had no experience in this application area. Hindsight later justified these considerations. The latter firm later secured a contract to build a student registration system for a research university having an enrollment of 56,000 students, but it failed.

Option	Capital Cost	Labor Cost	Technical Risk	Business Risk	Time to Implement
A: Retread mainframe apps	Low	High	Medium	High	Very high
B: Replace partially	Medium	Medium	Low	Low	Medium
C: Replace completely	High	Medium	Very high	High	High

Sometimes it's easier to cross a brook in two steps by using a stepping-stone in the middle than to make a great leap and risk falling into the water. The CIO, MIS director, and system development director recommended and implemented Option B and successfully completed the new system on time and within budget. Did they make the best decision? Examine the results for sensitivity. Could the risk of a complete replacement solution have somehow been managed?

Problem 2: Managing Software Complexity in a High-Tech Start-up Enterprise

In 1990 a technology transfer program was set up under a NASA contract at a small university to make technology developed at 1,200 national laboratories available to American business entrepreneurs. The goal of this system was to allow the vice president of technology or chief technologist of a small, high-tech American company to e-mail a query to the technology transfer center. The reformatted query would be forwarded to the appropriate national lab technology transfer databases. The center would return a suitable response and licensing information as a package. The query engine employed a technical thesaurus of 5,000 terms and an ancillary fuzzy logic processor with 30,000 terms. The CIO of the start-up center was faced with the following choices, in order of complexity:

- Use conventional RDBMS technology to access the laboratory databases (which were running Oracle, anyway), and then use fax, e-mail, FedEx, and so on to convey unstructured data. This choice was low-tech, clunky, and highly manual.

- Purchase a high-performance, novel, fully featured (but unproven) object-oriented database system (OODBMS) from a high-tech start-up firm. Implement the entire technology transfer system as truly state-of-the-art technology. It would return to the user a package of objects and unstructured data types, including patents, test data, reports, photographs, film clips, revisions, and updates.

- Choose a multiapplication approach with a fit of the best *proven* technology in available library and RDBMS software packages for each aspect of the application. Stitch them together to make the overall system as automatic and electronic as possible, essentially emulating OODBMS technology.

The following table summarizes the options considered by the developers. The first choice was considered the easiest means of getting a national technology transfer system operating as soon as possible. The system would essentially be manual in that it required making hard copies of documents and sending them to potential users using traditional media transfer methods. The start-up process would be short. However, there was a great danger that if it was successful, the system probably would not be able to handle the expected volume, and costs would increase disproportionately.

The second choice, which the CIO chose, was to employ novel but untested object-oriented database management technology to develop an ideal system that could obtain multimedia files from the national laboratories and package them as unstructured data objects for electronic transmission. The primary risk was that the OODBMS product would not come to market. Or, even if it did, the vendor would fail, or the product would not perform well. In fact, all three happened a few months into development, forcing the third option to be used.

The third choice was to emulate OODBMS technology by a more-or-less compatible suite of proven but older technology products. All the development team's programming skills would then be employed in stitching together these tools around an object-oriented front end that dealt with the remote user by furnishing unstructured data objects in the reply to the original query.

Option	Capital Cost	Labor Cost	Technical Risk	Business Risk	Competitive Advantage	Time to Implement
A: RDBMS technology	Medium	Medium	Low	Low	Low	Low
B: OODBMS technology	Medium	High	Medium	Medium	Medium	Medium
C: OODBMS emulation	Medium	Low	High	High	High	Low

The CIO of this start-up activity chose Option B but was forced to retreat to Option C when the novel OODBMS could not meet the required performance goals. The new software was plagued by internal complexity issues and turned out to be a bit beyond state of the art. Run an analysis with this data, and rank for yourself the complexity of the three options in terms of combined technical risk and business risk. If the passage of 25 years has managed to lower technical risk to medium and business risk to low for Option B, would Option B now be viable—that is, *significantly* less complex than it was?

Problem 3: Complexity in Patient Record Systems

So far, the complexity of medical patient record (PR) systems has eluded electronic automation. Such systems are an unsolved problem given today's medical and computer technology. A complex patient record in a large medical center may contain manually completed forms, computer forms, medical test results, handwritten notes, referral letters, photographs, X-rays, CAT scans, MRI scans, PET scans, EKGs, and EEGs, and may be 5 inches thick! A major medical research center at a large state university won a grant to use OODBMS technology to package this amalgam of unstructured data types and their revisions into a 100% machineable (electronically packaged and transmitted) object. The goal was clear, but it was deemed very high-risk. However, a useable system *was* required at the end of the project. The project investigated three options, in perceived order of complexity:

- Index electronically the physical file of multimedia documents and transmit only a highly abstracted index electronically. The physical documents would be forwarded manually as needed to support medical decisions. This approach was low-tech and *very* clunky, but it was much better than the existing PR system.

- Develop an OODBMS-based PR system from scratch, optimized for medical records and the developing medical center. This was high-tech but very high-risk at the time (and probably still would be today!).

- Choose hybrid relational/object technology such as the then newly announced Informix Datablade™ technology.

The following table summarizes the salient factors among these choices. The first choice would be a very low-risk approach to get something working that would provide some improvement. But it would not honor the grant's intent—to truly automate a patient record system. It was considered not as a realistic choice but as a baseline for risk, cost, and time to implement.

The second option was the ideal or the goal of choice but was a truly pioneering effort. The significant risk of failure as a research project alone would alienate the medical staff, who would not be content with a negative or vacuous result. The team had to produce *something* useful! Note that they could design to this goal and back off if complexity or lack of suitable technology rendered it infeasible.

The third option, although it was considered seriously from the beginning, was rejected as not being the stretch objective that the granting agency expected. Fortunately, it was carefully evaluated and well understood, because the development team was forced to default to it in the end.

Option	Development Cost	Capital Cost	Technical Risk	Business Risk	Competitive Advantage	Time to Implement
A: Index manually	Low	Low	Low	Low	Low	Low
B: OODBMS	High	Low	High	High	High	High
C: Relational/ object	Medium	High	Medium	Low	Low	Medium

Rank the true complexity of these options by performing an analysis and choosing one or more indicators of complexity in your formula.

The center chose to attempt Option B to honor the grant's intent. It included 25 NeXT workstations on a peer-to-peer network. The project was unsuccessful, primarily because of the medical staff's inability to agree on the system's functional requirements. Although this may be termed organizational complexity rather than software complexity, it was certainly a major design factor. The system developers fell back to Option C to get something working in the grant period. However, Option C lacked competitive advantage, because it could not be licensed to other medical centers or third-party vendors. From the sensitivity analysis chart, estimate what the Option B factors would have to become to make this project viable. (Assume that you could somehow convince the physicians to agree on a functional specification.)

Problem 4: Oil Well Drilling Decision System

Drilling for oil is a high-risk endeavor. Each well costs at least $10 million to drill, but on average only 35% of the information available is used to make a drilling decision. Oil well database persistence may be a worst case in the computer field. Some of the historical data that needs to be kept may go back 150 years to Indian treaties, letters patent, legal titles, geological data and reports, geological tomography, and test drill logs. In addition, any new drilling data must be kept for 50 years. Petroleum prospectors agree that drilling decisions would be very well-informed if 85% of the available data was used. However, the data is not readily accessible because it is in many different forms (media) at many different locations. A major U.S. petroleum company with significant computer resources undertook a research study with the goal of developing a drilling decision system using the latest available software technology at the time. It would attempt to include as much of the multimedia data as available. The options considered were as follows:

- Build a sophisticated worldwide index to all available data, based on both location and similarity to other data sets and their drilling results. Abstract the data for later electronic transmission, irretrievability, and analysis, but leave it where it is until it's needed for the drilling decision process for a new well.

- Build an OODBMS that can incorporate all unstructured multimedia data as objects so that the drilling decision team has all the data available to make a fully informed decision.

- Build a relational system that automates as much of the machineable data as possible but merely indexes the data elements that are not readily machineable to electronic form.

The factors employed in making this decision are summarized in the following table. The first choice was to simply automate only the index of data available and use it to retrieve data manually in either hard copy or electronic form at the time it was needed to make a drilling decision. Although this approach offered some improvement over the current state, it did not represent a suitable goal for a research project and would not have had a significant return on investment (ROI).

The second choice was truly a stretch objective given the state of software technology at the time. The Norwegian Research Defense Establishment had invented object-oriented technology in the form of Simula™ to manage Norway's forest reserves in the 1960s. Simula and other similar packages were not equipped to handle the kind of multimedia data sets involved in petroleum exploration. Still, if this project could be carried to success, the competitive advantage it would give the company would be incalculable.

The third choice was to push relational database management technology to the limit in spite of its inability at that time to handle complex and unstructured data types and to do revisions rather than just data set updates. The team knew it could be done and would be a major improvement, but would it be good enough?

Option	Development Cost	Technical Risk	Business Risk	Competitive Advantage	Estimated Complexity	Time to Implement
A: Index	Low	Low	Low	40%	1	Low
B: OODBMS	High	High	High	85%	9	High
C: RDBMS	Medium	Medium	Medium	55%	5	High

The team chose Option C but did not go into implementation because the ROI for such a system was not convincing to senior management. Which decision do you think was best then? How about today?

Problem 5: The ROI Issue

Note that the analysis in Problem 4 did not include an estimate of financial payback for the effort because there was so little experience with drilling decisions made with better information. What column(s) would you add to this table to be able to estimate the payback for each option? How sensitive is each analysis to the abstract estimate of system complexity in column 6?

Problem 6: An Abstract Complexity Analysis

Consider the perspective on complexity presented in Problem 2. Assume that a certain enterprise application could be built with three levels of modularity, as summarized in the following table. Option A uses relatively few large components, each of which is of rather high complexity. Option B uses five times as many smaller and much less complex components but involves a slightly higher degree of technical risk and more testing. Option C uses many small and simple or "atomic" components but has high extrinsic complexity due to the intercomponent communication required.

Option	Module Size	Number Required	Relative Complexity	Technical Risk	Testing Effort	Time to Implement
A: Subsystem functionality	Large	30	7	Low	Low	Low
B: Business functions	Medium	170	4	Medium	Medium	Medium
C: Atomic functions	Small	2500	9	High	High	Medium

Which is the preferred implementation strategy? Why? (Note that time to implement may be dramatically reduced in high-granularity or atomic module systems by a sophisticated proprietary development environment such as JD Edwards OneWorld™.)

Problem 7: Sensitivity to Complexity

How sensitive is the analysis of Problem 6 to the estimated complexity? Are the decision choices or implementation options well-differentiated by the estimate of relative complexity? Are they equally well-differentiated by the number of modules needed to complete an application? Why does having more modules in an application require more testing time?

Endnotes

[1]T. L. Saaty, "Rank Generation, Preservation, and Reversal in the Analytic Hierarchy Decision Process," *Decision Sciences*, Vol. 18, 1987, pp. 157–177.

[2]http://eprints.cs.vt.edu:8000/archive/00000399/.

[3]B. W. Boehm, "Quantitative Evaluation of Software Quality," Proceedings of ICSE 2 (1976): 592–605.

[4]B. Littlewood and L. Strigini, "Software Reliability and Dependability: A Roadmap," Proceedings of ICSE 2000, the 22nd International Conference on Software Engineering, p. 2.

[5]http://www.gartner.com/DisplayDocument?doc_cd=116455. Gartner's Refined Hierarchical Analysis method is considered a proven best practice for making technology acquisition choices that fit an enterprise's long-term needs, as well as its immediate requirements.

[6]Expert Choice tutorial material at http://www.expertchoice.com.

[7]Op cit Saaty, p. 157.

[8]R. Fisher and W. Ury, *Getting to YES* (Penguin Books, 1983).

[9]Op cit Saaty, p. 159.

[10]D. R. Anderson, D. J. Sweeny, T. A. Williams, *Quantitative Methods for Business*, 6th Ed. (St. Paul: West Publishing Company, 1995), p. 814.

[11]T. L. Saaty, *The Analytic Hierarchy Process: Planning, Priority Setting, Resource Allocation* (New York: McGraw-Hill, 1980), pp. 165–197.

[12]T. L. Saaty, "How to Make a Decision: The Analytic Hierarchy Process," *Interfaces*, Vol. 24, No. 6, 1994, pp. 19–43. This article is also available on http://sigma.poligran. edu.co/politecnico/apoyo/Decisiones/curso/Interfaces.pdf.

[13]http://www.expertchoice.com/customerservice/faqs.htm#Possible_differences_in_ priorities_of_the_alternatives_in_the_model_view_and_the_data_grid.

[14]Op cit Anderson, et. al, p. 816.

[15]Op cit Saaty 1, p. 160.

[16]Op cit Anderson, et al., p. 817.

[17]M. Brassard, *The Memory Jogger Plus+* (Methuen, MA: Goal/QPC, 1989), pp. 103–116.

[18]Ibid, p. 111.

[19]T. L. Saaty, *Decision Making for Leaders* (Pittsburg: RWS Publications, 1990).

[20]http://www.expertchoice.com.

[21]E. Forman and M. A. Selly, *Decision by Objectives* (Singapore: World Scientific Publications, 2001), pp. 43–126.

CHAPTER 9

Complexity, Mistakes, and Poka Yoke in Software Development Processes

Defects = 0 is absolutely possible.
—Shigeo Shingo

Management is often so focused on finding solutions
that it fails to define the problems.
—Watts S. Humphrey

Overview

Poka yoke, a Japanese term that means mistake-proofing or fail-safing, recognizes that human errors are unavoidable but do not necessarily have to result in defects. It employs a set of proactive measures, particularly a 100% inspection at the source, to detect process errors before they cause defects. The emphasis is on prevention and quality measures at the source. This includes stopping the process upon detection of process errors that may cause defects downstream. The process is restarted only after the cause has been identified and eliminated. This relatively simple system can have a huge impact on software cost, quality, and development time. The five principles of effective poka yoke deployment are *100% inspection at the source, appropriate upstream control measures, rapid implementation, people focus and teamwork,* and *problem-solving approach*. Poka yoke should not be approached as a panacea for proofing all kinds of mistakes. It may be more suitable in certain situations than others.

Trustworthy software must be robust vis-à-vis the following three causes of defects: variations, mistakes, and, above all, complexity. The strategies for eliminating defects caused by these three are distinctly different: *statistical methods, poka yoke*, and *reduction of product and process complexity at design stages*, respectively. As process capability improves, mistakes play an increasingly crucial role in determining product quality. Furthermore, the collective impact of these mistakes, commonly prevalent in complex systems, can be potentially catastrophic. However, complexity is the "mother of all defects" and must be addressed before a poka yoke deployment. Poka yoke involves 100% inspection; the other two types of inspections, judgment and informative, especially judgment, are less effective in reducing defect rates.

The chapter establishes the link between complexity reduction, and variations and mistakes. It makes a case for controlling complexity as a crucial first step to eliminate the causes of potential mistakes substantially before mistake-proofing (poka yoke) is deployed. It identifies a practical measure of complexity and provides a framework for controlling product and process complexity in a software context. Finally, it presents a poka yoke system as a cost-effective quality control system to reduce defects further as part of a DFTS deployment.

Chapter Outline

- Poka Yoke as a Quality Control System
- Principles of Poka Yoke
- Causes of Defects: Variation, Mistakes, and Complexities
- Situations in Which Poka Yoke Works Well
- Mistakes as Causes of Defects
- Controlling Complexity in Software Development
- Mistakes, Inspection Methods, and Poka Yoke

- Deploying a Poka Yoke System
- Identifying a Poka Yoke Solution
- Key Points
- Additional Resources
- Internet Exercises
- Review Questions
- Discussion Questions and Projects
- Endnotes

Poka Yoke as a Quality Control System

Poka yoke, a Japanese term that means mistake-proofing or fail-safing, is a vital element of an effective process quality control (QC) system. Poka yoke is also called Zero (Defect) Quality Control (ZQC). It recognizes that human errors are unavoidable but do not necessarily have to result in defects. It was pioneered by a Japanese quality exponent and a key developer of the Toyota Production System, Shigeo Shingo. It employs a set of proactive measures, particularly a 100% inspection at the source to detect process errors before they cause defects. Shingo made one crucial distinction between a mistake and a defect. Mistakes are inevitable. People are human and make mistakes by failing to concentrate all the time, or by not completely understanding the instructions they are given, or by not following their instructions all the time without fail. Defects result from failure to prevent a mistake from reaching the customer; therefore, defects are entirely avoidable. The goal of poka yoke is to design the process so that mistakes can be prevented or immediately detected and corrected so that the customer does not receive a defective product even if mistakes have occurred.

The emphasis is on prevention and quality measures at the source. This includes stopping the process upon detection of process errors that may cause defects downstream. The process is restarted only after the cause has been identified and eliminated. The detection and elimination of errors can be either manual or automated. Empowered process workers can proactively detect process errors and initiate appropriate corrective measures. Or the error elimination can take place automatically upon detection of product or process deviation.

This chapter presents two powerful approaches to delivering defect-free software as part of a DFTS deployment: *controlling complexity* and *mistake-proofing (poka yoke)*. We have argued that mistakes are a major source of defects that requires even more attention than Statistical Quality Control (SQC), especially in a software development context. We will discuss how complexity reduction and mistake-proofing are linked and how controlling complexity is a smart way to eliminate the causes of potential mistakes substantially before a poka yoke deployment. Although poka yoke is a simple concept, it requires considerable discipline and competence across the process supply chain, involving not only the software development firm but also outsourcing firms and customers. In the absence of effective coordination with various partners, it will not only fail to deliver, but it also may cause unnecessary delays and bottlenecks. On the other hand, when managed properly, this relatively simple system can have a huge impact on software cost, quality, and development time.

Principles of Poka Yoke

Poka yoke emphasizes 100% inspections upstream for possible causes of defects, as well as rapid feedback and follow-up actions. This implies corresponding de-emphasis on expensive downstream inspection and Statistical Quality Control (SQC), which can be reduced dramatically or eliminated in many cases. Generally the "freedom from the spell of statistics" entails a more objective use of statistics. Poka yoke differs from SQC philosophically in that it does not accept the passive inevitability of defects. "Every defect that shows up is preceded by an earlier phenomenon—the error that was the cause of the defect." This is what led Shingo to arrive at the idea of zero (defect) QC methods.[1]

In an enterprise software development context, poka yoke is particularly pertinent for two broad reasons. First, SQC is difficult to apply given the low volume of statistical data compared to a mass-manufacturing environment. Second, external failure costs may far exceed internal failure costs. Poka yoke aims to correct the process rather than the product. Traditionally, poka yoke relies on inexpensive in-process quality control methods. It's closely related to the concept of *jidoka*, or autonomation—the low-cost "intelligent machines" that stop automatically when they detect an error. Error detection is followed by feedback and corrective action at the source to eliminate the error's cause and isolate its potential impact downstream. Effective implementation of poka yoke involves the following five principles:[1, 2]

- **100% inspection at the source:** Shingo argued that making inadvertent mistakes is only human and therefore is unavoidable. But what *can* be avoided are the product nonconformities that result from inadvertent mistakes. He propounded a fundamental concept in quality management: *Poka yoke, when supported by 100% inspection at the source, can, in effect, detect every mistake.* This concept is discussed in more detail later in this chapter.

- **Appropriate upstream control measures:** The monitoring, feedback, and corrective devices should be as close as possible to the source of the potential defect. Poka yoke control measures should be in relation to the degree of the problem's severity. Simplicity of measures is emphasized because they are easily developed and made available. Poka yoke also entails cost-effectiveness and lack of complexity. (Complexity is a major source of defects by itself.) Simple, economical, and adequate controls work best. In an enterprise software development context, appropriate control systems consist of simple checklists, error flags, prompts, self-check of programmed inputs, successive checks, data hiding, and protecting methods. Many measures comprise elements that should be deployed anyway. Poka yoke, therefore, often involves doing things right rather than doing something new or innovative.

- **Rapid implementation:** Many effective ideas can be implemented within hours of a problem's occurrence. Overanalyzing to find the perfect solution may not be the best resort. A better solution can, of course, be developed in due course.

- **People focus and teamwork:** Enterprise software development is a highly human-intrinsic and collaborative process. As such, quality software can be developed only by nurturing discipline, team spirit, and a sense of shared pride. It is important to involve software developers in identifying solutions and taking ownership of results. Issues related to developing a superior workplace environment are discussed in Chapter 10. Chapter 20 covers the need for teamwork and organizational preparedness.

- **Problem-solving approach:** Poka yoke is implemented by asking a series of questions—"5 Ws and 1 H." Ask "Why did the defect occur?" five times, followed by "How do we fix it?" This is a commonsense problem-solving approach to poka yoke deployment.

Causes of Defects: Variation, Mistakes, and Complexities

Numerous factors cause defects and determine product quality. Hinckley discusses a study to determine which elements of design have the greatest influence on product quality.[3] The study showed that defect rates were strongly linked to assembly time and the number of assembly operations over a wide range of industries. This led to the conclusion that the major source of defects could not be variation, the primary focus of quality improvement initiatives. Some 60 to 90% of all defects are created in production—and a similar percentage of defects escape to customers due to mistakes, either human or technological (mechanical) in origin.[4]

An often-overlooked reality is that a large number of organizations relying merely on variation-focused initiatives such as Six Sigma will fail to achieve the Six Sigma quality level unless they also find effective ways to address mistakes and complexities, the "mother of all defects." When seeking an extremely low rate of nonconformities, it is essential to eliminate mistakes in addition to controlling variation. Mistakes become even more crucial as organizations strive to achieve defects (nonconformities) lower than 1,000 defects per million opportunities (DPMO), which corresponds to 4.59σ. Both Six Sigma and Statistical Quality Control (SQC) are variation-focused and as such do not address mistake prevention—a major, if not the major, source of defects in most processes that have already attained high level of capability. Mistakes are discrete and probabilistic compared to variations, which are random. They cannot be measured by distribution models that describe process variation. Part-to-part variations in component properties and dimensions have been historically conceived as the major cause of defects. Consequently, SQC has been promoted as an adequate and absolute quality control system. The grounds for SQC's inherent limitations as a guide to quality control are well documented and can be summarized as follows:[5]

- Small sample sizes often fail to detect defects.

- A small number of readings obscures the skew of distribution.

- "Oddball" and "outlier" observations are often discarded.

- Traditional inspection methods are not perfectly reliable.

- Assumed distribution models may be invalid. (They may ignore the Pareto principle and the probability and impacts of the extremely rare—the "vital few.")

- SPC cannot deliver the highest levels of quality (lower than 50 DPMO, which corresponds to 5.39σ) by itself.

- Because the control mechanisms are downstream, many defects may still occur.

Both Juran and Gryna[6] and Hinckley and Barkan[7] state the inadequacy of the normal distribution. A Hinckley and Barkan study reveals that significant errors do occur in assessing the extreme limits of the (normal) distribution. As such, the normal distribution is of little help in predicting distributions 3σ beyond the mean.[7] SQC has yet another limitation when applied to software development: the volume of data may often be small for any meaningful statistical analysis. As such, Six Sigma, Taguchi Methods, and other statistics-based methodologies must be supplemented. This helps with not only monitoring, control, and elimination of defects caused by variation, but also mistakes and complexities in manufacturing and, even more so, in software development. To summarize, trustworthy software must be robust vis-à-vis all three causes of defects:

- **Variation:** Statistical methods are commonly used to measure variations. These are discussed in Chapters 6 and 15. But as Hinckley and Barkan have stated, understanding rare events (particularly those beyond the three standard deviations from the mean) and the limitations of conventional statistical methods is particularly important when the goal is to achieve extremely low nonconformity (below 10 DPMO, which corresponds to 5.76σ).[8] Variation-based defects (nonconformities) are discussed in Chapters 15 through 19. We will not discuss this topic in any depth in this chapter. Instead, we will focus on mistakes and complexity.

- **Mistakes** are one of the most common causes of defects in software development. In terms of severity, their impact is second only to defects caused by complexity. Mistakes are different from variations in that they are not characterized by the physical properties or dimensions of any attribute. They are conditions of being in one state or another. Mistakes and mistake-proofing (poka yoke) are discussed later in the book.

- **Complexity** is a major source of all kinds of defects, including variation- and mistake-based. The more complex a product, service, software, or system, the more opportunities it has for mistake and variation nonconformities. Complexity thus is the root cause of many nonconformities attributed to mistakes and variations. In a DFTS context, reducing both product- and process-related complexities should be an essential element of an overall defect-reduction strategy.

One important issue that comes out of the work of Hinckley and Barkan is identifying the tools that describe and manage these distinct sources of nonconformities. Variation is managed with SPC and statistics. Mistakes are tackled using poka yoke. Complexity is controlled during the design process.[8]

Even processes with high process capability need poka yoke. Human errors, although dependent on complexity, are independent of variance-based nonconformities. Where software nonfunction can be catastrophic, poka yoke is an indispensable tool. This chapter discusses mistakes and complexities; variation is presented in Chapter 15. We first discuss poka yoke systems, beginning with where poka yoke can be used effectively as a mistake-proofing system.

Situations in Which Poka Yoke Works Well

Poka yoke should not be approached as a panacea for all kinds of mistakes. It is important to understand that poka yoke may be more suitable in certain situations than others. Grout provides guidelines for situations where it works well and where it does not (see Table 9.1).[9]

Poka yoke can be very effective in software development processes. Its applicability is supported by the various considerations listed in Table 9.1. People affected by the process must be involved in designing a poka yoke system. Such systems should be simple and free of complexity (itself a cause of defects). Simple, commonsense tools work best. But poka yoke is not rocket science, nor is it a silver bullet, so it should not be approached as such.

TABLE 9.1
Applicability of Poka Yoke

Works Well	Does Not Work Well
In manual operations where worker vigilance is needed	Where destructive tests are used
Where mispositioning can occur	Where the production rate is very rapid
Where adjustment is required	Where shifts occur more rapidly than they can be responded to
Where teams need commonsense tools and not another buzzword	Where control charts are used effectively for successive and self-checks only
Where SQC is difficult to apply or apparently ineffective	
Where attributes, not measurements, are important	
Where training costs and employee turnover are high	
Where mixed-model production occurs	
Where customers make mistakes and blame the service provider	
Where special causes can reoccur	
Where external failure costs dramatically exceed internal failure costs	
Where product nonfunction can be catastrophic	

Mistakes as Causes of Defects

Hinckley and Barkan define a mistake as the execution of a prohibited action, or failure to perform a required action, or the misrepresentation of information essential for the correct execution of an action.[10] Rare mistakes do occur, even in high-capability processes. The fact that mistakes are rare in many processes means that traditional sampling and statistical methods are not useful in estimating their frequency:

> Mistakes can only be described effectively in terms of probability, which is the only universal means to describe both mistakes and variability.[11]

How critical are mistakes in determining quality of complex products such as enterprise software? The simple answer is: to a very large extent. Harris and Chaney have concluded that 80% of the nonconformities in complex systems can be attributed to mistakes.[12] Hinckley and Barkan have shown that mistakes can be effectively described only in terms of probability:

> Mistakes either occur or they do not. Further, as every distribution describing variation can be converted to probabilities, consequently, the only universal method of describing both variation and mistake is probability.[13]

In a software context, the causes of defects can be broadly classified as follows:

- **Wrong design:** This is the most serious error in software. It is a consequence of the software designer's not understanding the user's functional needs and the user's not understanding the technology and what it can and cannot do. This is a "language translation" problem, because the user as a domain expert speaks one "language," and the programmer as a computer expert speaks another. One of the solutions is to have two project leaders for each application development—one from the programming staff and one from the user staff. The system architect then serves as the conflict revolver between the two. QFD methodology can be extremely useful in capturing the voice of the users and other customers, internal as well as external. The DFTS process supports this methodology (see Chapter 11).

- **Wrong process/operation:** In program development, this can occur when the application is "out of scale" with either the computer intended for it, the programming language chosen to write it in, the operating system used, or the experience of the development staff.

- **Inadequate process/operation:** This is the most common error in programmed business applications. It usually occurs when the programmers do not fully understand the users' (implicit or unstated) requirements. The user expects an operation to do several things at once (which is logical to him or her as an accountant or supply chain expert) but fails to convey this to the programmer.

- **Skipping a process/operation:** This may happen in complex software and may produce mysterious results. It is a result of the programmer's not anticipating unusual or unexpected hardware situations, such as dividing by 0. So-called "bulletproof" programs employ many lines of code to predict and handle situations that may occur very rarely but can cause a great deal of trouble when they do. Protective codes or error handlers take a lot of human design and coding time and some program storage. But they cost very little in machine cycles because they, like the situations they handle, almost never happen.

- **Using the wrong software algorithms or components:** This happens in business applications when the wrong library routine is used to do a tax calculation, for example. In the case of NASA's Mars lander, a program used English units instead of metric units, causing the lander to crash into Mars instead of landing softly on it.

- **Lack of software component synchronization:** This happens in software when a library routine reads a file that has not yet been written and gets an error. Or perhaps file reads are not synchronized with writes, so a file is read before it has been rewritten, and the seeking program gets old data rather than current data.

- **Failing to properly initialize a software algorithm or component:** This is common in programming. It may occur, for example, as a result of failure to initialize a program algorithm or method so that, rather than beginning a sum with 0, it begins with some unknown leftover value. Modern programming languages try to protect the programmer from such errors, but they still occur, sometimes when the initialized variable is set to the wrong value. This is comparable to a bolt in a mechanical assembly being torqued to the wrong value, leaving it too loose or too tight and thus producing a failure.

Trustworthy software boils down to freedom from defects (nonconformance). As the process capability improves, mistakes play an increasingly crucial role in determining product quality. Furthermore, the collective impact of these mistakes, commonly prevalent in complex systems, can be potentially catastrophic. It is no wonder that avoiding mistakes rather than SQC-based variation control has been the key instrument of conformance quality in nuclear power plants and air traffic control systems, where the consequences of failure could be catastrophic. A key strategy in mistake-proofing is controlling complexity, as discussed next.

Controlling Complexity in Software Development

As we stated, complexity is the mother of all nonconformities. It must be addressed before poka yoke deployment. Chapters 1 and 3 discussed complexity as a challenge to developing trustworthy software from the software developer's perspective. From the user perspective, the question "Why does software have bugs?" will not go away. The response to that question is, software is intrinsically more complex than hardware because it has more states, or modes of behavior. An integrated enterprise business application system, for example, is likely to have 2,500 or more input forms. No machine has such a large number of operating modes. Computers, controlled by software, have more states (that is, larger performance envelopes) than do other, essentially mechanical, systems. Thus, they are intrinsically more complex.

Two vital questions from the developer's perspective are "Do we understand the nature of complexities in software?" and "Can we measure them?" The fact is that we do not and are not likely to understand or measure complexities anytime soon. A number of approaches have been taken to calculate or at least estimate the degree of complexity, but the simplest is lines of code (LOC), which is a count of the executable statements in a computer program. Although this metric began in the days of assembly-language programming, it is still used today for programs written in high-level programming languages. Most procedural third-generation memory-to-memory languages such as FORTRAN, COBOL, and ALGOL typically produce six executable ML statements, whereas register-to-register languages such as C, C++, and Java produce about three. Recent studies show a curvilinear relationship between defect rate and LOC; defect density appears to decrease with program size and then increase again when as program modules become very large (see Chapter 3). Curiously, this result suggests that there may be an optimum program size leading to a lowest defect rate—depending, of course, on programming language, project, product, and environment.

McCabe proposed a topological or graph-theory measure of cyclomatic complexity as a measure of how many linearly independent paths make up a computer program (see Chapter 3). Kan has reported that, other than module length, the most important predictors of defect rates are number of design changes and complexity level.[14] We may never fully comprehend complexity and measure it as such, but we now have a number of identifiable surrogates:

- Number of inputs
- Number of outputs
- Number of states
- Number of executable statements in a program (LOC)
- Module length
- Number of design changes

- Complexity level
- Number of features
- Defect rates
- Number of components
- Lack of discipline on the part of software developers
- Duration of development process

All these are related to complexity, so where do we start? Hinckley reports a link between assembly time and defect rate. Furthermore, he proposes assembly time as a measure of complexity:[15]

> Every change that reduces product or process complexity also reduces the total time required to procure materials, fabricate parts, or assemble products. Thus, time is a remarkably useful standard of complexity because it is fungible, or, in other words, an

interchangeable standard useful in measuring and comparing the complexity of different product attributes. As a result, we can use time to compare the difficulty of installing a bolt to an alternative assembly method based on a snap-fit assembly. In addition, time has a common international value that is universally recognized and easily understood. It would result in fewer mistakes. The product design for reduced complexity involves addressing time.

He cautions that care must be taken when using time as a measure of complexity, because worker skill, training, and the workplace strongly influence how long it takes to perform similar tasks.[16]

Task complexity can be reduced by product designs that take less time to complete. This involves addressing two fundamental issues:

- **Software product concept:** The TRIZ and Pugh concept selection methodologies presented in Chapter 12 provide opportunities to come up with the right product concept for reducing complexity, with development time as a measure of complexity. The concept itself has to be grounded in customer requirements, as identified by QFD and the Kano model, presented in Chapter 11.

- **Software product optimization:** This involves software design optimization with development time as a requirement using Taguchi Methods, presented in Chapters 16 and 17.

Reducing process complexity is as important as reducing product complexity. But unlike manufacturing, software product design is intricately linked to its development process. Reducing process complexity involves asking three basic questions: Is a robust software process in place to attain the complexity reduction objective? Is the process adequately supported by value analysis, standardization for best practices, and necessary documentation? Are the process and its supportive elements being used and observed in practice? This broad framework consists of the following:

- **Robust Development Model:** This ensures that a defined process is in place that lets the software team identify, develop, and deliver software that meets customer requirements with focus and discipline. The DFTS model (see, for example, Figure 2.6 in Chapter 2) provides such a framework.

- **Value analysis:** Value analysis keeps the development process focused on the product value as defined by the customer. It identifies the product and process activities that add value as perceived by the customer, those that do not but are required by the process, and those that neither create any value nor are required by the process. The last is called *muda* (waste) in Japanese and must be eliminated.

- **Standardization:** This ensures that standardized procedures support the development process. These should be monitored and improved. They should be based on the best practice available, including those coming from the internal development team as well as the supporting personnel.

- **Documentation:** Adequate documentation of the process as well as its changes and improvements are critical in meeting software development objectives.

- **5S system:** The 5S system (discussed in Chapter 10) is a key methodology for workplace organization and visual controls developed by Hiroyuki Hirano.[17] The 5 S's refers to five Japanese words: *seiri* (sort or clean up), *seiton* (straighten), *seiso* (shine), *seiketsu* (standardize), and *shitsuke* (sustain). Sort means to separate needed and unneeded materials and remove the latter. Straighten means to neatly arrange and identify needed materials for ease of use. Shine means to conduct a cleanup campaign. Standardize means to do sorting, straightening, and shining at frequent intervals and to standardize your 5S procedures. Sustain means to form the habit of always following the first four S's. The 5S system supports the software development process as a whole to be disciplined and productive.

- **Decomposition:** Simplicity is attained when tasks are comprehended. One of the major causes of complexity is cognitive. The idea of decomposing tasks into smaller, manageable segments cannot be overemphasized.

- **Smarter domain-specific languages and formally based tools:** We expect deployment of smarter domain-specific languages like Lawson software's Landmark™ (see Chapter 16). We also expect formally based tools that in the future can automatically expose certain kinds of software errors by producing evidence that a software system satisfies its requirements. Such tools then can allow practitioners to focus on development tasks best performed by people, such as obtaining and validating requirements and constructing high-quality requirements specifications.[18]

Managing complexity is one of the most critical software quality assurance tasks and is also one of the major challenges in software development. It is one of the root causes of variation- as well as mistake-based nonconformities. It must precede any poka yoke deployment, because its correct deployment reduces mistake-based nonconformities substantially.

Recognizing flaws in design that result in complexity and detecting mistakes are best done early in the design phases and should be planned accordingly. Complexity, in particular, can be corrected only upstream in the concept development and design stages. For mistake detection, the payoff from 100% inspection upstream at the source is substantially higher than inspections downstream. This sets the stage for mistake reduction using poka yoke.

Mistakes, Inspection Methods, and Poka Yoke

There are three types of mistakes:

- Ones that have occurred and that resulted in defects

- Ones that have occurred but that haven't yet resulted in defects

- Ones that have not yet occurred but may occur if corrective measures are not taken

The payoff increases as we move from prevalence of the first type to the third type, presumably as a result of proactive measures such as complexity reduction. All three need inspection to identify, but the implications are totally different. Shingo places inspections in the following three categories:[19]

1. **Judgment inspections:** This is what he calls a *postmortem inspection*. Whether it is 100% inspection or sample-based, it cannot reduce the defect rate. Furthermore, it is wasteful, because it inspects all goods, whether they are defective or not.

2. **Informative inspections:** An informative inspection involves feeding back information on defect occurrences for corrective measures. This is done with the purpose of gradually reducing the defect rate. There are three types of informative inspections:

   - **Statistical Quality Control (SQC):** We discussed the limitations of SQC earlier in this chapter. It also plays a limited role in software development, because the volume of data for statistical analysis may be limited in many cases. The biggest limitation of SQC is that it is reactive and accepts the notion that if it is not statistical, it is not quality control. SQC was discussed in Chapter 6 and is covered further in Chapter 15.

   - **Successive Check System (SuCS):** Shingo concluded that feedback and corrective actions are too slow to be effective. His remedy was successive inspections throughout the production process before further value-adding. He also concluded that 100% inspection in SuCS could even be economical compared to SQC if a low-cost inspection could be devised. "That is why a (low-cost) effective poka yoke ought to be used!"[20] SuCS, a 100% inspection, performs immediate feedback and action.

   - **Self-Check System (SeCS):** Shingo argued that SeCS could be even faster than SuCS for feedback and corrective action. It has two flaws, however. First, workers may compromise when doing the self-check. Second, they might occasionally forget to perform the self-check. SeCS can work if appropriate poka yoke devices can provide immediate feedback if abnormalities occur. This kind of inspection is a higher-order approach than SuCS.[21] To encourage self-check, imaginative incentives should be devised that reward people for reporting their own defects.

3. **Source inspections:** This involves discovering errors in conditions that give rise to possible defects. This is based on 100% inspection at the source and immediate feedback and corrective actions using suitable poka yoke devices. The payoff here is the highest, because feedback and corrective actions are taken before defects can occur. Only 100% source inspection with appropriate poka yoke measures can make zero defects possible. Both SuCS and SeCS are only informative inspections; they cannot prevent the occurrence of even one defect. It is therefore desirable to deploy 100% inspection at the source with poka yoke. The use of SuCS and SeCS should be limited to instances constrained by technical or financial limitations.[22]

Michael Fagan's Defect-Free Process includes one of the most effective software inspection methodologies. We strongly recommend Fagan's important work, particularly its powerful inspection methodology.[23, 24]

Deploying a Poka Yoke System

The poka yoke system consists of 100% inspection and use of poka yoke devices. The inspection process provides detection, and poka yoke provides feedback and corrective actions. Poka yoke measures must be customized. Although numerous examples of poka yoke for manufacturing exist,[25, 26, 27] software examples are not as well documented. Tables 9.2 and 9.3 list poka yoke measures. Understanding causes of mistakes is important in devising poka yoke measures. But almost all mistakes are caused by human errors:[28]

1. Forgetfulness

2. Errors due to misunderstanding

3. Errors in identification

4. Errors made by amateurs

5. Willful errors

6. Inadvertent error

7. Errors due to slowness

8. Errors due to lack of standards

9. Surprise errors

10. Intentional errors

TABLE 9.2

Common Poka Yoke Measures in Enterprise Software Development

Type of Poka Yoke Approach	Examples of Typical Poka Yoke Measures
Preventing human errors	**Designing components with unique signatures:** This is done by carefully documenting software components or library programs so that the user knows what he is getting. The Java language has a capability called introspection that allows the using program to ask an object what it does and how it does it, to prevent such errors.
	Using linking procedures that respect signatures: The program can be given preambles that will prevent them from being misused, and objects can hide data and protect methods so that using programs cannot change or modify them in error.
	Use of error flags: Signaling an error condition by an error flag or exception so that an error handler can prevent transaction failure or database corruption.
	Root cause analysis and corrective measures required before work resumes: This is done in business applications by careful input editing and rejection of suspicious transactions to an exception file that is examined by a human expert, corrected, and reprocessed later.
Warning about sources of defects	**Component labeling and documentation:** Documenting, classifying, and labeling software components.
	Determinate component hierarchies: Object hierarchies and object interfaces like Java uses.
	Flagging hierarchy violations: Java can do this if the object class is properly specified.
Designing preventive mechanisms	**Eliminating error-prone components:** Use well-tested computer Library programs or classes or components.
	Amplification of human senses: Robotic and neural net programming technology.
	Redundancy in design (backup systems): Coding several versions of an algorithm to handle a variety of data input.
	Simplification by using fewer components: This is a major goal of program design; it is called reusability.

Type of Poka Yoke Approach	Examples of Typical Poka Yoke Measures
	Enhancing product producibility and maintainability: Design programs so that they are lucid, easily understood, and easily maintained and modified, typically by programmers much less experienced than the original authors. **Selecting components that are proven:** This is a very important aspect of reusable programs and is one of the main goals of object-oriented programming.
Bug-prevention mechanisms	**"Next operation as customer":** All programmers thoroughly test their own work. **Test prior work before adding any more value:** Don't add anything to a program that has not been tested and may have faults. Test early and frequently. **Install programmer's command:** Real-time check or "automatic program correction." **Use object-oriented programming:** This helps avoid errors. **Get rid of defect-prone software:** If a software unit exceeds an error threshold, throw it out and let a different developer do the recoding. Early errors predict late errors. Statistical sampling can predict how many faults are left, but it cannot locate them. (The preceding steps cannot eliminate bugs, but they leave fewer and less complicated errors.)
Preventive inspections	**Source inspection:** To check process errors and correct them at the source. **Self-check inspection:** Self-check by the software developer and fixing the product before handing it over. **Successive check methods:** Checks by the next person in the process and correcting problems before proceeding.

TABLE 9.3
Examples of Poka Yoke in a DFTS Process

DFTS Phase	Common "Defects"	Mistakes That Cause Them	Mistake-Proofing Measures
Requirements development	Erroneous requirements development	User can't express requirements clearly User undervalues or overexpects User changes application requirements frequently	QFD-based requirements development
Design	Over-designing or a wrong design may result in the following: • Wrong solution • Features not needed • High technical/ business risk • High maintenance • High cost • Low utility • Delay • Loss of business/ competitive advantage	Features are added/ asked for because they are easy to add/ask for Inadequate communication between users and developers	QFD-based requirements development Team-based development led by application and programming leaders with the system architect as conflict revolver Taguchi Methods for design optimization FMEA/FTA for risk appraisal
Coding	Programming bugs	Simple oversights on the part of programmers Misunderstanding of specifications Inexperience	Coding standards and hierarchy controls Team walkthroughs More-precise specifications Improved programmer training
Test	Cannot check all the data paths	Application is too complex	More componentization More hierarchy levels

DFTS Phase	Common "Defects"	Mistakes That Cause Them	Mistake-Proofing Measures
Evaluation	Inconsistent results	Incomplete testing criteria	Improved testing standards and procedures
Verification	Results are not verifiable	Incomplete or defective test data and/or procedures	Better test plan
Validation	Cannot make program produce correct result from verified test data	Error(s) during development	Error analysis to isolate process stage(s) where error(s) likely were made
Implementation	Inconsistencies with two or more cooperating programs	Mistakes in human and machine communication	Error isolation by staged testing of partial results
Integration	Individually correct components will not work together	Inconsistent or poorly specified interstitial component communications	Systematic review of component/object method invocation
Maintenance	Lack of customer satisfaction	Maintenance programmer inadequacy vis-à-vis programmer creator	Training Adequate documentation Supervision

Identifying a Poka Yoke Solution

Hinckley has proposed the following six-step methodology, quality by control of mistakes (QCM), for an efficient approach to identify a poka yoke measure for problem-solving:[26]

1. Identify the problem.

2. Analyze the problem.

3. Generate solutions.

4. Compare, select, and plan the solution.

5. Implement the solution.

6. Evaluate.

In this chapter we have presented two powerful approaches to deliver defect free software as part of a DFTS deployment: controlling complexity and mistake-proofing (poka yoke). We have argued that mistakes are a major source of defects that requires even more attention than Statistical Quality Control (SQC). This is especially so in a software development context.

We have shown that complexity reduction and mistake-proofing are linked and how controlling complexity is a smart way to eliminate the causes of potential mistakes substantially before poka yoke is deployed. We have identified a practical measure of complexity and provided a framework for controlling product and process complexity in a software context. Finally, we have introduced poka yoke system as a cost-effective quality control system to reduce defects further as part of a DFTS deployment.

Key Points

- *Poka yoke*, which means mistake-proofing or fail-safing, recognizes that human errors are unavoidable but do not necessarily have to result in defects.

- Pioneered by Shigeo Shingo, poka yoke employs a set of proactive measures, particularly a 100% inspection at the source to detect process errors before they cause defects. It emphasizes prevention and includes stopping the process upon detection of process errors that may cause defects downstream. The process is restarted only after the cause has been identified and eliminated.

- Complexity and mistakes are strongly linked. As such, it is best to eliminate the causes of potential mistakes substantially by complexity reduction before a poka yoke deployment.

- The five principles of effective poka yoke deployment are 100% inspection at the source, appropriate upstream control measures, rapid implementation, people focus and teamwork, and problem-solving approach.

- Organizations that rely merely on variation-focused initiatives such as Six Sigma will fail to achieve a Six Sigma quality level unless they also find effective ways to address mistakes and complexities (the "mother of all defects"). Trustworthy software must be robust vis-à-vis all three causes of defects: variations, mistakes, and complexities.

- Poka yoke should not be approached as a panacea for all kinds of mistakes. It is also important to understand that poka yoke may be more suitable in certain situations than others.

- Mistakes can be defined as executing a prohibited action, failing to perform a required action, or misrepresenting information essential for the correct execution of an action.

- Rare mistakes do occur, even in high-capability processes. The fact that mistakes are rare in many processes means that traditional sampling and statistical methods are not useful in estimating their frequency.

- As many as 80% of the nonconformities in complex systems can be attributed to mistakes.

- Mistakes can be effectively described only in terms of probability: Mistakes either occur or they do not. Because every distribution describing variation can be converted to probabilities, the only universal method of describing both variation and mistakes is probability.

- Trustworthy software boils down to freedom from defects (nonconformance). As the process capability improves, mistakes play an increasingly crucial role in determining product quality. Furthermore, the collective impact of these mistakes, commonly prevalent in complex systems, can be potentially catastrophic.

- Avoiding mistakes rather than SQC-based variation control has been a key instrument of conformance quality in nuclear power plants and air traffic control systems, where consequences of failure could be catastrophic.

- A key strategy in mistake-proofing is to control complexity.

- Software is intrinsically more complex than hardware because it has more states, or modes of behavior. An integrated enterprise business application system, for example, is likely to have 2,500 or more input forms. No machine has such a large number of operating modes. Computers, controlled by software, have more states (that is, larger performance envelopes) than do other, essentially mechanical, systems. Thus, they are intrinsically more complex.

- We do not understand the nature of complexities in software and are not likely to understand or measure complexities anytime soon. A number of approaches have been taken to calculate or at least estimate the degree of complexity, but the simplest is LOC.

- Even though we may never fully comprehend complexity and measure it, a number of identifiable surrogates exist: number of inputs, number of outputs, number of states, LOC, module length, number of design changes, complexity level, number of features, defect rates, number of components, lack of discipline on the part of software developers, and the duration of the development process.

- Hinckley reports a linkage between assembly time and defect rate and proposes time as a measure of complexity. Care must be taken when using time as a measure of complexity, because worker skill, training, and the workplace strongly influence how long it takes to perform similar tasks. Generally, task complexity can be reduced by product designs that take less time to complete.

- The complexity reduction framework consists of the Robust Development Model, value analysis, standardization, documentation, the 5S system, decomposition, and smarter domain-specific languages and formally based tools.

- There are three types of mistakes: ones that have occurred and that resulted in defects, ones that have occurred but have not yet resulted in defects, and ones that have not yet occurred but may occur if corrective measures are not taken. The payoff increases as we move from prevalence of the first type of mistake to the third type.

- These three mistakes require inspection to identify, but the implications are totally different. Shingo categorizes inspections as judgment inspections, informative inspections (SQC, SuCS, SeCS), or source inspections. The payoff in source inspection is the highest; only this can make zero defects possible. Both SuCS and SeCS are only informative inspections and cannot prevent the occurrence of even one defect. It is therefore desirable to deploy 100% inspection at the source with poka yoke. The use of SuCS and SeCS should be limited to instances constrained by technical or financial limitations.

- Almost all mistakes are caused by human errors: forgetfulness, slowness, misunderstanding, lack of standards, errors in identification, errors made by amateurs, intentional errors, inadvertent errors, and surprise errors.

- Hinckley has proposed a six-step methodology, quality by control of mistakes (QCM), for an efficient approach to identify a poka yoke measure for problem-solving.

Additional Resources

http://www.prenhallprofessional.com/title/0131872508

http://www.agilenty.com/publications

Internet Exercises

1. Read the article at http://csob.berry.edu/faculty/jgrout/pokasoft.html, and present a summary of it to the class. (This article, by Harry Robinson, was originally presented at the Sixth International Conference on Software Testing Analysis and Review [STAR 1997].)

2. Browse through the articles on poka yoke application in software development at http://csob.berry.edu/faculty/jgrout/pokayoke.shtml. Suggest their possible applications in a software development context you are familiar with.

Review Questions

1. Explain the term *poka yoke*. What are the principles for effective deployment of this quality system?

2. List and describe the three major causes of defects. Explain their significance in a software development context. How are these sources of defects typically controlled?

3. What are the limitations of variation-focused quality systems? What are the limitations of SQC, and how can they be overcome?

4. What are some typical situations in which poka yoke works well? When is it unsuitable?

5. Explain Hinckley and Barkan's definition of a mistake. Why might statistical methods not be useful in estimating their frequency? What is the significance of mistakes in a complex system such as enterprise software?

6. Provide a broad classification of causes of software defects. What is the significance of mistakes in a high-capability software development process?

7. Give an example of a simple estimate of software complexity. How is it different from McCabe's and Kan's predictors for the same?

8. What are the surrogates for software complexity? Comment on Hinckley's proposal to use development time as a measure of complexity. What are its possible limitations?

9. What are the measures for reducing software complexity? Explain their significance and effectiveness.

10. List Shingo's categorization of inspections. What is their relative merit in tackling the three types of mistakes?

11. List the most common human errors that are responsible for mistakes.

12. What are the typical mistakes in each of the various phases of a DFTS process? What mistake-proofing measures are suggested?

Discussion Questions and Projects

1. Discuss the merits of the poka yoke quality system in a software development context.

2. Devise a poka yoke system for a software project you are currently involved with.

Endnotes

[1] Shigeo Shingo, *Zero Quality Control: Source Inspection and the Poka-Yoke System* (Portland, OR: Productivity Press, 1986), p. 278.

[2] Connie Dyer, "Robust Quality," in Genichi Taguchi and Don Clausing, *Harvard Business Review*, January-February 1990, p. 73.

[3] C. Martin Hinckley, *Make No Mistakes! An Outcome-Based Approach to Mistake-Proofing* (Portland, OR: Productivity Press, 2001), p. xi.

[4] Gene E. Wiggs, ibid, p. xii.

[5] Op cit Hinckley, pp. 6–10.

[6] J. M. Juran and F. M. Gryna, *Juran's Quality Control Handbook*, 4th Ed. (New York: McGraw-Hill, 1988), 16.19–16.21, 24.6, 31.1–31.24.

[7] C. Martin Hinckley and Philip Barkan, "The Role of Variation, Mistakes, and Complexity in Producing Nonconformities," *Journal of Quality Technology*, 27(3), July 1995, p. 243.

[8] Ibid.

[9] J. R. Grout, "Mistake Proofing Promotion," *Production and Inventory Management Journal*, 1997, 38(3):33–37.

[10] Op cit Hinckley and Barkan, p. 243.

[11] Ibid, p. 244.

[12]D. H. Harris and F. B. Chaney, *Human Factors in Quality Assurance* (New York: John Wiley and Sons, 1969).

[13]Op cit Hinckley and Barkan, p. 244.

[14]S. H. Kan, *Metrics and Models in Software Quality Engineering* (Singapore: Pearson Education, 2003), p. 327.

[15]Op cit Hinckley, pp. 37–41 (p. 41).

[16]Ibid, p. 46.

[17]Hiroyuki Hirano, *5 Pillars of the Visual Workplace: The Source Book for 5 S Implementation* (Portland, OR: Productivity Press, 1990).

[18]Constance Heitmeyer, "Managing Complexity in Software Development with Formally Based Tools," http://chacs.nrl.navy.mil/publications/CHACS/2004/2004heitmeyer-FESCA04.pdf.

[19]Op cit Shingo, p. 57.

[20]Ibid, p. 69.

[21]Ibid, p. 77.

[22]Ibid, p. 93.

[23]http://www.mfagan.com.

[24]David A. Wheeler, Bill Brykczynski, Reginald N. Meeson, Jr., *Software Inspection: An Industry Best Practice* (IEEE Computer Society Press, 1996).

[25]Op cit Shingo, pp. 135–261.

[26]Op cit Hinckley, pp. 109–344.

[27]NKS/Factory Magazine (Ed.), *Poka Yoke: Improving Product Quality by Preventing Defects* (Cambridge, MA: Productivity Press, 1988), pp. 29–270.

[28]Op cit Hinckley, pp. 76–77.

CHAPTER 10

5S for Intelligent Housekeeping in Software Development

Managers who do not accept responsibility for maintaining the 5 S's are not entitled to complain if their workers feel the same way.

—*Hiroyuki Hirano*

Be as conventional as possible in your dress, manner, and lifestyle so you can reserve your creativity for your work.

—*Honoré de Balzac*

Overview

5S is a methodology that helps ensure a productive workplace environment. It was developed by Hiroyuki Hirano, who concluded that a large number of organizations embarking on Just in Time (JIT) fail to realize its potential in the absence of workplace discipline and a clutter-free environment. 5S supports Toyota Production System (TPS) and the principles of lean. It helps reduce non-value-added activities, standardize tasks, and increase work efficiency and productivity in diverse work environments. 5S stands for Sort, Straighten, Shine, Standardize, and Sustain. In a DFTS context, 5S can help address the following issues:

- Streamlining documentation
- Sorting customer orders
- Sorting current and old development software
- Avoiding "feature multiplication"
- Optimizing supply costs

329

- Standardizing processes and practices
- Creating an orderly development process
- Managing a technology repository
- Housekeeping
- Improving productivity
- Improving the work environment

Hirano has identified 12 types of resistance to 5S. These must be anticipated and handled well for 5S to succeed. The key steps of a successful 5S deployment are *management buy-in, training and implementation, link to a reward system,* and *follow-up and continuous improvement.* Effectively communicating the benefits of 5S is critical for a successful and lasting deployment.

Chapter Outline

- 5S: A Giant Step Toward a Productive Workplace Environment
- Implementation Phases of the 5S System
- The 5S System and the DFTS Process
- Overcoming Resistance
- Implementing 5S

- Key Points
- Additional Resources
- Internet Exercises
- Review Questions
- Discussion Questions and Projects
- Endnotes

5S: A Giant Step Toward a Productive Workplace Environment

5S is a methodology that helps create a productive workplace environment. It was initially used in Japan to lay foundations for introducing JIT. It was developed by Japanese manufacturing consultant Hiroyuki Hirano. He concluded that a large number of organizations embarking on JIT fail to realize its potential in the absence of workplace discipline and the clutter-free environment that systematic housekeeping can provide.[1] JIT, an integral component of what has come to be known as TPS, is based on a philosophy of complete elimination of waste. 5S is an integral part of what is broadly called lean concepts. It supports TPS and the principles of lean and helps reduce non-value-added activities, standardize tasks, and increase work efficiency and productivity in diverse work environments. We will discuss a little later how a 5S system meshes with powerful organization-wide interventions such as TPS and DFTS.

5S stands for the following five Japanese words, all beginning with S (see Figure 10.1):

- *Seiri* (sort or clean up or organize) means to separate needed from unneeded materials and equipment, document them, and remove unneeded items.

- *Seiton* (straighten or set orderliness) means to neatly arrange and identify needed materials for ease of use and access.

- *Seiso* (shine or cleanliness) means to clean up the workplace and keep it tidy.

- *Seiketsu* (standardize) means to sort, straighten, and shine frequently and to standardize this procedure to maintain the preceding three S's.

- *Shitsuke* (sustain or discipline) means to sustain the preceding four S's with discipline.

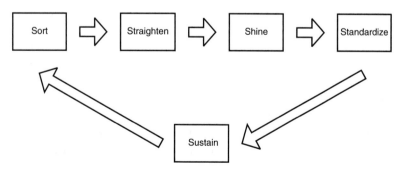

FIGURE 10.1
The Five Phases of the 5S System

Often a sixth S is added that stands for **safety**. This implies that safety should be an integral part of procedures and work habits in an organization and that safety procedures should be defined. The 5 S's (we prefer the 6 S's) support software development as a whole to be disciplined and productive. Introduced correctly, a 6S system can greatly improve operational efficiency in a workplace. It creates discipline and a clutter-free environment, thus redirecting energy to focus on vital operational goals. It also helps reduce costs of various supplies and improves safety and productivity in the workplace in addition to providing a simple housekeeping procedure. The results can be visible immediately and can lay a foundation for a major intervention such as DFTS.

Implementation Phases of the 5S System

This section discusses in more detail the five phases of the 5S system implementation.

Phase 1: Sorting/Cleaning Up

The main objective of the first phase is getting rid of junk mail, documents, clutter, and unneeded tools, fixtures, and equipment. In a software development environment, this also means broken and unneeded hardware, including equipment that has not been used in a long time and that is unlikely to be used in the future.

5S can be applied to electronic as well as paper documents. Unneeded documents cause you to waste time when you have to shuffle through them, looking for a needed document. They also occupy physical and memory space. By getting rid of such unused items, you can free up space, reduce the number of obstacles to productivity you have to walk around, and find important items quickly. Often people debate whether a particular item can be thrown away. Such items can be "red-tagged" with a date. The item is disposed of if it is not used by that date (normally one to six months from now).

After sorting has been carried out, the stage is set for tidying the workplace.

Phase 2: Straightening/Orderliness

This phase involves keeping documents, tools, and equipment in the right places. The key consideration is ease of access and use for all personnel concerned, with due consideration to safety and security of equipment, documents, data, and users. Aesthetics as well as ergonomics should be taken into account when items are placed in various locations. Consideration should also be given to weight, size, and the items' value.

Phase 3: Shine/Cleanliness

This phase of 5S concerns maintaining the newly found order after the unneeded items and rubbish have been disposed of and everything has been rearranged. A major shift here is that now the owners of the workplace (this includes the physical work space as well as the "virtual" work space on the screen) assume the responsibility for keeping it clean and orderly. They understand that this means devoting 5 to 10 minutes daily to cleaning and tidying-up routines. They are responsible for their own work areas, and responsibility for common areas is shared. A simple written procedure is established, with input from all concerned during the procedure development process. Employees are adequately trained and clearly understand what it takes to keep the workplace tidy.

Phase 4: Standardize

This is a crucial phase of 5S. It is important not to underestimate the likelihood of people reverting to their old ways. This phase is simply about maintaining the routine established in the first three phases. It is quite challenging to maintain the new standards. Needless to say, appropriate training is important. To keep from losing the gains that have been made, companies should carry out regular, detailed, established audits. Such audits should be followed by appropriate feedback and corrective measures if needed. Left to themselves, people will backslide. Often companies link such audits to regular performance reviews, but this approach can breed resistance if not handled properly. On the whole, the success of the initiative depends on the value it creates for the employees and their correct perception of the same.

Phase 5: Sustain/Discipline

In this phase the objective is to further improve. This means *kaizen*, or continuous improvement. The previous phases of 5S dealt with creating and maintaining a clean and orderly working environment. This phase of 5S is about further improving the 5S implementation. It means understanding the causes of a disorderly workplace and clutter. What causes the workplace to be disorderly and dirty in the first place? This requires making observations and keeping records of problems. A Pareto analysis could help prioritize and identify the most important issues that need attention.

To sustain a 5S system, the organization must deal with people's mind-sets, and that's the toughest part. Often this involves initiating measures for bringing about transformative changes based on systematic methodologies (see Chapter 5). Accepting meaningful changes and embracing continuous improvement is powerful indeed. But as Fujio Cho, former president of Toyota Motor Company, has said, "You have to address employees' fundamental way of thinking." This clearly requires commitment and leadership.

The 5S System and the DFTS Process

5S is often perceived by managers as just being about good housekeeping. However, Hirano had larger objectives in mind when he developed this system. He strongly believed that in the absence of a system like 5S, JIT did not have much chance of succeeding. In a manufacturing environment, 5S plays a critical role in eliminating various waste related to excess inventory, unnecessary motion, and unproductive processes. Furthermore, by reducing complexity, it also helps reduce product and process defects. Thus, 5S has become an integral part of JIT management in manufacturing industries. It can similarly play a crucial role in a DFTS initiative by helping address the following issues:

- **Streamlining documentation:** Multiple and outdated copies of documents are a great source of risk and can adversely affect software cost, quality, and delivery schedule. This must be addressed such that one electronic copy is kept in a central repository. Someone from the team should be assigned to update and inform the necessary people about changes if and when they occur. Similarly, someone should be responsible for managing memory on C and C++ projects (Java does this automatically).

- **Sorting customer orders:** Much programming time is lost as more program development code is discarded than is ever used. This has a severe effect on cost, schedule, and developer morale. A streamlined process to sort customer orders eliminates all whimsy from the development environment. All the managers who say "I don't know what I want, but I'll know it when I see it" should be reassigned.

- **Sorting current and old development software:** All software should be sorted. The current versions should be separated from the old versions, which are archived. This ensures that the development staff uses the latest standards.

- **Avoiding "feature multiplication":** This is a serious problem in software development. Needed and unneeded features should be clearly earmarked so that development time is not lost on developing unneeded features.

- **Optimizing supply costs:** A systematic analysis of the development process provides information about supply needs for the required software development tools. Thus, only needed development tools are licensed. Furthermore, such analysis identifies the need to license a second copy, if needed, for developers working from home. Thus, supply costs for software development tools are optimized.

- **Standardizing processes and practices:** 5S when implemented properly invariably results in simplified procedures and processes, thus reducing complexity. This is of huge importance in mistake-proofing (see Chapter 9).

- **Creating an orderly development process:** Process analysis also helps build a program development environment that can maintain catalogs of current and prior project builds.

- **Managing a technology repository:** Often, you have versions of software and technology that are no longer used but that need to be preserved as a backup and as support for customers who may not have updated.

- **Housekeeping:** 5S provides a system that keeps all software versions current during development using a database-oriented grandfather/father/son system. Using a UML-based flowchart system can help you keep high-level documentation current. A specialist could be assigned to each programming team to maintain this documentation.

- **Improving productivity:** The preceding practices result in improved overall productivity. They also provide an opportunity for optimum planning of space requirements for programmers, including those who work at home. This may, in turn, reduce space requirements.

- **Improving the work environment:** A streamlined, clutter-free environment is a useful by-product of a 5S system. It should be further strengthened to encourage communication within and between programming teams. It also releases space for meetings and other group activities.

Sidebar 10.1: From 5S to the Lean DFTS Process

The word "lean" is at the heart of the Toyota Production System (TPS). It was first used by Womack and Jones in their 1991 book *The Machine That Changed the World*.[2] The authors surveyed and benchmarked manufacturing companies around the world and concluded that Japanese manufacturing companies were typically much more productive and efficient than their Western counterparts.

A few years before this book, Taiichi Ohno, the man behind TPS, had published *Toyota Production System*, which explained the foundations of "lean manufacturing."[3] Ohno devised seven categories of *muda* ("waste" in Japanese) that cover virtually all the various ways in which manufacturing organizations waste or lose money. These came to be known as the "The Seven Wastes." The purpose of JIT management, a key component of TPS, is to identify and eliminate waste by making it visible and measurable. Organizations that have a relatively small proportion of wasteful activities are lean enterprises.

What is waste? Ohno defined waste as the use of all resources that do not produce the product as defined by the customer. If the customer does not need it or will not pay for it, it is waste. This includes material, machines, energy, and labor. He classified waste into the following seven categories:

- Overproduction
- Waiting
- Transportation
- Inventory
- Motion
- Overprocessing
- Defective products

Ohno reasoned that anything that does not create value for the customer, even items that are needed by the producer to meet production or regulatory requirements, is waste from the customer's perspective. The producer cannot do without meeting regulatory or other service requirements of a business, but the waste associated with them must be contained to the absolute minimum. Ideally, the waste must be eliminated, not just reduced. Even in highly efficient Japanese organizations, the true value added is often less than 3 to 4%, which means 96 to 97% is *muda*—a chilling revelation.

Identifying waste is not enough. TPS consists of a range of tools that are used to identify and eliminate waste. Some of the most important tools are JIT, *jidoka* (autonomation), *poka yoke* (mistake-proofing), and *kaizen* (continuous improvement). Hirano believed that such unprecedented and unrelenting effort to identify and eliminate waste at every level in an enterprise would hardly stand a chance without the workplace discipline that a 5S system provides.

Lean production is beyond the scope of this book, but a DFTS system embraces the TPS philosophy of identifying and eliminating waste. A wasteful enterprise cannot deliver quality products. Table 10.1 compares seven major categories of waste in both manufacturing and enterprise software development. It reveals the striking similarities in challenges regarding elimination of waste in manufacturing and the software development process. A lean software development process is a natural progression for an enterprise that has embraced DFTS. It is also possible to deploy lean and DFTS processes in tandem. All such enterprises (those going for DFTS and Lean DFTS) would be well advised to build a solid organizational foundation for such ventures by implementing a 5S system first.

TABLE 10.1
A Comparison of Seven Wastes in Manufacturing and Software Development

Manufacturing		
Type of Waste	Cause of Waste	Basic Corrective Tool(s)
Overproduction	Quality problems cause loss along the way	Voice of the customer (VOC) Quality Function Deployment (QFD) Improved design *Poka yoke* (Mistake-proofing) Statistical Process Control (SPC) Complexity reduction Just-in-time (JIT) Single-Minute Exchange of Dies (SMED)
Waiting	Need for work-in-progress (WIP) finished goods due to large batch size	Theory of Constraints (TOC) Cellular layout SMED
Unnecessary transportation	Due to functional layout	Cellular layout
Excess inventory	Quantity discount Quality issues	True-cost analysis Cellular layout JIT Root-cause analysis SPC *Poka yoke*
Unnecessary motion	Cluttered and untidy workplace	5S
Overprocessing	Rework because of quality issues	Root-cause analysis SPC *Poka yoke*
Defective units	Rework because of quality issues	Root-cause analysis SPC *Poka yoke*

TABLE 10.1
continued

Software Development		
Type of Waste	Cause of Waste	Basic Corrective Tool(s)
Too many program modules rewritten Too many unasked features	Poor planning and design	VOC QFD Improved design *Poka yoke* Complexity reduction
Waiting—unable to complete next build	One or more program modules are not ready	Better program planning Support for overloaded team (TOC)
Too much movement of code and/or personnel	Dispersed development team	Improve locality of effort as needed (cellular layout)
More development tools licensed than needed Wrong module development	Poor planning and design	Maintain tighter controls on development tool licensing Better program planning 5S
Too much team communication	Too many programmers on team	Clarify relationships 5S
Overprocessing due to faults	Too much rework due to poor design or implementation	Better design and improved testing criteria Root-cause analysis *Poka yoke*
Defective modules in development	Inadequate software development tools	Better design and improved testing criteria Root-cause analysis *Poka yoke*

Overcoming Resistance

You should anticipate resistance to a 5S implementation. 5S involves considerable change in how people go about their work. It is not so much about clutter and mess on people's desks. It has more to do with the discipline and clarity with which work is approached and organized. Clutter, or lack of it, is just a by-product. The fact that 5S is simple in concept does not help much with its acceptance; on the contrary, there may be skepticism as to how it can move mountains. Experience, however, shows that a 5S system prepares an enterprise for more ambitious, organization-wide interventions such as JIT and DFTS.

Hirano has identified 12 types of resistance to 5S (Table 10.2).[4] You may add one or two of your own. As you can see, skepticism can come from a variety of sources, including senior executives. You must anticipate and handled these well for 5S to succeed. In a larger sense, this is a classic case of resistance to change (see Chapter 5).

TABLE 10.2
Twelve Types of Resistance to 5S Deployment[4]

Resistance # 1:	"What's the big deal about Organization and Orderliness?"
Resistance # 2:	"You want me, the president, to be 5S chairman?"
Resistance # 3:	"Why clean up when it will soon get dirty again?"
Resistance # 4:	"Implementing Organization and Orderliness will not boost output?"
Resistance # 5:	"Why concern ourselves with such trivial matters?"
Resistance # 6:	"We already implemented them."
Resistance # 7:	"I know my filing system's a mess but I know my way around it."
Resistance # 8:	"We did 5S 20 years ago."
Resistance # 9:	"5S and improvement stuff is just for the factory."
Resistance # 10:	"We're too busy to spend time on Organization and Orderliness."
Resistance # 11:	"Why should anyone tell me what to do?"
Resistance # 12:	"We don't need 5S. We're making money, so let us do our work the way we want to."

Reprinted with permission from *5 Pillars of the Visual Workplace: The Sourcebook for 5S Implementation* by Hiroyuki Hirano (English Translation Copyright © 1995 Productivity Press) www.productivitypress.com.

Implementing 5S

Chapter 5 presented some critical issues in managing change. The challenge of introducing change systematically is pertinent here too. A systematic plan to introduce 5S consists of four key steps, as discussed in this section.

Step 1: Management Buy-in

It is imperative that the initiative has the support of top management, including the CEO. If that is the case, the 5S initiative could be linked to a broader objective of a DFTS initiative or undertaken as a stand-alone initiative. Management must understand the initiative's benefits, including cost and the bottom line. Before the initiative goes anywhere, management must state its commitment and appoint a project manager/master black belt (MBB) for the 5S execution. (The MBB reports to the Vice President of Software Development and the Chief Quality Officer, as discussed in Chapter 5.) The decision to implement 5S should be properly communicated to all concerned.

Step 2: Training and Implementation

Training should be provided as appropriate. It is best imparted around personal 5S projects that trainees carry out as part of the training process. In other words, people must learn and implement the system themselves. The senior management team should be trained to implement their own 5S projects. They all must discover the system's benefits. The projects themselves should be customized to individual priorities. This can go a long way in overcoming resistance and ensuring robust implementation.

Step 3: Link to a Reward System

The 5S implementation must be linked to individual performance appraisal for the next few years. People should understand that 5S is not a fad; it is how the workplace will be organized. Only then will they learn and improve it on a continual basis. People should be given clear 5S-related goals and expectations. They should also understand its benefits (Table 10.3).

Step 4: Follow-up and Continuous Improvement

Regular audits should be carried out to ensure that the system is working. Feedback should be provided with the goal of maintaining and improving 5S. Individual difficulties should be looked into and appropriate assistance provided. As we stated in Chapter 5, it is best to provide positive incentives for change. Theoretically, the desired changes may be attained by either increasing the driving forces or diminishing the restraining forces. However, it is desirable to introduce changes by strengthening driving forces rather than diminishing the opposing ones (see Figure 5.3 in Chapter 5).

TABLE 10.3
Benefits of a 5S System

Benefit # 1:	It lays the foundation for a more productive and efficient organization.
Benefit # 2:	It enhances the possibility of success for future quality initiatives.
Benefit # 3:	It initiates a culture of continuous improvement (*kaizen*).
Benefit # 4:	It lowers costs and improves profitability due to waste elimination.
Benefit # 5:	It improves quality due to lower defects.
Benefit # 6:	It improves product design due to a reduction in mistakes and process complexity.
Benefit # 7:	It reduces inventory and costs associated with development tools.
Benefit # 8:	It improves safety (especially when deploying 6S).
Benefit # 9:	It reduces space and memory storage requirements.
Benefit # 10:	It lowers maintenance costs.
Benefit # 11:	It helps create a clutter-free work environment.
Benefit # 12:	It improves employee morale.

The value of 5S system lies in its simplicity and practical value. It is bolstered by visual standards and devices. Properly deployed, it can be a key component of a robust quality management system in an organization. It can help introduce a culture of learning and continuous improvement. The 5S system is substantial and yet manageable. That is not to say that it is easy to implement. The opportunities and challenges of a 5S system are listed in Tables 10.1, 10.2, and 10.3. It can be an excellent tool to initiate a DFTS process in an organization.

Key Points

- 5S is a methodology that helps create a productive workplace environment. It was developed by Hiroyuki Hirano, who concluded that a large number of organizations embarking on JIT fail to realize its potential in the absence of workplace discipline and a clutter-free environment.

- 5S supports TPS and the principles of lean. It helps reduce non-value-added activities, standardize tasks, and increase work efficiency and productivity in diverse work environments.

- 5S stands for sorting the needed from the unneeded, straightening needed materials for ease of use and access, shining the workplace to keep it clean and tidy, standardizing the procedure to maintain the preceding three S's, and sustaining the preceding four S's with discipline.

- 5S lets an organization introduce discipline and a clutter-free environment, thus refocusing energy on vital operational goals. It helps reduce the cost of various supplies, improves safety and productivity, and provides a simple housekeeping procedure. The results can be visible immediately and can lay the foundation for a major intervention such as JIT and DFTS.

- In a DFTS context, 5S can help address the following issues: streamlining documentation, sorting customer orders, sorting current and old development software, avoiding feature multiplication, optimizing supply costs, standardizing processes and practices, creating an orderly development process, managing a technology repository, housekeeping, improving productivity, and improving the work environment.

- Hirano has identified 12 types of resistance to 5S. It is important that you anticipate these and handle them for 5S to succeed.

- The key steps for a successful 5S deployment are management buy-in, training and implementation, linking to a reward system, and follow-up and continuous improvement.

- Effectively communicating the benefits of 5S is crucial for a successful and lasting deployment.

Additional Resources

http://www.prenhallprofessional.com/title/0131872508

http://www.agilenty.com/publications

Internet Exercises

Watch the slide show at the following Web site, and suggest how you can use these ideas in a software development context:

http://quality.dlsu.edu.ph/trainings/5s_0506.pdf

Review Questions

1. Explain what 5S stands for.

2. List and explain what issues 5S can address in a DFTS context.

3. Describe some important software development issues that 5S can address.

4. Give two examples of waste in a software context for each of the seven categories classified by Ohno. What are their underlying causes, and what measures can be taken to address them? How does a 5S deployment help address any of these?

5. List six major types of resistance to a 5S deployment.

6. Explain the four steps of a successful 5S deployment.

7. List the major benefits of a 5S deployment.

Discussion Questions and Projects

1. Explain an application of 5S in a software development context, giving specific examples of what each S stands for and value it creates.

2. Discuss detailed application of a 5S deployment to address three software development issues. Explain how each of the five phases plays an important role in ensuring effectiveness of deployment.

3. Discuss a framework to overcome resistance to a 5S deployment.

4. Discuss how a 5S deployment can be made successful by required training, an imaginative reward system, appropriate follow-up, and continuous improvement.

5. Suggest a plan for communicating the benefits of a 5S deployment effectively across an organization.

Endnotes

[1]Hiroyuki Hirano, *5 Pillars of the Visual Workplace: The Sourcebook for 5S Implementation* (Portland, OR: Productivity Press, 1990), pp. 25–31.

[2]James P. Womack, Daniel T. Jones, Daniel Roos, *The Machine That Changed the World: The Story of Lean Production* (New York: Harper-Collins, 1991).

[3]Taiichi Ohno, *Toyota Production System: Beyond Large-Scale Production* (New York: Productivity Press, 1988).

[4]Op cit Hirano, pp. 13–18.

CHAPTER 11

Understanding Customer Needs: Software QFD and the Voice of the Customer*

Doing a "House of Quality" matrix is not doing QFD. That is just doing a matrix. QFD is a quality system for the assurance of customer satisfaction. The use of multiple tools is required for that.

—Yoji Akao

What is impossible to do in one paradigm, may be easy to do in another.

—Joel Barker

Overview

Leading companies around the world, among them Toyota and General Electric, have practiced Quality Function Deployment (QFD) for decades. Developed in Japan by Dr. Yoji Akao and Dr. Shigeru Mizuno, QFD has two aims: to ensure that true customer needs are properly deployed throughout all phases of the development process, and to improve the development process itself. The application of QFD to software (**Software QFD**) began in Japan in 1982, in North America in 1988, and in Europe in 1990. Today many leading software organizations around the world use Software QFD and it is an essential part of such organization-wide quality approaches as Total Quality Management (TQM) and Design for Six Sigma (DFSS) at those companies.

---

* This chapter was authored by Richard Zultner, International Akao QFD Prize recipient, certified QFD Red Belt, and director of training and research at the QFD Institute.

As a quality system, QFD employs, but is not limited to, the Seven Management and Planning (7 MP) Tools and has *deployments*, or subsystems, to address customer concerns such as quality, technology, cost/schedule, and reliability/risk, among others. Although QFD is known for the "House of Quality" matrix, organizations that simply use this matrix alone neither meet the aims of QFD nor are considered to be "doing QFD" by leading QFD experts. Further, because of unfortunate historical errors in understanding, many published QFD examples are incorrect and are not suitable as models for software development. Such mistakes are corrected in the overview of Blitz QFD presented in this chapter.

Chapter Outline

- QFD: Origin and Introduction
- Problems with Traditional QFD Applied to Software
- Modern QFD for Software
- The Blitz QFD Process
- Implementing Software QFD
- Conclusion

- Key Points
- Additional Resources
- Internet Exercises
- Review Questions
- Discussion Questions
- Endnotes
- About the Author

QFD: Origin and Introduction

This book advocates moving the quality-related aspects of development as far upstream in the development process as possible. QFD provides tools and techniques to help with even the "fuzzy front end" of the development process. The Robust Software Development Model (RSDM) presented in this book provides a powerful framework for developing trustworthy software in a time- and cost-effective manner. A key aspect of Specification or Functional Design, performed by systems analysts in concert with the potential end users of the software, is to determine *who* the targeted customers or intended users are for the software solution we are developing, *why* the customers or users need a solution (what user problems the software must solve), and therefore *what* the software should do and *how well* it should do it.

So, what role can QFD play in an RSDM? QFD's contributions to the Seven Components of RSDM are as follows:

1. QFD can make interactions with customers more efficient and productive, and it offers tools and techniques for identifying spoken and unspoken requirements throughout the software development process.

2. QFD can make feedback and communication more effective between developers and across development phases.

3. QFD enables the optimization of design for reliability (or other software quality attributes) from a customer perspective, and it has methods for reducing the time (and therefore the cost) of development.

4. QFD supports the identification of opportunities for "quick hits" with incremental development methods, and better "aiming" of such methods.

5. QFD can be performed in a step-wise fashion and can be tailored as needed by an organization or a project team.

6. QFD offers tools and techniques for risk analysis from a customer perspective throughout the development process.

7. QFD enables object-oriented development to be customer focused and value driven.

In Chapter 2's discussion of the Design for Trustworthy Software (DFTS) process, **software quality** is defined as the degree to which a system, component, or process meets customer or user needs or expectations. Although all five major components of trustworthy software are areas where QFD can play a role, the most significant area is customer responsiveness. If the software is of no value to the customer, the reliability, safety, security, or maintainability

of the software is *irrelevant* to the customer. Customers are only interested in the trustworthiness of software that is worth something to them. To understand customers' definitions
of *value*, we have to "listen to the voice of the customer"—a concept that QFD created and
introduced.

To develop trustworthy software and to gain customers' trust, we must first meet customers' needs, whether stated or unstated. We must be able to identify these needs correctly
on an iterative basis throughout all phases of the software development process.

But how can we meet unstated needs? And how can we ensure that our software, when
delivered, will actually be trustworthy in the eyes of its users? QFD was created to address
exactly such questions.

What's Different about QFD as a Quality System?

The traditional role of methods such as Statistical Process Control and the DMAIC
problem-solving approach of Six Sigma has been to improve the quality of a product or
process *after* it has been produced or established. Methods such as Statistical Process
Control (SPC) and the DMAIC problem-solving approach of Six Sigma are excellent in
such situations. They can take an existing situation and efficiently reduce "negative quality"
such as defects, problems, and variability. In the late 1960s in Japan, Dr. Yoji Akao saw that
such methods were not enough, however. Two fundamental insights led to the development
of QFD:

1. It is important to design in quality; that is, to produce quality from the
   beginning, and not to design or produce something and *then* correct it.

2. It is necessary to consider quality from the perspective of the *customer*—
   not just from the technical perspective of the engineer or developer.

These insights ultimately led to the development of QFD as a modern quality system,
focused on understanding what *value* means to the customers or users we intend to satisfy.[1]
Therefore, QFD uses tools and techniques that take customer statements and actions as
input, in addition to the traditional methods based on measurements of what's wrong with
what already exists (see Figure 11.1).

Traditional quality-improvement and problem-solving methods focus on reducing
defects. Dr. Deming described such approaches as "scraping burnt toast." And even with
all defects removed (zero defects), are we assured that our customers will be satisfied? No.
Satisfaction is not merely the absence of defects. Rather, satisfaction requires the presence
of value, as determined by the customer. Modern quality methods, such as QFD, focus on
adding value to the customer, which requires new tools and techniques.

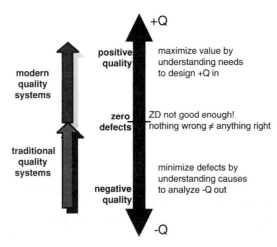

FIGURE 11.1
Traditional versus modern quality systems.

Traditional quality-improvement and problem-solving methods use **data** (measures from an *existing* product or process) to find the root cause of defects or problems and remove them or solve them. In order to use these approaches, you must first develop something—then you can test it and improve it. In contrast, QFD's aim is to understand the customer's needs and use that understanding to drive design and development—to ensure customer satisfaction on the first pass through development.[2] So, you can use QFD for new-product development, even for the initial development of products and software that are new to a customer, a company, or the world.[3]

Further, in contrast to the assumptions of many approaches to software requirements, QFD does *not* assume that customers understand their needs, or that customers can tell us all of their needs. Note that many iterative or evolutionary development approaches begin with an assumption that it is not possible or practical to get a sufficient set of requirements from customers such that developing to those requirements would satisfy customers. Thus, iteration is used as a strategy to obtain feedback from customers on an ongoing basis in order to redirect the development effort in mid-flight. This series of small build-and-correct cycles allows developers to proceed even when only a weak understanding of what is needed is available (from customers or analysts). The application of QFD tools and techniques to requirements discovery creates a much better understanding of requirements, much more quickly. Therefore, the need for and the number of iterations required during development is drastically reduced (see Figure 11.2).[4]

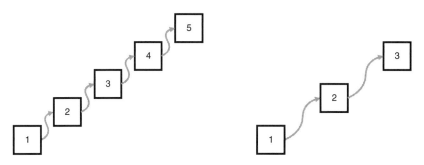

FIGURE 11.2
Iterative methods alone, and with QFD. Fewer iterations require less effort and take less time. QFD tools, applied to better discovery of customer needs at the front end of the development process, can reduce the number of iterations required, and thus development time and effort.

The History of QFD

QFD originated more than 20 years ago in Japan for the efficient development of products and services that satisfy customers. Dr. Yoji Akao and other leading quality experts in Japan developed the QFD tools and techniques and organized them into a comprehensive quality system.[5]

Organizations throughout North America have used QFD since 1984, with cross-functional teams and concurrent/simultaneous engineering, and on services, products, and the product development process.[6, 7, 8] In certain industries, such as the automobile industry, QFD use is now practically universal. And as companies such as Toyota and Ford demonstrated the effectiveness of QFD, its use in the software industry became inevitable (see Figure 11.3).

The History of Software QFD

Why apply QFD to software? In almost all cases, software is developed to produce a result for the organization(s) that funded the software's development. And in most of those cases, software is built to satisfy customers, both internal and external. To satisfy customers better (and/or faster), we must deliver value to them more efficiently. To do this, we need a framework for value, and a process to ensure its efficient delivery. QFD was developed over the past 40 years for this purpose[9] and it has been applied to software for almost two decades.[10]

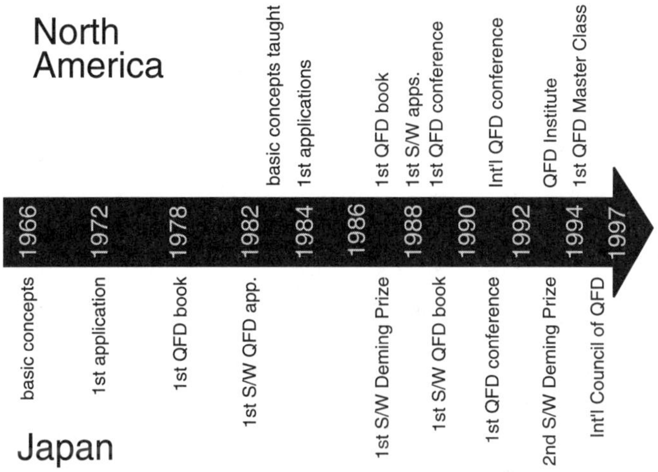

FIGURE 11.3

The first 20 years of QFD in Japan and North America. Note that QFD development preceded its use at Toyota in the 1970s and the first use of a matrix came before Mitsubishi Heavy Industry's application at its Kobe shipyards. The first QFD book written in English was Bob King's *Better Design in Half the Time*, published in 1987.

In Japan

Since 1982, Japanese software organizations have been using QFD with impressive results.[11] Dr. Tadashi Yoshizawa and other leading software quality experts in Japan pioneered Software QFD.[12] NEC IC Microcomputer Systems Ltd., which received a Deming Prize in 1987 for its world-class software-quality efforts, is a sterling example of the power of Software QFD.[13] In 1989, with support from the Ministry for International Trade and Industry (MITI), the Information Processing Promotion Industry Association released a two-volume, 360-page book on Software QFD to further the development of high-quality software by Japanese firms.[14] These impressive efforts to combine sophisticated software engineering[15] with state-of-the-art quality systems, such as QFD, are continuing.[16]

In North America

Since 1988, North American software organizations have been using QFD.[17] Firms such as AT&T Bell Laboratories,[18] DEC,[19, 20] Hewlett-Packard,[21, 22] IBM,[23] Texas Instruments,[24] and others have reported good results with Software QFD. QFD has become an essential part of TQM for world-class software organizations[25] and today it is part of DFSS as well.

So, What Is QFD and Why Do We Need It?

To understand what QFD is and why we need it, it helps to consider a very simple model of the development process.

- **Analysis phase.** What the customer wants, documented in a specification.

- **Design phase.** How the product will work, documented in a design.

- **Development phase.** Make the product and test it.

- **Implementation.** Deliver/install the product and begin supporting it.

Now consider two organizations with the same resources and the same time pressures to develop a product to satisfy a customer.

Incoherent Development

The first organization proceeds as usual (see Figure 11.4a). It gathers requirements, documents them in a specification, and attempts to meet all the requirements throughout the development process. But like most software development organizations, this organization does not have enough resources or time to meet *all* customer requirements and provide best efforts throughout development. Even if the spec notes the high importance of some of the customer's requirements, there is no method to communicate such information to all the developers and through all the phases. Nevertheless, some items in each phase receive special attention, but this decision is made independently by those involved in each step of development; furthermore, by chance, some items that received best efforts in one phase also receive best efforts in a later phase. The result is a product that does not fully represent the effort the team put in, as most of the team's best efforts are wasted by lesser efforts upstream or downstream. Also, the product is strong in terms of meeting the requirements of greatest importance to the customer, but only by luck. Because the results depend on chance, a large organization with many development teams will have a few successes due to good luck, and a few clear failures due to bad luck. In both cases, the efforts of the team are not responsible for the result.

Coherent Development

The second organization proceeds with QFD (Figure 11.4b). It uses QFD to discover the customer's voice and to gather the customer's requirements, including the priority the customer places on those requirements. There are not enough resources or time for all customer requirements to receive best efforts throughout development, so the team concentrates on the small number of high-value requirements. It uses specific formal and informal methods to communicate the high-value needs and their priority to all developers and through all phases. The high-value items receive best efforts in every phase, consistently.

The result is a product that shows the team's true capability. They performed at their absolute best, end to end, on the items that mattered most to the customer. For the same amount of resources and time as the first organization, the second organization has produced a result that is clearly superior. And because they used a systematic process to produce this result, they can repeat their success, as can all other development teams in the organization.

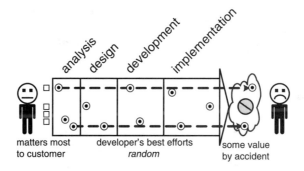

matters most   developer's best efforts   some value
to customer   *random*   by accident

FIGURE 11.4A
An incoherent development process. The boxes on the left represent customer needs. Within each phase, best efforts are applied based on local judgments (and without regard to best efforts in the preceding phase). Over the life of the project, some best efforts align by chance, producing a product with strengths that are not predictable and that align with customer importance only by luck. Without a method to communicate what is most important to the customer end to end, alignment of best efforts to customer priority, and across phases, will be random.

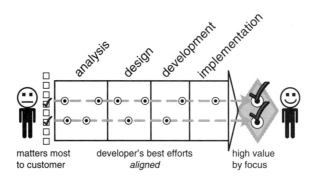

matters most   developer's best efforts   high value
to customer   *aligned*   by focus

FIGURE 11.4B
A coherent development process. QFD is used to discover truer customer needs including their importance. This is communicated end to end throughout the development process by both formal and informal means, and everyone concentrates their best efforts where it matters most to the customer. The result is a product with predictable strengths on items of greatest importance to the customer: a high-value solution, produced efficiently.

A Focus on Priority

Why is focus so important to QFD? In order to satisfy customers when our time and resources are limited, we must be efficient. Consider a customer with many requirements, as shown in Figure 11.5.

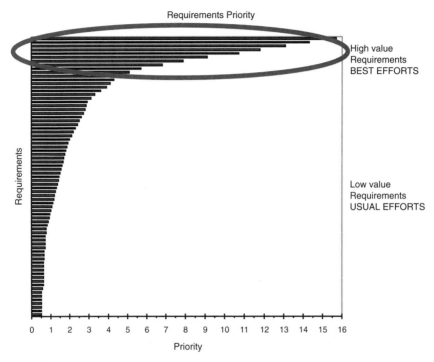

FIGURE 11.5
Accurate measurement of requirements priority reveals a Pareto distribution.

So to improve our development process for greater customer satisfaction, we need to apply our best efforts on the small number of high-value requirements. Much of the effort spent on doing a great job on the many low-value requirements has no impact on customer satisfaction.

Some customer needs are more important than others. When the importance of needs is accurately measured, such as with the Analytic Hierarchy Process (see Chapter 8), it is clear from the priorities that a vital few requirements are as much as an order of magnitude more important than the many requirements of almost trivial importance. Performance on the trivial requirements doesn't matter. Only performance on the important requirements has a significant effect on customer satisfaction. With limited resources or time, it is essential to do your best on what matters most to customers. On the many trivial requirements, do what you can, time and resources permitting.

Most analysis approaches concentrate on requirement *completeness*. The assumption is that we should discover, document, and deliver *all* the customer requirements, and that this will satisfy the customer. In contrast, QFD focuses on requirement *sufficiency*. The assumption in this case is that if we concentrate our available efforts on the most important requirements, we have our best chance at satisfying the customer. The aim is to deliver a *sufficient* level of performance on a *sufficient* number of high-value requirements to satisfy the intended customer.

In Software QFD, software requirements of low value, but requiring high effort to develop, will be set aside to free up effort for the high-value requirements.[26] They are intentionally not implemented. If low-value requirements are missing, customers may notice, they may complain, they may even insist they be added in the next upgrade, but they will still buy, accept, and use the software. The customer's interest, choice, and loyalty are won or lost on how the software performs on the small number of high-value requirements. Most requirements will have no significant impact on customer satisfaction because they just aren't that important to the customer—they're of low value.

QFD Defined

So, what is QFD? Japan Industrial Standard Q 9025 defines QFD as follows:

> ... [a] supporting technique for organizations to achieve effective and efficient performance improvement of management system and provides methods for deployment and realization of the voice of the consumer from product quality characteristics and product elements to process elements. Furthermore, it provides methods for identifying operation or job function that is important in assuring product quality. This standard has been designed for use by organization requiring the following.

Items from the perspective of new product development are the following:

- Identification of voices of the consumer toward new product to be developed and compilation of such voices in the form that can be viewed easily

- Identification of the design elements necessary to realize markets needs

- Quantitative assessment of required quality and quality characteristics to be prioritized in product to be developed

- Determination of design quality of the product in the planning and development stage

- Early identification of technology to become bottleneck in development and review into solution of the problem

- A grasp of management of the new product development process from a total perspective including quality, cost, productivity, and reliability[27]

QFD is a modern quality system composed of deployments (subsystems), each focused on one dimension of the development process (such as reliability). These deployments in turn are composed of a series of tools, organized in a sequence to address the questions and concerns of that dimension throughout the project and the development process.[28]

QFD Deployments

In this chapter, the term *QFD* refers to the entire quality system shown in Figure 11.6, not just to the first box, which represents the "House of Quality" matrix.

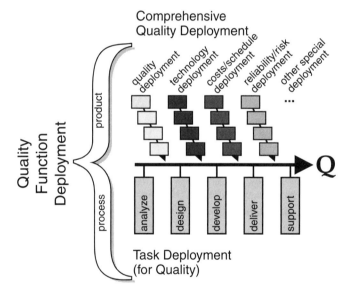

FIGURE 11.6
Deployments of QFD. QFD is a quality system with many subsystems. Task deployment is the application of QFD to the development process itself. It is used to tailor QFD to a specific organization. Comprehensive quality deployment refers to the QFD activities applied during a project. Specific deployments address the dimensions of development that are important for that project, such as quality, reliability, safety, security, and maintainability in a DFTS organization.

The Four-Phase Model of QFD

The four-phase model of QFD was popularized by a *Harvard Business Review* article, "The House of Quality."[29] Presenting an early understanding of QFD, the model was widely adopted by automotive suppliers, for whom it had been developed. Parts suppliers at the time were operating in a build-to-print environment. Their auto company customers supplied them with a detailed design and asked them to build the corresponding parts.[30] Figure 11.7 shows the four-phase model.

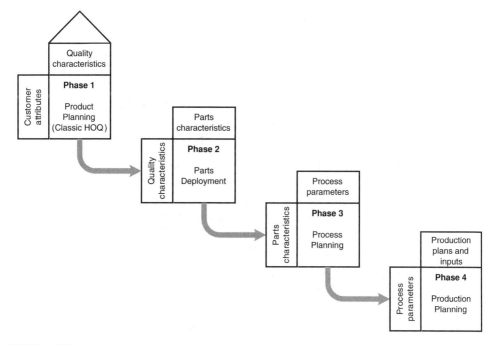

FIGURE 11.7
The four-phase model begins with the "House of Quality" and deploys quality characteristics into parts, the specific equipment to make those parts, and the settings and procedures for those parts-making machines. As this is a tailored QFD process for parts suppliers in a build-to-print environment, no design activities are supported, making this an inappropriate model for software development.

When the design is a given and cannot be changed, the only decision a parts supplier needs to make is how to build the part better—how to best upgrade an existing model of the product. The four phases in this approach are as follows:

1. **Phase 1: The "House of Quality" customer attributes/quality characteristics matrix.** This matrix answers the question, what does a "good product" mean to our customers? The definitions of *goodness* contained in the customer attributes are mapped into the quality characteristics of the product. So this is where the "voice of the customer" represented by the product attributes is translated into the language of the product quality characteristics.

2. **Phase 2: The Parts Deployment quality characteristics/parts characteristics matrix.** This matrix answers the question, what parts of the product deliver the quality characteristics our customers want? Critical quality characteristics are mapped into parts and their characteristics. (Note that the design, and therefore the necessary parts, is already determined. There is no design in the software development sense in this model, as a parts supplier in a build-to-print environment cannot do systems design; it can only upgrade the existing product. It is constrained to *only* make changes within parts or within its production process.)

3. **Phase 3: The Process Planning part characteristics/process parameters matrix.** This matrix answers the question, where in our manufacturing process can we affect the critical parts characteristics? Critical parts characteristics are mapped into process steps and parameters. So this is where the "voice of the customer," translated into critical process steps and parameters, reaches the factory floor.

4. **Phase 4: The Production Planning process parameters/production requirements matrix.** This matrix answers the question, what should the production plans, procedures, and inputs be for the key process operations to produce the key parts (with their critical characteristics) to satisfy the customer? So now the "voice of the customer" has reached the machine operators, and it determines the settings on the production machinery.

At each phase, only the most important items are deployed to the next phase. (Otherwise, the matrices can become unmanageably large.) In this way, QFD is helping the entire production process end to end to focus best efforts on what matters most to the customers. So what is actually conveyed by the "voice of the customer" is not the content of what the customer said—that changes from customer attributes to engineering characteristics, and so on, to machine settings—but the *importance to the customer*, the *priority*. So across the dimensions of development, represented by the rows and columns of the matrices in the model, the knowledge of what's most important to the customer is communicated.

The "House of Quality" Matrix

When they think of QFD, many people think of the "House of Quality" matrix. So named because it resembles a house (if you use your imagination), this matrix is intended to be the bridge between the world of the customer and the world of the developer. It is here that traditionally the "voice of the customer," or customer needs, are translated into the corresponding quality characteristics and capabilities that the solution will require (see Figure 11.8).

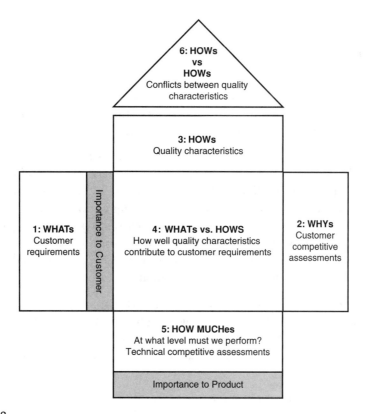

FIGURE 11.8
Components, or "rooms," of the traditional "House of Quality" matrix. When first introduced to North America in the mid-1980s this was how the matrix was described for hardware and model upgrade applications. Today modern QFD uses a more sophisticated approach that leads to smaller and more focused matrices with greater accuracy that take less time and effort to produce.

The "House of Quality" matrix is an analysis matrix, and it is created before any design activities are performed. The matrix has several components, often referred to as *rooms* (listed here in order of completion):

- **Room 1.** Traditionally, this room represents customer requirements (the *whats*). It is more accurate to say that this is the hierarchy of customer needs (the *whys*) with quantification (magnitude and priority).

- **Room 2.** Traditionally, this optional room of customer competitive assessments is a table with fixed ordinal or interval scale weights. It is much more accurate (and valid) to use the Analytic Hierarchy Process (AHP) from Chapter 8 throughout this room. If there are no customer competitive concerns, such as for an internal project, this component is unnecessary.

- **Room 3.** Traditionally, this room represents quality characteristics (the *hows*). It is more accurate to say that this is the hierarchy of the characteristics or capabilities that the solution must have to satisfy the customer (the *whats*).

- **Room 4.** This room is the heart of the matrix. It maps the customer needs to the quality characteristics and capabilities, clearly showing the contributions the quality characteristics and capabilities make to customer needs. In Japan, Quantification Method III is used to reorder the rows and columns of this matrix, to enhance the patterns represented with symbols. Certain patterns of symbols are significant. Traditionally, the contribution strength was represented by a fixed 1-2-3 or 1-2-4 or 1-3-5 or 1-3-9 ordinal or interval scale. It is much more accurate (and valid) to use the AHP from Chapter 8 throughout this room.

- **Room 5.** Traditionally, this optional room of technical competitive assessments is a table using fixed ordinal or interval scale weights. It is much more accurate (and valid) to use the AHP from Chapter 8 throughout this room. If there are no technical competitive concerns, such as for an internal project, this component is unnecessary.

- **Room 6.** Traditionally, this optional "roof" of the "House of Quality" matrix is completed much later in the development process, by designers considering technical and physical conflicts among quality characteristics and capabilities for a given design. It is important to note that a "conflict" applies only to a particular design, and you can dissolve it using methods such as *Teoriya Resheniya Izobreatatelskikh Zadatch* (TRIZ; see Chapter 12 for an introduction to this powerful method for systematic innovation). If there are no technical or physical conflicts, such as for a software project, this component is unnecessary. (Most published case studies with roofs are poor examples of this very specialized component, and are good arguments for the use of TRIZ and other innovation methods to eliminate the conflict.)

Software QFD does not use the "roof" of the "House of Quality" matrix. The columns in the matrix are software or technical requirements—the characteristics and capabilities which any solution must have in order to satisfy the customer, and therefore to be a "quality" solution. And these should be implementation free, or devoid of any assumptions of design or implementing technology. (Such design decisions occur later in the development process and are supported by subsequent QFD matrices and tables.) Therefore, the items in the columns cannot conflict, unless we have already created the design or are constrained in what design we can use (as may be the case for an upgrade of an existing product). In order for a conflict to exist, a design or implementing technology must be assumed. For example, in the classic hardware example of a car door, a conflict is presented between "ease of opening" and "sealing against rain". But this conflict exists only with a conventional door design. For tilt-forward doors, as on a Lamborghini Countach or Toyota Sera, no conflict exists. For gull-wing doors, such as on a Bricklin or DeLorean, no conflict exists. Also note that such conflicts are fundamentally physical conflicts, and there are no physical conflicts in software.

In software development, when we are making design decisions during the design phase and are choosing which implementing technology to use, it is useful and appropriate to examine logical or design conflicts—and the roof can be helpful. But that is in the design phase, not in the analysis phase, and the "House of Quality" is an analysis phase matrix.

The "House of Quality" ≠ QFD

You are not performing QFD if all you are doing is creating a "House of Quality" matrix. This is the forceful pronouncement of Dr. Yoji Akao, the developer of QFD and still the foremost authority on QFD:

> When a baby takes their first step, they are "learning to walk." But clearly they are not "walking" in the usual sense we use the word. A child of four can walk, run, skip, and jump. They are mature at walking. If they are still taking one step and falling down, it is cause for serious concern. Doing just a House of Quality for a first QFD project is unexceptional. Still just doing a House of Quality years later is unfortunate.

A "House of Quality" matrix is just one tool, only one step, and it could be the basis for QFD if you keep going, but just doing one matrix (of any kind) is not QFD. It is just creating a matrix. And a matrix is just one of the seven tools in the 7 MP toolbox of QFD (see Chapter 7 for information on all of the basic QFD tools).[31]

"Kindergarten QFD"

Some software organizations have succeeded with Software QFD, only to stagnate and become a case of arrested development. These organizations learned about the "House of Quality" matrix of QFD and applied it successfully to their software projects. Then they expanded the number of projects using QFD, but not the amount of QFD that they were using. Some software organizations are still only using the "House of Quality" matrix years after learning about QFD. They crawl, but they have never learned to walk. They don't even know what walking *is*.

QFD Maturity

Once a team or an organization learns a bit about QFD, we can look at several factors to assess their success. We can look at the **breadth** or the extent of their use of QFD throughout the organization. We can examine the **depth**, or the degree to which they integrate and use QFD end to end throughout the development life cycle. We can see the **height** or **power** of their QFD process, by checking the number of deployments (subsystems) they use and the number of tools they employ in each. (This simple metric has limitations, but it works well for immature QFD organizations.) Combined, these measures tell us the team or organization's **QFD maturity**.

In competitive situations, a company using just one tool (such as the "House of Quality" matrix) will have a difficult time competing with an organization using several tools in an integrated way. And a company using just one deployment will wither in the face of organizations using multiple deployments. A **deployment** is a subsystem of the QFD system, with a series of tools sequenced to address one dimension of the development process, throughout the development process. For example, technology, or the means of implementing functional requirements, is one common deployment. Generally this deployment involves several tools applied at the architecture, application, subsystem, and module levels of detail. As a point of comparison, comprehensive QFD approaches contain the five basic deployments shown in Figure 11.6, plus additional special deployments.

One cause for concern is that in many U.S. software organizations, QFD development has halted at a low level; often at just the "House of Quality" stage. Is QFD so difficult to implement that only excellent organizations can succeed with it?

Consider the tools and techniques of structured analysis (SA), which were developed at about the same time as QFD. Although they were a tremendous step forward for software development (providing a structured approach to requirements specification), they were unwieldy, were labor intensive, and had numerous rough edges. (Many people just used data-flow diagrams.) Only good and determined organizations succeeded in mastering SA at that time. During the next decade, significant refinement and development occurred.

These changes did not invalidate the initial concepts of SA, but they did give practitioners greater power and assurance for less effort. This "next-generation" SA reduced the risks and made SA accessible and successful for a much wider audience.

QFD Evolution

QFD has evolved since it emerged in Japan, and moved to North America and then to the rest of the world.[32] In the twenty-first century, QFD has been applied to QFD itself, to produce a "next-generation" Modern QFD. The basis for Modern QFD is the Blitz QFD approach—a QFD method designed to be a better, faster, and cheaper QFD process than the traditional QFD approach.

Let's first look at some of the problems software organizations have experienced with traditional QFD in practice, and the causes of these problems. Then we'll consider how Modern QFD, based on Blitz, can prevent or minimize them, and why it is better, faster, and cheaper.

Problems with Traditional QFD Applied to Software

Traditional QFD applied to software had a number of problems. Some of these were not problems with QFD itself, but rather, with a limited understanding of QFD or a weak implementation approach. What went wrong, at times, when traditional QFD was applied to software?

Traditional QFD Failures

Some software project teams failed in their attempt to apply QFD because they lacked training and they had no support by experienced Software QFD practitioners during their first Software QFD project. Of course, any powerful method can fail with inadequate training or support, so this is not a fault of QFD, but there were a number of failures of this type when software organizations first tried to do Software QFD. It is important to obtain good training in Software QFD (not in Hardware QFD, as there are too many tricky details that are different) and appropriate support for those using Software QFD for the first time.

QFD is not magic. You can certainly do it so poorly that is a complete waste of time. But QFD's track record over 40 years for hardware applications, and over 20 years for software, is clear. If you learn it and apply it correctly, QFD can work, and work well.

In fact, QFD's reputation is so great that some organizations experience *false positives* when they try QFD. Knowing that Software QFD is a "best practice" in leading software organizations, a team may claim (and believe) that QFD worked great on their project. When asked whether they will use it again, they will say, "Yes, on a *larger* project." Upon further questioning, they will say it was a little too much for the size of their project. This means QFD really failed—the team would not, on their own, use it again on a similarly sized or smaller project. This is not a solid foundation for QFD to grow on in an organization. But failure, or a false positive, is not the only danger in implementing QFD.

"The Matrix Is Too Big"

The "House of Quality" matrix usually has about 50 percent more columns than rows. That is, for 100 rows, you will typically generate about 150 columns. And that means there are 15,000 cells to examine—even though typically only 20 percent to 30 percent of them take on values. This is too much effort to spend in one place in the development process. Why does the matrix get this big?

Garbage In...

The concept of "garbage in, garbage out" is the cause of many oversized "House of Quality" matrices. Unfortunately, some books and seminars still describe the rows and columns as *what*s and *how*s. This is a description, not a definition, and it allows people to put anything that they would consider a *what* in the rows and any answer to a *how* in the columns. This leads to the situation where newcomers make avoidable mistakes.

This is a special problem for software, as the terms *what* and *how* have been widely used in methods as far back as SA to explain the distinction between logical or essential (technology-and-implementation-free) models done in analysis and appearing in a functional spec, and physical or design (technology-and-implementation-specific) models done in design and appearing in a design spec.

That QFD continues to flourish despite these challenges is perhaps the best testimony to the method's robustness. Even poor QFD is significantly better than no QFD, so QFD continues to grow and spread anyway.

Criteria versus Solutions

If you have *how*s, or design solutions, in the columns, you will likely put the criteria for choosing the solutions in the rows. For technical people these are usually **technical requirements** or **design requirements**—the characteristics or capabilities that the design/technology/implementation must satisfy. So we wind up with what should be the columns in the rows, and the customer needs never appear. This is a very common situation, and you will find this situation in the well-known car-door case study. Although this is a useful matrix, it is a design matrix, not a "House of Quality" matrix, produced to bridge the world of the customer and the world of the developer. (And it may not be the most important matrix for you to do, if for some reason you are doing only one.)

"It Takes Too Long"

One of the most common complaints of applying traditional QFD to software is that it can take a great deal of time. Worse, once people begin the detailed analysis that any QFD matrix requires, they often lose sight of the reason QFD exists: to ensure customer satisfaction *efficiently*.

In the next section, we'll see how Modern QFD addresses the purpose of QFD, but without using the matrix as the primary tool to do so and thereby avoiding this problem. The QFD framework will still aid us in keeping our focus on the "voice of the customer" and on cross-functional team communication concerning what matters most to customers, and it will act as an aid in discovering high-value customer needs and corresponding product requirements and features.

To address this problem, some practitioners of traditional QFD tried to "speed up" or "streamline" traditional QFD by

- Doing only the "House of Quality" matrix

- Doing a size-limited "House of Quality" matrix, with a restricted number of rows and columns, or by using the secondary level of the customer needs hierarchy instead of the tertiary level

- Focusing on only portions of the product where critical trade-offs occur, when doing a model upgrade

- Terminating the QFD process when it has provided "enough" answers to critical questions

Unfortunately, such approaches did not succeed and are not pursued today. Instead, by going back to the fundamentals of QFD and applying QFD to itself, a more efficient form of QFD was developed, whereby the matrix is an optional tool and is used only when specifically required. Another benefit of this analysis was to clearly show the power of QFD for new-product development, including products that are new to the company and are new to the world.

"We Knew That Already"

A common complaint concerning Software QFD is that the results were not of sufficient value—in other words, they weren't worth the effort required to produce them. As many people are still only doing the "House of Quality" matrix for their software development projects, this means that the "House of Quality" matrix required too much effort and yielded too few insights. The common complaint is, "We knew that already. The answers were obvious."

Weak Content

A major cause of lack of value in the "House of Quality" matrix is weak content. Several things cause content to be weak, and the most common is not having a clear understanding of the project's strategy—in other words, not having a clear idea of the project's success factors and how the project fits with the organization's overall strategy. This can lead to irrelevant QFD results. The second cause of weak content is not defining what types of customers the project has to satisfy, and how much it has to satisfy them—that is, which customers are most important to the project's success, and why. This leads to the wrong customers being visited, a greater proportion of customer needs from the least important customers, and a lack of important needs from the most important customers. The final cause of weak content is not having a strong upstream "voice of the customer" process prior to doing the "House of Quality" matrix—that is, not being clear, trained, or skilled at observing the context of the customers, gathering their statements, and organizing and prioritizing their needs. This leads to important needs being lost or misunderstood by the time they get to the "House of Quality." Before you invest time and effort in doing a "House of Quality" matrix, make sure the inputs are correct.

But even if the content was correct, there were other problems...

Weak Understanding

If QFD was a newly developed technique, we could understand why certain errors are so common. But despite the fact that QFD is a mature method, an almost random pattern of learning and dissemination of bits and pieces of QFD occurred in the first 15 years of QFD's spread to North America and Europe.

The problem is further aggravated by QFD's role as a key component in both TQM[33] and DFSS.[34] Because too few people in the Six Sigma community have acquired a comprehensive understanding of QFD, the biggest benefits to using QFD are still ahead for most organizations that use DFSS.

Filter the Input

The "House of Quality" matrix should have *only* customer needs in the rows, and *only* the related software characteristics and capabilities in the columns. Nothing else should be in this particular matrix. To ensure this, you should sort out the customer statements using a Customer Voice Table (CVT), organize them using an Affinity Diagram, structure them using a Hierarchy Diagram, and prioritize them using the AHP (we will discuss all of these issues shortly). After this upstream processing is done, you will have good input to your "House of Quality" matrix.

This will prevent the problem of mixed items in your matrix, but what about the sheer size of the matrix. What if we have lots of customer needs?

Control the Size

There are several aspects to making sure you are not overwhelmed in the QFD process, and the first aspect is to focus on your most important customers, by prioritizing your strategy and your customers, and then having the *customers* prioritize their needs. This allows you to concentrate on the top *n* customer needs. The second aspect is to plan what matrices you should do (if any), and limit their size. There is no point in working through a matrix with many more customer needs than you can act on with best efforts. Take the top *n* customer needs and choose *n* to be within what the team can tackle. Finally, do not exhaust all of your QFD efforts in one shot at one point in the project. It is far better to do ten 10x10 matrices (or other QFD tools) to address ten key dimensions during your project at ten carefully chosen points in time, than it is to do one 100x100 "House of Quality" matrix at one point.

If at any time, you feel that your matrix (or any QFD tool) is "too big," it means you have not managed the size of your work objects properly. In software engineering, we have to do *complete* work objects. You have to put all the objects in your system on your class hierarchy diagram, not just the most important ones. But in Software QFD, we are focused on value, so working on the top *n* of anything is not only allowed, but also is essential for focus and efficiency.

Check the Matrix

Every step in the QFD process involves procedures for checking the step, catching errors, and assuring correctness. (This is a basic property of any good quality method.) QFD matrices can contain a variety of structural errors, and methods for checking for such errors do exist, as do methods for conducting simple mathematical checks on the values in the matrix. Learn how to do the work right, and how to check that you have done so.

Modern QFD for Software

In response to feedback from both software and nonsoftware organizations using QFD in the early 1990s, a group of experienced practitioners at the QFD Institute[35] (QFDI) applied QFD *to* QFD to develop a better QFD product.[36] What resulted was Blitz QFD: a faster, better way to do QFD, especially for those just starting to use the method. This is an engineered initial subset of QFD designed to provide maximum gains from a minimum of effort. In practice, Blitz QFD turned out to be the perfect way to get the benefits of QFD on very rapid development projects, and any time that time or resources were tightly limited. The aim is to deliver essential value to key customers rapidly and efficiently.

Blitz QFD

In order to do the least QFD and get the most gains, we must focus on QFD fundamentals and apply them to software development.

- **Exploration.** What are the most important things for us to know about satisfying our customers' needs? We need requirements exploration to answer this.

- **Execution.** What are the most important things for us to do to deliver value to customers? We need requirements deployment to plan this.

So what does Blitz QFD have that allows us to answer these questions quickly during software development?

The Seven Management and Planning (7 MP) Tools

The "official" tools for QFD are the Seven Management and Planning (7 MP) Tools (see Chapter 7)[37] as shown in Figure 11.9. While you are not limited to these tools, it is necessary to be familiar with them to take full advantage of Modern QFD.[38]

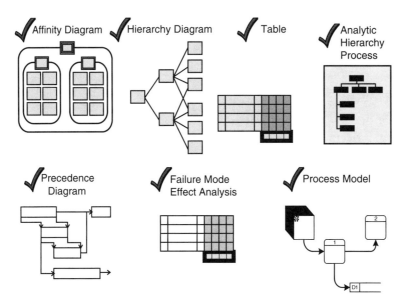

FIGURE 11.9
The 7 MP Tools for Blitz QFD. The basic tools for traditional QFD are modified for Blitz QFD. Gathered from a variety of disciplines, these tools support rapid requirements exploration and deployment. Note that matrices, which are for detailed analysis, are not used.

Customer Satisfaction and Value

Customers are satisfied when they receive value: benefits greater than the effort or cost to them of achieving those benefits.[39] Customers determine the amount of benefits and costs, and therefore, the value they received.

What Is Value?

In QFD, **value** is recognized when customers perceive benefit, either by a *problem* of theirs that has been solved or minimized; an *opportunity* they want to seize, maximize, or enable; themselves *looking good* to significant others; or themselves *feeling good* about themselves.[40] If a software package does nothing for any of your problems, does not enable you to seize any of your opportunities, does not help you to impress others whose opinion you care about, or does not help you feel better, it is of no value to you.

Even a single customer will desire multiple benefits (problems, opportunities, and look good and feel good issues) with different magnitudes and priorities. These are **customer needs** in QFD terms. A group of customers with similar perceptions of value (benefits and costs) and similar judgments about their magnitudes and priorities is a **customer segment**.

How Is Value Delivered to Customers?

Out of the large number of software work objects (objects, data, functions, scripts, and so on) produced during development, only a few directly or strongly relate to *any* high-priority customer need.[41] This does not suggest that unnecessary items are worked on during development. All the items are there for a reason. And if none of them was delivered, the customer would certainly not be satisfied. But many "necessary" items have no significant effect individually on the amount of value a customer receives. Whether they are done superbly well—or are absent entirely—individually they do not comprise the difference between customer satisfaction and customer dissatisfaction. In examining ten recently developed Information Technology (IT) development projects in a large retail organization, such "necessary" but nonessential (non-high-value-added) items averaged 73 percent of the items delivered.[42] Doing a great job on items that don't matter to customers is inefficient.

What Is Essential to Our Success?

A small number of items individually have a *very* significant effect on the amount of value a customer receives. Done well, they can deliver sufficient value to ensure customer satisfaction. Such high-value items are *essential* to satisfying the customer. In a large retailer study, the number of essential items in the ten systems studied ranged from 3 to 17.[43] If we could identify these *essential items* upfront, we could concentrate our best software engineering attention on them. Doing a great job on items of high value to the customer is very efficient development.

Further, out of the many development tasks we perform on a software project, only a few are truly critical to performing the essential tasks well. If we could identify these *essential tasks* upfront, we could concentrate our best project management attention on them. On the few essential tasks, managing for speed is counterproductive; the risk to value is too high. On the many nonessential tasks, managing for speed is very productive.

Being able to quickly see which development items are high value and in which project tasks they are performed gives us a framework to efficiently ensure the satisfaction of our targeted customer segment(s).

The Blitz QFD Process

Figure 11.10 shows the nine steps of the Blitz QFD process. As you can see, the few first steps in Blitz QFD are aimed at understanding the project's context. We will discuss each of the nine steps of the process in the following subsections.

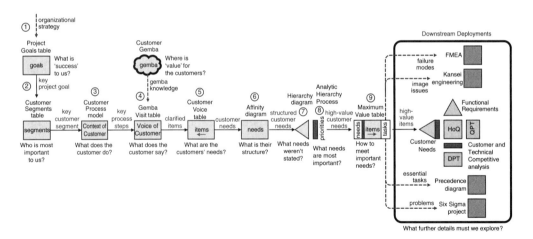

FIGURE 11.10
The Blitz QFD process has nine steps and no matrices (although it may lead to matrices, such as the "House of Quality" matrix shown behind step 9). From the Maximum Value Table (MVT), a wide range of project-specific concerns can be followed up. Four common ones are shown with branches: FMEA (for detailed analysis of high-risk items), Kansei Engineering (for analysis of interface design and look-and-feel-related issues), essential tasks on a Precedence diagram (for Schedule Deployment with Critical Chain project management), and problems (for solving with Six Sigma DMADV or DMAIC methods).

Step 1: Key Project Goal

Why are we doing this project? In what part of our organization's strategy is this project expected to play? To answer these questions we need to understand some aspects of strategy. One method that can help with strategic issues for software is the New Lanchester Strategy.[44]

The New Lanchester Strategy

The New Lanchester Strategy is based on the Lanchester Laws, discovered by the British aeronautical engineer, F. W. Lanchester. After the outbreak of World War I in 1914, Lanchester, with great interest, witnessed battles in which aircraft he had worked on were used. He became convinced of the need for a mathematical analysis of the relative strengths of opposing battlefield forces to describe aircraft effectiveness. By conducting quantitative studies of the number of casualties on both sides in land, sea, and air battles, he arrived at the Lanchester Laws.[45, 46]

Lanchester's work was introduced in Japan in 1952 in a book on operations research sent by W. Edward Deming: *Methods of Operations Research* by P. M. Morse and G. E. Kimball. Dr. Nobuo Taoka restructured Lanchester's military strategies into marketing and sales strategies. The books Dr. Taoka wrote were unprecedented business best-sellers in Japan. The Japanese adopted Lanchester's Laws, his ideas on concentration, and his military terminology in their marketing terminology. The strategies provided unique insights into competition between companies, and rules for selecting a strategy depending upon whether the company was attacking a new market or defending an existing market position were found to be quite useful. The Japanese also extended Lanchester's work to powerful and practical methods for planning market segmentation, market structure, and market position.[47, 48]

From an analysis of the goals of our project, we should have a clear definition of what *success* means for the project. And we should understand that the team's performance will be evaluated when the project is finished.

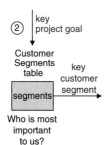

Step 2: Key Customer Segment

Which customers or users can help us the most, to achieve our key project goal? Which can block our success? Whomever we must satisfy to succeed, or whomever must not be dissatisfied, we fail as a potential *customer* in QFD. Therefore, the next step is to consider the types of customers we are aiming to please, and their relative importance to the project, so that we can focus on the key segment.

Customer Segments Table

Because we will usually not have time to interview, survey, or visit all of our customers or users, we will have to work with a subset of them. So it is critical that we understand what subsets, or types, of customers we are dealing with so that we can make sure we investigate some users in each segment.

There are a variety of ways to perform segmentation.[49] From an analysis of our customer segments, we should understand which customer segments are critical for us to succeed, and whom we must satisfy with our software.

Step 3: Key Process Steps

If we understand the meaning of success and we understand our key customer segments, we need to know where our software should add value to these key customers. To do this we will have to go to the *gemba*. But first it is useful to model what we already know, or expect to find, in a customer context model. A process model, such as a data-flow diagram, is useful for this.

Customer Process Model

We can use any process modeling method here, but for software developers, methods that are already familiar and are supported by drawing or CASE tools are best. A data-flow diagram is well suited to modeling the situation where the customer or user does whatever we are trying to support with our software.

From an analysis of the customer context, we should understand what customers do, and why, as well as what their problems are and the magnitude of those problems. But at this point our model is based on what we already know. How can we fill in what we don't know and validate what we think we do know?

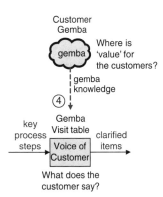

Step 4: Go to Gemba

We must go the "real place"—the *gemba*—where customers would benefit from the software we will build, and observe firsthand their situation, their problems, and their opportunities. We will use interviews, observations, and situation analyses in the *gemba* to gather the "voice of the customer."

Gemba Visit Table

Our aim is to observe what our customers do, and to understand why they do these things. We will also talk to our customers, but we won't get requirements—we'll get **verbatims**, or actual words. With their verbatims, we want to understand what they say (their meaning), and why they say it.

We can use a simple table to record our observations and the customers' actual words when we interview them in the *gemba*. Audio and video recordings are also valuable, as not everyone will be able to visit every *gemba*. If we can record what we see and what is said, we can share the experience with others on the team.

Why Go to the Gemba?

Most software developers build software for others—for customers or users. The developer will have a mental model, or a surrogate, of the customer in his head and will often refer to this model when interpreting requirements or making design decisions.[50]

But what does this mental model of a customer look like? In the absence of any other influence, it looks just like the developer. And this leads to statements such as, "Our customers won't want to do that; I never do."

The best software developers have accurate mental models of their customers in their heads, and they obtained those mental models because they had direct contact with real customers, in real situations. There is no substitute for seeing the customers firsthand in their work environment, and the means they use to perform their work. You learn about a customer's job, goals, and problems. And this knowledge does not develop without actually visiting the customer.

I have seen many cases where major design decisions were stymied because none of the designers had ever spent any time in the customer's world. When they finally were persuaded to "go see" (instead of "go ahead and guess"), they were able to resolve their quandary, with confidence, in less than an hour.

When key developers have never been to the *gemba*, inevitably they will make unfortunate assumptions about what the customer needs, or how the customer will use the software. Often this will result in a system that is overburdened with features (just in case they are ever necessary) and is overdesigned for unnecessary performance.

Too often, specification writers work with features rather than benefits—but customers buy benefits, not features. For example, in writing a specification for a fax machine it may be tempting to specify a stepper motor or servo drive to move the paper or print head. But is that a benefit? Can the customer perceive it directly? If not, we should specify what the customer will actually notice, such as speed, print quality, and noise level.

This is where we get the "voice of the customer" in QFD. Once we have collected the verbatims and observations, the next step is to analyze them so that we get more than just the stated, surface requirements.

Step 5: What Are the Customer Needs?

What does the customer need? We have to analyze their clarified statements before we can clearly understand what we must do to satisfy them. Statements about reliability, cost, technology, usability, portability, and so on, are very different from **customer needs**, which are solution-independent statements of the benefits customers desire. As such, different people using different tools deal them with at different times during development.

To capture our customers' voices, we must begin by listening to raw customer expressions—the verbatims. What customers say are not requirements. They are statements that we must understand, classify, organize, and prioritize. Only then do we have customer requirements as rigorously defined by QFD. What are their problems, opportunities, and strategic directions? What does the customer want, or need to do, about these concerns? The answers to these questions are true requirements.

Stated Requirements

Stated requirements begin as verbatims from multiple sources. Direct sources are interviews and observations. Indirect sources are mail and phone surveys. Historical sources are complaints and compliments concerning prior products and processes. You must carefully translate these raw customer expressions into positive, clear, and concise requirement statements using the CVT (or the voice of the customer table in Table 11.1). The customers then review and confirm these requirements, and you must sort statements that are not requirements, such as capabilities, features, functions, data, tasks, costs, schedule dates, technologies, and so on, into appropriate columns. Deployments following quality deployment address each of these thoroughly with a focused series of matrices and tables. You should organize the customer requirements alone by the customer using the Affinity Diagram[51] to uncover the customer's conceptual organization of their requirements.

Unstated Requirements

You must uncover unstated requirements by going to the *gemba*—the place where your product/process adds value for the customer—and observing with your own five senses the context of product/process use. Then you must organize these observations in a customer context table. Such context analysis techniques are an extension of existing problem analysis approaches. You may uncover additional unvoiced requirements by using some of the five types of relations diagrams.[52] This tool allows you to discover significant requirements that no customer may have mentioned. Exciting and expected requirements are frequently found in this way—as well as with systems dynamics analysis.

In working through these steps, it is necessary to recognize and define each type of requirement as you encounter it. A requirements dictionary can be invaluable for this.

Changing Requirements?

One common refrain in software development is that the "user's requirements are vague or continually changing." To deal with this various incremental, iterative, and prototyping methods are available. But are the requirements actually changing, or is just our understanding of the requirements changing? Is the ambiguity of the specification due to some fundamental instability of the user's needs, or is it caused by a weak requirements discovery process? Customer needs originate from the customer's problems, opportunities, and the look-good-and-feel-good issues the customer faces in their situation. If the customer's situation is not changing in frequent or unpredictable ways, if their problems or opportunities are not suddenly emerging or vanishing, we cannot blame the problem on "change." (By the same token, unless the customer continues to require changes at the same rate *after* their system is delivered, the cause of the original "ambiguity" was not "change," but our own weak ways of obtaining requirements.) Part of the power of the requirements discovery methods in QFD is that they don't require or expect the customer to understand or articulate their own needs. They just have to allow us to visit their *gemba*, observe their situation, and listen to their verbatims. All these are inputs to the "voice of the customer" analysis process.

Customer Voice Table

We use the **Customer Voice Table** (CVT) for this analysis. (The CVT also acts as a good diagnostic tool: a "requirements Pareto chart").[53] Figure 11.11 depicts a typical CVT.

In the CVT we analyze the verbatims (as well as our observations and customer *gemba* analyses) to uncover the customer need(s) that underlie their verbatims and their actions. The columns consist of all the types of "requirements" that the customers are concerned about—and thus they represent the dimensions of our project that are critical for success. So the table offers a high-level look at what will be important to address on a project.

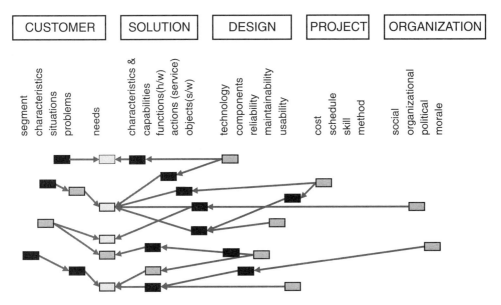

FIGURE 11.11
The CVT is where we analyze the customer verbatims to discover the customer's underlying
needs. Customers may tell us anything, but only solution-independent benefit statements
represent true customer needs. Using the CVT, we work with the customer to understand
what their needs are and why they are asking for them. This table is a powerful requirements discovery tool.

Specifications: Features or Needs?

In QFD we don't focus on features. We don't even ask customers what features they want.
Instead, we ask about the benefits they desire; their needs. What problems do they need
to solve? What opportunities do they need to seize? From understanding such benefits,
we can derive by analysis the best set of features to efficiently deliver the most value to our
customers.

Certain features may be unnecessary to deliver desired benefits. But if you ask the customer, they may not realize that, and they may insist that they need it. Including such a
feature only adds an unnecessary burden on development, with no increased satisfaction for
the customer. Features are concrete. They are software capabilities or characteristics implemented in a particular way (with a certain design and implementing technology). The customer is not an expert on design or technology, so we should not be asking them to decide
on those issues. The customer is an expert on their needs, and that's what we should be asking about.

When developers concentrate on needs, they understand why a user has a particular need and why it is important to them, and they preserve the full range of options for the design and choice of implementing technology. Customers buy benefits, not features. And when they are presented with a new feature, they try to figure out whether the feature will help them with any problems they have or opportunities they want to seize. But even if they can't see a benefit, they may still ask for it, as it may come in handy upon further analysis. It is much better to direct our inquiry to their problems and opportunities where they are truly knowledgeable and expert.

Perhaps the biggest failure of most software specifications is that they don't clearly distinguish customer needs from software characteristics and capabilities (or features), and they do not indicate what is most important to the customer, and why. Actually, this is not surprising. Developers can put into the spec only what they understand, and what tools and techniques do they have to understand customers' needs and priorities?

The CVT is where the analysis occurs to help developers understand customers, after going to the *gemba*. The output of the CVT is the column of customer needs, most of which were extracted from the verbatims and observations of the customers (that were in other columns). *Only* the customer needs are used in the next steps.

Step 6: Structure the Customer Needs

The customer needs in the CVT are just a list, and we know the list is incomplete. What we want to do is somehow bring to the surface the needs we are missing that are important to the key customer segment. How can we do that? Two steps are required.

The Affinity Diagram

After analyzing and sorting out the customer needs, we engage the customer in a simple exercise to bring to the surface the way *they* think about *their* needs. The result is an **Affinity Diagram** produced by using the KJ Method developed by cultural anthropologist, Jiro Kawakita. This nonrational "right brain" method comes from the field of cultural anthropology. Using the KJ Method to produce the Affinity Diagram reveals the **natural structure** of the customer's needs: the cognitive structure the customer uses to think about their own requirements.[54]

With the structure of the customer's needs revealed, we will use that structure to refine needs and fill in missing and unstated needs.

Hierarchy diagram

structured ⑦ customer needs

What needs weren't stated?

Step 7: Analyze Customer Needs Structure

A simple procedure transforms the Affinity Diagram into a first-cut "skeleton" **Hierarchy Diagram**. You use the Hierarchy Diagram to analyze the structure of the customer's needs and to uncover missing and unstated needs. A key part of the analysis is to quantify the *magnitude* of the customer's needs. We *must* know what level of performance is currently available and what improvement is required to satisfy the needs.[55]

The Hierarchy Diagram

Also known as *tree diagrams* or *systematic diagrams*, Hierarchy Diagrams are one of the 7 MP Tools used throughout all QFD deployments.

You can organize almost all key project concerns, including reliability, cost, and customer needs, into hierarchies with primary, secondary, and tertiary levels. Technically these are hierarchies, not trees, as "child" nodes may have more than one parent. They are useful for functional analysis and to show the hierarchy and decomposition of customers, requirements, objects, functions, and so on.

Hierarchy Diagrams make the structure of the high-value customer requirements visible. A three-level hierarchy works well even for very complex situations. Traditionally, requirements are organized in lists. It is difficult with lists to know whether you have a complete set of requirements. A properly organized and prioritized hierarchy can tell us whether we have sufficient requirements to satisfy our customers.

We analyze the hierarchical structure of our customer's needs to uncover **unstated** requirements, which are requirements that no customer mentioned but that the customers confirm are important. This **needs hierarchy analysis** is a requirements discovery method especially valuable for new and unprecedented software. It's difficult for customers to provide requirements for software they've never seen or used before, but we still have to develop such software.[56]

A hierarchy is a natural representation of needs, and it is a very efficient format for analysis. Once we know the structure and magnitude of the customer's needs, we can prioritize them.

Analytic Hierarchy Process

⑧ high-value customer needs

priorities

What needs are most important?

Step 8: Prioritize the Customer Needs

Given the customer's needs and their magnitude, we also need to know how important they are to the customer—their **priority**. And since we will use the priorities as weights, we need ratio-scale priorities. What is the simplest way to get ratio-scale priorities?

The Analytic Hierarchy Process (AHP)

The Analytic Hierarchy Process (AHP) is the simplest prioritization method that provides accurate results on a ratio scale. (Other methods are available, but either they are less accurate or they don't produce ratio-scale numbers. To use the priorities as multipliers, they *must* be on a ratio scale.)[57]

You use AHP to prioritize the customer requirements in the Hierarchy Diagram. Although customer requirements were traditionally prioritized with a simple 1 to 5 scale, advances in Japan led to the use of the AHP.[58] The AHP requires slightly more effort, but it provides superior accuracy of results along with consistency checking and sensitivity analysis.[59] This method employs pairwise comparisons on hierarchically organized elements to produce a very accurate set of priorities. Developed more than 20 years ago in North America, AHP has been used in a wide variety of settings to establish priorities and improve the accuracy of decision making.[60, 61] Further, users can carry out the calculations required by using a spreadsheet, or through the use of specialized AHP software.

The efficiency of the process comes from using AHP to prioritize the customer needs hierarchy from the top down. That allows us to identify the top 10 or 20 customer needs while analyzing less than 30 percent to 40 percent of the total requirements. We *must* have a detailed understanding of the vital few high-value customer needs. If we get them wrong, we cannot satisfy the customer, and we will fail. We do not need such detail on the trivial low-value needs. Getting them wrong, or even leaving them out, will not have the same effect on customer satisfaction.

Discover Only Sufficient Requirements

Note that this means that we do *not* need a complete set of requirements in order to satisfy the customer. In Modern QFD, the aim is to discover a **sufficient** set of requirements, or the smallest subset of customer needs necessary to satisfy the customer. In other words, can we deliver enough value for enough high-value needs so that the customer will be satisfied with our solution? If so, we don't need anymore requirements. This **essential value** approach to requirements definition is well suited to very rapid development efforts. We don't waste time building what we don't have to build.[62]

In traditional QFD, we use Matrix Data Analysis Charts (one of the 7 MP Tools) to present the results of multivariate data analysis. Particularly for customer segmentation, techniques such as conjoint analysis, cluster analysis, factor analysis, multiple regression analysis, and others are useful, when substantial quantitative customer data exists. This is the most mathematically sophisticated quality tool.

In Modern QFD, the AHP has replaced Matrix Data Analysis Charts. Now we know what the customers what. So what should we do to satisfy their needs?

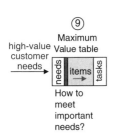

Step 9: Deploy Prioritized Customer Needs

We use matrices and tables to **deploy** (visibly communicate) value and priority throughout the development process in traditional QFD. We use matrices to explore in depth the relationship between two (or more) key project concerns simultaneously. We use tables to adjust priorities, set performance target levels, and document the details of processes and decisions. In Modern QFD, we use tables for deployment as well.

We use matrices to examine two (or more) dimensions simultaneously in any QFD deployment. Most commonly used to deploy value in QFD, matrices can also be used for prioritization using the AHP to focus on critical items. We can use a variety of matrices beyond the traditional L-matrix (such as the T-, Y-, X-, and C-matrices) for multidimensional analysis in QFD deployments.

With an essential set of high-value customer needs identified (along with their magnitudes and priorities), we then must plan how to deliver them. To do this we can use a table similar to the CVT: the Maximum Value Table (MVT).

The Maximum Value Table

On a CVT we begin with items that can come from any dimension of the development process, and we end up with just customer needs as our output. On an MVT we begin with just customer needs as inputs, and we may end up with items from any dimension of the development process as our output (see Figure 11.12).

When we have identified and connected the relationships between the high-value needs and related items throughout the project, we have discovered the *essential items* for development. On essential items we should use our best people, our best tools, and our best methods. Here is our best chance to do well and have it matter to the customer.

The MVT gives us a way to plan how to deliver the most important customer needs. This is where we identify the dotted lines in Figure 11.4b. The essential tasks that are the output of the table are where we need to apply consistent best efforts end to end on our project.

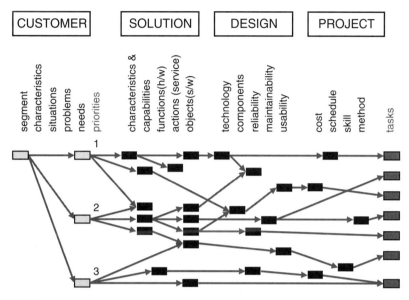

FIGURE 11.12

The MVT is where we analyze the top high-priority needs of our targeted customer segment in terms of whatever vital, special, or difficult items are required to meet the customer's needs. The result is the identification of those items across the project that are essential to satisfying the most important customer needs, and those project tasks where the essential items are worked on. This table is a powerful requirements deployment tool.

TABLE 11.1

Comparison of CVT and MVT. There are many tables and matrices in QFD, but Blitz QFD uses only tables (no matrices). Although these two tables are "cousins" with many apparent similarities, they have different purposes and produce different outputs.

CVT	MVT
Works right to left	Works left to right
Columns: all the types of customer concerns	Columns: all important project dimensions
Input: customer verbatims	Input: top n prioritized customer need
Output: customer needs	Output: essential items and tasks
Diagnostic: requirements	Diagnostic: project focus

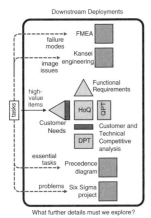

What further details must we explore?

Downstream Deployments: Analyze (Only) Important Relationships in Detail

At this point, we can use selected tools from the set of 7 MP Tools to analyze in detail any items of special concern for the project. For example, we can examine the relationship between customer needs and solution capabilities with a "House of Quality" matrix. All of the QFD tools are available for use here, on those items (and columns) that are most important.

Failure Mode Effect Analysis

We use Process Decision Program Charts along with fault trees and failure mode effect analysis to analyze reliability issues. This tool comes from reliability engineering.

Kansei Engineering

Kansei Engineering is a technology that translates human *kansei* and images into physical design elements for designing a product satisfying *kansei*. For example, in order to realize *kansei* as expressed in "spacious western style room," we can analyze what "spacious" means, and using the results we can determine the square footage of the room, ceiling height, total area of windows, ceiling and wall colors, floor colors, and drapery colors that are also relevant to that *kansei*. Designing the room based on the data obtained through such a procedure will enable us to materialize a western room that makes you feel "spacious."

Today our basic needs for clothes and food are already satisfied. Now people want quality in their products. We are no longer satisfied with simply having a filling meal; rather, we demand delicious food and are willing to spend more for better food and nicer goods. As such, people today are looking for better-quality "goods" that meet their *kansei*. In this era, pursuing and addressing *kansei* is a must, and without it no product that meets the needs of the time can be developed. *Kansei* Engineering has gained attention as a tool to realize this aim.

We can apply *Kansei* Engineering in industry and in organizations. It provides a scientific analysis as well as design tools for architects to use on the houses and buildings they are working on; for the furniture industry to use in their sofa, bed, or chest designs; for the textile industry to use in fashion design; for auto manufacturers to use in their car designs; for the appliance industry to use in their appliance designs; and so on.

—Mitsuo Nagamachi, Hiroshima University

The "House of Quality" and Beyond

Blitz QFD is fast and efficient, but there is a limit to how many items you can address with it. If you must handle a large number of items, matrices are necessary. As such, one of the additional tasks you can perform is to apply the Kano model to your quality characteristics.

The Kano Model

The Kano model, developed in the 1980s by Dr. Noriaki Kano, deals with "attractive quality creation" and the impact on customer satisfaction that a product may have if certain types of quality characteristics are present or absent, and to what degree.[63] You can apply the Kano model as an advanced technique after you have translated customer needs in quality characteristics, or even features.[64] It is a useful tool for designers who need to design a superior product in a competitive environment, and have marketing research support.

The Kano model requires that you complete interviews or surveys for a sufficient number of people from a segment, in order to draw a legitimate inference from the sample data to the segment response. The number of interviews or surveys required means that this is not a quick or simple analysis to carry out. It is critical that you validate and test the survey before you use it, as the wording on a Kano survey is very critical to proper evaluation of results. Figure 11.13 depicts the Kano model.

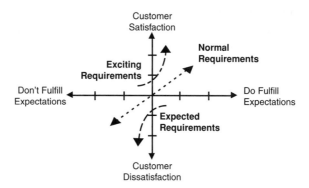

FIGURE 11.13
The Kano model has three levels of customer satisfaction on the vertical axis: satisfied, neutral, and dissatisfied. On the horizontal axis, a feature is present and meets expectations, or is absent and doesn't meet expectations.

The three main types of "requirements" in the Kano model are as follows:

1. **Expected requirements.** Features that are expected will dissatisfy if absent, but are neutral if present. Customers usually do not mention such features (unless they have recently experienced their absence). Delivering increased performance of expected requirements does not increase customer satisfaction.

2. **Normal requirements.** Features that are expected will dissatisfy if absent, but will satisfy if present. Customers usually mention features of this type (but don't expect customers to be able to tell you *all* of their normal requirements). Delivering increased performance of normal requirements does increase customer satisfaction, and decreased performance decreases customer satisfaction. On normal features relating to high-value customer needs, we want to be competitive and have a few where our performance is superior to the competition.

3. **Exciting requirements.** Features that are exciting will satisfy if present, but are neutral if absent. Usually customers do not mention these features (because they are often not aware of them, or that it is possible to get them). Delivering decreased performance of exciting requirements does not decrease customer satisfaction. On exciting features relating to high-value customer needs, we have an opportunity for a distinct competitive advantage. These features are often innovative and may be the result of applying new technology.

Precedence Diagrams

Precedence diagrams are the newer relatives of their older cousins, arrow diagrams and activity network diagrams. Project managers have used them for many years, and they are particularly powerful in the schedule deployment component of Software QFD using Critical Chain project management.

For dealing with project schedules and budgets, project managers have a variety of project management tools and techniques. For dealing with value, they have … what?

Modern QFD identifies the **essential path** for a project, which comprises the "most value-adding" activities. These determine the value our project can deliver to our customers. The **critical path** comprises the longest series of dependent activities in the activity network. These determine the project's elapsed time. Which is more important to your success in software development? **Project QFD** is the continuation of Modern QFD by the project manager to control the project and assure the delivery of value to customers.[65]

Six Sigma Projects

When the "voice of the customer" analysis identifies a customer problem we must solve, we need to apply a problem-solving method. The QI Story approach from TQM and the DMAIC approach from Six Sigma are effective methods for doing this. In some cases, we may need to use the initial steps of these methods to study the context of the customer and determine what improvements we can make.[66]

Follow-Up: Apply, Evolve, and Improve the Process

We must continuously improve our development process. With Blitz QFD, we have a basic framework for becoming more sophisticated at delivering value to our customers better and faster. Beyond this lies the entire Comprehensive QFD process and tools. This last step is essential for avoiding arrested development of the QFD process. (Some software organizations have been using "Kindergarten QFD" for years. They have never gone beyond a rudimentary application of QFD, and so today spend more effort than necessary to get fewer gains than what Modern QFD could provide them.)

Blitz QFD is an engineered way to get started with value. Once you have this base, there are many ways to extend it further.[67] This last step is essential for avoiding arrested development of the QFD process.

Blitz QFD is a better place to start QFD than the "House of Quality" is. If it is appropriate for your project, you will get a better "House of Quality" matrix faster and with less effort than if you started off there. The "House of Quality" matrix will be sized and scoped to fit your project's strategy, your customers, and the relative importance of the relationship of customer needs to functional requirements compared to other relationships of other dimensions of your project.

Rapid Development

In software development there are many approaches to rapid application development (RAD).[68] Most of these methods lack focus—they have no "aiming mechanism" to customer satisfaction. Although fast feedback, rapid prototyping, iterative development, and other techniques are excellent for "midcourse corrections," they work even better when Blitz QFD helps to reduce the number of unnecessary iterations.

One of the largest software development organizations in the world, when developing its rapid development methodology, was concerned about the "full speed ahead into a brick wall" risk it found in most rapid development methods. It chose Blitz QFD to "aim" its rapid development approach and formally incorporated it into its global methodology. Its experience was that this enhanced the effect of its rapid development software engineering and project management methods.[69]

Schedule Deployment with Critical Chain Project Management

Perhaps the best follow-up to Blitz QFD, which gives us excellent technical focus on the essential items, and Project QFD, which gives us excellent project management focus on the essential tasks, is QFD Schedule Deployment.

The Schedule Deployment subsystem of QFD uses the **Critical Chain** approach to project management (from the Theory of Constraints) to reduce the elapsed time of most software projects by 15 percent to 25 percent (15 percent for small projects and 25 percent for big projects).[70] However, Critical Chain implementation is challenging, as it requires a paradigm shift in project management. There are also some very powerful methods for proactive risk management that are possible only with Critical Chain.[71]

Although you can use QFD Schedule Deployment and Blitz QFD completely independently, it is important to use Schedule Deployment *with* Blitz QFD to ensure that projects are shorter *and* satisfying to the customer.

Several software organizations are currently implementing Blitz QFD with Schedule Deployment, and results to date have been so good that they have so far refused permission to even summarize their results.[72] This is a very promising avenue for any software group looking to make substantial improvements in their performance.

Implementing Software QFD

In the first ten years of the use of Software QFD in North America, QFD was refined and fit to the special needs of software development. But how have software organizations fared in implementing Software QFD? Figure 11.14 shows where QFD adds value in the software development process.

The People Side of QFD

QFD addresses the entire software development process, end to end. As software development is a managed, socio-technical system, so QFD considers management, social, and technical aspects (see Figure 11.6). QFD works best if managers empower their development teams. QFD works best with full, cross-functional representation on the project team—including customers. QFD works best with a concurrent sequencing of project phases. QFD works best if the team spends time in the *gemba*—the place where the software adds value to the customer. QFD works best with heavyweight project managers with authority over cross-functional resources for the entire project. Although the technical aspects are most commonly addressed in QFD literature, some of the most successful Software QFD organizations use only the social side of QFD (so far). It is also easier, once started, to maintain the social aspects of QFD throughout the duration of the project. You should neither neglect nor underestimate the power of the people side of QFD.

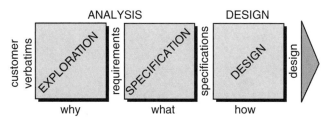

FIGURE 11.14
Where does QFD add value in software development? Primarily at the "fuzzy front end."

With a limited number of items of great importance to the customer, it is possible for a team to focus its efforts on only social mechanisms. Software startups often use this approach. Once they succeed and begin to grow, they must add formal and technical tools in order to maintain their ability to deliver customer-satisfying software with a rapidly increasing workforce.

QFD Challenges and Pitfalls

Software organizations have taken a variety of approaches in implementing QFD. The three large organizations profiled in the following subsections were selected to illustrate the *range* of implementation possibilities, not best or worst practices. In most cases, a software organization implementing QFD does not have open to it an "ideal implementation" path as described in some of the QFD articles published recently. They must make do with their situation, and their organization, as they find it. They must use an opportunistic approach to implementation.

Case 1: Basic QFD

In this case, QFD was brought in by the Software Development Group in 1988. They saw QFD as a way to improve their requirements-gathering process. In this organization, they started with the basic "House of Quality" matrix and began using it for software. They developed a short course for developers and proceeded to broadly roll out QFD among their development community. Training and consulting assistance was available on a limited basis from a handful of part-time QFD practitioners. Software QFD spread, and stagnated at a basic level.

The strength of this approach is that QFD has become a routine part of software development. QFD has been "installed" in the software development process. The penetration of QFD in this organization is truly impressive. The weakness of this approach is that since developers did not see QFD as an area of expertise, no experts arose to lead the organization beyond their initial use of what today can be called "Kindergarten QFD." Today, although they have had good overall success with QFD, in certain competitive sectors they have been beaten by competitors using a more comprehensive, more sophisticated, and more powerful QFD process.

Case 2: Facilitator QFD

In this case, the Quality Group brought in QFD in 1988. They saw QFD as another service their facilitators could offer to their internal customers, the software development teams. Developers were already accustomed to requesting assistance with team building, decision making, testing, standards, and other quality-related tools and techniques, so QFD became just another offering. The process started with the Quality Group's decision to adopt QFD as an "official" quality technique. Then, some members of the Quality Group were trained in Software QFD. These QFD facilitators then began working with project teams and attending conferences to learn more about QFD.

In this organization, QFD is considered a quality technology, and teams wishing to use QFD arrange for a QFD facilitator to work with their team on an as-needed basis for the duration of the project. When the facilitators are not busy, they engage in "QFD evangelism" to spread the word about QFD and line up future projects to work with. The Quality Group highlights projects using QFD, and publicizes successes internally and externally. Every year, some people on the teams that used QFD become enthusiastic about it and request a transfer to the Quality Group to become QFD facilitators.

The strength of this approach is that a small group of trained QFD experts works with project teams. This is a good way to get a small number of high-quality QFD efforts going quickly. The weakness of this approach is that since the project teams are led through the QFD process, they often don't learn it themselves, and they become dependent on the facilitators for any QFD use. Rarely is any formal developer training performed. Further, the process is critically dependent upon the knowledge of the facilitators. In some cases, facilitators were pressed into service without adequate training and experience. For those projects fortunate enough to get a knowledgeable facilitator, the results can be most impressive. But the small number of facilitators prevents that from being the case for the majority of project teams. (Also, the best facilitators tend to leave and become consultants…)

Case 3: Guerrilla QFD

In this case, top management had very little understanding of quality, especially quality systems such as QFD. They did permit their project managers and project teams wide latitude in selecting their approach to software development. Such empowerment extended to obtaining training and consulting assistance without the express approval of higher-level managers. Thus, at the team level, any particular project manager and team could choose a "new and radical" approach (such as Software QFD in 1988) and use it on their project.

In this organization, the spread of QFD is very much in the spirit of Francis Marion ("the Swamp Fox" circa 1780), Mao Tse-tung,[73] and Ernesto (Che) Guevara. Developers or team leaders with good experience with QFD persuade their colleagues to give QFD a try. Some training and consulting assistance is obtained, if possible, and the most appropriate parts of QFD are applied to the project. Rarely is the term *QFD* applied to their efforts, and generally no effort is made to highlight that they are using any new tools or techniques. Depending on the degree of success that results, more developers become QFD *partisans*, and some become actual QFD *provocateurs*—secretly spreading QFD throughout their organization.

The strength of this approach is that it is virtually unstoppable. People who use QFD tend to do better than those who do not (even with partial mastery), and so they spread out and rise up in the organization. Even if management wished to, they could not suppress this "no name" QFD approach. To suppress it management would first have to be able to recognize it in its many forms and variations, and that would require extensive training. (In that training, they would see the benefits of QFD and cease their persecution of it, we hope.) The weakness of this approach is that since the spread of QFD is unplanned, unmanaged, and unsupported, it occurs haphazardly as the partisans move from one project to the next. Also, some of the provocateurs tire of the lack of support and appreciation from their management and leave to work at other organizations which embrace and value their QFD experience. This is a setback for the partisans in that particular area of the firm, and more time is lost until a new provocateur emerges.

In each of these cases, software organizations were faced with a new and powerful method: Software QFD. In all cases the initial champions within the organizations had limited knowledge of QFD and faced unique challenges in implementing it in their organization. All three organizations "succeeded" in implementing QFD in the view of those who initially brought it into the organization. All three have now reached a plateau, where further progress appears to require that they change their implementation approach.

How to Implement Software QFD

How you implement Software QFD depends on a number of factors. Where is the highest "QFD Champion" in the software organization? Has there been any exposure to QFD in other areas of the company, or by managers who came from other organizations? Are competitors using QFD to good advantage? (That is what drove the North American automotive community quickly and deeply into QFD in the mid-1980s.) How many project teams are just starting a development or enhancement project, and how many would volunteer to try QFD? Is there an accepted software engineering process (also known as a methodology, or system development life cycle)? Are software engineering analysis and design activities done according to current best practices? How are project managers trained? What is their authority? What tools do they use?

All of these issues, and more, answer a number of questions:

- *Who* needs to know what about QFD so that we can get started?
- *What* projects should pioneer QFD? (More than one is highly recommended.)
- *Where* do you start with QFD? (The "House of Quality" is *not* the best place to begin for software.)
- *When* do you start using QFD on a project? (It's nice to start at the beginning, but much value can be gained by applying QFD to a project already underway.)
- *How* do you start with QFD? (What combination and sequence of training and consulting are required?)
- *How much* QFD should you use on your first project? (You will *not* be able to do "all of QFD" on a first project.)

It is also important to understand *why* the organization is considering QFD, so the decisions on the aforementioned issues result in a positive final assessment of the pioneer QFD projects.

By examining the experiences of some of the software organizations that have pioneered QFD in North America, we can learn to reduce the initial effort required and increase the rate of success.

Conclusion

Blitz QFD allows you to apply the power of QFD to software, with greater efficiency than traditional QFD approaches. It draws from the early roots of QFD in Japan before 1972, when matrices were not yet common. Blitz QFD was designed to prevent stagnation with low-power "Kindergarten QFD." As you grow in experience with QFD you will follow a migration path to the "House of Quality" matrix, and beyond to more comprehensive QFD.

Blitz QFD takes an end-to-end view of the development process for your project, and seeks to spend scarce person hours on the most important dimensions of your project. It delivers maximum value for the effort invested. This is a good deal for development teams.

Dr. Deming said we must view the development process as a system and look at how we satisfy our customers as an organization. Blitz QFD has precisely that aim: to effectively satisfy the most important needs of our most important customers through the efficient delivery of value. Results to date are exciting, and further refinement is still occurring.

Modern QFD in the DFTS Process

QFD is a key methodology in DFTS and is shown in Figure 11.15 in its critical role. Central to successful DFTS deployment is the understanding of the central role Blitz QFD plays for customer responsiveness. Modern QFD is deployed across the whole DFTS process to ensure that the software development process remains customer focused and that value is adequately analyzed and addressed throughout the various phases of software development. The focus of QFD changes in different phases according to the objectives of those phases. Other tools, techniques, and methodologies are utilized in one or more phases of the DFTS process as needed. QFD's value as a quality management methodology enhances tremendously when used effectively and in conjunction with other quality management systems, including the following:

- Pugh Analysis and TRIZ: Concept Selection and Creativity (Chapter 12)

- FMEA and FTA: Risk Analysis and Prevention (Chapter 13)

- Taguchi Methods: Design Optimization (Chapters 2, 16, and 17)

DFTS is a robust total product development methodology that includes other systems in addition to QFD. Some of the tools and techniques introduced in this book include B7, 7 MP, AHP, *poka yoke*, 5S, Object and Component Technologies, Software Quality Metrics (SQM), quality measures, and statistical methods.

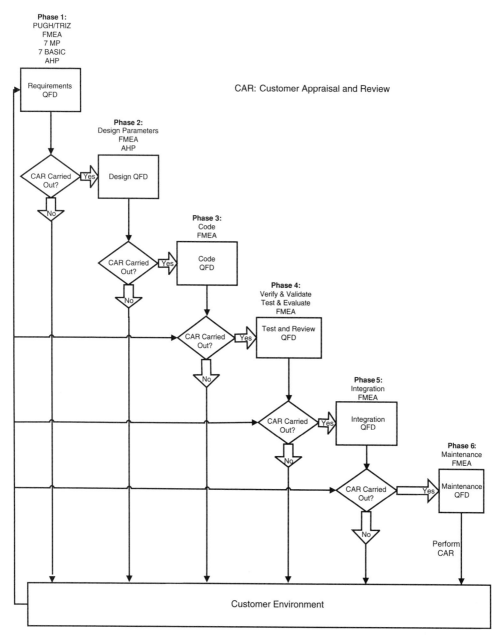

FIGURE 11.15
QFD and DFTS. This is an example of how QFD can drive the DFTS process where it is critical to satisfy customers with not only the content of the software, but also the process of development.

Key Points

- QFD is a quality *system*. QFD is not "doing a 'House of Quality' matrix." "Kindergarten QFD" is just doing a "House of Quality" matrix, especially if no one can explain why that matrix (and not any of the other matrices in QFD) was done, and done first. QFD is not a canned method, and you should tailor it to the project's needs and the organization's development process. Stagnation occurs when the QFD process in an organization remains substantially unchanged for many years.

- QFD has deployments (subsystems) to address any aspect of product or process that is important to the intended customers. Especially important for DFTS projects are deployments for quality (customer responsiveness), reliability, safety, security, and maintainability. Another important deployment is that of schedule (cycle time or delivery time), which QFD addresses with critical chain project management.

- Project goals and strategies are important for developers to understand at a very early stage. If the project charter does not state this clearly, you can use methods such as the New Lanchester Strategy to help clarify it. Also note that not all projects are strategic.

- Understanding what type of customers you intend to satisfy is necessary in order to focus your requirements discovery. You can devise customer segments in many ways, but the team must have a common understanding of who the customer is.

- Much of the apparent ambiguity in customer requirements stems from the developers not understanding the customer's situation. If you cannot accurately model the customer's process, how can you expect to build the right software?

- The *gemba* is the actual place where your software should add value to the customer or user. The *gemba* is not a conference room, unless you are developing conferencing software. Go where the user actually does what they need help with. Observe.

- Whatever the customer tells you is not a requirement or a need, but a *verbatim* (an actual statement of their "raw words"). We must analyze their statements (and actions) to derive their needs, which we should confirm with them.

- To structure the confirmed customer needs *the customer* develops an Affinity Diagram. We need to understand the way the customer thinks about their needs (we don't care what developers think about customer needs).

- A Hierarchy Diagram, once it is quantified, prioritized, and confirmed, is the most important single work object in the entire development process. It is the definition of *value* to the customer. Understand that, and you have a chance to build software that will satisfy your customers.

- You must scale priorities by ratio or nomalized before using them as weights. AHP is the simplest, currently known method for obtaining ratio-scale priorities. Priorities that are not ratio scaled cannot legitimately be used as weights or multipliers. And benefit/cost analysis cannot be done if the benefits are not quantified on a ratio scale.

- The MVT defines on one page, over the entire project, your plan for how you intend to satisfy your target customers efficiently. It is an extremely valuable result to focus a project team, and an experienced cross-functional team can produce it in one day when guided by a capable QFD facilitator.

- You should perform downstream deployments in QFD only when required, and only to the extent required, not by default. Match the size and investment of effort to the project's need for the answers they can provide. The complaints that QFD is "too big" or "takes too long" reflect traditional or poor practice, not best current practice of modern QFD.

- The reduction in schedule made possible by the methods in QFD Schedule Deployment—namely, Critical Chain project management—can free up enough time (within 12 months of implementation) to recoup even a very substantial investment in QFD training and education, and the Blitz QFD approach presented here is very efficient with respect to training and application time. The excuse of "we don't have time to do QFD" simply doesn't hold up on serious consideration.

Chapter 3 elaborates on the issue of metrics and quantification, which this chapter only considers for the Hierarchy Diagram. Chapter 7 deals with the 7 MP Tools in greater depth. Chapter 12 provides further ideas for design decisions and concept selection. Chapter 13 covers risk and Failure Mode Effect Analysis in greater detail. Chapter 16 considers other issues concerning requirements, Chapter 24 covers the case of defining customer needs for brand-new (new to the company) products, and Chapter 26 addresses the application of QFD to project management.

Additional Resources

You can obtain additional information about most of the topics in this chapter from the following source:

The QFD Institute, 1140 Morehead Ct., Ann Arbor, MI 48103; www.qfdi.org

The QFD Institute, a not-for-profit organization, offers both public and in-house courses on basic QFD for hardware, services, and software (known as the QFD Green Belt program). They also provide courses on QFD for Design for Six Sigma and for academics, as well as a QFD Black Belt program for organizations that are serious about ensuring customer satisfaction with QFD. They also offer an annual conference and periodically host the international QFD symposium.

The following sites provide additional material for this chapter:

www.prenhallprofessional.com/title/0131872508

www.agilenty.com/publications

Internet Exercises

Read the "House of Quality" article by Hauser and Causing, located at the following URL:

www.amazon.com/gp/product/B00005RZ1Z/104-1647300-7414354?v=glance &n=551440

After reading the article, you should be prepared to discuss the following:

1. **"What's so hard about design."** Discuss the barriers and obstacles to understanding what customers really want. Are cross-functional teams the answer? What does QFD offer to help cross-functional teams?

2. **"Building the house."** Customer attributes are phrases customers use to describe product characteristics. Distingish true customer needs as opposed to mistaking product characteristics for customer needs in new product development (that is, not upgrading an existing model).

3. **"Building the house."** The row items are described as *whats* and the column items as *hows*. In software development, at the end of the analysis phase a functional specification is supposed to contain the *whats* and the design spec is supposed to contain the *hows* reflecting the decisions made during design. So the "House of Quality" matrix would then connect the analysis and design phases. Is this necessary in software development? What about the inputs to the creation of the functional spec? Can the "House of Quality," as described here, be of any use at the front end of the development process?

4. **"Using the house."** The roof "matrix" for the car-door example claims that the engineering characteristics of "peak closing force" and "door seal resistance" have a strong negative relationship. For which type of car-door design is this true? Discuss at what point in the development process a designer decides on a design, and therefore whether engineering characteristics conflict. When can you finish the "House of Quality" matrix by completing the roof matrix?

5. **"The houses beyond."** The linked series of houses convey the customer's voice. But this example was completed at a time when car-door suppliers built to car company specifications. So the four houses explore *only* the decisions open to the door supplier, and redesigning the door is not one of them. Discuss the danger of using a QFD model tailored for parts suppliers as a general model for QFD, especially for software development.

The "House of Quality" article is also available from the following three sources:

1. Hauser, John R., and Don Clausing. "The House of Quality," *Harvard Business Review*, Vol. 66, No. 3, May–June 1988, pp. 63–73.

2. http://harvardbusinessonline.hbsp.harvard.edu/b01/en/common/item_detail.jhtml;jsessionid=RUL5ABFLWLQLUAKRGWDSELQBKE0YIISW?id=88307

3. Reprinted in *The Product Development Challenge*, Kim B. Clark and Steven C. Wheelwright, Eds. (Boston: Harvard Business Review Book, 1995).
Reprinted in *IEEE Engineering Management Review*, Vol. 24, No. 1, Spring 1996.
Translated into German and published in Hermann Simon and Christian Homburg, *Kunderzufriedenheit* (Gottingen, Germany: Hubert & Co., 1998).

Review Questions

1. How important is it to satisfy customers? How important is it to satisfy internal customers? What is the benefit if we succeed in satisfying them? What is the cost if we fail?

2. As a modern quality system, QFD uses the new 7 MP Tools. Traditional quality systems use the basic seven quality control (7QC) tools. From a comparison of the tool sets, what type of problems will QFD be good at? What type of problems will QFD be poor at?

3. The New Lanchester Strategy is a simple framework for considering strategic issues at the beginning of a project. What difference does it make if the project manager, or project team, understands or does not understand the expected strategic contribution of their project?

4. What is the difference between an incoherent and a coherent development process? In which environment would you expect employee satisfaction to be higher and turnover lower? Why?

5. The "voice of the customer" analysis is not simply a recording of what the customer says they want. Rather, it involves understanding why they are asking for those things, and then offering expert solutions to meet those needs. How would you proceed if you don't have the expertise to provide the kinds of solutions the customer needs?

6. QFD takes a very different approach to requirements, compared to traditional software engineering. What problems with software requirements can QFD help with? Where would it not be useful?

7. This chapter argues that only a few high-priority needs determine customer satisfaction. Consider a recent purchase you made. On what basis did you decide to buy? Are you satisfied with your purchase? Why or why not? Does your personal experience support the claim that a vital few needs drive satisfaction?

8. *Kansei* Engineering is a systematic approach to engineering look-and-feel (sensory engineering). What aspects of software development could benefit from this approach? (For what type of software would this be very important?)

9. QFD Schedule Deployment, if implemented properly, has the power to reduce the elapsed time of projects by 15 percent to 25 percent in less than a year. What other methods can reduce project schedules? What were the results of those methods when implemented? (Do they involve a paradigm shift?) If you could invest some of this reduction back into the development process, what would you do with it? (What "extra" methods would you use if a "free" 5 percent of the project could be spent on them?)

Discussion Questions

1. In this chapter, to focus on a key customer segment, you have to first focus on the most important goal of the project. Pick a software project and a primary goal, and then identify the key customer segment. Now change the primary goal and explain why a different customer segment is the most important.

2. In this chapter, following the Blitz QFD approach, only one key customer segment is given as an example. For software you are familiar with, identify at least three customer segments and give an example of a unique customer need for each segment. Can the needs of all segments be met with a single software product? (Do you think it is easier or harder to meet the unique needs of customer segments in software or hardware products? Why?)

3. This chapter mentions only a data-flow diagram as an example for modeling a customer process. What other software engineering representations could you use to model the context of a customer?

4. This chapter stresses the importance of visiting the customer's *gemba*. What would be an example of a software product, and a customer segment, where it would not be possible to "go to *gemba*"? (And what would you do in that case?)

5. The CVT was not introduced into North America until QFD was already popular and many poor practices were well established. Why is it important to sort the verbatims and only bring customer needs into a "House of Quality" matrix? (What common problems does this prevent?)

6. Affinity Diagrams are very commonly misused. When developers arrange the items, different patterns emerge than when customers arrange them. Take a set of items you are familiar with and arrange them. Then give the same items to a colleague and ask him to arrange them. Were the patterns the same? (What would happen if your colleague built a system for you, but based on his pattern?)

7. You use Hierarchy Diagrams to capture the structure of customer needs. They explain the "decision" the customer makes about whether to be satisfied, or dissatisfied, with your software. Prepare a hierarchy of your needs for software you are familiar with. Ask a colleague to do the same. Then exchange and discuss your hierarchies. What did you learn about your colleague's needs, and the way he thinks about them?

8. Accurate priorities are important for proper focusing. Using the AHP method explained in Chapter 8, prioritize a few items familiar to you. Then prioritize the same items using another common method. What explains the difference in the results? (Has the second method you tried ever been validated?)

9. The MVT for a DFTS project will have columns for customer needs (customer responsiveness), reliability, safety, security, and maintainability. What other dimensions of development would the type of software you are involved with require? Why?

Endnotes

[1]Y. Akao, and G. Mazur. "The Leading Edge in QFD: Past, Present, and Future," in *International Journal of Quality and Reliability Management*, Vol. 20, No 1, (2003).

[2]R. E. Zultner, "Blitz QFD Tutorial," in *Transactions from the 10th Symposium on QFD Tutorials* (Ann Arbor, MI: QFD Institute, 1998).

[3]R. E. Zultner, "Defining Customer Needs for Brand New Products: QFD for Unprecedented Software," in *Transactions from the 11th Symposium on QFD* (Ann Arbor, MI: QFD Institute, 1999).

[4]R. E. Zultner, "Project Estimation with Critical Chain: Third-Generation Risk Management," *Cutter IT Journal*, Vol. 12, No.7, July 4–12.

[5]Y. Akao, Ed. *Quality Function Deployment: Integrating Customer Requirements into Product Design*. Translated by Glenn Mazur (Cambridge, MA: Productivity Press, 1990).

[6]L. P. Sullivan, "Quality Function Deployment," *Quality Progress*, Vol. 19, No. 6, June 1986, pp. 39–50.

[7]B. King, *Better Designs in Half the Time: Implementing QFD Quality Function Deployment in America*, 3rd Ed. (Methuen, MA: GOAL/QPC, 1989).

[8]J. Terninko, G. Mazur, and R. Zultner. *The Facilitator's Guide to Better Designs in Half the Time* (Methuen, MA: GOAL/QPC, 1994).

[9]Op. cit., Akao and Mazur.

[10]R. E. Zultner, "Software QFD: The North American Experience," in *Proceedings of the 1st Pacific Rim Symposium on Quality Deployment*, held at Sydney, Australia on February 15–17, 1995, pp. 163–174.

[11]S. Aizawa, *et al.* "General Purpose Wave Form Analysis Program Development" (in Japanese), *Quality Control*, Vol. 33, Special Issue, November (Tokyo: Japan Union of Scientists and Engineers, 1982), pp. 360–366.

[12]T. Yoshizawa, *et al.* "Software Quality Deployment and Supporting Systems" (in Japanese), in *27th Research Conference Transactions,* 1-9 (Tokyo: Japan Society for Quality Control, 1985).

[13]NEC, *NEC IC Micon Deming Prize Application* (in Japanese) (Kawasaki City, Japan: NEC IC Microcomputer Systems Company, 1987).

[14]IPPA, *High Quality Software Production through Quality Function Deployment* (in Japanese) (Tokyo: Information Processing Promotion Industry Association, 1989).

[15]M. A. Cusumano, *Japan's Software Factories: A Challenge to U.S. Management* (New York: Oxford University Press, 1991).

[16]T. Yoshizawa, Y. Akao, M. Ono, and H. Sindo. "Recent Aspects of QFD in the Japanese Software Industry," in *44th Annual Quality Congress Transactions* (Milwaukee: American Society for Quality Control, 1990), p. 465.

[17]R. E. Zultner, "Software Quality Deployment," in *Goal/QPC 5th Annual Conference Proceedings* (Methuen, MA: GOAL/QPC, 1988).

[18]D. M. M. Thompson, and M. H. Fallah. "A Systematic Approach to Product Definition," in *A Symposium on QFD Transaction,* (Novi, MI: ASI, ASQC, and GOAL/QPC, 1989), pp. 279–285

[19]L. Cohen, "Quality Function Deployment," *National Productivity Review*, Vol.36, No. 2, Summer 1988, pp. 197–208.

[20]R. J. Thackeray, and G. Van Treeck. "QFD for Embedded Systems and Software Product Development," in *GOAL/QPC 6th Annual Conference Proceedings* (Boston: GOAL/QPC, 1989).

[21]M. Betts, "QFD Integrated with Software Engineering," in *2nd Symposium on QFD Transactions* (Novi, MI: ASI, ASQC, and GOAL/QPC, 1990), pp. 442–459.

[22]K. I. Shaikh, "Thrill Your Customer, be a Winner," in *A Symposium on QFD Transactions* (Novi, MI: ASI, ASQC, and GOAL/QPC, 1989), pp. 289–303.

[23]A. I. Sharkey, "Generalized Approach for Adapting QFD for Software," in *3rd Symposium on QFD Transactions* (Novi, MI: ASI, ASQC, and GOAL/QPC, 1989), pp. 380–416.

[24]J. Moseley, and J. Worley. "Using QFD to Gather Customer Requirements for Products that Support Software Engineering Improvement," in *3rd Symposium on QFD Transactions* (Novi, MI: ASI, ASQC, and GOAL/QPC, 1991), pp. 244–251.

[25]R. E. Zultner, "Software Total Quality Management: What does it take to be World Class?" *American Programmer*, Vol. 3, November 1990, pp. 2–11.

[26]R. E. Zultner, "Software Quality Deployment: Applying QFD to Software," in *2nd Symposium on QFD Transactions* (Novi, MI: ASI, ASQC, and GOAL/QPC, 1990), pp. 132–149.

[27]Japanese Industrial Standards Committee. *Performance Improvement of Management Systems—Guidelines for Quality Function Deployment*, JIS Q 9025 (Tokyo: Japan Standards Association, 2003).

[28]S. Mizuno, and A. Yoji, Ed. *Quality Function Deployment: The Customer-Driven Approach to Quality Planning and Deployment*, Rev. Ed. (Tokyo: Asian Productivity Organization, 1994).

[29]J. R. Hauser, and D. Clausing. "The House of Quality," *Harvard Business Review*, Vol. 66, No. 3, May–June 1988, pp. 63–73.

[30]G. Mazur, *Comprehensive QFD for Service Organizations* (Tokyo: Japan Business Consultants, Ltd., 1995).

[31]D. P. Clausing, *Total Quality Development: A Step by Step Guide to World Class Concurrent Engineering* (New York: ASME, 1994).

[32]K. Ozeki, and A. Tetsuichi. *Handbook of Quality Tools: The Japanese Approach* (Cambridge, MA: Productivity Press, 1990).

[33]N. E. Ryan, Ed. *Taguchi Methods and QFD: Hows and Whys for Management* (Dearborn, MI: ASI Press, 1998).

[34]Y. Nayatani, E. Toru, F. Ryoji, and M. Hiroyuki. *The Seven New QC Tools: Practical Applications for Managers*, translated by J.H. Loftus (Tokyo: 3A Corporation, 1994).

[35]QFD Institute (www.qfdi.org) has been organizing an annual symposium on QFD in North America since 1989. The proceedings of the symposia, based on case studies and research from organizations worldwide, provide a rich resource on QFD. You can obtain the proceedings from QFDI.

[36]G. Watson, *Design for Six Sigma: Innovation for Enhanced Competitiveness* (Milwaukee: ASQ Press, 2005).

[37]Op. cit., Japanese Industrial Standards Committee.

[38]Op. cit., Akao and Mazur.

[39]R. E. Zultner, "Before the House: The Voices of the Customers in QFD," in *Transactions from the 3rd Symposium on QFD*, held at Novi, MI, June 24–25, 1991 (Novi, MI: QFD Symposium Committee, 1991), pp. 450–464.

[40]L. D. Miles, *Techniques of Value Analysis and Engineering* (New York: McGraw-Hill, 1982).

[41]R. E. Zultner, "Priorities: The Analytic Hierarchy Process in QFD," in *Transactions from the 5th Symposium on QFD*, held at Novi, MI, June 21–22, 1993 (Novi, MI: QFD Symposium Committee, 1993), pp. 459–466.

[42]Op. cit., Zultner, 1991.

[43]R. E. Zultner, "Project QFD: Blitz QFD for Project Managers," in *Transactions from the 9th Symposium on QFD* (Ann Arbor, MI: QFD Institute, 1997).

[44]T. Lewis, "Surviving in the Software Economy," in *Upside Magazine*, March 1996, pp. 67–78.

[45]N. C. G. Campbell and K. J. Roberts. "Lanchester Market Structures: a Japanese Approach to the Analysis of Business Competition," *Strategic Management Journal*, Vol. 7 (1986), pp. 189–200.

[46]N. C. G. Campbell, "Market - Share Patterns and Market Leadership in Japan," Int. Studies of Mgt. & Org., Vol. XVIII, No. 1 (1987), pp. 50–66.

[47]S. Yano, *New Lanchester Strategy*, Vol. 1 (Sunnyvale, CA: Lanchester Press Inc., 1995).

[48]S. Yano, *New Lanchester Strategy - Sales and Marketing Strategy for the Weak*, Vol. 2 (Sunnyvale CA: Lanchester Press Inc., 1996).

[49]G. Mazur, *QFD for Service Organizations* (Tokyo: Japan Business Consultants, Ltd., 1993).

[50]D. Olson, *Exploiting Chaos: Cashing in on the Realities of Software Development* (New York: Van Nostrand Reinhold, 1993).

[51]S. Mizuno, *Management for Quality Improvement: The 7 New QC Tools* (Cambridge, MA: Productivity Press, 1988).

[52]Ibid.

[53]Op. cit., Zultner, 1999 (3).

[54]J. Kawakita, *The KJ Method: Seeking Order out of Chaos* (Tokyo: Chuokoron-sha, 1986).

[55]Op. cit., Zultner, 1993.

[56]Ibid.

[57]A. Griffin, and J. R. Hauser. "The Voice of the Customer," in *Marketing Science*, Winter 1993, pp. 1–27.

[58]K. Tone, and R. Manabe, *Analytic Hierarchy Process Applications* (in Japanese) (Tokyo: Japan Union of Scientists and Engineers, 1990).

[59]Op. cit., Zultner, 1993.

[60]T. L. Saaty, *Decision Making for Leaders: The Analytic Hierarchy Process for Decisions in a Complex World*, Rev. 2nd Ed. (Pittsburgh: RWS Publications, 1990).

[61]T. L. Saaty, *Fundamentals of Decision Making and Priority Theory with the Analytic Hierarchy Process* (Pittsburgh: RWS Publications, 1994).

[62]Op. cit., Zultner, 1997.

[63]N. Kano, N. Seraku, F. Takahashi, and S. Tsuji, "Attractive Quality and Must-be Quality," in *The Best on Quality*, edited by John D. Hromi. Volume 7 of the Book Series of the International Academy for Quality (Milwaukee: ASQC Quality Press, 1996).

[64]N. Kano, *Guide to TQM for Service Industries* (Tokyo: Asian Productivity Organization, 1996), pp. 127–132.

[65]Op. cit., Zultner, 1997.

[66]Op. cit., Watson.

[67]J. B. ReVelle, , J. W. Moran, and C. A. Cox. *The QFD Handbook* (New York: John Wiley & Sons, 1998).

[68]C. Gane, *Rapid Systems Development using Structured Techniques and Relational Technology* (New York: Rapid System Development, Inc., 1987).

[69]M. P. McDonald, "Achieving Software Quality in a RAD Process," in *4th International Conference on Software Quality Proceedings* (Milwaukee: ASQ Software Division, 1994).

[70]E. M. Goldratt, *Critical Chain* (Great Barrington, MA: North River Press, 1997).

[71]R. E. Zultner, "Schedule Deployment Tutorial," in *Transactions from the 11th Symposium on QFD Tutorials* (Ann Arbor, MI: QFD Institute, 1999).

[72]Ibid.

[73]M. Tse-tung. *Guerrilla Warfare*, translated by Brigadier General Samuel B. Smith, USMC (New York: Praeger, 1961).

About the Author

Richard E. Zultner is an international consultant, educator, author, and speaker. Applying powerful improvement methods, such as QFD, to high-tech software-intensive products and processes has been his primary focus for over ten years.

He is a founder and director of the QFD Institute—a nonprofit organization dedicated to the advancement of the theory and practice of QFD. For his pioneering work in Software QFD, he received the International Akao Prize in 1998. He is also a certified "Jonah" in the Theory of Constraints (TOC), and is a Six Sigma Master Black Belt, specializing in Design for Six Sigma.

Richard provides consulting and training in Software QFD, Design for Six Sigma, and Critical Chain Project Management.

Richard holds a master's degree in management from the J. L. Kellogg Graduate School of Management at Northwestern University, and has professional certifications in quality, project management, software engineering, and theory of constraints. He has taught QFD and Critical Chain project management in the graduate program at Stevens Institute of Technology as an adjunct professor.

CHAPTER 12

Creativity and Innovation in the Software Design Process: TRIZ and Pugh Concept Selection Methodology

Invention is man's oldest occupation.
—Genrich Altschuller

The wrong choice of concept in a given design situation can rarely,
if ever, be recouped by brilliant detailed design.
—Stuart Pugh

Overview

Design for Trustworthy Software (DFTS) requires innovative "outside-the-box" thinking, but Genrich Altschuller has shown that creativity can be learned—it is not an inborn characteristic limited to only a few people. His TRIZ theory of innovative problem solving has been developed from a careful analysis of more than two million engineering patents worldwide to discover the fundamental *patterns* of innovation. We report here on the adaptation of the highly structured and well-tested TRIZ methodology to the design of computer software, which has already shown excellent results for applications to parallel processing. The essence of the TRIZ methodology is to take a problem you cannot solve in your real-world problem space and map it to a similar generic problem in the TRIZ space. Then you follow the very explicit

405

TRIZ methodology to find the generic solution to the generic problem in the TRIZ space. Finally, you map that solution back to a candidate solution for the specific problem in the designer's problem space. This chapter covers the relationship between and interoperability of TRIZ with QFD and Taguchi Methods. It also discusses the application of brainstorming and the Pugh concept selection method to clearly identify the smallest solutions that meet the customer's needs and that are also technically and economically feasible. The role of software patents in protecting the intellectual property inherent in software is discussed, with warnings that the patent law is too weak to protect software.

Chapter Outline

- The Need for Creativity in DFTS
- Creativity and TRIZ
- TRIZ in Software Development
- TRIZ, QFD, and Taguchi Methods
- Brainstorming
- Pugh Concept Selection Methodology

- Software as Intellectual Property
- Key Points
- Additional Resources
- Internet Exercises
- Review Questions
- Discussion Questions and Projects
- Endnotes

The Need for Creativity in DFTS

Trustworthy software development processes, like most human endeavors, thrive in innovative development environments. Innovation can create breakthrough values for customers in terms of cost, quality, and delivery requirements. This is especially true at upstream stages of the process, which present vast opportunities for meeting customer requirements innovatively—more so than is the case downstream. This chapter focuses on Phase 1 of the DFTS process (see Figure 2.6 in Chapter 2). In particular, we discuss issues related to the *hows* of the software development process after customer requirements, the *whats,* have been identified following QFD. We are concerned here with the concept and architectural issues of the software development process rather than detailed design activities that are undertaken from Phase 2 onward. As soon as a particular software concept has been agreed upon, the stage is set to carry out risk assessment of the proposed development concept, using FMEA and other techniques (see Chapter 13) before proceeding to Phase 2.

The ability to innovate has long been recognized as depending on three human qualities: creativity, tenacity, and serendipity. The story is often told about Thomas Alva Edison, who combined these qualities to such a high degree that he obtained 1,082 U.S. patents for his inventions. This record never has been excelled (although a handful of his successors at General Electric have passed the 500 mark). As the story goes, the pile of failed experiments thrown out Edison's second-story office window in Menlo Park reached to the windowsill by the time he discovered tungsten as the ideal material for the filament of the incandescent lightbulb. So although creativity may be learned, success may also depend on the inborn quality of tenacity and circumstances that promote serendipity (see Sidebar 12.1). This chapter discusses three common innovation methodologies that can be used in the software development process: *TRIZ, brainstorming*, and the *Pugh Concept Selection Methodology.* The first two provide a means to generate concepts, and the third one provides a methodology to select from a list of workable concepts.

Creativity and TRIZ

TRIZ (pronounced "treez," for *Teoriya Resheniya Izobreatatelskikh Zadatch*) is the Russian acronym for the *Theory of Inventive Problem Solving (TIPS)*. TRIZ is a systematic approach to solving a variety of system problems creatively. Its roots can be traced to the Russian engineer and inventor Genrich Saulovich Altschuller, who discovered that the evolution of systems is not a random process, but is governed by certain objective laws. These laws, proposed by Altschuller, in turn can be used to consciously develop a system based on discovering innovative ideas and implementing them. He states that inventiveness can be taught. Creativity is not instinctive, and one does not have to be born with particular traits to be creative; rather, creativity can be acquired by learning.[1, 2, 3]

Sidebar 12.1: What Is Serendipity?

Serendipity is the ability to recognize a valuable result that occurs when you're actually looking for something else. The word was introduced into the English language by Sir Horace Walpole in 1754. It was derived from a legend called "The Three Princes of Serendip." (Ceylon was called Serendip by medieval Arab explorers from whom the legend comes.) At a rare truce meeting between their incessant wars, the princes decided that each year they would meet and compare their inventions, and a committee of their combined advisers would elect as king for a year the prince with the best invention. The three princes soon discovered that their best inventions often turned out to be not what they were trying to create, but accidental discoveries they had not intended. In a letter to a friend, Walpole called this situation "serendipity" and thereby added this useful neologism to the English language (*Oxford English Dictionary*, Volume IX). Stories of serendipity abound in American technology. Perhaps the best known is the discovery of a transparent bulletproof plastic later named Lexan at General Electric R&D Laboratories by Drs. Bendler and French when they were only seeking to create a scratchproof form of Plexiglas. Of course, the oldest serendipity stories are the "Eureka!" experience of Archimedes, much later the discovery of X-rays by Roentgen, and the discovery of penicillin by Sir Alexander Fleming.

When one of the authors was vice president and director of a computer architecture program at a company led by a retired military officer, he had the occasion to note to the CEO that innovation inhered in three qualities: creativity, tenacity, and serendipity. The CEO, ever the military commander, leaned across his large desk and inquired intently, "Yes, but how do you *manage* serendipity?" The author, realizing that he was on the spot, improvised, "You 'manage' serendipity by providing inventors a laboratory environment in which it is very likely to happen." It was a narrow escape. However, the CEO shortly later led the design of a new research laboratory for the firm in which the physical layout maximized opportunities for serendipity. He really got it!

In English, TRIZ is sometimes called by the tantalizing apparent nonsequitur *systematic innovation* rather than by its Russian acronym.[4] *Systematic* conjures the image of an algorithmic sequence of activities that are performed to achieve a known result. In contrast, *innovation* is the result of heuristics, which are the opposite of algorithms, and which are erratic and unpredictable. Writers on the subject do not intend an oxymoron and thus carefully define the term to make it precise. The essence of the theory is that contradictions can be resolved methodically by the application of innovation solutions. The premises on which the theory is based are that the ideal design is a goal, that contradictions can actually lead to improved solutions, and that innovation as a process can be structured systematically.[5] Practitioners of TRIZ have shown that applying common solutions to resolve contradictions improves the design of products and systems. Use of TRIZ has shown it to be far more effective than the ultimate heuristic known as trial and error. This method was favored by Edison, who was fond of saying that genius is "1% inspiration and 99% perspiration." Edison could afford the luxury of doing thousands of experiments to reach a single goal because he surrounded himself with bright young men he trained and supervised closely as co-inventors (see Sidebar 12.2). His methods worked for the incandescent lightbulb, but he wasted a fortune at the peak of his career trying to separate iron ore magnetically.

Actually, all the processes for enhancing creativity are limited, because their usefulness decreases as the goal's complexity increases. At some point all heuristics reduce to trial and error, and the number of trials increases dramatically as complexity increases. Altschuller was motivated to develop TRIZ by two questions: How can the time required to invent a needed product be reduced? and How can a process be structured to encourage breakthrough thinking? He soon realized that scientists are simply not trained to "think outside the box"—that is, outside their own field of reference. He and his colleagues then analyzed innovative solutions to problems stated and solved on the worldwide patent base to develop the patterns of innovation. They studied 200,000 patents and selected 40,000 of them as being particularly good exemplars of the methodology they were seeking to develop. These demonstrated that the development of an engineering system is not a sequence of random (heuristic) events but rather is governed by certain patterns. Since then, TRIZ practitioners have reviewed more than two million patents to further refine the method. It is a systematic and orderly way to help engineers think outside the box by giving them examples from beyond their own narrow discipline and experience.

TRIZ has developed a large tool set over the past five decades, beginning with the 40 inventive principles (adapted for software in Table 12.1, shown later), and then the 39 engineering parameters, the four separation principles, the concept of ideality, and the 76 standard solutions.[6]

The natural objective function of innovative system development with TRIZ is ideality, which is defined as follows:

ideality = Σ benefits / (Σ costs + Σ harm)

in which evolution toward the ideal system is guaranteed by increasing benefits while reducing costs and harm. To provide direction to the design evolution, the design team usually imagines the ideal final result, which provides an *ideal*, if unrealistic, goal but gets the team focused on the same "out of the box" goal. This tends to remove both real and perceived barriers by offering alternative solutions. Starting with perfection encourages breakthrough thinking, inhibits backsliding toward less-ideal solutions, and leads to defining clear boundaries for the project.

In spite of this complexity, the method can be most easily understood as a mapping. As shown in Figure 12.1, all the TRIZ tools support this process. You identify a specific problem and its parameters, and then you map it to a generic TRIZ problem. Using the appropriate TRIZ tools, you find the generic TRIZ solution to the generic TRIZ problem. Finally, you map the generic solution from the TRIZ solution space back to the original specific problem space as a specific solution.

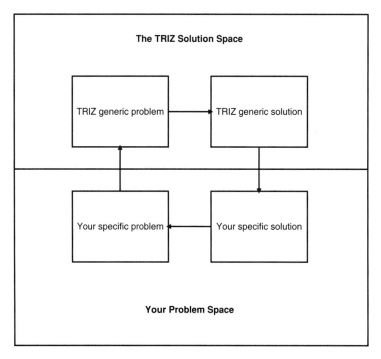

FIGURE 12.1
The TRIZ Solution Process

The first of the inventive principles is *segmentation* (see Table 12.1). Using this tool allows the user to apply the process shown in Figure 12.1 *iteratively* on the various subsystems or their components. Principle 7 in the list is *nesting* (see Table 12.1), which allows the user to employ the process shown in Figure 12.1 *recursively* on the whole system under design. The genius of the TRIZ inventive problem-solving or design methodology is that it combines at different levels both algorithmic and heuristic problem-solving techniques. It is a curious way of applying knowledge and experience to produce wisdom. Herbert Hoover, a noted hydraulic mining engineer before he became U.S. President, once said, "Wisdom is not knowing the ultimate, but rather knowing what to do next." TRIZ uses an algorithmic process to lead the inventor toward which heuristic to apply next. As always with heuristics, it is in the end a trial-and-error process, but a highly focused trial-and-error process informed by the experience of three million successful inventions documented as patents.

If you're interested in the development and practice of this sophisticated development methodology, we encourage you to read *Systematic Innovation: An Introduction to TRIZ* (see endnote 4), written by three experienced practitioners and illustrated with many examples from manufacturing. In this book we want to discuss more-recent applications of the method to software development.

Sidebar 12.2: Being There When the Page Was Blank

When one of the authors was an engineering undergraduate, he took an electrical engineering (EE) course on rotating machinery from a 72-year-old professor emeritus. Needing a professor's signature to pursue an opportunity to participate in the International Geophysical Year in 1956, he went to the professor's secretary to get the form signed. He asked if she would have "the doctor" sign the form. She told him that the correct title was Professor, not Doctor, because the professor had no degree. In fact, he had not even attended high school. Shocked, the author asked how the professor could teach at Harvard without a formal education. The secretary replied that when the professor was 13, his father had apprenticed him to Mr. Edison, and the professor's name was also on the patents for almost all the machinery in the school's EE laboratory. She noted wisely that if you invented it, you don't need to go to school to learn about it.

TRIZ in Software Development

Programming has long been considered the engineering equivalent of writing literature, or perhaps composing music. Thus, creativity is an important aspect of the programmer's craft. In the early days of computing, programmers were very scarce, so tests were devised to identify which trainees would likely develop into effective programmers. Those who created the programmer qualifying tests at first assumed that software development would require the same intellectual capabilities that hardware design required. However, this turned out not to be the case. In fact, efforts to retread engineers, draftsmen, time-and-motion study experts, and even physicists were mostly failures (see Sidebar 12.3). IBM, for whom a rapidly growing supply of capable programmers was very important, developed a test that really worked. Surprisingly, it identified musicians as the most promising candidates. After this discovery, it did seem intuitive after all. A program is a statically coded linguistic representation of a dynamic process or performance, just like a musical score when "executed" produces a musical listening experience or performance. The ability to manipulate or read codes or symbols on a piece of paper while imagining what the result will sound like (or, in the case of a program, what the numerical result will be) is a highly creative process. Our interest here is in how TRIZ can be applied to enhance the effectiveness of this process within a given programming staff working on a given project.

Sidebar 12.3: Lingua Latina Non Mortus Est

In the early 1960s, when one of the authors was principal programmer at Univac Defense Systems, he was asked to "retread" a group of 50 mechanical draftsmen as programmers. They had become redundant with the switch from vacuum tube logic to transistor-logic-based computers. The boss asked the author to include his secretary in the class as well. She often found and corrected programming errors when typing assembly-language programs for the programming staff, so he thought she must have some degree of latent talent for this craft. The 50 draftsmen never learned to program, in spite of the author's best efforts to teach them, but the secretary did so well that she was immediately transferred from a clerical pay grade to a professional pay grade as a junior programmer.

The author's next assignment was to write a FORTRAN compiler for the U.S. Air Force to run on a specialized military mainframe that did not have a commercial programming language compiler. The boss's former secretary, now a fledgling junior programmer, was assigned to the team of seven. Each week on Monday, module assignments were handed out with expected input and output. Each week the new programmer showed up early Friday afternoon with a perfect program that could do all the inputs the author had suggested, plus a few pathological cases she had added to the test. She would then ask for the rest of the afternoon off to take her three teenage daughters shopping. After several weeks of this spectacular performance, the author decided to test her skills with an especially complex module. As always, she was in his office right after lunch on Friday with an elegant, documented, and tested solution. The author commented after quickly reading the program as she sat near his desk that she programmed as if she had a degree in Latin, to which she responded, "I do; my BA degree is in Latin." As Paul Harvey would say, the rest of the story is that she was immediately promoted to programmer. She retired from the Univac Defense Systems Division some 20 years later as Director of Systems Programming.

The application of TRIZ to software development was pioneered by Graham Rawlinson (TRIZCON 2001) and Kevin Rea (TRIZCON 2002).[7] Rea took the 40 TRIZ principles that Altschuller and his early colleagues developed and crafted analogical principles that apply to software engineering, similar to the application of the original principles to mechanical engineering. The results are so elegant and useful that they are summarized in Table 12.1 as today's state of the art in applying TRIZ to software design:

TABLE 12.1
Rea's Analogies for Altschuller's Inventive Principles[8]

Principle Number	Principle Name	Description	Software Analogy	Example
1	Segmentation	Divide an object into independent parts	Separate similar functions and properties into self-contained program modules	C++ templates and OOP generally
2	Extraction	Separate an interfering part or property from a system	Define the grammar of a programming language to enable interpretive extraction	Extract text from image files
3	Local quality	Change a system's structure from uniform to non-uniform	Change an object's classification from a homogenous hierarchy to a heterogeneous hierarchy	Nonuniform access algorithms
4	Asymmetry	Change the shape of a design from symmetrical to asymmetrical	Change the program to nonuniformly affect a computation's result	Second-order hashing function to even out a hash table
5	Consolidation	Make operations in a system contiguous or parallel	Make processes run concurrently	Synchronize execution of threads in time
6	Universality	Make a part perform multiple functions	Make a program support multiple functions based on context	Polymorphism
7	Nesting	Place an object inside another, then another, then another	Inheritance in OOP	Nested objects in OOP

TABLE 12.1
Continued

Principle Number	Principle Name	Description	Software Analogy	Example
8	Counterweight	To counter a system's weight, merge it with other objects that provide "lift"	Use sharing to support large numbers of fine-grained objects efficiently to counter dynamic loads on a system	A shared object that can be used in multiple contexts simultaneously
9	Prior counteraction	Preload counter tension to reduce excessive stress	Perform a preliminary process or actions to improve a later computation	Multiply by a precomputed reciprocal in a loop rather than dividing by a constant
10	Prior action	Carry out all or part of an action in advance	Same	Java translation to interpretive language for a Java Virtual Machine (JVM)
11	Cushion in advance	Prepare a means beforehand to compensate for unusual events	Use an algorithm that handles worst-case harmful effects	Exception handling in Java
12	Equipotentiality	In a potential field, limit position changes	Change an algorithm's operating conditions to control the flow of data in and out	A transparent persistent data store
13	Do something in reverse	Invert the action to solve a problem	Store transactions in reverse order for backing out	Database recovery
14	Spheroidality	Replace linear parts with curved parts	Replace linear data structures with circular ones	Circular buffer

Principle Number	Principle Name	Description	Software Analogy	Example
15	Dynamicity	Design the characteristics of an object or process to change to be optimal	Same	DLLs
16	Partial or excessive action	If 100% is hard to achieve, try for less or more by dithering	Increase algorithmic performance by perturbation	Synchronization in Java
17	Transition to a new dimension	Difficulty with moving an object in a line may be solved by moving it in a plane	Use multilayered assembly of class objects	Interfaces in Java
18	Mechanical vibration	Use oscillation	Change the frequency of an algorithm's execution	Change an object's invocation rate to maximize overall application performance, such as updating balances on accounts after each transaction
19	Periodic action	Use periodic rather than continuous actuation	Perform a task periodically rather than continuously	Time scheduled backups
20	Continuity of useful action	Maximize a system's duty cycle	Develop a fine-grained solution that utilizes the processor at full load	Asynchronous nonpreemptive multitasking
21	Rushing through	Conduct a process at high speed	Transfer data in burst mode before a worst-case scenario	Allocate network bandwidth on a priority basis

TABLE 12.1
Continued

Principle Number	Principle Name	Description	Software Analogy	Example
22	Convert harm into benefit	Eliminate a harmful action by adding it to another harmful action	Invert the role of a harmful process and direct it back	Defeat denial-of-service attacks on a network server
23	Feedback	Introduce feedback to improve a process or action	Introduce a feedback variable into a closed loop to improve subsequent iterations	Rate-based feedback in an asynchronous transfer mode (ATM) system
24	Mediator	Use an intermediary process	Use a mediator to provide a view of the data in a different context	Mediators can be used in XML to enhance semistructured data
25	Self-service	Make an object serve itself by performing auxiliary functions	Same	Automatic updating of applications over the Internet
26	Copying	Use an inexpensive copy instead of the real thing	Instead of creating a new object, use a shallow copy	A shallow copy constructs a new object and inserts references to the original object in it
27	Dispose	Replace an expensive object with multiple inexpensive objects	Same	Use rapid or throwaway prototypes
28	Replacement of a mechanical system	Replace a mechanical system with sensory means	Same	Voice recognition versus typing and reading
29	Pneumatic or hydraulic construction	Use gas or liquid parts instead of mechanical parts	None	None

Principle Number	Principle Name	Description	Software Analogy	Example
30	Flexible films or membranes	Isolate the object from its environment	Isolate the object with wrapper objects	Wrappers in Java
31	Porous materials	Make an object porous	None	None
32	Change color	Change an object's transparency	Same	A transparency function in a photo program
33	Homogeneity	Make objects interacting with a given object out of the same material	Create pure objects of a certain type, ensuring identical properties	Container data object, such as an array
34	Rejecting and regenerating parts	Discard portions of an object that have fulfilled their function	Discard unused memory	Garbage collection in Java
35	Transformation properties	Change the degree or flexibility	Same	Software can be transformed to provide a different service based on properties changing by time of day
36	Phase transition	Use phenomena that change during a phase transition	None	None
37	Thermal expansion	Use thermal expansion of materials	None	None
38	Accelerated oxidation	Replace common air with oxygen-enriched air	None	None

TABLE 12.1
Continued

Principle Number	Principle Name	Description	Software Analogy	Example
39	Inert environment	Replace the normal environment with an inert one	None	None
40	Composite materials	Change from uniform to composite materials	Change from uniform software abstraction to a composite one	Software design patterns are the core abstractions behind successful recurring problem solutions in software architecture

So far, the application of TRIZ to software has started with algorithms and improved them by making them run faster, especially on parallel processors. Work has also been reported on the use of a TRIZ-based software tool for software process improvement at Motorola.[9] This tool, TechOptimizer from Invention Machine Corp. (http://www.invention-machine.com/), was intended for manufacturing applications. This project's objectives were to improve quality and cycle time. The following parts of the system were modeled:

- Development life cycle
- Project management
- Software quality assurance
- Process improvement

One limitation is that budgeted product development cost should not increase. The Principles module of TechOptimizer was found to be the most useful in generating concepts along the lines of Rea's analogical extensions. The Prediction module was less useful but still helpful, and the Effects module was found to be too closely linked with the physical world to be useful in a software process improvement study. The firm's generally available product, the Goldfire™ Innovator's Optimizer Workbench, is a unique problem-solving environment that delivers a structured process for inventive problem solving. It brings focus and clarity to problem definition and analysis, helps generate incremental and innovative ideas, and helps evaluate, validate, and prioritize solutions. Thus, it is a semantic knowledge engine providing precision research, knowledge management, and innovation trend analysis capabilities. The use of the Innovator's Optimizer Workbench indicates that although the transition of TRIZ from the manufacturing world to the software development world may be a bit awkward, it is still promising enough for further research and consideration.

Some of the other early software users of the method seem to think that the method will not really pay off until it can be applied to software architecture or high-level design, and software engineering generally. The pessimists among them think that software TRIZ practitioners must start over using Altschuller's methodology by analyzing thousands of software architecture patents to discover the particular patterns of creativity and innovation that pervade this field in contrast to those of a mechanical nature. Although Rea has done a brilliant job of constructing analogous principles for most of the 40 original TRIZ Inventive Principles, clearly some simply do not apply to software design and development. The 39 Engineering Parameters of TRIZ are even less suitable for analogical transformation from mechanical engineering to software engineering. The last section of this chapter discusses the issue of software patents as a vehicle for intellectual property protection. Although patents might not survive in that role, their precise specifications make good grist for the Altschuller mill to discover how innovation has historically come about in software engineering. The claims are of no interest for such analysis, but every patent begins with a list of its prior art and a recitation of "horribles"—the things that are so bad in the prior art that the inventors were led to the invention described in the following specification. Meanwhile, Rea's analogies for the 40 Inventive Principles for Software Design are certainly an adequate starting point to apply the method.

TRIZ, QFD, and Taguchi Methods

TRIZ, QFD, and Taguchi Methods are indeed three separate quality-enhancing technologies, but they often are logically related by a Venn diagram, as shown in Figure 12.2. The basic idea here, one commonly stated in the TRIZ literature, is

QFD + TRIZ + Taguchi Methods = customer-driven robust innovation

Figure 12.3 shows the relationship of these tools. A filled-in circle shows that a column has a significant impact on a row. Lightly filled-in circles indicate a moderate impact, and empty circles indicate a weak impact.

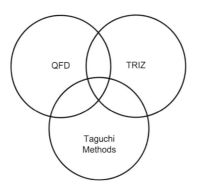

FIGURE 12.2
TRIZ, QFD, and Taguchi Methods

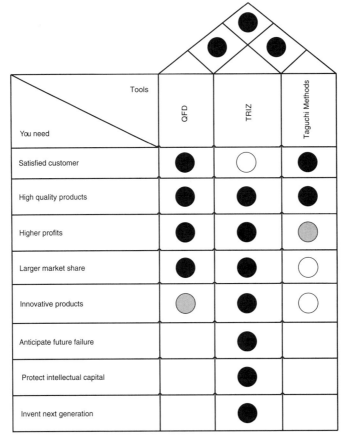

FIGURE 12.3
The Relationship Between QFD, TRIZ, and Taguchi Methods

QFD, TRIZ, and Taguchi Methods are all clearly very much upstream methods, but the order of their application in a robust design process seems to be QFD, and then TRIZ, and then Taguchi. QFD systematically translates the customer's needs and desires into the engineer's language. Product qualities important to the customer are linked to the design's engineering requirements and target values. TRIZ then provides a methodology to develop a creative solution, and Taguchi Methods determine the design's parameter values. Each of the three tool sets has its particular focus in the design stage of a product or process, but together they form a complete and balanced methodology to support robust design. John Terninko presents a workshop with several case studies for hardware engineering and manufacturing, illustrating the synergy between these three interlinked methodologies.[10]

Brainstorming

Brainstorming was introduced in connection with the *cause-and-effect diagram* in Chapter 6 and the *affinity diagram* in Chapter 7. It has been used for problem solving and idea generation in a wide variety of contexts. In a DFTS context, it has to be customized in that it follows QFD where customer requirements have been identified. The QFD data thus generated must be available to the brainstorming team so that it generates specific software design concepts that respond to these requirements. Needless to say, it should be carried out in quick succession to QFD and must include the people involved with QFD and *gemba* visits (see Chapter 11). The other major difference here is that the customer must always be apprised of the concepts and the final selection made from them.

The brainstorming format is basically the same as described in Chapters 6 and 7. The group size should be between five and nine people. If you have more people, it might be best to break them into groups of five or six; small size enhances communication and informality. It is important to invite people with diverse backgrounds and especially those with customer contacts. The sessions should not be longer than 30 to 40 minutes. If satisfactory ideas have not been generated within that time, it is best to adjourn and meet again. It is just fine to meet a number of times, depending on the problem's nature and severity. Table 12.2 summarizes brainstorming best practices.

TABLE 12.2
Brainstorming Best Practices in a DFTS Context

Brainstorming Phase	Best Practices
Before brainstorming	1. Document VOC and customer requirements. 2. Form the brainstorming team. Look for both experience and diversity. Break people into groups if you have more than ten. It is advisable not to group people of different management levels. 3. Appoint an experienced moderator and an assistant for record keeping. 4. Formulate the purpose of the brainstorming in a question form. 5. Circulate the brainstorming rules, such as the following: • Encourage the generation of as many ideas as possible (up to a maximum of 50). • Give everyone the opportunity to speak. • Encourage participants to combine their ideas with those of others. • Don't criticize any idea (all criticisms are to be red-flagged). • Refrain from discussing unrelated matters.
During brainstorming	1. Post the meeting's purpose on the meeting room wall. 2. Restate the meeting's purpose and context. 3. Use sticky notes for written ideas and interactive whiteboards for spoken ideas. Save them all for analysis and follow-up. 4. Keep the pace swift, with short answers and statements, to generate a lot of concepts without getting bogged down in any particular one initially.
After initial brainstorming and during follow-up session(s)	1. Group the concepts in terms of similarity of cost, quality, delivery, and other implications. 2. Send them to all the participants before the next session. 3. The participants should be asked to choose the three best concepts and why they chose them before the next session. 4. Discuss the chosen concepts in the subsequent session(s). Make a short list of the most promising ones for evaluation by Pugh Concept Selection Methodology or other evaluation techniques.

Pugh Concept Selection Methodology

The triad of design methods described in Figure 12.3 (QFD, TRIZ, Taguchi Methods) is about as far upstream as you can get in the design and development of a new product or process. But perhaps one matter is still logically prior—concept selection (what needs to be invented). The customer more often talks in terms of desiderata or vague needs. He or she is not an engineer and often cannot provide clear, unambiguous input for the QFD process. The Scottish engineering design professor Stuart Pugh has developed a formal design concept selection method that we will feature here as the preferred method in its context as a utility function method. Design concept selection, although logically prior to QFD, does not strictly precede the QFD process. Instead, it's contemporaneous. It comes before, during, and after, because it is highly iterative. Concept selection is picking the idea (actually, ideas) that best satisfy the product requirements as they emerge from QFD and the voice of the customer. Concept selection is the first attempt (or attempts, actually) to map the user's needs to a viable software architecture. Durfee argues that concept selection implies that the design team in consort with the customer actually weeds out bad ideas rather than trying to select the best one.[11] He also notes that concept must be a structured process:

- Customer needs drive the process.

- All criteria are considered.

- Choices are documented.

- Choices can be defended later in the design cycle.

- The process should be immune from the influence of a champion.

The principal steps of the Pugh process more precisely define a structured process as follows:[12]

1. Identify relevant user requirements.

2. Develop engineering specifications for requirements.

3. Develop weight criteria for requirements.

4. Generate several viable design requirements.

5. Rank the concepts using Pugh analysis.

6. Synthesize the best elements of each concept into an optimal design.

7. Iterate until a clearly superior concept emerges.

We will return to the Pugh method shortly. First, to set it in context, we consider the general utility function method. The *utility*, or total effectiveness, of each design alternative is obtained by summing the numerical scores assigned to the individual evaluation criteria weighted for its importance to the final result.[13] The utility equation is

$$U_i = \Sigma\, w_i\, x_{ij}\ (j = 1, 2, 3,..., m)$$

U_i is the utility of the jth design concept alternative. w_i is the weighting coefficient or measure of importance for the ith evaluation criterion, x_i. m is the number of concept alternatives considered. The sum is from 1 to n, the number of criteria.

Utility function analysis is used in cases where it is necessary to evaluate both quantitative and qualitative considerations at the same time. The evaluation criteria are derived from customer requirements, engineering specifications, and insights developed during concept generation. It is important to have a reasonable number of clear, independent criteria to support a good design decision. Because not all criteria are equally important, it is necessary to weight them for relative importance. Normally the sum of the weights is normalized to 1.0. The various candidate criteria are usually scored from 1 to 5. However, if more resolution is needed, and the data can support it, a scale of 1 to 10 may be used. In many cases you may use a reference scoring method whereby a best in class or standard design of some sort is chosen as a reference and is given a score of 3 out of 5 or 2 out of 3. Surprisingly, the utility scores for the various methods usually show clear ranking and separation. Everything else is then the same as, better than, or worse than the reference. If two or three design alternatives are closely ranked in utility, they may all be continued into the next design phase if the budget allows. Utility function analysis is quite amenable to computer spreadsheet analysis. This allows the design team to vary weights and criteria scores to achieve separation between utility values until a clear concept winner emerges. Stuart Pugh's method is a simplified version of the utility function method. Pugh's simplifications may be summarized as follows:[13, 14]

- All evaluation criteria are assumed to be of equal importance.
- The alternatives are scored using the reference-based scoring method.
- Instead of a point scale, alternatives are scored with respect to the reference as better than, the same as, or worse than.
- The overall score is determined by counting the better, same, and worse values for each alternative.

Pugh's method facilitates concept selection in several ways:

- Scoring is simple. Deciding on whether something is the same as, better than, or worse than some characteristic is much simpler than assigning it a numeric value.

- The method is easy to use and adapt as the team gains insight. It is more repeatable than numeric schemes.

- The matrix or spreadsheet tableau of concept alternatives versus evaluation criteria shows which evaluation criteria are driving the decision, a fact often obscured by numeric schemes.

- The method makes it easier to evaluate a large number of alternatives using a variety of evaluation criteria.

All utility function methods, as well as other decision support algorithms, are essentially qualitative analysis done with a quantitative cast. Curiously, Pugh's method remains strictly qualitative right up to the last moment, when the pluses, minuses, and sames are added up to produce a score. This allows a qualitative backtrack through the data, even up to the final matrix to allow the team to see which criteria are really driving the decision.

After a particular software concept has been selected from a list of possibilities generated from TRIZ and brainstorming techniques, the stage is set to carry out risk assessment of the proposed development concept, using FMEA and other techniques (see Chapter 13), before proceeding to Phase 2, which deals with Robust Design (see Chapters 16 and 17).

Software as Intellectual Property

In the Agrarian Age, arable land was the primary source of wealth. In the more recent Industrial Age, capital was the primary source for the production of wealth. In the Information Age, the source of wealth is information, or knowledge. It is packaged in the form of either static databases or computer-based files that are accessed by software. Increasingly, information will be packaged as computer simulations in which very complex scientific and engineering relationships can be demonstrated in an operational way (see Sidebar 12.4). There is a fundamental difference, however, in information as a source of wealth as opposed to arable land or capital, either of which are committed resources. I cannot use my 800 acres to both grow soybeans and lease to another farmer to grow corn. I cannot invest my $10,000 in both GE shares and T-notes. But if I understand some novel software-based Information Age technology, I can explain it to you, and then we will both know it and can use it as a source of wealth. Dr. Richard Stallman, a Macarthur Fellow at MIT, and his colleagues have noted this fundamental difference and argue for all software to be "open-source" like Linux rather than proprietary like Windows XP. The vehicle they have devised for this is the *copyleft* (as opposed to the *copyright*). Stallman's own software, such as GNU (recursively defined as "GNU is Not UNIX"), and his remarkable editor, Emacs, are available only under a copyleft in which the user warrants that he or she will provide the software without cost to others and inform Stallman of any bugs or errors in the code.

But software truly is intellectual property in the age of computers. It can be protected in order of relative security, as trade secrets, by copyrights, or by patenting it. Actually, the Trade Secrets Act is strong but has a trapdoor. If the software engineer who knows your secret tries to make money using it on his own, you can get a permanent injunction to prevent him from doing so. However, if he retaliates by going to a developer's conference and disclosing your secret technology, it is now no longer a secret and therefore is no longer protected by the Act. The copyright appears to be the logical protection mechanism for something like software, which is created and transferred as a written document. In fact, integrated circuit designers have found that copyrighting their masks as images provides more effective protection than patenting the chip's architecture as a mechanism. Clearly a software-based algorithm or process is a mechanism. In fact, some of the pioneers of software patenting, such as John Rooney, patent counsel of Univac in the 1960s and later chief patent counsel at Medtronic, got the first software patents by a back door process using this fact. Rooney, in his Socratic questioning style, would ask the designer of a novel software technology at Univac if it could also be implemented as microprogrammed firmware. The answer was always yes. Then he would ask if it could be implemented as firmware, couldn't it also be implemented in hardware as combinatorial logic or a programmed logic array (PLA). Again the answer was yes, but the software engineer would admit that he didn't know how to do that. So then Rooney would offer to provide a hardware designer to assist as co-inventor by designing the hardware implementation. He would then apply for a patent on the hardware as the preferred implementation, and the firmware and software as alternative implementations. Indirect, perhaps, but protected by patent law they were.

In the 1980s it became possible to patent software directly after the U.S. Patent Office was able to recruit examiners who could deal with it. Many of the early software patents were quite solid, but more recent patents and their failure to stand up under challenge in the courtroom have cast doubt on the use of patents to protect intellectual property cast as software. In a series of two articles in the *IEEE Spectrum*, Ben Klemens has argued that no clear boundary between software and mathematics exists and that software is better protected by copyrighting it rather than patenting it.[15] Dr. Klemens is a guest scholar at the Brookings Institution working on the forthcoming book *Math You Can't Use: Patents, Copyright, and Software*, to be published by the Brookings Institution Press. His thesis is well illustrated by numerous examples of mathematical formulas and numeric methods that have been granted patents as the patent office pendulum has swung too far the wrong way. Although mathematical algorithms were never patentable as scientific principles, what happened was recent developments in mathematical methods that are totally dependent on high-performance computers for their execution. This has opened a back door to patenting them due to blurring the distinction between mathematics and machinery. To a mathematician, Dr. Klemens' argument is simple: a modern computer is equivalent to a Turing or state machine; all modern programming languages can turn any computer into a state machine; and Church's *Lambda-calculus* can express any mathematical procedure, and likewise any software process, as a set of purely mathematical Lambda-calculus expressions. Therefore, it is impossible to distinguish between software and mathematics.[16] Incidentally, this was the major theme of the late Prof. Edsker Dykstra's work and is the basis of functional programming and any other denotative programming technology.

If software is formally equivalent to mathematics and mathematics cannot be patented, every software patent is a legal contradiction. In his second article (and presumably in his forthcoming book), Dr. Klemens argues that software patents are not viable and that the system will collapse under its own weight because it will soon prove to be unworkable. There is no way of reconciling a highly decentralized industry such as software, dependent on massive independent invention, with a law that makes independent invention a liability.[17] So, what is the alternative? His answer is clearly the copyright. Although the copyright does not offer a patent's monopoly protection, it provides adequate protection for software as intellectual property and is much simpler and much less expensive.

Sidebar 12.4: A Picture Is Worth...

Some years ago, when one of the authors was director of the Minnesota Supercomputer Center, he hosted a National Science Foundation (NSF) sponsored conference on "The Role of Supercomputers in Observational Astronomy." The last speaker in the plenary session was Professor Joan Centrella of Drexel University, who showed her famous eight-minute video on the creation of the universe. The author was standing at the back of the auditorium at the University Radisson Hotel, waiting to herd the attendees onto waiting buses to go to a party at the Supercomputer Center. The session had run a half-hour over. A "Minnesota swede" janitor was leaning on his broom beside me at the rear door, waiting to clean up and rearrange the room for another event. As Professor Centrella was receiving her well-deserved standing ovation, I leaned over and asked the janitor what he thought of the presentation. He replied: "Vell, dat vas pruddy gud. I can't vait to get home and tell my vife how the universe vas created." This is the power of a visual simulation of a complex natural event (or, in this case, the Big Bang, a "supernatural" event, since it cannot be described by the laws of physics as we know them). A visual simulation communicates with everyone, whereas the relativistic or quantum equations it is modeled with can communicate with only a few hundred specialists. The future of scientific communication lies in the use of simulation models like these, even for specialists.

Key Points

- Design for Trustworthy Software requires innovative, out-of-the-box thinking.

- Altschuller, the developer of TRIZ, has shown that creativity isn't an instinctive capability but rather one that can be learned.

- TRIZ practitioners have examined more than two million engineering patents to find the patterns that guide innovation.

- The highly structured TRIZ methodology has been adapted to the software development process and has shown encouraging results, especially for parallel processing applications.

- TRIZ methods work in concert with QFD and Taguchi Methods for innovation in software architecture and design.

- Conventional brainstorming and Pugh concept selection methods can be used together with TRIZ, QFD, and Taguchi Methods to identify the design approaches that will best meet the customer's needs.

- Software has become a major vehicle for intellectual property in the Information Age. It can be protected by the Trade Secrets Act, copyright law, or patent law.

- Patent law is becoming an increasingly fragile protection mechanism for software as intellectual property.

Additional Resources

http://www.prenhallprofessional.com/title/0131872508

http://www.agilenty.com/publications

Internet Exercises

1. Look up Genrich Altschuller on the Internet, and trace his development of TRIZ.

2. Find URLs dealing with the application of TRIZ to software architecture and development.

3. Can you find any Russian URLs for TRIZ?

Review Questions

1. Explain the difference between creativity and innovation.

2. What role does serendipity play in innovation?

3. In what ways is TRIZ simply highly organized "common sense"?

4. Find all the places in Table 12.1 where the analogues for TRIZ principles fail to apply to software. Why do they not succeed in the software domain?

Discussion Questions and Projects

1. "A new idea is worth a dollar, but a new idea and a development plan to bring it to market is worth a million dollars." Discuss.

2. Why do you think Altschuller's work was rejected in the USSR but widely accepted in the United States?

3. Take a software problem you have already solved innovatively, and map it through the TRIZ process shown in Figure 12.1 in a *pro forma* manner. Did you instinctively apply TRIZ principles?

4. Take one of the failed analogies from Review Question 4, and try to make it work. If software is a mechanism in the abstract sense, why doesn't a mechanical analogue work? How could you make it work?

Endnotes

[1] G. S. Altschuller, *Creativity as an Exact Science: The Theory of the Solution of Inventive Problems* (New York: Gordon and Breach, 1984).

[2] G. S. Altschuller, *40 Principles: TRIZ Keys to Technical Innovation* (L. Shulyak, Trans.) (Worcester, MA: Technical Innovation Center, 1998).

[3] G. S. Altschuller, *And Suddenly the Innovator Appeared: TRIZ, the Theory of Inventive Problem Solving* (L. Shulyak, Trans.) (Worcester, MA: Technical Innovation Center, 1996).

[4] J. Terninko, A. Zusman, B. Zlotin, *Systematic Innovation: An Introduction to TRIZ* (New York: St. Lucie Press, 1998), p. 5.

[5]Ibid, p. 3.

[6]Ibid, p. 10.

[7]K. C. Rea, http://www.triz-journal.com/archives/1999/08/d/index.htm.

[8]K. C. Rea, *TRIZ and Software: 40 Principle Analogies Part 1 and Part 2*, http://www.globalplatforms.com/. See http://www.triz-journal.com/archives/2001/09/e/index.htm and http://www.triz-journal.com/archives/2001/11/e/index.htm.

[9]T. Stanbrook, *TRIZ for Software Process Improvement*, COMPSAC02, Oxford, August 2002, pp. 466–468.

[10]J. Terninko, *Step-by-Step QFD: Customer-Driven Product Design* (Boca Raton: St. Lucie Press, 1997).

[11]W. Durfee, "Concept Selection," ME 4054 lecture notes, http://www.me.umn.edu/courses.me4054.lecnotes/select.html.

[12]D. Warburton, *Getting Better Results in Design Concept Selection*, http://www.devicelink.com/mddi/achive/04/01/mddi0401p66a.jpg.

[13]H. W. Stoll, *Product Design Methods and Practices* (New York: Marcel Dekker, 1999), pp. 122–130.

[14]S. Pugh, *Total Design: Integrated Methods for Successful Product Engineering* (Workingham, England: Addison-Wesley, 1990).

[15]S. Klemens, "Software Patents Don't Compute," *IEEE Spectrum*, July 2005, pp. 56–59, and "New Legal Code," August 2005, pp. 60–62.

[16]Op cit Klemens, "Software Patents Don't Compute," p. 59.

[17]Op cit Klemens, "New Legal Code," p. 62.

CHAPTER 13

Risk Assessment and Failure Modes and Effects Analysis in Software

The current system cost trend is approaching software domination over hardware ...
the relative frequency could be as high as 100:1 software to hardware failures.

—*Way Kuo*

Twenty years from now you will be more disappointed by the things that
you didn't do than by the ones you did.

—*Mark Twain*

Overview

Risk of failure in software products can be estimated by Failure Modes and Effects Analysis (FMEA) and potential failures eliminated by Software Failure Tree Analysis (SFTA). FMEA was developed by the Germans for the V1 rocket bomb program and later was applied more generally by the defense industry worldwide and more recently by the automotive industry. We find that a simplified version of FMEA is applicable to risk assessment in software development when applied as far upstream as possible during the design phase. SFTA allows the designer to anticipate potential software defects or bugs from the later stages of design documentation or pseudocode but before investment in coding and testing has begun. Grady's method is applied to tracing potential failures identified by SFTA back to their most likely source so that they can be eliminated by redesign. It is far less expensive to catch what may become bugs at this stage of development, essentially the first design review, than to catch them downstream in product testing, or worse, by the customer or end user. This chapter discusses the five most common categories of software failure modes and their elimination in design by FMEA and SFTA.

Chapter Outline

- FMEA: Failure Modes and Effects Analysis

- Upstream Application of FMEA

- Software Failure Tree Analysis

- Software Failure Modes and Their Sources

- Risk Assignment and Evaluation at Each Stage of DFTS

- Key Points

- Additional Resources

- Internet Exercises

- Review Questions

- Discussion Questions and Projects

- Endnotes

FMEA: Failure Modes and Effects Analysis

Much has been written about the analysis of failure modes and their effects (FMEA) for hardware design, development, and manufacture. Here we want to apply this proven, effective technology to software design and development. A system integrating both software and hardware functionality may fail due to the capabilities of the software component or components that are invoked by external control, by a user, or by another device. Software may also fail when used in an unfamiliar environment or by an inexperienced, impatient, or clumsy user. A software failure is defined by many designers as a departure from the expected "output" result or action of a program's operation, which differs from the requirement or specification. The program may either run or fail to run when called upon. This failure may be due to user or "pilot error" (referred to as "smoke in the cockpit" by software designers, who have little faith in the end user's ability to operate software properly), by a hardware or network communications error, or by an actual problem (defect or bug) in the software itself.

Hardware design is often constrained by engineering trade-offs that can be totally overcome only by a cost-is-no-object approach, which is rarely used, for obvious reasons. Software design is constrained by the same cost and time factors as hardware design projects but is not so vulnerable to the need for intrinsic functional capability or engineering trade-offs common in hardware design. Software design is done in more of an "anything is possible" context, so there is a great temptation for the designer to multiply functions beyond what the end user needs or actually requested. This leads to the same risk that an overly complex machine design would have. Software designers and programmers often must be reminded of the rule that mechanical designers try to follow: "Any part that is not designed into this machine will never cause it to fail." In other words, the programmer's chief canon of either elegance or reliability is simplicity!

Unlike building rococo late-medieval cathedrals, writing reliable computer programs *is* rocket science! The rocket designer quickly learns that the weight of any feature added to the rocket increases the rocket's final weight by 10 times the weight of the added feature. Computer programming does not suffer such a severe penalty for redundancy or gratuitous functionality, but simplicity and economy of program expression nonetheless are very highly desired. Curiously, FMEA literally *is* rocket science, because it began with the German V1 rocket bomb. The first models of this weapon were notoriously unreliable, but the development of the first version of FMEA and its application eventually produced a success rate of 60%. That doesn't sound very impressive by today's quality standards, even for rockets, but the V1 was the *first* production rocket vehicle. What became FMEA in the American aerospace industry came with the German rocket scientists and their second model, or version V2, which was the basis of the later American Redstone rocket.[1]

Here we will begin with a review of FMEA applied to hardware and examine the potential for its use at each stage of the DFTS methodology described in Figure 2.6. FMEA is a systematic step-by-step process that predicts potential failure modes in a machine or system and estimates their severity. The initial design can then be reviewed to determine where and how changes to the design (and, in the case of mechanical systems, operations, inspection, and maintenance strategies as well) can eliminate failure modes or at least reduce their frequency and severity. FMEA is also sometimes applied to identify weak areas in a design, to highlight safety-critical components, or to make a design more robust (and expensive) but less costly to maintain later when in service.[2] Some of FMEA's key features and benefits are not applicable to software design. However, those that are will be very beneficial in our effort to build quality and reliability into software as far upstream in the design and development process as possible.

An extension of FMEA called FMECA adds a criticality analysis. It is used by the Department of Defense and some aerospace firms. The criticality analysis ranks each potential failure mode according to the combined influence of its severity classification and probability of failure based on the data available. Criticality analysis is used for complex systems with many interdependent components in mission-critical scenarios. It is not used by the automotive industry, as is the basic FMEA, and it is not generally applicable to enterprise software design and development.

Functional FMEA is normally applied to systems in a top-down manner in which the system is successively decomposed into subsystems, components, and ultimately units or subassemblies that are treated as the "black boxes" that provide the system with essential functionality. This approach is very well suited to analyzing computer programs for business applications, which naturally decompose in a hierarchical manner, right down to the fundamental subroutines, functions, or software objects. (These elements are also referred to as "black boxes" by software designers and testers.) The hardware reliability engineer considers the loss of critical inputs, upstream subassembly failures, and so on for the functional performance of each unit. This helps the engineer identify and classify components as to the severity of their failure modes on overall system operation. There also exists a dual or bottom-up FMEA approach that is not as applicable to software systems design.

Much has been written on FMEA, and we could quote many authors and as many variations of procedure, but a good basic paradigm is that of Andrews and Moss,[3] which we repeat here as a seven-step process:

1. Define the system to be analyzed and its required performance reliability.

2. Construct a functional system hierarchy showing how the subsystems and components interconnect.

3. Identify any assumptions made in the analysis of system and subsystem failure modes.

4. List components, identifying their failure modes and rates (or ranges) of failure.

5. Complete a set of FMEA worksheets analyzing the effect of each sub-assembly or component failure mode on system performance.

6. Enter severity rankings and failure rates or ranges on the worksheets, and evaluate the criticality of each failure mode on system reliability.

7. Review the worksheets to identify the reliability-critical components, and make recommendations for design improvements.

You can surely already detect the aroma of a typical mechanical or civil engineering process that has been "reduced to code" as the saying goes. FMEA is supported by basic tutorial manuals giving all the forms and instructions on how to fill them out and perform an analysis,[4] by training courses teaching automotive engineers the technology,[5] and by handbooks that help the engineer keep the many details of the process in mind.[6] We do not need to go through a sample analysis here, because much of it is not applicable to software, but it is useful to show a typical FMEA worksheet such as that shown in Figure 13.1.

As you can see from this worksheet, the difficult stage is determining failure severity and its frequency or range. Because the system is typically under design, the analyst has no way to assign precise values, but he or she can deal with subjective estimates and ranges. For example, severity in mechanical systems and continuous processes can be estimated as follows:

- **Minor:** No significant effect

- **Major:** Some reduction in operational effectiveness

- **Critical:** Significant reduction of performance with a dramatic change of state

- **Catastrophic:** Total loss of system, with significant property damage, personal safety hazards, and/or environmental damage

Range estimates of failure probability for mechanical systems are typically as follows:[7]

- **Low:** Fewer than 0.01 failures per year

- **Medium:** 0.01 to 0.1 failures per year

- **High:** More than 1 failure per year

System ....   Date ....

Indenture Level ....   Sheet ....of................

Ref. Drawing....................   Originator ....

Operating State.................   Approved ....

Identification	Function	Failure Mode	Failure Effect		Failure Detection Method	Compensating Provisions	Severity	Remarks
			Local Effect	System Effect				

FIGURE 13.1
A Typical FMEA Analysis Worksheet

These levels of criticality and ranges are typical of large mechanical systems but are not directly applicable to the reliability of enterprise application software. We need to develop a more dynamic range in the middle of the severity scale, because real application software reliability problems run from major to critical. Catastrophic errors are of a serious business-risk nature that would hopefully be caught during an audit. The failure frequency ranges seem benign by software standards. High in our field would be several times a day and very low something that occurred once in ten years. Recently such an error came to the attention of one of the authors when an accounts-payable module that had run without problems for ten years blew up when in use by a large construction company. The vendor's testing expert coded a stress test to discover the problem and let it run all night to perform 250,000 transactions. The next morning the run had finished without error. The next evening he ran it 500,000 times and discovered the problem. A storage leak in a C program module had returned to the storage manager one fewer byte than it had requested for each transaction. The error did not produce an application failure until the program was used by a very large international construction company that purchases many thousands of items. This would rate as a minor problem with a low frequency of occurrence on the typical FMEA scales, but it would be a very rare combination of circumstances for software errors.

Upstream Application of FMEA

FMEA is not limited to evaluating a finished or even provisional design by trained reliability engineers. Using FMEA as far upstream as possible can influence a system's early architectural concept, but it's less precise and less predictive because it is even further from any actual experience with the system. Figure 13.2 illustrates the use of FMEA at several levels during design and development. Although it is taken from the hardware design and development arena,[8] it will later be seen to be applicable to software practice. Clearly the risks identified for concept FMEA are very different from those that may occur for design FMEA or process FMEA. The point is that failure modes resulting from design errors and failure modes resulting from implementation or process errors result in very different kinds of risk and subsequent failure.

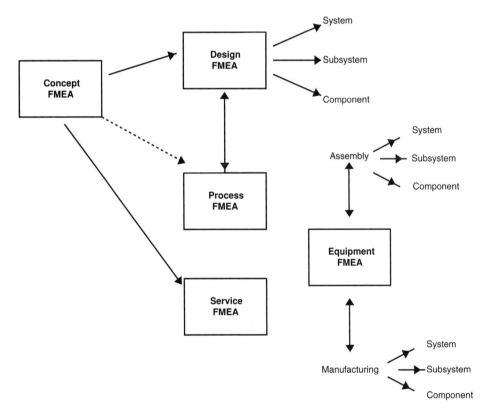

FIGURE 13.2
Types of FMEA That Apply to Software as Well as Hardware Architecture

Adapted from G. S. Wasserman, *Reliability Verification, Testing, and Analysis in Engineering Design* (New York: Marcel Dekker, 2003), p. 41.

Concept or architectural FMEA is applied at the beginning of a development project when the system's feasibility or application is first being assessed. It is used to clarify and define intended functions and their interdependencies, to assess design feasibility and implementation technology, and to determine whether redundancy is required or desirable. The scope of architectural FMEA begins at the system's top functional level but may be applied recursively throughout the system hierarchy all the way to the component level.

Design FMEA is the classical application level for the method and is still the place where it provides the most benefit as far upstream in the development process as possible. Concept, equipment, and process FMEA forms are similar in structure but differ in terms of guidelines for entering ratings. At the design level the entries can be defined most crisply.

A *failure mode* is the manner in which a component or system failure occurs—the way in which the component or subsystem does not or might not meet the design intent or specification. It is simply the answer to the question "In what ways could this subsystem or component fail?" Naturally a failure mode can propagate through the system hierarchy, and the failure observed at each level must be noted in the form. Potential failure modes are usually considered to fall into one of four categories:[9]

- **No function:** Complete absence of the intended function

- **Partial function:** Does not meet some of the required functions

- **Intermittent function:** Sometimes performs the function properly

- **Unintended function:** Some unintended function is performed

Potential *effects of failure* are defined as the effects of the failure mode on the function *as perceived by the customer*. There may be four types of customers:

- An internal customer, or the next stage in the development process

- An external customer or buyer of the system—in our case, of an enterprise business application (say, the CFO)

- The application's end user (say, an accounting clerk)

- A government agency/standard (abroad, the local Generally Accepted Accounting Practices [GAAP]) or regulatory body (in the United States, the Financial Accounting Standards Board [FASB])

Severity defines the seriousness of the failure effect on the customer. Table 13.1 is adapted from the severity ratings used by FMEA practitioners in the auto industry.

TABLE 13.1
Adaptation of the Auto Industry Severity Rating System[10]

Severity	Description of Failure Rate	Rating	Reliability Target
Safety	Fails to meet federal safety standards	9 or 10	100%
Major	Stops the product's operation (catastrophic)	7 or 8	95%
Moderate	Product fails to perform one or more functions	4, 5, or 6	80 to 90%
Low	Causes customer annoyance	2 or 3	—
Minor	Customer use problem	1	—

Although developed by the automobile industry, this FMEA severity scale is already more suitable for software and shows more dynamic range than the earlier example. Of course, automobiles have a number of computers in them these days, from three to nine or more, so software error modes are becoming a factor in their reliability as systems as well.

The occurrence scale of failures has likewise been extended by the automobile industry to provide the spectrum shown in Table 13.2.

TABLE 13.2
Occurrence Rating System Used by the Auto Industry[11]

Probability of Failure	Possible Rates	Rating
Very high (inevitable)	1 in 2 1 in 3	10 9
High (repeated failures)	1 in 8 1 in 20	8 7
Moderate (occasional)	1 in 80 1 in 400 1 in 2,000	6 5 4
Low (few failures)	1 in 15,000 1 in 150,000	3 2
Remote (failure unlikely)	1 in 1,500,000	1

This table also is more representative of software, again perhaps because automobiles today are complex electromechanical machines controlled by computer software.

FMEA can be viewed as a Pareto chart, as described in Chapter 6, for prioritizing the allocation of resources for design improvements, modifications, and/or upgrades. The design FMEA team should prioritize actions based on those failure modes with effects that have the highest severity ratings and with causes that have the highest severity times occurrence ratings. In spite of the numerical trapping of FMEA and its strong basis in mathematical and statistical analysis (see Modarres, Kaminskiy, and Krivtsov for a rigorous mathematical treatment of reliability engineering),[12] FMEA is still an art, not a science. The further upstream in the development process it is applied, the more prescient and less scientific it becomes, yet at the same time it is more useful and insightful for motivating design changes.

Software Failure Tree Analysis

Software Failure Tree Analysis (SFTA) is like FMEA in that its purpose is to anticipate failure *a priori* in a program rather than to prove that it works properly in an *a posteriori* or testing procedure. In manufacturing it is called Fault Tree Analysis (FTA). Several software reliability experts have used it for software reliability analysis, and it has become known as SFTA.[13, 14] SFTA may begin in the program's detailed design phase, not quite as far upstream as FMEA, because it needs a dynamic expression of the program's function in the form of a flowchart or high-level pseudocode to begin the analysis. The fault tree is a static mapping of the program's flow into a static tree diagram that lists the operational possibilities at each stage of the program's dynamic process. Used at the design phase, it identifies some of the top-level hazards. Used at the coding phase, it identifies some test paths that should be implemented to verify that lower-level hazards will not occur. Like FTA, SFTA begins by identifying potential failures during the design phase. Although it is done during design, the hazards or potential failures in operation and maintenance are also considered and forecast. The term *hazard* is often used to denote a potential failure, because we cannot call a problem a failure before it actually happens!

Although the terminology differs from one author to another, a hazard has three basic characteristics:

- Whether an intended service occurs or does not

- Whether it occurs on time or too early or too late

- Whether it provides the correct answer or not

Table 13.3 illustrates the fundamental hazard opportunities.

TABLE 13.3
Hazard Opportunities for SFTA

Characteristic	No Hazard	Commission Hazard	Omission Hazard
Service provision	Occurs	Occurs when it should not	Does not occur when it should
Service timing	Timely	Occurs too early	Occurs too late
Service value	Correct	Obvious fault	Obscure fault

To build a fault tree, you draw a graph whose nodes are hazards of either single components, subsystems, or the entire system. Relationships among the nodes are represented by edges in the graph. Each edge is labeled AND if both components must fail, OR if one or the other must fail, or N of M if N of M redundant components must fail.[15] Each node in the graph must represent an independent event. When the graph is complete, the failure tree can be scanned to identify the following:

- Single points of failure for which the system's integrity rests on a single component

- Uncertainty for which there are not enough constraints on the variable values or conditions to branch to

- Ambiguities for which the graph is disconnected

- Missing components

Figure 13.3 shows an example of an SFTA graph with AND and OR connectors for a simple scenario. A method call fails to produce a result because hidden variable or object-state data was not stored properly, resulting in a consequent data read error, or because the method throws an exception. The low-level design changes required to prevent these hazards would start with catching any method exceptions and then would add code to ensure that sequential data is properly stored and recast upon recall.

Such an analysis can be applied to any system, whether hardware or software or both, but it's especially suitable for software systems because a software design can be expressed as sequences, decisions or branches, and iterations. As soon as the fault tree for a design is available, we can assume that a certain fault will occur. But if we cannot find a set of events in the tree that will produce it, we may conclude that it cannot occur. However, if points of failure do appear in the design's fault tree, they can be removed, components or conditions can be added to prevent that hazard's enabling conditions to arise, or components can be added to correct the problem if the failure inevitably does arise. Some hazards in computation are inevitable, and modern languages such as Java have exception-handling capability to deal with them. Examples are floating-point underflow or overflow, division by 0, and numbers out of range. Earlier programming languages allowed the programmer to laboriously code avoidance or hazard/exception handling for such events, however unlikely. But modern languages "throw" exceptions automatically and encourage the programmer to "catch" them in code blocks that prevent the program from either halting or producing an incorrect result. Fault trees have been used in mechanical design to calculate the probability that a given fault will occur, but such a practice has not yet been applied to computer software to our knowledge.

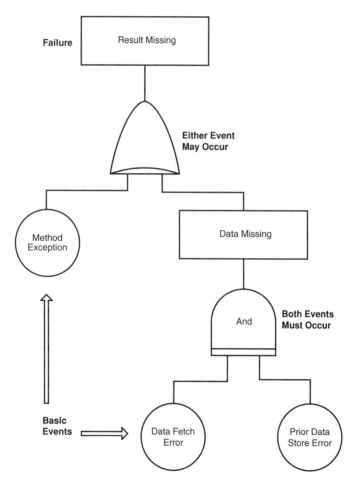

FIGURE 13.3
A Simple SFTA Graph for a Method Invocation

For large application programs having many dependencies or time and rate dependencies, the failure trees can be very time-consuming to draw, so the analysis may become quite tedious. The research frontier for this methodology is automating the construction of the tree and its graph from a design-level specification of the program, as well as automating the analysis of the graph for potential hazards. As soon as the failure points are identified, redesign to correct them is neither difficult nor costly. In fact, it occurs so far upstream in the development process that it is essentially part of the first-level design review.

Software Failure Modes and Their Sources

Machines fail because of wear among parts, environmental hazards, metal fatigue, corrosion and rust, and operator misuse. Systems fail because of unit failures, communication glitches, and operator misuse or configuration errors. The failure modes for software are quite different, because software does not *wear* or age as do mechanical or even electrical components. Most software failures are actually written into the script like a villain is written into a melodrama. However, they are usually unconsciously programmed *side effects* that produce unintended consequences. Over the past 40 years, programming language and operating system designers have given a great deal of attention to eliminating opportunities for programmers and users to provoke unintended side effects. The structured programming movement of the 1970s and the elimination of the GOTO command in modern programming languages have been a great help. More recently, the development of object-oriented programming languages, object-oriented design technology, and integrated program development environments have made a huge difference.

An excellent paradigm for software failure opportunities and the ultimate sources of these failures is given in Robert Grady's book *Successful Software Process Improvement*. Figure 13.4 is adapted from his schema and description.[16] It is important to have a schema like this to be able to identify the most likely source of a program failure, or to at least narrow it down to a few possibilities. The apparent failure is exhibited as doing nothing when it was supposed to do something, or doing the wrong thing, or loss of control, or shifting the process sequence to the wrong place, or simply halting. Today's operating systems often can give programmers or testers valuable clues to help them identify the failure mode and its potential source(s). Early operating systems were not very helpful. One of the first operating systems, IBJOB on the IBM 7090 computer, simply halted when it lost program control. It sent the following cryptic message to the line printer:

THE MACHINE HAS ENCOUNTERED A CATASTROPHIC ERROR; NO
FURTHER INFORMATION IS AVAILABLE AT THIS TIME.

All this message told the user was that the program did not come to a normal stopping point. The user would spend the rest of the night looking at a machine-language dump of his program's state when it halted due to an unknown failure.

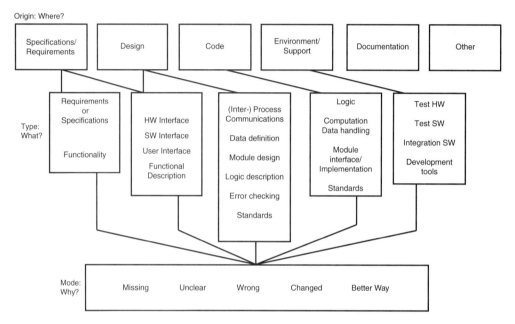

FIGURE 13.4
Mapping Failure Modes to Their Sources

Adapted with permission from R. B. Grady, *Successful Software Process Improvement* (Upper Saddle River, NJ: Prentice-Hall, 1997), p. 199.

The schema shown in Figure 13.4 takes the failure mode source analysis back to one of the four program development stages: specification/requirements, design, coding/implementation, or environment/support. Its failure modes fall into five categories:

• The intended result may be missing due to a data input error or program error.

• It may be unclear, ambiguous, or unexpected.

• It may simply be wrong.

• It may have changed during processing when it shouldn't have.

• It may have been inefficiently obtained and could be computed by a better method.

Grady's schema allows the FMEA analyst to work backwards through the diagram from the failure mode, to the type of error, to its most likely source. In our experience, the largest source of failure in new programs is the high-level designer's misunderstanding of the functional specification. Second is the detailed designer's choice of algorithm (including data definitions and data handling) to compute a result. Third is the implementer or coder's expression of the algorithm in the programming language as implemented on the host computer hardware. Experience with Grady's paradigm has shown it to be very effective for analog electronics systems and software-controlled digital electronic systems. The most subtle and difficult-to-discover and -correct failures are those that are intermittent either in time or in some data element range of values. This is true of electrical systems, whether analog or digital, but it's less common in purely mechanical systems.

Risk Assignment and Evaluation at Each Stage of DFTS

Figure 2.6 in Chapter 2 illustrates the overall DFTS process advocated by this book. Note that each feedback step in the process has one or more major quality tools in the feedback loop.

Starting at the top of the figure, they go down the chart as six levels. FMEA is applied at each level, as shown in Table 13.4, where the FMEA scope at each level is shown in Figure 13.2. FMEA is a hierarchical risk analysis tool and may be as well applied to a hierarchical software system as a hardware system or complex machine.

TABLE 13.4
Quality Tools Applied at Various Levels of DFTS (See Figure 2.6)

Level	Quality Tool(s)
Phase 1: Requirements	QFD and Voice of the Customer Pugh Concept Development TRIZ Inventive Problem Solving Concept FMEA: Analyze concept for risks
Phase 2: Robust Design	QFD on the functional and technical design features Design FMEA: Analyze design for risks SFTA detailed software tree analysis
Phase 3: Coding/Implementation	Component FMEA: Component risk analysis
Phase 4: Verify, Validate, Test, and Evaluate	Subsystem FMEA: Subsystem risk analysis
Phase 5: Integration	System FMEA: System integration risk analysis
Phase 6: Maintenance	Service FMEA: In-service risk analysis

The failure modes and their likely sources are different at each level of feedback in a DFTS methodology. The appropriate level of FMEA or, in some cases, SFTA is applied at the indicated feedback level of the DFTS model shown in Figure 2.6 to discover remaining failure modes in the system and subsystems. It is usually an architectural/design team brainstorming process to come up with a list of potential failures or hazards at each level. The identifiable and justifiable hazards are mapped backward through a Grady Sources-to-hazards schema, as shown in Figure 13.3, as far back in the design process as possible. Then the hazards are eliminated by redesign. Failure modes in mechanical and electrical systems may offer a dazzling array of possibilities, but fortunately in programming, they are most often limited to five categories:

A really catastrophic failure in a new program is known as a fatal error—one that causes the program to halt with no indication of why it did so. Fortunately, failures of this nature are usually detected in testing and rarely occur on the customer's premises. But fatal errors can happen when an unexpected or unusual data error not caught by an input edit forces a program down a control path that has not been tested.

Key Points

- Failure Modes and Effects Analysis (FMEA) is literally rocket science. It was developed for the German V1 rocket bomb project.

- FMEA has been used primarily in the defense industry since then. More recently, it has been used in the automobile industry.

- Our interest is in adapting a simplified version of FMEA to software development and as far upstream in the design and development process as possible.

- This may be done as a seven-step process based on the standard-practices manuals used for FMEA by the automobile industry.

- Whereas FMEA can be applied at all levels of design development and usage, for software it is most useful at the design level as Design FMEA.

- Software Failure Tree Analysis (SFTA) may be used in conjunction with FMEA as a means of anticipating errors in the final software product at the earliest possible stage of design.

- Potential failures can also be mapped back to their likely sources, and redesign can be done to keep them from occurring later.

- There are only five categories of common software failure modes. FMEA and SFTA are effective at catching them early in design.

Additional Resources

http://www.prenhallprofessional.com/title/0131872508

http://www.agilenty.com/publications

Internet Exercises

1. Look up FMEA on the Internet, and identify sites that are related to its application to software development.

2. Look up SFTA on the Internet, and trace its development and current usage.

Review Questions

1. Why is FMEA for software similar to its application to automobile design and development?

2. Why is FMEA for software simpler than for mechanical products? In the preceding chapter you saw that some of the analogies for mechanical TRIZ failed to reach into the virtual world of software.

3. Explain why Design FMEA is more useful for software risk assessment than Concept FMEA or Process FMEA.

4. Describe the five most common software failure modes. Can you think of other less-common or second-tier failure modes you have encountered?

Discussion Questions and Projects

1. Draw a software failure tree for the last program module you wrote. Does it reveal any risks you were not already aware of?

2. Trace through Grady's failure mode mapping schema in Figure 13.4 with this same program module in mind. Do you already instinctively use his method in a less formal way? Most such design tools are simply the distilled common sense and codified experience of the more articulate and thoughtful practitioners of any craft.

3. Which of the back-tracing paths in Grady's schema do you use most often?

Endnotes

[1]J. D. Andrews and T. R. Moss, *Reliability and Risk Assessment* (New York: ASME, 2002), p. 2.

[2]Ibid, p. 75.

[3]Ibid, p. 77.

[4]R. E. McDermott, R. J. Mikulak, M. R. Beauregard, *The Basics of FMEA* (Portland: Productivity, Inc., 1996).

[5]ASI, *FMEA Design and Process, Version 5.0* (Detroit: American Supplier Institute, 1998).

[6]K. W. Dailey, *The FMEA Pocket Handbook* (Detroit: DW Publishing Co., 2004).

[7]Op cit Andrews and Moss, pp. 84–85.

[8]G. S. Wasserman, *Reliability Verification, Testing, and Analysis in Engineering Design* (New York: Marcel Dekker, 2003), p. 41.

[9]Ibid, p. 45.

[10]Ibid, p. 46.

[11]Ibid, p. 48.

[12]M. Modarres, M. Kaminskiy, V. Krivtsov, *Reliability Engineering and Risk Analysis* (New York: Marcel Dekker, 1999).

[13]A. M. Neufelder, *Ensuring Software Reliability* (New York: Marcel Dekker, 1997), pp. 203–214.

[14]S. L. Pfleeger, L. Hatton, C. C. Howell, *Solid Software* (Upper Saddle River, NJ: Prentice-Hall, 2002), pp. 47–50.

[15]Ibid, p. 48.

[16]R. B. Grady, *Successful Software Process Improvement* (Upper Saddle River, NJ: Prentice-Hall, 1997), p. 199.

CHAPTER 14

Object and Component Technologies and Other Development Tools

The only thing in the world growing faster than computing technology today is computer end-user expectation.

—P. C. Patton

Overview

Computer programming development has long been stretched between two conflicting goals: improved productivity in terms of lower costs and reduced development time, and greater product reliability and thus software trustworthiness. Object-oriented analysis, design, and programming (OOADP) technology promises to resolve this tension and meet both goals by building software products in sophisticated program development environments using tested, proven components. This process is similar to building an automobile from an inventory of proven mechanical components and subsystems. The IBM SanFrancisco™ middleware product suite is presented in this chapter as an example of the future of software development with components. Alternative technologies such as Extreme Programming for enhanced productivity and N-Version Programming for increased reliability are also presented and contrasted. Several modern programming environments are compared and their URLs given, and trends in automatic software development are forecast.

Chapter Outline

- Major Challenges in Enterprise Business Applications

- Object-Oriented Analysis, Design, and Programming

- Component-Based Software Development Technology

- Extreme Programming for Productivity

- N-Version Programming for Reliability

- Modern Programming Environments

- Trends in Computer Programming Automation

- Key Points

- Additional Resources

- Internet Exercises

- Review Questions

- Discussion Questions and Projects

- Endnotes

Major Challenges in Enterprise Business Applications

The two major problems in enterprise business application development and perhaps in computer programming generally are how to increase productivity while increasing quality. Programming has always been tedious and painstaking but creative work. The productivity increase in programming in the development process has been about 500% over the past 50 years. This would be remarkable in any other labor-intensive craft. Sadly, it pales before the factor of 10^{10} increase in computer hardware performance during the same period—not to mention the proliferation of computers into applications not even imagined 50 years ago. At the same time development time and cost are unsatisfactory to the buyer of programming product development, the quality of computer programs is far from satisfactory to the end users of these products. Until recently these two demands were irreconcilable. Anything that would speed up development or reduce cost tended to reduce quality. And efforts to improve quality almost always required more time and money. This chapter presents the object-oriented revolution, which has been waiting in the wings for a long time. We'll review its ability to support component-based software development, which has been advocated for an even longer time. We will also discuss briefly productivity-based approaches such as Extreme Programming and quality-based approaches such as N-Version Programming. All of these new development technologies are well supported for individual users and small groups by programming development environments (PDEs) and for large groups by integrated development environments (IDEs). These are discussed in terms of a few leading examples. The computer end user is like the complaining cowboy in a Western saloon 150 years ago who expected stronger whiskey, louder music, and wilder women. The computer end user expects faster development at lower cost, more-capable software, and totally bug-free software. At last these expectations may be met.

Object-Oriented Analysis, Design, and Programming

In the year 2000, as they have said at the beginning of each decade for the past 30 years, object-oriented design and analysis advocates said, "This is the decade of objects." Although we hope this will be true in this decade, we can at least say that this is certainly the *century* of objects. One of the authors witnessed the birth of object-oriented computing. He must confess that even though he was already a programming veteran at the time, he was not completely sure what was being delivered at this blessed event. The inventors were not sure either, but as the baby grew, it became ever stronger and more recognizable as the revolution in computer programming technology it has become today.

Sidebar 14.1: The Birth of Object-Oriented Programming

In 1961, as scientific consultant for Sperry Univac International's Europe, Middle East, and Africa Division, one of the authors helped arrange a $50,000 discount on a Univac 1107 computer to be delivered in late 1962 to the Norwegian Defense Research Establishment. In return for the discount, Kristen Nygaard and Ole-Johann Dahl of the NDRE were to license to Univac the Simula event-oriented simulation package they had been developing in the ALGOL 60 high-level programming language. They had done the basic development and some limited small-scale testing on the small Danish Gier computer, which supported the best Algol 60 compiler available at the time. The initial application for the simulation package was to be management of Norway's forest reserves. Univac had gone to Europe with the large-scale Univac Scientific 1107 marketing program in 1961, together with compilers for the COBOL, FORTRAN, and ALGOL programming languages. Shortly thereafter, the vendor developing the Univac Algol 60 compiler announced that it would not be able to deliver this product so critical to marketing an American mainframe in Europe at that time.

Fortunately, another similar contract with a software license buy-back had been negotiated with Case-Western Reserve University, but the software to be delivered had not yet been specified. Upon hearing the bad news about the initial ALGOL package cancellation, we immediately flew to Sperry Rand Univac headquarters in New York to get permission to ask

Case-Western Reserve to do an Algol 60 compiler to fulfill their contract requirement. On arrival in Cleveland the next day, we were pleased to meet an academic development team headed by the world's best programmer, Donald Knuth, supported by undergraduate research assistants Nick Hubacker and Joe Speroni. They said they could deliver the desired compiler in the amazingly short time of six months. The author was stunned by this impossible time estimate but equally amazed by the team abilities. When the compiler was ready six months later, he flew from Sperry Rand International headquarters in Lausanne, Switzerland to Cleveland, Ohio to bring the compiler back to Paris. Univac had time available every night on the University of Paris' Univac 1107 at the Faculty of Sciences center in Orsay, a Paris suburb. Nygaard and Dahl planned to be there to make the final checkout runs for Simula when the compiler arrived.

Unfortunately, the "chicken war" between the United States and the European Economic Community (EEU) was on. The EEU, mainly France, had objected to U.S. chicken producers exporting "factory-grown" frozen chickens to Europe and had limited imports to "processed chickens" only. With typical Yankee ingenuity, the American producers had started putting a dollop of paprika on each chicken before shrink-wrapping and freezing it and then labeling it as "processed chicken." The French were furious, but they had not been specific as to what they meant by processed chicken, so the chickens had to be accepted as processed and therefore were legal imports. French customs officers responded by making entry into France difficult for Americans by dumping the contents of their suitcases on the counter or floor when they said they had nothing to declare upon entry. The author knew he would never get a computer magnetic tape reel with the new UNIVAC 1107 Algol 60 compiler on it past this gauntlet. So he asked the Case-Western Reserve team to punch out the compiler program code in binary on common 80-column punched cards. These cards would likely be perceived as having no commercial value, because they were no longer reusable. This turned out to be five boxes of 2,000 cards each, which filled a large suitcase.

Upon arriving at the Paris Orly airport at 10 p.m. with a small bag of clothing and a large suitcase full of cards, the author, who fortunately spoke fluent French, was confronted by a surly French customs officer. The card file was declared as a compiler for the University of Paris Univac computer. The agent said that the content of the card file was information, and information was taxed when entering or leaving France. The author offered to pay the tax. The inspector went on to suggest that perhaps the contents were a filthy novel that would not be allowed entry in any case. The author observed that filthy novels were exported from France to the United States but never the reverse, to which the agent agreed, with some amusement. The inspector then took about a half-inch of the binary cards from one box and offered to send them to the Ministry of Information for tax evaluation. The author held one of the lacey binary cards up to the light and told the agent that the information was in the holes, but since the holes were not there, how could the agent possibly tax him for something that did not exist? This peculiar Gallic logic prevailed, and he told the author to "Get out of here" (*Aller, Monsieur*) without even dumping his clothes on the floor.

The author rushed to Orsay by taxi, arriving in the computing center at midnight, where Nygaard and Dahl were nervously pacing. The new Algol 60 compiler was readily installed, and Simula, which had been written completely in ALGOL as its meta-language, was implemented and worked the first time. What a pleasure to be a facilitator for five of the world's best programmers—three from Cleveland and two from Oslo. Simula became the world's first object-oriented program. Years later, Nygaard and Dahl were knighted by the King of Norway and were acknowledged by the international computing community as the inventors of OOP. The author had the privilege of sponsoring Dr. Nygaard on a speaking tour of the United States in 2000, a year before he died at the age 73. Dr. Dahl died six months later.

The genius of Simula was turning each simulated event into what we know today as an object. The events had coded methods and hidden data, they were invoked by messages from other objects, they were polymorphic, and they had inheritance properties. The idea of generalizing them beyond a simulation package was readily accepted. But as with every other new software technology, there is a 20-to-30-year gestation period from the conception in the research laboratory to emergence in the marketplace. Naturally, much has been written about object-oriented analysis and development, which we will not attempt to review here. Our interest is the importance of the object revolution in the ability to deploy objects as components, and its influence on software quality, especially reliability. We will focus rather narrowly on the OOADP process and how it contributes to our two stated goals in tension. We'll note pitfalls and problems that any new technology and its use may engender. We'll also describe the promise of object frameworks with reference to the most ambitious framework attempted so far—IBM's SanFrancisco™ project. One of the authors was architect of an effort to reimplement a business system written in COBOL and C that was recast into Java using this framework. He can testify to the ability of an object framework to deliver quality software in much less time, at far less cost, and with a high degree of object componentization and code reusability (see Sidebar 14.2).

Objects are computational modules that have signatures, attributes or properties, and behaviors or methods that carry out computing tasks on data. They communicate with each other by sending and receiving messages. Each object, which is an operational unit of computation, is an instance of a blueprint from which it was constructed, called a class. The classes for an entire application are arranged in a hierarchy or tree-shaped blueprint "sheaf" for the whole application. The analyst specifying the functions for a new business (or any other) computer application builds use cases (as described in Chapter 1) for each function that the ultimate user of the application expects it to perform. From these use cases, what will become objects are defined as classes or abstract program blueprints. The classes are then organized into a hierarchy so that subclasses can inherit properties and methods from superclasses. This minimizes the number of different program pieces that must be written and checked out to complete the application. This feature of OOP maximizes reuse, which tends to resolve the tension between the conflicting software development goals of low time and cost on the one hand and high quality on the other. Reuse is further enhanced by an object characteristic called polymorphism—an object's ability to modify its behavior based on the data type in the message that invokes or calls it to perform one of its behaviors. For example, in Java, if the programmer wants to print a primitive data element, he or she can call the println method with a character as data. It will print the character with an integer, it will print the integer with a floating-point number, it will print a decimal with a string, and it will print the string of characters. Any object constructed from its class can inherit a method from a superclass and then override that method to make it specific to its own needs. Thus, reusability is not like making identical cookies with a cookie cutter. Each object can customize the attributes and methods it chooses to inherit from the hierarchy above it.

Having organized the objects defined from the analyst's use cases into a hierarchy, the software architect must then describe how they interact, again based on the use-case analysis. Having defined the interactions, the developer may now describe operations on objects, which are defined by the flow of the intended application. Each of these steps is dependent on the previous step, but as the process goes on, a high degree of iteration is required, because new discoveries at each level require revisiting previous levels. It has been noted that because water does not flow uphill, the spiral model soon replaced the waterfall model for OOADP.[1] If you're unfamiliar with this process, you might want to refer to Ivar Jacobson's book *Object-Oriented Software Engineering*, a thorough but very accessible reference.[2]

Lest you think that OOADP is the elixir that cures all software development ills, we want to recommend another book, *Pitfalls of Object-Oriented Development*, by Bruce Webster.[3] It describes the hazards that accompany the new technology for those who have not yet ventured far beyond their procedural program development heartland. This book is not at all discouraging, and it's quite slender compared to all the other OOP books on our shelves.

In our opinion, the best research project exploring the limits of OOADP technology was the IBM SanFrancisco™ (SF) project, which fortunately was well-documented for posterity. Sadly, this was not intended to be a research project, but a new technology middleware approach to enterprise business applications development. It was to be designed in the marketplace by the software vendors known as IBM Partners in Development with IBM funding and facilitation. A few successful deployments of the system were made before IBM abandoned the project, or actually folded it into its WebSphere™ business components product set.

SanFrancisco™ was a type of OOP middleware known as a framework, defined as "a set of cooperating object classes that make up a reusable design for a specific type of software application. Such a framework is typically customized to a particular application by creating application-specific subclasses of the abstract classes in the framework."[4] Figure 14.1 shows the amazing scale of SanFrancisco™. The SF layers lie between the applications to be developed and the hardware they will eventually run on. SF was designed to initially operate on the Windows NT Server, AIX, AS/440, and HP-UX platforms.[5] All of these hardware platforms and their operating systems supported the JVM and Java Libraries. SF was a Java-oriented middleware system. But the capability of Java Wrapper technology and the Native API allowed developers to simply wrap COBOL programs and compile and link C programs using the Native API. Thus, they could encapsulate working code modules and components as quasi-Java components into a Java-based application or system as it was being developed. SF was divided into three layers: Foundation, Common Business Objects, and Core Business Processes. Of the "towers," or Core Business Processes, only General Ledger, Warehouse Management, and Order Management were delivered in the product's first release. In Sidebar 14.2 we report our own experience with the GL tower. Note from the figure that an application can be built on the Foundation layer, the Common Business Objects layer, or a tower or towers of the Core Business Processes layer. However they are based, all SF applications are interoperable via the Foundation layer, which provides the fundamental infrastructure for any SF base application suite or system.

Initially the Foundation was CORBA- and CORBA Services-based. However, it did not include a CORBA object request broker (ORB), simply because it was 100% Java-based, and the ORB for Java is the remote method invocation (RMI) API.[7] The Foundation's function was to support distributed objects, concurrent access to objects, and persistent or database storage of objects. It also contains the basic services and defines the SanFrancisco Programming Model (SFPM). The services provided are naming, notification, query, and base classes.

The Common Business Objects (CBO) layer consists of general business objects, financial business objects, and generalized mechanisms that are shared by all business applications. General business objects include company, currency, and customer objects. Financial objects include bank, bank account, invoicing, and financial calendar, among others. The generalized mechanisms include the 16 basic patterns defined in SF, including commands, key, cached balances, policies, and keyed attribute retrieval.[8]

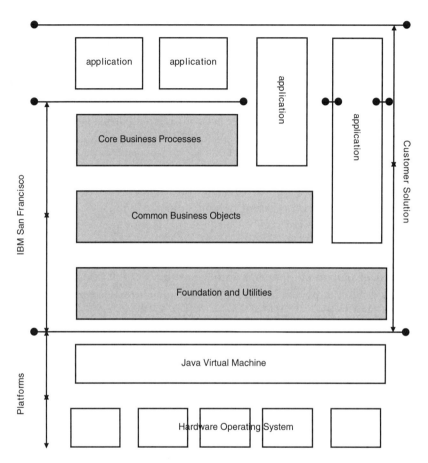

FIGURE 14.1
The SanFrancisco™ Architecture[6]

The initial Core Business Processes (CBP) were GL, Order Management, and Warehouse Management. AR and AP were under consideration. In fact, at least one Partner in Development firm had a proposal on IBM's table to develop these middleware towers. Figure 14.2 illustrates three types of applications built on SF middleware. The business's financial applications would be built on the financial towers of the CBP. A nonfinancial application such as insurance or transportation would be built on the CBO. A non-centrally-related business function such as patent portfolio management would be built directly on the Foundation. In our opinion, SF's Foundation layer was its true technical genius, but when the project was folded into IBM's Software Division, marketing force trumped technical finesse, and the Foundation was replaced by Sun Microsystems' Enterprise JavaBeans (EJB). As soon as SF's uniqueness and performance capability were compromised, it was "parted out" like an exotic automobile missing its engine, and the parts were shelved at IBM's WebSphere™ operation.

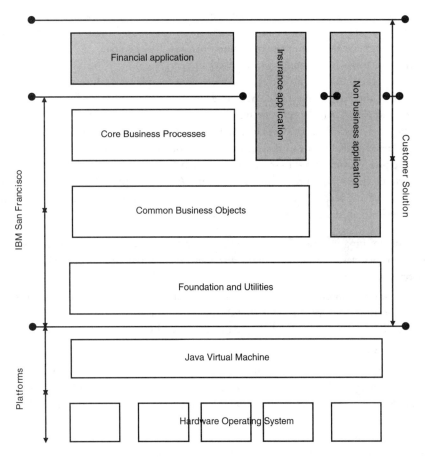

FIGURE 14.2
Building on IBM SanFrancisco™[9]

P. Monday, J. Carey, and M. Dangler, *SanFrancisco Component Framework: An Introduction*, p. 24, © 1999 by Paul Monday, James Carey, Mary Dangler. Reprinted by permission of Pearson Education, Inc. All rights reserved.

Sidebar 14.2: The Power of Java Middleware

When one of the authors was Chief Technology Officer of a tier-one business applications software vendor, he was invited to join the IBM SanFrancisco Technical Advisory Group as a representative of his employer. The firm was considering recasting its proprietary 4GL-based applications into object technology using C++ or Java. Naturally, the possibility of using SanFrancisco™ was attractive, because IBM's object framework was nearing completion after four years of development. The firm became the first licensee of the product. It opted to recast its Version 5.0 business software into Java objects, using the IBM framework technology, as a proof of concept or evaluation. At that time, the 4GL-based Version 7.2 was being released and Version 8.0 was in planning. Version 5.0 had just gone off support as obsolete because it did not support multiple currencies, electronic data exchange, or Internet clients. Because these were in the Foundation of the SF framework, they would be "free" and comparable to the same features that had been carefully implemented in Version 6.0. The first module or application to be recast was the General Ledger. Following a use-case analysis and design using SF, we came up with a time estimate of six months for five programmers, or 2.5 person years. When the plan was presented to senior management for go-ahead approval, it was noted that the last time GL was so reprogrammed was to the AS/400 from COBOL to RPG II, and it took 20 people one year. Naturally, the question arose as to how we could do this at one-eighth the cost and in half the time using Java. The answer was simple:

- Programming in Java was twice as efficient and productive as programming in RPG II.
- An object class library, particularly a framework, was twice as effective as a COBOL or RPG library.
- The value proposition of IBM's SF was that half the code shipped on any business application developed using it would come from the six-CD-ROM SF middleware distribution, as opposed to being manually coded by the project team.

Because $2 \times 2 \times 2 = 8$, and 20 person years divided by 8 is 2.5 person years, we should have been close to our estimate. This blithe arithmetic was greeted with considerable incredulity, but we met our goals over the ensuing six months. What was most remarkable, and is generally a beneficial side effect of OOADP, is that the application was developed in vertical "slices" rather than horizontal "layers." When we were half done, we could show management half of the final functionality (such as forms) working, because the functions ran all the way from GUI data entry to the underlying database and back through the computation to the output screen or report. This was no big deal for recasting a working application into a different language, even if it were from procedural languages (COBOL and C) to objects (Java). But for the development of a new application under the careful oversight of the buyers and/or future end users, it is a tremendous advantage. Not only can you meet users' expectations for functionality and usability, but you also reduce development time and cost, because specification misunderstandings can be corrected by the very effective WYSIWYG process. The users will get what they see, and if that isn't what they want, now is the time to fix it. This is one of the most important features of object-oriented programming for making sure that form really does follow function.

Component-Based Software Development Technology

Software components are not new. In fact, they date from the earliest days of programming the first electromechanical computer, the Harvard-IBM Sequence-Controlled Calculator, built for the U. S. Navy in 1938. The first programming forms were wide-lined yellow legal pads. Later, when it was noticed that new programs could often be prepared by modifying old ones, programmers at the Harvard Computation Laboratory started writing programs in the same leather-bound ledger books that undergraduates used to take classroom notes.

One of the authors once asked Betty Holberton how she came up with the idea of the first application generator, her sort-merge generator. She replied that she noticed that every time she was asked to write a new sort-merge program for the later Harvard Mark IV computer, she changed only a few parameters in one of her previously checked-out and recorded programs. After a number of times rewriting and reentering a program to change just a few numbers, she realized she could write a program that would use parameter data as input and actually output the new sort-merge program, which could then be loaded into the computer's program storage, the data tapes mounted, and the application run.[10] To our knowledge, this is the first use of a computer program to write another computer program.

It wasn't long after that Mrs. Holberton's colleague Dr. Grace Hopper came up with the idea of a compiler, which of course is a computer program that creates a machine-language computer program from a high-level language statement of the intended program's function. Dr. Hopper's compiler research was not popular at the Harvard Computation Laboratory, so she joined the Eckert and Mauchly Company when it did a spin-off from the University of Pennsylvania. The company created Math-Matic, the first compiler to generate mathematical programs from formulas, and Flow-Matic, the first compiler to generate business data processing programs from process or business procedural flow statements.[11]

As soon as fully tested computer programs could be stored on magnetic media or 80-column punched cards rather than being reentered from handwritten ledger books, the idea of components really took off. Some of the first commercial compilers, like the original FORTRAN for example, did not allow components or subroutines but with FORTRAN II the technology became a standard programming practice, and shared subroutine libraries became available for mathematical functions, linear algebra, differential equations, and so on. The ability to share such libraries was limited by the variety of computer architectures in the 1950s; there were three address, two address, and single address machines having either 1's compliment or 2's compliment binary arithmetic, with or without floating point hardware, or decimal or character oriented machines having a variety of word lengths of either 24, 27, 30, 32, 36, 40, and 48 bits. It was years before even the programming languages themselves were sufficiently standardized that users of different machines could share component libraries written in high-level languages.

But what have software components become today? The idea of software components has been around so long that they have become part of the wallpaper. Software designers talk about components and their properties with a dazzling diversity of semantics. Components, like objects, are seen as the key to software reusability. Moreover, reusing proven programs is an important way to reduce time to implement and cost to develop, while at the same time improving quality. But proponents rarely agree even on the scale or granularity of components. To use a chemical/biological metaphor, some components are the size of atoms, some are the size of inorganic molecules, some are the size of organic molecules, some are as large as amino acids, and some are as large as proteins. Some are even body parts stitched together like Frankenstein's monster. The smallest or atomic components/objects have the greatest reusability, but with the least advantage. The largest (like body parts) have the least reusability and the most complex interfaces, but the greatest advantage or gain when they actually work together.

Our own experience in developing activity-based accounting systems suggests that components should be sized, in our metaphor, larger than amino acids but smaller than proteins. A component's size or scope should relate to the modularity of the functional partitioning in the application domain. For example, our General Ledger had 169 components, Accounts Receivable had 219, and Accounts Payable had 209. The system supported nearly 2,000 forms, some of which had up to nine subforms, so clearly there was a high degree of reusability at this basic building-block level. Nonproprietary but domain-specific components like these are the most promising for technical quality, wide reusability, and market advantage.[12, 13] As reported in the preceding section, when we migrated or recast this application system into IBM SanFrancisco™ with its somewhat larger components, it went smoothly. Recasting into a more molecular component-sized framework such as JD Edwards OneWorld™ or Microsoft COM+ would have been much more difficult.

The Defense Advanced Research Projects Agency (DARPA), for whom components are very important, has sponsored the development of a Component Software Glossary in an effort to bring component technology out of the background and onto the design table as a set of proto-standards. The URL for this 27-page glossary is http://www.objs.com/survey/ComponentwareGlossary.htm.

The *raision d'etre* for this glossary was to move the field from a *descriptive* glossary of ambiguous terms to a more nearly *prescriptive* glossary of precise operational definitions that all software designers would be able to use in a standardized way. Some authors are beginning to emphasize standardized nomenclature for components and may devote an early chapter to the need for such standards.[14]

The Object Management Group was founded in 1989 as a consortium of all the software manufacturers save one (guess which one). Its function is to achieve interoperability on all levels of an open market for software objects.[15] The effort to gain a high degree of object interoperability led to the Common Object Request Broker Architecture (CORBA). CORBA 3 is the latest version of the suite of CORBA standards for the CORBA Component Model (CCM). Actually, CCM is an ambitious logical extension of EJB. The original JavaBeans specification called for a flat file of beans or Java components allowing only peer-to-peer connectivity. By connecting one bean instance's listener to another bean instance's event source, events flow. EJB is a hierarchical framework and has no provision for connection-oriented programming. One of the main extensions of CCM to EJB is adding a connection-oriented programming capability.[16] The CCM was explained in a recent paper[16] by Wang, Schmidt, and O'Ryan in a major handbook on component software engineering.[17]

Since the demise of SanFrancisco™, the major marketplace component models are COM+, EJB, and CCM—which, as just noted, is really an extension of EJB. Tier 1 enterprise application software vendors must choose between Microsoft's C# and COM+, or Sun Microsystems' Java and EJB. The smaller vendors and some of the tier 1 vendors are not in a position to dictate to their customers which clients they must use. Therefore, they have to make two business logic libraries—one in COM+ to support Microsoft desktop clients, and one in EJB to support Java-based and UNIX desktop clients. A recent evaluation and comparison of the three models by Longshaw[18] gives a side-by-side assessment of the three models, including robustness and security factors (see Table 14.1). Each table entry represents the extent to which a component technology satisfies a criterion on a scale of 1 to 5, with 5 being the best. By Longshaw's analysis, all three rank 4 out of 5 for security, but COM+ has a slight edge in robustness. Note also that despite all these factors, the component models still have a long way to go in achieving robustness.

TABLE 14.1
Side-by-Side Assessment of COM+, EJB, and CCM

	COM+	EJB	CORBA Components
Scalability	****	****	****
Ease of development	*****	****	***
Security	****	****	****
State management	***	****	****
Deployment	***	**	****
Robustness	***	**	**
Platform support	**	*****	None
Implementation	****	***	None

Adapted from Longshaw, "Choosing Between COM+, EJB, and CCM"

Extreme Programming for Productivity

Extreme Programming (XP) is a deliberate and disciplined approach to software development. Risky projects with volatile requirements are ideal for XP methodology. These projects experience greater success and developer productivity. XP works because it emphasizes customer involvement and promotes teamwork. One of the most surprising aspects of XP is its simple rules and practices. They may seem awkward and a bit naive at first, but they soon become a welcome change from more formal development models. Customers enjoy being partners in the software development process, and developers actively contribute, regardless of experience level. XP was developed eight years ago by Kent Beck and has been proven at a number of companies of different sizes and from varied industries worldwide. XP is successful primarily because it stresses customer satisfaction and early customer involvement far upstream in the design process. The methodology is designed to deliver the software the customer needs when it is needed. XP empowers developers to confidently respond to changing customer requirements, even late in the development cycle.

XP improves a software development project in four essential ways: communication, simplicity, feedback, and courage. XP programmers communicate with their customers and fellow programmers. They keep their design simple and clean. They get feedback by testing their software from day one. They deliver the system to the customers as early as possible and implement changes as suggested. With this foundation, XP programmers can courageously respond to changing requirements and technology. XP itself is also different.

It has many small pieces. Individually the pieces make no sense, but when they're combined, you can see a complete picture, as with a jigsaw puzzle. This is a notable departure from traditional software development methods. Beck's thesis is that software that is engineered to be simple and elegant is much more valuable than software that is complex and hard to maintain. His example is hard to gainsay:

> A typical software development project will spend about twenty times as much on people as on hardware. That means a project spending 2 million dollars on programmers per year will spend about 100 thousand dollars on computer equipment each year. Let's say that we are smart programmers and we find a way to save 20% of the hardware costs by some very clever programming tricks. It will make the source code harder to understand and maintain, but we are saving 20% or 20 thousand dollars per year, a big savings. Now what if instead we wrote our programs such that they were easy to understand and extend. We could expect to save no less than 10% of our people costs. That would come to 200 thousand dollars, a much bigger savings. This is certainly something customers will notice.[19]

Much of what went into XP was Beck's reevaluation of how software was created. The quality of the source code is much more important than you might realize. Just because our customers can't see our source code doesn't mean we shouldn't put effort into creating something we can be proud of. Thus, XP is not really the same as "quick and dirty." Instead, it is an attempt to develop programs "quick and clean." It is especially useful for programs that have relatively short lifetimes, or whenever requirements are volatile and rapidly changing.

N-Version Programming for Reliability

N-Version Programming (NVP) has been proposed as a method of providing fault tolerance in software. In practice it requires the independent preparation of multiple versions of a software component for some function or application. All the versions are executed in parallel in the application environment, each receiving the same inputs and each producing the required outputs. The N outputs are presented to a selection algorithm that chooses the final application output. If all outputs are expected to be the same, the selection algorithm would merely be majority decision logic. This programming model is clearly derived from hardware risk analysis, and a large body of experience applies it to hardware systems. In fact, the first electronic digital computer in the U.S., the ENIAC, built at the University of Pennsylvania from 1942 to 1946, used two interesting techniques to provide its fabled reliability. When J. Presper Eckert and John Mauchly designed the machine, consisting of 18,000 vacuum tubes, they were warned by electronic reliability engineers that the machine would not run for more than 30 seconds without a failure. Eckert, the engineer on the team, chose the military's rugged 6SN7 as the vacuum tube type and decided to run the tubes with 5.0 volts on the filaments rather than the design value of 6.3 volts. He then designed each logic gate in the machine to independently produce three results and used majority decision logic to accept the two that agreed as the correct answer (that is, 1 bit in the case of a logic gate). This was a very conservative design, but Mauchly and Eckert knew that if the first computer were unreliable, it would set back their effort to demonstrate the utility of electronic computing.[20] NVP is this same idea applied at the subroutine, component, or method level in software rather than at the bit level in hardware.

If numerical results at the function level in software result from the N versions, they may be expected to differ slightly, because different numerical methods may have been used. In this case the decision algorithm might be programmed to select the median value—or, more conservatively, the median value of all the answers that differ from one another by some tolerance less than a given epsilon value. It may occur, however, that no decision to output a result can be made, because all N versions of the program fail or for some reason produce answers that cannot be resolved in the decision logic. NVP's inability to come to a consensus may also result from the use of finite-precision or rational arithmetic.[21] All the theorems of real analysis were proven only for the real numbers, not the rational numbers. Although the rationals are dense in the reals, and a lot of work has been done in constructive real analysis, situations do arise where this seemingly theoretical distinction is important. Every numerical analyst knows that you cannot use Laplace's determinant method to solve linear systems on a computer for this reason. Many who have done a lot of linear algebra have computed left inverses to a matrix that turn out not to be right inverses. Whenever finite precision arithmetic is used, the result of a sequence of computations depends on the order of the computations and the actual arithmetic algorithms used by the hardware. This problem is known as the *consistent comparison problem*. It can be shown to occur in simple three-version control systems—exactly the kind of application you would expect to benefit from software redundancy.[22]

Advantages of NVP

NVP has some advantages for critical applications that must never be allowed to fail:[23]

- The independent design and build of functionally similar programs is more costly but does not add to system complexity.

- Due to this design, if diversity fails to deliver trustworthy operation, it does so independently and with very low risk of coincident failures.

- As Very Large-Scale Integration (VLSI) circuits (chips) become larger and more complex, it is more difficult to check out all possible failure modes. Different ways of computing the same critical function tend to reduce this risk.

- Verification and validation time of multiple versions are reduced because multiplicity does not add to complexity.

- Given an effective specification for multiple versions, the programs can be job-shopped to a variety of experts at competitive rates.

Disadvantages of NVP

NVP's disadvantages or challenges are fewer but well worth careful consideration:

- An unambiguous, precise specification is a *sine qua non* for contracting functional requirements to a diverse group of program version suppliers.

- The hope for NVP as a software reliability enhancement is based on faith that software designed and implemented in different ways will not cause similar errors at the decision point.

- The cost of NVP is a linear multiple of the cost of single-version software. Economy suggests that NVP be applied only to the critical paths in the program.

Modern Programming Environments

Many of the productivity and quality gains made available by objects and components are made possible by the use of modern development environments. We cannot catalog the whole spectrum of available products, but we will mention one or two leading or typical products in each class used for enterprise application development in Java. Some of these sophisticated tool sets support development in other programming languages as well, even COBOL. Many Java programmers simply use the current Java Development Kit (JDK), which can be downloaded for free from the Sun Microsystems Web site. For the individual developer it is adequate. For the solo programmer who prefers a window-oriented environment, the TextPad PDE can be downloaded from Sun's Web site for a free 30-day trial and/or can be purchased over the Internet for $29. The next step up from a PDE is a workgroup-capable IDE. The most readily available and lowest-cost of these is Sun Microsystems' Sun ONE Studio 4, which was formerly known as Forte. A number of commercially available products are in this capability range and a bit beyond. They include the widely used Borland JBuilder, which supports medium to large development workgroups. Finally, for large workgroups or enterprise-wide development, Eclipse and IntelliJ IDEA 4.5 are available. Eclipse is especially well documented and is supported by a number of textbooks, handbooks, and user guides. You can download it from the Eclipse Web site for free. It supports a number of programming languages other than Java, including COBOL.

The TextPad PDE is very popular in college computer science departments that teach Java. It's also popular among solo programmers who want a convenient Windows environment without needing to go to a command-line interface, even to run programs having command-line arguments. It doesn't let you test or run Java Servlets or Java Server Pages, but it can be augmented with Apache Tomcat if you need those services. TextPad cannot incorporate or deploy JavaBeans, because a true IDE such as Sun ONE is needed to do that. Site licenses are available for schools or commercial development groups. The URL is http://www.textpad.com/.

A similar PDE with a few more IDE-like capabilities, especially for the user of JavaBeans, is NetBeans. It is also popular in academic computer science programs based on the Java programming language. It can be downloaded and used for free. The URL is http://www.netbeans.org/.

Other products in this class of super-PDE but sub-full-IDE include Java Creator and Net Computing from Germany. Their URLs are http://www.jcreator.com/ and http://www.netcomputing.de/.

A similar product from Apache is Ant, which can be downloaded from http://ant.apache.org. The user manual for Ant can be read or downloaded from http://ant.apache.org/manual/index.html.

Sun ONE Studio 4 was derived from the earlier Forte IDE for Java. It simplifies testing and deploying code on application servers, but it lacks some features that more-advanced IDEs offer, including UML modeling, refactoring, Struts support, and profiling. It is built on Sun's NetBeans, which makes a number of third-party plug-ins available. It has a built-in update center wizard that checks for and installs new or updated IDE components. Templates for various types of classes, such as Enterprise JavaBeans, Java Server Pages, and Web services, help the user create classes and write code. Sun ONE Studio's code editor provides right-click context menus that create stubs for constructors, methods, and inner classes. But an application framework is not included with the basic IDE; Sun offers the Sun ONE Application Framework as a separate $1,495 product. Without this framework, implementing business logic requires that the developer write more code by hand than if using a more capable IDE. As you will see later, this is not always a disadvantage.

A GUI designer in the Sun IDE generates code for building Abstract Windows Toolkit and Swing interfaces but does not support two-way editing. Auto-generated GUI code is marked as guarded and protected from manual changes. This is unlike Eclipse, which reflects most manual changes of the Java automatically generated code back into the GUI specification. The IDE doesn't include a UML modeling tool, but wizards make it easy to generate a variety of entity beans from existing database tables. On the back end, a number of integrated components help make predeployment testing a quick and relatively painless process. The IDE does include Apache's Web server Tomcat and a hobbled PointBase database server. An EJB test application requires a few clicks to create, and it presents a Web form interface that lets the user invoke methods on newly coded beans and observe the results. Essential IDE features such as code completion and incremental search are built in, as is good support for Javadoc. Although Sun ONE Studio doesn't include some development life-cycle tools that other packages offer, it offers a solid, basic set of features that will meet the needs of most small enterprise development groups. An excellent series of textbooks for this product is popular in technical colleges and universities.[24, 25] There is also a textbook for rapid application development using Sun ONE Studio 4.[26] The Sun URL for this product, recently upgraded to version 5, is http://www.sun.com/software/sundev/jde/index.xml.

One of the big kahunas for Java (and other) language IDEs is Borland JBuilder from Imprise Software. Borland came out with JBuilder shortly after Symantec Cafe, one of the first Java IDEs. About the same time, IBM announced a Java IDE that soon became the basis of Eclipse and then shortly later became open-source. JBuilder is a capable fully featured product that supports a large development workgroup. Although it is rather expensive, a service contact provides in-depth user support. The URL for JBuilder's Web site is http://www.borland.com/jbuilder/foundation/.

One of the most popular IDEs for commercial development workgroups is Eclipse. Like JBuilder, it allows cross-platform development—which is Java's *raision d'etre*. It allows UML specification as well, but it is a very large-scale developer's tool set, not recommended for small or loosely integrated groups. Every Java program in the system is put into the Eclipse source file, and the whole system is recompiled every time each user changes his or her program and asks for a compile. It takes a patient programmer to deal with a small change that produces hundreds or even thousands of errors all over the developing system. The big advantage of Eclipse (other than its being a typical IBM product, offering everything for everyone) is that it can be downloaded for free. Eclipse is a big system, and a number of ponderous tomes describe its features and usage. Their essence has been distilled into a small, accessible book titled, oddly enough, *Eclipse Distilled*.[27] It's highly recommended for the development manager evaluating or planning an Eclipse installation. Many developers think that Eclipse is too much of a good thing. However, a senior software developer and former Eclipse user who recently switched back from IntelliJ made the following statement to one of the authors in a recent e-mail. We quote it here because it is typical of the experience reported by developers who have climbed this product's rather steep learning curve:

> Much of what I get from an IDE is one-stop shopping for doing all of my development. By that I mean I can compile, run, debug. I can edit and find the files that I want quickly. Other features that are very useful are reference searching, reference navigation,

and a whole host of re-factoring support. And those are just the basic features one would expect from a modern IDE. The learning curve at first seems steep, but what you get in return is enormous in terms of productivity.[28]

So, there is the testimony of a typical Eclipse heat-seeker and senior business applications architect. The URL for Eclipse is http://www.eclipse.org/.

IntelliJ IDEA 4.5 is the current version of the Java IDE developed in the Czech Republic. It is widely used in Europe and North America. It is comparable to Eclipse. It is not free, but it is significantly less costly per seat than most other commercial Java IDEs. The user interface is far less complex than Eclipse and much more developer-friendly. It has a large following in the United States. The vendor's URL is http://www.intellij.com/idea/.

Finally, we want to address the issue of whether you should use an IDE at all, and we'll point out some of the cons. You don't have to become dependent on the convenience of IDE automation; the use of public-domain software like Emacs is no more expensive than the use of IBM Eclipse. When a development group's productivity becomes tightly tied to a particular IDE and its magical shortcuts, this can be a limiting dependency. A change in organizational standards from one tool to another can reduce productivity overnight. Limiting the use of proprietary special features is difficult because programmers work around such rules. Also, an expensive IDE license is an easy target for cost-cutting. Many of the most capable IDEs have high licensing fees. The best programmers frequently develop at home as well and expect to use the same toolset both at work and at home. The more costly an IDE, the more likely a developer will not be able to afford a personal license, which means a divergence between the home and work tool sets. Site licenses allowing one person use from *either* the developer's home *or* office computer at any given time often can be negotiated.

Many serious programmers are very productive using only a simple text editor that is much less resource-intensive in its use of both memory and CPU time. A capable IDE with its many shortcuts and automatic code generation and wizards creates an abstraction from specification issues and takes at least 65MB of memory. It also requires a rather steep learning curve before the new user becomes proficient. Developers need to understand Java specifications in detail before taking shortcuts, but a good IDE encourages the opposite. It is not wise to automate what you do not understand how to do manually. An IDE also takes the effort out of performing certain tasks, such as compiling, generating Java archive (JAR) files, and generating RMI stubs. An IDE is convenient in isolation, but not always in a development team, where team members must interact regularly, in terms of both source code control and the build process. The development environment should be completely transparent to these two processes.

Thorough knowledge of source code control and build environments is key to understanding integration and addressing problems without bringing the whole development team to a halt when some minor fault occurs. A project configuration management engineer will not always be available, so team members should be familiar with the build process. Committed IDE users often do not understand these systems, because IDE automation effectively insulates them. Few IDEs support multiple languages, but the most capable ones all do. Although IDEs facilitate integration with third-party applications, such as source code control tools, such integration is often limited. Often the third-party integration doesn't include all of the third-party tool's features. By nature, IDE automation insulates the developer from the technology and typically produces project artifacts such as hierarchical directory structures or configuration files that must be properly in place to use the code in the project.

Trends in Computer Programming Automation

We think that not only third-party software vendors but also large internal development organizations will go the way of the automobile industry. Today, the largest vendors, such as SAP, among others, are vertically integrated, as was Ford Motor Company in its early years. Ford had its own taconite mines in Minnesota to produce iron ore that was made into iron and then steel by its own mills. It had ranches in Montana to raise sheep for the wool used to make mohair upholstery fabric. It had its own sand mines in New Mexico to manufacture of automobile glass. Many large European manufacturers of hard goods still have such vertical organizational structures, but today Ford Motor Company is one of the most horizontally organized manufacturers in the world. A multitude of small independent engineering and manufacturing firms in Michigan, Wisconsin, and Ontario make components for Ford automobiles. Most firms that make automobile parts do not sell automobiles. Instead, they sell components to firms that sell subassemblies that sell larger subassemblies to firms that assemble and sell automobiles. The supply chain is short and flat but is controlled by quality engineering and manufacturing standards along with sophisticated computer supply chain controls.

The earliest advocates of software standards and componentization argued that this industrial model would one day be possible if software design and engineering followed the path of hardware design and engineering. It is simply a recursive evocation of Henry Ford's specialization of labor applied to larger and larger components. The migration of Ford from a highly vertically integrated manufacturer to a highly horizontally integrated one was a consequence of this principle applied over time as automobiles became more complex. As the modularity characteristics of software components and their design and development become more similar to hardware components, we think the assembly of information *bits* into useful software "machines" will follow the pattern of the assembly of physical *atoms* (actually, molecules) into useful hardware machines.

The fruition of early software component advocates' dream in today's increasing use of object-oriented design and development technology is already an increasing trend. The development of the CORBA standard and its subscription by all of the software firms in the world save one has allowed small, highly specialized firms such as Iona in Ireland and Trax in Poland to develop and market sophisticated, high-quality software components (called middleware) all over the world. Indian firms are rapidly entering this market as well, having gained a great deal of experience as outsource developers during the Y2K turnover. Small software vendors in the United States are already buying components from smaller firms in India and selling or licensing their products to larger software vendors in the U.S. and Europe. As in the case of hardware component design and development, we may expect to see automation technology enter the picture as well. In fact, it already has, and in three different dimensions: object frameworks, specification-based design and development, and application generators.

Object frameworks were covered in the section "Object-Oriented Analysis, Design, and Programming." The SanFrancisco™ product was large and sophisticated, supported by nearly 3,000 IBM Partners in Development and ultimately decommitted by IBM. It demonstrated the technical feasibility and economic promise of framework technology. The software vendor ranks contain other examples, such as JD Edwards OneWorld™, as do numerous proprietary internal development frameworks. At least one firm has specialized in helping internal software development groups design and establish proprietary frameworks. It is truly a shame that SanFrancisco™ did not survive its patron's (CEO Gerstner) departure from IBM. Curiously, many of its components survived individually to become parts of other IBM software developments. Framework technology is intrinsically large-scale in its scope, but it doesn't have to be as large-scale and function-inclusive as SanFrancisco™ attempted to be. There were too many cooks in the kitchen, and their demands caused the scope and scale of the middleware product set to increase until the complexity was more than they could deal with in training and use. The learning curve became too steep for most of the many small firms (IBM Partners) that had themselves multiplied the product's functionality during the specification stage. Still, although this product was too early and perhaps beyond the scope of software automation at the time, the technology it employed will surface again as the scale of software development and the need for its development automation increases so that not only third-party software vendors but also large internal development organizations will use it.

Specification-based design and development of enterprise business application software has long been the Holy Grail of software development. The concept is simple enough, but its realization has been very elusive. You would like an application domain specialist (accountant, supply chain expert, clinical patient records manager, cost accountant, value engineer) to write an unambiguous specification of a functional component that will meet your computational and/or record-keeping requirements when finally committed to software. Of course, this must always be done, regardless of the implementation technology employed, but the most desirable course would now be to feed the specification language-defined application or component into a "supercompiler" that would create a working computer program that meets the domain expert's needs and expectations. The software vendor further along in developing this technology is Lawson Software, with its Landmark™ development system. Landmark™ promises to usher in a whole new technology in which domain experts become high-level programmers and former application programmers become metaprogrammers developing the supercompiler metasoftware middleware that enables and supports the new application development technology.

Application generation is not new; it began with Betty Holberton's sort-merge generator in the early 1950s. It has seen a resurgence more recently with Analysts International's Corvet™ application generator, Lawson Software's proprietary 4GL for UNIX and Bismarck for the AS 400, Univac's MAPPER™ for the 1100/2200 series, and Burroughs LINC™. The latter two application generators have been merged for the common product line resulting from the merger of the two firms into Unisys. Today LINC is still the largest-scale application generator available. It lets the developer create complete application systems totally in LINC. You can think of application generators as application-specific specification-based development systems. LINC has few limitations and may be, like Lawson's forthcoming Landmark™, a truly generic "find" in the search for the Holy Grail of application computer programming.

A new paradigm for productivity enhancement is coming from WesCorp, a software automation start-up firm in St. Paul, Minnesota. Eric Inman, the founder of WesCorp, has compared the conceptual apparatus of mathematics to that of programming. He believes today's programming languages and tools are fundamentally flawed in terms of their power of expression. Even the high-level specification languages and application generators, while providing limited gains, generally worsen long-term prospects. Instead of inventing just another set of incremental improvements, Inman has formulated a mathematically complete solution for making any programming language, or any other formal language, complete in terms of its expressive power. A complete language cannot be improved by any application generator. WesCorp's introduction of complete languages into the marketplace will revolutionize the art of programming, because these languages will impose no limits on the concepts and ideas that can be represented.

Key Points

- Software productivity and quality have lagged far behind the gains in hardware productivity and quality over the past 50 years.

- Object-oriented analysis, design, and programming promise to dramatically improve both software productivity and quality.

- The IBM SanFrancisco™ project is presented as an example of the promise of Java-based middleware for improving productivity and quality in OOP software development.

- Component-based software development is employed to maximize the reusability of proven software components to build large systems.

- Components can be defined at various sizes, from atomic to molecular, to function based on size.

- Small components maximize reusability, and large components reduce complexity and improve performance.

- Extreme Programming technology enhances programming productivity.

- N-Version Programming enhances program reliability.

- Modern programming environments harness the sophistication of modern programming languages and technology and improve both programmer productivity and program trustworthiness.

- Programming development will continue to enjoy greater and greater automation as application domain specialists become the application "programmers" using the tools developed by "metaprogrammers."

Additional Resources

http://www.prenhallprofessional.com/title/0131872508

http://www.agilenty.com/publications

Internet Exercises

1. Investigate one or two of the PDEs whose URLs are listed in this chapter.

2. Investigate one or two of the IDEs whose URLs are listed in this chapter.

3. Compare the IDE concept to the PDE concept.

4. Can you find IBM SanFrancisco™ on the Internet?

Review Questions

1. Is this the decade of objects? If so, why? If not, why not?

2. What is the promise of OOP for software trustworthiness?

3. How will OOP reduce the cost of software?

4. What is middleware, and how can it help the software developer?

5. Compare Extreme Programming and N-Version Programming.

Discussion Questions and Projects

1. It has been stated that the ability to create a computer model of a virus is a consequence of the 10^{10} increase in computer hardware performance plus the 10^{10} increase in computational chemistry algorithm development over the past 50 years. Can you find an analogue to this situation in business data processing?

2. Computer people are notorious for predicting the future of their discipline. What do you think the software industry will look like in five years? In 10 years? How do you expect to be involved personally?

Endnotes

[1] I. Jacobson, *Object-Oriented Software Engineering* (Harlow, Essex: Addison-Wesley, 1996), p. 72.

[2] Ibid.

[3] B. Webster, *Pitfalls of Object-Oriented Development* (New York: M&T Books, 1995).

[4] DARPA, *Component Software Glossary*, http://www.objs.com/survey/ComponentwareGlossary.htm, 2005, p. 13.

[5] R. Ben-Natan and O. Sasson, *IBM SanFrancisco Developer's Guide* (New York: McGraw-Hill, 2000), p. 150.

[6]P. Monday, J. Carey, M. Dangler, *SanFrancisco Component Framework* (Reading: Addison-Wesley, 1999), p. 23.

[7]M. Johnson, R. Baxter, R. Dahl, *SanFrancisco Life Cycle Programming Techniques* (Upper Saddle River, NJ: Pearson, 1999).

[8]Op cit Monday, pp. 33, 34.

[9]Ibid, p. 24.

[10]Elizabeth Holberton, personal communication, Washington, D.C., 1982.

[11]P. C. Patton, "The Idea of Computer Programming," QMCS white paper, St. Thomas University, 2004.

[12]C. Szypersi, *Component Software Beyond Object-Oriented Programming*, 2nd Ed. (Harlow, Essex: Pearson, 2002), p. 30.

[13]G. T. Heineman and W. T. Councill, *Component Based Software Engineering* (Upper Saddle River, NJ: Pearson, 2001), pp. 5–19.

[14]Op cit Szypersi, pp. 38–45.

[15]Ibid, p. 231.

[16]Ibid, p. 308.

[17]N. Wang, D. C. Schmidt, C. O'Ryan, "Overview of the CORBA Component Model," Chapter 31 of reference 13, pp. 557–571.

[18]A. Longshaw, "Choosing Between COM+, EJB, and CCM," Chapter 35 of reference 13, p. 639.

[19]K. Beck and C. Andres, *Extreme Programming Explained: Embrace Change*, 2nd Ed. (Lebanon: Addison-Wesley, 2004).

[20]J. Presper Eckert, personal communication, Philadelphia, 1993.

[21]S. S. Brilliant, J. C. Knight, N. G. Levenson, *The Consistent Comparison Problem in N-Version Software*, Department of Computer Science, University of Virginia.

[22]Ibid, pp. 2–5.

[23]V. Bharathi, "N-Version Programming Method of Software Fault Tolerance: A Critical Review," National Conference on Nonlinear Systems and Dynamics, IIT Kharagpur, Dec. 28–30, 2003.

[24]Y. D. Liang, *Tutorial for Sun ONE Studio 4* (Upper Saddle River, NJ: Pearson, 2004).

[25]Y. D. Liang, *Introduction to Java Programming with Sun ONE Studio 4* (Upper Saddle River, NJ: Pearson, 2003).

[26]Y. D. Liang, *Rapid Java Application Development Using Sun ONE Studio 4* (Upper Saddle River, NJ: Pearson, 2003).

[27]D. Carlson, *Eclipse Distilled* (Upper Saddle River, NJ: Pearson, 2005).

[28]Phillip W. Patton, personal communication, St. Paul, MN, 2005.

PART III

Designing for Trustworthy Software

CHAPTER 15

Quality Measures and Statistical Methods for Trustworthy Software

Trust is a broad concept, and making something trustworthy requires a social infrastructure as well as solid engineering.

—Craig Mundie

Statistics, like software development, is as much an art as it is a science.

—Katrina Maxwell

Overview

Trustworthy computing requires both trustworthy hardware and trustworthy software. Early computer hardware manufacturers supplied application software but soon retreated from such offerings for fear of contingent liability. This gave rise to the third-party software industry giving the user of enterprise software the choice of build or buy, or a combination of the two. Recently Microsoft, the dominant supplier of system and application software for desktop computers, started a trustworthy computing initiative. This initiative focuses on security, privacy, reliability, and business integrity. The development of enterprise application software has a long history of process management and improvement, and more recently has seen the use of statistical process control technology. Criteria are given for software performance measures and for measurable attributes of the development process. Consistent, measurable attributes are required to allow the process to be controlled by statistical methods. Statistical process control methods were developed for manufacturing process control, where they are used downstream in the manufacturing process to control the process by feedback. Software development has no analog to manufacturing, so statistical methods must be pushed as far upstream in the design process as possible. Current developments are pushing statistical process control methods into the architectural design stage of the development process. Software developers have a wide variety of packaged statistical tools available to support the development process.

Chapter Outline

- Trustworthy Software
- Microsoft's Trustworthy Computing Initiative
- Statistical Process Control for Software Development Processes
- Statistical Methods for Software Architects
- Key Points
- Additional Resources
- Internet Exercises
- Review Questions
- Discussion Questions and Projects
- Problems
- Endnotes

Trustworthy Software

Chapter 3 reviewed a range of software metrics and their history. Here we want to present and discuss statistical tools for measuring the software development process to ensure quality or, in the sense that we use the term in this book, its trustworthiness. Enterprise software is trustworthy if you can trust it with your business's data, which means that you can trust it with your business. In the early days of the computer revolution, after hardware manufacturers successfully offered their customers FORTRAN and COBOL compilers and the first operating systems, attention turned to the possibility of providing application software for the computer user as well. This wasn't meant as an additional business opportunity, but a means of encouraging the further proliferation of computers—especially into new application areas. It also was meant to encourage existing and potential users to purchase more computer hardware. Offering compilers for high-level programming languages had been a tremendous boon for hardware manufacturers and users alike, but still the development of applications was a long, laborious process, even using more-powerful programming languages. Offering application packages for accounting, order entry, mail-order merchandising, and the then-vastly-undercomputerized retail business arena seemed like the logical next step in the computer revolution. Unfortunately, the legal departments of the large hardware vendors that offered the first such application packages feared the contingent liability issues that could arise if a hardware vendor's application package failed and put one of its users out of business. Hence, early free vendor prepared or sponsored application packages that came out had disclaimers stamped in red ink across the title page of the documentation. They read something like this:

> DISCLAIMER: This software is not guaranteed or warranted in any way. It is not guaranteed to load; if it loads, it is not guaranteed to compile; if it complies successfully, it is not guaranteed to run properly; and even if it does, it may not be reliable. If your business suffers financial loss or ruin as a result of using this software, the XYZ Corporation is not responsible and cannot be held liable for your loss.

Naturally, such a disclaimer did not encourage confidence. A few pioneering (and trusting) computer users in the new retail applications arena actually did use hardware manufacturer-supplied application software, and without problems. It was not long, however, before the legal department in hardware vendor firms overruled the marketing department and such application software offerings disappeared—at least from manufacturers of computer hardware. Today the very companies that pioneered such offerings have strict policies against being too closely involved with business applications development. The closest that the more venturesome will get to application software is providing middleware to support the rapid development of new applications. The service bureau industry was pursuing new business application markets at this same time. It also experienced some nervous moments over contingent liability but wrote contracts for computer services with similar disclaimers and never suffered a successful legal challenge. This edginess on the part of computer manufacturers and service bureaus, together with a general shortage of application software developers, encouraged the emergence of the third-party software industry. Today it develops, sells, and supports most enterprise business software.

We relate this bit of history as a way of pointing out what trustworthy software *is not*. Today's computer user expects enterprise software to be trustworthy. Although they understand that it may not be perfect, they expect that the vendor will make a best effort to ensure quality and guarantee correct operation—at least to the product's specification and/or sales contract. The hardware manufacturer's free-software disclaimer would be a major affront today (although the license agreements that accompany desktop software these days can give you pause). But then enterprise application software is not free anymore, either. One of the authors was responsible for developing a new Y2K-compliant administrative system for a $2 billion enterprise in the early '90s. The cost of the hardware for the enterprise server was $1.2 million, the database management system for 650 concurrent users was $6 million, and the first three application packages cost $900,000. The total investment over five years was more than $18 million. The corporation's executive vice president exacted warranties from the software vendors and held them responsible for meeting contracted performance.

The increasing dependence of modern business on computers—ultimately, on enterprise applications software—demands ever-higher standards of quality—measurable and predictable quality. Quality software is trustworthy software, and trustworthy software is the *sine qua non* of trustworthy computing.

Microsoft's Trustworthy Computing Initiative

In October of 2002, Microsoft distributed a white paper titled "Trustworthy Computing" from a team headed by Craig Mundie, Senior Vice President and CTO, Advanced Strategies and Policy.[1] In December 2002 the company distributed a major policy statement based on industry response to the October white paper; it was called "Building a Secure Platform for Trustworthy Computing."[2] Review of these white papers was a major incentive for the authors' research leading to this book. We consider the Microsoft Trustworthy Computing Initiative to be a significant driver of the development of trustworthy enterprise business applications software. The initial white paper noted that not only must the industry learn to make software trustworthy, but because computers have already lost people's trust, "we will have to overcome a legacy of machines that fail, software that fails, and systems that fail."[3] Hence, Microsoft's Trustworthy Computing Initiative is a label for a whole range of advances that must be made for users to be as comfortable using devices powered by computers and their software as they are using devices or appliances powered by electricity. One of the authors once lived in a house in Wheeling, West Virginia built just after the turn of the 20th century. Each light fixture in the house had two globes—one powered by electricity and the other by gas illumination. When the new-fangled electricity failed, you could always light the gas lamp and not be left in the dark. A hundred years ago, electricity was not as trustworthy as it is today, but it became trustworthy as the requisite infrastructure and quality developed. This too will happen with computing, as it has with all new technologies.

In January 2002 Bill Gates issued a call to action, challenging his employees to build a trustworthy computing environment for customers that would be as reliable as our electrical networks (which, by the way, are not perfect and do fail, sometimes catastrophically). The four goals of trustworthy computing are as follows:[4]

- **Security:** The customer can expect that systems are resilient to attack and that the confidentiality, integrity, and availability of the system and its data are protected.

- **Privacy:** Customers can control data about themselves, and those who use this data faithfully adhere to fair information practices.

- **Reliability:** The customer can depend on the product to fulfill its functions when required to do so.

- **Business integrity:** A product's vendor behaves in a responsive and responsible manner.

At the same time, Microsoft created a framework to track and measure its progress in meeting the security goal. Because Microsoft was the leading vendor of desktop operating systems, its products were the primary targets of Internet attackers. We will present this framework and its objectives because they provide a good segue into this chapter's topic of measuring the software development process generally, from design through deployment, and, of course, the inevitable redesign.

The security goal can be factored into the software's being secure by design, secure by default, and secure in deployment, as well as communications. The goal of *secure by design* includes eliminating any security vulnerability at design time and adding any features needed to enhance security. The designer or architect has the best opportunity to eliminate both errors of commission and errors of omission at the very beginning of the development process by observing three practices:

- Building a secure architecture—that is, designing function around security requirements

- Adding security features, even if they are not necessarily demanded by end-user functionality

- Reducing vulnerabilities in the code

Secure by default means shipping software at a basic or default functional level. In other words, features that probably would be used only by an advanced user are turned off as the default condition. This means that the user who eventually turns on an advanced feature will more likely take responsibility for managing its use in his or her environment.

Secure in deployment results from adding capability in the software to support users in five distinct but related activities:

- *Protecting* systems by ensuring that data is accessible only to trusted users

- *Detecting* attempted intrusions, security violations, and unexpected behavior

- *Defense* by appropriate corrective action when an apparent security violation occurs

- *Recovery* of systems that have been compromised or experienced unexpected failures

- *Managing* the preceding activities by having appropriate policies and procedures in place to coordinate and manage these activities

Communications involves informing everyone in the user organization who uses the software of the appropriate policies and procedures. It also involves ensuring that the software vendor informs and trains users properly, releases patches promptly, and warns of new attacks, best practices, and changes in technology.[5] Although technology and sound engineering underlie software security, much of the solution lies in improved social infrastructure, which is merely enabled by technology.

Statistical Process Control for Software Development Processes

Statistical process control is a mainstay in manufacturing but is not yet common in software development. This isn't because software architects and programmers don't have a background in mathematics and statistics, because most do. Rather, the software development process does not naturally produce the kind of high-volume time-series data that is so natural a side effect of the manufacturing assembly line and of all continuous industrial processes. The software development process is any process or subprocess used by a software project or organization. It thus applies to any identifiable activity that may be undertaken to produce a software system or product. This includes planning, estimating, designing, coding, testing, inspecting, reviewing, measuring, and controlling, as well as the subtasks that comprise any of these undertakings.[6]

Software process management is all about managing the work processes involved in designing, developing, deploying, maintaining, and supporting both software products and today's increasing array of software-intensive or "digital" systems. The time-honored concept of a controlled process dates back to Walter Shewhart in 1931. It defines a process as being in control when, by using past experience, you can predict within limits how the process may be expected to perform in the future. Controlled processes are stable processes, and process stability lets you predict results. If a controlled process cannot meet changing customer requirements or industry standards, or if it no longer meets business objectives, it must be changed or improved. The four key goals of process management are process definition, process measurement, process control, and process improvement. Deming taught that these goals should be pursued iteratively in his famous Plan, Do, Check, Act (PDCA) approach that has been so successful in manufacturing process improvement. Figure 15.1 is adapted from Florac and Carleton [7] but is familiar to every practitioner of manufacturing process improvement. Our goal here is to apply the rich history of manufacturing process management to software development. The first step in doing so is to discover the measurable product and process characteristics that are important in enterprise business software development. These are presented in Table 15.1, also adapted from Florac and Carleton.[8] This static table suggests a dynamic framework for measuring process behavior; it involves the following:

- Clarifying business goals as they relate to software product development

- Identifying and prioritizing critical issues that inhibit goal attainment

- Selecting metrics (see Chapter 3) that characterize the product under development

- Making process measurements by collecting data

- Using the data to analyze process behavior

- Evaluating process performance

Such a framework is familiar to software architects and project managers, but they usually pursue it from a qualitative rather than quantitative perspective. This chapter is intended to give the software developer some new, more quantitative tools for managing the software development process.

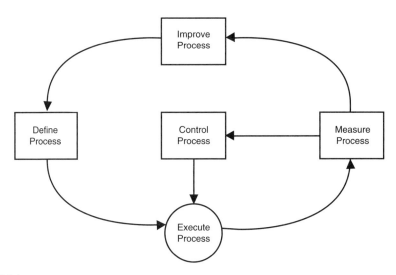

FIGURE 15.1
The Process of Process Management
W. A. Florac and A. D. Carleton, *Measuring the Software Process*, p. 6, Fig. 1.2. © Pearson Education, Inc. Reprinted by permission of Pearson Education, Inc. All rights reserved.

TABLE 15.1
Measurable Characteristics for Software Development[a]

Resources	Activities	Consumed	Retained	Products
Products and by-products from other processes Ideas, concepts Resources: • People • Facilities • Tools • Raw materials • Energy • Money • Time	Processes and controllers: • Requirements analysis • Designing • Coding • Testing • Configuration control • Change control • Problem management • Reviewing • Inspecting • Integrating	Resources: • Effort • Raw materials • Energy • Money • Time	People Facilities Tools Materials Work in process Data Knowledge Experience	Products: • Requirements • Specifications • Designs • Units • Modules • Test cases • Test results • Tested components • Documentation

Resources	Activities	Consumed	Retained	Products
Guidelines and directions: • Policies • Procedures • Goals • Constraints • Rules • Laws • Regulations • Training • Instructions	Flow paths Product paths Resource paths Data paths Control paths Buffers and dampers Queues Stacks Bins			• Defects • Defect reports • Change requests • Data • Acquired materials • Other artifacts By-products: • Knowledge • Experience • Skills • Process improvements • Data • Goodwill • Satisfied customers

[a]W. A. Florac and A. D. Carleton, *Measuring the Software Process*, p. 27, © Pearson Education, Inc. Adapted by permission of Pearson Education, Inc. All rights reserved.

The critical issue in setting up a measurable software process that will be amenable to statistical analysis is identifying measurable characteristics or attributes and selecting the measures. Because the characteristics and their measures differ from project to project, depending on the application and its requirements, we will not attempt to employ all the measures given in Chapter 3 here. Instead, we will define a typical set of measures and use them in an example to give you an overall appreciation of a quantitative framework for software process development. Table 15.2 gives the major criteria for measures to characterize software process performance. Table 15.3 lists a large number of measurable attributes of software development processes as an example only (not all of them are recommended for every project a development group undertakes).

TABLE 15.2
Criteria for Software Performance Measures[b]

Criterion	Selection Guidelines and Examples
Measures should relate closely to the issue under study.	Quality, resource requirements, time to deliver.
They should have high information content.	Attributes are sensitive to process results.
They should pass the reality test.	They should reflect the degree to which the process achieves results.
They should permit easy information content of data.	Choose attributes that have numerical measures that are readily available, consistent, and well-defined.
They should show measurable variation.	A numerical measure that never changes provides no information.
They should have diagnostic value.	For example, they should not only identify unusual occurrences but also indicate their causes.

[b]W. A. Florac and A. D. Carleton, *Measuring the Software Process*, p. 28, © Pearson Education, Inc. Adapted by permission of Pearson Education, Inc. All rights reserved.

TABLE 15.3
Measurable Attributes of Software Development Processes[c]

Givens	Activities	Utilized	Results
Changes: • Type • Date • Size • Number received Requirements: • Requirements stability • Number identified • Percentage traced to design • Percentage traced to code	Flow charts: • Processing time • Throughput rates • Diversions • Delays • Backlogs Length, size: • Queues • Buffers • Stacks	Effort: • Number of development hours • Number of rework hours • Number of support hours • Number of preparation hours Time: • Number of meeting hours	Status of work units: • Number designed • Number coded • Number tested Size of work units: • Number of requirements • Number of function points • Number of lines of code • Number of modules • Number of objects • Number of bytes in database

Givens	Activities	Utilized	Results
Problem reports: • Type • Date • Size • Origin • Severity • Number received Funds: • Money • Budget • Status People: • Years of experience • Type of education • Percentage trained in XYZ • Employment codes Facilities and environment: • Square feet per employee • Noise level • Lighting • Number of staff in office or cubicles • Investments in tools per employee • Hours of computer usage • Percentage of capacity utilized		• Start time or date • Ending time or date • Duration of process or task • Wait time Money: • Cost to date • Cost of variance • Cost of rework	Output quantity: • Number of action items • Number of approvals • Number of defects found Test results: • Number of test cases passed • Percentage of test coverage Program architecture: • Fan-in • Fan-out Changes: • Type • Date • Size • Effort expended Problems and defects: • Number of reports • Defects density • Type • Origin • Distribution by type • Distribution by origin • Number open • Number closed Critical resource utilization: • Percentage of memory utilized • Percentage of CPU capacity utilized • Percentage of I/O capacity utilized

As soon as a set of measurable attributes or characteristics has been selected for a software development project and numerical measures and a data collection system have been set up for them, data will surely begin to flow as work progresses. Figure 15.2, adapted from Florac and Carleton, presents a Venn diagram showing the overlap of problem identification with problem analysis. The methods employed go from qualitative to quantitative, from left to right. The "low-tech" methods on the left are already familiar to you. In the center, the Pareto chart is a commonly used form of the histogram; its use is explained in Chapter 6. The cause-and-effect diagram is another name for Ishikawa's fishbone diagram. The right side of the figure reviews statistical and other quantitative methods; their use is described in the next section. Scatter diagrams display empirically observed relationships between two process attribute measures. Any pattern in the plot may indicate a causal relationship in the data and thus is potentially grist for the statistical mill—in particular, correlation and regression analysis. Correlation analysis can tell us how closely correlated (corelated) two variables are, and regression analysis can tell us the nature of that relationship. In fact, regression analysis can tell us how much of the variability in one variable can be explained by variation in the other. Multiple regression analysis can tell us, given a large number of measurable influences on an outcome, which are the most significant, and how much of the variability in the result is explained by any chosen subset of them. Usually it's the two or three most significant, which may explain more than 80% of the variability in the result. We won't bore you with statistical formulas. Nobody programs these things anymore. Even high school students do them with a few button presses on a $100 graphing calculator. The serious user will purchase, download, and use the Minitab 14, a comprehensive statistical package. See the Minitab Release 14 URL, http://www.minitab.com/products/minitab/14/default.aspx, for a functional description and ordering information. For the most part, the software process manager can often do quite well using a spreadsheet such as Microsoft Excel. So, what do you need to know about statistics to control a software development process? Let's briefly review the software architect's statistical toolbox and consider an example related to quality.

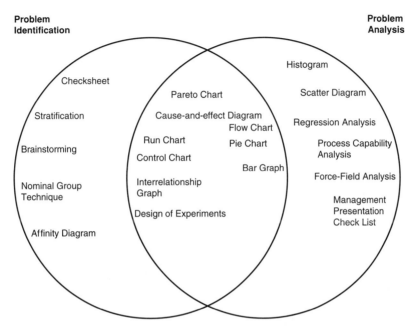

**Problem
Identification**

**Problem
Analysis**

Checksheet

Stratification

Brainstorming

Nominal Group
Technique

Affinity Diagram

Pareto Chart

Cause-and-effect Diagram
Flow Chart
Run Chart   Pie Chart
Control Chart
                   Bar Graph
Interrelationship
Graph

Design of Experiments

Histogram

Scatter Diagram

Regression Analysis

Process Capability
Analysis

Force-Field Analysis

Management
Presentation
Check List

FIGURE 15.2
The Analytic Toolkit
W. A. Florac and A. D. Carleton, *Measuring the Software Process*, p. 55, Fig. 3.4. © Pearson Education, Inc.
Reprinted by permission of Pearson Education, Inc. All rights reserved.

Statistical Methods for Software Architects

The major quantitative methodology in support of DFTS is Taguchi Methods and the application of orthogonal arrays, which are covered in Chapter 17. Here we will cover some basic concepts of statistical analysis deemed useful for the software development architect or project manager for managing the development process from a more quantitative perspective. If you want more details, refer to *Applied Statistics for Software Managers* for a very useful tutorial.[9] For more depth in statistical quality assurance methods, we recommend *Statistical Quality Assurance Methods for Engineers*.[10] For a standard-practices manual, we recommend the *Handbook of Statistical Methods for Engineers and Scientists*.[11] The latter two publications are not oriented to the software development process but are very good references for statistical process control in manufacturing generally.

We begin by reviewing a few basic definitions. The *variance* of a range of sample values measures the distance between each value and the mean of the sample. It is equal to the sum of the squared differences between observations over the range of values and the mean value of the entire sample, divided by the number of observations n minus 1 (n–1). The more commonly used measure of sample variability is the *standard deviation*, which is simply the square root of the variance. A data set can also be described by its *frequency distribution*, usually represented graphically by a bar chart or pie chart. Some frequency distributions occur so often that they have special names and equations. For example, the *normal distribution* is graphically represented by the familiar bell-shaped curve that is symmetrical about the average value of the data it represents. In a normal distribution, the mean, median, and mode all have the same value. The normal distribution can be described by only two parameters—the mean and the standard deviation. The bell curve's width is defined by the standard deviation; thus, the greater it is, the wider the curve. If the numerical data collected for some measurable attribute follows a normal distribution, 68% of the observations fall within plus or minus one standard deviation of the mean, 95.5% of them fall within two standard deviations of the mean, and 99.7% fall within three standard deviations.[12]

The analyst uses *correlation methods* to tell how well two sets of observations or distributions are related to each other. Calling for a correlation analysis on two sets of data produces a single number between –1 and +1, called the correlation coefficient. A value of 1.0 indicates a perfect correlation, –1.0 a perfect negative correlation, and 0 no correlation at all. A high correlation value between two sets of data does not necessarily demonstrate a functional relationship or even causality. Further analysis may indicate a *Spearman rank correlation* to compare the two variables' rank, or place, in an ordered list for the same observation. For example, if you wanted to study the relationship between a program's size and effort metrics, as described in Chapter 3, you would first rank the project's size. Suppose there are five projects, ranked in size from smallest to largest as 1 through 5. Ranking the effort the same way, you can call the statistical package for Spearman's rank correlation and compute the correlation coefficient. If it were 1.0, size and effort would be perfectly correlated, which is the usual case.[13] If the coefficient is less than 1, you would investigate which project enjoyed more or less effort than expected and inquire why. This analysis generally is used when the data is ordinal, as in our example, or when the data is far from normally distributed. When the data is normally distributed and linear, or when it is interval or ratio data, the *Pearson's correlation* is indicated. This method uses the actual values of the variables instead of their ranks. Calling the Pearson correlation method in Minitab 14 or another statistical package with the same data for Maxwell's example produces a correlation coefficient of 0.9745. Although this result may be more precise because it was computed with the actual size and effort data, it yields the same result. Size and effort are completely correlated for these five programs.

Regression analysis is an extension of the familiar least-squares method of fitting a straight line through a set of data points in the x-y plane. In the case of Dr. Maxwell's example of effort versus size, we can call for a regression analysis to get a straight-line fit to the data, which now gives us a formula for predicted effort in terms of program size:

predicted effort = A + B × program size

in which the coefficients A and B are returned by the statistical package. Such a formula is based on the actual experience of our development team and thus is a good predictor of the manpower required to create the next program given an estimate of its size.

Multiple regression analysis is similar to simple regression analysis, except that the dependent variable is some unknown but experiential function of two or more independent variables. For example, you could extend the preceding example to develop a formula for predicted effort as a function of program size and team size. Multiple regression analysis is particularly valuable in a situation in which you have a measurable process result or desideratum such as program performance, quality, time to build, cost to build, and so on, and you have a sea of historical data measurements describing the various aspects of your process and its subprocesses. Now the question is, which of the independent variables most influence cost, which influence quality, and which influence cycle time? Calling the multiple regression method for each of the process results as dependent variables, assuming the process measures to be the independent variables, shows that each result typically can be explained by a few (three to five) of the total group of measures. As shown in Table 15.2, any process can have measurable attributes, and it is unclear which of them influence the process outcomes and how much. One author's experience has shown that the bread-baking process has more than 350 variables, but only five are statistically significant. To predict cast-iron mold life in a Bethlehem Steel mill, data was collected for more than 200 measurable attributes for four years, but 98% of the variance in the fourth year's data could be explained with only six attributes, based on a multiple regression (MR) analysis of the first three years' data. It turned out that more than 90% could be explained by one variable—the mold's temperature at the time the steel was poured into it. A simple rerouting of the molds from the cold outside storage yard through a very warm steel mill before reuse dramatically lengthened mold life and reduced process costs. Manufacturing or continuous-material processes and software development have many observable, measurable, experiential variables, all of which contribute to the result in some way. But we rarely know which ones are the most important in influencing product attribute outcomes—such as quality, for example.

Some regression opportunities involve qualitative rather than quantitative variables and thus cannot employ MR. Instead, they must use *analysis of variance (ANOVA)*. Examples of such variables in software development might include business sector, programming language, hardware platform, operating system, and user interface. These could have significant influence on dependent variables such as effort, productivity, time to build, and cost. Typically ANOVA begins with a null hypothesis such as *The mean percentage of measurable-variable-x utilization is the same for all seven application software products the firm sells.* You have no idea starting out what the means in the population are, so you must use the sample data to estimate them. The larger the variance in *x* between the application types and the smaller its variance within application types, the more likely it is that *x* utilization differs between application types.

This brief summary of statistical tools for the computer architect is not meant to be complete or exhaustive. It's a review and hopefully a spark to encourage your interest in using quantitative methods to measure and improve software development processes. We'll close with a descriptive example adapted from Maxwell.[14] The goal of her example was to develop a predictive model or equation to estimate the effort required of a development group to produce a new software product. The independent variables might be, for example, *size*, *type* of application, *OS* platform, *user* interface, *lang*uage used, *p1–p15* for 15 different productivity factors, and *time* to build. The goal is a predictive equation such as

effort = f (size, type, OS, user, lang, p1–p15, time)

Some of these variables are quantitative data, and others are qualitative ordinal data. Maxwell begins by analyzing effort against each of the variables separately. Clearly effort is proportional to size. Among the productivity variables, effort increases with customer participation. It shows no relationship to staff availability, methods, or use of tools, but it does increase with logical complexity and probably with requirements volatility. Maxwell's multiple regression analysis using the numerical variables alone explains 78% of the variance in effort. After experimenting with two-, three-, and four-variable models, she ends up with a five-variable model that explains 81% of the variance in effort. Effort increases with increasing application size, requirements volatility, and application size; it decreases over time and depends on the user interface chosen.

You will find that although the Minitab 14 software is a benefit, almost everything you need to do with statistics for software design and development can be done using Microsoft Excel.

Key Points

- Trustworthy computing requires both trustworthy hardware and trustworthy software.

- Originally, computer hardware manufacturers supplied application software, but they retreated from such offerings for fear of contingent liability.

- This gave rise to the third-party software industry giving the user of enterprise software the choice of build or buy, or a combination of the two.

- Microsoft, the dominant supplier of system and application software for desktop computers, has started a trustworthy computing initiative.

- The Microsoft initiative focuses on security, privacy, reliability, and business integrity.

- The development of enterprise application software has a long history of process management and improvement. More recently, it has seen the use of statistical process control technology.

- Table 15.2 lists criteria for software performance measures, and Table 15.3 lists measurable attributes of the development process.

- Consistent, measurable attributes allow the process to be controlled by statistical methods.

- Statistical process control methods were developed for manufacturing process control, where they are used downstream to control process by feedback. Software development has no analog to manufacturing, so statistical methods must be pushed as far upstream in the design process as possible.

- Current developments are pushing statistical process control methods into the architectural design stage of the development process.

- Software developers have a wide variety of packaged statistical tools available to support the development process.

Additional Resources

http://www.prenhallprofessional.com/title/0131872508

http://www.agilenty.com/publications

Internet Exercises

1. Find examples of the use of application control charts on the Internet.

2. Review the Minitab Web site.

3. Do an Internet search to determine the current status of Microsoft's Trustworthy Computing Initiative.

Review Questions

1. What are the four goals of Microsoft's trustworthy computing initiative?

2. Distinguish between *trustworthy computing* and *trustworthy software.*

3. What are the criteria for software performance measures?

4. From your experience, select the five most important attributes of the software development process in Table 15.3.

Discussion Questions and Projects

1. Why was contingent liability for application software the bugaboo of the early days of computing?

2. If the manufacturer of a stepladder can be sued when a user gets hurt through improper use, why can't a software firm be sued when a user goes bankrupt through misuse of the software?

Problems

1. Review the capabilities of Minitab-14, and describe how you might have used it to support your last development project.

2. Table 15.3 is generic and attempts to cover all the possibilities. Simplify and reduce it by eliminating factors that are of secondary importance in your own experience and development area.

Endnotes

[1]C. Mundie, P. de Vries, P. Haynes, M. Corwine, "Trustworthy Computing" (Redmond, WA: Microsoft Corp., 2002), white paper, October, 12 pages.

[2]Microsoft, "Building a Secure Platform for Trustworthy Computing" (Redmond, WA: Microsoft Corp., 2002), white paper, December, 16 pages.

[3]Op cit Mundie, et al., p. 1.

[4]Op cit Microsoft, p. 3.

[5]Ibid, pp. 4–5.

[6]W. A. Florac and A. D. Carleton, *Measuring the Software Process* (Boston: Addison-Wesley, 1999), p. 4.

[7]Ibid, p. 6.

[8]Ibid, p. 13.

[9]K. D. Maxwell, *Applied Statistics for Software Managers* (Upper Saddle River, NJ: Prentice-Hall, 2002).

[10]S. B. Vardeman and J. M. Jobe, *Statistical Quality Assurance Methods for Engineers* (New York: John Wiley & Sons, 1999).

[11]H. M. Wadsworth, *Handbook of Statistical Methods for Engineers and Scientists*, 2nd Ed. (New York: McGraw-Hill, 1998).

[12]Op cit Maxwell, p. 281.

[13]Ibid, pp. 291–298.

[14]Ibid, pp. 125–182.

CHAPTER 16

Robust Software in Context

You gain virtually nothing in shipping product that just barely satisfies the corporate standard over a product that just fails. Get on target; don't just stay in-spec.

—Genichi Taguchi

A customer is the most important visitor on our premises. He is not dependent on us. We are dependent on him. He is not an interruption of our work. He is the purpose of it. He is not an outsider on our business. He is a part of it. We are not doing him a favor by serving him. He is doing us a favor by giving us an opportunity to do so.

—Mahatma Gandhi

Overview

The software industry stands on the brink of an era of dramatic change. We expect the industry to continue the restructuring process already begun, emerging as a much smaller number of horizontally structured firms mostly doing business with each other. As software becomes highly "componentized," the industry will begin to resemble the automotive industry, with many small firms making parts, but only a few large ones assembling them into finished products. Software automation in the form of application generation technology will become the norm as system analysts and other domain specialists become the new application programmers, writing in specification languages. Meanwhile, the more talented of today's application programmers will become system programmers, writing the meta-compilers that will transform specification language codes into Java and C application programs. It is still true that new technologies do not *replace* old technologies, at least not at first; in their infancy, they merely *supplement* them. The next four chapters address the transition period during which robust, trustworthy software is still created by current technology and processes as the new technology and its streamlined processes emerge.

Chapter Outline

- The Software Specification Process

- What Is Robust Software?

- Requirements for Software to Be Robust

- Specifying Software Robustness

- Key Points

- Additional Resources

- Internet Exercises

- Review Questions

- Discussion Questions and Projects

- Problems

- Endnotes

The Software Specification Process

When finally agreed upon and documented, the requirements for a new software application emerge in the form of a *specification*. This document tells exactly what will be expected of the software's functionality after it is completed and *meets* the specification. Until now, all software development methodologies depended on a multistage process involving specialists with different educational backgrounds, different work experience, and different development responsibilities who had very little contact with other stages in the development process. These multiple stages with high technological separation have made software development rather error-prone. Product and application opportunities are developed by marketing specialists. Requirements are then developed by functional domain experts called application or system analysts to produce a functional specification. This document is mapped into a technical design document by software architects, then is detailed component by component by software engineers, and finally is coded, tested, and certified by programmers. From the earliest days of the *application generator*, invented by Betty Holberton, and the *compiler*, invented by Dr. Grace Hopper, the possibility of *specification-based programming* has been the Holy Grail of the application programming craft. Reaching this elusive goal would entail domain experts—say, accountants or supply-chain specialists—writing a *precise* functional specification for an accounting or supply-chain application. This would then be fed into a sort of *meta-compiler* to produce a high-level language program that could be compiled to machine language by a conventional compiler and tested. Kristin Nygaard and Ole-Johann Dahl, the Norwegian inventors of Object-Oriented Programming, spent years trying to take application development to this next level. They used a generic technology that would ultimately be available to all members of the consortium funding its development. Unfortunately, both inventors passed away before their plans were fully realized. Richard Lawson and Richard Patton of Lawson Software in St. Paul, Minnesota have been working on a similar but proprietary middleware technology for more than 20 years. They recently announced their latest version of such a system, called Landmark™. The proprietary Landmark™ development system represents the ultimate *upstreaming* of software application development design decisions. These decisions will now be made as domain decisions by empowered domain experts, thereby eliminating the multiple layers of (mis)communication involved in traditional software development. The announcement of this new technology created quite a buzz on the Internet and in the MIS press. For example, a lead article in *Information Week* noted the following:

> Lawson Software Inc. last week unveiled a domain-specific language aimed at increasing software quality by reducing the massive amounts of code required in an application. Code-named Landmark, the technology has been under development for more than three years by founder Richard Lawson and chief architect Richard Patton. Lawson software architects will spend the next several years using Landmark to rewrite the company's

product line, which was originally written in COBOL. Unlike a general-purpose computer language, a domain-specific one is aimed at a particular kind of business need. Based on a services-oriented architecture, Landmark generates application-specific code in Java.[1]

Figure 16.1a illustrates the many steps of conventional application software development, with its implied technical language "translation" between each stage. Figure 16.1b shows the idealized specification-based development approach, with domain experts writing precise specifications in a specification language and domain experts evaluating and testing the results. Programmers are needed, but they are not directly involved in the development process. They are the very high-level system programmers who wrote and will later maintain the application software generator. Such a program has been called a "meta-compiler," but this term is not really appropriate. A meta-compiler is a compiler that produces a new compiler, such as Generalized ALGOL at Stanford[2] and ARGMAT at Stuttgart.[3] The best nomenclature for this kind of application generator would be "super-compiler," because it transforms one high-level language to another, which is then compiled by a conventional compiler.

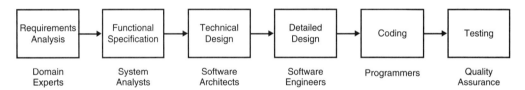

FIGURE 16.1A
Traditional Software Development Processes

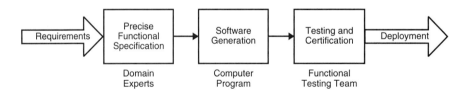

FIGURE 16.1B
Specification-Based Software Development

Comparing the two diagrammed processes does not fully indicate the difference between their final stages. In Figure 16.1b the testing is done by domain experts solely to determine whether the functional capabilities of the resulting application fulfill the specified requirements. In conventional development processes, the testing stage involves straightening out a tangled web of design errors, technical errors, coding errors, human miscommunications, and mistakes. This is best done following a disciplined DFTS approach like that shown in Figure 2.1 in Chapter 2.

It is the contention of the authors of this book that the future of application programming as a profession will include two groups: those who learn enough about the domain to write in the forthcoming novel specification languages by Lawson, Wescorp, and others, and those who learn enough about system programming to write the application generator programs. Application programming as we know it today will either disappear or be outsourced. Between now and then, however, we will have to invoke Taguchi and QFD methods to move design tasks upstream in the development process to achieve robust software architecture.

While the silver bullets are being molded by Lawson Software, Wescorp is getting its patents, and the Norwegian consortium left behind by Nygaard and Dahl is proceeding to a consensus, we must still write a lot of robust enterprise software applications in Java using a dependable multistage software development methodology.

Sidebar 16.1: A Precise Functional Specification

In the late 1960s, one of the authors was general manager of one of the first software companies. Its president had declared that the firm could no longer enter fixed-price contracts for programming due to runaway "scope" problems the firm had with some application development contracts with General Motors. They decided that the solution to this problem was writing more precise functional specifications and "attaching" such a customer-approved specification to the application development contract. The author soon got a call from the head of MIS for a major Minnesota-based railroad for which they had written numerous applications to run on her Univac III in COBOL. She needed a new application and had budgeted $60,000 for it. When he told her we no longer did fixed-price work, she exploded. Margaret was a size-40 scorpion with a vocabulary that would embarrass a Duluth stevedore. She exploded at his reluctance, which she termed a business relationship "betrayal." He proposed a compromise whereby they would write a precise functional specification for $15,000 and she could shop it out. If any other software firm would contract to write the COBOL application for less than $45,000, she would be under budget, and he would have no hard feelings. She agreed. However, the firm won the final bid. The approved new type of specification was attached to a contract calling for three $15,000 progress payments, all of which pleased the firm's president.

Some weeks later, the author visited Margaret at the railroad MIS center for the show-and-tell. They entered the Univac III machine room, which had "no smoking" signs posted; Margaret kept her cigarette in her mouth. They went to the line printer, where proud programmers from both groups were printing out the test report from Margaret's test data. She leaned her ample frame over the printer to get a closer look through her bifocals, dropping cigarette ashes into the printer. She said: "Not bad, Patton. Now, if your team will just move this column over here and that column back there, and change this caption to read like this, etc., etc., before I release the last progress payment." He replied, "But, Margaret, we agreed on a precise functional specification, and this program fully and accurately implements that specification." She looked at him incredulously over her bifocals, which had now slipped down her nose a bit, and replied, "Patton, who the *%$& ever reads a two-volume functional spec?" He realized that Margaret was just exercising her managerial prerogative of "marking territory." However, he could not agree to make the changes without the president's approval, because this was their first use of what was to become a new business model for the firm.

Naturally, the president was furious. He called in the firm's general counsel to discuss suing the railroad to make them live up to the contract and give us the final progress payment without making any changes. The lawyer asked the author how much it would cost to make the changes, and he estimated $300 to $400. He told the boss it would cost several times that to file a lawsuit, so they should just go ahead and please the customer.

Margaret's question has remained unanswered in the author's mind over the ensuing 36 years of application development experience: "Who the *%$& ever reads a two-volume functional spec?" Now we know the answer to her question: When it is "read," it is read by an application generator program!

What Is Robust Software?

A general but descriptive definition of robustness in product and process design is given in *Taguchi's Quality Engineering Handbook*: "Robust design (including product and process design) generally means designing a product or process that can function properly under various conditions of use or operation."[4] This definition can be extended to make it more prescriptive, which is the purpose of this book, at least for business enterprise applications software. Our contention is that robust software is trustworthy software, because it performs as *specified*, *expected*, and *desired* in spite of adverse circumstances, termed *noise* by Taguchi. The essence of the Taguchi method lies in measurements made in the product's functional space to calculate a signal's nearness to an ideal output function. Thus, its use in quality engineering or robust design involves a procedure for improving functionality to meet user needs (voice of the customer) and improved accuracy in prediction of outcomes by using measurement methods in both the functional space and multidimensional space. Each design feature or improvement is an individual engineering task. As long as the multidimensional data has sufficient accuracy, the *signal-to-noise ratio* may be calculated as the Mahalanobis distance from objects or phenomena that do not belong in the homogenous design space.[5] This distance measure was introduced by P. C. Mahalanobis in 1936 as a measure of similarity in a sample set based on the correlations between the samples. Robust software design classifies a signal into two types: the quality of an active signal for software that the user interacts with, and the quality of the Mahalanobis-Taguchi System (MTS) for a passive signal resulting from largely exogenous performance limiting factors that arise in complex systems, whether they be organic or automaton.[6] The Taguchi method assumes that all conditions of software use belong to either a signal (proper function) or noise (faulty operation, error, or bug), independent of whether the user depends on the software application actively or passively. At the design stage of the development process, the intended software functionality is considered the user's *active signal factor*. However, in the downstream stages of development, the inspection, testing, diagnostic, and prediction data is regarded as representing *passive signal factors*. Thus, robustness in software can be quantified at the earliest design stages in such a way that it can be analyzed, predicted, and even enhanced before the application detailed design is complete and coding has begun. The stages in the DFTS process (see Figure 2.6 in Chapter 2) allow continuous prediction and improvement during consequent development.

Requirements for Software to Be Robust

When we specify the function set of a new application, it is not necessary to identify robustness or trustworthiness as qualities explicitly in either quantitative or qualitative terms. These qualities are intrinsic. If the application carries out the intended function set without error (or without compromise by unanticipated exogenous influences, such as noise factors), the software is by definition trustworthy (always does what the user depends on it to do). Therefore, it is robust (its "signal" is never lost in the "noise" of daily use). The major requirement at this stage is *clarity* in describing the system's intended functions. The required degree of clarity can come only from the ultimate users of the system, not generally the buyers of the system or even the managers. Naturally, the needs of these groups for economy, performance, audit trailing, transaction logging, and so on must be met. However, the system's primary functionality must be declared by the active users. As Sidebar 16.2 illustrates, obtaining this degree of clarity has been a problem from the earliest days of computing. One of the earliest rules of thumb in business application development was that the first time an application was computerized, it was simply automating the paperwork. That is, the computer's intrinsic capability to improve or reengineer the business process was totally ignored. A second rule was essentially a corollary of the first: An information system must be developed three times before it really makes use of the computer in any intrinsic way.

Sidebar 16.2: Getting the End User's Input

One of the authors used to teach at the University of Minnesota and directed its control data Cyber 74/174 computer center. He was called back to his previous employer, a software firm, as a consultant to write a precise functional specification for a juvenile justice system for Ramsay County, Minnesota, where St. Paul is located. The local control data firm had been the unexpected low bidder with a Cyber 174 computer. This computer normally was sold for technical and scientific applications written in FORTRAN. However, the machine was blessed with one of the best COBOL compliers ever written. It was just beginning to appear in business and government installations. The author had just developed the Hennepin County (where Minneapolis is county seat) justice system before leaving the software firm to go to the university. Thus, he was familiar with the Law Enforcement Assistance Administration (LEAA) guidelines for such local government justice information systems.

At the first meeting with the juvenile justice department senior staff and board of governors, the author explained in detail how the design team would interview the juvenile probation officers to learn their needs and expectations for the system that would be serving them. The meeting quickly disintegrated. The management group asserted that they were in charge of this department, they had the budget, and they were buying the system, so there was no need for us to talk to the probation officers, who were just low-level employees anyway. They were obviously inexperienced buyers of this sort of technology, so the author began to ask them a series of "optometrist questions": Would you prefer to see A or B? Which would be better, C or D? What about the choice between E and F? Naturally, they had no idea what he was talking about. They reluctantly agreed that he could interview the junior staff, but they would still have to approve the specification. To this proposition he readily agreed! This anecdote illustrates that the people buying a computer application or system are not necessarily the ones who will be using it, but the software architect must accommodate the needs of both.

Specifying Software Robustness

Today's multistage development processes can anticipate downstream activities in support of robust design such as testing and debugging by grouping functions or signal factors into small homogeneous groups.[7] This vastly simplifies the analysis using orthogonal arrays (discussed in Chapter 17). It also recognizes that all the function points in a business software application interact or influence each other equally. Applications are naturally organized into functional hierarchies that partition the application in a natural way. In addition, Taguchi has proposed design as a three-step process:[8]

1. **System design** is intended to meet the end users' functional requirements.

2. **Parameter design** is intended to make product performance less sensitive to exogenous factors in its usage environment.

3. **Tolerance design** involves tightening tolerances on product or process parameters to reduce variability in performance.

For example, software system or application design involves new concepts, ideas, and methods to provide novel or improved software capability to users. Unless the technology offering a competitive advantage in the marketplace is patented, copyrighted, or held as a trade secret, it can quickly be copied by competitors, and competitive advantage is soon lost. Parameter design allows the development team to build the novel technology into the product in a uniform yet intrinsic way that is not easily isolated and copied. The product also will be less sensitive to user error and environmental hazards, such as errors in data or other related application programs. Parameter design is used to make a product robust, or less sensitive, to noise factors without trying to control or eliminate the noise. Sidebar 16.3 gives a simple example concerning musical instrument construction to illustrate this process. This example is a mechanical rather than a programming one, and it is implicit rather than explicit. However, it shows the essence of this *Taguchi insight* on using parameter design to dramatically improve quality at no cost. The best examples of trade-offs between parameter and tolerance design are naturally electronic circuits. The fastest but most expensive way to reduce performance variability in such circuits is to tighten tolerances on critical components. The best way is to change design point parameters in such a way that tolerances are not so critical. If parameter design is inadequate to meet performance robustness goals, the design team must turn to tolerance design.

Tolerance design requires the use of tighter tolerances or higher-quality, higher-cost materials to reduce performance variation or sensitivity to environmental or usage factors. For tolerance design, the quality loss function is used to substantiate the increased costs of higher-quality components by lower loss to society.[9] Opportunities for tolerance design do not occur as often in software development as they do in circuit design, in which they are a legendary design trade-off. Examples include the use of more time- and/or space- (or use license) costly algorithms for computing functions as opposed to a less accurate estimate of a computed value. A sensitivity or error analysis of an algorithm may lead the software designers to a parameter design to avoid the higher-cost software component.

The benefits of robust software specification for robust software development are technology readiness, flexibility, and reproducibility. Computer software development lends itself naturally to small-scale laboratory-like experiments of test data to optimize functionality. This quality technology allows an entire group of program products rather than just individual programs. As soon as a software function's robustness has been optimized, newly planned products within the same family can be designed using straightforward adjustments. This ensures one of the greatest benefits of software reusability: reduced cycle time and enhanced quality in downstream software development. Finally, all these benefits can be reproduced downstream for the benefit of both the software vendor and the user.[10]

Sidebar 16.3: An Example of Parameter Design

One of the authors bought a modern baroque-style harpsichord for his wife while teaching at the Technical University of Stuttgart in the mid-1960s. The instrument performed beautifully during the time they lived in Germany, but after they returned to the United States, he had to retune it every time it was played. A careful reading of the German instructions brought to light the requirements that the instrument was to be kept at a temperature of 60 to 65 degrees Fahrenheit (European room temperature), with relative humidity between 68 and 70%. This was no problem in a stone or concrete house in Southern Germany, but it was impossible in Minnesota, where winter humidity is 10 to 20% and in the summer is 60 to 80%. Controlling the ambient temperature and humidity by storing the instrument in a special cabinet is expensive enough for a cello, but it would be out of the question for an instrument as large as a baroque harpsichord. The author asked Dr. Layton James, harpsichordist of the St. Paul Chamber Orchestra, how he dealt with this problem. Dr. James had years earlier bought a Zuckerman harpsichord kit. He carefully laid it out in his basement, stacking the spruce and other wood parts to get good air circulation, and left them there for three years before building the instrument. He had no tuning problems with the finished instrument. So, for a given system design, his *implicit parameter design* approach produced the desired insensitivity to environmental factors. This would have been much more expensive to handle through tolerance design or by controlling for "noise" in the ambient storage or performance environment.

Key Points

- The many stages of current software development processes make it error-prone.

- Novel application generation technologies promise to simplify software development and make its creation much less error-prone.

- A truly precise functional specification is difficult to achieve due to the high degree of ambiguity in creative team-based human development activities.

- If a really precise functional specification can be written, it can be automatically transformed into an error-free working program.

- Software is robust if it can function to specification under any usage conditions.

- Software is trustworthy if it meets its users' expectations under any reasonable conditions of use.

- Robustness in software can be achieved by a three-stage Taguchi process: system design, parameter design, and tolerance design.

- System design is intended to meet the functional requirements of the final end users.

- Parameter design is intended to make the product less sensitive to exogenous ("noise") factors in its usage environment.

- Tolerance design involves tightening tolerance in product or process parameters to reduce variability in performance.

Additional Resources

http://www.prenhallprofessional.com/title/0131872508

http://www.agilenty.com/publications

Internet Exercises

1. Check the Internet for application generation products and systems.

2. Review the current status of Lawson's Landmark™ generated software.

Review Questions

1. What are the stages of the traditional software development process?

2. What makes the traditional process error-prone?

3. List the major ways in which errors creep into well-intentioned software developments, from your experience.

4. What characteristics would make an application software specification truly precise?

5. Why is this difficult to do in practice?

6. Define "robust software."

7. Define "trustworthy software."

8. How is robustness an intrinsic quality while trustworthiness is an extrinsic one?

Discussion Questions and Projects

1. Define the three steps Taguchi recommends for robust design.

2. Have you intuitively done a trade-off study in a past software development project that traded parameter design for tolerance design? Explain.

3. Why does parameter design save product cost while tolerance design adds to it?

Problems

1. Consider your last software design/development project. Analyze it in terms of the Taguchi triad: list the primary factors for its system design, those for its parameter design, and those for its tolerance design, if any. It has been said that most of consulting and engineering practice is the codified application of common sense and experience. Did you intuitively trade parameter factors for tolerance factors? How would the clarification of Taguchi's method have enlightened this process?

2. In the design considered in Problem 1, list the control and noise factors. How did you intuitively account for the latter to optimize your design or to make the program more robust and/or trustworthy?

Endnotes

[1] Laurie Sullivan, "New language cuts coding," *InformationWeek*, May 16, 2005.

[2] Niklaus Wirth, "A Generalized ALGOL Compiler," doctoral dissertation, Stanford University, 1962.

[3] P. C. Patton and H. R. Lawson, "ARGMAT: A Self-adaptive Matrix Interpretive Code," ISD Report No. 22, Technical University of Stuttgart, September 1965.

[4] G. Taguchi, S. Chowdhury, Y. Wu, *Taguchi's Quality Engineering Handbook* (Hoboken, NJ: John Wiley & Sons, 2005), p. 58.

[5] Ibid, p. 59.

[6] Ibid, p. 97.

[7] Ibid, p. 102.

[8] P. J. Ross, *Taguchi Techniques for Quality Engineering*, 2nd Ed. (New York: McGraw-Hill, 1996), p. 204.

[9] Ibid, p. 245.

[10] Y. Wu and A. Wu, *Taguchi Methods for Robust Design* (Fairfield, NJ: ASME Press, 2000), p. 11.

CHAPTER 17

Taguchi Methods and Optimization for Robust Software

Quality losses result mainly from product failure after sale; product "robustness" is more a function of product design than of online control, however stringent, of manufacturing processes.

—*Genichi Taguchi*

Many design engineers would not know what to do with the results from a Taguchi statistical analysis and need help to interpret the data.

—*Jiju Anthony*

Overview

Taguchi's quality loss function provides a measure of the overall loss to society when a product fails to meet its target functionality and reliability. His signal-to-noise ratio measures the positive quality contribution from controllable or design factors versus the negative quality contribution from uncontrollable or noise factors. Taguchi Methods involve seven steps, beginning with a clear statement of the design problem and ending with a confirming statistical experiment showing how parameter choices will enhance robustness. An example from electrical circuit design is presented, because it is much more similar to software design than mechanical design, where Taguchi Methods have found their largest application. A more-detailed example from software design or product improvement is given, building on the previous example. Taguchi further developed and applied an earlier technique involving Latin squares or orthogonal matrices to allow the evaluation on multiple parameters simultaneously. His use of orthogonal matrices permits a multifactorial analysis that is far more efficient than a conventional "bottleneck" analysis. It also allows the study of factor interactions.

Chapter Outline

- Taguchi Methods for Robust Software Design

- An Example from Engineering Design

- An Example from Software Design and Development

- Orthogonal Matrices for Taguchi Parameter Design Experiments

- Applications to the Design of Trustworthy Software

- Key Points

- Additional Resources

- Internet Exercises

- Review Questions

- Discussion Questions

- Problems

- Endnotes

Taguchi Methods for Robust Software Design

We will begin with a brief review of Taguchi Methods as they were developed over the past 50 years, originally for robust hardware design. Statistical quality control first began in manufacturing in the early 1900s by testing the output of production lines in an effort to reduce process and product variability. Deming and others soon concluded that although downstream testing might reduce the number of defective products shipped, it could never achieve any intrinsic process improvement or product quality. However, many years passed before it was accepted that upstream preproduction experiments done during design could contribute to the optimization of industrial processes, quality improvement of products, or reduction of cost and waste. As you will see, this is critical to the design of robust, trustworthy software. Software development really has no manufacturing component; it is the direct result of design and continual redesign and upgrading. Conventional wisdom dating from Aristotle says that in designing an experiment, you should change only one parameter at a time. This is the essence of the Western tradition of logical analysis. But this analytic approach can't discover parameter interactions, because if a system is more than the sum of its parts, analysis will always fail to discover its essence. Taguchi Methods let you change many factors at a time, albeit in a systematic way, to discover both that factor's major effects and its interaction or systemic effects. As soon as a factor (parameter) and its effects are well understood, the designer can take appropriate steps through parameter design to eliminate potential defects in the resulting product. This technology was developed by Professor Genichi Taguchi, director of the Japanese Academy of Quality and four-time recipient of the Deming Prize. He devised a quality improvement technique that uses statistical experimental design for the effective characterization of a process or product at design time, together with a statistical analysis of variability. This allows quality to be designed in as far upstream as possible, at the initial design and prototyping stages of product development.[1]

Taguchi defines quality in a negative manner as the loss imparted to society from the time a product is shipped. This includes the cost of customer dissatisfaction, including loss of reputation, and goodwill. Apart from direct loss due to warranty and service costs, an indirect loss occurs due to market-share loss and any costs needed to overcome consequent loss of competitive advantage. Taguchi's loss function establishes a value basis for the development of quality products. A product does not fail to exhibit quality only when it is outside specification, but also when it deviates from its *target value*. Thus, quality improvement now means minimizing the variation of product performance about its target value. Figure 17.1 depicts Taguchi's famous quadratic quality loss function, in which loss is proportional to the square of the deviation from the target value:

$$L(Y) = (M/D^2)(Y - t)^2$$

In the formula for this curve, L(Y) is the loss to society when a product's performance (Y) deviates from its target (t). M is the producer's monetary loss when the customer's tolerance (D) is exceeded. The objective of Taguchi Methods for product design improvement is to identify *controllable* (or design) factors and their values or parameters. By optimizing these parameters, any variation in product performance can be minimized and the product made robust with respect to changes in operating and environmental conditions. Also, the Taguchi approach deals with *uncontrollable* (or noise) factors in the product's operating environment that affect product performance. This too enhances product robustness.

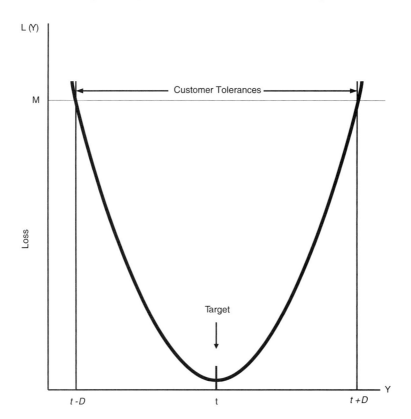

FIGURE 17.1
Taguchi's Loss Function L(Y)

Key to the design of statistical experiments in Taguchi Methods is the use of orthogonal matrices, which are described later. This technology was developed by Plackett and Burman in 1946 for multifactorial experiments and later was adopted by Taguchi.[2] Controllable factors that reduce performance due to noise factors but keep it on target are identified. The effect of the noise factors is reduced or eliminated rather than the noise factors themselves, because they are defined as uncontrollable. Performance variation is simulated in these statistical experiments by systematically varying noise factors for each of the settings of the controllable factors in the study. This is called a reduced multifactorial study in Taguchi Methods, because not all the factors of a complex product or system can be studied at once. Figure 17.2 is a simplified paradigm of the Methods that shows the parts and the process. Further technical details appear later in this chapter. In Figure 17.2, the rows of the *inner* (fractional orthogonal) *array* are controllable factor-level settings in which every level setting of each factor chosen for the statistical experiment with every other level of all the others chosen factors the same number of times. At every level combination of the controllable factors, observations are obtained while changing the settings of the noise factors. For the purposes of the experiment, we can change the uncontrollable factors to discover design tolerances, just as the electrical engineer changes margins on a circuit design to discover failure modes and improve robustness. The *outer arrays* shown in the figure are used to determine the level combinations of the noise factors. This allows the design engineer or her statistician to simulate the effect of variability and optimize the settings to minimize performance variability from the target value and thus make the design more robust. For each of the m rows in the inner array, the n rows of the outer array provide n observations on the response being investigated, or nm values for the entire experiment.

The outer array is not a random subset of values from the noise space but rather test levels of the noise factors chosen to cover or span the noise space. If the distribution of a noise factor is known with a mean M and standard deviation S, and the factor is linear, Taguchi suggests it be tested at two levels: (M – S) and (M + S). However, if its effect is not linear, it should be tested at three levels: $(M - S \sqrt{(3/2)})$, M, and $(M + S \sqrt{(3/2)})$. If a prototype hardware or software product is available, the parameter design experiment can be conducted by actual trials. If the product is unavailable, the experiment must be conducted on the design itself using a response model.[3] Such a model simply relates product performance to both signal (controllable) and noise (uncontrollable) factors. The results of the statistical experiment are the performance measures shown on the right side of the figure. The noise performance measures (NPM) give the variation in response at each setting to determine the controllable factors that can minimize the effects of noise on performance. The target performance measures (TPM) identify the controllable factors that have the largest effect on mean performance response and thus can be modified to bring mean response to the design target. Before Taguchi, such statistical experiments focused on the TPM only. Taguchi's major contribution was to include the NPM and a suitable measure for it—the *signal-to-noise ratio* (SNR), which estimates the inverse of the coefficient of variation, or ratio M/S—the mean divided by the standard deviation. Taguchi's formula for SNR is

$$SNR = \log_{10} (M^2/S^2)$$

in which M and S are the mean and the standard deviation of the Y_{ij}, or the data column in Figure 17.2.

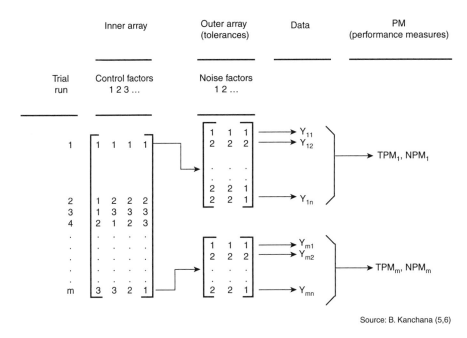

Source: B. Kanchana (5,6)

FIGURE 17.2
Experimental Paradigm for Taguchi Optimization

Table 17.1 lists the steps of Taguchi Methods for either hardware or software design. This chapter gives examples of both to illustrate the use of the Methods. The principal novel idea of Taguchi Methods is that the statistical testing of a new or improved product should be carried out at the design stage to make the product robust to variations in both its manufacturing and usage environments. Because software is not manufactured in the ordinary sense of the term, the focus here is on design for trustworthiness in use. Hence, we will not repeat or even summarize the vast literature on the successful application of Taguchi Methods in manufacturing, but rather focus on their application to the design of robust software.

TABLE 17.1
Steps in Taguchi Methods

Step Number	Step	Description
1	Define the problem.	Clearly state the problem to be solved.
2	Determine the objective.	Identify performance responses to be optimized.
3	Brainstorm.	Identify both signal and noise factors.
4	Design the experiment.	Choose factors and build orthogonal arrays.
5	Conduct the experiment.	Perform trials and collect data.
6	Analyze the data.	Evaluate TMP and NPM for each trial run.
7	Interpret the results.	Identify variability and target control factors and select their optima.
8	Confirm the experiment.	Prove that new parameter settings enhance robustness.

An Example from Engineering Design

Although our interest here is software design, a simpler yet realistic example from electrical circuit design may be very helpful in giving you insight into Taguchi Methods. This application shows the trade-off potential between the three stages of Taguchi design and also gives you insight into the increasing replacement of electronic circuits by software algorithms. Analog filters for radio and other signal processing have long since been replaced by digital (software-programmed) filters. Modern communication receivers are simply computer programs that tune to and receive signals on a chip-based computer. Similarly, the most advanced radio transmitters are computers that, rather than computing a number, prepare and transmit a signal at a chosen or preprogrammed frequency. As an example, we take a case study from the literature by Kanemoto.[4]

Much of electrical circuit design involves adjusting part values and their tolerances to achieve a target performance over a certain range with the minimum number of parts and the least constraint on part tolerances. Normally, electronic components have tolerance values of plus or minus 20%. High-quality parts with a 10% tolerance are very expensive. Parts having 1% tolerance are even more expensive and usually are reserved for laboratory or standards use. Figure 17.3a shows a simple frequency-modulated oscillator consisting of an inverter, a piezoelectric crystal, two resistors, two capacitors, and two voltage-dependent variable capacitors. Figure 17.3b shows the voltage variation resulting from a modulation signal V around a 2V dc bias value. Figure 17.3c shows the frequency deviation resulting from the signal voltage. Clearly the performance value of this circuit is to maintain a relationship between frequency deviation (output) and a varying signal voltage (input). This performance target can be disturbed by noise factors such as environmental temperature, time drift, and power fluctuation, but the latter is the principal noise factor, ranging from + or –0.5V. When designing an electronic circuit, it is simple enough to bench-test it to determine variation around the target value of zero deviation from a center frequency of 453.286 kHz for an input signal voltage of 0. In this case, you can do a full factorial study since there are so few parameters.

The experiments with Kanemoto's circuit showed an error variation of 12.763 Hz and an error variance of 1596. The control factors and their levels are shown in Table 17.2, in which power source voltage is the voltage input to the inverter. This data is put into an orthogonal array to carry out the statistical experiment. The results are shown in Table 17.3. It gives the SNR and sensitivity values for the original configuration, the optimal configuration, and the improvement or gain, along with the results of the follow-up confirmatory experiment. The factors for the original circuit are $A_1B_2C_2D_2E_2F_2H_2$—that is, the first crystal choice, a CSB-455 in column 1 of the factor table and the second or column 2 choice for all the other factors. The optimal circuit given these factors and the single noise factor of the small power supply voltage instability is $A_2B_3C_3D_3E_3F_2G_2H_3$. This would be the circuit with the second crystal choice, a B456-F15, R1 = 1 kOhm, Rd = 5.6 kOhms, C2 = C1 = 820 mfd, and both capacitors of chip type, and the bias on the inverter set at 7 volts. This is a rather simple problem, but it does show Taguchi Methods favorably. You can vary all the factors at once to optimize the circuit in one statistical experiment and its confirmation, rather than fiddling at the designer's bench for days or doing hundreds of circuit simulations, changing one part value at a time.

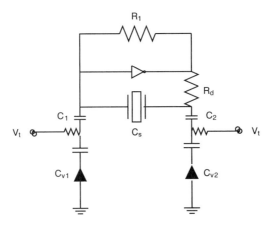

FIGURE 17.3A
Frequency-Modulated Oscillator: The Experimental Circuit

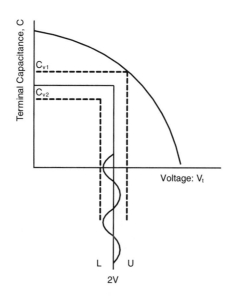

FIGURE 17.3B
Voltage Variation

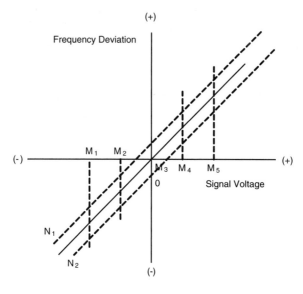

FIGURE 17.3C
Frequency Deviation

TABLE 17.2
Circuit Control Factors and Levels

Label	Control Factor Name	Level 1	Level 2	Level 3
A	Crystal type	Type A	Type B	Type C
B	Resistor R1	680 Ohms	820 Ohms	1 kOhm
C	Resistor Rd	3.3 kOhm	4.7 kOhm	5.6 kOhm
D	Capacitor C1	560 mfd	680 mfd	820 mfd
E	Capacitor C2	Two levels below C1	One level below C1	Same as C1
F	Capacitor type	Ceramic	Chip	Film
G	Capacitor type	Ceramic	Chip	Film
H	Power source voltage	3	5	7

TABLE 17.3
Analytical Results Optimizing the Frequency-Modulated Oscillator Circuit

Configuration	SNR		Sensitivity	
	Estimate	Confirmation	Estimate	Confirmation
Optimal	37.53	37.27	60.25	60.32
Optimal	29.78	29.77	57.32	57.24
Improvement	7.74	7.50	2.94	3.08

An Example from Software Design and Development

As our first example of a software design application of Taguchi Methods, we will consider a software program improvement project for the Indian government. It was created by B. Kanchana and published as his doctoral dissertation at the Indian Institute of Science at Bangalore.[5] Most software design projects start with an existing program rather than a blank sheet of paper (or a blank programming screen these days), so our example exhibits little loss of generality as a typical software design project. This Indian Defense Ministry project was to redesign the man-machine interface display (MMID) subsystem of the Airborne Surveillance Platform (ASP) system, which was programmed in the C language. The quality goal was to reduce the number of errors per module in the system shown in hierarchical form in Figure 17.4. This subsystem employs a user interface device to provide access protocol, equipment control, and operations oversight, and it displays the air surveillance situation on a color display.

Each engagement of the system lasts five or six hours and involves thousands of data words scanned every few seconds. Figure 17.5 shows part of the cause-and-effect diagram for typical design faults in the project's requirements, specification, and design phases. The two major modules of MMID, Receive_plot_data() and Command_proc_task(), are shown in Figure 17.6. Receive_plot_data() displays plot data in screen coordinates, and Command_proc_task() handles azimuth display, range ring display, and maximum range detection. The first factor is the number of requirements per module. The second is the cyclomatic complexity of each module. The third is coupling modes between modules, data coupling (call by value), stamp coupling (call by name), control coupling (method invocation), common data coupling (global data reference), and content coupling (remote method invocation), in increasing complexity. These parameters or control factors are listed together with their possible levels in Table 17.4.

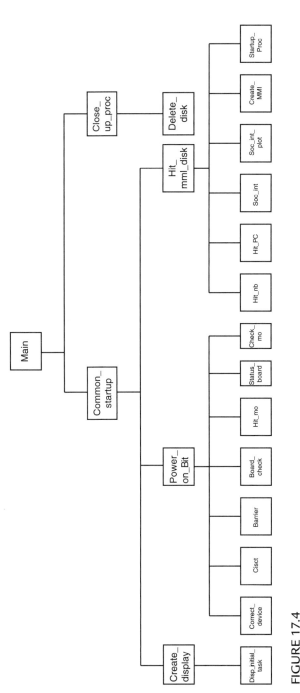

FIGURE 17.4
Architecture of the MMID Subsystem

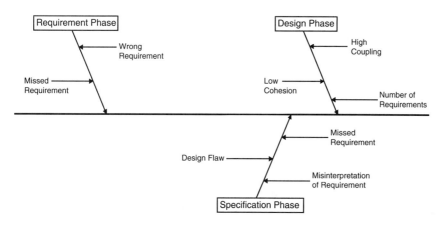

FIGURE 17.5
A Typical Cause-and-Effect Diagram for Design Faults

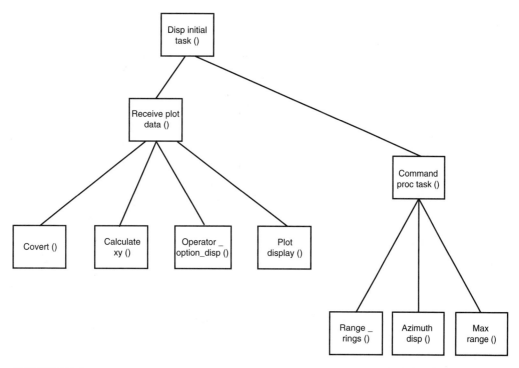

FIGURE 17.6
Major Modules of the MMID Subsystem

TABLE 17.4
Control Factors and Their Levels

Label	Control Factor Name	Level 1	Level 2	Level 3
A	Number of requirements per module	1	2	>2
B	Cyclomatic complexity	<5	5–10	>10
C	Coupling	Data, stamp, and control	Common, content	

A factorial experiment to consider all possible factor level combinations of these would require 18 experiments because A is at three levels, B is at three levels, and C is at two levels, and $3 \times 3 \times 2 = 18$. Taguchi has tabulated a series of orthogonal arrays for use in such experiments. L_9 (for a nine-row Latin square) is the appropriate array for this data set, as shown in Table 17.5.

TABLE 17.5
Taguchi's L_9 Orthogonal Array

Experiment	A	B	C
1	1	1	1
2	1	2	2
3	1	3	3 = 2
4	2	1	2
5	2	2	3 = 2
6	2	3	1
7	3	1	3 = 2
8	3	2	1
9	3	3	2

For each experiment, a number of modules are tested for errors, as shown in Table 17.6. Kanchana computed the SNR as

$$S/N(\theta) = -10 \log_{10} [\Sigma (y_i^2/n)], \ i = 1, n$$

in which $\theta = (\theta_1, \theta_2,...,\theta_k)$ is the vector of control parameters, and $y = (y_1, y_2,...,y_k)$ is the vector of performance statistics. You repeat each observation n times at each selected combination of design parameter sets in the orthogonal array. The best setting of the design parameters is the one that maximizes the SNR—in this case, the type 2 experiment. In other words, it's the case in which cyclomatic complexity is maintained at level 2, coupling is kept at level 2, and the number of requirements per module is kept at level 1.

TABLE 17.6
Experimental Results

Experiment	Module Name	Errors	Average Per Module	SNR
1	Azimuth()	2		
	Calc_xy_pos()	1	1.5	−3.98
2	Curr_opt_option()	1	1.333	−3.01
	Sector_proc()	2		
	Hndl_async_calls()	1		
3	Glb3_var()	2	2.0	−6.02
	Fan_out()	2		
	Fan_in()	2		
	Tx_sec_menu_proc()	3		
	Security_ clearance()	3		
4	Track_ret_opt()	2	1.5	−3.98
	Sys_data_in_out()	1		
5	Prev_curr_scan_disp()	1	2.0	−6.98
	Date_time_input()	3		
6	Elapsed_time()	1		
	Mod1_nam()	3	2.0	−6.98
7	Receive_data()	2		
	Current_status()	1	1.5	−3.98
8	Peridoc_hlth_task()	1	1.66	−4.77
	Handle_dbit_PRF()	2		
	Get_dbit_PRF_ack()	2		
9	Overlay()	1	3.33	−11.89
	Set_mission_time()	6		
	Receive_plot_data()	31		

To verify these results, Kanchana examined the error-prone module Set_mission_time() and discovered that it had a cyclomatic complexity of 18, two requirements per module, and employed common coupling. To improve MMID quality, this module was split into six smaller modules. After coding, they were tested to discover only one error in one of them rather than the six in the first version. Likewise, Security_clearance() was examined to discover a cyclomatic complexity of 12 and common coupling but only level 1 requirements. It was split into five modules, none of which showed any errors upon testing. The conclusion in Kanchana's dissertation and in a later presentation[6] was that the optimal design parameters for MMID are one requirement per module, coupling by data passing whenever possible, and limiting cyclomatic complexity to less than 10.

Orthogonal Matrices for Taguchi Parameter Design Experiments

This section presents more technical details for the use of the reduced factorial or orthogonal matrix method so central to Taguchi Methods. The full nomenclature for an orthogonal array is $L_a(b^c)$, in which L stands for Latin square, a is the number of test trials, b is the number of levels for each column, and c is the number of columns in the array. An orthogonal matrix is a generalized Latin square. For example, the $L_4(2^3)$ orthogonal array is shown in Table 17.7.

TABLE 17.7
An $L_4(2^3)$ Orthogonal Array

Number	1	2	3
1	1	1	1
2	1	2	2
3	2	1	2
4	2	2	1

Appendix B of the *Robust Engineering Workshop Manual* from the American Supplier Institute gives schemata for orthogonal arrays up to $L_{54}(3^{35})$.[7]

We want to use such matrices to represent the design values and trade-offs over which the design engineer has a choice, as well as the noise factors that may cause the product to deviate from the target (and thus quality) when used in its operational environment. This is the second stage in a Taguchi robust engineering design process. The first is designing to meet user-expressed functional requirements. The third stage is tolerance design, in which the engineer must tighten tolerances on components that cannot be made adequately robust by parameter design. Successful parameter design is the essence of Taguchi Methods. We start with a product that is designed to meet the user's requirements, but now we want to ensure that it will do so all the time, and thus exhibit robustness in the face of adverse real-world environmental and usage factors. The great advantage of parameter design is that it adds robustness without adding cost; in fact, it reduces costs by eliminating unnecessary components, and of course future warranty claims and later rework. Tolerance design is employed only when parameter design does not meet all the implicit robustness requirements and almost always adds cost to the actual product, even though it does contribute positively to the quality loss function itself.

Figure 17.7, adapted from a popular and readily available statistical handbook,[8] presents a small L_9 orthogonal matrix that is large enough to support a more detailed discussion of the parameter design or optimization process for a product, whether hardware or software. The columns of the design parameter matrix represent the design parameters, and its rows represent different combinations of test settings. The noise factor matrix specifies the test levels for the noise factors. Its columns identify the noise factors, and its rows represent the different combinations of noise factors applied simultaneously. In reality, the engineer has no control over either the levels or combinations of noise factors. But in the parameter design experiment, he can try different levels and combinations in such a way as to stress his design and optimize its robustness against such uncontrollable factors. Each test run of the design parameter matrix is crossed with every row of the noise factor matrix. In this way, virtual product performance mimics future real product performance variation at given design parameter settings. The result of the statistical experiment is a performance statistic that estimates or predicts the effect of the noise factors on expected performance for the controllable parameter combinations. A preferred combination of design parameters is identified by an objective function such as the SNR. The prediction then is verified by a confirmation experiment, and several iterations may be required to minimize the object function. Parameter design experimental data may be gathered by actual physical experiments or by simulation trials using a performance model.

A performance statistic estimates the effect of noise factors on a performance characteristic. If $\theta = (\theta_1, \theta_2 ... \theta_k)$ is the vector of design parameters and $w = (w_1, w_2 ... w_t)$ is the vector of noise factors, and the performance factor Y is a function of θ and w, $Y = f(\theta, w)$. We can further define the following functions of θ:[9]

Mean	$\eta(\theta) = E[Y]$
Variance	$\sigma^2(\theta) = E[\{Y - \eta(\theta)\}^2]$
Coefficient of variation	$CV(\theta) = \sigma(\theta)/\eta(\theta)$
Mean squared error	$MSE(\theta) = E[(Y - \tau)^2]$
Bias of distribution of Y	$B(\theta) = \eta(\theta) - \tau$

in which τ is the target value. Three possible optimization situations occur, depending on the target value. If the target value is 0, if Y has a nonnegative distribution, and if the loss function L(Y) increases as Y increases, the expected loss is proportional to

$$MSE\ (\theta) = E[(Y - 0)^2] = E[Y^2]$$

In this case, Taguchi recommends the performance measure $-10 \log MSE(\theta)$. If the target value is infinity, if the distribution of Y is positive, and if the loss function decreases as Y decreases, Taguchi recommends using 1/Y as the performance characteristic so that the target value of 1/Y becomes 0. On the other hand, if a specific target value $\tau = \tau_0$ is desired, and the loss function increases symmetrically and Y deviates from the desired target value τ_0 in either direction, the loss function L(Y) is proportional to $MSE(\theta) = E[(Y - \tau_0)^2]$, so that $MSE(\theta) = \sigma^2(\theta) + [B(\theta)]^2$ and $\sigma(\theta) = CV(\theta)\ \eta(\theta)$.

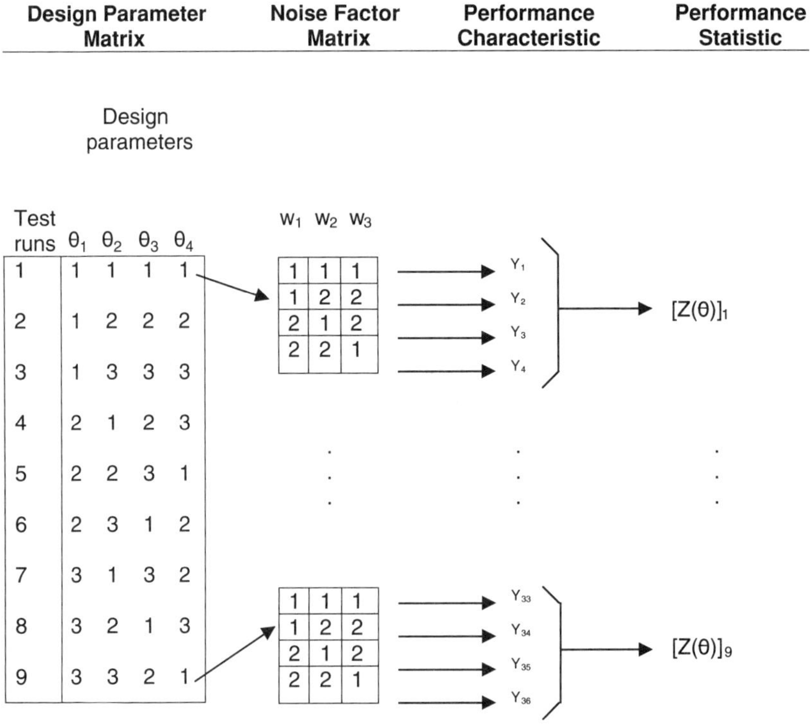

FIGURE 17.7
Taguchi Parameter Design Schema

529

Applications to the Design of Trustworthy Software

Having reviewed the elements of Taguchi Methods as they relate to software design, we now want to pull everything together as a set of guidelines for the use of these Methods in the earliest stages of design. Chapters 18 and 19 show how Taguchi Methods can be adapted for validation, verification, testing, evaluation, integration, extension, and maintenance to ensure trustworthy software. For software development, design is the primary activity, but we include requirements development, functional specification, and technical design as the three phases of the design process. Clearly Taguchi Methods apply only after the first round of these three phases and after a design is proposed that satisfies the user's requirements, meets the specification, and now needs to be "bulletproofed," as the programmer usually puts it. Every Taguchi optimization is different because every product's performance target is different. Thus, the design engineer and his or her team need to pursue the steps shown in Table 17.1. They are the best equipped to identify software performance characteristics and noise factors, determine their levels, and, with the help of statistics, analyze the performance statistics and validate the experiment(s) with a follow-up run to confirm the predications.

Key Points

- Taguchi's quality loss function provides a measure of the overall loss to society when a product fails to meet its target functionality and reliability.

- Taguchi defines a signal-to-noise ratio (SNR) to measure the positive quality contribution from controllable or design factors versus the negative quality contribution from uncontrollable or noise factors.

- Taguchi Methods involve seven steps, beginning with a clear statement of the design problem and ending with a confirming statistical experiment showing how parameter choices enhance robustness.

- An example from electrical circuit design was presented because it is much more similar to software design than mechanical design, where Taguchi Methods have found their largest application.

- An example from software design or product improvement was given, building on the previous example.

- A cause-and-effect or "fishbone" diagram was presented to guide fault analysis for the software example.

- Taguchi developed an earlier technique involving Latin squares or orthogonal matrices to allow an evaluation on multiple parameters simultaneously.

- Orthogonal matrices permit a multifactorial analysis that not only is far more efficient than a conventional "bottleneck" analysis but also allows the study of factor interactions.

Additional Resources

http://www.prenhallprofessional.com/title/0131872508

http://www.agilenty.com/publications

Internet Exercises

1. Find Internet sites that deal with the quality loss function. Now limit the results to sites that deal with it in a software product context.

2. Find Internet sites that refer to the Taguchi seven-step method.

Review Questions

1. Describe the quality loss function and its application.

2. Review and explain the seven steps in a Taguchi analysis.

3. Which steps of this analysis may be iterated to gain a design optimization?

4. What is the contribution of "orthogonality" in Taguchi's use of orthogonal arrays?

5. Review the statistical terms used in this chapter, and try to come to an intuitive understanding of them.

Discussion Questions

1. Why is the choice of a signal-to-noise ratio formula special for each application of Taguchi Methods?

2. If a formal methodology is merely the codification of experience and common sense, why is it helpful? List the pros and cons of using a formal method such as Taguchi's seven-step process.

Problems

1. Consider the last software application you debugged, enhanced, modified, or upgraded. Analyze it following the paradigm that is used for Kanchana's example, and construct the appropriate orthogonal array for the statistical experiment.

2. Define a suitable signal-to-noise ratio for your problem, and perform the statistical experiment to rank the error-prone modules. Now compare the results of this formal statistical paradigm with your intuitive experience. Do you arrive at the same result? If not, why not?

Endnotes

[1] N. Logothetis, *Managing for Total Quality: From Deming to Taguchi and SPC* (New York: Prentice-Hall, 1992), p. 298.

[2] R. L. Plackett and J. P. Burman, "The Design of Multifactorial Experiments," *Biometrica*, 33 (1946), pp. 305–325.

[3] Op cit Logothetis, p. 302.

[4] Y. Kanemoto, "Robust Design for a Frequency Modulation Circuit," *Quality Engineering*, Vol. 6, No. 5, pp. 33–37. This paper is also in G. Taguchi, et al., *Taguchi's Quality Engineering Handbook* (New York: Wiley, 2005), pp. 741–745.

[5] B. Kanchana, *Software Quality and Dependability Issues for the Airborne Surveillance Platform: A Systems Engineering Study*, doctoral dissertation, Indian Institute of Science, Bangalore, India, December 1998, p. 107.

[6] B. Kanchana and V. V. S. Sarma, *Software Quality Enhancement Through Software Process Optimization Using Taguchi Methods*, Proceedings of the International Conference and Workshop on Engineering of Computer Based Systems, IEEE, Nashville, TN, March 7–12, 1999, pp. 188–193.

[7] ASI Consulting Group, *Robust Engineering: Week I Workshop Manual* (Detroit: ASI, 2001), pp. B1–B19.

[8] R. N. Kacker and S. Ghosh, "Robust Design Methods," Chapter 20 of *Handbook of Statistical Methods for Engineers and Scientists*, 2nd Ed. (New York: McGraw-Hill, 1997), pp. 20.1–20.29.

[9] Ibid, p. 20.16

CHAPTER 18

Verification, Validation, Testing, and Evaluation for Trustworthiness

*The software development process doesn't prevent bugs; it merely
puts off dealing with them until the end of the project.*

—*Peter Amey*

Good (software) design ought to keep errors out in the first place.

—*Philip Ross*

Overview

The software development process includes testing, verification, validation, and code debugging to ensure proper function and reliability. Verification is the process of ensuring that programs meet their design specifications. Validation is the process of ensuring that a program meets its functional specification. Case studies demonstrate the use of Taguchi Methods for both program verification and validation. Seven types of software tests are described to verify and validate software; however, it is impossible to explicitly test every execution path through a large program. Black-box testing strategies test the functionality of each unit of code, and white-box testing methods are used to test the fidelity to design for each unit of code. Integration testing tests the interoperability of previously tested units of code. Bottom-up integration testing is an intuitive process of testing assemblies as the system is built. Top-down testing is a structured, algorithmic process that begins with the control program coded as a series of stubs or pseudo-programs that are replaced in a top-down fashion by actual code. Regression testing is employed to ensure that new versions of the program do not lose functionality over previous ones.

Chapter Outline

- Continuing the Development Cycle
- Verification
- Validation
- Testing and Evaluation
- Key Points
- Additional Resources

- Internet Exercises
- Review Questions
- Discussion Questions and Projects
- Problems
- Endnotes

Continuing the Development Cycle

You have heard the voice of the customer in a Taguchi-focused requirements study. You have met the customer's expectations and approval in a Taguchi-centered design specification. You have designed a software product that has been subjected to a Taguchi parameter analysis and optimization against all the adverse but uncontrollable noise factors the team can imagine. Now it is time to complete the development process and actually build the product with software trustworthiness as the goal. However, perhaps we should call the software development process a cycle, because it is the nature of software to be constantly in a state of redesign. The life cycle of any version of a typical enterprise software application is about three years. Conventional wisdom in the field says that when a software product or application is released to the marketplace as version 1.0, the design team should already have version 2.0 in the later stages of technical design and should be working on the requirements for version 3.0. To a hardware designer, such a product-planning process appears to be a rather cynically managed effort to achieve planned obsolescence, but such is the nature of successful software development. The flexible nature of software and the escalating expectations of its users are such that the designer's reach must always exceed his or her grasp. The authors consider this constant improvement and extension process or cycle to be a natural application for Taguchi Methods, because they allow the development group to become a learning organization. In other words, as each version of the product becomes more capable, it becomes at the same time less complex internally and less prone to errors, and thus more robust and trustworthy.

This chapter describes how Taguchi Methods can support each of the verification and validation stages of the development cycle and gives an example or case study of their application to these phases. Until more software vendors employ formal methods in software design, conventional software development processes will continue to be the mainstay of development. Formal methods such as Lawson's Landmark™ and Praxis High Integrity Systems Z require that application developers begin not by writing code but rather by arranging symbols in logical propositions. In the case of Landmark™, the application or specification language is the logical language of accounting, or supply chain, or purchasing, or payroll. In the case of Z (pronounced "zed"—it's British, don't you know!), it is essentially the language of mathematical logic: the propositions can be examined for correctness and logical consistency or even proven valid, like a theorem.[1] As soon as the developer is certain the specification has no logical flaws or bugs, he or she can convert it to a nearly bug-free program semimanually (Z) or automatically (Landmark). The actual cost of bugs delivered in software is truly incredible. More than 18% of software projects are canceled before completion.[2] But the greater potential losses come from projects that are completed, installed, and then compromise the future of the business using them. The urban legend discussed in Sidebar 18.1 is such a mild case compared to reality that it has become a standing joke among developers.

Here we will start with the definitions supplied by Watts Humphrey of the Software Engineering Institute, which he took from the pioneering work (1976) of G. J. Myers.[3, 4] However, it is our intention to bring these concepts into the context of the process as a whole with Taguchi as a backdrop.

- **Testing:** The process of executing a program or part of a program with the intention of finding errors.

- **Verification:** An attempt to find design errors by executing a program in a test or simulated environment. Whenever possible, it is the process of proving a program's correctness.

- **Validation:** An attempt to find functional problems by executing a program in a test environment.

- **Debugging:** Diagnosing the precise nature of a known error and correcting it.

These are very early definitions, but they provide a good starting point for making the concepts more precise. Note that testing is a *means* for verification and validation, and that debugging is a corrective activity, not a testing activity.

Sidebar 18.1: An Urban Legend About Business Software

A story has been floating around the information technology industry for more than 20 years. Although it's probably apocryphal, it is so plausible that it refuses to die. It goes like this: A major retailer with a complex multi-warehouse distribution system experienced a software glitch that caused one of its warehouses to suddenly "disappear" from the system. The company was in the midst of simplifying its supply chain and had recently closed several warehouses as a cost-cutting measure, so no alarm was raised when no new goods arrived at the missing warehouse. Nor, of course, were any requested for dispatch. Goods originally sent to this warehouse were automatically redirected to others in the system since it no longer "existed" (was no longer a viable destination for purchased inventory). The employees at the warehouse were given no instructions, so they just kept reporting for work each day as always. Given no information, they kept the place shipshape and awaited new instructions, which never came. The firm's payroll system was not linked to the supply chain/warehousing system, so the employees of the ghost warehouse kept receiving paychecks. When the software glitch finally came to light, the aging inventory in the missing warehouse was sold off by a factoring firm. The employees were transferred to other sites in the company, with instructions to tell no one about the problem. Apparently, all the employees have kept their silence, because no one has come forward to verify this story. Even if it's true, it would not even make the list of major supply chain software failures. In 2004, Sainsbury lost $527 million, and in 2001 Kmart canceled a new supply chain system after spending $130 million on it.[5] Lack of an adequate supply chain system soon drove Kmart into bankruptcy.

Verification

This section defines verification in a Taguchi context as the process of ensuring that programs meet their *design* specifications. Verification is carried out primarily through unit testing as opposed to system or subsystem testing. With Taguchi Methods, the first stage of verification is actually validating the parameter optimization. The next step is verifying the design. The most important part of conventional software development processes is verifying the code itself as a unit, component, module, or subsystem. Much has been written about program verification, much of which has been summarized by Humphrey.[6] The current research on formal methods is a descendant of early efforts to prove programs correct (to *verify* them), as you would prove a mathematical theorem. This can be done for small programs of about 150 lines of code. But it is as difficult and painstaking as proving a mathematical theorem, and it usually requires the same degree of training and talent. So-called "straight-line code" is usually transparent to its creator. If it's well-documented, it is equally transparent to any trained reader of computer program codes. Most low-level programming errors are introduced when a loop, branch, or function call is introduced. Structured methods have been developed to verify for loops, while loops, and repeat-until loops, but they are rather clunky and are seldom used by programmers, who usually just execute the loop in their heads as an intuitive verification. Use of these structured methods is like solving an algebra problem by following all the steps explicitly and quoting the rules. Such analysis is not very interesting, but it always exposes any errors (just as it does in algebra).

Clearly, such methods verify code rather than design, but the promise of Taguchi Methods is that the developers may verify design directly. Case Study 18.1 illustrates an early such Taguchi application. Only about half a dozen Taguchi software design case studies have been published, most of which are quoted as examples or referred to in this book.

Case Study 18.1: Taguchi Methods for RTOS Design Verification[7]

This case study illustrates the use of a series of L_8 parameter design experiments as a strategy for selecting a set of real-time operating system features that provide optimum performance against the stated goals. The parameters were chosen for a radio set controller architecture and were tried in a test-bed environment. The use of Taguchi Methods ensured that the product would behave in a predictable and optimal fashion. The developer of this application and author of the case study presents it as a template to help any software engineer enhance real-time operating system (RTOS) performance for other applications.

The application is to computer scheduling and operation of a tactical VHF (very high frequency) radio set. For some years, advanced military radios have been more like computers that send and receive both digital and analog signals, rather than solving equations and presenting their solutions. Early systems had the digital control logic distributed through the radio circuitry, but the emergence of inexpensive powerful microprocessors led to their use as stored-program controllers for such complex multifunction radio systems. As these programs grew in size and complexity, they began to require operating systems, and because radio communication takes place in real time, hence RTOS. It is a little-known fact that most of the microprocessors sold each year do not appear in desktop computers or enterprise servers. Instead, they go into dedicated or embedded applications like this case. Some automobiles today have as many as nine. Just as the engineer can purchase a general-purpose microprocessor off the shelf and customize it to his application, he can buy an RTOS for that same chip and customize or parameterize it for a particular application functionality. The VHF radio in this case study carries out a set of independent concurrent processes under preemptive priority scheduling. Because radios today are basically digital computers, they generate interrupts, which must be handled by the control microprocessor and its RTOS's interrupt scheduling routine (ISR). The control software running in the controller depends on the RTOS to provide communication between software tasks and hardware interrupts (as software ISRs). The three communication requirements are ISR to program task, task to task, and task to hardware (such as turning a virtual knob or making a menu selection). Each of these three cases has two different operating system "mechanisms" for interprocessor communication. For ISR-to-task or task-to-task communication, you can specify either a mailbox or a queue, but for task-to-hardware, the choices are a semaphore or a resource lock.

During design, control and data flows were constructed for radio and traffic operations and their primary communication mechanism, messaging, signaling, and resource lock. The goal was to optimize these communication flows without any possibility of multitask contention, which could lock up the radio in the middle of a critical message. An experiment was designed to determine the correct parameters for optimal RTOS performance for this embedded application. The following control factors over which the designer has some influence were chosen:

- **Processor speed:** Choice of 12MHz or 30MHz clock speeds
- **Messaging:** Choice of mailboxes or circular queues
- **Signaling:** Two methods for messaging between tasks are events and mailboxes
- **Resource locking:** Use of either resource locks or semaphores to prevent simultaneous access to hardware resources by competing tasks

The exogenous noise factors over which the designer has no control, but that result from the radio's operation in its tactical environment, were as follows:

- **Interrupt mix:** The mix of various interrupts generated by the system
- **Interrupt rate:** The rate at which interrupts are received by the RTOS

For the experimental design, the control factors were as follows:

Factor	Level 1	Level 2
Processor speed (MHz)	12	30
Messaging	Mailbox	Queue
Signaling	Event	Mailbox
Resource locking	Resource	Semaphore

The input signal is a series of events entered as interrupts (t_{ISR}). Output is measured as when an event is queued, when it starts execution, and when it finishes (t_{end}). Ideally the system should process the messages as fast as possible, so a smaller-the-better method with a signal-to-noise (SN) ratio is

$$SN = -10 \log \{\Sigma \ (t_{end} - t_{ISR})^2 \ / \ N\}$$

The average case was 7 times per second, the worst case was 30 times per second, and failure was defined as an interrupt rate of N times per second.

The L_8 matrix for this Taguchi parameter design was as follows:

Case	Speed	Messaging	Signaling	Resource Lock
1	12	Mailbox	Event	Resource
2	12	Mailbox	Semaphore	Semaphore
3	12	Queue	Event	Semaphore
4	12	Queue	Semaphore	Resource
5	30	Mailbox	Event	Semaphore
6	30	Mailbox	Semaphore	Resource
7	30	Queue	Event	Resource
8	30	Queue	Semaphore	Semaphore

The SN ratios for data rates of 7 and 30 messages per second were as follows:

Case	SN 7	SN 30
1	−27.7	−27.7
2	−27.7	−27.7
3	−32.0	−32.3
4	−32.0	−32.6
5	−21.7	−21.8
6	−21.8	−21.8
7	−28.7	−28.4
8	−28.5	−28.3

A study of these results indicates that the dominant factors are processor speed and messaging, which were comparable in amplitude. Thus, the optimal choice is a 30MHz clock speed and the use of mailboxes for messaging. The author of this case study goes on to validate the results of his choice of 30MHz and mailboxes with 12MHz and queues. The performance difference was 10.3 db at 7 events per second and 10.7 db at 30 events per second. 10 db amounts to a significant performance difference. The other factors, signaling and resource locking, did not contribute in any significant way to the optimal results, so they can be chosen at the designer's convenience.

The 10 db performance enhancement caused by choosing a processor having 2.5 times the clock speed is a noteworthy optimization. This is primarily because of the RTOS's ability to run its timer loop, the main overhead in the system, twice as fast. In fact, it reduced message latency from 40.6 ms to 12.1 ms. But at what cost? The author computed the Taguchi quality loss function associated with use of the more expensive part. He discovered that the quality loss for the current radio system, using the slower, less-expensive chip, is $78 and for future systems would be $215. The cost of upgrading from the 12MHz chip to the 30MHz chip is minor. Compared to the quality loss, it is a very desirable design option.

Verification should be done as early in the design process as possible, before any code is written and available for testing of validation. To do this, the design logic must be represented precisely. In the early days of computing, flowcharts were used and verified before coding began. Today, pseudocode is often employed to serve the same function. Automatically produced flowcharts are not only used by reverse-engineering tools such as Xcellerator and Texas Instruments TEI but also are the mainstay of large-scale design support systems such as Rational Rose. The design of large, complex software systems is hardly possible without some sort of pseudocode or graphical design tool employing UML to allow design verification at the precoded logic level stage. The ability to model logic for the various loop constructs is critical, because that is where most errors are introduced. As long as the intended behaviors of all the program's high-level architectural constructs are known, design verification can take place.[8] A precise specification of the design's intended function helps you define the preconditions and thus ensures that the logic handles every case properly. It is desirable to consider all possible cases at the logic level and be sure they are handled. In large development projects, design reviews are generally used as an intuitive verification process as design and development proceed. After 50 years of program design and development, no single method for program verification has become commonplace. Until formal methods are more widely available, the developer's best option is to use conventional means supplemented by Taguchi Methods.

Validation

This section defines validation in a Taguchi context as the process of ensuring that the program meets the *functional* specification. In other words, no functions have been left out, and gratuitous (unspecified) features and unintended side effects are not present. It's not possible to test all the combinations the program will encounter. Therefore, you must consider which ones to test, how to test them, and what degree of confidence these tests can produce in the program's validity.

Case Study 18.2: Taguchi Methods for Software Validation[9]

This case study was used by Taguchi et al.[9] to show how the method can be used for a software validation application. It is common knowledge that not all the paths or threads of even a simple program can actually be tested, due to combinatorial explosion. This case study illustrates this fact for a rather simple program and yields insight into how to validate such a program with a high degree of confidence.

Consider a shared printer that serves a number of users over an office LAN. Server printers like this typically have a lot of options. This printer has five paper trays, five print ranges, six choices of the number of pages per sheet (1, 2, 3, 4, 6, 8), four duplex options, two collation choices (stapled or not), two orientations (portrait or landscape), and six possible paper scales. This yields 144,000 combinations that the program must be able to deal with—but it gets worse. There are yes/no choices for 11 print options, or $2^{11} = 2,048$ combinations. Multiplied by 144,000, this gives us 294,912,000 possible operational modes for this shared printer.

The developers cannot check them all, so which ones should they choose, and with what confidence of validation? Even if it were possible to check out one every minute, 24 hours a day, 365 days a year, it would take 561 years. If a program could be written to check out one combination every second, it would still take almost ten years—at least three times the product's expected market life. By the time the automated testing were finished, the product would be two generations out of date! And this is pretty simple as computer programs for enterprise software go. In the past, test plans aimed at the most common or likely user choices and checked them out over a month or two. Testing was complete when the time was up, when the product shipped, when the error rate went down, or when a week went by with no new errors discovered. Taguchi Methods for software testing employ an orthogonal array to improve both area coverage and detection rate. The Taguchi case study chose eight factors at three levels:

Factor Letter	Factor Name	Level 1	Level 2	Level 3
A	Staple	No	Yes	
B	Side	2 to 1	1 to 2	2 to 2
C	Number of copies	3	20	50
D	Number of pages	2	20	50
E	Paper tray	Normal	Tray 5	Tray 3
F	Darkness	Normal	Light	Dark
G	Enlarge	100%	78%	128%
H	Execution	From PC	At machine	From memory

These test parameters attempt to cover the range on each factor. They produce the following L_{18} orthogonal matrix:

	A	B	C	D	E	F	G	H
1	1	1	1	1	1	1	1	1
2	1	1	2	2	2	2	2	2
3	1	1	3	3	3	3	3	3
4	1	2	1	1	2	2	3	3
5	1	2	2	2	3	3	1	1
6	1	2	3	3	1	1	2	2
7	1	3	1	2	1	3	2	3
8	1	3	2	3	2	1	3	1
9	1	3	3	1	3	2	1	2
10	2	1	1	3	3	2	2	1

	A	B	C	D	E	F	G	H
11	2	1	2	1	1	3	3	2
12	2	1	3	2	2	1	1	3
13	2	2	1	2	3	1	3	2
14	2	2	2	3	1	2	1	3
15	2	2	3	1	2	3	2	1
16	2	3	1	3	2	3	1	2
17	2	3	2	1	3	1	2	3
18	2	3	3	2	1	2	3	1

The case study reports the results of only 18 tests, according to each row in the orthogonal test array. For each test, if the system provides the proper response, the result is 0. If it fails, the result is 1. After the tests are run and the data collected, a set of two-way response tables are generated—an A×B table, an A×C table, and so on. The entry in each table is the sum of the 1s in its responses. For example, there are nine combinations of $B_i C_j$ (for i = 1,2,3 and j = 1,2,3), and there are two runs of $B_2 C_3$ in an L_{18} array. The result in the tests was 2 in $B_2 C_3$, and 2 out of 2 is 100%. In contrast, there were two failures in $A_1 B_2$ out of three occurrences, or 66.7%. Finally, the 100% failure combinations are investigated to see why they occurred. Note that this method localizes the failures to a program segment of code but does not necessarily identify them. Taguchi reports that three international firms have used this method in this application. All three achieved 400% improvement in both area coverage and failure detection rate.

Reliability and validity are closely related, because the valid implementation of a responsive, verified design meets its user's requirements. Furthermore, predictive validity in a software system is tantamount to software trustworthiness. Reliability refers to the consistency of a number of measurements using the same measurement methods. Validity means that the measurement taken measures what you intended to measure.[10] Obviously, a measurement may be reliable but not valid. Software metrics researchers classify validity into *criterion-related validity* and *content validity*. The former is often called *predictive validity* and measures how well the software will perform to its user's requirements in the future, clearly a primary measure of trustworthiness. The latter is a measure of how well the validity measurement covers the subject. Kan uses the analogy of a rifle accuracy test to show the difference between reliability and validity.[11] If you take several test shots with a new rifle, and they produce a neat 1-inch grouping at 100 yards at the edge of the target, the rifle has reliable accuracy. On the other hand, if they produce a 10-inch scatter group with its center in the middle of the target, the rifle has valid accuracy. The ideal is a small grouping in the center of the target; this shows that the rifle is both reliable and valid. Having gained this result by careful adjustment, the target shooter can go to his or her next match certain of the gun's trustworthiness, or the hunter can take the rifle into the field confident that it will be a trustworthy firearm. With software testing, we want to establish tests that show that the software is both reliable and valid and thus will be found completely trustworthy by its users. Like sighting in the rifle, there is a bit of tension between reliability and validity, and testing metrics need to respond to both requirements. Of course, such measurements in software are multidimensional compared to sighting in a simple mechanical device such as a firearm.

Testing and Evaluation

Testing and evaluation usually begin after the coding is done. This phase is intended to ensure that the coded application actually does the things it purports to accomplish, and to the users' satisfaction. Testing and evaluating test results are the means employed to validate and verify the final software application. Watts Humphrey, again following the pioneering G. J. Myers, defines seven types of software tests:[12]

- **Unit or module tests** *verify* single programs or modules. These are typically conducted in isolation and in special test environments.

- **Integration tests** *verify* the interfaces between system parts—subsystems, modules, and components.

- **External function tests** *verify* the external system functions as stated in the external specifications.

- **Regression tests** *validate* the system's previous functionality, ensuring that improvements and corrections have not resulted in the loss of previous functionality.

- **System tests** both *verify and validate* the system to its initial objectives.

- **Acceptance tests** *validate* the system to the user's requirements.

- **Installation tests** *validate* the system's installability and operability.

Much has been written about the software system testing that has grown up in the three decades since Myers. We make no attempt to summarize these writings here. We're content to describe the seven testing methods or means as they contribute to the verification and validation of a software system under development. In the Taguchi context, we seek to evaluate by testing the software's trustworthiness as well.

Testing methods at any level are often called either *black box* or *white box* tests. The term *black box* originated in engineering labs when a student was given a sealed box that had two input terminals and two output terminals and that contained some combination of resistors, inductors, and capacitors. The student was told to determine the precise network in the box by external testing alone. He would usually start with input from a sine wave generator, and then, by increasing frequency and observing the output on an oscilloscope, measure the unknown circuit's response. Then he would use a square wave input, and then an impulse input, and so on. The idea was that the student had to learn the *functional performance* of the network in the black box without knowing what was in it, and then construct a hypothesis regarding its contents. White-box testing arose in the early days of software testing as a metaphorical chiasmus to black-box testing. Here the goal was to verify the *design performance* of the box's contents knowing exactly what was in it and having full access to the designer's documentation. In a well-designed and well-documented system, members of the development team can apply both types of methods in support of design verification and functional validation as the system develops, starting with units, going to components, then modules, then subsystems, and finally the system itself. Integration testing follows the assembly of components and in many ways is a bridge between black-box and white-box testing.[13] The many aspects of integration testing are covered in the next chapter.

Software testing presents an interesting problem: Because more testing almost always yields more bugs, when should you stop? The law of diminishing returns applies at a certain point, but if testing and consequent debugging go beyond that, the law of increasing returns often pops up (see Sidebar 18.2). While the number of bugs goes down exponentially with testing, the time to find them goes up exponentially. Experts estimate that testing may uncover only 50 to 70% of the bugs in a program.[14] Until the use of formal methods and specification-based program development becomes widespread, testing after coding will continue to be required.

Sidebar 18.2: Testing and Debugging Anomalies

In the 1950s, one of the authors worked with a team to convert a large assembly language-coded linear programming package from the Univac 1105, which was a two-address architecture, to the Univac 1107, a single-address architecture. The original program contained only three comments in 25,000 lines of code, and all three of them were false. The program was manually converted line by line by a team of programmers who knew a lot about linear programming and who were familiar with both computers. The computer center had an 1105 with the code running properly, as well as a brand-new 1107, so we could do functional-level whole-system black-box tests. The first test run indicated 166 coding errors. As the testing of improved versions progressed, the number of errors fell exponentially until only three bugs were left. The team set a cigar box on the 1107 computer console. They invited members and curious onlookers to put in a dollar bill and a slip of paper inscribed with their name and the number of bugs they thought would appear on the next run. Most guessed one or two. One cynic guessed eight. The author guessed 18. He was sneered at by the others, who had less testing experience and were not prepared for the outcome. The result was 15 new bugs!

Also to be noted is the fact that as the number of bugs goes down exponentially with testing, the time to find them goes up exponentially. In 1956, Bell Labs brought out an interpretive floating-point system for the IBM 650 computer that occupied 1,200 of its 2,000 magnetic drum memory locations. The structures programming group at Boeing-Wichita set a goal of providing the same functionality in only 600 locations. It took three programmers three months to achieve all this functionality, but they used 616 memory locations. It took a month to remove eight lines of code, another month to remove five more, and yet another month to remove the last three.

Unit testing is usually white-box testing aimed at testing as many of the internal paths as possible through a small piece (unit) of code. A path is a sequence of instruction executions or a *thread* that leads from the unit program's entry to its exit. The use of functions in C and objects in C++ and Java has dramatically simplified unit testing and made it much more effective. Unit testing by the programmer who knows it best has the fault of its virtue. Because the programmer designed and/or wrote it, he or she may be blind to unexpected actions or side effects. The person who created the faults in a program is the person least likely to recognize them. The person most likely to recognize them has a steep learning curve to get to the same point of understanding as the program's creator. It is generally not possible to test all the possible paths of even a simple program. Even if it were, that would not guarantee correctness in the face of unexpected or pathological inputs. In addition to object-oriented technology, the conscious anticipation of later white-box unit testing during design has advanced the ability to test almost every aspect of a program's behavior.[15] As products become more complex, testing becomes more expensive and time-consuming. Defects tend to mask other defects or problems. They may even interact to make their discovery and correction more difficult, or even mask the effects of yet other defects. Thus, as noted in Sidebar 18.2, as programs become larger and more complex, unit testing finds fewer defects, and it costs more to find them.

Although it's usually thought of as a late process, *integration testing* may be employed whenever a developer tries to get two program units or modules to work together, the most elementary being a function call or object invocation. Testing pioneer G. J Myers proposed two types of integration testing—bottom-up and top-down, which are described in Tables 18.1 and 18.2.[16] We will turn to the details in the next chapter, which discusses integration testing of the entire system. It's clear that integration testing is best done at each stage of code accumulation, because errors undiscovered at integration points are much more difficult to find and correct later. Here we simply note that bottom-up testing is heuristic, intuitive, personal, and localized, whereas top-down testing is algorithmic, structured, team-based, and global. The former is often used for small development projects, and the latter is almost always required for large programming projects.

TABLE 18.1
Bottom-Up Integration Testing

Approach	Early testing to both verify and validate modules. Modules can be integrated in clusters. Emphasis on module performance and functionality.
Advantages	Test stubs are not needed. Errors in critical modules are found early. Manpower requirements are low.
Problems	Test drivers are required. Modules are usually not yet working programs. Interface errors are discovered late.
Remarks	At any point in the process, more code is available than with top-down testing. Bottom-up testing is more intuitive than top-down testing. The strategy is relatively ad hoc as modules become available.

TABLE 18.2
Top-Down Integration Testing

Approach	The control program must be completely tested first. Modules are carefully integrated one at a time. The major emphasis is on interface testing.
Advantages	No test drivers are needed. The control program and the first layer of modules constitute an early prototype of the whole system. Interface errors are discovered early. Modular features aid debugging.
Problems	Test stubs are needed at each level in the program hierarchy. A planned, structured approach slows manpower buildup. Errors in critical modules at low levels are found late.
Remarks	A "working" program early on builds both team and management confidence. It is difficult to maintain a purely top-down integration testing strategy practice.

External function testing is employed to *verify* the external system functions as stated in the external specifications. It is a significant part of any test plan and the ultimate user's major criterion of satisfaction. As noted earlier in this chapter, it is the major component in verification of any software system. The major requirements for an external function test are a file of input data and corresponding expected (and hence, specified) output data. The respective input and output data files may be generated by the program being replaced by the new application, by a competitive program, by a previous noncomputer-based system, or by a manual analysis. In any case, the external function test indicates the cases for which the program works to specification and the cases for which it does not. It is always wise to include in a test plan pathological examples or data cases intended to exercise the exception handling capability of the system under test. This latter type of testing is particularly important in numerical applications such as linear programming, integer programming, mixed integer programming, crew scheduling, or any other application in which a small numerical error in input can result in a costly or inappropriate business decision.

Regression testing validates the system's previous functionality, ensuring that improvements and corrections in the new version have not resulted in the loss of previous functionality. Naturally it is employed only when an existing system is upgraded or replaced with a later version. Over the years, some complex systems have been literally maintained or upgraded out of existence. It may be done after major maintenance or installation of the vendor's bug fixes as well. It is common practice to employ novice programmers to maintain existing program inventories for obvious reasons: it is less costly, it gives trainees experience, and it teaches them how the firm's data processing applications work. Unfortunately, these programs were written by much more highly skilled programmers, who may have employed software technology and techniques the new programmers do not understand. Regression testing is the organization's best defense against negative maintenance, as discussed in the next chapter.

System testing is done to both *verify and validate* that the system satisfies its initial objectives. This is the final test made by the software's designers and developers. Success means that the product is ready for the marketplace.

Acceptance testing is done to *validate* that the system meets the user's requirements. Such testing is almost purely functional. However, performance aspects depending on technical decisions and trade-offs may also play a role.

Installation testing is done to *validate* the completed system's installability and operability. This type of testing is done by and for the system's operators as opposed to the users. The payroll department may be completely happy with the functionality of a payroll system that takes 12 hours every Friday to run the payroll using one processor. However, the MIS department would surely prefer a system that employed two processors and that completed the payroll in only one shift. That would not only simplify operations and shift assignments but also would allow the payroll to be rerun on second shift in case a glitch or power failure occurred.

An excellent objective for software development process improvement would surely be the withering away of testing as a component of the overall development process. Formal methods will be a big step toward this goal but will not completely eliminate testing.[17] Testing is so large and costly a part of the development process that we should do everything possible to reduce it to a minimum. The French automotive engineer Rene Panhard and Emile Levassor built their first automobile in 1890. Upon seeing the first Rolls-Royce Silver Ghost in 1911, Panhard is said to have remarked, "Mon Dieu, it is a triumph of craftsmanship over good design." The goal of using Taguchi Methods upstream in software design and development is to make the software creation process a triumph of good design over downstream craftsmanship and expensive rework. Craftsmanship in the form of "build and fix" has been used for 50 years. It is too slow and too expensive and has never worked very well. Moreover, it does not support the development of the increasingly larger and more complex software systems that our technological future will depend on.

Key Points

- The software development process includes testing, verification, validation, and code debugging to ensure proper function and reliability.

- Verification is the process of ensuring that programs meet their design specifications.

- A case study demonstrated the use of Taguchi Methods for program verification.

- Validation is the process of ensuring that a program meets its functional specification.

- A case study demonstrated the use of Taguchi Methods for program validation.

- Seven types of software tests verify and validate software.

- It is impossible to explicitly test every execution path through a large program.

- Black-box testing strategies test the functionality of each unit of code.

- White-box testing strategies test the fidelity to design for each unit of code.

- Integration testing tests the interoperability of tested units of code.

- Bottom-up integration testing is an intuitive process of testing assemblies as the system is built.

- Top-down testing is a structured, algorithmic process that begins with the control program coded as a series of stubs or pseudo-programs that are later replaced in a top-down fashion by actual code.

- Regression testing is employed to ensure that new versions do not lose functionality over previous ones.

Additional Resources

http://www.prenhallprofessional.com/title/0131872508

http://www.agilenty.com/publications

Internet Exercises

1. Investigate the contributions of Watts Humphrey and G. J. Myers to software trustworthiness.

2. Find the current state of development and utilization of Praxis High Integrity Systems Z on the Internet.

Review Questions

1. Define software verification, validation, and debugging.

2. Describe the seven types of tests done to verify and validate software during development.

3. What is integration testing?

4. Describe the pros and cons of bottom-up integration testing.

5. Describe the pros and cons of top-down integration testing.

Discussion Questions and Projects

1. Why is it difficult to maintain a purely top-down integration testing strategy in practice?

2. If testing is so critical to software function and reliability, why is eliminating it a desirable objective in improving software trustworthiness?

Problems

1. Replicate the paradigm of Case Study 18.2 for a program, preferably a device driver you have written.

2. Compare top-down and bottom-up testing for efficiency, effectiveness, and ease of use. Which would you use in your next development project? Why?

Endnotes

[1]P. K. Ross, "The Exterminators," *IEEE Spectrum*, September 2005, pp. 36–41.

[2]R. N. Charette, "Why Software Fails," *IEEE Spectrum*, September 2005, pp. 42–49.

[3]W. S. Humphrey, *Managing the Software Process* (Reading, MA: Addison-Wesley, 1990), p. 192.

[4]G. J. Myers, *Software Reliability, Principles and Practices* (New York: John Wiley and Sons, 1976).

[5]Op cit Charette, p. 47.

[6]W. S. Humphrey, *A Discipline for Software Engineering* (Reading, MA: Addison-Wesley, 1995), pp. 418–439.

[7]H. S. Forstrom, "Robust Optimization of a Real-Time Operating System Using Parameter Design," in G. Taguchi, S. Chowdhury, Y. Wu, *Taguchi's Quality Engineering Handbook* (New York: John Wiley and Sons, 2004) pp. 1324–1344.

[8]W. S. Humphrey, *Introduction to the Personal Software Process* (Reading, MA: Addison-Wesley, 2004), p. 240.

[9]ASI, "Application of Taguchi Methods to Software System Testing," in G. Taguchi, S. Chowdhury, Y. Wu, *Taguchi's Quality Engineering Handbook* (New York: John Wiley and Sons, 2004) pp. 425–433.

[10]S. H. Kan, *Metrics and Models in Software Quality Engineering* (Reading, MA: Addison-Wesley, 1995), p. 68.

[11]Ibid, p. 70.

[12]Op cit Humphrey (1990), p. 194.

[13]Ibid, p. 193.

[14]Ibid, p. 194.

[15]W. S. Humphrey, *Introduction to the Team Software Process* (Reading, MA: Addison-Wesley, 1999), p. 131.

[16]Op cit Humphrey (1995), p. 198.

[17]Op cit Ross, p. 41.

CHAPTER 19

Integration, Extension, and Maintenance for Trustworthiness

It doesn't matter how many parts a machine has as long as each one is made perfectly.
—Sir Henry Royce in 1938

Mon Dieu, it is a triumph of craftsmanship over good design.
—The French automotive engineer Panhard on first seeing a Rolls-Royce in 1911

Overview

Enterprise business software is designed for particular applications but always runs in the context or environment of an overall business data processing system. Applications thus must be integrated by testing in an actual operating environment or a virtual test version of it. In some cases critical new software may be run in parallel to ensure that all situations are tested with real data. Successful applications software is often extended or upgraded to meet new application requirements. The new version must be tested for functionality, regression-tested for continuity, and integration-tested for conformity. Maintenance programmers often are less experienced than the team that wrote the software and thus must be well led and supplied with good tools. Taguchi Methods are well suited not only for software extension but also for software maintenance.

Chapter Outline

- Completing the Development Cycle

- Integration

- Extension

- Maintenance

- Key Points

- Additional Resources

- Internet Exercises

- Review Questions

- Discussion Questions and Projects

- Problems

- Endnotes

Completing the Development Cycle

The last three phases of the development cycle close the cycle's loop and bring what has been learned in development and the marketplace back to the "drawing board" for the next version. Successful software may enjoy many cycles of revision and regeneration over its total life-cycle design lifetime. For business enterprise application software, seven or eight versions of a fundamentally good design over 20 years is not unknown. Although software is not manufactured like hard goods, it is designed, redesigned, and redesigned again, many times. This holds true not only for applications software sold by third-party vendors, but also for software developed by management information system (MIS) organizations for use by a single company. The two rules of thumb from the earliest days of business software development were as follows:

- A new application must be developed three times to get it right.

- An application's maintenance cost over five years is equal to the package's initial development cost.

The first may not be so different from the situation with hardware engineering and development, but the second is very different indeed.

Integration

Applications are designed as integral functional subsets of a system, but they always run in the context of an integrated business system. Thus, they must be tested at a system level to ensure that even though they may run to specification, they do not also cause unintended problems or side effects in other software applications in the same system. Software application testing is generally done in several steps:

- Unit testing of individual components or modules to specification

- Subsystem or application testing to the application's overall functional specification

- System testing to ensure compatibility of the new or improved application with the whole business system

- Regression testing to ensure that while the new or improved software does what it is supposed to, it doesn't fail to do properly the things it has always done correctly before

The basic problem with system-level software integration is how to assemble hundreds of components that are not necessarily working properly yet into a complete system that must now be validated to do so. Even if you could be sure that, as Sir Henry said, "Each part is working perfectly," this would not necessarily guarantee that the whole system will do so. From the earlier unit-testing phases, you can assume that 50 to 70% of the bugs have been found and corrected. From the later low-level integration testing, you can assume that most of the interface bugs have been found, and perhaps another 10% of the intrinsic unit-level problems.

Sidebar 19.1: The Supermarine Spitfire

Rolls-Royce was founded by an aviation enthusiast early in the 20th century. It was then, and is still today, primarily a manufacturer of aircraft engines. In 1938 the firm designed a radical new V-12 double overhead-cam aircraft engine named the Merlin to go in a pylon racing float-plane called the Supermarine Spitfire. The chief engineer, Henry Royce, was criticized for designing so complex an engine with so many moving parts. His famous response was, "It does-n't matter how many parts a machine has as long as each one is made perfectly." The airplane won the race, and this remarkable engine went on to power the famous Spitfire fighters that won the Battle of Britain in World War II. Later in the war the North American P-51 Mustang was designed as a long-range fighter to escort Boeing B-17 bombers over Germany. It used the Merlin engine design made under license by Allison in the United States, but the American-made engines were not made to RR standards of perfection and did not hold up as well. Over time, the Britain-based Mustang planes' engines were replaced by the RR version. Sir Henry is both right and wrong. He is right if "each part is made perfectly," but the ability to make each part perfectly at an acceptable price is rarely possible. The cost of "making each part perfectly" is also part of the RR motorcar legend. In any era, a Rolls-Royce automobile costs as much as or more than the average American home. When his automotive customers complained about his high prices, Royce was known to comment, "If you purchase a Rolls-Royce, you only cry once." Sir Henry seems to have had a powerful command of the ontological "if."

Extension

Software is usually released in major numbered versions, such as 1.0, 2.0, 3.0. However, circumstances may require a minor extension, updating, or upgrading to meet the terms of a new union contract, a new tax law or other legal record-keeping requirement, a new Financial Accounting Standards Board (FASB) recommendation, an acquisition, a challenge to the vendor's competitive advantage, or for many other reasons. Such extensions or upgrades are usually called something like version 3.1 or even 3.4.2 in some rapidly changing business application areas. Upgrades and extensions of software functionality are a promising application area for Taguchi Methods, which are ideal for product improvement or redesign. Taguchi Methods excel when design data is already available. So naturally an enhancement allows the designer to evaluate the value of modifications with the quality loss function and thus see what the real value of an enhancement will be in the next release and later releases. New features can also be evaluated for their functional enhancement to the product by parameter analysis, which works best in a test-bed environment. What better test bed for any upgrade than the current product?

Case Study 19.1: Extending the Capability of an Electronic Warfare System[1]

Electronic countermeasure (ECM) systems are multiplexed computer-controlled microwave (radar) transceivers that intercept an enemy's radar signal. They send back in real time a masking signal only slightly stronger than the expected reflection that tells the enemy radar operator the wrong signature, the wrong distance, and even the wrong number of potential targets. You cannot hide a carrier fleet group, but if you make all 28 destroyers appear to have the same signature as the carrier, the enemy cannot aim a missile accurately at the real carrier.

The software for such systems must be continually upgraded to be able to detect and counter new enemy radars, new radar frequencies, and new targeting and scanning techniques. This is a natural application for Taguchi Methods, because the software extensions are additions to a tested library of proven countermeasure software algorithms. Also, tactical ECM systems must work properly in the presence of uncontrollable noise factors. Robustness is critical in such systems, and trustworthy software is essential, because the alternative is assured destruction! For the system under analysis in this case study, software upgrades are made on a weekly basis, but checking them against all the recognized emitter types takes 16 hours. The goal of the Taguchi analysis was to enhance robustness while reducing weekly testing time. The noise factors in the study were variation in emitter characteristics over the range of recognized emitter types; variation in emitter position, including amplitude (nearness) and azimuth (direction of received signal arrival); variation in emitter mode; and actual background (electrical atmospheric) noise.

An L_{18} orthogonal array was selected to model one two-level factor and up to seven three-level factors. The factors in the array are as follows:

Factor	Level 1	Level 2	Level 3
Overall mean	—	—	—
Frequency diversity	Single	Multiple	—
Frequency	Low	Medium	High
Emission type	Continuous wave (CW)	Stable	Agile
Scan type	Steady	Circular	Raster
Peak power	Nominal	Medium	Low
Arrival angle	Bore sight	Offset 1	Offset 2
Illumination	Short	Medium	100%
Background	None	Low density	High density

Next, 18 emitters or Taguchi experiments were selected to cover the parameters represented in the factors. The major characteristics were single radio frequency (RF), high RF, stable emission mode, circular scan, and short illumination time. For example, the first 2 of the 18 experiments went as follows:

Number	Mean	Diversity	Frequency	Emission	Scan	Power	Illumination
1	0	Single	High	CW	Steady	Nominal	100%
2	1	Single	High	Stable	Circular	Medium	Short

The developer's choice of experimental parameters was informed by extensive experience with the system and a history of weekly upgrades to the software. We will not try to explain the case study at this level of technical detail, because we are merely focusing on the methodology. You're encouraged to read the referenced article.[1] The signal-to-noise (SN) ratio for this experiment was calculated as follows:

SN = −20 log {(total defects) / (n + 1)}

Because the problem type is "maximum is best," the SN for a perfect system is 0 dB. Any performance error will result in a negative SN ratio. The "defects plus 1" expression was used because log (0) is undefined and log (1) = 0. To compute the SN ratio for all 18 experiments in the array, the value of n would be 18. However, to compute the SN for RF diversity alone, n would be 9, because "multiple" appears in nine of the experiments and "single" in the other nine. The author calculates the SN ratio for multiple diversity as −10.6 dB and for single source as −7.8 dB, based on the errors detected in a particular testing session.

This case study confirmed that each week's upgraded software can be tested in only four hours for the 18 emitter types modeled. This was considered significant, because sensitivity to test results did not show any additional system weakness when the more-extensive monthly test was carried out later. The use of a Taguchi analysis to reduce testing time for the weekly software upgrades by a factor of 4 is quite remarkable. However, the most amazing result of this application of the method was that the careful choice of 18 emitter types by the designer, together with the operational noise factors, surpassed the performance results of testing for each radar type individually!

Maintenance

Maintenance must be done when bugs are found in the software by vendor staff or client users. An enterprise resource planning (ERP) software vendor with 400 software engineers in its development organization may have 80 or 100 staff in its support organization. Many of these support staff are domain experts who advise client user staff on the best use of the firm's software. They must be sensitive to situations in which the software is not performing to the client's requirements. Most of their work is of a true support nature, referred to as "hand holding" or, in really messy cases, "diaper changing." In some fraction of cases it amounts to documenting errors in such a way that they can be repeated in a laboratory test setting. Many, if not most, of the support situations are in the broader context of the vendor's software, as modified or customized by the client. It runs with a database management system (Oracle, DB2, Informix, Microsoft SQL Server), on an operating system (Microsoft Windows XP, OS/400, UNIX, Linux). It suddenly exhibits a glitch because a change in some component of the support software exhibits an unexpected and unintended inconsistency. In more complex corporate global networked environments, multiple vendor ERP software applications run on machines from multiple manufacturers, each with a different operating system. A minor upgrade or bug fix from one vendor can make ripples throughout the whole pond. While the client firm running such a system has long since had to assume system responsibility, it may need vendor software expert backup at a moment's notice. This kind of support goes far beyond calling someone and asking, "What do I do if...?" Usually one or two people from the client firm have the unpublished telephone numbers of one or two experts from the software vendor firm, plus the implicit authorization to call one of them to travel around the world at a moment's notice to help in an emergency.

In any case, what is learned in these situations must be shared first within the vendor's support and development groups and then with all the potentially affected client users of the software. Bug and change reports are posted on vendor Web sites subscribed to by clients or often are broadcast to client MIS groups to be inserted. This happens only after they have been thoroughly tested to make sure that they cause no further "ripples" themselves by introducing unintended consequences. This may mean testing every combination of computer version, database management system (DBMS) software, and operating system. This is clearly a situation that calls for the Taguchi Methods to test a combination of parameters for a combination of noise factors all in one go with special sensitivity to any possible interactions.

Case Study 19.2: Field Maintenance of Software Systems[2]

The ability to perform major bug fixes over the Internet, and even "ship" software over the Internet, has a downside backlash on final testing before shipping by software vendors. Of course, every attempt is made to fix known bugs, but at this stage the remaining bugs are mostly unknown and soon to be discovered by the new users. The authors of this case study were inspired by a paper titled "Evaluation of Signal Factor and Functionality for Software" by Genichi Taguchi.[3] If a Taguchi final vendor test and debugging session is carried out using the method of this case study, it can become the basis for later field maintenance of the software on the many customers' premises. The approach is to allocate items of concern or signal factors to an L_{18} or L_{36} orthogonal array, run the software for a combination of signal factors in each row of the array, and assign a result of 0 or 1, depending on whether the result is normal or an error. Later, you can calculate a variance or interaction to identify which combination of factors was most likely to appear as a bug.

In this case, the process began with the beta version of the firm's software, because the beta version was known to have several bugs. This allows the process to start with a known "bug baseline," allowing the developers to certify its efficacy. As the software is maintained in the field, the new bug reports are added to the corrected software profile, and the experiments are rerun to provide a continuing maintenance profile. This is especially important in maintenance, because new bugs are often a result of the use of two ostensibly "bug-free" features used in combination with a particular data set. The Taguchi orthogonal array method is used in lieu of complete testing of all combinations. Therefore, evolving an L_{18} or L_{36} array over time to discriminate in favor of testing certain combinations (profiling?) is a powerful maintenance technique. As signal factors, the authors chose eight factors that can be selected by users and allocated them to an L_{18} array. Because this is a case study of a company's actual software product, naturally the authors chose not to tell their readers what bugs their software exhibited and what multiple bug profiles they should search for in maintenance.

Sidebar 19.2: Maintaining Sophisticated Software Functionality Out of Existence

In 1961 Sperry Univac announced the Univac 1107 computer, the largest, fastest, most powerful commercially available machine of its day. It came with a capable but rather "plain vanilla" system software ensemble provided by the manufacturer. However, buyers of such major mainframes already had come to expect a powerful, interactive, open-shop, user-friendly operating system, FORTRAN IV, COBOL, ALGOL 60 compilers, and a sophisticated assembly-language processor.

The inventor of FORTRAN, Roy Nutt, had left United Aircraft and helped found Computer Sciences Corporation, a firm on the West Coast that wrote such software for computer manufacturers and the Department of Defense. They were contracted to write a state-of-the-art FORTRAN compiler. They chose to write it in a new 1107 assembly language, which they also contracted to prepare. This language, called SLEUTH II (because it replaced the manufacturer's SLEUTH I), was a remarkable language, perhaps the best assembler ever written, and certainly the best assembler ever made for writing compilers. Among other advanced features, it allowed recursive programming (at the assembly language level!) and even supported mutual recursion between two separate programs. In addition, it had numerous other abstruse features that were not all that well documented—at least, not well enough for new maintenance programmers, who didn't even know what recursion was, let alone mutual recursion.

SLEUTH II had been written by the best programmers in the world for their own use, with little consideration for the non-computer-literate masses.

One of the authors had occasion to use SLEUTH II as a scientific consultant to Sperry Rand International while on a five-year assignment in Europe. He employed these tricky features to develop programming languages for aircraft structural design applications at the Technical University of Stuttgart[4] involving hyper-matrices, or matrices with matrices as elements down to several levels. He eventually returned to the United States and took up a new position as scientific consultant in the Univac Scientific Computing Division in Roseville, Minnesota. Here he tried to run some of these programs to test the double-precision floating-point arithmetic capability of the Univac 1108, successor to the 1107. Unfortunately, they no longer worked. Naturally the maintenance staff for SLEUTH II was consulted. It was discovered that because the programmers didn't understand what these features were, they simply "maintained" them out of existence. Because their managers didn't understand the features either, they not only allowed them to do it, but they institutionalized the newly devolved versions as corporate standards. Thus was a work of genius lost forever.

Key Points

- Enterprise business software is designed for particular applications but always runs in the context or environment of an overall business data processing system.

- Applications thus must be integrated by testing in an actual operating environment or a virtual test version of it. In some cases, critical new software may be run in parallel for months to ensure that all situations are tested with real data.

- Successful applications software is often extended or upgraded to meet new application requirements. The new version must be tested for functionality, regression-tested for continuity, and integration-tested for conformity.

- Maintenance programmers are often less experienced than the team who wrote the software and can introduce problems.

- Taguchi Methods are well suited not only for software extension but also for software maintenance.

Additional Resources

http://www.prenhallprofessional.com/title/0131872508

http://www.agilenty.com/publications

Internet Exercises

1. The British Spitfire fighter aircraft was an amazing engineering development. Although almost 70 years have passed since its development began, it is well-documented on the Internet. Learn about this remarkable machine. When Reichmarshall Herman Goering asked General Galland what he needed to hold off an invasion of Fortress Europe, covered by Allied air power, he replied curtly, "A squadron of Spitfires."

2. Search the Internet for tools for application software maintenance.

Review Questions

1. List the steps in the conventional software development cycle, drawing feedback loops to the various "reentry" points.

2. What are the issues of software integration? Extension? Maintenance?

Discussion Questions and Projects

1. Why are Taguchi Methods especially suitable for software application package extension?

2. Lay out the design for a Taguchi-based software maintenance paradigm or process in which maintenance programmer inexperience will be overcome.

Problems

1. Much of the maintenance of noncurrent but still-supported business application software may be outsourced, often to companies abroad. The rule of thumb here is: "If you can move it across the hall, you can move it around the world." What are the issues in writing a statement of work to outsource the maintenance of an application package you are familiar with?

2. Review the entire development cycle, and list the Taguchi applications at each stage. How would you introduce a Taguchi-based trustworthy software development program at your firm? Start upstream and move downstream, or start with maintenance and move upstream as the methods prove themselves in practice.

Endnotes

[1]S. Goldstein and T. Ulrich, "Robust Testing of Electronic Warfare Systems," in Taguchi, et al., *Taguchi's Quality Engineering Handbook* (New York: John Wiley and Sons, 2004), pp. 1351–1359.

[2]K. Takada, M. Uchikawa, K. Kajimoto, J. Deguchi, "Efficient Debugging of a (sic) Software Using an Orthogonal Array," *Quality Engineering*, Vol. 8, No. 1, pp. 60–69. Also summarized in Taguchi, et al., *Taguchi's Quality Engineering Handbook* (New York: John Wiley and Sons, 2004), pp. 1360–1364.

[3]G. Taguchi, "Evaluation of Signal Factor and Functionality for Software," *Standardization and Quality Control*, Vol. 62, No. 6 (1999), pp. 68–74.

[4]P. C. Patton and H. R. Lawson, "ARGMAT: A Self-adaptive Matrix Interpretive Code," ISD Report No. 22, Technical University of Stuttgart, September 1965.

PART IV

Putting It All Together: Deployment of a DFTS Program

CHAPTER 20

Organizational Preparedness for DFTS

The methodologies of Six Sigma we learned from other companies, but the cultural obsessiveness and all-encompassing passion for it is pure GE.

—Jack Welch

You're right not because others agree with you, but because facts are right.

—Warren Buffett

Overview

After the CEO and the top management team have bought into the DFTS initiative, the team must assess its preparedness before a formal launch. Although the DFTS principles, tools, and techniques are relatively straightforward, they are not easy to implement. Realizing their full potential may be even more challenging and requires competence as well as leadership commitment. This chapter commences with two case studies that illustrate some key elements of successful quality initiatives. They illustrate that quality initiatives are major long-term commitments and that such appreciation is vital for their successful implementation.

The *lean* methods, originally developed for automobile assembly, have been successfully adapted for transaction processes and service industries. The leadership challenges for achieving organizational excellence and delivering transformational results are not industry-specific. Although industry experience is a valid managerial issue, leadership challenges transcend industry specificity. Leadership research illustrates that there is no one ideal characteristic of a great or even good leader. The characteristics to inspire, motivate, and lead to lofty heights are needed in all leaders. Beyond that, it all depends on particular era, situation, and cultural contexts. In software development contexts, the ability to inspire on a personal level may be a highly desirable trait, particularly in small organizations and small software development teams. Rarely, if ever, do leaders possess all the characteristics by themselves. But great leaders always recognize their own shortcomings and have others within the organization lead in areas where they lack capabilities.

The key elements for assessing organizational preparedness are creating leadership commitment, understanding the leadership role, assessing strategic linkages, ensuring organization-wide participation, understanding the need for customer focus, and assessing current quality management capability. Such analysis creates awareness of organizational challenges during preparatory stages. Invariably, such analysis leads to identification of critical deficiencies that need to be addressed. Asking the right questions is the key.

Chapter Outline

- Time to Ponder

- Leadership Challenges for Transformational Initiatives

- Assessing Key Organizational Elements

- Key Points

- Additional Resources

- Internet Exercises

- Review Questions

- Discussion Questions and Projects

- Endnotes

Time to Ponder

After the CEO and the top management team have bought into the DFTS initiative (Step 1 in Table 5.1 in Chapter 5), the team must assess its preparedness to launch the initiative. Such an exercise provides an opportunity to take stock of key organizational issues before a formal launch. DFTS can be conceived, mistakenly, merely as a technology to develop robust software. Such a flawed conception must be corrected. Just like Six Sigma, TPS, and TQM, it is essentially a leadership initiative. The principles, tools, and techniques of DFTS were described in earlier chapters. Although they are relatively straightforward, they are certainly not easy to implement. Realizing their full potential may be even more challenging and requires competence as well as leadership commitment, as discussed in Case Studies 20.1 and 20.2. They illustrate that quality initiatives are major long-term commitments and that such appreciation is vital for their successful implementation. It may be worth your while to read these case studies before proceeding. This pause may enable you to take a step back and reflect on where your organization stands and to what extent it is ready to embark on a major initiative that may be may be transformative, even for the best-run organizations. The two case studies reflect just that.

Case Study 20.1: Striving for a Perfect Production Process

The Toyota Production System (TPS) is widely considered to be the world's most advanced production system. Also known as *lean,* it has been developed by Toyota Motors Corporation over a period of nine decades and is still a work in progress. It embodies the totality of Japanese quality management practice unlike any other system. What is remarkable about TPS is its steady progression and its zealous custodianship by four generations of Toyota leadership. TPS is based on the following five core principles:

- Elimination of waste (*muda*)
- Just in time (*kanban*)
- Continuous improvement (*kaizen*)
- Mistake-proofing (*poka yoke*)
- Worker involvement

Within Toyota, four key people are credited with developing the system:

- Sakichi Toyoda, who founded the Toyoda Group in 1902
- Kiichiro Toyoda, son of Sakichi Toyoda, who headed the automobile manufacturing operation from 1936 to 1950
- Eiji Toyoda, Managing Director from 1950 to 1981 and Chairman from 1981 to 1994
- Taiichi Ohno, the father of the Kanban System

Two other men helped shape the Toyota Production System:

- Shigeo Shingo, a quality consultant hired by Toyota, who helped implement quality initiatives
- Edwards Deming, who brought Statistical Process Control to Japan

Operationally, TPS is characterized by the 4 Ps: philosophy, planning, production, and people.[1]

Philosophy

The keystone of Toyota's quality control system is the critical role of the team members in the manufacturing process. The key principles on which TPS is established are as follows:

- Encouraging employees to play an active role in the quality control process
- Using employee ideas and opinions in production processes
- Practicing *kaizen*—striving for continuous improvement

Toyota team members treat the next person on the production line as their customer and will not pass a defective part on to that customer. If a team member finds a problem with a part of the automobile, that person stops the line and corrects the problem before the vehicle goes any farther down the line.

Planning

In the planning stages, it is important to note that new-product planning emphasizes a product that is as defect-free as possible. In other words, Toyota designs quality into the automobile.

Technical advances such as computer-aided design (CAD) have helped designers create and modify their specifications much faster than before, while improving design quality. CAD allows designers to see their ideas as they take shape on a monitor display, in addition to clay models.

Quality is an essential part of the preproduction process. Quality is the driving force in establishing a system that meets the goals of design, cost, and production volume. The planning phase also establishes a plan that outlines all details of the inspection process. Quality control involves close cooperation of many production departments.

Production

Toyota's quality control during production ensures that the correct materials and parts are used and fitted with precision and accuracy. This effort is combined with thousands of rigorous inspections performed by team members during the production process.

Team members on the line are responsible for the parts they use. They are inspectors of their own work and that of their coworkers. When a problem on any vehicle is spotted, any team member can pull a rope—called an *andon* cord—strung along the assembly line to halt production. Only when the problem is resolved is the line restarted. This process involves every team member in monitoring and checking the quality of every car produced.

After the vehicles are completed, the tests really get tough. At the end of final assembly, the vehicles are started and then driven to functional inspection. Here, every aspect of the vehicle is put through a demanding set of tests and inspections.

People

Through quality circles and a suggestion system that rewards employees for ideas, team members strive to achieve the Toyota principle of *kaizen*, or continuous improvement. (A quality circle is a small group of workers, doing similar tasks, who meet voluntarily and regularly during normal working hours under the leadership of their immediate supervisor. They discuss work-related problems with a view toward making recommendations to management.)

Toyota strives to institute its best practices throughout its assembly plants worldwide. At its U.S. manufacturing facility in Kentucky, more than 90,000 employee suggestions are adopted each year. Some individuals have contributed more than 1,000 suggestions. Each team member is a quality inspector. At any time during the production process, any team member who spots a problem can stop production by pulling the *andon* cord. Each year about 60% of the employees achieve perfect attendance—being present and on time every day. They are rewarded with a gift, a special evening of entertainment, and a chance to win a new automobile. Every year, in a random drawing, 15 Kentucky-built Toyotas are given to team members with perfect attendance.

TPS has transformed Toyota beyond recognition. As Eiji Toyoda observed, "When I went to Detroit in 1950, we were producing 40 cars a day. Ford was making 8,000 units, a 200-times difference. The gap was enormous."[2] Some 50 years later, Toyota has overtaken Ford as the world's second-largest auto manufacturer, now within striking distance of being the top auto manufacturer in the world. Both its market capitalization and profitability are higher than that of GM, Ford, and DaimlerChrysler combined. Top management's commitment to quality has been critical in Toyota's remarkable ascent as the leader in automotive quality globally. Although TPS is based on ideas that may appear deceptively simple, its implementation has required four generations of committed leadership that have involved people at all levels. Toyota's "Five Values" form an action guide for its employees to enforce its basic philosophy, as shown in Table 20.1.

TABLE 20.1
Toyota's Five Corporate Values

Value	Description
Globalization	Learning from the best in the world, we aim to become the best in the world.
Customer orientation	We forge partnerships with our customers and strive to exceed their expectations.
Challenge to change	Unbound by convention, we embrace the challenge of creation.
Professional excellence	We develop our strengths and think and act responsibly.
Teamwork	We recognize the human worth of each individual and collaborate to achieve goals.

Although corporations all over the world have attempted to emulate Toyota, not all have obtained that kind of result. It requires more than just addressing process deficiencies. People across the organization must think, act, and behave differently before attempting to improve the development process. As Toyota's former president Fujio Cho said, "…no mere process can turn a poor performer into a star. Rather, you have to address employees' fundamental way of thinking." Or, if you like, it's the people, stupid!

Case Study 20.2: Institutionalizing Six Sigma at GE

It is amazing how General Electric "came from behind," bought into Six Sigma, and produced breathtaking results across the spectrum of its vast businesses globally. GE's Six Sigma implementation has become the hallmark of organization-wide quality initiatives in the West, just as Toyota's TPS embodies Japanese quality management practices. Above all, it clearly illustrates the critical role CEOs play in a major organizational initiative. Jack Welch has admitted with characteristic candor, "I was very slow to buy into Six Sigma. I thought the quality movement was bull. Larry Bossidy is the one who got me into Six Sigma, after he had been running AlliedSignal for a while. Larry hated quality more than I did. And then one day he said, Jack, this works. I'm getting all kinds of results."[3]

What made the GE Six Sigma deployment so robust is that it not only produced transformative results for GE but also unleashed sweeping interest in Six Sigma globally. The following are the critical elements of GE's formidable Six Sigma initiative:

CEO-Driven

The most important reason for Six Sigma's roaring success at GE is that it was passionately driven by Jack Welch, who called it the most important initiative of his 40-year career at GE. After he was convinced of its inherent value, Welch led it with typical commitment, passion, and zest. The initiative evolved and expanded from its initial deployment in manufacturing operations to subsequently include transactions to service businesses to DFSS to Six Sigma support for customers and suppliers, and lately Lean Six Sigma. It is now a decade-long global initiative. It has been led passionately by two successive CEOs, Jack Welch and Jeff Immelt. They both understand its colossal value in improving bottom-line performance, preparing customer-focused leadership, and being "the centerpiece of our dreams and aspirations for this great company."[4]

Early on, Welch clearly saw Six Sigma's potential as a transformative intervention—even for GE, with its highly competitive performance culture—and he conveyed his belief vociferously. He understood that for Six Sigma to succeed, he must bring his total commitment: "To make an initiative successful, you've got to commit yourself to it totally, and stay committed. The last thing you want is to turn these programs into the 'flavor of the month.' You have to be relentlessly persistent. That's why, after a meeting on one of these things, I will send out my notes to all the participants, to make sure we're on the same page. Clearly, it has slowed us down to make sure that each of these initiatives stuck. We'd stay with an initiative two to three years before bringing the next one in, doing them deliberately one after the other, in sequence. Between Six Sigma and e-commerce, for instance, three years passed."[5]

Jack Welch understood that Six Sigma is essentially a leadership initiative rather than a set of tools and techniques. He also realized that it requires leaders at all levels to implement and sustain it. He therefore took his senior leaders into his confidence to ensure that they understood its value and were enthusiastic about it. To accomplish that, he invited Larry Bossidy to address GE's 30 top executives who constituted its Corporate Executive Council (CEC). He also selected the very best talents available to drive this initiative: "We put great people on our initiatives. The effort blossoms with great people, with their intellect, their ideas. Then we take the successes, and make these people the role models who talk about it to others."[6]

Cultural Compatibility

At GE Six Sigma was rapidly adapted to its performance-driven culture. It has been seen as a follow-up to initiatives such as Work-Out that empowered workers closest to work that leads to rapid problem-solving and product, process, and workplace improvements. Six Sigma was also compatible with GE's ethos of an action-driven learning organization: "Our behavior is driven by a fundamental core belief: the desire, and the ability, of an organization to continuously learn from any source, anywhere—and to rapidly convert this learning into action—is its ultimate competitive advantage."[7]

Although GE did not invent Six Sigma, it embraced and transformed it into a typical GE initiative: "The methodologies of Six Sigma we learned from other companies, but the cultural obsessiveness and passion for it is pure GE."[8] Most notably, the Six Sigma initiative was congruent with larger GE values and leadership principles, which helped GE easily assimilate Six Sigma into its cultural milieu:[9]

- Create a clear, simple, reality-based, *customer-focused vision*, and communicate it straightforwardly to all constituents.
- Understand *accountability and commitment* and be decisive...set and meet aggressive targets...always with unyielding integrity.
- Have a *passion for excellence...hate bureaucracy* and all the nonsense that comes with it.
- Have the *self-confidence to empower others* and behave in a boundaryless fashion...believe in and be committed to *Work-Out* as a means of empowerment...be *open to ideas from anywhere.*
- Have, or have the capacity to develop, *global brains and global sensitivity*, and be comfortable building diverse global teams.
- Stimulate and relish change...don't be frightened or paralyzed by it. *See change as opportunity*, not just a threat.
- Have enormous energy and the ability to *energize and invigorate others*. Understand *speed as a competitive advantage*, and see the total organizational benefits that can be derived from a focus on speed.

Strategic Compatibility

By mid-1990s, GE with some 15 years of Welch stewardship possessed the strategic clarity of a vast multibusiness global enterprise. The key element of GE's strategy is well-documented and had been executed successfully over the years. This simply meant being "No. 1 or No. 2—or fix, sell, or close." Welch had restructured GE businesses over the years based on market leadership. He knew that this gave GE a competitive advantage. Six Sigma was totally supportive of GE's key strategy.

Enabling Management Infrastructure

Welch's strategy of market leadership was supported by a management system meant to create the agility of a small enterprise. It consisted of the following:[10]

- **Delayering:** This was meant to create a nimble enterprise free of stifling bureaucracy.
- **Small-company culture:** GE built a culture of small business based on "self-confidence, simplicity, and speed."
- **Work-Out:** A system involving people closest to the work. They are empowered to solve a problem or tap an opportunity for improvement, usually on the spot in a town-style meeting involving all those concerned. If a quick solution cannot be

reached, those responsible must provide credible reasons and direct further study. Work-Out helps overcome bureaucracy, embrace "boundaryless behavior," and decimate a "Not Invented Here (NIH)" mentality while encouraging teamwork and participation and enhancing speed of problem-solving and execution of decisions.

- **Change Acceleration Program (CAP):** This is GE's change management program using a set of specific tools. These tools enable accelerated transition from current state to improved state starting with the change champion *leading* to *creating a shared need* to *shaping a vision* to *mobilizing commitment* to *making change last* to *monitoring progress*. Finally, you have to ensure that *supporting systems, structures, and management practices* such as staffing, development, rewards, communication, organizational design, and IT systems complement and reinforce change (see Figure 20.1).[11]

- **Operating System:** This is a year-round series of intense learning sessions in which the business CEOs, role models, and initiative champions from GE as well as outside companies meet and share the world's intellectual capital: its best ideas.[12] All GE initiatives, such as Six Sigma, globalization, and e-business, go through this yearly learning cycle for several years with a view toward improving, enriching, and implanting them as "a way of life."

- **Stretch:** This means striving to be "as good as you can possibly be" in every organizational endeavor.

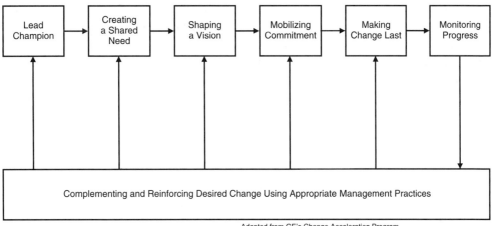

Adapted from GE's Change Acceleration Program
http://www.geinsurancesolutions.com/erccorporate/theinstitute/pc/cust_cap.htm

FIGURE 20.1
GE's Change Acceleration Program

Supportive Reward System

GE supported its Six Sigma initiative by an appraisal and compensation system clearly linked to its success:

- 40% of every manager's bonus is tied to his or her progress on Six Sigma quality.
- All hiring and promotions are based on Six Sigma competence and performance.

The reward system has been further reinforced by the fact that Six Sigma was the top item on every agenda in every discussion in every business globally for the first three years of the initial deployment. Furthermore, Six Sigma was among the three big initiatives of the 1990s; the other two were globalization and services. Welch viewed Six Sigma as a leadership-development process and thought that the next GE CEO would most certainly be a black belt or a master black belt. Such emphasis clearly communicated that Six Sigma was indeed a big deal.

Investment in Human Capital and a First-Rate Teaching Infrastructure

Welch invested heavily in organizatio1n-wide formal learning to help GE employees acquire Six Sigma leadership, technical, and teaching skills. It meant creating teaching skills at an unprecedented scale, even for a large corporation like GE. Some 10,000 black belts and 100,000 green belts were trained and drove more than 20,000 projects during 2000. That helped generate additional financial return of some $2.4 billion.[13]

The investment in human resources and management infrastructure has built a massive capability that continues to make a huge contribution to GE's performance, even after Welch's departure in 2001. GE completed some 50,000 projects in 2002, took Six Sigma to customers in 2003, and introduced Lean Six Sigma in 2004.

The focus of Six Sigma has expanded to help seek improvements innovatively in previously unexplored areas. For example, GE achieved $2.7 billion of improvements in working capital in 2003–2004. During 2002–2004, GE Transportation improved inventory turns from seven to nine, GE Advanced Materials improved accounts receivable by six turns, and GE Commercial Finance expanded its returns through a "Lean Six Sigma"-like focus on margin expansion, risk management, and lower cost.[14]

It has taken GE a decade to learn, implement, and assimilate Six Sigma. It is still a work in progress. It has evolved and expanded across every GE business across the world. But the quest for improvement and perfection continues, just like Toyota's quest for perfection in quality improvement and waste elimination (see Case Study 20.1). Beyond measures of improvement, Six Sigma's true and enduring success lies in how it is now an integral part of GE's culture. It defines how GE works.

Leadership Challenges for Transformational Initiatives

Having read these case studies, you might say, "Well, Toyota and General Electric are great examples of producing quality products, but how can I extrapolate their methods and leadership challenges to fit my software development scenario?" We have often faced such questions. The *lean* methods, originally developed for car assembly, have been successfully adapted for transaction processes and service industries. As far as leadership, the fact is that leadership challenges for achieving organizational excellence and delivering transformational results are not industry-specific. Although industry experience is a valid managerial issue, leadership challenges transcend industry specificity. The Toyota and GE case studies illustrate the tasks that corporate leaders face in leading an organization to commanding heights and enduring results. Leadership research illustrates that there is no one ideal characteristic of a great or even good leader. The characteristics to inspire, motivate, and lead to lofty heights are needed in all leaders. Beyond that, it all depends on the particular era, situation, and cultural context. Eiji Toyoda, Akio Morita, Jack Welch, and Andy Grove have all been great corporate leaders, but with remarkably different personal characteristics, styles, and attributes.

In a software development context, the organization's size can vary from a few to tens of thousands. In such workplaces, creativity and the ability to inspire at a personal level may be highly desirable traits—particularly in small organizations and small software development teams. Because software development is a highly human-centric craft, the ability to extract the best from individuals and groups is a highly desirable leadership trait. In such a context, leaders may also need to be technically savvy. In this regard, we will refer to Sony's famous duo, Akio Morita and Masaru Ibuka, who formed a formidable team but with remarkably different leadership attributes. Morita was outgoing, charismatic, and forceful. Ibuka was detail-oriented and technically brilliant but also a dreamer who could always be counted on to inspire his engineers to overreach themselves. They fulfilled two distinct leadership needs for their organization. Rarely, if ever, do leaders possess all the leadership characteristics by themselves. But great leaders always recognize their own shortcomings and have others within the organization lead in areas where they lack capabilities. So, as far as what are the distinguishing features of a great leader in the software area, we say, it all depends.

Assessing Key Organizational Elements

Now that you have read the two case studies, pondered them, and discussed them with top management, you may be ready to address the following issues vis-à-vis your proposed DFTS initiative:

- Leadership commitment
- Understanding the leadership role

- Understanding strategic linkage

- Ensuring organization-wide participation

- Understanding the need for customer focus

- Current quality management capability

As mentioned in Chapter 5, DFTS requires strong leadership and infrastructural support to be successful. This chapter attempts to emphasize the critical importance of taking another look at the state of leadership commitment and capabilities. This involves assessing the following key organizational elements (see Table 20.2): *creating leadership commitment, understanding the leadership role, assessing strategic linkages, ensuring organization-wide participation, understanding the need for customer focus,* and *assessing current quality management capability.* These elements determine the degree of preparedness for a major intervention such as DFTS. You may either carry out a traditional assessment based on brainstorming or use AHP methodology (see Chapter 8) to assess overall preparedness. These elements are discussed in the following sections.

TABLE 20.2
Assessing Key Elements of Organizational Preparedness in a DFTS Initiative

Organizational Element	Assessment: Strong (S), Medium (M), or Weak (W)
Creating leadership commitment	
Understanding the leadership role	
Assessing strategic linkages	
Ensuring organization-wide participation	
Understanding the need for customer focus	
Assessing current quality management capability	

Creating Leadership Commitment

Genuine commitment and involvement of top executives, led by CEOs, are *sine qua non* for successful implementation of a DFTS initiative. Without these, such initiatives are doomed to failure. As Case Study 20.1 illustrates, Toyota's quality initiatives were driven by generations of successive chief executives over nine decades. In such rare cases, organizations develop strong beliefs, systems, procedures, and often their own lexicons and folklores. That is very powerful, cannot be easily taken away, and becomes a self-sustaining source of competitive advantage. Performance cultures based on positive beliefs and ideas can be bedrocks of quality and performance for long periods of time much beyond executive life spans. This is the nature of organizations with strong-performing cultures. For such cultures to be fostered, CEOs must lead—there is no substitute for that. Toyota's is a formidable case in that four generations of leaders have led the organization with a consistent message. The message has been based on customer focus, worker empowerment, waste elimination, and continuous improvement of products and processes. These now constitute Toyota's deep-rooted corporate philosophy and are manifested in its operations worldwide.

Organizational cultures based on transforming ideas become part of the institution-building process and are central to an organization's core beliefs, whether stated or not. Although formative years provide great opportunities for fostering such ethos, strong cultures can also be cultivated by committed CEOs in companies without compelling histories, like Toyota's. The most celebrated quality management intervention in the West is GE's formidable Six Sigma initiative, led by Jack Welch (as discussed in Case Study 20.2).

Although GE's Six Sigma initiative is exemplary, the lesser-reported cases of Samsung, Hyundai, and Caterpillar are remarkable too. We have studied a number of major corporate initiatives across a variety of industries and cultures. We have found a common denominator in every case of successful deployment: the total commitment and involvement of the CEOs. We cannot overemphasize this simple fact.

Understanding the Leadership Role

The CEO and top managers must do a number of things. But the one thing they must never do is launch the initiative without adequate preparation and without understanding the challenges involved. Do we understand how it works? Is the CEO committed enough to bet his job on the initiative's resounding success? Are we ready collectively, and will we give it our emotional energy? Can we drive it collectively with enthusiasm and as a top priority for the next two to three years and support it much beyond that? All these questions are part of executive buy-in, discussed in Chapter 5. As stated throughout this book, DFTS is all about leading change. The CEO, together with top management, should be prepared for the following:

- **Change yourself:** First and foremost, you must understand the need to change and be willing to do so elegantly. Top management must embrace change before asking anybody else to change. This means accepting new priorities, methods, systems, and processes as needed. In short, it's a new way of doing things.

- **Learn:** Learning is crucial to improvement. In the absence of actually understanding how the initiative works, commitment and support will be phony, if they exist at all. The return on learning is highest at the top executive level in that it makes everything else possible. The state of mind that "learning is for the guys down the line" must be discarded.

- **Communicate:** The CEO and his team must communicate their message clearly and enthusiastically with each other as well as others in the organization. A robust communication plan must be prepared. They should work diligently to share information and encourage empowerment down the organizational hierarchy. The people closest to the development process and to the customers must own and be able to influence the new development process.

- **Provide resources:** DFTS requires human, technical, and financial resources. These must be planned and budgeted for. But the most important resource DFTS needs is top management's time, focus, and attention. That's a precious commodity and should be budgeted for too!

- **Initiate organization-wide learning:** The initiative requires leadership as well as technical skills. These were introduced in Chapter 5 and are discussed further in Chapter 21.

Assessing Strategic Linkages

It is important to understand how the initiative supports the company's strategic objectives, such as growth, market share, and profitability, and how they are related to cost, quality, and customer satisfaction. At GE, Welch saw Six Sigma in the following three strategic contexts:

- As a common learning system to prepare future leaders across the large, multi-business, global organization

- As a means to provide customer-focused products and services

- As a way to improve cost and quality competitiveness

It is important to understand these in an organizational context and also vis-à-vis other initiatives and priorities. Doing so creates clarity as to whether, why, and when the organization should launch such an initiative.

Ensuring Organization-Wide Participation

The best solutions often come from the workers—the software developers in this context. Top management must involve them and make them enthusiastic. Doing so will ultimately determine whether the implementation succeeds. It is important to prepare the workers for the new process as well as provide them with the training they need to be active participants. Top management must address two additional issues to create credibility:

- **Willingness to take risks:** More than anything else, this demonstrates management's commitment to the initiative. Occasional delays and even setbacks will occur. It is vital to impart an atmosphere that tolerates innovation—even if it is not always successful. Zero tolerance for failure and mistakes will shut down creativity.

- **Be realistic in setting targets:** It is wise not to drive people crazy by setting impossible targets and schedules when DFTS is first implemented. Enthusiasm for learning is critical for successful deployment.

Understanding the Need for Customer Focus

DFTS is a customer-focused quality initiative. Therefore, it is important that the organization as a whole understand the business imperatives of being customer-focused. In absence of such clarity, it is likely to become a mere slogan. The top management team can help create such a milieu by doing things such as regularly visiting customers in their work environment.

Structured *gemba* visits are of immense value (see Chapter 11). The objective should be to obtain valid customer input for software design as well as enrich the customer experience during the software development cycle. Many managers visit customers only when prospecting business or fire-fighting. The best opportunities are provided when things are going fine, when the product is being conceived, and during all the upstream activities associated with the development process. Top management should have regular and structured interaction with the customers and expect the same from others. Simply calling customers regularly and responding honestly and adequately to their concerns cannot be overemphasized. Every meaningful customer interaction must be documented and disseminated. In the absence of such commitment to customers, the initiative may not go very far. Such cultural change must be initiated and sustained by the CEO and the top management team. A structured, customer-focused approach requires building competence in four areas:[15]

- **Customer relationship management** deals with building trust and expectations so that the customers call when they have a need.

- **Interaction management** focuses on the interaction that takes place after the customer calls. Customers need to be assured that the firm is more interested in meeting their needs than just making a sale. The interaction should be hassle-free.

- **Diagnosis management** focuses on best-practice guidelines for diagnosing customer needs when the customer contact person (CCP) interacts with the customers. This involves CCP experts developing methods for defining what the customer really wants.

- **Customer-service management** consists of the ongoing dialogue that occurs when service is requested during and after delivery.

Assessing Current Quality Management Capability

You must assess the organization's quality capabilities as part of the preparatory steps. This can be linked with the assessment of training needs discussed in Chapters 21 and 22. An assessment of quality capability addresses the following:

- Has the organization undertaken other quality initiatives in the past? What was the outcome? Why? What was learned? What can be done to improve the initiatives? How can DFTS be integrated with existing quality systems?

- Does the organization have a quality system in place such as a Software Quality Metrics System (SQMS) or a Cost of Software Quality (CoSQ) system? If so, how have they helped? How can we improve them?

- Do we have any CMM™ competencies?

- What is our human resources inventory as far as quality management capability? How are individual (PSP™) and team software (TSPi™) competencies? How can we use these resources more effectively? How can we enhance these capabilities?

- What are the organization's values regarding learning, customer focus, and quality? Have they been helpful in creating a quality-conducive culture? How can we reinforce our quality culture?

This chapter has presented two case studies, involving Toyota and GE, that indicate the enormity of leadership challenges in establishing sustainable quality leadership. They also indicate the sheer centrality of committed and consistent leadership. We have discussed organizational preparedness issues that need to be looked into and addressed before a formal launch. Such an assessment creates awareness of leadership and organizational challenges during preparatory stages. It is not about the decision to go ahead with the initiative or not because that would have been decided on at the "buy-in" stage. It is about when and how to best launch the initiative. Invariably, such an analysis leads to the identification of important organizational deficiencies that need to be addressed. The leadership asks the following questions at this stage: Are we ready to launch the DFTS initiative? If not, what needs to be addressed to prepare us to do so? Asking the right questions is the key.

Key Points

- After the CEO and the top management team have bought into the DFTS initiative, the team must assess its preparedness to launch the initiative. Such an exercise provides an opportunity to take stock of key organizational issues before a formal launch.

- DFTS sometimes is mistakenly thought of as merely a technology to develop robust software. Such a flawed conception must be corrected. Just like Six Sigma, TPS, and TQM, DFTS is essentially a leadership initiative.

- Although the DFTS principles, tools, and techniques are relatively straightforward, they are not easy to implement. Realizing their full potential may be even more challenging. It requires competence as well as leadership commitment.

- TPS is widely considered to be the world's most advanced production system. It has been developed over a period of nine decades, and it is still a work in progress. What is remarkable about TPS is its steady progression and its zealous custodianship by four generations of Toyota leadership.

- TPS is based on five core principles: eliminating waste, Just in Time, continuous improvement, mistake-proofing, and worker involvement.

- TPS is characterized by 4 P's: philosophy, planning, production, and people.

- The critical elements of GE's Six Sigma initiative are CEO-driven, cultural compatibility, strategic compatibility, enabling management infrastructure, supportive reward system, and investment in human capital and first-rate teaching infrastructure.

- It has taken GE a decade to learn, implement, and assimilate Six Sigma. It is still a work in progress. It has evolved and expanded across every GE business around the world. Beyond measures of improvement, Six Sigma's true and enduring success lies in the fact that it is now an integral part of GE's culture. It defines how GE works.

- The leadership challenges for achieving organizational excellence and delivering transformational results are not industry-specific. Although industry experience is a valid managerial issue, leadership challenges transcend industry specificity.

- The Toyota and GE case studies illustrate the tasks that a corporate leader faces in leading an organization to commanding heights and delivering enduring results. Leadership research illustrates that there is no one ideal characteristic of a great or even good leader.

- The characteristics to inspire, motivate, and lead to lofty heights are needed in all leaders. Beyond that, leadership depends on the particular era, situation, and cultural context. Eiji Toyoda, Akio Morita, Jack Welch, and Andy Grove have all been great corporate leaders, but with remarkably different personal characteristics, styles, and attributes.

- In a software development context, creativity and the ability to inspire on a personal level may be highly desirable traits, particularly in small organizations and small software development teams. Because software development is still a highly human-centric craft, the ability to extract the best from individuals and groups is a highly desirable leadership trait.

- In a software development context, leaders may also need to be technically savvy. Sony's famous duo, Akio Morita and Masaru Ibuka, formed a formidable team, but with remarkably different leadership attributes. Morita was outgoing, charismatic, and forceful. Ibuka was detail-oriented but also a dreamer. He was technically brilliant and could always be counted on to inspire his engineers to overreach themselves. Morita and Ibuka fulfilled two distinct leadership needs for their organization.

- Rarely, if ever, do leaders possess all these characteristics. But great leaders always recognize their own shortcomings and have others within the organization lead in areas where they lack capabilities. So what are the distinguishing features of a great leader in the software area? We believe it all depends.

- The key elements of assessing organizational preparedness are creating leadership commitment, understanding the leadership role, assessing strategic linkages, ensuring organization-wide participation, understanding the need for customer focus, and assessing current quality management capability.

- Such analysis creates an awareness of leadership and organizational challenges during the preparatory stages. Invariably, such an analysis leads to the identification of important organizational deficiencies that need to be addressed. Asking the right questions is the key.

Additional Resources

http://www.prenhallprofessional.com/title/0131872508

http://www.agilenty.com/publications

Internet Exercises

1. Download and read the article "It's All About Leadership: Engaging People in Evolving a Lean Culture" by Janet Riley of The Boeing Company. It appears on the following Web site:

   http://lean.mit.edu/index.php?option=com_docman&task=cat_view&Itemid=88&gid=144&orderby=dmdatecounter&ascdesc=DESC

   Summarize the article for the class.

2. From the same Web site, download and read the article "Small Problems Become Big Problems Without Immediate Problem Solving" by Jerrel Smith of Boeing. Present a summary to the class.

Review Questions

1. List and explain the key principles that TPS is based on. Which ones are more significant in a software development context, and what are their implications?

2. What are the 4 P's of TPS? Explain them in a software development context.

3. Explain the key elements of GE's Six Sigma initiative. What would you recommend for your organization that is planning to deploy DFTS?

4. What are the distinguishing features of a great leader in a software development organization? Why?

5. What are the key elements of assessing organizational preparedness? Who should be involved in carrying out such an assessment?

Discussion Questions and Projects

1. Discuss the reasons why DFTS may be difficult to implement, and suggest measures an organization may take to overcome these odds.

2. Describe how the 4 P's work in Toyota. How can you adapt them in a software development organization?

3. Prepare to carry out a mock assessment for organizational preparedness before a DFTS initiative. Discuss this with the class. Assign specific roles to class (team) members for the mock exercise. Present the findings to the class.

Endnotes

[1]http://www.toyotageorgetown.com/qualdex.asp.

[2]http://www.time.com/time/asia/asia/magazine/1999/990823/toyoda1.html.

[3]Noel M. Tichy and Stratford Sherman, *Control Your Destiny or Someone Else Will* (New York: HarperBusiness, 2001), p. 303.

[4]Letter to share owners, GE 1997 Annual Report.

[5]Op cit Tichy and Sherman, p. 307.

[6]Ibid.

[7]Letter to share owners, GE 1996 Annual Report.

[8]Ibid.

[9]Letter to share owners, GE 1991 Annual Report.

[10]Letter to share owners, GE 1995 Annual Report.

[11]http://www.geinsurancesolutions.com/erccorporate/theinstitute/pc/cust_cap.htm.

[12]Op cit Tichy and Sherman, p. 341.

[13]Op cit Tichy and Sherman, p. 336.

[14]Letter to share owners, GE 2004 Annual Report.

[15]Frank W. Davis and Karl B. Manrodt, *Customer-Responsive Management* (Cambridge, MA: Blackwell, 1996), pp. 143–167.

CHAPTER 21

Launching a DFTS Initiative

...it is more difficult to tell what problems will emerge—as they certainly will.
—John Maddox

Stay hungry. Stay foolish.
—Steve Jobs

Overview

This chapter is a sequel to Chapters 2, 5, and 20. The PICS implementation framework is revisited and its four phases are examined in turn. The chapter emphasizes building organization-wide competencies to launch and sustain a DFTS initiative. It starts with a review of various *planning* activities and a summary of deliverables. It is followed by a detailed presentation of the two *implementation* steps (Steps 11 and 12). Step 11 deals with establishing overall learning objectives, designing and customizing learning curricula, and providing training for support personnel. Step 12, the core of DFTS implementation, consists of black belt and master black belt training and the ensuing application of such learning to an actual software development project. This is followed by a discussion of monitoring and control mechanisms. A defining aspect of the DFTS learning process involves self-appraisal, successive appraisal, and review of work carried out to date with the customers. Here customers are not only the external customers but also the internal ones—the next person(s) in the development process.

Simon's *Levers of Control* consists of four constructs—*belief systems*, *boundary systems*, *diagnostic control systems*, and *interactive control systems*—that deal with strategic control of the enterprise. Another set of control mechanisms, *internal control systems*, are not used to control strategy but are fundamental to ensuring the integrity of data used in strategic control systems. It is therefore essential that those responsible for the organization's internal control systems be involved to safeguard the integrity of DFTS process and quality data, especially Cost of Software Quality (CoSQ) and other financial data. Finally, the process has operational controls. These are accomplished through *feedback control systems*, which are an integral part of the PICS framework, and through *project management*, with its own control mechanisms. The DFTS feedback control system must be designed to measure variables that are important, measurable, and actionable. They meet five different sets of objectives: *learning and teaching capabilities*, *CoSQ capabilities*, *customer satisfaction*, *process robustness*, and *improvement opportunities*.

A case study of GE's Operating System is introduced as a vehicle to launch a new initiative and enrich it through several yearly cycles. Effective management of the software development process is emphasized using sound project management principles. This is followed by a discussion of the two steps that comprise the "secure" phase of the PICS model: *freezing the improvements and gains* and *integrating the initiative*. Next is Case Study 21.2, "Quality Initiatives and Their Integration at TCS." A brief discussion of *application in small software firms and e-cottages* is provided. The chapter ends with a brief discussion of the future course of a DFTS initiative.

Chapter Outline

- DFTS and the PICS Framework
- Plan
- Implement
- Control
- Secure
- Application in Small Software Firms and e-Cottages

- What's Next?
- Key Points
- Additional Resources
- Internet Exercises
- Review Questions
- Discussion Questions
- Endnotes

DFTS and the PICS Framework

This chapter is a sequel to Chapters 2, 5, and 20. Chapter 2 introduced the Robust Software Development Model (RSDM), which defines Design for Trustworthy Software (DFTS) as an iterative six-stage development process (see Figure 2.6). Chapter 5 presented a 15-step PICS implementation framework; it's repeated here in Figure 21.1. It identifies organizational infrastructure and leadership support systems that are key to a successful DFTS implementation. Chapter 20 emphasized the need to assess organizational preparedness before embarking on a DFTS implementation (see Table 20.3). An organization will be better prepared to implement the initiative following an honest appraisal of its preparedness and taking remedial measures that may be needed.

This chapter discusses how to launch the DFTS process effectively. It particularly emphasizes building organization-wide competencies to launch and sustain DFTS. The PICS implementation framework consists of four phases: *plan, implement, control,* and *secure* (Figure 21.1). The following sections look at each of these in turn.

Plan

The first ten steps of DFTS represent various planning activities. They constitute both the "software" of the implementation process, such as creating awareness and securing commitment, and its "hardware," such as designing a supportive organizational structure and communication and reward systems. These collectively constitute an organization's infrastructure and management practices. Table 21.1 describes the planning process and its deliverables.

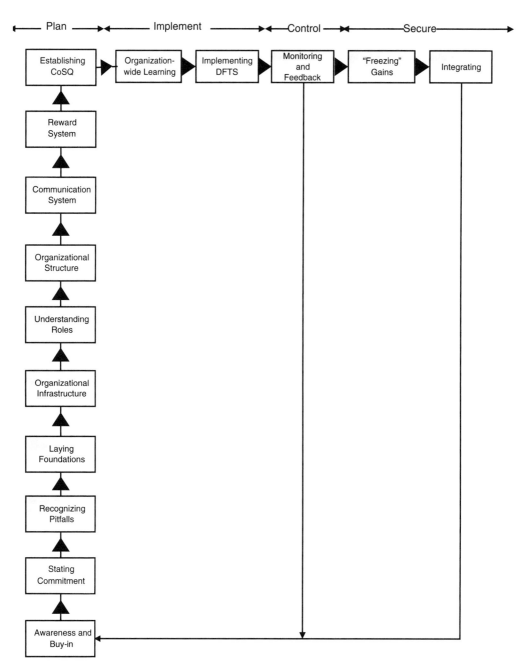

FIGURE 21.1
PICS Implementation Framework

TABLE 21.1
DFTS Planning Activities and Their Deliverables

Step Number	Step Name	Deliverables
1	Creating management awareness and buy-in	Understanding the DFTS process Management buy-in DFTS Steering Committee Appraisal of existing quality capabilities Outline plan and budget
2	Communicating top management's commitment	Communication strategy and plan
3	Recognizing pitfalls	Understanding potential pitfalls Identifying implementation strategies and support systems
4	Laying philosophical foundations for a quality-focused enterprise	Awareness of current shortcomings Understanding the need to change Strengthening the quality culture
5	Building the organizational infrastructure	Understanding current shortcomings Identifying remedial measures
6	Understanding the roles and responsibilities of the key players	Creating a quality-supportive environment Understanding roles and expectations
7	Designing a supportive organizational structure	Creating a customer-, process-, and network-based structure
8	Establishing an effective communication system	Plan for robust internal and external communication
9	Creating an appropriate reward system	DFTS-supportive reward system
10	Establishing a CoSQ reporting system	Providing visibility of cost and causes of poor quality Identifying opportunities for improvement Providing a common language for communicating the consequences of poor quality

As stated in Chapter 5, the ten planning activities are critical elements of the DFTS deployment process. They reinforce the initial launching of the initiative, help integrate it into the organization, and build foundations for continuous improvement. Strong management systems and practices are crucial to a successful implementation. GE and Toyota have a history of excellent management systems and practices that have helped them immensely in their various quality initiatives (see Case Studies 20.1 and 20.2). GE's sound management systems, such as Work-Out™, Operating System™, and Change Acceleration Program (CAP™), as well as its performance culture based on *speed, simplicity, self confidence*, and *worker empowerment*, have been instrumental in its enormously successful Six Sigma initiatives. Organizations should learn and adapt best practices rather than trying to copy them. We cannot overemphasize the need for the CEO and top management to work together to strengthen the organization's quality culture, infrastructure, and management practices before implementing the DFTS initiative. These issues are discussed at length in Chapter 5.

Implement

DFTS implementation consists of Steps 11 and 12 in the PICS framework (see Figure 21.1). It involves two broad sets of activities: launching organization-wide learning and implementing the DFTS process. These constitute this chapter's main focus. They involve designing and delivering formal DFTS learning and training for the organization as a whole.

Step 11: Launching Organization-Wide Learning

Organization-wide learning helps build capabilities to inspire and sustain the DFTS initiative as well as build foundations for continuous learning and improvement. To attain those goals, the organization has to transform itself into a learning entity that can continually identify opportunities for improvement and innovation. Such capabilities can be powerful instruments in making quality initiatives self-sustaining and for launching future initiatives. It takes years of committed leadership to build corporate cultures in which continuous improvement and innovation thrive (see Case Studies 20.1 and 20.2). It is important to identify both long- and short-term objectives and to ensure that they are complementary. The training program should be designed to meet the following long-term objectives:

- Build foundations for a customer-focused quality culture

- Develop a strong learning and teaching infrastructure

- Acquire the ability for continuous improvement as well as innovation

- Develop human capital and build a knowledge base

Long-term objectives help sustain the initiative and produce lasting results, but an organization also needs to focus on short-term objectives that reflect customer expectations as well as the organization's short-term internal objectives. Short-term results must focus primarily on the customer's quality, cost, and schedule requirements identified during QFD. These objectives should be measurable and included in the project charter. The following capabilities are needed to attain short-term objectives and to get started with the DFTS process:

- Develop skills to listen to and understand customer requirements.

- Acquire competence to translate customer requirements into measurable metrics.

- Learn DFTS technology.

- Overall, develop the ability to deliver the customer's cost, quality, and schedule requirements throughout the product life cycle at the lowest cost to the software development organization deploying DFTS technology.

The first software project that the team develops using the DFTS technology should be comprehensive enough to provide adequate learning opportunities without being unduly complex. The learning curricula as well as assessment and certification should be structured to meet both short- and long-term objectives.

Designing Learning Curricula: Customization and Differentiation

The priorities of specific objectives may differ from organization to organization, as revealed by the preparedness appraisal. "One size fits all" is not the best DFTS learning strategy. The learning curricula must be customized to specify an organization's short- and long-term objectives and priorities given its strengths and deficiencies as well as its competitive and strategic contexts. To do that, the organization's current capabilities, short- and long-term objectives, and competitive and strategic challenges must be assessed. Much useful data is generated during the preparedness appraisal, as discussed in Chapter 20. These must be made available for curricula design.

In addition to customization, the training programs should also be differentiated as per the roles and needs of the trainees concerned. The training is imparted in two stages, as described in Steps 11 and 12 of the PICS framework (see Figure 21.1).

Training Support Personnel

As stated in Chapter 5, Step 11 involves training those who are largely in supporting roles, such as senior executives, Executive Champions (ECs), and various personnel in sales, marketing, finance, and human resources (HR), who provide support services including costing, customer liaison, documentation, and training. Their understanding of the DFTS process is important for its successful implementation and integration.

DFTS training tends to be much more inclusive than a typical Six Sigma and DFSS program given the pervasiveness of the software development process in such organizations. Step 11 involves two customized and differentiated training programs. Senior executives and ECs attend the senior executives and champions seminar, and other support personnel undergo white belt training.

Senior Executives and Champions (SEC) Seminar

This seminar is meant for the members of the steering committee and other senior executives. It includes the CEO and senior executives from software development, quality, finance, planning, sales, marketing, internal IS, and HR, as well as ECs and project champions, as applicable.

The seminar is organized following the decision to introduce DFTS as the software development technology. It should be practical but also intense in that it delivers meaningful zest. The participants, led by the CEO, must display their enthusiasm for learning and launch the initiative. Needless to say, it should be prepared and designed well.

A typical SEC seminar takes four to five days and consists of the following key components:

- Review organizational preparedness, objectives, and the implementation plan.
- Identify the first project, project team, and other resources.
- Establish broad deliverables and a timeline.
- Overview the DFTS philosophy and technology.
- Establish a framework linking the executive reward system and growth to individual and collective contributions in the implementation process.
- Set up a robust framework for monitoring project progress.
- Establish an organization-wide DFTS communication plan.

All the senior executives must attend this seminar. A few senior executives, such as Vice President of Software Development/Chief Software Architect, Chief Quality Officer, and various ECs and project champions, must undergo more intensive training meant for black belts. This equips them with additional "hands-on" skills to lead a DFTS implementation process.

White Belt Training

White belt training should be organized after the SEC seminar and should be designed to strengthen the process. It is meant for personnel who provide support in the organization. This includes support personnel from HR, sales and marketing, finance, and information systems. White-belt participants should be introduced to the metrics, tools, and techniques of the DFTS process and acquire an awareness of the methodology and its value.

A typical white-belt seminar may take two to three days and consists of the following key components:

- Understand the organizational context of the DFTS initiative.

- Overview the DFTS philosophy and technology.

- Understand the roles in successful implementation.

- Understand the link between rewards and growth with individual and team contributions in the implementation process.

Step 12: Implementing DFTS Technology: Learning and Application Process

This step is at the heart of the trustworthy software development process. It involves training and applying DFTS methodology (see Figure 2.6) to an actual software development project. Classroom learning and application are interspersed over the project development cycle and constitute an integrated learning system, as shown in Figure 21.2. Step 12 consists of training the team members and leaders in the DFTS technology and then having them apply it to an actual software development project. It consists of two training programs—DFTS black belt training and DFTS master black belt training.

DFTS Black Belt Training

This training program involves software developers and project leaders. It is scheduled as part of the implementation process. It enables effective learning acquired during project implementation and classroom learning. All software professionals, from Vice President of Software Development/Chief Software Architect down to young software engineers, must undergo black belt training. It should also be required training for all quality professionals, from Chief Quality Officer downward. Such organization-wide training is essential, because quality management is usually not included in software engineering curricula in colleges or graduate schools. The team undergoing Black Belt training should have an approved software development project already assigned, together with a project charter.

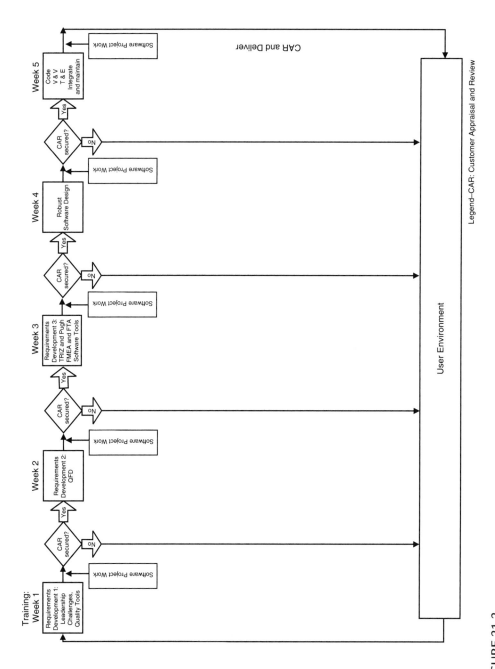

FIGURE 21.2
DFTS Black Belt Training and Project Work Schedule

Black belt training constitutes the core body of knowledge for the DFTS process. We also emphasize the importance of acquiring Personal Software Process (PSP™) and Team Software Process (TSP™) skills.[1, 2] Training consists of five sessions of one week of formal classroom learning followed by five sessions of actual software development activities. The duration of the software development activities between classroom training may vary from a few weeks to several months in an enterprise software context.

Black Belt Training Curriculum

DFTS black belt training must be customized to organizational needs. Typically the curriculum consists of the following key learning components:

Week 1: Requirements Development 1

DFTS technology in context

Software models and metrics

Financial perspectives of trustworthy software

DFTS infrastructure and PICS implementation framework

PSP™ and TSP™ processes

Seven Basic Tools and Seven Management and Planning Tools

Analytic Hierarchy Process

Poka yoke and 5S

Week 2: Requirements Development 2

Quality Function Deployment

Week 3: Requirements Development 3

TRIZ and Pugh

FMEA and FTA

Object and component technologies and other development tools

Week 4: Robust Software Design

Software quality measures

Robust software requirements

Taguchi Methods and optimization for robust software

Week 5: Coding, T and E, V and V, and I and M

Coding

Testing and evaluation

Verification and validation

Integration and maintenance

DFTS Master Black Belt Training

DFTS Project Leaders are trained to be master black belts (MBB) who provide technical, teaching, coaching, mentoring, and leadership support to the project team, as discussed in Chapter 5. MBBs undergo the same training classes as black belts (BBs), along with other software and quality professionals. In addition, they should acquire advanced skills in at least two DFTS bodies of knowledge, such as CoSQ, Software Quality Metrics System (SQMS), QFD, TRIZ, FMEA, and Taguchi Methods. Additional advanced training programs for MBBs can be designed given a software developer's specific training needs.

MBBs should be proficient to help BBs and other software and quality professionals in a wide range of software development issues.

Training Evaluation and Certification

In a Six Sigma or DFSS project, team members possess green belt skills and are led by BBs, who in turn are mentored by MBBs. DFTS BBs and MBBs play roles that are more intense and that have comparatively higher skill sets than their counterparts in Six Sigma and DFSS. For example, BBs are team members in a DFTS project rather than project leaders, a role assigned to MBBs. DFTS MBBs also carry the teaching and mentoring responsibilities of Six Sigma/DFSS MBBs. As such, DFTS MBBs play three critical roles: lead the project teams, teach/train BBs and others throughout the organization, and act as mentors to BBs and white belts. (They can also be mentors to senior executives, much like senior executives at GE had young mentors to help them during the launch of GE's e-business initiative.[3]) Comparatively, BBs and MBBs need broader skill sets in a DFTS context compared to Six Sigma and DFSS. Software developers (BBs) and team leaders (MBBs) both must be proficient in the whole DFTS development process—not just coding, but also various upstream and downstream development activities (see Figures 2.6 and 21.2).

The leadership must make training and learning a big deal. Everyone with any link to the DFTS process must undergo training—and that starts with the CEO. Successful completion of training and subsequent contribution in DFTS deployment and integration must be made the major requirement for individual rewards and growth for everyone, including the CEO and top management. The quality and HR departments should come up with a certification scheme for the DFTS trainees in consultation with academia and possibly outside consultants. Trainee participants must meet a specified level of proficiency for certification purposes. Table 21.2 shows typical certification requirements.

TABLE 21.2
Typical Certification Requirements for Various DFTS Training Programs

Training Level	Duration/ Course(s)	Minimum Attendance Requirement	Minimum Exam Requirement	Project and Other Requirements	Certification
Senior executives	Three-day SEC seminar	85%			Certificate of attendance
Support personnel	Three-day white belt seminar	85%	Grade B in an hour-long exam		White belt certificate
Project team members (black belts)	Five-week black belt training	85%	Grade B in a three-hour exam	Participation in one or two software projects (Evaluated by MBBs on stated criteria)	Black belt certificate of attendance (upon satisfying attendance and exam requirements only) Certified black belt (upon satisfying all requirements)
Project leaders (master black belts)	Five-week black belt training	85%	Grade B in a three-hour exam	Lead one or two project(s) Mentor at least four people Train team members (Evaluated by immediate supervisor)	Certified master black belt (upon satisfying all requirements)
	One- to two-week advanced training in a specified area	85%	Grade A in two three-hour exams in specified DFTS body of knowledge (BOK)		

Each week-long DFTS training phase is followed by software project work and Customer Appraisal and Review (CAR) before the next phase of training and further development work. The duration of the development activities varies from a few weeks to several months in an enterprise software context. This is a process of action learning in that the team learns not only in the classroom but also during the actual software development process (see Figure 21.2).

A defining aspect of the DFTS learning process is the practice of self-appraisal, successive appraisal, and review of work carried out to date with the customers. This ensures that customer needs are understood as they evolve throughout the development process. The customers are kept abreast of the state of the development process, thus avoiding costly surprises and revisions. Here customers are not only external but internal—the next people in the development process.

Control

Step 13 constitutes control activities in the PICS framework. At a minimum, control systems in a DFTS process involve monitoring of and feedback for variations in process and software product quality for taking necessary corrective actions (see Figure 21.1). But in a larger organizational context, a solitary control mechanism such as these would hardly be effective, especially if DFTS is meant to be a key element of an organization's overall competitive posture. Simons, in his landmark work *Levers of Control*, proposes a system of four control constructs to successfully implement a competitive strategy:[4]

1. **Belief systems** are an explicit set of values, beliefs, and purposes as expressed in mission and vision statements, credos, and statements of purpose. Commitments to customers, employees, and other stakeholders have to be clearly stated and practiced for them to be credible. They provide stability, character, and strength to organizations and serve them especially well in turbulent times and times of crisis. Johnson & Johnson's famous credo, listed in Figure 21.3, has been an anchoring influence for the company. It has changed little since it was penned by Robert W. Johnson, Jr., in 1943. It places responsibility to stockholders last; doctors, nurses, patients, and their families, employees, and the community all precede it. In more recent times, corporate leaders such as Medtronic's Bill George have argued against the futility of maximizing shareholder value as a sustainable strategy. He states: "Motivating employees with a mission and a clear sense of purpose is the only way I know to deliver innovative products, superior service, and unsurpassed quality to customers over an extended period of time. Over time, an innovative product or a service will be copied by your competitors. Creating an organization of highly

motivated people is extremely hard to duplicate."[5] Emphasizing customer and employee interests above stockholder return as a sound corporate practice is a recent trend in corporations globally. The Indian IT software outsourcing provider Infosys Technologies, which makes a lot of money for its stockholders, does not even mention stockholder interests in its mission statement while including clients, employees, vendors, and society at large (see Figure 21.4). Belief systems invariably transcend particular initiatives or performance cycles. They direct the behavior of senior executives seeking new opportunities or facing strategic choices that may alter an organization's course. Although belief systems constitute the most powerful control mechanism, their true significance is probably least understood.

2. **Boundary systems** are formally stated sets of rules, limits, and proscriptions tied to defined sanctions and credible punishments. Such control mechanisms consist of codes of conduct, strategic planning systems, asset acquisition systems, and operational guidelines. These are meant to help senior executives in their conduct on issues involving the organization's reputation. They also define strategic boundaries to protect resources in opportunity-seeking behavior.

3. **Diagnostic control systems** measure and monitor outcomes to correct deviations from preset standards of performance as expressed in budgets, best practices, standards, goals, and metrics. The preset standards are set by senior executives or are negotiated between senior executives and those who report to them. To be effective, these standards must be based on the collective understanding of the beneficiaries of the outcomes, such as customers and other stakeholders. In a DFTS context, measures such as CoSQ (see Chapter 4) and SQMS (see Chapter 3) monitor process and software product quality. These are fed back upstream for corrective measures, as shown in the PICS framework (see Figure 21.1).

4. **Interactive control systems** require regular and personal involvement of managers in the subordinates' decision activities. Such systems include project management systems, customer appraisal and review, and profit planning systems. Such systems ensure that managers remain engaged and that the discussion is based on real and validated data that constitutes the agenda of discussion between managers and subordinates: the essence of fact-based decision making.

Another set of control mechanisms, internal control systems, are not used by managers to control strategy.[6] However, they are fundamental in ensuring the integrity of data used in strategic control systems. It is therefore essential that those responsible for the organization's internal control systems also be involved in safeguarding the integrity of DFTS process and quality data, especially CoSQ and other financial data (see Chapter 4).

Our Credo

We believe our first responsibility is to the doctors, nurses and patients, to mothers and fathers and all others who use our products and services. In meeting their needs everything we do must be of high quality. We must constantly strive to reduce our costs in order to maintain reasonable prices. Customers' orders must be serviced promptly and accurately. Our suppliers and distributors must have an opportunity to make a fair profit.

We are responsible to our employees, the men and women who work with us throughout the world. Everyone must be considered as an individual. We must respect their dignity and recognize their merit. They must have a sense of security in their jobs. Compensation must be fair and adequate, and working conditions clean, orderly and safe. We must be mindful of ways to help our employees fulfill their family responsibilities. Employees must feel free to make suggestions and complaints. There must be equal opportunity for employment, development and advancement for those qualified. We must provide competent management, and their actions must be just and ethical.

We are responsible to the communities in which we live and work and to the world community as well. We must be good citizens - support good works and charities and bear our fair share of taxes. We must encourage civic improvements and better health and education. We must maintain in good order the property we are privileged to use, protecting the environment and natural resources.

Our final responsibility is to our stockholders. Business must make a sound profit. We must experiment with new ideas. Research must be carried on, innovative programs developed and mistakes paid for. New equipment must be purchased, new facilities provided and new products launched. Reserves must be created to provide for adverse times. When we operate according to these principles, the stockholders should realize a fair return.

Johnson & Johnson

FIGURE 21.3
The Johnson and Johnson Credo
Courtesy of Johnson & Johnson. Reproduced with permission.

Infosys' Vision, Mission and Values

Vision

"To be a globally respected corporation that provides best-of-breed business solutions, leveraging technology, delivered by best-in-class people"

Mission Statement

"To achieve our objectives in an environment of fairness, honesty, and courtesy towards our clients, employees, vendors and society at large"

The values that drive us: C-LIFE

- **Customer Delight:** A commitment to surpassing our customer expectations.

- **Leadership by Example:** A commitment to set standards in our business and transactions and be an exemplar for the industry and our own teams.

- **Integrity and Transparency:** A commitment to be ethical, sincere and open in our dealings.

- **Fairness:** A commitment to be objective and transaction-oriented, thereby earning trust and respect.

- **Pursuit of Excellence:** A commitment to strive relentlessly, to constantly improve ourselves, our teams, our services and products so as to become the best.

FIGURE 21.4
Infosys's Belief System (http://www.infosys.com/about/vision_and_mission.asp)

Finally, the process has operational controls. These are accomplished through *feedback control systems*, which are an integral part of the PICS framework, and through *project management*, which has its own control mechanisms. Organization-wide control systems are beyond the scope of this book. We will discuss feedback control systems and project management in a DFTS context.

Step 13: Feedback Control Systems

This is a crucial element of the PICS framework and is the equivalent of the "check" phase of Deming's PDCA Cycle (Deming called it the Shewhart Cycle).[7] If you fail here, the whole process becomes erroneous and out of control. It therefore must be designed to operate well. A reliable feedback control system provides appropriate measures of key variables in a time- and cost-effective manner for learning the state of the development process and for taking subsequent corrective and improvement measures. The variations are measured from product as well as process appraisal and involve both internal review and interaction and appraisal with customers, both internal and external. These constitute a major learning opportunity for improvement and may consist of a cycle of review meetings and corrective measures. Such a mechanism is effective if it is an ongoing activity of continuous learning and improvement year after year until the initiative is effectively internalized as part of an organization's culture.

Case Study 21.1 illustrates GE's Operating System, which has proven to be a powerful tool for continual appraisal and enrichment. It transforms initiatives across several dozen businesses rapidly such that all the initiatives become operational across the company within one month of launch and produce positive financial results within their first cycle. GE's various initiatives undergo successive cycles of year-round review and enrichment through its Operating System. By 2002, Globalization had been enriched through more than a dozen cycles, Six Sigma had gone through five cycles, Product Services had gone through six, and e-Business had gone through three.[8]

We propose a DFTS feedback review framework as part of the control mechanism, as discussed next.

Elements of DFTS Feedback Control System

Using multiple performance measures, financial and operational, was proposed by Kaplan and Norton in "The Balanced Scorecard."[9] The DFTS feedback control system, shown in Figure 21.5, must be designed to measure variables that are important, measurable, and actionable. They must provide visibility of process and products meeting five sets of objectives (as you will see, they are interrelated): *learning and teaching capabilities, CoSQ capabilities*, *customer satisfaction*, *process robustness*, and *improvement opportunities*. Here are some important questions they help address:

- **Learning and teaching capabilities:** Do we understand the DFTS process well and feel comfortable using it? Are we developing a required internal teaching infrastructure and resources to improve and expand it? If not, why not? What can be done to improve our learning and teaching capabilities?

- **CoSQ capabilities:** Are we measuring the cost of poor quality accurately throughout the software development cycle? (See Figure 2.6.) Have we developed capabilities to use such information correctly? If not, why not? How can we improve our CoSQ capabilities?

- **Customer satisfaction:** Have we specifically met the customer's cost, quality, and delivery schedule, as measured by relevant metrics? Have we exceeded them or fallen short? If we haven't succeeded, why? What can we do to improve customer satisfaction?

- **Process robustness:** How capable is our DFTS process, as determined by a process feedback loop, in meeting stated and unstated customer requirements, as determined by CAR? What opportunities have been identified to improve our use of various tools, techniques, and methodologies that constitute DFTS technology? What steps should we take to improve the process capability before integrating the revamped DFTS process and expanding it further? How can we improve our DFTS process capabilities?

- **Improvement opportunities:** What are further opportunities for improvements, identified from internal idea generation and emergence of best practices, and as measured by the gap between the customer needs and process performance? (Process capability improves as the gap diminishes; this also implies less room for improvement.)

FIGURE 21.5
Elements of Feedback Control Systems

Establishing a Feedback Control System

Control systems essentially provide visibility on cost, quality, and other measures of performance. They often become sociopolitical in nature because the people involved may feel insecure or perceive a loss of power as a result of such visibility of their performance. A feedback system therefore must have the support of the CEO and top management to be viable. Another problem with such systems is that although they have been in use for all kinds of control purposes, they are not always perceived and designed well. The system should be developed by a team assigned by the DFTS steering committee. For any control system of this nature to work, it must be customized. Establishing the DFTS feedback control system involves the following steps:

1. Obtain management commitment and support.

2. Obtain the cooperation of users and other stakeholders.

3. Establish a development team.

4. Identify control system requirements and measures (see Figure 21.5).

5. Determine sources of data.

6. Establish procedures to collect data.

7. Design control system reports.

8. Collect data and conduct control runs.

9. Eliminate bugs from the system.

10. Implement, monitor, and improve.

11. Expand the system.

DFTS Feedback Review Framework

A well-structured review system should be more than just a control mechanism. It should enrich and energize the initiative across the organization by providing required measures to improve the product and the development process. These measures let an organization improve and upgrade the system continually until the system has been perfected, integrated, and expanded. For that to happen, the CEO must drive the review process, involving the organization as well as its customers. It must be made a big deal and its success a defining undertaking for the business. The control system will be effective only if it is a hands-on, year-round process involving key persons within the organization as well as customers.

The measures needed at different phases of the DFTS process must be correctly identified. The control system should be integrated with the DFTS launch and its subsequent appraisal throughout the year. Any such new initiative needs the organization's CEO to be its champion for several years (see Case Study 21.1).

Case Study 21.1: GE's Operating System for Continual Learning and Enrichment[8]

General Electric's Operating System is led by its CEO and provides a vehicle to launch a new initiative and enrich it through several yearly Operating System cycles (see Figure 21.6).[12] We do not recommend that an organization blindly copy this system, because it is unique and an integral part of GE's culture. It is best that you learn from it and adapt it to your needs and context, rather than trying to copy it.

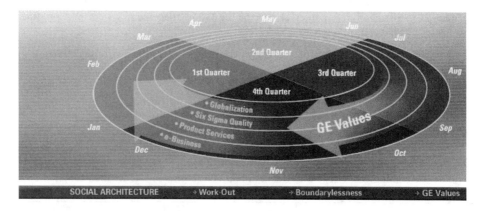

FIGURE 21.6
The Yearly Cycle of GE's Operating System
Reproduced with permission from http://www.ge.com/en/company/companyinfo/operating_system/main.html.

What Exactly Is GE's Operating System?

The Operating System is a review and learning mechanism and is "GE's learning culture in action." It is a year-round series of intense learning sessions in which CEOs, role models, and initiative champions from GE, as well as outside companies, meet and share intellectual capital.

The central focus is always on sharing, and putting into action, the best ideas and practices from across the company and around the world.

How Does It Work?

Meetings take place year-round, in an endless process of enrichment. Learning builds from previous meetings, expanding the scope and increasing the momentum of GE's company-wide initiatives.

Driven by the company's values—trust, informality, simplicity, boundaryless behavior, and a love of change—the Operating System allows GE businesses to reach speeds and performance levels unachievable on their own.

What Are the Results?

The Operating System translates ideas into action across three dozen businesses so rapidly that all the initiatives became operational across the company within one month of launch and have always produced positive financial results within their first cycle.

Globalization has been enriched through more than a dozen cycles. Six Sigma is in its fifth cycle, Product Services is in its sixth, and e-Business is in its third.

The Operating System is closely linked to GE's other management tools and systems, such as its Social Architecture, Work-Out, Boundarylessness, and GE Values (see Case Study 20.2 in Chapter 20). All these are an integral part of the GE management system and produce a uniquely synergistic effect.

Table 21.3 lists the key elements of the yearly cycle spread over four quarters.

TABLE 21.3
Key Elements of GE's Operating System

First Quarter			
600 global GE business leaders gather each January to evaluate last year's performance and to determine the coming year's key initiative(s). Subsequent events in GE are then centered on making these initiatives happen.			
Month	Main Task	Who Participates	Subtasks/Activities
January	Operating managers meeting	600 leaders	Initiative launch Case for new initiative Outside company initiative experience One-year stretch targets Role model presentations Relaunch of current initiatives
February			Intense energizing of initiatives across businesses
March	Corporate Executive Council	35 business and senior corporate leaders	Early learning? Customer reaction? Initiative resources sufficient? Business Management Course (BMC) recommendations

Second Quarter			
People leading and practicing the year's key initiatives present their progress to GE leadership. At the same time, an anonymous CEO survey is sent to 11,000 GE employees for candid feedback on the initiatives' progress.			
Month	**Main Task**	**Who Participates**	**Subtasks/Activities**
April	Anonymous online CEO survey	11,000 employees	Do you "feel" the initiative yet? Do customers feel it? Sufficient resources to execute? Messages clear and credible?
May	Leadership performance reviews at business locations	All business staffs	Initiative leadership review Level of commitment/ quality of talent on initiatives Differentiation (20%/70%/10%) Promote/reward/remove
June	Corporate Executive Council	35 business and senior corporate leaders	Initiative best practices Review of initiative leadership Customer impact BMC recommendations

Third Quarter			
Role models and heroes from across GE (and across the world) present to the 150 corporate officers at an annual meeting—a platform where each business can measure its progress against the best of its peers.			
Month	**Main Task**	**Who Participates**	**Subtasks/Activities**
July	Session I: A three-year strategy		Economic/competitive environment General earnings outlook Initiatives update/strategy Initiative resource requirements
August			Informal idea exchanges at corporate and businesses
September	Corporate Executive Council	35 business and senior corporate leaders	BMC recommendations Clear role models identified Outside company best practices presented Initiative best practices (all businesses) Customer impact of initiatives

TABLE 21.3
Continued

Fourth Quarter			
As one cycle ends, another begins. Budgets, personnel, and business plans are finalized for the coming year. Continued review and analysis ensure that the right people are in the right jobs for long-term success.			
Month	Main Task	Who Participates	Subtasks/Activities
October	Corporate officers meeting	150 officers	Next-year operating plan focus Role models present initiative successes Executive Development Course (EDC) recommendations All-business dialog: What have we learned?
November	Operating plans presented	All business leaders	Initiatives stretch targets Individual business operating plans Economic outlook
December	Corporate Executive Council	35 business and senior corporate leaders	Set agenda for January's operating managers meeting Individual business initiative highlights BMC recommendations

Each initiative goes through several yearly cycles of Operating System review and learning until it is *embedded in the company's DNA.*[12]

Project Management

Project management competence is an important skill set for a successful DFTS implementation. The Project Management Institute (http://www.pmi.org) offers a Project Management Professional (PMP) certification program that covers the following body of knowledge:[10, 11]

- The project management framework
- The standard for project management
- Project integration management

- Project scope management

- Project time management

- Project cost management

- Project quality management

- Project human resources management

- Project communication management

- Project risk management

- Project procurement management

Several brands of project management software are available, and a number of them do a fine job. However, they are not a panacea and cannot rescue ill-conceived projects. Such projects will result in poor quality and will cause time and cost overruns despite the excellent project management software. Most project management software delivers just fine in conjunction with DFTS technology.

Any detailed treatment of this topic is beyond the scope of this book. We recommend that project leaders (MBBs) develop such competence and earn PMP certification. Other members and champions must acquire project management competence as well. MBBs with project management skills could also be the internal training resource in this important area. Chapter 26 addresses the application of Quality Function Deployment (QFD) to software project management.

Secure

Steps 14 and 15 constitute the last phase of the PICS model. They consist of freezing the improvements and gains and integrating and expanding the initiative, respectively. These two sets of activities are meant to *secure* the initiative as the organization's way of life. This is what Jack Welch calls *embedding in the company's DNA*.

Step 14: Freezing the Improvements and Gains

Chapter 5 discussed Kurt Lewin's Force Field Model and his Three-Step Model of Permanent Social Change (see Figures 5.2 and 5.3). We believe these are powerful tools to analyze and drive change in large social systems. They remain our preferred means of doing so. As we stated in Chapter 5, such changes are difficult to introduce and sustain without positive driving forces such as the organization's reward system and leadership support. At GE, 40% of bonuses and promotions are dependent on Six Sigma project results.

Furthermore, MBBs and BBs are accorded high standing. Such changes can be accomplished much more easily if the CEO and the top management team embrace those changes and make the initiative a big deal. They should start by linking their own reward system and promotion prospects to successful implementation of the initiative and by embracing the changes it entails: *change yourself first.* That works unlike anything else we know of.

Step 15: Integrating and Expanding the Initiative

This is a crucial last step. Successful integration determines the initiative's ultimate success. Chapter 5 introduced the broad issues related to DFTS integration, and they merit elaboration. The need for integration is best understood if you consider the following:

- Different quality systems have a different format, structure, and objectives.

- It is not clear which system serves a given purpose best (such as in selecting outsourcing partners).

- Maintaining different systems may result in duplication, cause confusion, and cost resources.

Integration may become quite complicated if it was not part of the initial deployment planning and if the organization has competing quality systems in place. It is perfectly fine for an organization to have a number of quality systems, so long as they serve particular needs that are not unduly conflicting. Table 21.4 describes different quality systems common in software companies. These may serve distinctly different needs. They can coexist and create synergy if integrated properly so that they serve customers and other needs even better. Integration also provides opportunities to eliminate duplication and redundant practices. It is advisable to have an internal quality management framework that all new deployments can be integrated into (see Case Study 21.2). Yang proposes an integration model consisting of *management principles*, *implementation practices*, and *cultural changes.*[13]

TABLE 21.4
DFTS Vis-à-Vis Other Quality Initiatives in the Software Industry

Quality Initiative	Description	Focus of the System
DFTS	An integrated software development methodology that includes the Iterative Robust Software Development Model, Robust Software Design Optimization Engineering, and Object-Oriented Design Technology. Uses a six-phase RDCVIM model. Meant specifically for trustworthy software development. Led by the CEO and top management, with emphasis on optimizing total life-cycle cost, quality, and cycle time.	Upstream phases, iteration with users and between phases, early risk analysis, design optimization, and use of appropriate software technology.
DFSS	A generic methodology for product, service, and process design. Uses the five-phase MADV/IDDOV model. Meant for design/redesign of high-impact projects. Led by the CEO and top management.	Upstream phases, interaction with users, early risk analysis, and design optimization.
Six Sigma	Generic customer-focused process improvement. Uses the DMAIC model. Meant for any product or process improvement. Led by the CEO and top management.	Key bottom-line-driven short projects. Involves rapid change. Works best when short-term goals are aligned with long-term goals and strategy.
TQM	Customer-focused quality management system. Origins in the Japanese CWQC. Decentralized—led by managers across the organization. Quite popular in 1980s and 1990s. In decline now.	Organization-wide continuous improvement in all products, processes, and systems affecting customer satisfaction. Focus on the long term.

TABLE 21.4
Continued

SEI Capability Maturity Models		
Model	Description	Focus of the Model
CMMI®	Helps integrate separate functions, set improvement goals and priorities, provide guidance for quality processes, and serve as a reference for appraising capability. Consists of four integrated models: System Engineering (SE), Software Engineering (SW), Integrated Product or Process Development (IPPD), and Supplier Sourcing (SS). Incorporates SCAMPI Appraisal Method and Six Capability Levels. SCAMPI Lead Appraisers™ and appraisal for maturity levels are available.	Improvements to attain higher capability maturity across the four models: SE, SW, IPPD, and SS
PCMM®	Helps address critical people issues in a software context. Introduced in 1995. Replaced by version 2 in 2001. PCMM Lead Assessors and appraisal for maturity levels available.	Best practices in HR, knowledge management, and organization development. Five maturity levels.
ISO Standards		
Standard	Description	Focus of the Standard
ISO 9001:2000	An international quality management system. The most popular generic quality standard worldwide. Replaces the 1994 version. Independent third-party audits and certification are available.	A set of five quality standards based on eight principles: customer focus, leadership, involvement of people, process approach, systems approach to management, continual improvement, factual approach to decision making, and mutually beneficial relationships with suppliers.

ISO Standards (continued)		
Standard	Description	Focus of the Standard
ISO 17799:2005	Information security techniques. Replaces the 2000 version. Contains code for best practices for information security management. Not designed to be a certification standard.	Establishes guidelines and general principles for initiating, implementing, maintaining, and improving information security management in an organization.
ISO 14001	A generic international environmental management system consisting of standards and tools. A few software developers have implemented the system with a view to understanding their clients' environmental management activities and requirements. Independent third-party audits and certification are available	What the organization does to minimize harmful effects on the environment caused by its activities and to continually improve its environmental performance.
Other Standards		
Standard	Description	Focus of the Standard
BS 15000-1: 2002	Provides recommendations for IT service management. Is relevant for those responsible for initiating, implementing, or maintaining IT service management in their organization. It specifies a number of closely related service management processes.	Promotes the adoption of an integrated process approach to effectively deliver managed services to meet business and customer requirements. It specifies a number of closely related service management processes.
BS 15000-2: 2003	Describes the best practices for service management processes within the scope of BS 15000-1. BS 15000-2 represents an industry consensus on quality standards for IT service management processes.	Delivers the best possible service to meet an organization's business needs within agreed-upon resource levels—service that is professional, cost-effective, and with risks that are understood and managed.

TABLE 21.4
Continued

Quality Awards		
Award	Description	Focus of the Award
Malcolm Baldrige	An award for U.S.-based organizations or units for outstanding achievements in seven areas. The winner gets a review, feedback, and a competition-based award.	Based on a review by business and quality experts of the following reward criteria: leadership; strategic planning; customer and market focus; measurement, analysis, and knowledge management; human resources focus; process management; and business results.
EFQM	An award for European or Europe-based firms for excellence based on the EFQM Excellence Model that can be used for self-assessment, benchmark, improvement, vocabulary, and management structure.	Based on a review of the TQM framework of five "enablers" (leadership, people, policy and strategy, partnerships and resources, processes) and four "results" (customers, people, society, and key performance).
RGNQA	An award for organizations based in India. The criteria are similar to those for Malcolm Baldrige, the Deming Prize, and the European Quality Award.	Based on nine criteria: leadership; policies, objectives and strategies; human resources management; resources; processes; customer-focused results; employee satisfaction; impact on environment and society; and business results.

Integration of Management Principles

The integration of management principles involves asking the following questions:

- What are the differences and similarities between DFTS tools, techniques, and methodologies and those of existing systems?

- What new best practices have emerged from the DFTS deployment that have a substantial impact on quality, life-cycle cost, delivery schedules, internal efficiency, and motivation of people?

- What changes can substantially improve the value of other quality initiatives?

- What changes can substantially enhance DFTS effectiveness and value by using best practices from other systems?

- What tasks can be eliminated or merged as a result of this analysis?

- What synergies can be identified between DFTS and other systems, and what are their values?

This analysis can be further enhanced by including external best practices.

Integrating Implementation Practices

Here we are concerned with how we can integrate and share the elements of DFTS and other quality systems. The elements that should be considered are employee participation, teamwork, training, human resources management, reward system, communication system, quality principles, objective, strategies, project management, statistical tools, and CEO support. It is also important to identify elements that are not common.

Integrating Cultural Changes

This has to do with identifying the organization's underlying vision, mission, values, and beliefs and how they are congruent with the DFTS process and other initiatives and practices within the organization. More specifically, it involves determining what behavioral and cultural issues are critical to performance. These are not always formally addressed, but their understanding is crucial to the initiative's viability and often the enterprise's long-term vitality as well. Case Study 21.2 illustrates how these changes relate to an organization's strategic differentiators and various quality initiatives over several decades. Chapter 27 is a case study in which well-known quality and other management tools such as Consumer Encounters, New Lanchester Strategy, Kansei Engineering, Theory of Constraints, TRIZ, Voice of the Customer Analysis, FMEA, SPC, and other methods can be integrated into the new-product development process.

Another important aspect of integration has to do with the initiative's total assimilation into the organization's way of life. GE accomplishes that through its Operating System, discussed in Case Study 21.1. The CEO and the top management team must give the initiative their total and undivided attention for a number of years to facilitate its integration methodically into the organization.

Case Study 21.2: Quality Initiatives and Their Integration at TCS[14, 15]

In August 2004, Tata Consultancy Services (TCS) achieved an integrated enterprise-wide Maturity Level 5 assessment on both the Capability Maturity Model Integration (CMMI®) and the People Capability Maturity Model (PCMM®). A subsidiary of the Tata Group, the largest Indian conglomerate, TCS thus became the first company globally to achieve that double feat.

TCS is the largest IT services company in India. It has been a pioneer in the offshore IT delivery model since 1974. Over the years it has grown into a global IT services organization employing over 45,000 associates in 47 counties across five continents. It has a market capitalization of over $14 billion and serves organizations worldwide, including seven of the top ten Fortune 500 companies. Its diverse services include consulting, IT services, asset-based solutions, IT infrastructure, engineering and industrial services, and business process outsourcing (BPO). TCS has long been admired as an outstanding organization and was ranked number 1 across industries in the Hewitt-CNBC India Survey for 2004. Its IPO was named "Best India Deal" by *Finance Asia*, Hong Kong.

TCS enjoys a strong corporate culture emphasizing "helping the customer achieve their business objectives by providing best-in-class services." More than 75% of TCS's customers reward the company's reliability, passion, creativity, and unique ability to handle the broadest range of their IT needs by continually extending and deepening their partnerships with TCS.[16]

Vision

Global Top 10 by 2010

Mission

To help customers achieve their business objectives by providing innovative, best-in-class consulting, IT solutions, and services. Make it a joy for all stakeholders to work with us.

Values

Integrity
Leading change
Excellence
Respect for the individual
Learning and sharing

Key Differentiators

Truly global
Superior execution
Ability to deliver large-scale integration projects globally
Ability to scale
Strong people management
Superior client relationships
Continuous investment in R&D

The company's quality initiatives can be traced to the early 1980s, when internal quality standards began to be formalized. In 1993, the company received ISO 9001 certifications for a few units, which subsequently were extended enterprise-wide. It has held to ISO 9001 corporate-wide certification through yearly audits. In 1994, the company decided to build CMM capabilities. In 1998 one of its units was assessed at Level 5. Subsequently, it also got assessed successfully for PCMM at Level 5. During the intervening years, the company adopted its internal Tata Business Excellence Model (TBEM) and won the Tata Group's internal JRD QV Award and Rajiv Gandhi National Quality Award (RGNQA) for 2003 for three of its development centers in India. TCS has also implemented and maintained ISO 14001 and BS 7799 over the years.

All along, TCS has integrated its various quality initiatives through iQMS, its internal quality management system, which is based on IEEE, CMMI®, SW-CMM®, ISO 9001:2000, and PCMM. This integration and a relentless quest for excellence have enabled TCS to set global benchmarks in quality standards by becoming the first company in the world to achieve an integrated enterprise-wide Maturity Level 5 on both CMMI® and PCMM®. That also made the Level 5 assessment for its centers in China and Uruguay the first Level 5 assessments in China and South America, respectively.

Over the years, TCS has launched various initiatives and their upgrades:

- ISO 9001
- ISO 9001:2000
- ISO 14001
- BS 7799
- SW CMM® Level 5
- PCMM® Level 5
- TBEM
- JRD QV
- RGNQA
- iQMS
- CMMI® Level 5
- PCMM® Version 2 Level 5

How has TCS benefited from the multitude of quality initiatives? How does it create synergy? How does it remain customer-centric? Is its quality strategy deliberate, or has it emerged over the years? We still have work to do on all this. But the key to successful multiplatform quality deployments may well be effective integration of various platforms as you go. TCS has accomplished that just fine.

Application in Small Software Firms and e-Cottages

Most of what has been discussed in the case studies and examples in this book relate to large corporations. This is primarily because management research has focused on such organizations. We are reminded that software development groups tend to be small, particularly in new models that are emerging in China and India, which are dubbed *cottage industry models*. Here the software is grown or created by small groups (e-cottages)—an open-source system take-off—at the stated specifications of a larger proprietary organization. Even in large software organizations, development teams tend to be small. How can you mend and blend DFTS technology to help these small groups? Are DFTS tools, techniques, and methodologies applicable to such environments? We believe they are. In fact, quality initiatives thrive in small groups. Many quality tools, such as quality circles and brainstorming, work only in small groups. It is not so much a question of DFTS's applicability in small software organizations. It's more a question of whether small enterprises led by software techies have awareness of and timely access to knowledge and learning that larger organizations may have. That is as true of DFTS as it is for any idea and innovation.

For larger organizations, DFTS fits perfectly in their small development team environment. This has been emphasized elsewhere in this book, including this chapter. DFTS master black belts and black belts would have the required technical and leadership skills and would work in their small "autonomous" teams. When outsourcing to other software firms, including e-cottages, organizations need to ensure that their development partners meet and understand their quality needs. They owe it to themselves to provide necessary support and training. These small (or not so small) "independent" cells need to be fully integrated in their development and delivery process without losing or compromising any quality gains attained upstream. Many manufacturing firms in Japan and elsewhere provide such support to their suppliers. This needs to be better managed in software outsourcing.

We have discussed leadership challenges elsewhere in this book (see, for example, the section "Leadership Challenges for Transformational Initiatives" in Chapter 20). Great leaders are not the monopoly of large organizations. Sony's Morita and Ibuka, and even Toyota's Eiji Toyoda, began their remarkable industrial careers in rather humble circumstances. So have many corporate leaders in technology and software, such as Bill Gates, Steve Jobs, and Narayan Murthy, among many others.

What's Next?

In the final analysis, DFTS technology is about building and honing your competitive capability. This gets done only when committed and competent leadership drives it relentlessly and passionately. DFTS technology, when learned, implemented, and internalized effectively into your corporate genes, creates a formidable competitive advantage. The essence of

DFTS lies in its framework of organization-wide learning. The significance of rigorous learning can hardly be overstated. As Peter Senge emphasized in his remarkable work *The Fifth Discipline*, "the organizations that will truly excel in the future will be the organizations that discover how to tap people's commitment and capacity to learn at all levels."[17]

The next step in the DFTS process is to expand it further into all subsequent software development projects. Every new development must benefit from the learning in previous projects. This should roll on a continual basis. The learning and enrichment that come from ongoing review, appraisal, and learning about the DFTS deployment must become a way of life. These two suites of activities—expansion and continual appraisal and enrichment—must be institutionalized. Along the way you will develop new tools and techniques or come up with a new delivery model or breakthrough software technology, but all effective processes will entail constancy of customer-centricity and continual learning and enrichment. The real learning starts not by reading this book, but by launching the initiative. As Jack Welch says, "(we) launch and learn."[18]

Key Points

- PICS is a 15-step implementation framework for DFTS deployment. It identifies major activities and issues in the deployment process along its four phases: plan, implement, control, and secure.

- It is important to identify both long- and short-term objectives for DFTS training programs and to ensure that they are complementary.

- All training programs must be customized for a particular organization as well as differentiated along specific roles and responsibilities of the participants.

- Organization-wide learning starts with training two groups of support personnel: the senior executives and the support staff in HR, sales and marketing, finance, IS, and so on.

- All software professionals, from Vice President of Software Development/Chief Software Architect down to young software engineers, must undergo black belt training. It should also be required training for all quality professionals, from Chief Quality Officer downward.

- The leadership must make training and learning a big deal. Everyone with any link to the DFTS process must undergo training—and that starts with the CEO.

- Successful completion of training and subsequent contribution to DFTS deployment and integration must be made the major requirements for individual rewards and growth for everyone, including the CEO and the top management team.

- The quality and HR departments should come up with a certification scheme for the DFTS trainees in consultation with academia and possibly outside consultants. Trainee participants must meet a specified level of proficiency for certification purposes.

- Each week-long DFTS training phase is followed by software project work and Customer Appraisal and Review (CAR) before the next phase of training and further development work. This is a process of action learning in that the team learns not only in the classroom but also during the software development process.

- A defining aspect of the DFTS learning process is the practice of self-appraisal, successive appraisal, and review of work carried out to date with the customers. Here customers are not only external but internal—the next person(s) in the development process.

- Simon's *Levers of Control* consists of four constructs: belief systems, boundary systems, diagnostic control systems, and interactive control systems. They deal with strategic control of the enterprise.

- Another set of control mechanisms, internal control systems, are not used to control strategy but are fundamental in ensuring the integrity of data used in strategic control systems. It is therefore essential that those responsible for the organization's internal control systems also be involved in safeguarding the integrity of DFTS process and quality data, especially CoSQ and other financial data.

- Operational controls of the process are accomplished through feedback control systems, an integral part of the PICS framework, and through project management, which has its own control devices.

- The DFTS feedback control system must be designed to measure variables that are important, measurable, and actionable. They meet five different sets of objectives: learning and teaching capabilities, CoSQ capabilities, customer satisfaction, process robustness, and improvement opportunities.

- Feedback control systems essentially provide visibility on cost, quality, and other measures of performance. They often become sociopolitical in nature because the people involved may feel insecure or perceive a loss of power as a result of such visibility on their performance. Therefore, these systems must have the support of the CEO and the top management team to be viable.

- Although feedback control systems have been in use for all kinds of control purposes, they are not always perceived and designed well.

- A well-structured review system should be more than just a control mechanism. It should enrich and energize the initiative across the organization by providing required measures to improve the product and the development process. GE's Operating System is an excellent example of an innovative review and learning system.

- Project management competence is an important skill set for a successful DFTS implementation. We recommend that MBBs earn Project Management Professional Certification, offered by the Project Management Institute.

- Transformative changes are difficult to introduce and sustain without positive driving forces such as the organization's reward system and leadership support. At GE, 40% of bonuses and promotions are dependent on Six Sigma project results. Furthermore, MBBs and BBs are accorded high standing.

- A solid assimilation of an initiative involves integration at three levels: management principles, implementation practices, and cultural changes.

- DFTS tools, techniques, and methodologies are applicable to both large and small organizations. In fact, quality initiatives thrive in small groups. It is not so much a question of DFTS's applicability in small software organizations. It is more a question of whether small enterprises have awareness of and timely access to knowledge and learning that larger organizations may have. That is true for both DFTS and any idea or innovation.

- Large organizations, when outsourcing to other software firms, need to ensure that their development partners meet and understand their quality needs. They owe it to themselves to provide the necessary support and training. Many manufacturing firms in Japan and elsewhere provide such support to their suppliers. This needs to be better managed in software outsourcing.

Additional Resources

http://www.prenhallprofessional.com/title/0131872508

http://www.agilenty.com/publications

Internet Exercises

1. Read the article on the following Web site and present a summary of it to the class:

   http://www.sbaer.uca.edu/research/dsi/2001/pdffiles/PAPERS/Volume1/pt5/0628.pdf

A later version of this article is available as "Six Sigma: A Goal-Theoretic Perspective," Kevin Linderman, Roger G. Schroeder, Srilata Zaheer, Adrian S. Choo, *Journal of Operations Management*, 2003, Vol. 21, Num. 2, pp. 193–203.

In particular, discuss the following propositions suggested in the article:

Proposition 1: Six Sigma projects that employ specific challenging goals tend to result in a greater magnitude of improvement than projects that don't employ specific challenging goals.

Proposition 2: Specific Six Sigma goals tend to result in more team member effort than vague goals.

Proposition 3: The use of a structured method tends to increase performance on complex tasks.

Proposition 4: Employees who receive Six Sigma training tend to perform better on complex tasks than employees who do not receive training.

Proposition 5: Goal commitment increases with a mandate from senior leadership.

2. Read the PMI's *Project Management Body of Knowledge* on the following Web site:

   http://www.pmi.org/prod/groups/public/documents/info/
   pp_pmbokguidethirdexcerpts.pdf

   A printed version is available as *A Guide to the Project Management Body of Knowledge*, ANSI/PMI 99-001-2004 (Newtown Square, PA: PMI, Inc., 2004).

   Present a brief summary of the nine Knowledge Areas to the class.

Review Questions

1. What are the key deliverables of the planning steps in the PICS model? Explain their significance.

2. List and describe short- and long-term learning objectives of the DFTS training program.

3. Compare and contrast the training programs for senior executives with that for other support personnel.

4. Describe the roles of black belts (BBs) and master black belts (MBBs) in a DFTS deployment context. How do these roles differ from those of BBs and MBBs in a typical Six Sigma deployment context?

5. Describe the certification requirements for various levels of DFTS training. Are they adequate as described in this book?

6. Describe the role the CEO and the top management team play in securing the gains attained following a DFTS implementation.

7. Is DFTS applicable to small software enterprises? What role does a large organization play in securing its quality requirements from outsourcing partners?

Discussion Questions

1. Discuss the strengths and weaknesses of the PICS model vis-à-vis traditional software development models such as a waterfall model.

2. Explain the significance of customization and differentiation in designing DFTS curricula.

3. Describe and examine the significance of each of the four control constructs as proposed in Simon's *Levers of Control*. Is any construct really redundant in an origination that you are familiar with?

4. Discuss the elements of feedback control systems for a DFTS deployment. What important questions do they address, and what is their significance?

5. Make a critical appraisal of GE's Operating System (see Case Study 21.1), and present it to the class.

6. Make a critical appraisal of TCS's quality initiatives and their integration (see Case Study 21.2), and present it to the class.

7. Prepare a page-long memo for the CEO of your organization about launching a DFTS initiative in your organization.

Endnotes

[1] W. S. Humphrey, *Introduction to Personal Software Process*™ (Boston, MA: Addison-Wesley, 1997).

[2] W. S. Humphrey, *Introduction to Team Software Process*™ (Boston, MA: Addison-Wesley, 2000).

[3]N. M. Tichy and S.Sherman, *Control Your Destiny or Someone Else Will* (New York: HarperBusiness, 2001), p. 305.

[4]R. Simons, *Levers of Control* (Boston, MA: Harvard Business School Press, 1995), pp. 7, 178–181.

[5]W. George, "Address Given to the Academy of Management," *Academy of Management Executive* 15, No. 4 (November 2001), pp. 39–47.

[6]Op cit Simons, p. 181.

[7]W. E. Deming, *Out of the Crisis* (Cambridge, MA: MIT, Center for Advanced Engineering Studies, 1986), p. 88.

[8]http://www.ge.com/en/company/companyinfo/at_a_glance/operating_system.htm.

[9]R. S. Kaplan and P. Norton, "The Balanced Scorecard: Measures That Drive Performance," *Harvard Business Review*, January–February 1992, 70 (1): 71–79.

[10]http://www.pmi.org/prod/groups/public/documents/info/pp_pmbokguidethirdexcerpts.pdf.

[11]*A Guide to the Project Management Body of Knowledge*, ANSI/PMI 99-001-2004 (Newtown Square, PA: PMI, Inc., 2004).

[12]General Electric, annual report, 1999.

[13]C-C Yang, "An Integrated Model of TQM and GE-Six Sigma," *International Journal of Six Sigma and Competitive Advantage*, Vol. 1, 2004, pp. 97–111.

[14]http://www.tcs.com.

[15]http://www.tcs-america.com/investors/pdf/TCSPresentation-Equitymaster.pdf.

[16]http://itresearch.forbes.com/detail/ORG/1114710658_184.html.

[17]P. M. Senge, *The Fifth Discipline: The Art and Practice of Learning Organization* (New York: Doubleday Currency, 1990), p. 4.

[18]N. M. Tichy and S. Sherman, *Control Your Destiny or Someone Else Will* (New York: HarperBusiness, 2001), p. 305.

PART V

Six Case Studies

The following six case studies are included to illustrate and provide more sophisticated examples of some of the methods advocated by this book. These examples were provided by the leading developers of each methodology. We begin with Cost of Software Quality (CoSQ), which illustrates that quality assurance is not a cost issue in software development but rather a methodology that more than pays its own way. This book is devoted to the development of trustworthy business enterprise applications software, with only the occasional reference to the computing or data processing environment in which the application will run. That environment within a business enterprise is characterized by the information technology application portfolio—that is, the set of all the applications that must run together successfully in a viable enterprise. Quality Function Deployment (QFD) is a very important part of the DFTS process and one that most of today's developers are unfamiliar with. Here we include four case studies of QFD to give you a broad perspective on this powerful methodology. They further support the material introduced in Chapter 11.

Case Study 1 (Chapter 22), "Cost of Software Quality (CoSQ) at Raytheon's Electronic Systems (RES) Group," by Herb Krasner

This case study describes a benchmark software development organization that uses CoSQ to document the results of an improvement program and to observe how CoSQ concepts relate to the consistent production of high-quality software. This case study is meant to supplement the concepts developed in Chapter 4 with a realistic large-scale application in a major software development organization. The organization chosen for this case study showed specific, measured benefits. Although part of a large corporation, this development group was typical of a contract software development group in any large organization. Such an organization can be successful only if it can satisfy customers by delivering high-quality software on time and within budget. CoSQ is used to show the costs and benefits of its investments over the time span of the improvement program and provides a good example of how CoSQ is used in leading software development organizations today. Although this case study pertains primarily to large, mostly military, real-time, mission-critical, and embedded software applications, Raytheon breaks the costs into those associated with con-formance and those associated with nonconformance. They can then be classified more generally into costs for taking proactive or preventive measures and costs associated with repairs and cleanups needed to fix design/implementation errors and other rework costs. But the conformance costs are due to taking precautions to prevent or mitigate the effects of threats or probable failure patterns. In most cases these are ambiguous or ill-structured requirements, inadequate designer training, or trying to integrate components built with conflicting assumptions. Raytheon's use of CoSQ occurred within the context of its contract-oriented systems business. Thus, the approach reported in this case study was adapted to the specifics of that situation. A more general approach will likely be required in a different business setting, but we believe this case study presents a useful and general-izable example of CoSQ.

Case Study 2 (Chapter 23), "Information Technology Portfolio Alignment," by Ernest H. Forman

The impact of information technology has led to significant changes in the operation of most organizations. The resource demands for both maintaining and enhancing an organi-zation's information technology portfolio are insatiable, and they almost always exceed the available resources. Early decisions about what information technologies to implement and maintain were made by technologists. Today, however, organizations have realized that these decisions, while requiring a solid understanding of technology, also must involve senior management from throughout the organization to ensure alignment with the organization's strategic and tactical objectives. In the early days of MIS, the most critical applications were automated first. But before the needs of the entire organization could be satisfied, technology change demanded that the first five or six highest-priority applications be redone to meet the challenges of new hardware technology, new software technology, or a changed organization or business model. The result was that even after 20 years, the twelfth and thirteenth most important applications never were implemented. In practice, a wide range of processes have attempted to complete an IT applications portfolio that meets the organization's needs. The results of such processes vary widely because what might be intuitive isn't always effective. For example, assigning weights to criteria and projects and then allocating funds to the highest-ranking projects until available resources are consumed may seem logical, but actually this is far from optimal. In fact, the sum of the local optima is rarely the global optimum. This case study looks at the necessary requirements of a best-practices process for deciding what to include in an organization's portfolio of information technologies. This case study takes you beyond the quality issues involved in designing and developing a particular application, to the interactions of that application with existing and future applications in the user's portfolio. The case study illustrates the authors' approach with a specific example, but the case study is presented with such clarity and detail that you will be able to apply the method to your own situation. One well-worked example is often much more valuable than a theory! This case study illustrates an application of AHP introduced in Chapter 8.

Case Study 3 (Chapter 24), "Defining Customer Needs for Brand-New Products: QFD for Unprecedented Software," by Richard E. Zultner

QFD has traditionally been employed not only for new-product development but also for revisions or model upgrades to existing products. Listening to the voice of the customer is especially valuable when the customer has experience with a product that is to be upgraded. This case study deals with the problem of getting input from the future customers of a new, as-yet-undeveloped product with which they do not have experience. Most of the examples of Taguchi Methods application in this book are to product upgrades and improvements for which the method really works well and for which its application is easiest to visualize. Several times throughout this book we have noted that the enterprise business application designer or software architect rarely gets the opportunity to specify and design a whole new product from scratch, but it does happen. When it does, tools such as Concept Selection and QFD come to the rescue. This case study is a valuable adjunct to the methods taught in this book, because it focuses precisely on those situations. Existing approaches to QFD are reviewed, and new methods based on them are developed. The "mind of the customer" approach is used by the Theory of Constraints (ToC), which identifies the customer's core problem and core conflict. These can then lead to a solution beyond the customer's experience and help you plan for its acceptance and implementation. Applying ToC involves breakthrough solutions or paradigm shifts, and thus may involve overcoming the natural resistance of many people to change. This case study reviews the six layers of resistance to change and describes the specific tools to break through each layer. When the software architect starts with a blank sheet of paper to design a whole new product from scratch, he or she may have to deal with fewer constraints, but the novelty that situation permits will very likely engender organizational resistance. This case study, written by the leading consultant on QFD, teaches the designer how to deal with that resistance.

Case Study 4 (Chapter 25), "Jurassic QFD: Integrating Service and Product Quality Function Deployment," by Andrew Bolt and Glenn Mazur

QFD is a unique system for developing new products. It aims to ensure that the initial quality of the product or service satisfies the customer. In today's fast-paced economy, traditional design methods that rely on extensive concept and market testing and multiple rollouts take too much time and increase the risk that copycat products may enter the market first. Best efforts driven by internal requirements risk failing to recognize important customer needs. The tools and methods described in this chapter show you how these risks can be minimized with proper planning. This case study shows you how QFD can be customized to a specific project, in this case to design a tangible product—an animatronic dinosaur to be used in a theme park. Although the product development described in this case study is not software only, but a program-enabled robotic device, the case study deals with planning and requirements determination before the product or service is designed and implemented, as Chapter 11 recommends. It is an important topic that has not been covered in software engineering books so far. It is included here as a clear example of the technology. The ideas and approaches used are innovative, yet all can be realized in different ways, depending on the target applications. Even though this case study is not strictly in the software engineering area, it amply illustrates ideas behind the QFD approach that could form the front end of a systematic design of any complex product. Although it is instructive in many ways, this case study also shows that QFD can be a lot of fun—especially when it's used to design really big toys!

Case Study 5 (Chapter 26), "Project QFD: Managing Software Development Projects Better with Blitz QFD®," by Richard E. Zultner

QFD has been used for software development for more than a decade, and its popularity is increasing. This case study reviews the value of QFD for the software manager and the management process as well as the benefits to product quality improvement. After reviewing what can go wrong with a software development project, this case study suggests an initial use of QFD called Blitz QFD®. The idea is for project managers to manage value just like they manage time—by spending time on activities that are truly essential rather than those that are merely desirable. With this form of QFD, the manager can manage value in the same way he or she manages time, money, and people. This ensures that the product delivered to the customer is the first priority of the development project. Project QFD takes a portal-to-portal view of the development project and tells the project manager where to spend scarce person-hours on the most important activities in the project. This is the second case study written by the leading practitioner of QFD. It shows how QFD may be used effectively with a minimum of quantitative or computational overhead.

Case Study 6 (Chapter 27), "QFD 2000: Integrating QFD and Other Quality Methods to Improve the New-Product Development Process," by Glenn Mazur

Competitive advantage in the new millennium may belong more to those who can integrate a multitude of disciplines into a system, rather than to those who expect a single nuanced tool to do it all. The House of Quality is really more of a "great room" to which various "outbuildings" and other structures must connect. This is really a "meta" case study that shows where well-known quality and other management tools can be integrated into the New Product Development Process. These tools include Consumer Encounters, New Lanchester Strategy, Kansei Engineering, Theory of Constraints, TRIZ, Voice of the Customer Analysis, FMEA, and SPC. As such, it presents an array of tools and resources for the development team that wants to integrate various quality methods to build an appropriate organization software development strategy. Designing and developing new products is a multidisciplinary activity that involves different people at different times. It varies according to the company, its customers, and its product.

CHAPTER 22

Cost of Software Quality (CoSQ) at Raytheon's Electronic Systems (RES) Group[*]

Herb Krasner
University of Texas at Austin
hkrasner@ece.utexas.edu

Chapter Outline

- Introduction

- RES and Its Improvement Program

- Cost of Software Quality

- Experiences and Lessons Learned

- Case Study Implications

- Endnotes

Reproduced by permission of Jack Campanella, editor, *Principles of Quality Costs: Principles, Implementation, and Use, Third Edition* (Milwaukee: ASQ Quality Press, 1999), pp. 169-77.

Introduction

The intent of this case study is to provide visibility into a benchmark software development organization that currently uses CoSQ to document the results of its improvement program and to observe how CoSQ concepts relate to the consistent production of high-quality software. The Raytheon Electronic Systems (RES) organization was chosen as a case study subject because, using a CoSQ approach, it was able to show specific, measured benefits from its software improvement activities. See the discussion of RES CoSQ activities in Chapter 4's section on Software Quality Costs.[1]

Although RES is in the contract systems business, it is similar in many ways to the commercial software supplier who wants to achieve a successful and profitable business by satisfying customers with a high-quality software (or system) product delivered on time and within budget. Although there are many reasons to use CoSQ in an organization, RES used it to measure and demonstrate the effects of its ongoing software improvement program. Specifically, CoSQ was used to show the costs and benefits of its investments over the chronology of its improvement program. This is a good example of the way in which a few leading organizations are using CoSQ today.

RES and Its Improvement Program

Raytheon Electronic Systems (previously Raytheon Equipment Division) builds real-time, mission-critical, embedded software systems under contract to defense and commercial customers. It builds these systems in the domains of air traffic control, vessel traffic management, digital communications, ground and shipboard radar, satellite communications, undersea warfare, military command and control, and combat training. The systems it builds are large and typically range from 70–500 KDSI (thousand delivered source instructions).

Since 1988 RES has been engaged in a software improvement initiative which was driven by the need to overcome overrunning schedules and budgets, and the crisis-driven environment that resulted. Subsequently, once budgets and schedules came under some control, it turned its attention to the goal of reducing rework.

The RES improvement initiative covered roughly 350–600 professionals. The investment for the initiative has been steady at about $1 million per year. The SEI CMM (Software Engineering Institute Capability Maturity Model)-based approach was later adopted and used to help focus its improvements. Following this approach, it was self-assessed at CMM Level 1 in 1988, Level 2 in 1990, and Level 3 in 1992, and as of 1995 it operated all new projects starting at Level 4. (For a description of the SEI CMM levels, see Table 4.3 in the Software Quality Costs section of Chapter 4.)[2] In 1995, RES won the coveted IEEE Computer Society's Software Process Achievement Award.

RES's improvement program strategy included a dual focus on product and process. The product focal point areas included system definition, requirements definition, inspections and integration, and qualification testing. The process focal point areas included development planning and management controls, training, and pathfinding.

Cost of Software Quality

CoSQ was chosen as one of four measures to track, because it provided a framework to determine rework levels, as well as the overall return on investment (ROI) or RES's improvement program. The other measures chosen were software productivity, cost performance index, and overall product quality.

The following describes how RES used CoSQ as a method for tracking rework and calculating ROI in their software improvement program. It is adapted from previously published sources.

RES's CoSQ Model

Cost of software quality was considered the sum of two components: the cost of nonconformance (rework costs) and the cost of conformance (prevention and appraisal costs). RES determined that they needed to track these quality cost categories. The model shown in Figure 22.1 was used to accumulate them.

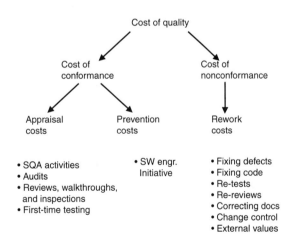

FIGURE 22.1
RES's CoSQ Model

In this model, CoSQ is the sum of the costs of appraisal, prevention, and rework. The focus on rework is important, because it represents the major component of waste and scrap of software development. One of the most costly activities in software development today is reworking or redoing what has already been done. There are many underlying reasons why this happens, but mostly because of flawed requirements, changing conditions, and unexpected problems. For some reason, software professionals have come to accept mountains of rework as part of their everyday activities—in some cases, they do not think of it as rework. For example, precious schedule time is spent on fixes for code defects when software doesn't perform as expected, or on redesign of a user interface because the customer expects something different from what is provided. Many software engineers think of this as the way things are supposed to happen.

The definitions of each subcategory (within the CoSQ categories of appraisal, prevention, and rework), which were rather brief for reasons of simplicity, were subject to misinterpretation. This was addressed by refining the definitions as experience was gained in using them. This required five iterations of the initial data-gathering exercise before a satisfactory level of consistency was obtained.

Breaking these basic quality cost categories (rework, appraisal, and prevention) into subcategories, defining the subcategories, and assigning project activities and costs to them proved to be a difficult task for RES. This was because the existing work breakdown structure used on the software projects did not correspond well to the CoSQ categories.

CoSQ Data Gathering

Project costs were collected using the conventional work breakdown structure, and project leaders periodically manually reassigned all costs to the cost of quality subcategories. The projects' CoSQ data was then combined. The improvement initiative costs were factored in as a separate prevention project. These were then used to produce the organizational CoSQ average and trend data.

Long-term plans were to develop a common work breakdown structure to provide as close a mapping to the cost of quality as possible. This would also entail a revision of the cost accounting system and possibly the time card reporting system as well.

Experiences and Lessons Learned

CoSQ Model Usage Lessons

RES encountered a number of experiences using the CoSQ model. Many questions arose about how to allocate costs to subcategories. There was quite a variation in the methods used to break down the actual costs to the defined cost bin. This was resolved by refining the subcategory definitions and by analyzing and comparing the sub-allocation algorithms used by the six target project leaders. It was necessary to have the project leader, rather than an administrator, generate the data because the project leader possessed the firsthand knowledge of project particulars, as well as good engineering judgment.

Using the CoSQ Data to Understand the Impact of Improvement

Table 22.1 shows the RES distribution of total project costs into CoSQ categories, to track the impact of its improvement program over the years. Starting at CMM Level 1 in 1988, RES introduced its software process improvement (SPI) program. Using the results of tracking 15 projects, it achieved CMM Level 3 practices in a little over three years. As seen in Figure 22.2, at the Level 1 stage, RES's CoSQ fluctuated between 55 percent and 67 percent of total project costs and, by the time of reaching Level 3 process maturity in 1991, its CoSQ had dropped to approximately 40 percent of total project cost. In 1990, when RES was approaching CMM Level 3, RES's total CoSQ was about 45 percent of total project costs, and its ratio of conformance to nonconformance costs was approximately 1.5. In 1994, when RES was adopting a goal of CMM Level 4, RES's total CoSQ was about 24 percent of total project costs, and its ratio of conformance to nonconformance costs was approximately 3.0.

TABLE 22.1
CoSQ Tracking at Specific Points in Time

	Other Project Costs	Rework (Non-conformance)	Appraisal	(Conformance)	Prevention
1988	34%	44%	15%		7%
1990	55%	18%	18%		12%
1992	66%	11%	—	23%	—
1994	76%	6%	—	18%	—

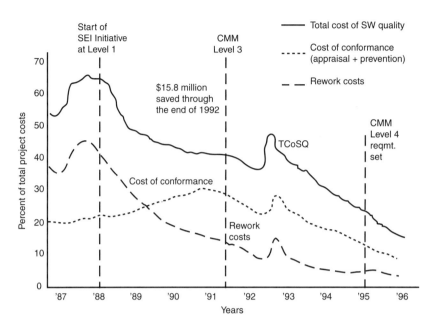

FIGURE 22.2
Tracking the Cost of Software Quality at RES

Rework Cost Savings

Figure 22.2 also shows the trend in the average costs of rework from the start of the improvement initiative. In the two years prior to the initiative, the rework costs had averaged about 41 percent of total project costs. In the two years following, that value had dropped to about 20 percent, and the trend was continuing downward. In 1995, CoSQ was approximately 25 percent of total project costs, and the rework due to both internal and external failures had been reduced to around 6 percent of total project costs.

Rework savings were achieved at the expense of a small increase in conformance costs. For example, appraisal costs rose when informal reviews were replaced by formal inspections, and prevention costs rose when inspection training was instituted. Also, rework costs associated with fixing defects found during design rose from about 0.75 percent to about 2 percent of project cost, and those associated with fixing defects found during coding rose from about 2.5 percent to about 4 percent of project costs.

The major reduction in rework costs was that associated with fixing source code problems found during integration, which dropped to about 20 percent of its original value. The second largest contributor to the rework reduction was the cost of retesting, which decreased to about half its initial value. This clearly indicates that the additional costs of performing formal inspections and the training that must precede it are justified on the basis of finding problems earlier in the process.

Software Quality

The ultimate measure of quality is the contribution that software made to RES's success with software-intensive systems. Improvements made have enabled success on several major software-intensive programs and have allowed RES to tackle larger software projects. This was concretely demonstrated on several complex system projects by removing software from the critical path, and even delivering early, thus earning incentives. The primary quantitative measure that RES uses to assess overall product quality is the defect density in the final software products. This density factory is measured as the number of software trouble reports (STRs) per thousand lines of delivered source instructions (KDSI) on each project. The project densities are combined to compute a monthly weighted average to yield a time plot (trend chart) of the Software Quality Level (STRs/KDSI). As shown in Figure 22.3, the average level of quality improved from about 17.2 STRs/KDSI to about 4 STRs/KDSI, about four times improvement.

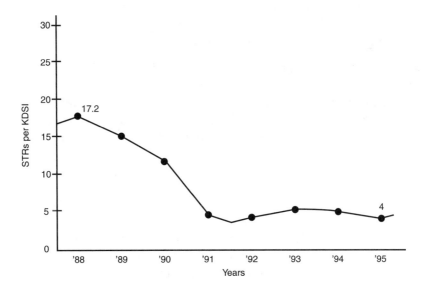

FIGURE 22.3
Tracking the Level of Software Quality at RES

Productivity

Data was collected from individual projects on their productivity in terms of equivalent delivered source instructions (EDSI) per man-month of development effort. The data was combined from all projects using a weighting function, and the results showed the average productivity was, in fact, increasing as a function of time—meaning that jobs were costing less. Overall, RES achieved a 170 percent increase in software productivity, as measured on 24projects over seven years.

Predictability

Management needed to be reassured that the improved productivity figures were being used to bid new jobs. This issue was addressed by collecting CPI (Cost Performance Index) data on the project's budgeted (predicted) cost and actual cost at completion (CAC). This CPI ratio (CAC/Budget) for each project was then used to compute the monthly weighted average (using the same approach as the cost of quality) to yield a plot of this time-variant measure. The results were encouraging, showing that the cost performance index was improved dramatically from about 20 percent overrun prior to the start of the initiative to the 1 percent to 2 percent range by early 1993. Overall, the CPI (CAC/Budget) went from about 1.43 to 1.00 in the first three years and has been steady at about 1.00 since.

Other ROI Results

RES has won additional business based on its process maturity results (no amount reported). Software personnel work less overtime than before, and this has led to lower turnover rates. The overall payoff of its improvement program was reported to be 7.5 times (not including a $9.6 million schedule incentive award in 1991)—for example, in 1990, it spent $1.1 million on improvements and determined that the cost of nonconformance was reduced by $8.2 million in that year. Other leading organizations have realized similar bottom-line benefits.

CoSQ Costs and Benefits

CoSQ analysis cost RES about $25,000 of overhead for the first-time exercise. It repeated the CoSQ analysis exercise about a year later and added the analysis process to the normal senior management process reviews on a semi-annual basis.

The CoSQ analysis used by RES was determined to be a viable mechanism for them to measure the overall effect of software process improvement. It can be used to isolate software waste/scrap and to try to drive it to zero. The information learned in applying the approach benefited the projects involved in the analysis by providing early feedback. The improvement of the organization's standard process was also facilitated.

Institutionalization of CoSQ Tracking

By 1993, after three years, the data-gathering exercise for CoSQ had become more routine. Although the full analysis was being made semi-annually, some department managers were requiring their project leaders to provide the CoSQ data along with their normal monthly tracking data. In retrospect, more emphasis could have been placed on transitioning to a common work breakdown structure geared to the collection of CoSQ.

Case Study Implications

RES's use of the CoSQ approach was pioneering and, as such, they learned many lessons that others do not have to learn the hard way. CoSQ was primarily used as an after-the-fact measure of its SPI program's cost and benefits, rather than as a tool to guide its SPI program (which was the CMM). It is expected that other organizations using the CMM approach to SPI will want to do likewise. Therefore, a detailed analysis of the CMM versus CoSQ will be needed so that investment opportunities can be better focused on high-impact areas. This analysis should be focused on the impact of prevention activities in the 18 CMM key process areas on internally and externally induced rework.

RES encountered specific difficulties in the following areas:

- When and how the CoSQ data was gathered, analyzed, reported, and used
- How the model clashed with other models that were already in use
- The lack of an existing Work Breakdown Structure (WBS) with well-defined categories that correspond easily to CoSQ
- How the model was defined at the detailed levels
- How the model was implemented in the organization
- How CoSQ was used for root cause analysis
- How the model was used to stimulate SPI and quality improvements

These difficulties can be overcome with appropriate training and coaching.

RES's use of CoSQ occurred within the context of its contract-oriented systems business; therefore, the CoSQ approach was adapted to the specifics of that situation. A more general approach will likely need to be modified for use in other situations, with different business success parameters. These situations include:

- Standard product-oriented businesses
- Service delivery situations
- Technology-based start-ups

Endnotes

[1]J. Campanella (Ed.), *Principles of Quality Costs: Principles, Implementation and Use* (Milwaukee: ASQ Quality Press, 1998).

[2]Ibid.

CHAPTER 23

Information Technology Portfolio Alignment

Ernest H. Forman
Professor of Management Science, School of Business
George Washington University, Washington, DC 20052
forman@gwu.edu

Overview

The enormous impact of Information Technology (IT) has led to significant changes in how most organizations operate. The resource demands for both maintaining and enhancing an organization's IT portfolio are insatiable—almost always exceeding the availability of resources. At first, technologists decided what forms of IT to implement and maintain. It wasn't long, however, before organizations realized that these decisions, although requiring a good understanding of the technologies, had to involve senior management from throughout the organization to ensure that the decisions aligned with the organization's strategic and tactical objectives. In practice, a wide range of processes attempt to do this. The results of such processes vary widely because what might be intuitive isn't always effective. For example, assigning weights to criteria and projects and then allocating funds to the highest-ranking projects until available resources are consumed may seem logical, but in fact is far from optimal. This chapter will explore the necessary requirements of a best-practice process for deciding what to include in an organization's IT portfolio.

Chapter Outline

- Part One—The Challenge
- Part Two—A New, Rational Approach
- Risk
- Extensions
- Summary
- Endnote

Part One—The Challenge

This case study outlines the advantages of a best-practice approach to deciding what to include in an IT portfolio. A well-thought-out process based on fundamental principles developed over the past 100 years can result in the following benefits to traditional seat-of-the-pants or rack-and-stack methods of portfolio composition.

- **Strategic focus** An IT portfolio *must* reflect the organization's mission and objectives. You can do this by aligning projects and resources with the organization's goals and objectives. A "good" portfolio for one organization might be ill conceived for another. An organization's direction, as set by senior management, *must* set the course for what goes into the portfolio.

- **Better, faster, more competitive decisions** Put in another way, this means "win or lose by *how* you choose." You must address risk and uncertainty. Prioritization is a key element of the "how you choose" portion of this equation, and there are good ways and poor ways (often evident in practice) to prioritize. Priorities based on color schemes (red/yellow/green), adding ranks, and other mathematically meaningless combinations of numbers are sometimes worse than no priorities at all.

- **Improved communication** Decision makers at all levels of the organization are involved, applying their knowledge and experience where it is most effective.

- **Convince others you are right** It isn't enough to just conceive an IT portfolio that is well aligned with an organization's objectives; you *must* communicate it in a way that convinces others that this is indeed the case. A best-practice process reduces battles and breaks deadlocks.

- **Build organizational buy-in** Although it is rarely possible to please everyone, it is almost always possible to have everyone feel they were part of the decision and can commit their energies to successful implementation.

The Five Phases of an Iterative Process

The best practice that we describe is based on an iterative process consisting of five distinct but related phases: design, structuring complexity, measurement, synthesis, and optimization. We will not discuss the details of each phase here, but rather, will focus on the essential nature of each phase and their relationships.

1. **Design** Organizations receive project proposals from numerous sources. There are numerous approaches to designing and articulating projects, including the identification of objective benefits, subjective benefits, risks, and costs. An analysis of what alternatives were considered in the design of each project is often helpful in understanding the proposed benefits.

2. **Structuring complexity** Evaluating benefits, costs, scenarios, and risks is an elusive business that you *must* structure carefully. There are almost always numerous competing factors to consider and just assigning weights in a spreadsheet is a futile exercise. Instead, a best practice entails structuring complexity by organizing these factors into a hierarchy of homogeneous clusters of scenarios, objectives, and subobjectives so that those involved in the decision process do not get lost in a maze of complexity and become hampered by miscommunication.

3. **Measurement** In the past, many organizations made decisions based primarily on financial projections. Portfolio decisions *should* involve both quantitative and qualitative factors. No matter how good the "data" is, there is always a need for keen human judgment, both to interpret the data and to establish priorities. Einstein observed that "Not everything that counts can be counted, and not everything that can be counted, counts." Peter Drucker observed that "We have to measure, not count." Data, no matter how complete and accurate, is not adequate. **Analysis** (breaking things down into parts and studying the parts) is not enough. *Judgment*, as well as data and analysis, is required and judgment *must* be applied in meaningful ways. Portfolio decisions *must* involve decision makers at all levels of the organization. Judgments cannot come solely

from the "top" or "bottom" of the organization. Judgments *must* be made, aligned, and synthesized from the top of the organization down, or from the technical levels of the organization up. An organization's portfolio *should* be shaped by the judgments that top management makes. These judgments reflect the direction the organization should take in order to be faithful to its core ideology. The portfolio should also be shaped by judgments of middle management that reflect the relative importance of objectives that will achieve the elements of its core ideology as well as meet competitive pressures, and judgments of middle and technical management about the activities or projects that can be included in the portfolio in order to achieve these objectives. The result is a consolidation of corporate information and judgments that produces a portfolio that is aligned, from top to bottom, with the organization's goals and objectives. Engaging all levels of an organization's knowledge base is easier said than done. Meetings can be endless and can involve considerable bickering—unless judgments are properly applied to "derive" measures that lead to a coherent, optimal portfolio. But you *must* be careful to ensure that the measures are based on human judgment as well as on data, and that the measures accurately reflect such judgment, are justifiable, and are mathematically sound. *The typical weights-and-scores approach, which many organizations use today, is far from adequate.* A sound IT portfolio alignment requires the following:

- Measures that factor in judgment about data (data alone is rarely adequate)

- Measures that accurately reflect human judgments

- Measures that synthesize judgments from personnel throughout an organization, from executive judgments about strategic objectives to technical judgments about the contributions of specific projects toward specific objectives

- Measures that can be justified because they are derived, rather than arbitrarily assigned

- Measures that can be justified because they are based on a sound mathematical process such as the Analytic Hierarchy Process (AHP)

- Measures that are proportional, or possess "ratio scale" properties that are necessary in order to use powerful optimization techniques in deciding what the IT portfolio *should* and *should not* include

A best practice methodology *must* also be capable of accommodating subtleties that can arise. Unless you incorporate subtleties such as rank reversals, ideal alternatives, and structural adjustment into the methodology, the veracity of the measures can be challenged and the credibility of the process diminished.

4. **Synthesis** The development of a best-practice IT portfolio requires a meaningful synthesis or "fusion" of data, information, analyses, and judgment. This can be a formidable task, especially when some of the information is subjective and some is objective, when there are conflicting objectives, and when expertise and perspectives are distributed throughout an organization. Beware that there are numerous ways to synthesize poorly and to produce a synthesis that does not meaningfully reflect its constituent parts. Examples include adding or averaging ranks, using simple 1 to 5 scales, "normalizing" data so that it appears to be comparable, and color coding. However, if you are careful with your measurements (as noted in step 3), you can avoid these mistakes and achieve a meaningful synthesis that produces ratio scale priorities reflecting proportional measures for the alignment of projects with objectives. Such a synthesis is necessary in order to determine an "optimal portfolio." You can perform sensitivity analysis to ascertain that the results are not only mathematically meaningful, but also logical and consistent. The need for iteration to accommodate additional information, creativity, redesign, or changes in judgment becomes apparent.

5. **Optimization** Optimization is often misunderstood. Optimization is not a search for a preordained "optimal" portfolio, such as searching for a needle in a haystack. Instead, an **optimal portfolio** is the identification of a subset of proposed projects that, in combination, aligns with an organization's objectives better than any other possible subset of projects. The measure of "better than" is based on the structuring, measurement, and synthesis described earlier. The "optimization" involves determining which subset of proposed projects is "best" and entails an efficient search for the "best" subset from a very large number of possible combinations of proposed projects that adhere to myriad monetary, physical, organizational, and political constraints.

The optimal portfolio is guaranteed to be

- Better than a portfolio negotiated using what is sometimes referred to as the BOGSAT (Bunch of Old Guys/Gals Sitting Around Talking) approach, in which benefits are not even measured, or are assessed with whatever can be quantified, omitting important qualitative considerations.

- Better than a portfolio in which benefits are derived based on a structuring of objectives and ratio level measurement, but where the projects are sorted by benefit and funds allocated until the budget is expended.

- Better than a portfolio in which benefits are derived based on a structuring of objectives and ratio level measurement, but where the projects are sorted by benefit/cost ratios and funds allocated until the budget is expended.

- An efficient optimization algorithm is required to identify an optimal portfolio because typically, the number of possible combinations is so large that an exhaustive search of all possible combinations would take hundreds or thousands of years for even the fastest known computers. Furthermore, equally important to the efficiency of the optimization algorithm is the ability for managers to understand and control the optimization process so that the resulting "optimal portfolio" is not only mathematically best, but also intuitively appealing—adhering to the organization's monetary, physical, organizational, and political constraints.

Objectivity, Subjectivity, and Quality

The word *objective* has different meanings in different contexts and people are often confused about the difference between an objective, an objective decision, and an objective decision process. An **objective**, as a noun, is something someone seeks. As an adjective, an **objective experiment** is one in which the outcome is not subjective—that is, it doesn't depend on any of the subjects. A scientific experiment that is objective will have the same results (plus or minus some measurement error) regardless of where it is performed and who performs it. Also as a noun, an **objective process** is one that commonly means systematic and fair.

In making complex decisions (such as deciding what projects *should* be included in an IT portfolio), we try to align the portfolio projects with the objectives that we seek to achieve. Because there are numerous objectives, we *must* prioritize them. There will never be any "data" or magic formulas to do this. We *must* do it on the basis of human (subjects') judgment. Consequently, the decision or portfolio will always be "subjective." Subjectivity in this sense does not say anything about the quality of the decision. The quality of such decisions can range from excellent to poor—depending on the quality (knowledge and experience) of the subjects, the way the decision is structured, and the measurement that is used to synthesize knowledge, data, and judgments.

The quality of an optimal IT portfolio involves much more than the accuracy of any data that is used in the process. In particular, an optimization is meaningless (and very possibly misleading) unless the measurements are in "proportion" to what we expect will happen. This "proportion" requires ratio level measurement. Simple 1 to 10 scales, such as those used in the Olympics to evaluate gymnasts, seldom produce ratio level measurements. An Olympic judge that rates a gymnast's performance a perfect 10.0 would consider that performance to be 2, 5, 10, or more times better than a 9.5 performance, not simply the ratio of 10/9.5 = 1.05 times better. Ratio level measurements mean that the measures of benefits are in proportion to the benefits that are expected to occur. It does not mean that the measures are accurate to so many decimal places. The accuracy of the measurements obviously depends on the accuracy of the available data and the quality of the judgments that are applied to the data as well as to the relative importance of the organization's objectives. Although an organization *should* continually strive to improve this "accuracy," it *must*, at any given time, proceed with what is then available. It must not fall into the trap of thinking that just because the measurement is not "precise" simplistic schemes producing ordinal or interval measurements are adequate for identifying an optimal portfolio. They are not.

Part Two—A New, Rational Approach

In this section, we will illustrate a best-practice approach to IT portfolio alignment with an example application using Expert Choice to develop a portfolio of projects from those shown in Figure 23.1.

Step 1: Design

Each project you propose for a portfolio should be the result of careful consideration by those proposing the project. Alternative project designs almost always exist, and quickly deciding on one design without searching for creative alternatives is usually short sighted. Each design will have its pros and cons, and a thorough evaluation of the alternatives with a process such as AHP not only will lead to the selection of the most preferred design, but also will lay a foundation for communicating the details and rationale for the project when it is evaluated as part of the project portfolio process. In some cases, it makes sense to design some projects at different levels of funding. If you do this, the benefits of the optimal designs at each funding level are evaluated and the subsequent optimization will determine not just whether to fund a particular project, but also at what level.

Alternative	Costs
AS/400 Replacements	990
Cisco Routers	500
Customer Service Call Center	980
Desktop Replacements	800
EMC Symmetrix	4220
Firewall and Antivirus Licenses	120
Iron Mountain Backup Service	430
Laptop Replacements	1340
Mobile Workforce Pocket PCs	230
Oracle 9i Upgrade	1890
PeopleSoft Upgrade	1670
Plumtree Corporate Portal	1345
ProServe System Upgrade	2300
Sales Force Laptops	150
SRDF Site/Service	3440
Thin Client Implementation	2100

FIGURE 23.1
IT Project Proposals

Step 2: Structuring Complexity—Focusing on Objectives

After the design phase is complete, the next step is to identify IT objectives to address the organization's strategic objectives from the IT perspective. Top-level decision makers then structure these objectives into an objectives hierarchy, as shown in Figure 23.2.

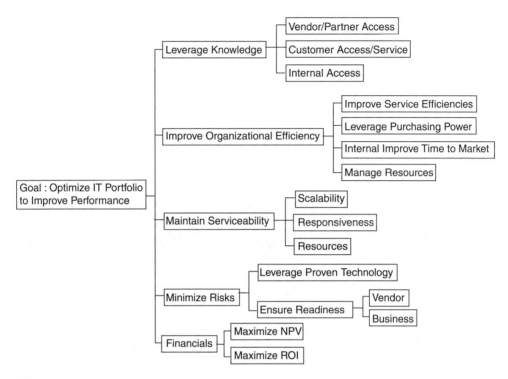

FIGURE 23.2
Objectives Hierarchy

Step 3: Measurement

The decision makers met to discuss the relative importance of the objectives. Using radio frequency keypads, they enter judgments about the relative importance of objectives, taken two at a time, from which they derive priorities for the objectives and subobjectives. Important aspects of this process include discussing and arriving at shared definitions of the objectives, as well as sharing information relative to the objectives, the organization's current capabilities and needs, and the competitive environment. Decision makers make pairwise judgments using a variety of input modes. The "verbal" mode, shown in Figure 23.3, entails stating which one of a pair of objectives is more important and, using the verbal scale shown in the figure, by how much.

For example, the judgment of one of the participants shown in Figure 23.3 was that Leveraging Knowledge was "equal to moderately" more important than Improve Organizational Efficiency.

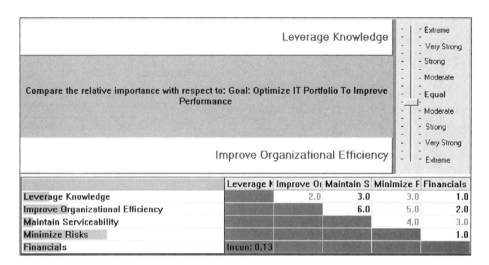

FIGURE 23.3
Pairwise Judgments of One Decision Maker for Top-Level Objectives

The verbal scale is essentially an ordinal scale, with "equal" represented by 1, "moderate" by 3, "strong" by 5, "very strong" by 7, "extreme" by 9, and intermediate judgments by even numbers. However, as explained earlier, ordinal measures are *not* adequate for allocating resources.

Ratio level measures are necessary! Fortunately, Expert Choice, which is based on Saaty's AHP, can derive ratio level measures from ordinal verbal judgments, provided there is enough variety and redundancy in the cluster of elements being compared.[1] Even when this is not the case, you can use Expert Choice's graphical pairwise comparisons, as shown in Figure 23.4, to derive ratio level priorities.

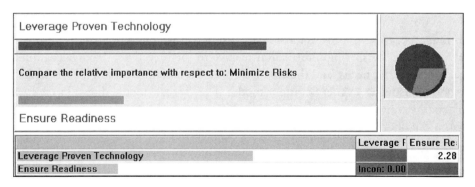

FIGURE 23.4
Pairwise Graphical Judgment for Two of the Subobjectives

An "inconsistency" measure is displayed for each cluster of judgments (0.13 in Figure 23.3) to identify inconsistencies that can be caused by clerical errors (pressing the wrong key), lack of concentration or information, inadequate model structure, or real-world inconsistencies. The decision makers can examine which judgment is most inconsistent with their other judgments, and reflect whether they should revise this or any of their other judgments. The objective is *not* to achieve the lowest inconsistency, but to *derive* ratio measure priorities that best reflect the decision makers' knowledge and understanding. Figure 23.5 shows the priorities derived for the top-level objectives from the judgments shown in Figure 23.3.

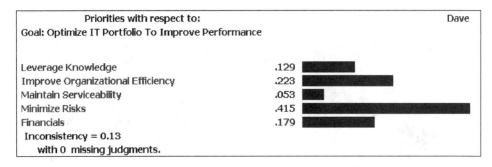

FIGURE 23.5
Priorities Derived from Judgments in Figure 23.3

Each participating decision maker can enter his judgments about the relative importance of a pair of objectives simultaneously. These are then displayed (see Figure 23.6) and discussed. Geometric averages of the judgments are computed for each objective pair and priorities are derived that reflect the best judgments of the decision makers (see Figure 23.7). It is common that in large hierarchies, different decision makers participate in making judgments at different levels, corresponding to their responsibilities and knowledge. This process produces a synthesis of knowledge that is virtually impossible to achieve in other ways.

The pairwise measurement process produces priorities, such as those shown in Figure 23.7. These priorities possess rank information as well as meaningful intervals and *ratios* (or proportions). The ratio level meaning of these priorities is particularly important because it would be mathematically meaningless to multiply priorities that were only interval or ordinal level measures by interval or ordinal level priorities at lower levels of the hierarchy. It would also be mathematically meaningless, and misleading, to use interval or ordinal measures in optimizing the IT portfolio of projects. Unfortunately, many organizations don't appreciate this requirement of their measures and wonder why the results don't make sense. They eventually become disillusioned with all numerical methods, opting to use their intuition to decide what should go in their portfolios. However, the complexities of competing objectives, trade-offs, and constraints preclude an organization that uses an intuitive allocation of resources to be competitive with an organization employing well-founded methods that include ratio level measures.

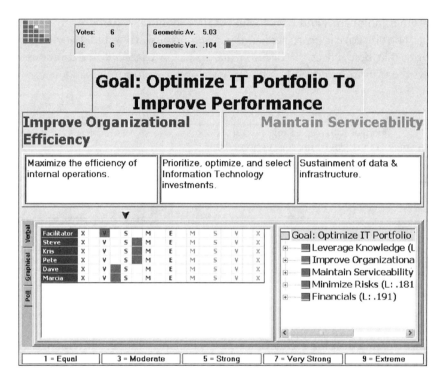

FIGURE 23.6
Individual Decision Makers' Judgments for One of the Pairwise Comparisons

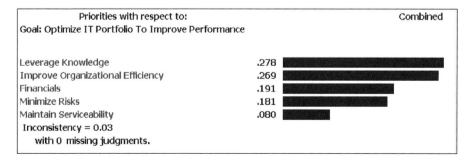

FIGURE 23.7
Priorities of Top-Level Objectives

After the decision makers derive priorities for their objectives and subobjectives in the objectives hierarchy, they evaluate the anticipated contributions of the proposed projects with respect to the lowest-level subobjectives in the hierarchy. They can do this in a variety of ways. Figure 23.8 shows a ratings approach whereby a panel of decision makers uses a verbal ratings scale to evaluate the anticipated contribution of a customer service call center project to the customer access/service objective. Prior to using the ratings scale shown in Figure 23.8, the decision makers performed pairwise comparisons for the words or "rating intensities" in this scale—for example, Excellent, Very Good, and so on—to derive ratio level priorities for the intensities. Respondents could, if they so desired, enter any priority between 0 and 1 if they chose not to use the scale provided. You also can derive priorities for the projects with respect to each covering objective with pairwise comparisons, or by translating data using linear or nonlinear, increasing or decreasing utility curves, or step functions.

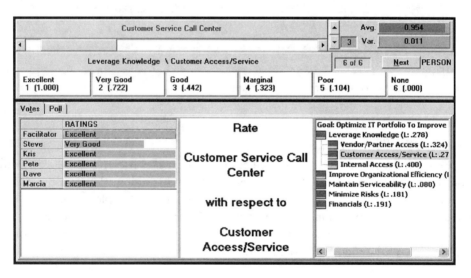

FIGURE 23.8
Ratings Approach

Figure 23.9 shows a datagrid reflecting some of the ratings for one of the participants. The data can contain hard data as well as verbal ratings. Regardless, the verbal ratings or data are translated into ratio scale priorities and then combined with the priorities for other participants, as shown in Figure 23.9.

Excellent	Very Good	Good	Marginal	Poor	None
1 (1.000)	2 (.722)	3 (.442)	4 (.323)	5 (.104)	6 (.000)

	Ideal mode				RATINGS	RATINGS	RATINGS	RATING⌃
AID	Alternative		Total	Costs	Leverage Knowledge Vendor/Partner Access (L: .333)	Leverage Knowledge Customer Access/Service (L: .333)	Leverage Knowledge Internal Access (L: .333)	Improve Organizati Efficiency Improve Service Efficiencie (L: .209)
A7	☑AS/400 Replacements		.351		None	Good	Good	Good
A2	☑Cisco Routers		.414		Good	Marginal	Marginal	Margin
A16	☑Customer Service Call Center		.422		Poor	Very Good	Very Good	Excelle
A12	☑Desktop Replacements		.220		None	None	Good	Good
A3	☑EMC Symmetrix		.359		Poor	None	Good	Margin
A11	☑Firewall and Antivirus Licenses		.270		None	None	Good	Good
A4	☑Iron Mountain Backup Service		.273		None	None	None	Excelle
A10	☑Laptop Replacements		.208		None	None	Good	Margin
A14	☑Mobile Workforce Pocket PCs		.206		Poor	Marginal	Good	Margin
A8	☑Oracle 9i Upgrade		.373		Marginal	Good	Marginal	Very Go
A6	☑PeopleSoft Upgrade		.258		Poor	Poor	Good	Good⌄

FIGURE 23.9
Datagrid of Ratings for One of the Participants

Step 4: Synthesis

The measurement processes, if performed as described, makes it easy to produce a synthesis or fusion of priorities using simple multiplication and addition. (Note: If the priorities are not ratio scale measures, as might be the case using simple weights-and-scores approaches, the multiplication and addition may be mathematically meaningless and lack credibility.) The priorities in the "Total" column in Figure 23.10 are proportional or ratio scale measures of the total anticipated *benefits* to all relevant objectives, qualitative as well as quantitative, of each project. The "units" of the benefits are immaterial—all that matters is that they are proportional. Multiplying all of the benefits by a constant would result in the same proportions. Figure 23.10 also shows the project costs.

Excellent		Very Good		Good		Marginal		Poor		None	
1 (1.000)		2 (.722)		3 (.442)		4 (.323)		5 (.104)		6 (.000)	

AID	Alternative	Total	Costs	RATINGS Leverage Knowledge Vendor/Partner Access (L: .324)	RATINGS Leverage Knowledge Customer Access/Service (L: .276)	RATINGS Leverage Knowledge Internal Access (L: .400)	RATING Improve Organizati Efficiency Improve Service Efficiencie (L: .209)
A7	☑AS/400 Replacements	.516	990	.000	.307	.343	.469
A2	☑Cisco Routers	.604	500	.383	.363	.422	.270
A16	☑Customer Service Call Center	.570	980	.141	.954	.469	.861
A12	☑Desktop Replacements	.456	800	.000	.255	.562	.383
A3	☑EMC Symmetrix	.531	4220	.035	.017	.536	.089
A11	☑Firewall and Antivirus Licenses	.529	120	.017	.052	.363	.363
A4	☑Iron Mountain Backup Service	.571	430	.000	.000	.000	.954
A10	☑Laptop Replacements	.322	1340	.000	.035	.422	.214
A14	☑Mobile Workforce Pocket PCs	.313	230	.070	.323	.536	.326
A8	☑Oracle 9i Upgrade	.572	1890	.363	.676	.402	.516
A6	☑PeopleSoft Upgrade	.457	1670	.177	.104	.363	.413

FIGURE 23.10
Datagrid of "Combined" Priorities for All Participants

Step 5: Optimization

Now that we have ratio scale (or proportional) measures of the project's benefits and their costs, it might seem intuitive to determine our portfolio by sorting by the benefits and funding projects until the budget is exhausted. This is *not* advisable for two very important reasons. First, it will lead to a suboptimal portfolio of projects. By this we mean that the total anticipated benefit will be less than a procedure that seeks to find a combination of projects that maximizes the total anticipated benefit. Looking at Figure 23.11, we see that such a procedure would, with a budget of $10,000, result in a portfolio of projects with a funding of $9,545 and an anticipated benefit of 4.339 "units," or 4.339/8.428 = 51 percent of what the anticipated benefit would be if the budget were enough to fund all of the projects. If we contrast this portfolio with one obtained using an "optimization" algorithm to identify a combination of projects that results in the highest possible total benefit without exceeding the specified budget, we have a portfolio (shown in Figure 23.12) that has an anticipated benefit of 6.127 "units," or 6.127/8.428 = 72.7 percent of what the anticipated benefit would be if the budget were enough to fund all of the projects. Thus, the optimized portfolio is 41 percent more effective (and at a cost that is slightly less) than the "intuitive" approach!

Alternative	Total	Costs	Cum Cost	Cum Ben.
Plumtree Corporate Portal	0.773	$1,345	$1,345	0.773
Thin Client Implementation	0.706	$2,100	$3,445	1.479
Cisco Routers	0.604	$500	$3,945	2.083
Oracle 9i Upgrade	0.572	$1,890	$5,835	2.655
Iron Mountain Backup Servic	0.571	$430	$6,265	3.226
Customer Service Call Cent	0.570	$980	$7,245	3.796
ProServe System Upgrade	0.543	$2,300	**$9,545**	**4.339**
EMC Symmetrix	0.531	$4,220	$13,765	4.870
Firewall and Antivirus Licens	0.529	$120	$13,885	5.399
Sales Force Laptops	0.517	$150	$14,035	5.916
AS/400 Replacements	0.516	$990	$15,025	6.432
PeopleSoft Upgrade	0.457	$1,670	$16,695	6.889
Desktop Replacements	0.456	$800	$17,495	7.345
SRDF Site/Service	0.448	$3,440	$20,935	7.793
Laptop Replacements	0.322	$1,340	$22,275	8.115
Mobile Workforce Pocket P	0.313	$230	$22,505	8.428

FIGURE 23.11
Suboptimal Portfolio Obtained by Sorting and Allocating until Budget of $10,000 Is
Exceeded

Budget Limit: 10,000; Benefits: 6.127; % = 72.7; Funded Cost: 9,535; Base Case Maximum: 8.428

Set Base Case ☐ Feasibility Switch ☑ AutoSolve ☑

Ignore: ☐ Musts ☐ Must Nots ☐ Custom Constraints ☐ Dependencies ☐ Groups ☐ Funding Pools ☐ Risks

Alternative	Funded	Benefit	Cost	Partial	Must	Must Not
Plumtree Corporate Portal	YES	.773	1,345	☐	☐	☐
Thin Client Implementation	YES	.706	2,100	☐	☐	☐
Cisco Routers	YES	.604	500	☐	☐	☐
Oracle 9i Upgrade	YES	.572	1,890	☐	☐	☐
Iron Mountain Backup Service	YES	.571	430	☐	☐	☐
Customer Service Call Center	YES	.570	980	☐	☐	☐
ProServe System Upgrade	NO	.543	2,300	☐	☐	☐
EMC Symmetrix	NO	.531	4,220	☐	☐	☐
Firewall and Antivirus Licenses	YES	.529	120	☐	☐	☐
Sales Force Laptops	YES	.517	150	☐	☐	☐
AS/400 Replacements	YES	.516	990	☐	☐	☐
PeopleSoft Upgrade	NO	.457	1,670	☐	☐	☐
Desktop Replacements	YES	.456	800	☐	☐	☐
SRDF Site/Service	NO	.448	3,440	☐	☐	☐
Laptop Replacements	NO	.322	1,340	☐	☐	☐
Mobile Workforce Pocket PCs	YES	.313	230	☐	☐	☐

FIGURE 23.12
Optimal Portfolio Anticipated Benefit 41 Percent Greater at Lower Cost

A second reason that the "rack and stack" or intuitive approach is deficient is that it is extremely difficult (if not impossible with a large number of projects) to ensure that various constraints, such as funding pools, dependencies among projects, and limits on other resources besides money (such as personnel, machinery, building space, and so on) are taken into account. On the other hand, accounting for such constraints is straightforward and efficient when you determine the portfolio using an optimization approach. Figure 23.13 shows an optimal portfolio of the projects in our example, when sundry constraints are taken into account.

Budget Limit	Benefits			□ Set Base Case	☑ Feasibility Switch	☑ AutoSolve
10,000	5.182	%				
Funded Cost	Base Case Maximum	=	61.49			
8,935	8.428					

Ignore

□ Musts □ Must Nots □ Custom Constraints □ Dependencies □ Groups □ Funding Pools ☑ Risks

All   None

Alternative	Funded	Benefit	Cost	Partial	Must	Must Not			Network	Project Mgrs
Plumtree Corporate Portal	YES	.773	1,345	□	□	□		Plumtree	1.0	1.0
Thin Client Implementation	YES	.706	2,100	□	□	□		Thin Client	2.0	1.0
Cisco Routers	YES	.604	500	□	□	□		Cisco Routers	2.0	0.5
Oracle 9i Upgrade	NO	.572	1,890	□	□	□		Oracle 9i	1.0	1.0
Iron Mountain Backup Service	YES	.571	430	□	□	□		Iron Mountain	0.5	0.0
Customer Service Call Center	YES	.570	980	□	□	□		Customer	2.0	0.0
ProServe System Upgrade	NO	.543	2,300	□	□	□		ProServe	1.0	0.5
EMC Symmetrix	NO	.531	4,220	□	□	□		EMC	3.0	1.0
Firewall and Antivirus Licenses	YES	.529	120	□	□	□		Firewall and	1.0	0.0
Sales Force Laptops	NO	.517	150	□	□	☑		Sales Force	2.0	0.5
AS/400 Replacements	YES	.516	990	□	□	□		AS/400	5.0	1.0
PeopleSoft Upgrade	YES	.457	1,670	□	□	□		PeopleSoft	1.0	0.0
Desktop Replacements	YES	.456	800	□	□	□		Desktop	5.0	1.0
SRDF Site/Service	NO	.448	3,440	□	□	□		SRDF	1.0	0.5
Laptop Replacements	NO	.322	1,340	□	□	□		Laptop	1.0	0.0
Mobile Workforce Pocket PCs	NO	.313	230	□	□	□		Mobile	0.5	0.0
								Min		
								Max	20.0	5.0
								Actual	19.5	4.5

FIGURE 23.13
Optimal Portfolio with Additional Constraints

Not only can the optimization approach ensure that all relevant constraints are satisfied, but it also can tell decision makers how much an individual or a set of constraints reduces the portfolio's anticipated benefits. For example, since the optimal portfolio with a budgetary constraint of only $10,000, shown in Figure 23.12, has anticipated benefits of 72.7 percent of the base case maximum, and the optimal portfolio with additional constraints shown in Figure 23.13 has anticipated benefits of 61.49 percent of the base case maximum, the additional constraints reduce the anticipated benefits by (72.7–61.49)/(72.7) or 15.4 percent.

Decision makers sometimes impose constraints without realizing the impact of such edicts. For example, a decision maker might demand that the Oracle Upgrade project is a "must." Doing so results in the optimal portfolio shown in Figure 23.14, where the anticipated benefits are reduced from 61.49 to 28.39, or by 54 percent! If this constraint is political rather than absolutely necessary, the decision maker would most likely give some serious thought to imposing such a "must." On the other hand, decision makers could find comfort when imposing political constraints in situations where it is shown that the impact on anticipated benefits is minimal.

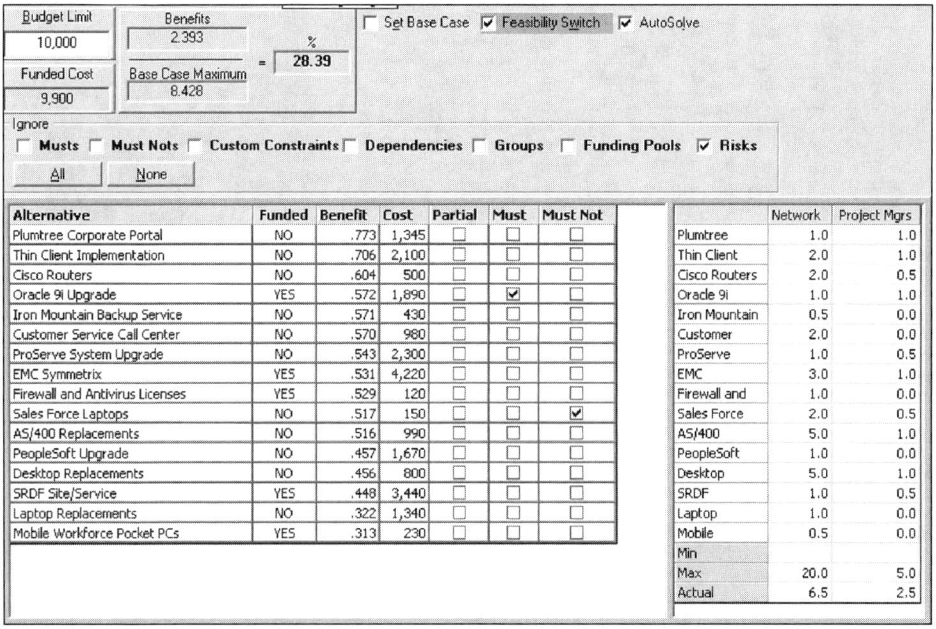

Alternative	Funded	Benefit	Cost	Partial	Must	Must Not			Network	Project Mgrs
Plumtree Corporate Portal	NO	.773	1,345	☐	☐	☐		Plumtree	1.0	1.0
Thin Client Implementation	NO	.706	2,100	☐	☐	☐		Thin Client	2.0	1.0
Cisco Routers	NO	.604	500	☐	☐	☐		Cisco Routers	2.0	0.5
Oracle 9i Upgrade	YES	.572	1,890	☐	☑	☐		Oracle 9i	1.0	1.0
Iron Mountain Backup Service	NO	.571	430	☐	☐	☐		Iron Mountain	0.5	0.0
Customer Service Call Center	NO	.570	980	☐	☐	☐		Customer	2.0	0.0
ProServe System Upgrade	NO	.543	2,300	☐	☐	☐		ProServe	1.0	0.5
EMC Symmetrix	YES	.531	4,220	☐	☐	☐		EMC	3.0	1.0
Firewall and Antivirus Licenses	YES	.529	120	☐	☐	☐		Firewall and	1.0	0.0
Sales Force Laptops	NO	.517	150	☐	☐	☑		Sales Force	2.0	0.5
AS/400 Replacements	NO	.516	990	☐	☐	☐		AS/400	5.0	1.0
PeopleSoft Upgrade	NO	.457	1,670	☐	☐	☐		PeopleSoft	1.0	0.0
Desktop Replacements	NO	.456	800	☐	☐	☐		Desktop	5.0	1.0
SRDF Site/Service	YES	.448	3,440	☐	☐	☐		SRDF	1.0	0.5
Laptop Replacements	NO	.322	1,340	☐	☐	☐		Laptop	1.0	0.0
Mobile Workforce Pocket PCs	YES	.313	230	☐	☐	☐		Mobile	0.5	0.0
								Min		
								Max	20.0	5.0
								Actual	6.5	2.5

Budget Limit 10,000 Benefits 2.393 % = 28.39 Funded Cost 9,900 Base Case Maximum 8.428

☐ Set Base Case ☑ Feasibility Switch ☑ AutoSolve

Ignore ☐ Musts ☐ Must Nots ☐ Custom Constraints ☐ Dependencies ☐ Groups ☐ Funding Pools ☑ Risks   All   None

FIGURE 23.14
Optimal Portfolio with "Must" for Oracle Upgrade

Risk

The portfolio optimization process described thus far incorporates anticipated project benefits (measured proportionally on a ratio scale), anticipated costs of the projects, as well as operational and political constraints. It can also incorporate risk, which you can include in the process in two ways. First, you can include risk minimization objectives in the objectives hierarchy by making pairwise comparisons as to the relative importance of these objectives compared to others, and the relative risks with respect to each risk objective. The total benefit of each project would then incorporate the risk minimization objectives.

A more formal and precise way to include risk considerations when determining an optimal portfolio of projects is to incorporate a subsidiary risk analysis that derives estimates of the relative probabilities of success (or failure) of the projects under consideration. The risk analysis, not discussed in detail here, can include every conceivable risk factor, both quantitative and qualitative, and derives relative risks or probability of success of the projects under consideration. You then determine the expected benefit of each project by multiplying its anticipated benefit by the probability of its success, as shown in Figure 23.15.

Alternatives	Benefits	Risks	Probability of Success	Expected Benefits
Plumtree Corporate Portal	.773	0.114	0.886	0.685
Thin Client Implementation	.706	0.161	0.839	0.592
Cisco Routers	.604	0.025	0.975	0.589
Oracle 9i Upgrade	.572	0.133	0.867	0.496
Iron Mountain Backup Service	.571	0.002	0.998	0.570
Customer Service Call Center	.570	0.054	0.946	0.539
ProServe System Upgrade	.543	0.128	0.872	0.473
EMC Symmetrix	.531	0.113	0.887	0.471
Firewall and Antivirus Licenses	.529	0	1	0.529
Sales Force Laptops	.517	0.051	0.949	0.491
AS/400 Replacements	.516	0.087	0.913	0.471
PeopleSoft Upgrade	.457	0.137	0.863	0.394
Desktop Replacements	.456	0.009	0.991	0.452
SRDF Site/Service	.448	0.079	0.921	0.413
Laptop Replacements	.322	0.033	0.967	0.311
Mobile Workforce Pocket PCs	.313	0.294	0.706	0.221

FIGURE 23.15
Multiplying Benefits by Probability of Success to Determine Expected Benefits

You then alter the portfolio optimization to determine a portfolio that maximizes the total *expected benefit*, as shown in Figure 23.16. The portfolio in this example does not differ from that derived earlier where there was no explicit consideration of risk, but in situations where one or more alternatives are relatively risky, the impact can be significant.

Budget Limit	Expected Benefits			
10,000	4.8216	%	=	62.64
Funded Cost	Base Case Maximum			
8,935	7.6976			

☐ Set Base Case ☑ Feasibility Switch ☑ AutoSolve

Ignore

☐ Musts ☐ Must Nots ☐ Custom Constraints ☐ Dependencies ☐ Groups ☐ Funding Pools ☐ Risks

[All] [None]

Alternative	Funded	E.Benefit	Cost	Partial	Must	Must Not		Network	Project Mgrs
Plumtree Corporate Portal	YES	.6849	1,345	☐	☐	☐	Plumtree	1.0	1.0
Thin Client Implementation	YES	.5923	2,100	☐	☐	☐	Thin Client	2.0	1.0
Cisco Routers	YES	.5889	500	☐	☐	☐	Cisco Routers	2.0	0.5
Oracle 9i Upgrade	NO	.4959	1,890	☐	☐	☐	Oracle 9i Upgrade	1.0	1.0
Iron Mountain Backup Service	YES	.5699	430	☐	☐	☐	Iron Mountain	0.5	0.0
Customer Service Call Center	YES	.5392	980	☐	☐	☐	Customer Service	2.0	0.0
ProServe System Upgrade	NO	.4735	2,300	☐	☐	☐	ProServe System	1.0	0.5
EMC Symmetrix	NO	.4710	4,220	☐	☐	☐	EMC Symmetrix	3.0	1.0
Firewall and Antivirus Licenses	YES	.5290	120	☐	☐	☐	Firewall and	1.0	0.0
Sales Force Laptops	NO	.4906	150	☐	☐	☑	Sales Force	2.0	0.5
AS/400 Replacements	YES	.4711	990	☐	☐	☐	AS/400	5.0	1.0
PeopleSoft Upgrade	YES	.3944	1,670	☐	☐	☐	PeopleSoft	1.0	0.0
Desktop Replacements	YES	.4519	800	☐	☐	☐	Desktop	5.0	1.0
SRDF Site/Service	NO	.4126	3,440	☐	☐	☐	SRDF Site/Service	1.0	0.5
Laptop Replacements	NO	.3114	1,340	☐	☐	☐	Laptop	1.0	0.0
Mobile Workforce Pocket PCs	NO	.2210	230	☐	☐	☐	Mobile Workforce	0.5	0.0
							Min		
							Max	20.0	5.0
							Actual	19.5	4.5

FIGURE 23.16
Optimal Portfolio Considering Project Risks

Extensions

The process described earlier is extremely flexible, and it must be in order to "fit" an organization's culture. Improved communications, both among and between every level of the organization, result from the explicit statement and focus on objectives, the application of hard data, expert interpretation of that data, and judgments about the qualitative aspects of the process. Political dictates can shape the portfolio to whatever extent the participants deem desirable, but their implications are clear enough so that only those dictates that "make sense" are applied. Changes to assumptions, such as the portfolio budget limit, can be explored. For example, Figures 23.17 and 23.18 show an efficient frontier of portfolio solutions, wherein a series of optimal portfolios is computed and displayed as a function of the budget limit. Top management can set the budget limit much more effectively with such information. Looking at Figure 23.17, you can see that it would make little sense to increase the budget from $10,000 to $15,000, as the incremental benefit is minimal.

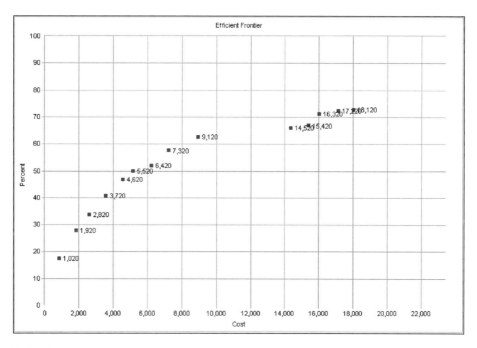

FIGURE 23.17
Efficient Frontier of Optimal Portfolios

Alternatives/Budget	1,020	1,920	2,820	3,720	4,620	
Benefit %	17.4%	27.8%	29.3%	36.7%	43.7%	
Cost	850	1,850	2,765	3,195	4,175	
Plumtree Corporate Portal			FUNDED	FUNDED	FUNDED	FU
Thin Client Implementation						
Cisco Routers	FUNDED	FUNDED	FUNDED	FUNDED	FUNDED	FU
Oracle 9i Upgrade						
Iron Mountain Backup Service		FUNDED		FUNDED	FUNDED	FU
Customer Service Call Center					FUNDED	FU
ProServe System Upgrade						
EMC Symmetrix						
Firewall and Antivirus Licenses	FUNDED	FUNDED	FUNDED	FUNDED	FUNDED	FU
Sales Force Laptops						
AS/400 Replacements						FU
PeopleSoft Upgrade						
Desktop Replacements		FUNDED	FUNDED	FUNDED	FUNDED	FU
SRDF Site/Service						
Laptop Replacements						
Mobile Workforce Pocket PCs	FUNDED					

FIGURE 23.18
Portfolio Components on Efficient Frontier

Summary

The best-practice approach to planning an IT portfolio provides a strategic focus and results in better, faster, and more competitive decisions—decisions that are aligned with the organization's overall and IT strategies. Improved communication and organizational buy-in are intrinsic in the process, reducing or eliminating costly battles and deadlocks. Is a formal approach that embodies this best practice right for every organization? The Gartner Group reports that the five most common reasons customers cited for not using a more formal approach are as follows:

- The economic consequences of a suboptimal decision are too low to justify such an investment.

- The number of choices or criteria being examined is too low to justify the approach.

- Insufficient IT skills or committed resources are available to make a difference.

- Because of political or technical biases, senior managers do not support a formalized approach.

- Decision makers are reluctant to commit to a formalized approach because of cultural or organizational issues.

The report also suggests that enterprises will need to determine when these reasons are simply excuses for making a better-informed decision, as opposed to sound business "exceptions to the rule."

Endnote

[1] Despite the fact that the fundamental verbal scale used to elicit judgments is an ordinal measure, Saaty's empirical research showed that the principle eigenvector of a pairwise verbal judgment matrix often does produce priorities that approximate the true priorities from ratio scales such as distance, area, and brightness. This happens because, as Saaty (1980) has shown mathematically, the eigenvector calculation has an averaging effect—it corresponds to finding the dominance of each alternative along all walks of length k, as k goes to infinity. Therefore, if there is enough variety and redundancy, errors in judgments, such as those introduced by using an ordinal verbal scale, can be reduced greatly. See Forman and Gass, "The Analytic Hierarchy Process—An Exposition," *Operations Research,* Vol.49, no. 4, July–Aug 2001, pp. 469–486.

CHAPTER 24

Defining Customer Needs for Brand-New Products: QFD for Unprecedented Software

Richard E. Zultner
Zultner & Co.
richard@zultner.com

Can we successfully get requirements for software new to the customer?

Overview

Quality Function Deployment (QFD) has traditionally been employed for "new" product development, but generally it has been applied to revisions, or model upgrades, not to brand-new products. Methods such as "listening to the voice of the customer" are not very useful when the customer has never seen the type of product you are trying to develop. So how can you successfully learn the requirements for products that are new to the customer? This chapter will review the existing approaches in QFD, and some new methods for defining customer needs for brand-new products.

One promising approach is the "Mind of the Customer" approach employed by the Theory of Constraints (TOC). The TOC Thinking Process tools can identify the customer's core problem and core conflict. Then you can use them to develop a solution beyond the experience of the customer, and plan the solution's acceptance and implementation.

This complementary approach shows the synergy between TOC (traditionally used for "tweaking the deal") and QFD (traditionally used for "tweaking the details") in developing brand-new products.

Chapter Outline

- Introduction
- Defining Brand-New Needs
- Tools
- Last Steps
- Layers of Resistance

- Conclusion
- Acknowledgments
- References
- About the Author

Introduction

QFD is a Quality system [Mizuno and Akao 1994]. The task of QFD in the overall framework of Total Quality Management (TQM) is to *ensure* customer satisfaction (see Figure 24.1) [Zultner 1993]. In order to achieve, or leverage, customer satisfaction, it is necessary to deliver and explain *value* to customers. To do this requires that the product/service be designed with value and produced with value. In order to develop such value *into* the product, we must start by discovering what value is for the customers we are trying to satisfy. We must understand from the customer's point of view what is valuable to them.

Definition of Value

There are only four sources of value for customers of software, and software-intensive products and services [Zultner 1996].

1. **Solve problems.** A problem is a current, negative situation. If we can minimize, or even eliminate, a customer's problem with a solution we provide, then we have delivered value proportional to the magnitude of the problem.

2. **Seize opportunities.** An opportunity is a future, positive situation. If we can advance, or even maximize, a customer's achieving an opportunity with a solution we provide, then we have delivered value proportional to the magnitude of the opportunity.

3. **Look good.** Customers want to look good to significant others. If we can significantly improve a customer's chances of impressing whomever they want to impress, with a solution we provide, then we have delivered value proportional to the importance of the impression to the customer.

4. **Feel good.** Customers want to feel good about themselves, their work, and their lives. If we can significantly improve a customer's feelings of confidence and satisfaction, with a solution we provide, then we have delivered value proportional to the level of the customer's feelings.

Any product, service, or software that does not address at least one of the preceding sources of value is valueless to customers. So how can we find the four sources of value for our own customers?

To satisfy customers today (so that they choose our product) and tomorrow (so that they are loyal to us) we must deliver value to them. To do this we must design and produce products and services that meet customer needs better than any other competitor. QFD ensures this during development.

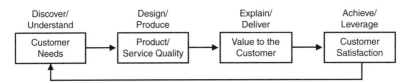

FIGURE 24.1
QFD as a quality system.

Why Not Ask?

The most direct way to get answers from customers is to ask them. But they won't be able to tell us all of their requirements. The Kano model (see Figure 24.2) tells us that we are likely to miss whole classes of requirements [Kano *et al.* 1984]. The basic types of requirements are as follows:

- **Expected requirements.** These requirements can dissatisfy if not fulfilled, but do not satisfy if fulfilled. Most customers won't even mention these—unless you don't meet them, in which case they will be very vocal about what's missing.

- **Normal requirements.** These requirements can dissatisfy if not fulfilled, or satisfy if fulfilled. Most customers will mention these—but only the ones they think of. Even with trained interviewers, it is difficult to reach as high as 80 percent discovery of these requirements.

- **Exciting requirements.** These requirements can satisfy if fulfilled, but don't dissatisfy if not fulfilled. Most customers won't mention these, because they haven't seen them before. If you meet these needs, customers will be very vocal about how much they like them.

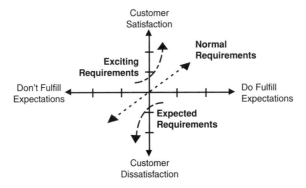

FIGURE 24.2
The Kano model.

So requirements differ in their effect upon customer satisfaction. And we won't get a complete set of requirements, because customers have no systematic way to sweep through their requirements space and download it to us. Yet we still must satisfy our customers!

Unprecedented Products

If we cannot rely on customers to tell us all their requirements, even for familiar products, what can we do for unprecedented products? For products that customers have never experienced before?

CUSTOMER NEEDS: Solution-independent benefits that customers desire to possess.

Defining Brand-New Needs

A number of methods for defining customer needs have been tried with QFD over the past decade. Which ones can you use to deal with brand-new products?

Methods for Defining Customer Needs

You can divide the various methods for defining customer needs into five general categories (see Figure 24.3):

1. **Emotions of the Customer.** Methods that concentrate on the affective, or sensory needs of the customer.

2. **Voice of the Customer.** Methods that concentrate on the customer's statements, or needs expressed in the language of the customer.

3. **Mind of the Customer.** Methods that concentrate on the logical, or perceived needs of the customer.

4. **Context of the Customer.** Methods that concentrate on the behavioral, or situational needs of the customer.

5. **Environment of the Customer.** Methods that concentrate on the strategic, or external needs of the customer.

Each category of method is best suited to developing certain types of products, in certain situations. Let's examine their application to software.

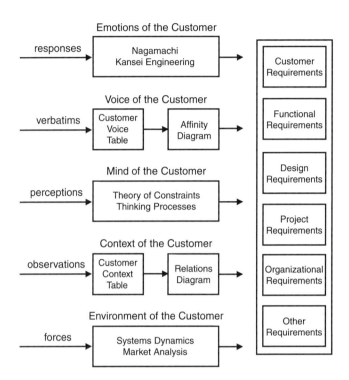

FIGURE 24.3
Methods for defining customer needs for various types of requirements.

Emotions of the Customer

Some methods for defining customer needs concentrate on the affective, or sensory needs of the customer. Kansei Engineering [Nagamachi 1999] is an example of such an approach. You can determine customers' emotional responses by using structured questionnaires and multivariate statistical analyses.

Perhaps the best example of a software product that has only emotional value and no functional value is that of a screensaver. Although at one time such software did perform a useful function—that of preventing burn-in on screens—monitor technology has rendered this original purpose obsolete. So today the value of a screensaver comes from its ability to make the user feel good (by displaying images they like) and look good (by displaying images their peers think are *cool*).

You could use Kansei Engineering to understand the factors of "coolness" and design a "way cool"er set of screen (and other) displays.

Kansei Engineering has a solid track record of refining existing products, and you certainly could apply it to a screensaver. Conceivably this could ultimately lead to an entirely new kind of software product that would no longer even be called a screensaver. Games are another attractive software application for Kansei Engineering.

BRAND-NEW PRODUCTS: QFD has traditionally been applied to upgrades of existing products.

Voice of the Customer

Some methods for defining customer needs concentrate on the customer's statements, or their needs expressed in their own language. The Voice of Customer Analysis within QFD is an example of such an approach [Akao 1990]. Even the most streamlined version of QFD, Blitz QFD [Zultner 1996], is heavily oriented toward Voice of Customer Analysis (see Figure 24.4). Through the use of the Customer Voice Table (CVT), you can translate customer verbatims into *customer* needs—solution-independent benefits that customers want to possess. Then you can organize these customer needs in a natural structure by taking the customer through the KJ Method to produce an Affinity Diagram. At this point, you create the customer needs hierarchy, and analyze, quantify, and prioritize it. This then becomes the left side of the "House of Quality" matrix.

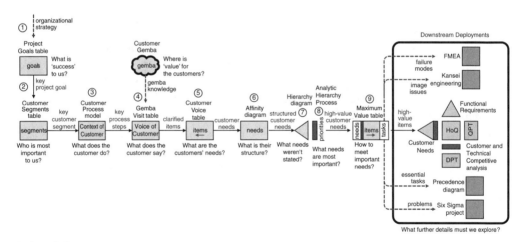

FIGURE 24.4
The "voice of the customer" begins by focusing on which customer(s) we need to satisfy to be successful.

There are many examples of Software QFD [Zultner 1994], and some cases of QFD being used to create brand-new software products. For example, one well-known software company developed a new package specifically for one segment of customers: travelers. It was the first product of its kind on the market, and it received good reviews. Another company used QFD to enter a market where there were entrenched competitors. Its first release was chosen "Editors' Choice" at the Milwaukee ASQC *Annual Quality Congress* ahead of software that had been on the market for years. In this case, the software was familiar to the customer, but it was new to the development organization. Yet the organization was able to build a superior product with its first release—using QFD.

Mind of the Customer

Some methods for defining customer needs concentrate on the logical, or perceived needs of the customer. The Theory of Constraints (see Sidebar 24.1) [Goldratt 1990] is an example of such an approach. Through the use of the Thinking Processes (the tools of TOC, see Figure 24.5), three questions are addressed: what to change, what to change to, and how to [cause the] change. These questions may be answered with logic, either necessity logic or sufficiency logic.

Even for the easiest-to-obtain normal requirements, it is difficult to get more than 80 percent of customer needs by asking—even for familiar products.

First (see Figure 24.5), you must analyze the customer's perceived problems, or undesirable effects (UDEs), that make up their current reality, to identify the core problem that causes 80 percent of the perceived problems. Next, the core problem is assumed to result from a core conflict. You examine this conflict, the assumptions behind the conflict surface, and then you break one or more of the assumptions with injections that dissolve the conflict. Then you use the injections as a starting point for a future reality with the undesirable effects turned into desirable effects (DEs), or benefits. Additional injections are often required to complete the model of the future reality to the customer's satisfaction. At this point, some of the injections may require planning to establish intermediate objectives, and their sequence. Finally, some of the injections and/or intermediate objectives may require detailed planning so that you can carry out the transition from the current reality to the desired future reality.

There are a number of case studies of companies using TOC to improve an existing product line. The focus on improvement when applying TOC is often on the price, delivery terms, turnaround, or other ways of "tweaking the deal." This is in comparison to QFD, where the focus is often on changing the product or "tweaking the details."

TOC attempts to create an "unrefusable offer" (URO) by dissolving and leveraging the core conflict. On some development projects, addressing the core conflict may lie outside the scope of the project.

QFD attempts to create a competitive offer by focusing on enough high-value needs to gain a competitive advantage. Those who practice QFD do not even consider whether a core conflict could cause a core problem. So for some QFD development projects, they may be overlooking a major opportunity to add value in an exciting way using TOC techniques.

There are many types of requirements, and many methods to obtain them:

- You can obtain requirements by analyzing the emotional responses of the customer, as in Kansei Engineering. You can obtain requirements by analyzing the statements, or verbatims, of the customer, as in traditional QFD practice.

- You can obtain requirements by analyzing the perceived current reality of the customer, as in the Theory of Constraints Thinking Processes analysis.

- You can obtain requirements by analyzing the context of the customer, as done in contextual inquiry and user interface design methods.

- You can obtain requirements by analyzing the forces at work to decide the future of the customer, as done in systems dynamics scenario modeling and market analysis approaches.

And there are many dimensions of product development to which to apply the requirements.

Voice of Customer Analysis is a core method of doing QFD. The customer verbatims are converted to needs, structured, inspected, filled in, quantified, prioritized, and used in the "House of Quality" matrix.

Several software organizations have used TOC to improve by permanently reducing their elapsed time for development [Zultner 1998], but not to create a brand-new product. Given the potential of the method, it is only a matter of time until this happens.

Context of the Customer

Some methods for defining customer needs concentrate on the behavioral, or situational needs of the customer. Customer context analysis [Marsh *et al.* 1991] is an example of such an approach in QFD. Through the use of a Customer Context table and Relations diagrams, you can analytically uncover customer needs that are required because of the customer's work process [Zultner 1991, Hakos and Redish 1998].

A major CAD vendor applied context analysis to its product, and was able to generate three years' worth of enhancements in one week. Although the vendor provided these features to its customers as enhancements to its existing software, the features were so novel that they could have been packaged as a separate product. To be able to generate this many new customer needs in a mature product is evidence of the power of these methods.

One of the traditional principles of QFD is to "go to *gemba*" and observe directly the place where your product adds value to the customer [McQuarrie 1993]. Even for software, this can lead to customer needs that the customer is unaware of—and a significant competitive advantage for the first firm to find these needs [Beyer and Holtzblatt 1997, Robert *et al.* 1998]. If you are not going to *gemba* now, consider doing so—even if just for a day. If you are going now, why not take full advantage of your observations by doing context analysis?

Environment of the Customer

Some methods for defining customer needs concentrate on the strategic, or external needs of the customer. Systems dynamics [Senge 1990] is an example of such an approach. Through the use of causal-loop structures and simulation analysis, you can forecast the future states that would lead to new needs.

One small software company foresaw that the rapidly decreasing price of hard disks would lead to most people having large amounts of storage available. As a result, everyone would be able to store everything, from *all* their applications. But could they then *find* anything? The rather basic facilities available for finding files based on name and file attributes would soon prove inadequate. So this company developed a new kind of software product to track and find a wide variety of information, stored in a wide variety of native application formats. The company conceived the product based on a forecast of needs that would exist once technological and economic forces acted. Currently the company has a successful product that still has no competitors.

An example of a software category that possibly could have been realized much earlier is Web auction software. People have held, and attended, garage sales for many years. With the advent of the Internet, it became possible to hold, and attend, a global garage sale. And with more people offering their items for sale than could attend any one physical garage sale, a critical mass was created for people with very specific interests, leading to more items available, more people interested, and more sales.

eBay could have happened earlier. The technology was waiting for the need to be recognized. What are some other examples that have yet to be recognized?

Tools

One way to compare the methods of traditional QFD and TOC is to examine their tools.

QFD's Seven Management and Planning (7MP) Tools

The tool set for QFD comprises the 7 MP Tools (see Figure 24.5) [Mizuno 1988, Nayatani *et al.* 1994]. Selected from a wide variety of disciplines, these tools are wildly different, ranging from the right-brain no-numbers tool of the Affinity Diagram to the heavily quantitative matrix data analysis chart. So broad is the range they cover that most QFD projects do not use the entire set of tools.

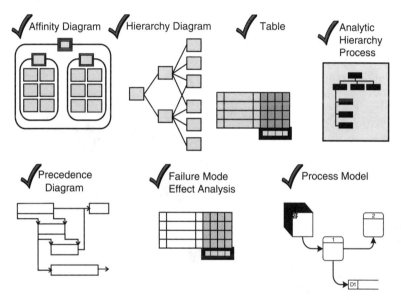

FIGURE 24.5
The tools of QFD, the Seven Management and Planning (7 MP) Tools, were taken from a variety of disciplines. Although each tool has a specific role to play in the Comprehensive QFD process, most individual QFD projects don't use all the tools.

The 7 MP Tools translate problems (undesirable effects) to benefits (desirable effects) right away, and then concentrate on focusing on the highest-value benefits. From there the QFD framework is tailored specifically for product development, so there is a great deal of structure to help plan exactly how to deliver the planned value.

One theme that all the tools have in common is that they are data driven. The content is produced through data collection, and the results are validated by additional data. In contrast to the TOC tools, there are no well-defined logical checks, and the logic is not strongly scrutinized.

Because the tools are data based, they have no requirement that the customers (or the developers) have any experience or intuition. This is most likely to be the case for a brand-new product.

Sidebar 24.1: What Is the Theory of Constraints (TOC)?

The **Theory of Constraints**, as developed by Dr. Eliyahu M. Goldratt, is the application of the methods of the hard sciences to human systems. At its core, it uses two concepts of the hard sciences that are quite different from their ordinary use: *complexity* and *problem*.

Complexity in ordinary language refers to the *amount of data* required to describe a system. In the following figure, System B requires many words to describe, so we'd ordinarily say it's "complex."

Complexity in the hard sciences refers to *degrees of freedom*—the number of points you need to interact with to impact the whole system. System A is "complex", because you must interact with four elements to affect the whole system.

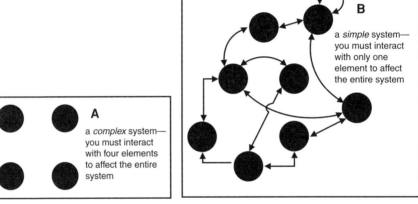

In the hard sciences, a *problem* is viewed as a conflict between two necessary conditions. Ordinarily, we seek to "solve" problems by compromise—trading off both conditions to get the "best" result we can. Sometimes this is even called "optimization," as if to suggest that it is not possible to do better. In Theory of Constraints, we "dissolve" problems by eliminating the conflict with a win-win "no compromise" result. By not compromising, it is possible to get big gains quickly—if you are willing to shift your paradigm.

To solve the problem in System A, it is necessary to develop and implement four solutions. Anything less cannot impact the entire system. This will be difficult.

To solve the problems in System B, we will work to discover the one core problem that causes the numerous symptoms we see. We will determine the conflict underlying the core problem, and break it. So we will have to develop and implement only *one* solution—impacting the entire system.

TOC's Thinking Processes

The tool set for TOC is the Thinking Processes [Dettmer 1997, Scheinkopf 1999]. These tools (Figure 24.6) share a rigorous use of logic. All the tools examine relationships for either necessity or sufficiency. All the tools share a common structure and syntax.

The Thinking Processes concentrate on undesirable effects (problems) right away, and only later, after the conflict has been broken, are the desirable effects (benefits) examined. From there the TOC framework provides a general structure to realize the benefits, so there is a great deal of flexibility when planning how to get to any future reality [Schragenheim 1998].

One theme that all the tools have in common is a careful scrutiny of the logic they represent. TOC has well defined "Categories of Legitimate Reservation" that provide a checklist of ways to confirm (or challenge) the logical structure [Scheinkopf 1999]. In contrast to the QFD tools, these tools do not use data, and data is not generally used to check the logic.

Because the tools are logic based, they are easier to present, and easier to use for buy-in than most of the 7 MP Tools. The absence of data as a check is perhaps least important when these tools are used for breakthrough results, where current data would hardly be relevant. If your project charter allows for your brand-new product to allow "thinking outside the box," you should definitely consider using Theory of Constraints Thinking Processes on your project.

The full Thinking Process Analysis uses all five TOC tools to analyze a situation and identify a core problem, develop a solution, and plan how to implement that solution.

1. Create a Current Reality Tree with UDEs to identify a Core Problem.

2. Create an Evaporating Cloud with the Core Problem. This is the Core Conflict. Identify the assumptions behind the cause-effect relationships, and surface injections to dissolve the conflict.

3. Create a Future Reality Tree with the injection as a starting point. This robust solution to the Core Problem should eliminate the UDEs, cause DEs, and block negative consequences.

4. Create a Prerequisite Tree to determine the Intermediate Objectives and their sequence.

5. Create Transition Trees for needed detailed action plans for accomplishing selected Intermediate Objectives and/or Objectives. A Communication Current Reality Tree (not shown) is also used to communicate a Current Reality Tree in a nonthreatening manner in order to get buy-in to the solution by those who are responsible for the core problem.

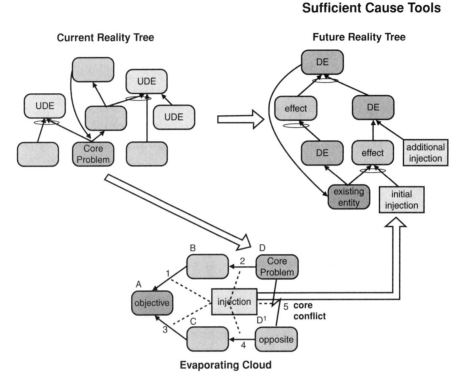

FIGURE 24.6
The Thinking Processes: the Theory of Constraints tools.

Last Steps

Developing brand-new products is not the last step. Before we are finished, we have to market the new product to our customers. This is a special challenge for unprecedented products. Not only do we have to deal with the issues of choice and loyalty, but first we have to get the interest of the customer.

Marketing Brand-New Products

This may require a paradigm shift—and for any significant change in the customer's world, there will be resistance. To work through the resistance effectively, we must understand the *layers of resistance* (see the next section).

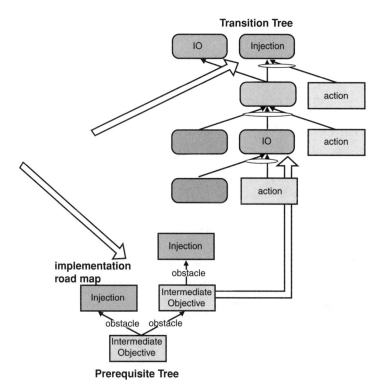

A classic software example was when Lotus Notes first entered the marketplace. The term *groupware* was not widely understood, and the package initially had only the basic capability to build applications. It is very difficult to demonstrate the value of groupware when no one in your group is using it yet.

Think of the layers of resistance as the customer's defense-in-depth against bad innovations—so they won't harm them. "No resistance" to innovation is not good—for people or for organizations. Good new products will (eventually) make it through the resistance, but we can accelerate the process. The layers of resistance will need to be worked through, carefully, point by point.

Layers of Resistance

Applying the Theory of Constraints often involves breakthrough solutions—paradigm *shifts*. It is not easy to persuade people to accept solutions that are very different from anything they know.

For this reason, the Theory of Constraints includes a method for shifting paradigms—on purpose, and efficiently. The key is to understand why people resist change, and what systematic defense they employ against change.

People raise objections to new ideas in a pattern: the layers of resistance. The marketing of an unprecedented product must be carefully structured to move people through all five layers successfully and efficiently. Only then can sales be sustained.

Table 24.1 summarizes the layers of resistance. For each layer, specific tools and techniques are used to efficiently work through the resistance and achieve buy-in to the solution.

TABLE 24.1
The 9 Layers of Resistance to Change

PoOGI Steps	Obstacles	Intermediate Objectives	Actions
What to Change? **What is the Problem?**	1. "I don't have that problem" That problem does not exist here	Agree on the goal Agree current situation is not good enough Agree problem exists, not their fault	Show they suffer from UDEs Show conflict underlying their problem Do single-UDE cloud
	2. "My problem is different" We have other, more serious problems	Agree their problem is caused by generic conflict Agree on core problem	Do generic cloud from single-UDE cloud
	3. "The problem is not under my control" So there is no point to even discussing solutions	Agree they can impact the problem	Clarify problem, do [communication] CRT Surface assumptions of generic cloud Identify assumptions they make, they can change

PoOGI Steps	Obstacles	Intermediate Objectives	Actions
What to Change to? **What is the Solution?**	4. "I have a different direction for a solution" You are offering me more of the same old things	Agree on the direction for a solution Agree on need for a win-win solution	Explore their solution (or compromise) Show how injection removes UDEs and does not compromise the objectives
	5. "The solution does not address the whole problem" There are still some undesirable effects	Agree the solution addresses the whole problem	show how solution addresses single-UDE clouds do Future Reality Tree
	6. "The solution has negative outcomes" yes BUT…	Agree tailored solution will not have negative outcomes	tailor solution, trim negative branches do Negative Branch Reservations
How to Change? **How to implement the Solution?**	7. "There are obstacles to implementing the solution" yes, BUT…	Agree on strategy to implement solution	identify Obstacles blocking solution and Intermediate Objectives to overcome them do Prerequisite Tree
	8. "I'm not clear how to implement the solution" So how do we proceed?	Agree on tactics to implement solution	do Transition Tree
	9. "Now we have to change what we're used to…" I'm afraid to start the change…	Agree to implement solution	overcome fear of uncertainty overcome fear of going first

Content compiled from Rami Goldratt, "Overcoming the Nine Layers of Resistance to Change," 4th International Conference on TOC for Education, Monterrey, Mexico, 10 August 2000.
The presentation summarized the work done by Efrat Goldratt in her doctoral research on resistance to change.

Conclusion

Practitioners using QFD have a variety of methods to address the challenge of unprecedented products—products no customer is familiar with. Although most development projects are upgrades of existing products, sometimes something truly new must be developed. And QFD's powerful framework can still help.

The Theory of Constraints offers QFD practitioners a complementary set of methods that concentrate where QFD does not—and vice versa. By using both approaches, you can analyze both the deal and the details to produce an unrefusable competitive product—even a brand-new product.

Acknowledgments

I would like to thank Dr. Eliyahu M. Goldratt, the developer of the Theory of Constraints, and other *Jonahs* in the TOC community who have educated me in the theory and practice of the Thinking Processes over the past few years. And I would especially like to thank my *Jonah's Jonah,* Frank Patrick, for his Socratic guidance and wisdom.

References

Akao, Yoji (Ed.). *Quality Function Deployment: Integrating Customer Requirements into Product Design* [translated by Glenn Mazur] (Cambridge, MA: Productivity Press, 1990).

Beyer, Hugh, and Karen Holtzblatt. *Contextual Design: A Customer-Centered Approach to Systems Designs* (Academic Press, 1997).

Dettmer, H. William. Goldratt's *Theory of Constraints: A Systems Approach to Continuous Improvement* (Milwaukee: ASQ Quality Press, 1997).

Goldratt, Eliyahu M. *Theory of Constraints* (Croton-on-Hudson, NY: North River Press, 1990).

Goldratt, Eliyahu M. *The Haystack Syndrome: Sifting Information out of the Data Ocean* (Great Barrington, MA: North River Press, 1990).

Goldratt, Eliyahu M. *What is this thing called THEORY OF CONSTRAINTS and how should it be implemented?* (Great Barrington, MA: North River Press, 1990).

Hakos, Joann T., and Janice C. Redish. *User and Task Analysis for Interface Design* (New York: John Wiley & Sons, 1998).

Kano, Noriaki, Nobuhiko Seraku, Fumio Takahashi, and Shinichi Tsuji. "Attractive and Must-Be Quality" (in Japanese). *Quality* 14 (February 2): p. 3,948 (Tokyo: JSQC, 1984).

Marsh, Stan, John W. Moran, Satoshi Nakui, and Glen D. Hofferr. *Facilitating and Training in Quality Function Deployment* (Methuen, MA: GOAL/QPC, 1991).

McQuarrie, Edward F. *Customer Visits: Building a Better Market Focus* (Newbury Park, CA: Sage Publications, 1993).

Mizuno, Shigeru. *Management for Quality Improvement: The 7 New QC Tools* (Cambridge, MA: Productivity Press, 1988 [1979]).

Mizuno, Shigeru, and Yoji Akao (Ed.). *Quality Function Deployment: The Customer-Driven Approach to Quality Planning and Deployment*. Rev. Ed. (Tokyo: Asian Productivity Organization, 1994 [1978]).

Nagamachi, Mitsuo. "Kansei Engineering Tutorial," in *Transactions from the 11th Symposium on QFD Tutorials*. Held in Novi, Mich., June 12, 1999 (Ann Arbor, MI: QFD Institute, 1999). Available from QFDI.

Nayatani, Yoshinobu, Toru Eiga, Ryoji Futami, and Hiroyuki Miyagawa. *The Seven New QC Tools: Practical Applications for Managers* [translated by John H. Loftus] (Tokyo: 3A Corporation, 1994 [1984]).

Robert , Dave (Ed.), Dick Berry, Scott Isensee, John Mullaly, *et al. Designing for the User with OVID: Bridging the Gap Between Software Engineering and User Interface Design* (Macmillan Technical Publishing, 1998).

Senge, Peter. *The Fifth Discipline: The Art & Practice of the Learning Organization* (New York: Doubleday, 1990).

Scheinkopf, Lisa J. *Thinking for a Change: Putting TOC Thinking Processes to Use* (Boca Raton, FL: St. Lucie Press, 1999).

Schragenheim, Eli. *Management Dilemmas: The Theory of Constraints Approach to Problem Identification and Solutions*. Foreword by William H. Dettmer (Boca Raton, FL: St. Lucie Press, 1998).

Zultner, Richard E. "Before the House: The Voices of the Customers in QFD," in *Transactions from the 3rd Symposium on QFD*. Held in Novi, Mich., June 24–25, 1991, pp. 450–464 (Ann Arbor, MI: QFD Institute, 1991).

Zultner, Richard E. "TQM for Technical Teams." CACM 10 (October 1993): pp. 79–91.

Zultner, Richard E. "Software QFD: The First Five Years," in *Annual Quality Congress*. Held in Las Vegas in May 1994 (Milwaukee: ASQC, 1994).

Zultner, Richard E. "Blitz QFD for Software: A Next Generation Approach for Delivering Value," in *7th International Conference on Software Quality Tutorials*. Held in Ottawa, Ontario, October 28-30, 1996 (Milwaukee: ASQ, 1996).

Zultner, Richard E. "QFD Schedule Deployment: Doing Development Faster with QFD," in *Transactions from the 10th Symposium on QFD*. Held in Novi, Mich., June 14–17, 1998 (Ann Arbor, MI: QFD Institute, 1998).

About the Author

Richard E. Zultner is an international consultant, educator, author, and speaker. QFD applied to high-tech and software-intensive products and processes has been his primary focus for the past 15 years. In 1998, he received the International Akao Prize for his contributions to the QFD field. He is one of 12 people so honored. In addition to providing consulting and training on Software QFD, Software SPC, and coaching executives on The Deming Way to Software Quality, Richard also acts as a Paradigm Guide to organizations willing to pioneer powerful new methods, such as the Theory of Constraints. Richard holds a master's degree in management from the J. L. Kellogg Graduate School of Management at Northwestern University, and has professional certifications in quality, software quality, project management, and software engineering. He is a certified *Jonah* in the Theory of Constraints from the Averham Y. Goldratt Institute.

CHAPTER 25

Jurassic QFD: Integrating Service and Product Quality Function Deployment

Andrew Bolt
MD Robotics, Canada

Glenn Mazur
QFD Institute

Japan Business Consultants, Ltd.
University of Michigan College of Engineering
glenn@mazur.net

Overview

Quality Function Deployment (QFD) is a unique system for developing new products which aims to ensure that the initial quality of the product or service will satisfy the customer. In today's turbo economy, traditional design methods that rely on extensive concept and market testing and multiple rollouts take too much time and increase risk that copycat products will enter the market first. Best efforts driven by internal requirements risk failure to recognize important customer needs. The tools and methods described in this chapter will show how you can minimize these risks with proper planning. This chapter will also show how you can customize QFD to a specific project, especially to design a tangible product, an animatronic dinosaur, to be used in a service operation (a theme park attraction).

Chapter Outline

- Company Profile of MD Robotics
- Why QFD?
- Triceratops Encounter at Universal Studios Florida Island of Adventure
- Summary
- About the Authors
- References

Company Profile of MD Robotics

MD Robotics, formerly known as the Spar Space Systems division of Spar Aerospace, Ltd., is a Canadian supplier to NASA with a well-established reputation for creating the world's most futuristic space robotics. The company's skill in precision movement robotics made it the supplier of choice to re-create one of nature's most fascinating and magnificent creatures ever—the dinosaur. MD Robotics, in cooperation with Universal City Development Partners (UCDP) of Orlando, Florida, designed and built three state-of-the-art robotically animated dinosaurs, the first of which it delivered in February 1999.

MD Robotics gained its initial expertise in the development of the space shuttle Canadarm used to manipulate cargo in and out of the shuttle's cargo bay. Although they had no previous experience with theme park attractions or dinosaur robots, the MD Robotics team accepted the challenge to combine their talents with Universal Creative and Hall Train Studios to provide life-like, large-scale, highly realistic "animals brought back from extinction."[1]

Andrew Bolt, the program manager, assembled a cross-functional team consisting of himself; some key engineers with experience in mechanics, hydraulics, controls, software, and electrical design from MD Robotics; the paleo-artist, Hall Train; and the customer. Bolt considered QFD to be an important tool for translating the vague, imagery-based requirements from the animator's storyboards into the detailed specifications needed to accurately budget resources, and then to design and build the creatures. In conjunction with QFD expert, Glenn Mazur, of Japan Business Consultants (Ann Arbor, MI), the team executed and formed a unique QFD template in just three weeks.

Why QFD?

QFD is a unique system for developing new products which aims to ensure that the initial quality of the product or service will satisfy the customer. In today's turbo economy, traditional design methods that rely on extensive concept and market testing and multiple roll-outs take too much time and increase risk that copycat products will enter the market first. Best efforts driven by internal requirements risk failure to recognize important customer needs. QFD tools and methods can reduce these risks with a robust, traceable, and structured system of planning. Further, you can customize QFD to a specific project, whether it is software, a product, a service, or as in this case, a combination of all three.

QFD is the only comprehensive quality system aimed specifically at satisfying the customer and, as in this case, the customer's customer (the theme park visitor). It concentrates on maximizing customer satisfaction (positive quality) and eliminating dissatisfaction (negative quality). QFD differs from traditional quality methods that focus on zero defects; after all, when *nothing is wrong it does not mean that anything is right.*

QFD focuses on delivering positive value by seeking out both spoken and unspoken needs, translating them into actions and designs, and communicating them throughout each organization on the value chain to the end customer (the theme park visitor). Further, QFD allows customers to prioritize their requirements and benchmark us against our competitors. Then QFD directs us to optimize those aspects of our products and services that will deliver the greatest competitive advantage. No business can afford to waste constrained financial, time, and human resources on things customers don't value or where they are already the clear leader.

History of QFD

QFD began 30 years ago in Japan as a quality system focused on delivering products and services that satisfy customers. To efficiently deliver value to customers, it is necessary to listen to the "voice of the customer" throughout the product or service development process. The late Dr. Shigeru Mizuno, Dr. Yoji Akao, and other quality experts in Japan developed the tools and techniques of QFD and organized them into a comprehensive system to ensure quality and customer satisfaction in new products and services [Mizuno and Akao 1994, Akao 1990].

In 1983, a number of leading North American firms discovered this powerful approach and have been using it with cross-functional teams and concurrent engineering to improve their products, as well as the design and development process itself [Akao 1983, King 1987]. Service organizations have also found QFD to be helpful. One of the authors of this chapter, Mazur, used QFD in 1985 to develop his Japanese translation business, Japan

Business Consultants, and saw revenues increase 285 percent the first year, 150 percent the second year, and 215 percent the third year [Mazur 1993]. QFD was an important part of Florida Power & Light's successful bid to become the first non-Japanese Deming Prize recipient in 1990 [Webb 1990] and in the 1994 Deming Prize awarded to AT&T Power Systems. Leading institutions such as The University of Michigan Medical Center [Gaucher and Coffey 1993, Ehrlich 1994], Baptist Health System [Gibson 1994, 1995], and others have applied QFD successfully in healthcare since 1991. Interesting service applications also include the development of an engineering Total Quality Management (TQM) curriculum at The University of Michigan College of Engineering [Mazur 1996a] and the application to employee satisfaction and quality of work life at AGT Telus [Harries *et al.* 1995], as well as in small and medium-size enterprises [Mazur 1994]. Integrating service and product QFD was a hallmark of the study Host Marriott completed to improve its breakfast service at U.S. airports [Lampa and Mazur 1996, Mazur 1996b].

Organizations have heralded QFD for such benefits as promoting cross-functional teams, improving internal communications between departments, and translating customer requirements into the language of the organization. Understanding customer requirements appears to be one of the weakest links in product and service design. In a survey of 203 projects at 123 industrial companies, managers rated 13 typical new-product development process activities in terms of what percentage of projects actually did the activity, and on a ten-point scale, how well they performed the activity. Least performed (25.4 percent of the projects) was a detailed market study of customer requirements, and when it was done, the quality of work was graded a 5.74 out of 10 [Cooper 1993].

Many product developers explain this by saying that customer requirements are often too vague, are never mentioned, change during the project, and even when met, are frequently not what customers want to buy. In QFD, you can employ several tools to clarify vague requirements, discover hidden ones, and prevent changes or misunderstandings by correctly analyzing their root benefits [Mazur 1997, Rings *et al.* 1998]. Prompting the development of these tools was a study done in Japan in 1984 that demonstrated that different types of requirements needed different approaches to understand [Kano *et al.* 1984].

Kano's Requirements

You must consider three types of customer requirements to understand how meeting or exceeding customer expectations affects satisfaction (see Figure 25.1).

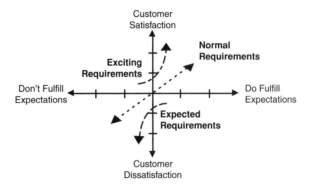

FIGURE 25.1
Kano's Model of Customer Requirements

- **Normal Requirements** are typically what we get by just asking customers what they want. These requirements satisfy (or dissatisfy) customers in proportion to their presence (or absence) in the product or service. Fast delivery is a good example. The faster (or slower) the delivery, the more customers like (or dislike) it.

- **Expected Requirements** are often so basic the customer may fail to mention them—until we fail to perform them. They are basic expectations without which the product or service may cease to be of value; their absence is *very* dissatisfying. Further, meeting these requirements often goes unnoticed by most customers. For example, if coffee is served hot, customers barely notice it. If it's cold or too hot, dissatisfaction occurs. Expected requirements *must* be fulfilled.

- **Exciting Requirements** are difficult to discover. They are beyond the customer's expectations. Their absence doesn't dissatisfy; their presence excites. For example, if caviar and champagne were served on a flight from Detroit to Chicago, that would be exciting. If they were not served, customers would hardly complain. These are the things that wow customers and bring them back. Since customers are not apt to voice these requirements, it is the organization's responsibility to explore customer problems and opportunities to uncover such unspoken items.

Kano's model is also dynamic in that what excites us today is expected tomorrow. That is, once introduced, the exciting feature will soon be imitated by the competition and customers will come to expect it from everybody. An example is the ability to have pizza delivered in 30 minutes. On the other hand, expected requirements can become exciting after a real or potential failure. An example might be when passengers applaud after a pilot safely lands an airplane in rough and stormy weather.

The Kano model has an additional dimension regarding which customer segments the target market includes. For example, the caviar and champagne that are exciting on the domestic flight might be expected on the Concorde from New York to London. Knowing which customer segments you serve is critical to understanding your customers' requirements.

Thus, eliminating problems handles expected requirements. You can gain little satisfaction or competitive advantage when nothing goes wrong. Conversely, you can gain great value by discovering and delivering on exciting requirements ahead of the competition. QFD helps ensure that expected requirements don't fall through the cracks and points out opportunities to build in excitement.

In summary, Kano found that the exciting needs, which are most tied to adding value, are invisible to both the customer and the provider. Further, they change over time, technology, market segment, and so on.

The QFD team understands these requirements best when going to the *gemba* (where the customer interfaces with the service) to observe, listen, and record the problems customers experience and the opportunities they wish to seize. Going to the *gemba* can be difficult for those who are used to seeing things from an internal point of view. They tend to see more process problems and solutions than customer needs. QFD tools help the team see the world from the customer's point of view.

Triceratops Encounter at Universal Studios Florida Island of Adventure

The movie *Jurassic Park* included an encounter with a sick triceratops lying on her side. In the theme park attraction, a veterinarian attends to a sick but standing "Sarah" who seems to acknowledge visitors to her paddock where she is being examined. The 24-foot triceratops looks, feels, acts, and even smells like a real animal, complete with actions such as breathing, blinking and pupil dilation, flinching, sneezing, drooling, and excreting. Visitors are never more than six feet away and can even pet her.

Given these encounters, the team's overall goal was to make a creature more believable and lifelike than any before. The state of the art at that time was the "DinoAlive" exhibit at an Osaka Japan museum that relied on hydraulics to give the creature smooth, quick movements. Vickers Inc. of Troy, Michigan [Horgan, Gottschalk] designed the creature and set a very high benchmark for realism of motion and appearance. For example, the 40-foot-high Tyrannosaurus Rex could move from a resting position to fully erect in only 1.5 seconds. The Jurassic ride in Hollywood also reflected where the industry was in June of 1996. The animals were fairly realistic but not convincing, especially if you were able to stop the show and examine them closely. There was also a great concern with reliability. Thus, very stringent requirements were made so that close encounters such as petting would be thoroughly convincing.

QFD Template

As a design method, QFD is no cookie-cutter approach. A project worth doing well deserves to have QFD tailored to the needs of the company, the team, the customers, and the customers' customers. The team used QFD in the conceptual stage to bridge the gap between the artist and the engineer so that the process was really tailored to suit the "skunk works" fast-turnaround working environment in which the program ran.

The conceptual design Scope of Work document that the team used to drive the QFD study specified that the outcome should include such specifications as degrees of freedom of movement, maximum velocity, range of motion, skin characteristics, and so on. These were to correspond to various scenarios that the animators portrayed in some 60 storyboards which included such activities as sneezing, playing, and moving legs. Given the time and cost budgets, the MD Robotics team wanted to put its earliest efforts on the dinosaur's most important aspects. The scope of work, however, did not indicate that any one storyboard activity was more critical than another—they were all equally important. Also problematic was the fact that for a company that builds space and defense components, translating the requirement of "sneezing" into an animatronic design was not something their engineers had done before.

After an initial QFD introduction, Mazur's task was to customize the QFD process to deliver these needs. Bolt led a review of the Scope of Work document, and three key elements emerged:

1. Achieve a clear understanding of the experience/benefits Universal wished to achieve.

2. Trace these benefits into engineering requirements.

3. Translate the engineering requirements into cost-effective conceptual designs.

To clarify the customer's requirements, we began a Voice of Customer Analysis of the Scope of Work document. First we used the Voice of Customer Table 1 (Customer Context Table) to break down the details of the scope of work into singular statements and to then reword them with regard to the context of use. Then we used the Voice of Customer Table 2 (Customer Voice Table) to sort the statements, first as benefits versus features and then detailing the features into additional categories that became the axes of the subsequent matrices. Figure 25.2 shows a deployment flowchart.

Voice of Customer Analysis

The Voice of Customer Table 1 (VOCT1) is commonly used to clarify complex customer requirements, particularly in the context of use of the product or service. Context is easily described by the 5W1H (who is using it, what they are using it for, and when, why, and how they are using it). Table 25.1 shows an excerpt from the VOCT1 for end-product requirements.

The Voice of Customer Table states the requirement of "animal-like reactions to the guests," who are described as families with elementary school-age children visiting the Triceratops Encounter paddock after experiencing the park's thrill rides. The reworded data reduces the complex requirement into singular terms to address the contextual concerns. Simply put, this attraction must not be a let-down after the park's action rides, and it must keep the interest of children ranging from young enough to be amazed by seeing a "live" dinosaur to young teens amazed to see something so lifelike in terms of both appearance and behavior. The reworded data begins the process of analyzing the voice of customer data into the details in the table.

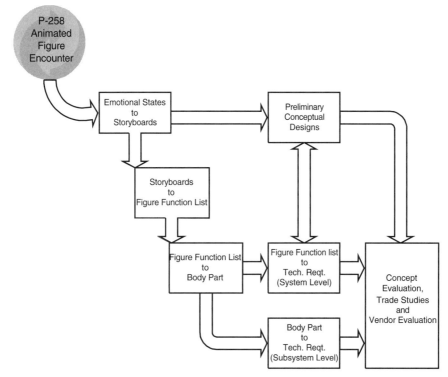

FIGURE 25.2
QF5 Flowchart for Triceratops Encounter

TABLE 25.1
Partial Voice of Customer Table 1 (Customer Context Table)

VOC from Scope of Work	Context of Use (5W1H)	Reworded Data
The close proximity of guest-to-dinosaur dictates fluid movements, noncyclical programs, low noise, realistic skins, animal-like odors, and animal-like reactions to the guests.	Who: Families with K–8 children. What: Entertainment. When: After thrill rides. Where: An animal paddock area behind the discovery center in Isla Nublar, home of Jurassic Park. Why: Amaze children. How: Guests are allowed limited, upervised interaction (close contact and some direct contact of specific body areas) with dinosaurs.	Smooth movement. Quiet movement. Looks realistic. Smells realistic. Reacts realistically to guests. Responds to touch. Nonrepetitive movement. One-on-one personal experience. Like a zoo. Interacts with guests. Appears alive. Appears alert.

The Voice of Customer Table 2 (VOCT2) sorts this reworded data on whether it describes a product feature or the customer benefit the feature must provide. Product features are broken down further into performance measurements, functions, reliability, safety, technologies, materials, components, and so on. In this case, for conceptual design, the categories were storyboards, body motions, technical requirements, and concepts (see Table 25.2).

TABLE 25.2
Partial Voice of Customer Table 2 (Customer Voice Table)

Benefit	Storyboard	Body Motion	Technical Requirement	Concept
Looks realistic	Variable, so revisits are different	Nonrepetitive	Resistant to outdoor elements	Concealed controls

These VOCT tables structured and analyzed both hidden and known requirements of the final product. The Voice of Customer Analysis in QFD also has the tools and methods to move up and down the customer value chain and can translate and link the requirements of end users (guests), the attraction operator, the maintenance crew, the installers, theme park management, and animators. One method for doing this is called **going to the *gemba*** or to the place where the product is used. Here we have features and benefits for the end product, but what about the benefits to the consumer? Since no consumer had ever seen a moving dinosaur, their interpretation of "realistic" was limited to their imagination based on illustrations, cartoons, or other robotics. It was relatively easy to see that you could visit the operator, maintenance, installer, management, and animator *gembas* at an existing amusement park, but what about the dinosaur *gemba*?

As vendors to the space industry, MD Robotics engineers were adept at simulating environments. It is well known that you can use swimming pools and high-altitude drops to simulate the microgravity of space, and that aerospace vendors use them frequently during design. To simulate the Triceratops Encounter, the engineers visited a petting zoo in Toronto where they observed children encountering live animals. This helped them better understand the expectations and interactions children would be familiar with. They learned that the general public looks for anthropomorphic qualities in the animals; in other words, they attach human emotional states to the animals' actions. They also noted that with the dawn of the information age, people and, specifically, children are incredibly knowledgeable when it comes to dinosaurs. For an animal to be convincing, its stance, motion, and look must be correct with the state of knowledge within the paleontology world today.

From this *gemba*, the engineers structured the emotional states they detected with an Affinity Diagram and a Hierarchy Diagram (see Table 25.3). They presented these emotional states to the animators for prioritization based on how each emotional state contributed to making the attraction popular and enjoyable. An interesting dichotomy arose because the animators placed a higher priority on a natural-looking effect which tended to emphasize gross body motion associated with distant viewing, while guests at the zoo wanted more contact with the head which tended to emphasize detailed head sub-mechanisms such as tongue, nostrils, and so on. Mazur recommended using sales points in the "House of Quality" to reemphasize those emotional states that were oriented more toward visitor contact.

The main means the animators used to convey the creative requirements to the MD Robotics team was storyboards. Figure 25.3 shows an example.

TABLE 25.3
Hierarchy of Emotional States (Partial)

Quiet	Bored
	Sleepy
	Shy
Agitated	Aggressive
	Distressed
	Startled
	Surprised
	Frightened
	Nervous
	Defensive
Active	Nosy
	Curious
	Playful
	Happy

FIGURE 25.3
Example of a Storyboard

© Storyboards by Hall Train (August 1996).

Emotion Deployment

The engineers then used the emotional states that both the Hall Train animators and the petting zoo guests prioritized to prioritize their 65 storyboards in order to determine which postures and positions most strongly correlated with the most important emotional states. Using this process they formed the emotional state versus storyboard matrix. This enabled the design team to get a feeling for how important each storyboard was to the show. Table 25.4 shows this deployment matrix.

In this matrix, the emotional states are weighted on a 1 to 5 scale, with 5 being the most important. The degree of correlation between each body motion and emotional state is indicated in the intersecting cells of the matrix, using the values of 1 for some correlation, 3 for average correlation, and 9 for strong correlation. The emotional state weight is then multiplied by the correlation value in each cell, and the results are summed column by column (absolute weight). This tells which body motion has the most and the strongest overall contribution to the most important emotional states.

TABLE 25.4
Emotional State versus Storyboard Matrix (Partial)

Storyboard #	7		8	52/54/55	53	56	59/60/29/58	61	62/63	1 to	8/64/65	
Emotional States	defensive posture		angry/aggressive	visual response	blinking	nostril flare/sniffing	Skin twitching/flexing motions 1/2	skin temperature	breathing 1/2		poses and views	IMPORTANCE
Distressed	9		9	9	9	9	9		9			2
Startled				9	9	9	9		3			3
Surprised				9	9	9	9		3			3
Playful				9	9	9	9		· 3			3
Happy				9	9	9	9		3			4
Absolute weight	83		69	339	351	327	351	0	201			
Sales Point weight	1		1	1.2	1.5	1.5	1	1	1.2			
Storyboard weight	**1.5**		**1.2**	**7.2**	**9.3**	**8.6**	**6.2**	**0.0**	**4.2**			

As mentioned earlier, there was a dichotomy between the animators and the petting zoo visitors we observed, and so we factored in a "sales point" to add more importance to head contact storyboards. In QFD, sales points further emphasize exciting requirements multipliers (1 is "not exciting," 1.2 is "exciting," and 1.5 is "very exciting"). Then we multiplied the absolute weights by the sales points, and normalized to a percentage to yield the storyboard weights. The storyboards with high weights are critical to conveying an exciting show to visitors. For example, the triceratops flaring its nostrils is crucial to conveying whether it is happy or startled (see Figure 25.4).

Body Deployment

Next, we used the QFD process to take this down another level to get the relationship between the storyboards and body motion, and then from the body motion to detailed body parts. Our main benefit in doing this was to see the relevance of the body parts to the emotional states. Because the emotional states were now weighted, this assured us that we would spend our time on the dinosaur's most relevant physical components.

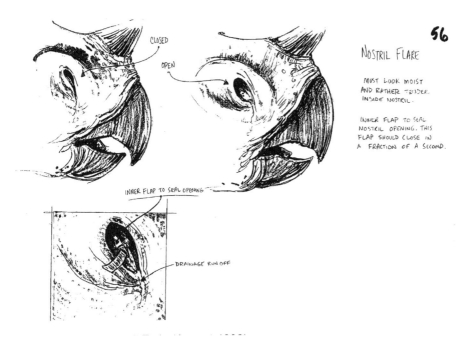

FIGURE 25.4
Storyboard 56. Nostril Flare.

© Storyboards by Hall Train (August 1996).

We structured body motions with an Affinity Diagram and a Hierarchy Diagram (see Table 25.5) and then we joined them in a matrix with the weighted storyboards.

TABLE 25.5
Body Motion Hierarchy (Partial)

Muscle	Skin	Shudder
		Twitch
		Temperature change
	Buttocks	Tense/release
		Bulge/expand
Appendages	Front toes	Spread
		Curl
	Neck	Yaw
		Roll

Facial parts	Nostrils	Flare
		Sniff/inhale
		Air blast
		Spray
		Moisten
	Eyes	Translate

The Storyboard versus Body Motions Matrix (see Table 25.6) shows the correlation of each body motion to displaying the theme of the storyboard and then weights the body motions using the same process as in Table 25.4. The first row, for example, shows that "left front leg 3 pitch" plays an average role in a defensive posture. In Table 25.6, the body motions have been rearranged in descending order of importance.

TABLE 25.6
Storyboards vs. Body Motions Matrix (Partial)

Body Motions		left front leg 3 pitch	lfl yaw	lfl roll		Skin articulation		Storyboard weight
Storyboards								
7	defensive posture	3	3	3				1.5
8	angry/aggressive	9	9	9				1.2
42								
	step backwards	9	9	9				4.2
49	throat movement							2.3
50	tongue movements							4.2
51/57	jaw movement							5.2
52/54/55	visual response							7.2
53	blinking							9.3
56	nostril flare/sniffing							8.6
59/60/29/58	skin twitching/flexing motion							6.2
62/63	breathing 1/2							4.2
to 6/18/48/64/65	poses and views							0.0
	Absolute Wt.	397.4	397.4	397.4		0.0		
	Body Motion Weight	2.93	2.93	2.93		0.00		

At this point, we deployed body motions into specific body parts indicated in the primary structure of the triceratops shown in Figure 25.5. A Body Motion to Body Parts Matrix translated the body motion weights into body part weights (see Table 25.7). This would tell us, among other things, how big a role the head base structure would play in the body motion function of head movement.

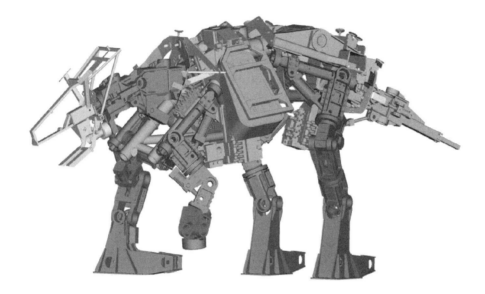

FIGURE 25.5
Primary Structure of Triceratops

Engineering Requirements Deployment

Our next step was to develop engineering requirements that would lead to design specifications and structure them in a Hierarchy Diagram (see Table 25.8).

TABLE 25.7
Body Motion versus Body Parts Matrix (Partial)

Body Parts	Head Assembly												Neck			U
Body Motion	head base structure	eye mechanism	tongue mechanism	nostril mechanism	mouth mechanism	breathing mechanism	jaw muscle mechanism	cheek muscle mechanism	frill muscle mechanism	ear muscle mechanism	head shell and skin	neck mechanism	upper neck muscle	lower neck muscle	neck shell and skin	
left front leg 3 pitch																
lf yaw																
right front leg 3 pitch																

TABLE 25.8
Engineering Requirements Hierarchy (Partial)

	Static balance	
Static mech.	Tip deflection	
	Mass	
	Reaction loads	Geometry
		Bearing loads
Kinematics	Joint angle of travel	
	Joint acceleration	
System design and architecture	Pneumatic power	Pneumatic flow rate

We deployed both the weighted body motions and the weighted body parts in matrices to determine which engineering requirements required the most exacting specifications. These matrices are not shown in this chapter. Additionally, we created matrices to identify and design out potential failure modes. Later in the study, these charts helped simplify certain systems and components resulting in lower cost, faster design, and improved reliability.

The May 1999 opening of the new Triceratops Encounter at Universal Studios' Jurassic Park attraction prompted *U.S. News & World Report* to write "these three creatures snort, stomp their feet—even pee. Ask the 'keeper' if you can pet them. It's up to him or her to decide."[2] (See Figure 25.6.)

FIGURE 25.6
The Prototype of "Sarah" Being Reviewed by the Customer

Summary

Quality-conscious organizations around the world have used QFD for more than 30 years. Its adaptability to nearly any product development project has earned QFD the reputation of being a methodical approach to ensure customer satisfaction with the quality of new products and services.

QFD has migrated upstream steadily since Akao introduced the method in the 1960s. For its first ten years, QFD focused on internal deployments within the company's operations to ensure that quality requirements were accurately communicated throughout the development and production processes. In its second decade of use, QFD incorporated external analyses of customer requirements based on examining actual uses by customers.

In its third decade, we now see QFD in the initial phases of product concepting [Rings *et al.* 1998]. Further, QFD is now being used to integrate the hardware, software, service, and process aspects that are common in most products today.

MD Robotics has continued to apply QFD to other products in its traditional lines of business with great success. Unlike what happened with dinosaurs, it is expected that the company's use of QFD will continue to evolve in order to ensure that its customer-driven focus will never become extinct.

About the Authors

Andrew Bolt has worked in the aerospace industry for 15 years, initially as a consultant to Spar Aerospace and then as a member of the management team. He managed the design of the next-generation space station robotic arm. He also was responsible for the design and build of the mobile base on which the space station arm is stored and performs maintenance tasks. Andrew managed the Mechanical Engineering division and was executive assistant to the director of operations within Spar Aerospace. This is where his exposure to the QFD process occurred. The Triceratops Encounter program was an excellent application of this process. It combined Andrew's engineering, process, and sculpting interests. Andrew managed that program from inception to completion and now is managing the strategic development of theme park robotics within the newly renamed MD Space and Advanced Robotics Company. You can reach him at 905-790-2800, extension 4095; by fax at 905-790-4430, or by email at abolt@spar.ca or abolt@mdrobotics.ca.

Glenn Mazur has been the "voice" of QFD since its early inception in the United States He has worked extensively with the creators of the QFD methodology, Drs. Shigeru Mizuno and Yoji Akao, since that time. He is a pioneer in the application of QFD and *Teoriya Resheniya Izobreatatelskikh Zadatch* (TRIZ) in service industries. He currently holds the following positions: president of Japan Business Consultants, Ltd., executive director of the QFD Institute, executive director of the International Council for QFD, chairman of the North American QFD Symposia, and adjunct lecturer of TQM at the University of Michigan College of Engineering. He is also a 1998 recipient of the Akao Prize for Excellence in QFD and is one of two designated trainers of QFD Black Belts in North America. You can reach him at 734-995-0847, by fax at 734-995-3810, by email at glenn@mazur.com, and on the Internet at http://www.mazur.net/.

References

[1] "Spar brings prehistoric creature to life." Canada NewsWire press release, March 10, 1999; www.newswire.ca/releases/March1999/10/c3114.html.

[2] Travel section. "Triceratops Encounter." *U.S. News and World Report.* May 10, 1999 p. 71.

Akao, Yoji, Ed. *Quality Function Deployment: Integrating Customer Requirements into Product Design.* Translated by Glenn Mazur (Cambridge, MA: Productivity Press, 1990a).

Akao, Yoji. *Company-Wide QC and Quality Deployment* (Chicago: The Cambridge Corporation, 1983).

Cooper, Robert G. 1993. *Winning at New Products, 2nd Edition* (Reading, MA: Addison-Wesley, 1993).

Ehrlich, Deborah. "Health Care: Tailoring a Service Industry." *Transactions from the Fourth Symposium on Quality Function Deployment* (Ann Arbor, MI: QFD Institute, 1994).

Gaucher, Ellen, and Richard Coffey. *Total Quality in Health Care: From Theory to Practice* (The Jossey-Bass Health Series, 1993).

Gibson, Jeff. "Happy Feet Part II: Return of the Princeton Foot Clinic." *Transactions from the Seventh Symposium on Quality Function Deployment* (Ann Arbor, MI: QFD Institute, 1995).

Gibson, Jeff. "Health Care Services: Princeton Foot Clinic." *Transactions from the Fourth Symposium on Quality Function Deployment* (Ann Arbor, MI: QFD Institute, 1994).

Gottschalk, M. "Dino-Adventure." *Design News* (August 16, 1993, pp. 52–58).

Harries, Bruce, and Matthew Baerveldt. "QFD for Quality of Work Life." *Transactions from the Seventh Symposium on Quality Function Deployment* (Ann Arbor, MI: QFD Institute, 1995).

Horgan, M. "Hydraulics returns dinosaurs from extinction." *Hydraulics & Pneumatics* (July 1993, pp. 27–28).

Kano, Noriaki, Nobuhiko Seraku, Fumio Takahashi, and Shinichi Tsuji. "Attractive Quality and Must-Be Quality." (Translated by Glenn Mazur.) *Hinshitsu* 14, no. 2 (February 1984): pp. 39–48.

King, Bob. *Better Designs in Half the Time: Implementing QFD Quality Function Deployment in America* (Methuen, MA: GOAL/QPC, 1987 and 1989).

Lampa, Steve, and Glenn Mazur. "Bagel Sales Double at Host Marriott Using Quality Function Deployment." *Transactions from the Eighth Symposium on Quality Function Deployment/International Symposium on QFD '96* (Ann Arbor, MI: QFD Institute, 1996).

Mazur, Glenn. "Voice of Customer Analysis: A Modern System of Front-End QFD Tools, with Case Studies." *Proceedings of ASQC's 51st Annual Quality Congress* (Milwaukee: ASQC, 1997).

Mazur, Glenn. "The Application of Quality Function Deployment (QFD) to Design a Course in Total Quality Management (TQM) at The University of Michigan College of Engineering." *Proceedings of International Conference on Quality–1996 Yokohama.* JUSE (October 15–18, 1996a).

Mazur, Glenn. "Doubling Sales with Quality Function Deployment." *Proceedings of the ASQC's Fifth Annual Service Quality Conference* (Milwaukee: ASQC, 1996b).

Mazur, Glenn. "QFD for Small Business: A Shortcut through the 'Maze of Matrices'." *Transactions from the Sixth Symposium on Quality Function Deployment* (Ann Arbor, MI: QFD Institute, 1994).

Mazur, Glenn. "QFD for Service Industries: From Voice of Customer to Task Deployment." *Transactions from the Fifth Symposium on Quality Function Deployment* (Ann Arbor, MI: QFD Institute, June 1993).

Mizuno, Shigeru, and Yoji Akao, Eds. *Quality Function Deployment: The Customer-Driven Approach to Quality Planning and Deployment* Translated by Glenn Mazur (Tokyo: Asian Productivity Organization, 1994).

Rings, Cathy, Brian Barton, and Glenn Mazur. "Consumer Encounters of the Third Kind: Improving Idea Development and Concept Optimization." *Transactions from the Tenth Symposium on Quality Function Deployment* (Ann Arbor, MI: QFD Institute, June 1998).

Webb, Joseph L., and W. C. Hayes. "Quality Function Deployment at FPL." *Transactions from the Second Symposium on Quality Function Deployment* (Ann Arbor, MI: QFD Institute, 1990).

CHAPTER 26

Project QFD: Managing Software Development Projects Better with Blitz QFD

Richard E. Zultner
Zultner & Co.
richard@zultner.com

Can Quality Function Deployment help the Project Manager to assure project success?

Overview

Quality Function Deployment (QFD) has been used for software development for more than a decade, and its popularity is increasing. One important factor in the adoption of QFD for software development is the project manager's decision to try it. Although the benefits of QFD for developers are well established, many project managers are not aware of how QFD can benefit them. Can QFD directly benefit project managers? Should a project manager doing new-product development use QFD to help him manage projects better?

After considering what often goes wrong with software (and other) development projects, and what causes those problems, an efficient, initial use of QFD is suggested: Blitz QFD. Project managers can apply this "best way to start with QFD" to better focus their development projects on efficiently delivering maximum value to their customers, and to plan for best efforts by the team on those activities that are truly essential, rather than merely critical. With Project QFD, project managers can manage value like they manage time, money, and people. And assuring that the product they develop delivers value to the customer is the development project manager's first priority.

Chapter Outline

- Introduction
- Problems with New Development
- Focus on Value with Project QFD
- Summary
- Acknowledgments
- References
- About the Author

Introduction

QFD has been applied to software development for more than a decade, and its popularity is increasing. QFD as a comprehensive system for quality (see Figure 26.1) originated in Japan in the late 1960s and rapidly gained strength in the 1970s [Mizuno and Akao 1994, Akao 1992]. It spread to North America in the mid-1980s and to Europe in the late 1980s [Hauser and Clausing 1988, King 1989]. Software QFD began in Japan in 1982 [Aizawa 1982], in North America in 1988 [Zultner 1988], and in Europe in 1990. Today the use of QFD for software has spread to the point that most leading software organizations have tried it and are (at various rates) expanding their use of it [Zultner 1995]. But not all projects are successful.

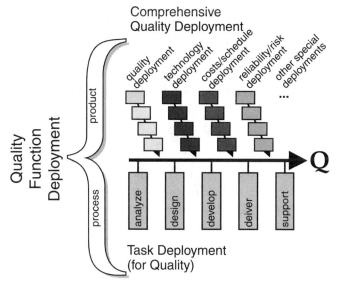

FIGURE 26.1
Comprehensive QFD is a powerful, mature quality system for efficiently delivering value in product development. Everyone applying QFD starts with just a small part. So what part of QFD should project managers start with?

Failure

Some software project teams have failed with QFD. They tried to do QFD based on a weak understanding of the method, or without understanding the differences between QFD for hardware and QFD for software. Encountering difficulties with no where to turn for assistance (or receiving ill-informed advice), they failed—and blamed QFD for their own mistakes.

Partial Success

Some software project teams have succeeded with QFD only to stagnate and become a case of arrested development. These teams typically learned about the "House of Quality" matrix of QFD and applied it with success. Then they used QFD on further projects, but they did not apply it at the level that they were previously. Some software project teams are still doing "Kindergarten QFD" (they are only using the "House of Quality" matrix) five years after learning about QFD. However you get started with QFD, you want to progress toward a more comprehensive use of QFD so that you are getting all the benefits QFD has to offer [Nakui 1991].

QFD Defined

QFD is a quality system made up of subsystems, or **deployments**, each focused on one dimension of the development process (such as reliability). These deployments in turn are composed of a systematic series of tools, organized in a specific sequence to address the questions and concerns of that dimension throughout the project. (Refer to Figure 26.1 for Dr. Akao's graphical definition of QFD.) **Comprehensive QFD** is the term used to clearly indicate that the entire quality system is being referred to, not just one little matrix.

Starting Right

QFD has been undergoing continuous improvement and refinement, and signs are now visible of a "second-generation" QFD emerging in Japan, North America, and Europe. One example of this trend is Blitz QFD, a QFD method designed to be a better, faster, and cheaper *initial* QFD process than what many software project teams are currently doing. But not counter to those approaches, Blitz QFD was designed so that you don't have to break any bad habits to progress to a more sophisticated application of Comprehensive QFD.

Let's first look at some of the problems software organizations have had with software development projects, and their causes. Then let's consider how Blitz QFD can help project managers better manage their product development projects.

Problems with New Development

Developing new software products is challenging. Among the most pervasive challenges are problems arising from difficulties with the development process. The project manager has the primary responsibility for dealing with these difficulties. What are they, and what can QFD do to help?

Incoherent Development Is Inefficient

On many development projects, when the project is over, it can appear that the team's best efforts were applied without any plan or pattern—that is, randomly. Indeed, there is often no correlation between how well the team did on any item, and how important it was to the customers. A simple test is to ask any developer on any project *what value their best efforts provided to the customer*. Most will be hard pressed to answer. Or you could ask a project manager to predict for his next phase which tasks will be performed the best. Most have no idea. So there is no plan for value, and there is no pattern to what is done best.

Random best efforts are terribly wasteful of a team's talents, and they are tremendously inefficient in terms of time (see Figure 26.2). Why does this happen?

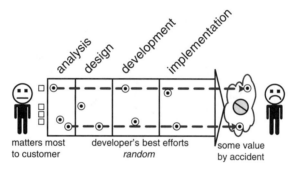

matters most to customer   developer's best efforts *random*   some value by accident

FIGURE 26.2
Incoherent development occurs when there is no focus during development on what matters most to the customers. Doing your best on activities that don't add value is an inefficient way of building lesser products than you are capable of.

Random Best Efforts—The Absence of Management

The simple answer is that there is no mechanism to direct the team toward what matters most to the customer. There are no tools or techniques for the project manager to use to *manage value*. Yet the whole purpose for new-product development is to deliver value to the customer. Without value, you have no chance of satisfying your customer (especially in a competitive environment).

In order to aim the team at value-adding activities, the project manager needs a way to find out what value is for this project, and this project's customers. Then the project manager needs a way to communicate that definition throughout the project—from start to finish.

The Critical Path Comes Second

What the project manager does have are tools to deal with his time, money, and people. He has a project schedule, with the critical path clearly determined (see Figure 26.3). Indeed, many project managers use the Critical Path Method (CPM), whereby they determine the critical path to see how long the project will take. Furthermore, many project managers spend more time and effort on the project schedule than on any other aspect of the project, and they are well supplied in this obsession with tools and techniques. They also have a project budget to track against, and they have assigned resources to the tasks in their project plan. But with no way to make value visible, they have no way to manage it. Schedule comes first by default.

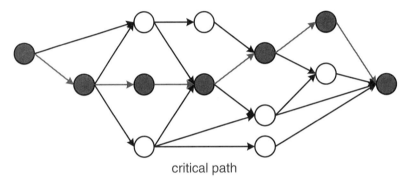

critical path

FIGURE 26.3
The critical path is the longest path through the activity network, and it determines the project duration. But finishing on time with a mediocre product is not success in product development. Schedule is important, but value is more important.

When managing a development project, a project manager will define a business case at the beginning of the project. The business case justifies performing the project by checking to make sure the project costs are outweighed by the customer benefits: In other words, is the value we intend to produce greater than the cost of producing it? Yet project managers frequently do not use this vital analysis to direct project management on a daily basis. With Project QFD, the project manager can directly connect the business case to the project so that he can concentrate on activities that have the largest effect on making the business case come true.

Finishing early or under budget will not make up for the fact that we have failed to deliver sufficient value to customers. Yes, time and money do matter, but delivering value matters more in product development. If we fail on value, then we fail—nothing can compensate. There is no substitute for value.

So what would be a better way to proceed?

Coherent Development Is Efficient

Instead of wasting our teams' time and talent doing a great job on things that don't matter to our customers, we must start by being clear about what matters to our customers. The development process must be coherent, like the light of a laser, and it must be aimed at value for customers: best efforts aligned end to end on what matters (see Figure 26.4).

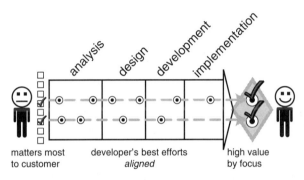

| matters most | developer's best efforts | high value |
| to customer | *aligned* | by focus |

FIGURE 26.4
Coherent development occurs when the project manager can focus the project on value, not just on the schedule. A small number of activities add the most value to the customer—the project manager must know which ones do that.

Best Efforts: Where They Matter to the Customer

We will need to use several tools and techniques to discover what really matters to our customers (refer to Figure 26.4). We cannot rely on our customers to simply tell us, as they are equally ill equipped to give us all of their requirements (and to tell us precisely how important each one is). It is our job to find out, but it is not their job to tell us. This is why value discovery methods are a key part of Project QFD.

QFD uses a set of tools, the seven new tools for management and planning, in a systematic sequence to uncover the "voice of the customer." The new tools are presented following. These methods are simple enough to learn and apply quickly, yet powerful enough to give us confidence that we can achieve a competitive advantage [Nayatani *et al.* 1994, Mizuno 1989]. These tools are not new—they are the result of refinement over 20 years of application. With these tools we have a reasonable hope of discovering what matters to our customers. But can we connect that to what we manage?

The Essential Path Comes First

Instead of focusing on only the critical path and on how fast we can do our work, we must also consider the essential path—how well we do what matters most (see Figure 26.5). And we must maintain that concern throughout the project. This **Essential Path Method (EPM)** is a new product development management method. Just as CPM focuses on time, EPM focuses on value. Both provide the project manager with tools and techniques to plan and manage those issues.

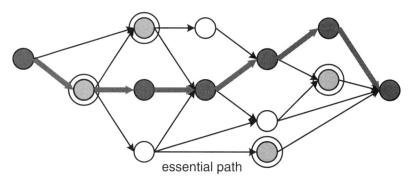

essential path

FIGURE 26.5
The essential path is defined by activities that add the most value to customers. These "steppingstones" show us where best efforts produce maximum value. For efficient product development, essential is more important than critical.

Value is the *prime directive* of product development. We must satisfy the customer, or we fail. We must deliver value, or we cannot satisfy the customer. And some tasks that are not on the critical path have a major effect on whether we deliver value. Some tasks add enormously more value than others. Those tasks are *essential* to our product development success.

With EPM, we first work on value, and the first step is to start with the customers. We start by discovery, and then we plan how to design and develop that thinking carefully about whom we are trying to satisfy: value *delivery*. QFD has an excellent set of tools for working with value. How can the project manager apply them?

Focus on Value with Project QFD

Learning from what software teams have learned as they applied QFD over the past ten years, let's consider the project manager as our "customer for QFD," and offer him the smallest subset of QFD that can deliver major benefits in better project management. The best place to start with QFD is Blitz QFD. What is it, and how can the project manager use it?

When someone "does Blitz QFD," it does not mean he has simply done the "House of Quality" really fast. Some teams have tried to reduce the time it takes to do QFD (really just the "House of Quality") by doing QFD work in joint application design (JAD) sessions. In this approach, a QFD facilitator rushes the team through the "House of Quality" in one or two days. The team feels good about doing QFD ("great, got that over with...") and is impressed with the facilitator's skills. Often a severe case of facilitator dependency develops, where teams must schedule their QFD work around a facilitator's availability. (Can you imagine having to wait for a "data flow diagram drawer" to become available so that you can complete your process models?) That is not good QFD.

Such a "Soviet-style" approach to implementing QFD is counter to the spirit of QFD. A multiskilled, cross-functional project team is the ideal vehicle for QFD. The project manager and his team should learn, and then be able to do, QFD by themselves (just like they do with their other software engineering and project management work). QFD is for project managers and developers, not just for QFD specialists. Where is the benefit of having development teams that do not know how to more efficiently deliver value and satisfy their customers?

So, what are the steps the project manager can use to discover and deliver value?

Seven Steps to Better Projects

The Blitz QFD path consists of a series of seven steps that use several tables, diagrams, and a mathematical method for sound prioritization [Zultner 1995]. See Figure 26.6 for a gestalt of the overall process.

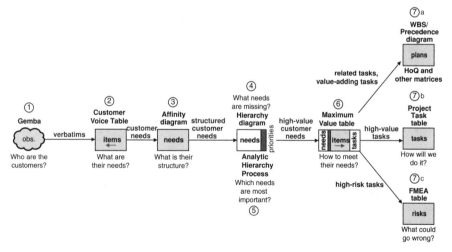

FIGURE 26.6
Project QFD is an application of Blitz QFD to the special needs of the project manager. It is fully upward compatible with Comprehensive QFD, and it gives the project manager the largest return for his efforts. Note that there are no matrices. Blitz QFD shows the project manager the essential path.

The first step is to start with customers. We start by thinking carefully about who we are trying to satisfy with our project: Who are our customers? This is a basic but crucial step that we must complete before we investigate customer needs. If we investigate the wrong people, the wrong customers, everything else will be wrong.

Step 1. Go to the Gemba

The *gemba* is the "actual place" where our product will add value to the customer (see Figure 26.7)—where our product will help solve our customer's problems and help them seize their opportunities. We must go there to learn what we cannot learn by any other method.

We can observe only by going to where our customers have their problems and opportunities, and seeing firsthand the context for our software. The context creates much of the opportunity for us to add value to our customers' work. By understanding the context, we can see opportunities to add value beyond what any customer might think of. We would use structured methods, such as in-context market research and contextual inquiry, at this point.

What we get from customers is not requirements, but verbatims, or statements that we must interpret and act on correctly. Customers don't give us needs; they give us hints that we must follow to find their needs.

FIGURE 26.7
Gemba means the "actual place." By going to the *gemba*, we listen to the "voice of the customer" and observe the context of the customer. Only then can we fully understand the customer's needs.

Step 2. Discover the Customer's Needs

Our customers will tell us many things, but they are untrained as requirements sources. It is our job to understand what they *mean* by their statements, and to understand *why* they are saying what they are saying. If we don't understand our customers, we have little chance of satisfying them. We must take their words and sort out what kind of statement they have made, and then discover the needs behind their words.

The Customer Voice Table (CVT) is the tool we use for this analysis (see Figures 26.8 and 26.9). The CVT provides a very simple but powerful way for us to see what kind of statements we have, and what could lie behind those statements. When we infer or generate an underlying need, we always confirm it with a real customer.

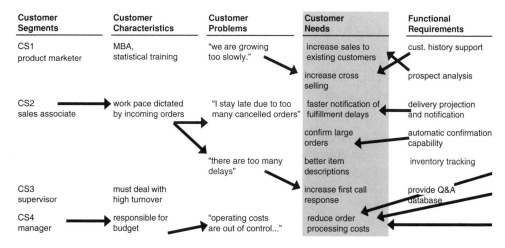

FIGURE 26.8
The CVT is a tool for sorting verbatims to discover underlying customer needs. We must understand what the customers mean by what they are saying, and why they are saying it. The result is a customer- and project-specific operational definition of value.

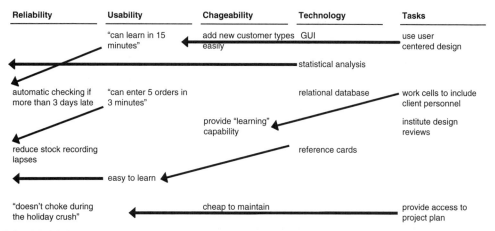

FIGURE 26.9
The CVT contains columns for any dimension of the project that the customer might mention. We can use it as a discovery tool, and as a diagnostic tool for "completed" requirements documents. The flow is from right to left, from verbatim to the underlying customer need.

Now that we have sorted our customer's needs from everything else, the next step is to take the list of customer needs that wind up in the Customer Needs column on the CVT and work with just those needs.

Step 3. Structure the Customer's Needs

From the list of customer needs, we must understand the way our customers think about their needs. Understanding the structure of their needs, as it is in their own mind, is a powerful basis for discovering unstated needs, or needs that they have implied by what they have said.

The customers produce an Affinity Diagram using the KJ Method (see Figure 26.10). This method from cultural anthropology is a fast and fun way to make visible how customers feel about the method they are performing. We want the actual customers to perform the KJ Method on their needs (and only on their needs).

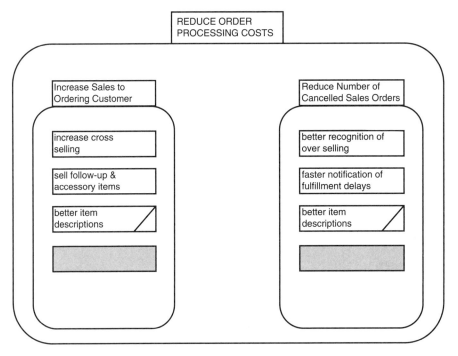

FIGURE 26.10
The Affinity Diagram, when created by actual customers, reveals the natural structure of their needs. Once we understand this structure, we can use it to uncover unstated but implied needs, which we can then confirm.

It is important that our customers perform the KJ Method and produce the Affinity Diagram. We want to know how they organize their needs. The way we think about our customer's needs is of only academic interest. We want to discover what we don't know about our customer's needs—not document our own irrelevant thoughts. (After all, the team isn't going to buy or use the software; they aren't the customers!)

The Affinity Diagram gives us the framework for how our customers think about their needs. Now we want to analyze that structure further.

Step 4. Analyze the Customer Needs Structure

Using the Affinity Diagram as a base, the team must now analyze the revealed structure, and fill in the missing needs.

The Hierarchy Diagram is the result of a simple transformation of the Affinity Diagram (see Figure 26.11). The Affinity Diagram shows us the skeleton structure of our customers' needs. Now we must analyze that structure, understand it deeply, and use it to uncover unstated (but implied) needs. The key is the rationale for why the items are arranged the way they are. We must carefully clarify and strengthen the natural structure.

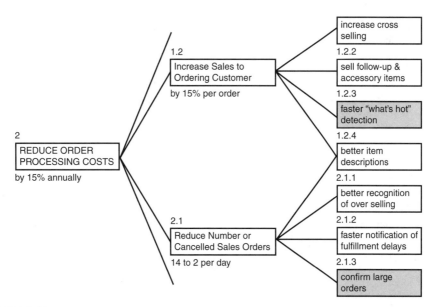

FIGURE 26.11
We use the Hierarchy Diagram to analyze the Affinity Diagram's structure and find the missing needs that the structure implies. Then we can prioritize this structure efficiently with the Analytic Hierarchy Process (AHP).

A properly analyzed hierarchy is one of the best and easiest methods to discover exciting customer needs that can provide a substantial competitive advantage.

Step 5. Prioritize the Customer's Needs

Blitz QFD is guided by a fundamental fact of project management: It is very difficult to focus on more than a few concerns throughout a project. To determine which few concerns would be most profitable for us to focus on, we must get our customers to prioritize their needs. Recognizing that priorities follow Pareto's Principle, we just want to know which vital few needs will deliver the most value to our customers.

The Analytic Hierarchy Process (AHP) is an elegant, efficient procedure that provides accurate ratio scale priorities of customer needs (or anything else; see Figure 26.12). With real customers, we work through the hierarchy of their needs from the top down. We pursue the high-priority branches first so that for a minimum of effort we can determine the highest-value needs of our customers. In many cases, we will not need to evaluate the majority of these needs because the structure of the hierarchy (and the priority of the primary and secondary needs) can't mathematically be of high value (see Figure 26.13).

You can use any spreadsheet to fairly closely approximate priorities using AHP. For exact answers, several AHP software products are available. (The lite or educational versions are more than adequate for QFD [for example, Expert Choice].)

Because we plan to use the priorities as weights to focus our best efforts, they must be accurate (tested and validated) and ratio scaled (so that we can properly multiply by them). The AHP is the simplest procedure known that meets these two criteria.

customer needs	1 increase cross selling	2 sell follow-up & accessory	3 faster "what's hot" detection	4 better item descriptions	normalized columns				row total	row avg.
1 increase crossselling	1	2	3	9	0.51	0.58	0.42	0.36	1.87	0.468
2 sell follow-up & accessory items	1/2	1	3	8	0.26	0.29	0.42	0.32	1.29	0.322
3 faster "what's hot" detection	1/3	1/3	1	7	0.17	0.10	0.14	0.28	0.69	0.172
4 better item descriptions	1/9	1/8	1/7	1	0.06	0.04	0.02	0.04	0.15	0.038
total	1.9	3.5	7.1	25.0	1.0	1.0	1.0	1.0	4.0	1.0

FIGURE 26.12
Pairwise evaluation is done on customer needs at the same level in the hierarchy, and ratio scale priorities are calculated by taking the row average of normalized columns. This is an approximation of the eigenvector, which you can determine exactly with AHP.

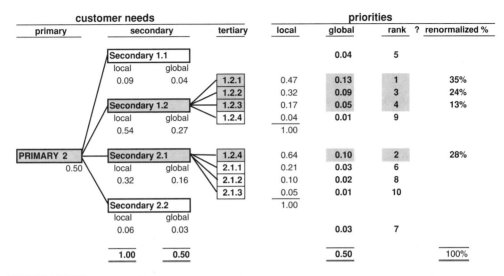

FIGURE 26.13
We use AHP to prioritize the hierarchy of customer needs from the top down. This allows us to find the highest-value needs without having to look at all the items, or even all the branches. A check on the consistency of the judgments is also part of the method.

Step 6. Deploy High-Value Customer Needs

Once we have identified the highest-value needs, we can select the top n needs (where n is a small number that you can actually focus your best efforts on end to end).

You use the Maximum Value Table (MVT) to deploy the highest-value customer needs (and their priorities) to whatever you must do during the project to deliver the most value you can to your customers (see Figures 26.14 and 26.15).

When you have identified the relationships between the prioritized needs and you have identified the items in the other columns by drawing linking arrows, you have identified *the most important items in every other column* in the table. This project-wide definition of value makes the MVT the single most powerful piece of paper in the QFD process. It shows all the most important items for all dimensions of the entire project.

The final result of the MVT is that we know which project tasks are essential to satisfying the customer—which tasks deliver the maximum value to the customer. On these tasks the project manager must do his best to plan and deliver the team's best efforts. On the performance of these tasks rests the best chance to satisfy the customer, and therefore the success or failure of the development project.

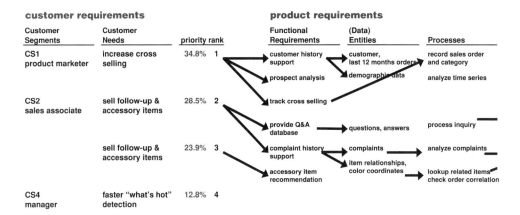

FIGURE 26.14

The MVT uses a framework similar to the CVT, but the MVT contains a column for all the project dimensions we must address to satisfy the highest-value needs. The flow is from left to right, from highest-value needs to the project tasks necessary to deliver those needs to the customer.

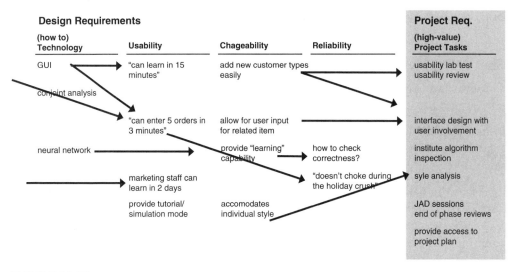

FIGURE 26.15

The MVT is the fastest way to identify which activities add the most value to customers. It summarizes on one page all the items that are most important to the project in terms of value. Now the project manager can identify what matters most; what is essential to success.

Step 7. Analyze Essential Tasks in Detail

A project manager should consider three basic analyses once he has defined the essential tasks. He must make sure the QFD analysis results are integrated into the master project plan; he must make sure he understands in detail how to perform the high-value activities; and he must consider how to avoid failure in performing the high-value activities. Three tools can help.

1. **Work Breakdown Structure (WBS).** The MVT shows us the most essential tasks. But some of these will not be in the project plan. (Because the project plan was created without any analysis of value, this is to be expected.) It is absolutely essential that the essential tasks be included in the project plan. After all, they are more important than any other tasks. We must update the WBS and/or the Precedence diagram with the high-value tasks. Project QFD does not replace existing project planning methods; it supplements them to include value, which is most the important issue on development projects.

2. **Project Task table.** Some of the essential tasks may be new to the team. They will require careful definition and detailed planning. The Project Task table is a simple, one-page framework for detailed task definition (see Figure 26.16). The checkpoints and control points are valuable contributions from the Quality field to the project manager. We should consider how the person performing the task can self-check his work so that he knows it is correct and complete, and what results the project manager can examine to control the performance and/or completion of the task. A comprehensive project management software package should support all the items in this table, and manage the relationships between them.

	What	Why	Who	When	Where	How	How much	How exp.		Check pt.	Control pt.
#	task, activity	priority	responsibility	date, precedence	unit, location	skill, method	target, standard	duration effort	difficulty	inputs, process?	results?
1.1	Review CBB database for reusable components	54.1	designer	Friday		know keywords	33% reuse	3 hrs	easy	cross checks	reuse %
1.2	Document calculation logic	21.5	analyst	next Wed.		logic tools	all calcs	1 week	moderate	inspection	# logic errors in test
1.8	Stifle management executeering	5.9	PM	throughout project	till end of project	feign insanity	90% fewer "shafts"	13 days total	hard	# puzzled looks	count no. of events
1.9	Improve module development process	12.7	developers	construction phase	S/W lab	clean-room	15% less time	10 weeks	hard	x, mR chart in real time	first, last 10 modules
	94.2										

FIGURE 26.16

The Project Task table provides the project manager with a way to define in detail the new high-value project tasks. The 5Ws, 3Hs, and 2Cs cover all the basic elements of a project task. The checkpoints and control points are especially important for detailed planning of essential tasks.

3. **Failure Modes and Effects Analysis (FMEA) table.** Managing risk is an important part of any development project, so which project activities should we examine first for risk? The essential tasks. One simple and well-tested tool for this purpose is the FMEA table (see Figure 26.17). Long used in reliability engineering, this tool is very useful when applied to high-value project tasks. The careful analysis of potential failure modes, and the preparation to prevent them, is one of the greatest strengths of a superb software development project manager. Active measures to mitigate risk are not new, but they are not applied widely enough in software development.

	Who	*Why*	*What*	*When*	*How much*		*Where*	*How exp.*	*How*		
#	source	threat	object	frequency?	impact?		detect?	overall risk	mitigating action	#	risk levels
FM 1.1	customer	changes	requirements	daily	small to large		easy	8	change control	MA2-12	9 extreme
											8
FM 1.2	customer	inconsistency in priorities		when prioritizing	small to large		hard	6	calculate inc. ratio	AHP-3	7 very strong
											6
FM 1.3	?	upsets (de-stabilizes)	process	rare	large		hard	3	X , mR chart data	SPC-1	5 strong
											4
FM 1.4	management	fails to support	Methlodgy	very rare	huge		easy	1	update resume	last	3 moderate
											2
									18			1 weak

FIGURE 26.17
The FMEA table gives the project manager a tool for risk management for high-value tasks. Anticipating problems and preplanning the prevention and mitigating actions is a powerful way to protect the essential tasks on the project, and to minimize loss of value.

Further Analysis

At this point, we can use any of the Seven Management & Planning (7 MP) Tools, including matrices, to analyze in depth any aspect of the project, if we have the time and resources to act on such analyses. For example, for many (but not all) projects, the relationship between customer needs and functional requirements is important. To examine in precise detail how all the top *n* customer needs relate (and how strongly) to the functional requirements, we can use the "House of Quality" matrix effectively. But there is no point in performing any detailed analysis, unless you believe your time and resources are sufficient to get the necessary results during your project.

With a well-stocked toolbox of QFD tools, it is easy to overanalyze. QFD can support more analysis than any single project can put to use. The project manager must discover the high-value customer needs, the important items on all dimensions of the project, and what tasks are essential to delivering the defined value. With limited time and resources, any analysis must provide a clear payoff. Don't fall into analysis paralysis.

The Blitz QFD process is designed to get projects off to a better start than just jumping in with a "House of Quality," which provides no direct benefits to the project manager. If it is appropriate for your project, you will get a better "House of Quality" matrix faster and with less effort from the foundation the Blitz QFD process provides. Prioritized customer needs allow you to control the size and scope of the "House of Quality" matrix, and avoid one of the leading causes of QFD project deaths: matrix gigantus.

Summary

The Project QFD process gives project managers the means to discover a customer- and project-specific definition of value. It then provides the means to plan how a team can efficiently deliver maximum value to the customer, given limited time, money, and resources. The essential activities on a project are steppingstones for the team to concentrate their best efforts where they matter the most for their customers.

This gives the project manager the tools to deal with value with the same skill and confidence that they already have for dealing with time (schedule), money (budget), and people (resources). Project managers with this knowledge have a substantial advantage over those without it. That is why some leading software development organizations have already trained many of their project managers in these methods, and have incorporated this approach into their development methodology. Their management said they must be able to develop market-leading products.

Project QFD takes an end-to-end look at the development process for a project, and shows you where to spend scarce person-hours on the most important items of your project. It delivers maximum value for the effort invested. Blitz QFD is an essential method for project managers.

Dr. Deming said we must view the development process as a system, and look at how we satisfy our customers—by what method? Project QFD has precisely that aim: to effectively satisfy the most important needs of our key customers through the efficient delivery of value. Results to date are exciting, and further refinement is still occurring. The author encourages anyone with comments, questions, or critiques to contact him, and participate in the ongoing improvement of Project QFD in theory and practice.

Acknowledgments

I would like to thank Dr. Yoji Akao, the co-developer of QFD, and the many others who educated me in QFD theory and practice over the past ten years. I would especially like to thank my colleagues at the QFD Institute for their time and energy in advancing the state of the practice of QFD in North America.

References

Akao, Yoji, Ed. *Quality Function Deployment: Integrating Customer Requirements into Product Design.* Translated by Glenn Mazur (Cambridge, MA: Productivity Press, 1990).

Akao, Yoji. "Origins and Growth of QFD in Japan," in *1st European Conference on QFD Proceedings.* Held in Milan, Italy, in March 1992, *11* (Milan: Galgano Formazione, 1992).

Arizona, S., *et al.* "General Purpose Wave Form Analysis Program Development" (in Japanese). *Quality Control 33* (Special issue: November 1982): *360366.*

AT&T Bell Laboratories. *Quality Function Deployment* (AT&T: 1990 Select Code *010-810-111*).

Carter, Donald E., and Barbara S. Baker. *Concurrent Engineering: The Product Development Environment for the 1990's* (Reading, MA: Addison Wesley, 1992).

Chalmers, Stuart. "Integration of Quality Assurance into Business Functions," in *Transactions from the 4th Symposium on QFD* (Novi, MI: QFD Institute, June 1992, pp. 218–235).

EC. *Expert Choice.* (Pittsburgh, PA: Expert Choice). Available from Expert Choice at 412-621-4492; http://ahp.net).

Gane, Chris. *Rapid Systems Development using Structured Techniques and Relational Technology* (New York: Rapid System Development, Inc., 1987).

Hammer, Michael, and Steven A. Stanton. *The Reengineering Revolution: A Handbook* (New York: HarperCollins, 1995).

Hauser, John R., and Don Clausing. "The House of Quality." *Harvard Business Review 66* (3 May–June 1988): pp. 63–73.

King, Bob. *Better Design in Half the Time: Implementing QFD in America.* 3rd Ed. Foreword by Yoji Akao (Methuen, MA: GOAL/QPC, 1989).

McDonald, Mark P. "Quality Function Deployment: Introducing Product Development into the Systems Development Process," in *Transactions from the 7th Symposium on QFD*. Held in Novi, Mich. 11–13 June 1995, pp. 435–448 (Novi, MI: QFD Institute, 1995).

Mizuno, Shigeru. *Management for Quality Improvement: The 7 New QC Tools* (Cambridge, MA: Productivity Press, 1988 [1979]).

Mizuno, Shigeru, and Yoji Akao, Ed. *Quality Function Deployment: The Customer-Driven Approach to Quality Planning and Deployment*. Rev. Ed. (Tokyo: Asian Productivity Organization, 1994 [1978]).

Nakui, Satoshi. "Comprehensive QFD System," in *Transactions from the 3rd Symposium on QFD*. Held in Novi, Mich. 24–25 June 1991, pp. 136–152 (Novi, MI: QFD Institute, 1991).

Nayatani, Yoshinobu, Toru Eiga, Ryoji Futami, and Hiroyuki Miyagawa. *The Seven New QC Tools: Practical Applications for Managers*, translated by J.H. Loftus (Tokyo: 3A Corporation, 1994 [1984]).

Porter, Michael E. *Competitive Advantage: Creating and Sustaining Superior Performance* (New York: The Free Press, 1985).

Saaty, Thomas L. *Fundamentals of Decision Making and Priority Theory with the Analytic Hierarchy Process* (Pittsburgh: RWS Publications, 1994).

Stalk, George. "Time—The Next Source of Competitive Advantage." *Harvard Business Review*, 41-51, 1988.

Takeuchi, Hirotaka, and Ikujiro Nonaka. "The New Product Development Game." *Harvard Business Review* 86 (1 January–February, 1986): pp. 137–146.

Zultner, Richard E. "Software Quality Deployment," in *5th Annual GOAL/QPC Conference Proceedings*. Held in Boston (Boston: GOAL/QPC, 1988).

Zultner, Richard E. "Software Total Quality Management: What does it take to be World-Class?" *American Programmer 3* (November 1990): pp. 2–11.

Zultner, Richard E. "Before the House: The Voices of the Customers in QFD," in *Transactions from the 3rd Symposium on QFD*. Held in Novi, Mich., June 24 and 25, 1991, pp. 450–464 (Novi, MI: QFD Symposium Committee, 1991).

Zultner, Richard E. "Task Deployment for Software Development: Process QFD," in *Transactions from the 4th Symposium on QFD*. Held in Novi, Mich., June 15–16, 1992, pp. 327–341 (Novi, MI: QFD Symposium Committee, 1992).

Zultner, Richard E. "Priorities: The Analytic Hierarchy Process in QFD," In *Transactions from the 5th Symposium on QFD.* Held in Novi, Mich., June 21-22, 1993, pp. 459–466 (Novi, MI: QFD Symposium Committee, 1993).

Zultner, Richard E. "Software SPC: What do our Metrics Mean?" in *4th International Software Quality Conference Proceedings.* Held in Washington, DC, in October 1994 (Washington, DC: ASQC Software Division, 1994).

Zultner, Richard E. "Software QFD: The North American Experience," in *Proceedings of the 1st Pacific Rim Symposium on Quality Deployment.* Held in Sydney, Australia, February 15–17, 1995, p. 163-174. Sydney, Australia: Macquarie Graduate School of Management. ISBN 1-86408-053-1.

Zultner, Richard E. "Blitz QFD: Better, Faster, and Cheaper Forms of QFD." *American Programmer 8* (October 1995): pp. 24–36.

Zultner, Richard E. "Blitz QFD." Presentation at QFD Forum. Held in Novi, Mich., June 14, 1995 (Novi, MI: QFD Institute, 1995b). Available from author at 609-452-0216.

About the Author

Richard E. Zultner is an international consultant, educator, author, and speaker. QFD applied to high-tech, software-intensive products and processes has been his primary focus for the past ten years.

In 1993, with several colleagues, he founded the QFD Institute, a nonprofit organization dedicated to the advancement of the theory and practice of Hardware, Service, Process, and Software QFD in North America. For information please contact the QFD Institute at 1140 Morehead Court, Ann Arbor, MI 48103, call 313-995-0847, or fax 313-995-3810. The QFDI home page is at www.qfdi.org.

Richard provides consulting and training in Project QFD, Blitz QFD, Software QFD, Software SPC, and Software TQM; and he coaches executives on The Deming Way to Software Quality.

Richard holds a master's degree in management from the J. L. Kellogg Graduate School of Management at Northwestern University, and he has professional certifications in quality, project management, and software engineering. He is currently working on his doctorate in software quality.

CHAPTER 27

QFD 2000: Integrating QFD and Other Quality Methods to Improve the New-Product Development Process

Glenn Mazur
QFD Institute
Japan Business Consultants, Ltd.
University of Michigan College of Engineering
glenn@mazur.net

Overview

Competitiveness in the new millennium may belong more to those who can integrate a multitude of disciplines into a system than to those who expect a single unnuanced tool to do it all. The "House of Quality" is really more of a "great room" to which various "outbuildings" and other structures must connect. This chapter discusses where you can integrate well-known quality and other tools, such as Consumer Encounters, the New Lanchester Strategy, Kansei Engineering, the Theory of Constraints, *Teoriya Resheniya Izobreatatelskikh Zadatch* (TRIZ), Voice of the Customer Analysis, Failure Modes and Effects Analysis (FMEA), Statistical Process Control (SPC), and other methods, into the new-product development process.

Chapter Outline

Demand for New Products

Modern consumerism has resulted in ever-increasing customer demands for differentiated products that meet individualized needs for convenience, functionality, and image. Manufacturers have become more adept at responding to this demand with such systemic changes as Lean Manufacturing [Womack], Flexible Manufacturing Systems, materials resource planning (MRP), and enterprise resource planning (ERP). Service providers such as financial institutions, retailers, and others are beginning to achieve this with software and high-tech solutions such as Web sites that deliver targeted messages to customers. In other words, technology is feeding this frenzy for individualized products and services, and the trend ought to continue as the number of households with personal computers and high-speed access grows.

Geography now plays an increasing role for both new markets and sources of new competition. Countries less invested in older technologies are often more willing to offer the improved functionality, performance, and reliability associated with new technology. Thus, there are opportunities for companies to sell in new geographical markets (provided they adapt to cultural differences [Ronney *et al.*]), and there are threats from new competitors with lower costs, newer technology, and so on.

Quality and New-Product Development

W. E. Deming, often named as the father of modern quality management, discussed consumerism as people's desire to improve their lives, especially in this Information Age where it is easy to see how others live. Trade is necessary to accomplish this, and trade depended on quality, which exists "if it helps somebody and enjoys a good and sustainable market." He warned that it is insufficient to merely satisfy customers, build loyalty, and eliminate defects. Customers access information and are rapid learners, and will switch if they think they will come out ahead. "It is necessary to innovate, to predict the needs of the customer, give him more" [Deming].

We must continuously investigate what product or service would help our customers more. They demand improvements in style, comfort, performance, and functionality, whatever these words mean in their minds. Traditional quality methods which focus on improving established products and processes have spawned new approaches, such as Quality Function Deployment (QFD), that better address the new-product development (NPD) process.

Traditional market researchers, long the bastion of NPD activities, are also finding that QFD can lead to a clearer definition of customer needs, better product concepts, and improved communication to internal operations that must then produce and deliver the product. Using tools and techniques from Comprehensive QFD

- Rubbermaid was able to significantly improve the consumer panel acceptance rate of its new-product concepts [Rings, Barton, and Mazur].

- Host-Marriott was able to identify an underserved market of business women air travelers and offer them a wide choice of bagels baked fresh in the airport concourse, resulting in sales doubling in just 30 days [Lampa and Mazur].

- MD Robotics, a supplier of robotic arms to NASA, was stymied in building an animatronic triceratops for Universal Studios Florida's new Jurassic Park attraction, until the MD Robotics team visited a children's petting zoo to see what customers really cared about [Bolt and Mazur].

QFD goes beyond the product, however. True to Deming's belief that quality requires management and leadership, QFD addresses both the quality of the product and the management of the process to develop it. The QFD tools for developing the quality of the product are well known and include the "House of Quality," Affinity Diagrams, Hierarchy Diagrams, and so on. Lesser known are those for managing the product development process.

In Mizuno and Akao's pioneering work in QFD in the 1960s, value engineering techniques such as function analysis were applied not just to the product functions, but also to improve the business and operation functions of the NPD organization [Mizuno and Akao]. Tables, hierarchies, flowcharts, and Quality Assurance Networks were the tools of choice. In more recent years, Akao has integrated ISO 9000 and related methods to improve NPD organizational effectiveness [Akao and Mazur], and to examine the internal back-office activities of service organizations [Akao and Inayoshi] and hospitals [Akao and Fujimoto].

Modern Quality Tools

In addition to QFD, numerous tools and techniques can aid new-product developers. This chapter will identify those I call "quality" tools because they meet the following criteria:

- They are measurable or use metrics.

- They systematically follow defined steps with input, analysis, and output.

- They create documentation for review and reuse.

This chapter does not provide an exhaustive list of tools and their utility to NPD, and readers may e-mail regarding omissions and errors to glenn@mazur.com. In this chapter, we will examine the following tools, listed here in alphabetical order (readers wishing to better familiarize themselves with them will find a list of resources at the end) of the chapter:

- The Analytic Hierarchy Process (AHP), including structure and prioritization of judgment criteria, prioritization of alternatives, and the Analytic Network Process (ANP)

- The Balanced Scorecard, a system that measures and manages corporate goals such as mission, vision, customer, and employee satisfaction

- Blitz QFD, a fast, matrix-less approach to addressing only the most critical customer needs

- Conjoint Analysis, a mathematical model of determining consumer preferences

- Consumer Encounters, which combines *gemba* visits and consumer panel testing

- Customer Integrated Decision Making (CIDM), a business front end to QFD

- de Bono's creativity methods, including Lateral Thinking, Provocation, and Six Thinking Hats

- Deming's approach to quality, including his 14 Points and System of Profound Knowledge

- The *Gemba* Visit, an observational approach to consumer behavior to uncover true requirements

- Hoshin Planning, to develop, target, and deploy strategic initiatives

- The Kano Model, a unique interviewing method using paired inverse questions to differentiate exciting, normal, and expected quality

- Kansei Engineering, a customer-driven approach to industrial design, including Semantic Differential, Quantification Methods, and Information Systems

- Lead User Research, a method for collaborating with technologically savvy users to develop breakthrough concepts for new products

- Lean Manufacturing, based on Toyota's Production System, which aims to cut the non-value-added "fat" out of manufacturing systems

- The New Lanchester Strategy, which uses war and game theory and operations research to identify strategic market and product opportunities, including market share profiling, strategies for the strong, and strategies for the weak

- Neural Linguistic Programming (NLP), a set of skills for psychologically influencing people, such as body language, verbal cues, and so on

- Project Management, including the Critical Path Method (CPM), Program Evaluation and Review Technique (PERT), and Gantt charts

- Pugh Concept Selection, a method to evaluate and improve new concepts

- QFD (Comprehensive), including its many deployments of Organization, Schedule, Core Competencies Matrix, Customer Segments Table, Customer Process Table, Voice of Customer Tables, "House of Quality," Function, Technology, Reliability, Capability (Tech. Map), Pugh Concept, Parts, Test, Manufacturing, Production, and Task

- Reliability, to prevent defects from being introduced during product design, including three types of FMEA and Fault Tree Analysis

- Seeds to Needs QFD, a technology-driven form of QFD

- The Seven Management and Planning (7 MP) Tools, a set of tools for managers to collect qualitative data and solve organizational and design problems

- The Seven Product Planning (7PP) Tools, a system to use market research tools more effectively

- The Seven Quality Control (7QC) Tools, a set of tools for frontline employees to collect quantitative data and solve quality problems

- Six Sigma, an update of Total Quality Management (TQM) methods, including SPC, Statistical Quality Control (SQC), and analysis of variance (ANOVA)

- Software Engineering tools to better understand processes

- Stage-Gate, which systematically applies go/no go decisions throughout the NDP process

- Strategic Information Systems (SIS) to use point-of-sale purchase information to seamlessly coordinate and forecast consumer purchases

- Supply Chain Management

- Taguchi Methods for Design of Experiments, Loss Function, and Design Optimization

- The Theory of Constraints to understand how to increase throughput of products into customers' hands, including Thinking Process, Trees, Layers of Resistance, and Critical Chain

- TQM methods for improving the quality of products and processes, including Daily Management, Kaizen, QI Story, 5S, *poka yoke*, Total Production Maintenance and Total Preventive Maintenance, quality control (QC), and quality assurance (QA)

- TRIZ, a Russian system of inventive problem solving, including Table of Contradictions, Problem Formulator, Innovative System Questionnaire, ARIZ, Anticipatory Failure Determination, Directed Evolution, and Su-Field Analysis

- Value Engineering, a dogged approach to uncovering cost reduction opportunities and improving product function, including FAST diagrams, value analysis, and function analysis

New-Product Development Process

New-product design and development is a multidisciplinary activity that involves different people at different times, and will vary according to the company, its customers, and the subject product. In a landmark study, Robert Cooper surveyed 123 industrial companies regarding how well they performed their new-product development process; the results showed that for the 13 most common NPD phases, companies averaged a rating between 5.27 and 6.96 on a scale of 10 [Cooper] (see Figure 27.1). The author believes that the quality tools mentioned earlier could help improve the NPD process.

Although Figure 27.1 is by no means exhaustive, marketers, engineers, and quality professionals should find it useful for improving the quality of the NPD process by integrating the traditional quality methods with marketing methods and creativity methods. No single project needs every tool because time-to-market would suffer. Rather, it is recommended that each organization review their NPD process, starting with the phases Cooper found weak (marked with a *), and apply whichever tools are necessary to strengthen this most important business activity.

Initial Screening	Preliminary Market Assessment	Preliminary Technical Assessment	Detailed Market Study	Pre-development Business/Financial Analysis	Product Development	In-house Product Tests	Customer Product Tests	Trial Sell	Trial Production	Pre-commercialization Bsn Analysis	Production Start-up	Market Launch
5.27	5.47	6.69	5.74	6.49	6.55	6.96	6.69	6.86	6.79	6.26	6.31	6.36

FIGURE 27.1
Self-evaluation of NPD efforts

NPD Stage	NPD Phase (*needs to improve)	NPD Task	Quality Tool
Idea	Generate Concept (not in Cooper's model)	Generate new product concepts to be screened	Consumer Encounter, Lead User Research, Seed to Needs QFD, 7PP, TRIZ
	Initial Screening*	Formalize Go/Kill criteria	Hoshin Planning, 7MP, Project Goals Deployment
		Prioritize Go/Kill criteria	AHP
		Multi-disciplinary evaluation	AHP
	Preliminary Market Assessment*	Determine market potential	CIDM
		Determine expected market penetration	New Lanchester Strategy
		Focused definition of market	Customer Segments Table, CIDM
		Contact customers directly	Consumer Encounters, Conjoint Analysis, Lead User Research, 7PP, CIDM
		Sales Force	New Lanchester Strategy
		Review Competitors Products	Consumer Encounters
	Preliminary Technical Assessment	First Technical Appraisal	AHP, Seed to Needs QFD, Lead User Research, House of Quality, Core Competencies Matrix, Technology Map
Detailed Investigation	Detailed Market Study *	Study competitive products and prices	Gemba Visits, Quality Planning Table (HoQ right room)
		Determine customer needs and wants	Voice of Customer Tables, 7MP, Customer Process Table, Kansei Engineering, NLP, S/W Eng Tools, TOC (Evaporating Cloud), VE (FAST), AHP
		Generate product specifications	Design Planning Table (HoQ basement), Taguchi Methods, Kansei Engineering, FMEA
		Market research objectives	Project goals deployment

FIGURE 27.1
Continued

Development		Clarify target segment	Customer Segments Table
		Determine market size	New Lanchester Strategy
		Test concept with customers	Conjoint Analysis, Kano, ANP
	Pre-development Business/ Financial Analysis	Multi-disciplinary input	Cross-Functional Management, Narrow QFD, Hoshin, 7MP, VE
		Confirm market information	New Lanchester Strategy
		Business analysis	Project Goals, Org Goals
	Product Development	Design Product	Blitz QFD, Kansei, CIDM, Lead User, HoQ, Function D., Reliability D., Parts Deployments, 7MP
		Resolve technical difficulties	deBono, Lead User, Pugh, Technology Deployment, Capability Deployment, FMEA, FTA, Taguchi, TRIZ, VE
		Resolve resource constraints	Schedule Deployment, VE, Task Deployment, TOC
		Develop Manuf Plan, Facilities Plan, Training	Manufacturing Deployment, Task Deployment, TOC, TRIZ, TQM, Lean Mfg
	In-house Product Tests	Strengthen test procedures	Test Deployment
		Test product	Taguchi, Pugh, Reliability Depl., FMEA, 7QC, TRIZ
Test & Validate	Customer Product Tests	Show customer sample or prototype	Conjoint Analysis, Kano
		Design customer test	
		Observe customer using product	Gemba Visit, Customer Process Table
	Trial Sell*	Gauge market acceptance	
		Define test market	Customer Segments Table
		Objectively measure results	Project Goals Deployment
	Trial Production	Test production system	Process FMEA, TRIZ, Production Depl., Taguchi, TPM
		Test production equipment	Process FMEA, 7QC, Poka yoke
		Check product against specs	7QC, SPC, SQC, Design review

			Confirm production volumes	Cross-Functional Mgt – Delivery, TOC
Full Production & Market Launch		Pre-commerci-alization Business Analysis	Detailed financial analysis	Project Goals Depl.
			Detailed market information review (sales forecasting, marketing costs)	New Lanchester Strategy
			Detailed cost review	VE, CFM – Cost, TOC, Supply Chain Mgt, Lean Mfg
			Final Go/Kill decision	Project Goals Depl., House of Quality
		Production Start-up	Review/change production facilities, operator training	Production Depl., QI Story, SPC, 7QC, Pokayoke, 5S, TPM, TOC, Lean Mfg, Supply Chain Mgt
		Market Launch	Advertise and promote product	New Lanchester Strategy
			Confirm marketing objectives	Project Goals Depl, Quality Planning Table (Rt room in HoQ)
			Communication among sales, marketing, production	Narrow QFD, 7MP, CFM-Delivery
			Train sales force	New Lanchester Strategy
Project/ Process Manage-ment		Manage New Develop-ment Process		Critical Chain Project Management, Stage-Gate, Balanced Scorecard

Resources for QFD and Other Quality Methods

Analytic Hierarchy Process (AHP) and Analytic Network Process (ANP)

Dyer, Robert F., and Ernest H. Forman. *An Analytic Approach to Marketing Decisions* (Prentice-Hall, 1991).

Saaty, Thomas L. *Decision Making for Leaders: The Analytic Hierarchy Process for Decisions in a Complex World.* Rev. 2nd Ed. (Pittsburgh: RWS Publications, 1990).

Balanced Scorecard

Kaplan, Robert S., and David P. Norton. *The Balanced Scorecard: Translating Strategy into Action* (Harvard Business School Press, 1990).

Blitz QFD

Zultner, Richard E. "Blitz QFD." *Tutorials of the Eighth Symposium on QFD/International Symposium on QFD '96—Novi* (Ann Arbor, MI: QFD Institute, 1996).

Zultner, Richard E. "Blitz QFD for Project Management of Software Development." *Transactions from the Ninth Symposium on Quality Function Deployment* (Ann Arbor, MI: QFD Institute, 1997a).

Conjoint Analysis

Bergman, Bo, *et al.* "Conjoint Analysis–A Useful Tool in the Design Process." *Transactions of the 8th Symposium on QFD/2nd International Symposium on QFD* (QFD Institute, 1996).

Gustafsson, Anders. "Customer Focused Product Development by Conjoint Analysis and QFD" (Linkoping University, 1996).

Consumer Encounters

Rings, Cathy, Brian Barton, and Glenn Mazur. "Consumer Encounters of the Third Kind: Improving Idea Development and Concept Optimization." *Transactions from the Tenth Symposium on Quality Function Deployment* (Ann Arbor, MI: QFD Institute, June 1998).

Customer Integrated Decision Making (CIDM)

Daetz, Douglas, William Barnard, and Richard Norman. *Customer Integration: The Quality Function Deployment (QFD) Leader's Guide for Decision Making* (New York: John Wiley & Sons, Inc., 1995).

de Bono

de Bono, Edward. *Lateral Thinking: Creativity Step by Step* (1970).

de Bono, Edward. *Serious Creativity* (Harper Business, 1992).

Deming

Deming, W. Edwards. *Out of the Crisis* (MIT-CAES: 1982, 1986).

Deming, W. Edwards. *The New Economics: For Industry, Government, Education* (MIT-CAES: 1993).

Gemba Visit/Voice of Customer Analysis

Bolt, Andrew, and Glenn Mazur. "Jurassic QFD." *Transactions from the Eleventh Symposium on Quality Function Deployment* (Novi, MI: QFD Institute, 1999).

Mazur, Glenn. "Voice of Customer Analysis: A Modern System of Front-End QFD Tools with Case Studies." AQC 1997 (Milwaukee: American Society of Quality Control, 1997).

Nelson, Dale. "The Customer Process Table: Hearing Customers' Voices Even If They're Not Talking," in *Transactions of the Fourth Symposium on Quality Function Deployment* (Ann Arbor, MI: QFD Institute, 1992).

Ronney, Eric, Peter Olfe, and Glenn Mazur. "Gemba Research in the Japanese Cellular Phone Market." *Transactions from the Twelfth Symposium on Quality Function Deployment/ 6th International Symposium on QFD* (Ann Arbor, MI: QFD Institute, June 2000).

Hoshin Planning

Akao, Yoji (Ed.). *Hoshin Kanri* (translated by Glenn H. Mazur) (Productivity Press, 1991).

Colletti, Joe. *A Field Guide to Focused Planning: Hoshin Kanri–American Style* (Woodledge Group, 1995).

Cowley, Michael, and Ellen Domb. *Beyond Strategic Vision: Effective Corporate Action with Hoshin Planning* (Butterworth Reinemann, 1997).

Mazur, Glenn, Hisashi Takasu, and Michiteru Ono. *Policy Management: Quality Approach to Strategic Planning* (IQD [www.qfdi.org/tut_hoshin.htm or 800-870-4200], 1998).

Melum, Mara Minerva, and Casey Collett. *Breakthrough Leadership* (American Hospital Publishing or GOAL/QPC, 1995).

Kano Model

Kano, Noriaki, Nobuhiko Seraku, Fumio Takahashi, and Shinichi Tsuji. "Attractive Quality and Must-Be Quality." *Hinshitsu* 14, no. 2 (February 1984): pp. 39–48.

Kansei Engineering

Mazur, Glenn. "Kansei Engineering." *Tutorials of the 12th Symposium on QFD/6th International Symposium on QFD* (Ann Arbor, MI: QFD Institute, June 2000).

Nagamachi, Mitsuo. "Kansei Engineering and Its Applications in Automotive Design." *SAE Technical Paper Series* 1999-01-1265 (1999).

Lead User Research

Cooper, Alex. "3M Uses Lead User Research to Pursue Innovation." *Product Development Best Practices Report,* Vol 6:5. May 1999, pp. 1–5.

Von Hipple, Eric. *The Sources of Innovation* (Oxford Univ. Press, 1994).

Lean Manufacturing

Kochan, Thomas A., *et al. After Lean Production* (Cornell University Press, 1997).

Liker, Jeffrey K. *Becoming Lean: Inside Stories of U.S. Manufacturers* (Productivity Press, 1999).

Womack, James P., *et al. The Machine That Changed the World: The Story of Lean Production* (HarperCollins, 1991).

New Lanchester Strategy

Taoka, N. *Lanchester Strategy: An Introduction* (Lanchester Press, 1997).

Yano, Shinichi. *New Lanchester Strategy* (Lanchester Press, 1995).

Yano, Shinichi. *New Lanchester Strategy: Sales and Marketing Strategy for the Weak* (Lanchester Press, 1996).

Yano, Shinichi. *New Lanchester Strategy: Sales and Marketing Strategy for the Strong* (Lanchester Press, 1996).

Neural Linguistic Programming (NLP)

O'Conner, Joseph. *Leading with NLP: Essential Leadership Skills for Influencing and Managing People* (Motorbooks International, 1999).

Project Management

Goldratt, Eliyahu M. *Critical Chain* (North River Press, 1997).

Kerzner, Harold. *In Search of Excellence in Project Management* (Van Nostrand Reinhold, 1998).

Pugh Concept Selection

Pugh, Stuart, *et al. Creating Innovative Products Using Total Design: The Living Legacy of Stuart Pugh* (Addison-Wesley).

QFD (Comprehensive)

Akao, Yoji (Ed.). *Quality Function Deployment: Integrating Customer Requirements into Product Design* [translated by Glenn H. Mazur] (Portland, OR: Productivity Press, 1990).

Mazur, Glenn. *Comprehensive QFD for Service Organizations v2000* (Ann Arbor, MI: Japan Business Consultants, Ltd., 2000).

Mazur, Glenn. *Comprehensive QFD for Products v2000* (Ann Arbor, MI: Japan Business Consultants, Ltd., 2000).

Mizuno, Shigeru, and Yoji Akao (Ed.). *Quality Function Deployment: The Customer-Driven Approach to Quality Planning and Deployment* [translated by Glenn H. Mazur] (Tokyo: Asian Productivity Organization, 1994).

Reliability
Stamatis, D. H. *Failure Mode and Effect Analysis: FMEA from Theory to Execution* (ASQ Press, 1995).

Seeds to Needs QFD
Koura, Kozo. "How to Connect Technology Seeds to Customer Needs." *Transactions of the 8th Symposium on QFD/2nd International Symposium on QFD* (QFD Institute, 1996).

Seven Management and Planning (7 MP) Tools
Brassard, Michael, and Diane Ritter. *The Memory Jogger II* (Methuen, MA: GOAL/QPC, 1994).

Mizuno, Shigeru (Ed.). *Management for Quality Improvement: The 7 New QC Tools* (Cambridge, MA: Productivity Press, 1988).

Nayatani, Yoshinobu. *The Seven New QC Tools* (3A Corporation/Quality Resources, 1994).

Seven Product Planning (7PP) Tools
Gustafsson, Anders, *et al.* "7 Product Planning Tools." *Tutorials of the Eighth Symposium on QFD* (QFD Institute, 1996).

Kanda, Noriaki, *et al.* "The Seven Product Planning Tools for New Product Development." *Hinshitsu Kanri* 45–46 (July 1994–May 1995; series of Japanese articles translated into English for QFD Institute Master Class, 1995).

Seven Quality Control (7QC) Tools
Brassard, Michael, and Diane Ritter. *The Memory Jogger II* (Methuen, MA: GOAL/QPC, 1994).

Hosotani, Katsuya. *Japanese Quality Concepts: An Overview* [translated by Glenn H. Mazur] (New York: Quality Resources, 1992).

JUSE Problem Solving Research Group. *TQC Solutions: The 14-Step Process* (Productivity Press, 1991).

Six Sigma, SPC

Wheeler, Donald J. *SPC at the Esquire Club* (SPC Press, 1992).

Wheeler, Donald J. *Understanding Variation: The Key to Managing Chaos* (SPC Press, 1993).

Wheeler, Donald J., and David S. Chambers. *Understanding Statistical Process Control* (SPC Press, 1992).

Software Engineering

Gane, Chris, and Trish Sarson. *Structured Systems Analysis: Tools and Techniques* (New York: Improved System Technologies, Inc., 1977).

Mazur, Glenn. "Elicit Service Customer Needs Using Software Engineering Tools," in *Transactions of the Seventh Symposium on Quality Function Deployment* (Ann Arbor, MI: QFD Institute, 1995b).

Stage-Gate

Cooper, Robert G. *Winning at New Products 2nd Edition* (Addison-Wesley, 1993).

Strategic Information Systems (SIS)

Shimada and Ebizawa. "Strategic Information Systems: Construction and Deployment" [in Japanese] (JUSE, 1989).

Supply Chain Management

Simchi-Levi, David, *et al. Designing and Managing the Supply Chain: Concepts, Strategies and Case Studie*s (Irwin/McGraw-Hill, 1999).

Taguchi Methods

Taguchi, Genichi. "Introduction to Quality Engineering: Designing Quality into Products and Processes" (APO, 1986).

Theory of Constraints

Dettmer, H. William. *Goldratt's Theory of Constraints: A Systems Approach to Continuous Improvement* (ASQC Press, 1997).

Goldratt, Eliyahu M. *It's Not Luck* (North River Press, 1994).

Goldratt, Eliyahu M., and Jeff Cox. 1992 Second Revised Edition. *The Goal* (North River Press, 1992).

Scheinkopf, Lisa J. *Thinking for a Change: Putting the TOC Thinking Processes to Use* (St. Lucie Press, 1999).

Total Quality Management (TQM)

Imai, Masaaki. *Kaizen: The Key to Japan's Competitive Success* (McGraw-Hill, 1986).

Imai, Masaaki. *Gemba Kaizen: A Commonsense, Low-Cost Approach to Management* (McGraw-Hill, 1997).

Kurogane, Kenji. *Cross-Functional Management: Principles and Practical Applications* (Asian Productivity Organization, 1993).

Mazur, Glenn. "TQM Virtual Course Pack, College of Engineering University of Michigan," ioe.engin.umich.edu/people/fac/gmazur.html

TRIZ

Terninko, John, Alla Zussman, and Boris Zlotin. "Step-by-Step TRIZ: Creating Innovative Solution Concepts," 1996.

The TRIZ Journal, www.triz-journal.com.

Value Engineering

Shillito, Larry. *Advanced QFD: Linking Technology to Markets and Company Needs* (Wiley-Interscience, 1994).

About the Author

Glenn H. Mazur has been active in QFD since its inception in North America, and has worked extensively with the founders of QFD on their teaching and consulting visits from Japan. His primary focus is in the service industry, as a manager for more than 15 years in automobile repair and parts warehousing, as a teacher, and as an owner of a translating and consulting business he started in 1982. He is one of North America's leaders in the application of QFD to service industries, sits on several advanced QFD research committees, and sits on the steering committee of the Symposium on Quality Function Deployment held annually in Detroit. He is also executive director of the nonprofit QFD Institute and the International Council for QFD. He is an adjunct lecturer of Total Quality Management at the University of Michigan College of Engineering. He lectures and trains in QFD worldwide. Mazur holds a master's degree in business administration and a bachelor's degree in Japanese language and literature, both from the University of Michigan. In 1998, he was awarded the Akao Prize for Excellence in QFD. You can reach him at glenn@mazur.com or via fax at 734-995-3810.

References

Akao, Yoji, and Glenn Mazur. "Using QFD to Assure QS-9000 Compliance." *Proceedings of the 4th International Symposium on QFD* (Sydney, Australia: 1998).

Akao, Yoji, and H. Fujimoto. "Applying QFD in a Hospital Setting: A Study in Medical Quality." *Transactions of the 6th International Symposium on Quality Function Deployment* (Novi, MI: 2000).

Akao, Yoji, and K. Inayoshi. "A Study of Service and Operational Quality—An Application of QFD in Library Services." *Proceedings of the 5th International Symposium on Quality Function Deployment* (August 24 and 25, 1999: Belo Horizonte, Brazil; pp. 200 and 211).

Bolt, Andrew, and Glenn Mazur. "Jurassic QFD: Integrating Service and Product Quality Function Deployment." *Transactions from the Eleventh Symposium on Quality Function Deployment* (Ann Arbor, MI: QFD Institute, June 1999).

Cooper, Robert G. *Winning at New Products 2nd Edition* (Addison-Wesley, 1993).

Deming, W. E. *The New Economics 2nd Edition* (MIT/CAS, 1994).

Lampa, Steve, and Glenn Mazur. "Bagel Sales Double at Host-Marriott Using Quality Function Deployment." *Transactions from the Eighth Symposium on Quality Function Deployment/International Symposium on QFD '96* (Ann Arbor, MI: QFD Institute, 1996).

Mizuno, Shigeru, and Yoji Akao (Ed.). *Quality Function Deployment: The Customer-Driven Approach to Quality Planning and Deployment* [translated by Glenn Mazur] (Tokyo: Asian Productivity Organization, 1994).

Rings, Cathy, Brian Barton, and Glenn Mazur. "Consumer Encounters of the Third Kind: Improving Idea Development and Concept Optimization." *Transactions from the Tenth Symposium on Quality Function Deployment* (Ann Arbor, MI: QFD Institute, June 1998).

Glossary of Technical Terms

5S
A quality system involving five tasks that all begin with S: *seiri* (sort), *seiton* (straighten or set), *seiso* (shine or cleanliness), *seiketsu* (standardize), and *shitsuke* (sustain).

ABC
Activity-Based Costing.

ABM
Activity-Based Management.

affinity diagram
A set of ideas about the topic in question, grouped in clusters based on their similarity.

AHP
Analytic Hierarchy Process.

ALGOL
International Algorithmic Language. An early high-level language for programming mathematical and engineering applications.

alpha testing
Initial testing of a new software release by the developer's staff.

ANOVA
Analysis of Variance.

AON
Activity on Node Diagram.

beta testing
Initial testing of a new release by advanced or experienced users.

Blitz QFD
A fast, matrix-free approach for addressing only the most critical customer needs.

BPR
Business Process Reengineering.

build
An operational software system at some level of functionality.

CAC
Cost at Completion.

CAD
Computer-Aided Design.

CAP
Change Acceleration Program.

CAR
Customer Appraisal and Review.

CASE
Computer-Aided Software Engineering.

CMM
Capability Maturity Model.

COBOL
Common Business-Oriented Language. An early high-level language for programming business applications.

CoPQ
Cost of Poor Quality.

CoQ
Cost of Quality. The expense of nonconformance—the cost of doing things wrong.

CORBA
Common Object Request Broker Architecture. A general open industry standard for working with distributed objects.

CoSQ
Cost of Software Quality. The total cost of conformance and nonconformance to the customer's quality requirements. Consists of direct and indirect expenses incurred for preventing, appraising, testing, discovering, analyzing, and fixing software faults, including maintenance.

CPI
Cost Performance Index.

CPM
Critical Path Method.

CQC
Corporate Quality Council.

CQO
Chief Quality Officer. An emerging position in many organizations where managing quality is considered essential to organizational success.

CVT
Customer Voice Table.

cyclomatic complexity
The number of linearly independent paths that make up a computer program.

DCF
Discounted Cash Flow.

design pattern
A general, repeatable solution to a commonly occurring problem in software design. This is not a finished design that can be transformed directly into program code. Rather, it is a description or template for how to solve a problem that can be used in many different situations.

DFSS
Design for Six Sigma.

DFTS
Design for Trustworthy Software.

DOE
Design of Experiments.

DPMO
Defects Per Million Opportunities.

DSDL
Domain-Specific Design Language.

EC
Executive Champion of a quality initiative.

EDSI
Equivalent Delivered Source Instructions.

Emacs
The text editor in GNU.

EPM
Essential Path Method. The essential path in a development project is the path that adds the most value for the customer.

ERP
Enterprise Resource Planning.

FASB
Financial Accounting Standards Board.

FMEA
Failure Modes and Effects Analysis.

FORTRAN
Formula Translator. An early high-level language for programming engineering and scientific applications.

framework
A set of cooperating object classes that makes up a reusable design for a specific type of software application.

function point
A collection of executable statements that performs a task, together with declarations of formal parameters and local variables manipulated by those statements.

GAAP
Generally Accepted Accounting Practices.

gemba
A Japanese term for the "actual place" where the product under development will add value for the customer.

GNU
Gnu is Not UNIX. A public-domain UNIX-like operating system.

HD
Hierarchy Diagram.

HoQ
House of Quality.

I.D.
Interrelationship Digraph. A tool that helps you explore and identify causal relationships between various ideas.

IDE
Integrated Development Environment.

ISR
Interrupt Scheduling Routine.

IT portfolio
The set of enterprise business applications used to run a business.

JIT
Just in Time.

JUSE
Japanese Union of Scientists and Engineers.

JVM
Java Virtual Machine.

Kano model
An advanced technique that may be used after customer needs are translated into quality characteristics, or even features.

kansei
A spacious Western-style room.

kansei engineering
A technology that translates human *kansei* and images into physical design elements to design a product satisfying *kansei*.

KDSI
One thousand Delivered Source Instructions (same as KLOC).

KJ method
A nonrational "right brain" method for discerning customer needs developed by cultural anthropologist Jiro Kawakita.

KLOC
One thousand Lines of Code.

Landmark™
A Lawson software specification-based design language for business domain expert use.

Latin square
Consists of n sets of the numbers 1 to n arranged so that no orthogonal (row or column) contains the same number twice.

LCC
Life-Cycle Cost.

LCL
Lower Control Limit.

Linux
A public-domain version of UNIX.

LOC
Lines of Code.

Mahalanobis distance
A statistical distance measure introduced by P. C. Mahalanobis. Based on correlations between variables for identifying different patterns to determine similarity in an unknown sample set.

MITI
The Japanese Ministry for International Trade and Industry.

MR analysis
Multiple Regression analysis.

MRP
Materials Resource Planning.

noise
The negative effects of uncontrollable factors in the use of a designed product.

NVP
N-Version Programming. A technique requiring the independent preparation of multiple versions of a software component for a function or application.

ODC
Orthogonal Defect Classification.

OOAD
Object-Oriented Analysis and Design.

OOP
Object-Oriented Programming.

orthogonal array
A matrix consisting of n sets of the numbers 1 to n arranged so that no orthogonal (row or column) contains the same number twice.

PAMPA
Project Attribute Monitoring and Prediction Associate visualization toolkit.

parameter design
The second stage of the Taguchi Robust Design process. The engineer uses orthogonal matrices to represent both design parameters and noise factors that may cause the product to deviate from its target.

PDE
Programming Development Environment.

PDM
Precedence Diagram.

PDPC
Process Decision Program Chart. A tree diagram that seeks to identify all the things that can possibly go wrong and specifies necessary countermeasures to prevent or correct them.

PERT
Program Evaluation and Review Technique.

PICS
Plan, Implement, Control, and Secure.

poka yoke
A Japanese term meaning mistake-proofing or fail-safing. Recognizes that human errors are unavoidable but do not necessarily have to result in defects. A vital element of an effective process quality control system. Also called Zero (Defect) Quality Control (ZQC).

PoNC
Price of Nonconformance.

QFD
Quality Function Deployment.

quality circle
A small group of workers doing similar tasks.

quality loss
The cost of product failure, which comes into the picture after products are shipped. It includes losses due to return, warranty, repair, and loss of goodwill resulting in loss of market share.

quality loss function
A function used for design decisions on financial grounds to decide whether additional costs of improved quality will actually prove worthwhile in the marketplace.

QWL
Quality of Work Life.

regression testing
Ensures that modifications and upgrades to a software version have not damaged prior functionality.

Robust Design
A methodology developed by Genichi Taguchi. Helps you develop products and processes that perform on target as per customer requirements despite the presence of factors that cause variability in the user and manufacturing environments at the lowest possible cost.

robustness
The state in which the technology, product, or process performance is minimally sensitive to factors causing variability (in either the manufacturing or user environment) at the lowest unit manufacturing cost.

ROQI
Return on Quality Investments.

round-tripping
The ability of an IDE to go from modified compiled Java code back to UML.

RSDM
Robust Software Development Model.

RUP
Rational Unified Process.

SA
Structured Analysis. A software development tool used before Software QFD.

SanFrancisco™
An IBM Partners in Development project to build a business application framework in Java.

SAP
The largest tier-one third-party ERP business application software vendor.

SDE
Statistical Design of Experiments.

SEC
Senior Executives and Champions.

SeCS
Self-Check System. Encourages a self-check, with imaginative incentives to reward people for reporting their own defects.

SEI
Software Engineering Institute.

SFTA
Software Failure Tree Analysis.

Six Sigma
A philosophy, system of management, and methodology used to improve products, processes, and service performance to make them defect-free and help them meet customer requirements in a cost-effective manner.

SN ratio
Signal-to-noise ratio.

software architecture
The description of elements from which a system is built, interactions among those elements, patterns that guide their composition, and constraints on those patterns.

software QFD
The application of quality function deployment technology to the software development process.

software quality
A software product's fitness for use. The degree to which a system, component, or process possesses a specified set of attributes necessary to fulfill stated or implied customer or user needs, expectations, and satisfaction.

software reliability
Software's ability to perform its functions under specified conditions for a specified time.

software safety
Freedom from conditions that can cause death; injury; illness; damage to or loss of access to and control over data, privacy, equipment, or property; or environmental harm.

software scalability
A computer application's ability to run on a larger machine or parallel processor to handle a larger transaction volume or throughput in such a way that performance scales linearly or nearly linearly with volume.

software security
A computer application's ability to operate without risk of compromise by error-prone programs or malicious activity by hackers.

SuCS
Successive Check System. Successive inspections throughout a process before further value-adding.

TCoSQ
Total Cost of Software Quality.

TCS
Tata Consultancy Services.

TOC
Theory of Constraints.

tolerance design
The third stage of the Taguchi Robust Design process. The engineer tightens tolerances on components that cannot be made adequately robust by parameter design.

TPOV
Teachable Point of View.

TPS
Toyota Production System.

TQM
Total Quality Management. A management approach to long-term success that is attained through focus on customer satisfaction.

TRIZ
Teoriya Resheniya Izobreatatelskikh Zadatch. The Russian acronym for Theory of Inventive Problem Solving (TIPS).

trustworthy computing
A hardware-software-network system that is dependable (including but not limited to reliability, safety, security, availability, and maintainability) and customer-responsive at various stages of the system life cycle.

trustworthy software
Software that is dependable (including but not limited to reliability, safety, security, availability, and maintainability) and customer-responsive. It can fulfill customer trust and meet the customer's stated, unstated, and even unanticipated needs.

UCL
Upper Control Limit.

UML
Uniform Modeling Language.

validation
The process of ensuring that programs meet their functional specifications.

verification
The process of ensuring that programs meet their design specifications.

VOC
Voice of the Customer.

WBS
Work Breakdown Structure.

XP
Extreme Programming.

ZQC
Zero (Defect) Quality Control. A technique for avoiding and eliminating mistakes. Poka yoke is the basis of ZQC.

Name Index

Index

performance sensitivity analysis,
274-275
ratio scale priorities for objectives,
264-267
General Electric (GE) Six Sigma initiative, 572
CEO-driven approach, 573
cultural compatibility, 573-574
investment in human resources, 576
management infrastructure, 574-575
reward system, 576
strategic compatibility, 574
teaching infrastructure, 576
General Electric (GE) Operating System,
606-610
IT portfolio alignment, 628, 643
challenges of, 644-645
design, 649
extensions, 662
IT project proposals, 650
iterative process phases, 645-648
measurement, 651-655
objectives hierarchy, 651
objectivity, 648-649
optimization, 657-660
risk, 660-661
structuring complexity, 650
synthesis, 656
MD Robotics, 630, 685-686
parameter design example, 508
QFD for new product development, 729
consumerism, 730
demand for new products, 730
examples of, 731
quality tools, 732-734
resources, 737-743
self-evaluation of NPD efforts, 734
QFD for unprecedented software, 629

railroad MIS functional specification,
503-504
Ramsay County, Minnesota justice
system, 506
RES (Raytheon Electronic Systems), 628,
634
CoSQ costs and benefits, 640-641
CoSQ data gathering, 636
CoSQ institutionalization, 641
CoSQ model, 635-636
CoSQ tracking, 637-638
difficulties encountered, 641
implications of, 641-642
lessons learned, 636
predictability, 640
productivity, 640
rework cost savings, 638-639
ROI results, 640
software improvement initiative,
634-635
software quality, 639
software field maintenance, 559-560
Submarine Spitfire, 556
Taguchi Methods for RTOS design
verification, 537-540
Tata Consultancy Services (TCS),
618-619
Toyota Production System (TPS),
569-570
people, 571-572
philosophy, 570
planning, 570
production, 570-571
catastrophic failure, 435
cause-and-effect diagrams
classifying processes with, 210-211
definition of, 194
elements of, 207
identifying causes with, 208-210

government agencies, 438
internal customers, 438
needs
  analyzing, 719-720
  analyzing customer needs structure, 378
  changing requirements, 375
  Customer Voice Table (CVT), 375
  defining for brand-new products, 669, 671-672, 674
  deploying high-value needs, 380, 721-722
  discovering, 716-718
  identifying, 374-375, 377
  logical or perceived needs, 672-673
  prioritizing, 378-379, 720
  stated requirements, 374
  structuring, 377, 718-719
  unstated requirements, 374-375
requirements, 89, 97, 668-669
  Kano's model of customer requirements, 688-690
segmentation, 371-372
Voice of Customer Analysis, 60, 671-672
CVTs (Customer Voice Tables), 375, 671, 692-696, 716-717
cyclomatic complexity, 79-80

D

DCF (Discounted Cash Flow), 117
debugging
  definition of, 536
  testing and debugging anomalies, 545-546
Decision Engine Products, 257
decision hierarchy, 261
decomposition, 315
defect removal effectiveness (DRE), 76
Defect-Free Process, 317

defective units, 337
defects, 3
  causes of, 307-312
  defect backlog, 76
  defect density, 78
  defect rate during formal system testing, 76
  defect removal effectiveness (DRE), 76
degrees of freedom, 676
delayering, General Electric (GE) Six Sigma initiative, 574
"delight-the-customer" (TQM), 74
demand for new products, 730
Deming, W. Edwards, 43, 118, 159-160
  consistent performance, achieving, 49-50
  fourteen points for management, 47-49
  quality philosophy, 50-51
deploying *poka yoke* systems, 317-321
DEs (desirable effects), 672
design, 46, 56, 506
  Design for Six Sigma (DFSS), 100, 613
  Design of Experiments (DOE), 50
  design patterns, 87-89
  design performance, 545
  DRE (defect removal effectiveness), 76
  FMEA (Failure Modes and Effects Analysis), 438
  IT portfolio alignment, 649
  iterative processes, 645
  parameter design, 46, 56, 506-508
  robust. *See* robust design
  system design, 46, 56, 506
  Taguchi Methods, 51
  tolerance design, 46, 56, 507
Design for Six Sigma (DFSS), 100, 613
Design of Experiments (DOE), 50
Design of Experiments, 44
design patterns, 87-89
desirable effects (DEs), 672

M

unintended function failure mode, 438
unique SLOC, 85
unit testing, 544-546
Univac 1107 computers, 560
Univac 1108 computers, 7
Univac Defense Systems, 412
Universal Studios robotic triceratops project.
    See MD Robotics case study
unnecessary motion, 337
unnecessary transportation, 337
unrefusable offers (UROs), 672
unreliability, causes of, 41-42
unstated requirements, 374-375
upper control limits (UCLs), 219
upstream internal failure costs, 106
upstreaming, 501
URO (unrefusable offer), 672
usability, 85
use cases, 21
users
    expectations, 86
    interaction with, 42
    obtaining input from, 506

V

validation, 533-535
    additional resources, 550
    content validity, 543
    criterion-related validity, 543
    definition of, 536, 541
    discussion questions, 550
    Internet exercises, 550
    key points, 549-550
    predictive validity, 543
    problems, 551
    reliability compared to validity, 543-544
    review questions, 550
    Taguchi Methods for software validation, 541-543

value
    of CoSQ analysis, 117-118
    definition of, 369, 667
    delivering to customers, 369
    essential items, 369-370
    value analysis, 314
    value management, 711
Value Engineering, 734, 743
variance, 491
verbatims, 373
verification, 85, 533-535
    additional resources, 550
    definition of, 536
    discussion questions, 550
    Internet exercises, 550
    key points, 549-550
    problems, 551
    program verification, 537
    pseudocode, 540
    review questions, 550
    Taguchi Methods for RTOS design verification, 537-540
    when to perform, 540
Virtuous Teaching Cycle, 156
visual simulations, 427
VOC (Voice of the Customer), 60,, 74, 375
    CVTs (Customer Voice Tables), 375, 671, 692-696, 716-717
    Voice of Customer Analysis, 671-672
volume, 84

W

waiting, 337
waste, 156, 335-338
waterfall software development model, 11-12
WBS (Work Breakdown Structure), 723
WesCorp, 471
What Is Total Quality Control? The Japanese Way, 199
white belt training, 595

BOOKS ONLINE

ENABLED

THIS BOOK IS SAFARI ENABLED

INCLUDES FREE 45-DAY ACCESS TO THE ONLINE EDITION

The Safari® Enabled icon on the cover of your favorite technology book means the book is available through Safari Bookshelf. When you buy this book, you get free access to the online edition for 45 days.

Safari Bookshelf is an electronic reference library that lets you easily search thousands of technical books, find code samples, download chapters, and access technical information whenever and wherever you need it.

TO GAIN 45-DAY SAFARI ENABLED ACCESS TO THIS BOOK:

- Go to **http://www.prenhallprofessional.com/safarienabled**
- Complete the brief registration form
- Enter the coupon code found in the front of this book on the "Copyright" page

PRENTICE HALL

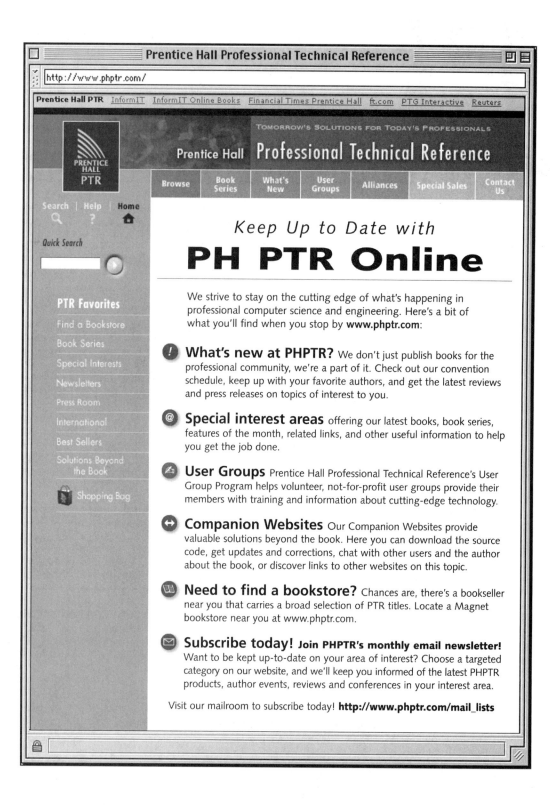